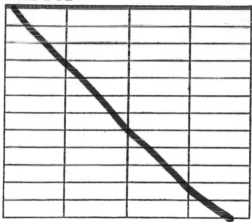

The Crowell Education Series

THEODORE L. RELLER, Advisory Editor

READINGS FOR
EDUCATIONAL PSYCHOLOGY

Readings for
EDUCATIONAL
PSYCHOLOGY

WILLIAM A. FULLAGAR
Associate Professor of Secondary Education
University of Florida

HAL G. LEWIS
Professor of Foundation of Education
University of Florida

CARROLL F. CUMBEE
Associate Professor of Child Development
University of Florida

New York   *1956*
THOMAS Y. CROWELL COMPANY

Preface

MOST teachers agree that effective learning involves more than listening to lectures and reading from a single textbook. College instructors, like other teachers, try to encourage their students to read broadly and to reflect on this reading. Often, however, they lack the time to choose worth-while readings from the welter of educational writings. And, when time is found for this task, the selections are not readily available to students. It was with these problems in mind that *Readings for Educational Psychology* was prepared.

Fifty selections by fifty-seven authors from education, psychology, psychiatry, mental hygiene, and related fields are arranged in three parts— "Learning and Learning Theory," "Understanding the Learner," and "The Learning Situation"—which are subdivided into ten sections. In almost every case the article or chapter is printed in its entirety, with the omission only of bibliographical references.

An interpretive headnote and a biographical footnote at the beginning of each selection serve to set the stage for the reader. In addition, other selections that relate to the subject under discussion are listed by number preceding each selection. If the student follows the careful reading of a selection with an equally careful perusal of the related selections, his breadth of understanding of the topic will be greatly enhanced. Finally, tables correlating the selections with the chapters of twenty-one educational psychology textbooks appear at the back of the book.

Because many teachers have found psychological learning theory of little value in their work with children, and some have felt it necessary to turn to the educational philosopher for a theory of mind and of learning that has meaning for classroom practice, emphasis is given to educational philosophy as learning theory. The selections by Dewey, Bode, and Kilpatrick should prove a valuable supplement to Part I, "Learning and Learning Theory." The book also contains many selections on personality development and mental hygiene, in keeping with the trend in today's

v

schools to give ever-increasing attention to these and other factors that influence the development and well-being of children.

To guide them in the selection of material, the editors established the following criteria:

1. The readings should complement and supplement, not duplicate, the material of the basic text.

2. They should stay well within the bounds of educational psychology.

3. A balance should be maintained between the "old," as represented by certain classic statements of the leaders of yesterday, and the "new," as exemplified by some of today's frontier thinkers.

4. The book should be oriented toward helping prospective and in-service teachers better meet their everyday problems.

5. The selections should be interesting and understandable, yet not superficial; challenging, yet not difficult.

If some readers feel that certain selections do not meet all of the criteria, that fact may serve to point up the broadness of the term *educational psychology* and the varied interests and expectations of those who teach and study in this area. The editors sought to bring into the selective process their own experience and interests in the fields of educational psychology, child development, educational philosophy, and curriculum.

Acknowledgment is made, in separate footnotes, to the authors and publishers of the selections used. However, the editors would like to express again their indebtedness for the privilege of reprinting these significant papers. Whatever merit this volume may possess is due to the scholarship and creativeness of the fifty-seven authors who generously consented to the inclusion of their previously published work. The editors claim credit only for many long months of searching, screening, choosing, and classroom testing of the selections used.

W. A. F.
H. G. L.
C. F. C.

Contents

I

LEARNING AND LEARNING THEORY

A. Some Concepts of Learning

II

UNDERSTANDING THE LEARNER

A. The Process of Growth and Development

III

THE LEARNING SITUATION

A. Organization for Learning

B. The Classroom Atmosphere

C. The Teacher's Role

READINGS FOR
EDUCATIONAL PHYSCOLOGY

I

Learning and Learning Theory

A. SOME CONCEPTS OF LEARNING

1. The Nature of Learning Theories*

Related selections: 2, 3, 5, 6, 8

BOTH THE teacher and the psychologist have regarded a study of learning and of the learning process as being of prime importance. An understanding of how people learn and under what conditions they learn best has been considered by many as being the first and major contribution of psychology to pedagogy. From many experiments and studies have come several different theories of learning with numerous variations within each theory. Getting deeply involved in these differences is one sure road to confusion for beginning teachers. Dr. Hilgard here classifies the theories into two families and describes their differences in respect to five critical aspects.

SOME TYPICAL PROBLEMS CONFRONTING LEARNING THEORIES

THE PREFERENCES of the theorist often lead him to concentrate upon one kind of learning situation to the neglect of the others. His theory is then appropriate to this situation, but becomes somewhat strained in relation

* Ernest R. Hilgard, *Theories of Learning,* Appleton-Century-Crofts, Inc., 1948, pp. 7–17. Reprinted by permission of the author and publisher.

Dr. Hilgard (1904—) is Dean of the Graduate Division and Executive Head of the Department of Psychology, Leland Stanford University. He is a former president of the American Psychological Association and an eminent scholar in the field of learning.

to other problems of learning.   A comprehensive learning theory ought to answer the questions which an intelligent non-psychologist might ask about the sorts of learning which are met in everyday life.   A few such questions will be listed here, and then used later in appraising the theories which different writers present.

1. *What are the limits of learning?*   Here is raised the question of the capacity to learn, of individual differences among learners of the same species and of unlike species.   There are questions not only of persistent differences in capacity, but of change in capacity with age.   Who can learn what?   Are the limits set at birth?   Do people get more or less alike with practice?   These are the sorts of questions which it is natural to raise.

2. *What is the rôle of practice in learning?*   The old adage that practice makes perfect has considerable racial wisdom behind it.   Surely one learns to roller skate or to play the piano only by engaging in the activity. But what do we know about practice in detail?   Does improvement depend directly on the amount of repetition?   If not, what are its conditions?   What are the most favorable circumstances of practice?   Can repetitive drill be harmful as well as helpful to the learner?

3. *How important are reward, punishment, or other motives in learning?*   Everybody knows in a general way that learning can be controlled by rewards and punishments, and that it is easier to learn something which is interesting than something which is dull.   But are the consequences of rewards and punishments equal and opposite?   Is there a difference between intrinsic and extrinsic motives in their effect upon learning?   How do goals and purposes affect the process?

4. *What is the place of understanding and insight?*   Some things are learned more readily if we know what we are about.   We are better off as travelers if we can understand a time-table or a road map.   We are helpless with differential equations unless we understand the symbols and the rules for their manipulation.   But we can form vowels satisfactorily without knowing how we place our tongues, and we can read without being aware of our eye movements.   Some things we appear to acquire blindly and automatically; some things we struggle hard to understand, and can finally master only as we understand them.   Is learning in one case different from what it is in the other?

5. *Does learning one thing help you learn something else?*   This is the problem of formal discipline, as it used to be called, or of transfer of training, to use a more familiar contemporary designation.   Some transfer of training must occur or there would be no use in developing a foundation for later learning.   Nobody denies that it is easier to build a vocabulary in a language after you have a start in it, or that higher mathematics profits

from mastery of basic concepts. The question is really one of how much transfer takes place and what its nature is.

6. *What happens when we remember and when we forget?* The ordinary facts of memory are mysterious enough, but in addition to familiar remembering and forgetting our memories may play peculiar tricks on us. Some things we wish to remember are forgotten; some things we would be willing to forget continue to plague us. In cases of amnesia there are often gaps in memory, with earlier and later events remembered. Then there are the distortions of memory, in which we remember what did not happen, as is so strikingly demonstrated in testimony experiments. What is taking place? What control have we over the processes involved?

These six questions will serve as useful ones to ask of each of the major theories. They suffice to illustrate the kinds of questions which give rise to theories of learning.

BASIC ISSUES ON WHICH THE MAJOR THEORIES DIVIDE

[In the discussion below, Dr. Hilgard groups the array of learning theories into two main families to avoid confusion.]

The two main theories may be designated *association* theories, on the one hand, and *field* theories on the other. Any naming in this way does some violence to the individual theories, but nevertheless the typical American theories of functionalism, connectionism, and behaviorism have a common underlying logic which permits them to be grouped together, and the other theories, stemming chiefly from gestalt psychology, have in turn a contrasting common ground. The theories here classified as association theories have been labelled *reflex arc* theories and *stimulus-response* theories. The field theories group together various varieties of *gestalt, neo-gestalt, organismic,* or *sign-significate* theories.

The distinctions between the families are not always sharp, and there are agreements and disagreements which cut across lines. That is, on some specific issues it would be possible to find association psychologists on opposite sides of the fence, paralleled by field psychologists divided on the same issue. But the total picture does not present such confusion. Although association psychologists do not comprise a single harmonious family, still any one adherent to that position tends to offer explanations more like those of another than like the explanations of any one in the field group. Correspondingly, the members of the field psychology family have in common their opposition to associationist conceptions. It is important to understand this basic cleavage, because there are profound differences in outlook, despite efforts of eclectics and mediators to harmonize the opposing camps.

The differences in systematic outlook may be summarized around five issues: environmentalism-nativism, the part-whole problem, emphasis upon reaction or cognition, the selected physical model, and the problem of historical versus contemporary explanation. These are differences not confined to learning theory, but they lie behind some of the cleavages reflected in learning theory. At the outset it should be stressed that the differences are matters of preference in the interpretation of a much wider range of data than those of learning. They are preferences in the interpretation of natural phenomena in general. Again, it is not that one of the contrasting preferences is exclusively right and the other exclusively wrong. Rather, each group believes that its point of view is scientifically the more fruitful.

1. *Environmentalism versus nativism.* The organism is born with sense organs, muscles and glands, and integrating structures. How its muscles and bones and sense organs and nervous elements function is closely related to their structure. But how they function is rapidly modified by learning. Because the evidence is often somewhat ambiguous, there is room for two interpretations of behavior, one which leans toward natural endowment as explanatory of behavior possibilities, and the other which attributes behavioral outcomes largely to learning.

The preference of associationists past and present has always been for environmentalism, that is, for attributing as much as possible to learning. In the field of perception, for example, the associationist makes much of Stratton's (1896) experiment in which, with experience, he became accustomed to the world as viewed through reversing lenses. The topsy-turvy world came to look all right and to provide cues for ready action. Hence the time-honored question as to how we could see the world right-side up when it is upside down on our retinas is solved by saying that we learn to use what visual cues we have to order our experiences of external reality. Gestalt psychologists (who may be taken as representative of field psychologists for this comparison) have a preference for nativism, in the sense that they account for the interaction of organism and environment largely in terms of the way in which the organism is made. In perception, for example, it is argued that seen motion, third dimension, and other such features attributed by associationists to learning are instead functions of contemporary arrangements, independent of prior experience.

It would be false to carry this distinction to extremes, for associationists do not usually accept the extreme environmentalism of a Watson (1925), nor do field psychologists go along with instinct psychologies like

McDougall's (1923). However, the preferences are found to hold in intermediate and ambiguous cases, when associationists give "the benefit of the doubt" to learning, gestalt psychologists to the nature of the organism as it interacts dynamically with the environment. These preferences are sufficiently strong to show themselves repeatedly in the controversial writings between association and gestalt psychologists.

2. *The nature of wholes and of parts.* Parts may be thought of as the substances out of which wholes are made. Houses are made of bricks and wood and plaster (or their modern equivalents in glass, metal, and plastics). The whole is composed of all its parts so conceived—no more, no less. Alternatively, a whole may be thought of as a unique pattern or organization of the parts, in which case the whole has properties beyond those of its parts, or is "more" than its parts. Thus a house has an architectural unity which is "more" than the materials of which it is composed. These alternatives—considering wholes according to their composition or according to their organization—represent a second difference in preference between association and field theories.

Association theories tend to consider wholes in terms of their composition. Complex habits are combinations of simpler habits. Complicated skills involve many "bonds" or "conditioned responses." Habit tendencies interact algebraically, so that several tendencies acting at once lead to greater or less vigor of response, depending upon the strengths and the signs of the tendencies. (Some tendencies have negative signs relative to others, that is, they are in conflict or inhibit each other.) Transfer of training, in one form of association theory, depends upon identical elements in the old and new learning situations. A comparison according to common elements is obviously a comparison according to composition. This preference for describing the whole according to its parts is referred to by critics of association theories as a form of *atomism,* said to be borrowed by associationism from nineteenth century physical science.

Field psychologies have as their most distinctive emphasis the primacy which they give to wholeness characters. That the whole is more than the sum of its parts represents to the field psychologist a basic viewpoint toward nature. Thus the standard illustration of a gestalt, that a melody is more than the tones and intervals of which it is composed, is taken to hold in learning also. Just as a melody is transposable, so something learned on one occasion may by transposition aid in the solution of a new problem. Solving a problem, while having some relationship to the solving of earlier problems, does not consist in the automatic running off of prior habits; even though prior habits may be discovered in the steps toward solution, the attack on the problem has individuality and novelty not describable by the habit components which can be found in it. The wholeness properties must not be lost by a faulty analysis. The field psychologist reverses the associationist approach: the wholes are not to be explained by the parts of which they are composed, but the parts are to be understood as differentiated out from a whole which has logical priority to them.

3. *Reaction and cognition.* The organism interacts with its environment by making sensory discriminations and by engaging in manipulatory, locomotor, and other energy interchanges with it. Some of the organism's interactions are covert, that is, not open to direct observation. Though quiet, the organism may be thinking. Because of the range of activities of interest to the psychologist, some psychologists prefer to lay emphasis on one segment of the organism's conduct, while others choose to emphasize other segments or aspects of its activity. Again there are family resemblances among contemporary associationists which differ from those among contemporary field psychologists.

The preference of the contemporary association theorist for a reaction psychology (laying emphasis upon movements) as over against a cognitive psychology (emphasizing perception-like and idea-like processes) is in part an aftermath of an earlier quarrel over the validity of introspection as a method in psychology. Most of the present day associationists (though not all of them) have been influenced by behaviorism, and share with the behaviorist an abhorrence of the subjective. Hence they prefer to speak of discriminatory reactions rather than of perceptions, avoiding the subjective or introspective connotations of the word perception. Thought processes tend to be interpreted according to their substantive basis in inner speech or other movements. A second root of the contemporary associationist's preference for a reaction-psychology is relatively independent of objections to subjectivity or to cognitive processes as such. It is based on what to the associationist appear to be the facts of the case so far as learning is concerned. That interpretation, stemming from Thorndike and supported by Pavlov and conditioned reflex theory, is that there is in fact a directness of connection between situations and the responses to them, with a minimum of mediation by ideas or idea-surrogates. It is a curious turn of history that the legatees of the doctrine of association of ideas should be the ones with the least use for ideational processes.

The field theorist, like the associationist, does not like to be considered a subjectivist. But unlike the reaction-psychologist he does not have the behaviorist's fear of contamination with subjectivity. He is likely to accept a form of introspection called *phenomenological* as contrasted with the introspections of trained observers. It is phenomenological observation which is used in the description of the difference in appearance between shadows and the surfaces on which they lie, which is used in experiments on seen movement, on the relative constancy of size of familiar objects seen at a distance, and so on. The field psychologist finds such observation important because of the prevalence in perception of organization, of figure-ground, of contours, and so on. While such observations could be translated into the discriminatory responses of reaction psychologists, the field psychologist is likely to believe that something is lost in this translation. Hence even in animal experimentation, in which cognitive processes are not observed, they are inferred by the field psychologist from the observable behavior. It is possible to prefer and to defend the preference for a cognitive psychology, even when all the data are behavioral. On the issue of fact in learning situations, the field theorist lies opposed to the associationist. It is his interpretation of learning experiments that a great deal of what might be called ideation goes on. The word *insight* is one which the gestalt psychologists brought prominently into the literature of learning. For most field psychologists something like insightful learning, be it called learning with understanding or learning under cognitive control, is the characteristic form of learning.

In the distinction between a reaction psychology and a cognitive psychology we have then a choice based both upon a preference as to the appropriate concepts to be used in a scientific psychology, and upon a preferred interpretation of what actually occurs in experiments. The former preference can persist, however experiments turn out. The latter preference, based on what is the case, is subject to change by experiments. If ideational processes are indeed necessary to explain what happens in experiments, the associationist can accept them in his reaction-psychology, although he will prefer to substitute for ideas some movement counterpart of them.

4. *Mechanism versus dynamic equilibrium.* Scientists believe the behavior of organisms to be lawful, at least within limits set by statistical approximations. In favoring some sort of cause-and-effect sequences, psychologists act like any other scientists. There is, however, a range of choice in the selection of the physical model after which we seek to design the laws to be used in psychological explanations. One physical model is provided by machines with rigid parts—with levers, pulleys, gears, motors—machines like typewriters or cash registers. When a key is pushed, the consequence is definitely predictable. The models may vary enormously in complexity, including automatic telephone switchboards and computing bomb-sights, but the principle is the same. A different model is provided by whirlpools, candle flames, and soap bubbles, in

which the parts are related to the whole in a less rigid manner. You can scoop a bucketful of water out of a whirlpool without changing it. The whirlpool, candle flame, and soap bubble are illustrations of dynamic equilibria, just as physical as the machines mentioned earlier, yet suggesting quite different analogies.

The preference of the associationist is for the machine model. The uses made of bonds, reflexes, and other isolatable activities which can be integrated into total habit systems more nearly resemble the model of the machine than of the whirlpool. Like his preference for environmentalism, it is a relative preference only, and the associationist is not bound by a strictly rigid model. Pavlov (1927), in spite of his essentially machine-like conception of conditioned reflexes, had doctrines of cortical action expressed by terms like irradiation and concentration which are not covered by the machine analogy. The same may be said of other associationist writers.

There is no ambiguity about the preference of the field psychologist. He is definitely on the side of the models of dynamic equilibria. Living things, unlike machines, are constantly interchanging their substance with the environment; they remain "the same" only because of a patterning or organization which persists in the midst of change. A single red corpuscle in the blood, as a carrier of oxygen, undergoes rapid change as it courses through the blood vessels. Its hemoglobin remains the "same" not because its molecules are the same after a few hours, but because it has maintained its organization as a separable something throughout the period of observation. There is no contradiction between treating the hemoglobin as so much chemical substance or treating it as a system in equilibrium. But there is a difference in point of view. By adopting the model of dynamic equilibria, the field psychologists warn against any effort to comprehend the totality of behavior in terms of component parts. The whole must always be viewed as a system, to which the parts are subordinate.

5. *Historical versus contemporary causation.* The decision to account for present behavior by its past history, or to explain it according to present circumstances, is not a decision forced by nature. Both approaches are possible; we need not even think that one is, in itself, better science than the other.

Consider a physical analogy. The storage battery fails in your car and the repairman wishes to make a diagnosis. He may take the historical approach. How old is the battery? How many miles have you driven it? Have you done much cold-weather starting, much night driving? Have you had trouble before? On the basis of such evidence he may decide, wisely, that it is time for a new battery. Or he may take the non-historical approach, considering the problem only in its contemporary aspects. He may examine the battery, test it, and decide solely in terms of its present operation whether or not it is worth retaining. Both methods are possible; often they would be used jointly. The historical approach might be more useful if it were a question of the condition of the plates which were not open to inspection. To use the analogy another way, suppose that the battery is in good condition and is now charged. Does it matter whether it was charged during a two weeks' trip you took into the country or whether it was charged in the garage? It does not matter, provided the battery is in the same present condition.

Confronted with a choice between historical and non-historical causation in the formulation of learning theory, the answer of the associationist is clear. He says that in order to account for the present you have to look to the past. What we do now is to act according to our repertory of habits built up in previous experience.

The field theorists believe it more profitable to be concerned with the present. They do not deny the influence of the past, any more than they would deny that a battery could be charged by a ride through the country. Of course you speak English now because you learned English in the past. From a scientific point of view, however, they believe it to be better to study you as the English-speaking person you now are than to concern themselves with what you did as you learned English. Whether or not one agrees with the field theorist, his position is a clear one and defensible as a possible one.

How the difference in preference expresses itself may be illustrated by the manner in which problem-solving is treated. The associationist finds in the solution of a novel problem that the learner assembles his experiences from the past appropriate to the new problem, responding either according to elements common to old and the new situations, or according to aspects of the new situation which are similar to old situations. The field psychologist points out, however, that even with appropriate past experience the organism may not solve the problem if it is presented one way and may solve it if it is presented in another way. Hence the contemporary structuring of the field is said to be more important than previous experience.

These five differences (environmentalism-nativism, part-whole problem, reaction-cognition, mechanism-dynamic equilibrium, and historical-contemporary causation) have been presented in an introductory way to make it clear that what seem to be diametrically opposed points of view may in fact turn out to be differences in preference, each being possible of clear statement, and to a point justifiable. The opposed cases are each made by intelligent men of good will.

---

2. Conditioned Emotional Reactions*

Related selections: 1, 6

OUT OF the experimental work of Pavlov, Watson, and others came a conditioned reflex theory of learning that had important implications for child rearing and schooling. Although many of their conclusions were later questioned and modified, one permanent contribution of this pioneer work was the placing of psychological study on a scientific basis. Students should understand the methods of this school and ask themselves if there are any kinds of learning for which it offers the best explanation. This selection reports one of a number of experiments by Watson and his associate during the first quarter of the century.

IN RECENT literature various speculations have been entered into concerning the possibility of conditioning various types of emotional response, but direct experimental evidence in support of such a view has been lacking. If the theory advanced by Watson and Morgan to the effect that in infancy the original emotional reaction patterns are few, consisting so far as observed of fear, rage and love, then there must be some simple method by means of which the range of stimuli which can call out these emotions and their compounds is greatly increased. Otherwise, complexity in adult response could not be accounted for. These authors without adequate experimental evidence advanced the view that this range was increased by means of conditioned reflex factors. It was suggested there that the early home life of the child furnishes a laboratory situation for establishing conditioned emotional responses. The present authors have recently put the whole matter to an experimental test.

Experimental work has been done so far on only one child, Albert B.

*John B. Watson and Rosalie Rayner, "Conditioned Emotional Reactions," *Journal of Experimental Psychology,* vol. III (February, 1921), pp. 1–14. Reprinted by permission of the authors and the American Psychological Association.
    Professor Watson (1878—), now retired, was director of the psychological laboratory at the Johns Hopkins University for many years. He was the foremost behaviorist in this country. Rosalie Rayner (Watson) collaborated with him in his research.

This infant was reared almost from birth in a hospital environment; his mother was a wet nurse in the Harriet Lane Home for Invalid Children. Albert's life was normal: he was healthy from birth and one of the best developed youngsters ever brought to the hospital, weighing twenty-one pounds at nine months of age. He was on the whole stolid and unemotional. His stability was one of the principal reasons for using him as a subject in this test. We felt that we could do him relatively little harm by carrying out such experiments as those outlined below.

At approximately nine months of age we ran him through the emotional tests that have become a part of our regular routine in determining whether fear reactions can be called out by other stimuli than sharp noises and the sudden removal of support. Tests of this type have been described by the senior author in another place. In brief, the infant was confronted suddenly and for the first time successively with a white rat, a rabbit, a dog, a monkey, with masks with and without hair, cotton wool, burning newspapers, etc. A permanent record of Albert's reactions to these objects and situations has been preserved in a motion picture study. Manipulation was the most usual reaction called out. *At no time did this infant ever show fear in any situation.* These experimental records were confirmed by the casual observations of the mother and hospital attendants. No one had ever seen him in a state of fear and rage. The infant practically never cried.

Up to approximately nine months of age we had not tested him with loud sounds. The test to determine whether a fear reaction could be called out by a loud sound was made when he was eight months, twenty-six days of age. The sound was that made by striking a hammer upon a suspended steel bar four feet in length and three-fourths of an inch in diameter. The laboratory notes are as follows:

One of the two experimenters caused the child to turn its head and fixate her moving hand; the other, stationed back of the child, struck the steel bar a sharp blow. The child started violently, his breathing was checked and the arms were raised in a characteristic manner. On the second stimulation the same thing occurred, and in addition the lips began to pucker and tremble. On the third stimulation the child broke into a sudden crying fit. This is the first time an emotional situation in the laboratory has produced any fear or even crying in Albert.

We had expected just these results on account of our work with other infants brought up under similar conditions. It is worth while to call attention to the fact that removal of support (dropping and jerking the blanket upon which the infant was lying) was tried exhaustively upon this infant on the same occasion. It was not effective in producing the fear response. This stimulus is effective in younger children. At what age such stimuli lose their potency in producing fear is not known. Nor is it known whether less placid children ever lose their fear of them. This probably depends upon the training the child gets. It is well known that children eagerly run to be tossed into the air and caught. On the other hand it is equally well known that in the adult fear responses are called out quite clearly by the sudden removal of support, if the individual is walking across a bridge, walking out upon a beam, etc. There is a wide field of study here which is aside from our present point.

The sound stimulus, thus, at nine months of age, gives us the means of testing several important factors. I. Can we condition fear of an animal, e.g., a white rat, by visually presenting it and simultaneously striking a steel bar? II. If such a conditioned emotional response can be established, will there be a transfer to other animals or other objects? III. What is the effect of time upon such conditioned emotional responses? IV. If after a reasonable period such emotional responses have not died out, what laboratory methods can be devised for their removal?

I. The establishment of conditioned emotional responses. At first there was considerable hesitation upon our part in making the attempt to set up fear reactions experimentally. A certain responsibility attaches to such a procedure. We decided finally to make the attempt, comforting ourselves by the reflection that such attachments would arise anyway as soon as the child left the sheltered environment of the nursery for the rough and tumble of the home. We did not begin this work until Albert was eleven months, three days of age. Before attempting to set up a conditioned response we, as before, put him through all of the regular emotional tests. *Not the slightest sign of a fear response was obtained in any situation.*

The steps taken to condition emotional responses are shown in our laboratory notes.

11 Months 3 Days

1. White rat suddenly taken from the basket and presented to Albert. He began to reach for rat with left hand. Just as his hand touched the animal the bar was struck immediately behind his head. The infant jumped violently and fell forward, burying his face in the mattress. He did not cry, however.

2. Just as the right hand touched the rat the bar was again struck. Again the infant jumped violently, fell forward and began to whimper.

In order not to disturb the child too seriously no further tests were given for one week.

11 Months 10 Days

1. Rat presented suddenly without sound. There was steady fixation but no tendency at first to reach for it. The rat was then placed nearer, whereupon tentative reaching movements began with the right hand. When the rat nosed the infant's left hand, the hand was immediately withdrawn. He started to reach for the head of the animal with the forefinger of the left hand, but withdrew it suddenly before contact. It is thus seen that the two joint stimulations given the previous week were not without effect. He was tested with his blocks immediately afterwards to see if they shared in the process of conditioning. He began immediately to pick them up, dropping them, pounding them, etc. In the remainder of the tests the blocks were given frequently to quiet him and to test his general emotional state. They were always removed from sight when the process of conditioning was under way.

2. Joint stimulation with rat and sound. Started, then fell over immediately to right side. No crying.

3. Joint stimulation. Fell to right side and rested upon hands, with head turned away from rat. No crying.

4. Joint stimulation. Same reaction.

5. Rat suddenly presented alone. Puckered face, whimpered and withdrew body sharply to the left.

6. Joint stimulation. Fell over immediately to right side and began to whimper.

7. Joint stimulation. Started violently and cried, but did not fall over.

8. Rat alone. *The instant the rat was shown the baby began to cry. Almost instantly he turned sharply to the left, fell over on left side, raised himself on all fours and began to crawl away so rapidly that he was caught with difficulty before reaching the edge of the table.*

This was as convincing a case of a completely conditioned fear response as could have been theoretically pictured. In all seven joint stimulations were given to bring about the complete reaction. It is not unlikely had the sound been of greater intensity or of a more complex clang character that the number of joint stimulations might have been materially reduced. Experiments designed to define the nature of the sounds that will serve best as emotional stimuli are under way.

II. When a conditioned emotional response has been established for one object, is there a transfer? Five days later Albert was again brought back into the laboratory and tested as follows:

11 Months 15 Days

1. Tested first with blocks. He reached readily for them, playing with them as usual. This shows that there has been no general transfer to the room, table, blocks, etc.

2. Rat alone.   Whimpered immediately, withdrew right hand and turned head and trunk away.

3. Blocks again offered.   Played readily with them, smiling and gurgling.

4. Rat alone.   Leaned over to the left side as far away from the rat as possible, then fell over, getting up on all fours and scurrying away as rapidly as possible.

5. Blocks again offered.   Reached immediately for them, smiling and laughing as before.

The above preliminary test shows that the conditioned response to the rat had carried over completely for the five days in which no tests were given. The question as to whether or not there is a transfer was next taken up.

6. Rabbit alone.   The rabbit was suddenly placed on the mattress in front of him.   The reaction was pronounced.   Negative responses began at once.   He leaned as far away from the animal as possible, whimpered, then burst into tears.   When the rabbit was placed in contact with him he buried his face in the mattress, then got up on all fours and crawled away, crying as he went.   This was a most convincing test.

7. The blocks were next given him, after an interval.   He played with them as before.   It was observed by four people that he played far more energetically with them than ever before.   The blocks were raised high over his head and slammed down with a great deal of force.

8. Dog alone.   The dog did not produce as violent a reaction as the rabbit. The moment fixation occurred the child shrank back and as the animal came nearer he attempted to get on all fours but did not cry at first.   As soon as the dog passed out of his range of vision he became quiet.   The dog was then made to approach the infant's head (he was lying down at the moment). Albert straightened up immediately, fell over to the opposite side and turned his head away.   He then began to cry.

9. The blocks were again presented.   He began immediately to play with them.

10. Fur coat (seal).   Withdrew immediately to the left side and began to fret.   Coat put close to him on the left side, he turned immediately, began to cry and tried to crawl away on all fours.

11. Cotton wool.   The wool was presented in a paper package.   At the end the cotton was not covered by the paper.   It was placed first on his feet. He kicked it away but did not touch it with his hands.   When his hand was laid on the wool he immediately withdrew it but did not show the shock that the animals or fur coat produced in him.   He then began to play with the paper, avoiding contact with the wool itself.   He finally, under the impulse of the manipulative instinct, lost some of his negativism to the wool.

12. Just in play W. put his head down to see if Albert would play with his hair.   Albert was completely negative.   Two other observers did the same thing.   He began immediately to play with their hair.   W. then brought the Santa Claus mask and presented it to Albert.   He was again pronouncedly negative.

11 Months 20 Days

1. Blocks alone. Played with them as usual.
2. Rat alone. Withdrawal of the whole body, bending over to left side, no crying. Fixation and following with eyes. The response was much less marked than on first presentation the previous week. It was thought best to freshen up the reaction by another joint stimulation.
3. Just as the rat was placed on his hand the rod was struck. Reaction violent.
4. Rat alone. Fell over at once to left side. Reaction practically as strong as on former occasion but no crying.
5. Rat alone. Fell over to left side, got up on all fours and started to crawl away. On this occasion there was no crying, but strange to say, as he started away he began to gurgle and coo, even while leaning far over to the left side to avoid the rat.
6. Rabbit alone. Leaned over to left side as far as possible. Did not fall over. Began to whimper but reaction not so violent as on former occasions.
7. Blocks again offered. He reached for them immediately and began to play.

All of the tests so far discussed were carried out upon a table supplied with a mattress, located in a small, well-lighted dark-room. We wished to test next whether conditioned fear responses so set up would appear if the situation were markedly altered. We thought it best before making this test to freshen the reaction both to the rabbit and to the dog by showing them at the moment the steel bar was struck. It will be recalled that this was the first time any effort had been made to directly condition response to the dog and rabbit. The experimental notes are as follows:

8. The rabbit at first was given alone. The reaction was exactly as given in test (6) above. When the rabbit was left on Albert's knees for a long time he began tentatively to reach out and manipulate its fur with forefingers. While doing this the steel rod was struck. A violent fear reaction resulted.
9. Rabbit alone. Reaction wholly similar to that on trial (6) above.
10. Rabbit alone. Started immediately to whimper, holding hands far up, but did not cry. Conflicting tendency to manipulate very evident.
11. Dog alone. Began to whimper, shaking head from side to side, holding hands as far away from the animal as possible.
12. Dog and sound. The rod was struck just as the animal touched him. A violent negative reaction appeared. He began to whimper, turned to one side, fell over and started to get up on all fours.
13. Blocks. Played with them immediately and readily.

On this same day and immediately after the above experiment Albert was taken into the large well-lighted lecture room belonging to the laboratory. He was placed on a table in the center of the room immediately under the skylight. Four people were present. The situation was thus very different from that which obtained in the small dark room.

1. Rat alone.   No sudden fear reaction appeared at first.   The hands, however, were held up and away from the animal.   No positive manipulatory reactions appeared.

2. Rabbit alone.   Fear reaction slight.   Turned to left and kept face away from the animal but the reaction was never pronounced.

3. Dog alone.   Turned away but did not fall over.   Cried.   Hands moved as far away from the animal as possible.   Whimpered as long as the dog was present.

4. Rat alone.   Slight negative reaction.

5. Rat and sound.   It was thought best to freshen the reaction to the rat. The sound was given just as the rat was presented.   Albert jumped violently but did not cry.

6. Rat alone.   At first he did not show any negative reaction.   When rat was placed nearer he began to show negative reaction by drawing back his body, raising his hands, whimpering, etc.

7. Blocks.   Played with them immediately.

8. Rat alone.   Pronounced withdrawal of body and whimpering.

9. Blocks.   Played with them as before.

10. Rabbit alone.   Pronounced reaction.   Whimpered with arms held high, fell over backward and had to be caught.

11. Dog alone.   At first the dog did not produce the pronounced reaction. The hands were held high over the head, breathing was checked, but there was no crying.   Just at this moment the dog, which had not barked before, barked three times loudly when only about six inches from the baby's face. Albert immediately fell over and broke into a wail that continued until the dog was removed.   The sudden barking of the hitherto quiet dog produced a marked fear response in the adult observers!

From the above results it would seem that emotional transfers do take place.   Furthermore it would seem that the number of transfers resulting from an experimentally produced conditioned emotional reaction may be very large.   In our observations we had no means of testing the complete number of transfers which may have resulted.

III. The effect of time upon conditioned emotional responses.   We have already shown that the conditioned emotional response will continue for a period of one week.   It was desired to make the time test longer. In view of the imminence of Albert's departure from the hospital we could not make the interval longer than one month.   Accordingly no further emotional experimentation was entered into for thirty-one days after the above test.   During the month, however, Albert was brought weekly to the laboratory for tests upon right and left-handedness, imitation, general development, etc.   No emotional tests whatever were given and during the whole month his regular nursery routine was maintained in the Harriet Lane Home.   The notes on the test given at the end of this period are as follows:

1 Year 21 Days

1. Santa Claus mask.   Withdrawal, gurgling, then slapped at it without touching.   When his hand was forced to touch it, he whimpered and cried. His hand was forced to touch it two more times.   He whimpered and cried on both tests.   He finally cried at the mere visual stimulus of the mask.

2. Fur coat.   Wrinkled his nose and withdrew both hands, drew back his whole body and began to whimper as the coat was put nearer.   Again there was the strife between withdrawal and the tendency to manipulate.   Reached tentatively with left hand but drew back before contact had been made.   In moving his body to one side his hand accidentally touched the coat.   He began to cry at once, nodding his head in a very peculiar manner (this reaction was an entirely new one).   Both hands were withdrawn as far as possible from the coat.   The coat was then laid on his lap and he continued nodding his head and whimpering, withdrawing his body as far as possible, pushing the while at the coat with his feet but never touching it with his hands.

3. Fur coat.   The coat was taken out of his sight and presented again at the end of a minute.   He began immediately to fret, withdrawing his body and nodding his head as before.

4. Blocks.   He began to play with them as usual.

5. The rat.   He allowed the rat to crawl towards him without withdrawing.   He sat very still and fixated it intently.   Rat then touched his hand. Albert withdrew it immediately, then leaned back as far as possible but did not cry.   When the rat was placed on his arm he withdrew his body and began to fret, nodding his head.   The rat was then allowed to crawl against his chest.   He first began to fret and then covered his eyes with both hands.

6. Blocks.   Reaction normal.

7. The rabbit.   The animal was placed directly in front of him.   It was very quiet.   Albert showed no avoiding reactions at first.   After a few seconds he puckered up his face, began to nod his head and to look intently at the experimenter.   He next began to push the rabbit away with his feet, withdrawing his body at the same time.   Then as the rabbit came nearer he began pulling his feet away, nodding his head, and wailing "da da."   After about a minute he reached out tentatively and slowly and touched the rabbit's ear with his right hand, finally manipulating it.   The rabbit was again placed in his lap.   Again he began to fret and withdrew his hands.   He reached out tentatively with his left hand and touched the animal, shuddered and withdrew the whole body.   The experimenter then took hold of his left hand and laid it on the rabbit's back.   Albert immediately withdrew his hand and began to suck his thumb.   Again the rabbit was laid in his lap.   He began to cry, covering his face with both hands.

8. Dog.   The dog was very active.   Albert fixated it intensely for a few seconds, sitting very still.   He began to cry but did not fall over backwards as on his last contact with the dog.   When the dog was pushed closer to him he at first sat motionless, then began to cry, putting both hands over his face.

These experiments would seem to show conclusively that directly conditioned emotional responses as well as those conditioned by transfer persist, although with a certain loss in the intensity of the reaction, for a longer period than one month.   Our view is that they persist and modify personality throughout life.   It should be recalled again that Albert was of an extremely phlegmatic type.   Had he been emotionally unstable probably both the directly conditioned response and those transferred would have persisted throughout the month unchanged in form.

IV. "Detachment" or removal of conditioned emotional responses. Unfortunately Albert was taken from the hospital the day the above tests were made.   Hence the opportunity of building up an experimental technique by means of which we could remove the conditioned emotional responses was denied us.   Our own view, expressed above, which is possibly not very well grounded, is that these responses in the home environment are likely to persist indefinitely, unless an accidental method for removing them is hit upon.   The importance of establishing some method must be apparent to all.   Had the opportunity been at hand we should have tried out several methods, some of which we may mention.   (1) Constantly confronting the child with those stimuli which called out the responses in the hopes that habituation would come in corresponding to "fatigue" of reflex when differential reactions are to be set up.   (2) By trying to "recondition" by showing objects calling out fear responses (visual) and simultaneously stimulating the erogenous zones (tactual). We should try first the lips, then the nipples and as a final resort the sex organs.   (3) By trying to "recondition" by feeding the subject candy or other food just as the animal is shown.   This method calls for the food control of the subject.   (4) By building up "constructive" activities around the object by imitation and by putting the hand through the motions of manipulation.   At this age imitation of overt motor activity is strong, as our present but unpublished experimentation has shown.

INCIDENTAL OBSERVATIONS

(a) Thumb sucking as a compensatory device for blocking fear and noxious stimuli.   During the course of these experiments, especially in the final test, it was noticed that whenever Albert was on the verge of tears or emotionally upset generally he would continually thrust his thumb into his mouth.   The moment the hand reached the mouth he became impervious to the stimuli producing fear.   Again and again while the motion pictures were being made at the end of the thirty-day rest period, we had to remove the thumb from his mouth before the conditioned response could be obtained.   This method of blocking noxious and emotional stimuli (fear and rage) through erogenous stimulation seems to persist from birth onward. Very often in our experiments upon the work adders[1] with infants under ten days of age the same reaction appeared. When at work upon the adders both of the infant's arms are under slight restraint. Often rage appears. They begin to cry, thrashing their arms and legs about. If the finger gets into the mouth crying ceases at once. The organism thus apparently from birth, when under the influence of love stimuli is blocked to all others.[2] This resort to sex stimulation when under the influence of noxious and emotional situations, or when the individual is restless and idle, persists throughout adolescent and adult life. Albert, at any rate, did not resort to thumb sucking except in the presence of such stimuli. Thumb sucking could immediately be checked by offering him his blocks. These invariably called out active manipulation instincts. It is worth while here to call attention to the fact that Freud's conception of the stimulation of erogenous zones as being the expression of an original "pleasure" seeking principle may be turned about and possibly better described as a compensatory (and often conditioned) device for the blockage of noxious and fear and rage producing stimuli.

(b) Equal primacy of fear, love and possibly rage. While in general the results of our experiment offer no particular points of conflict with Freudian concepts, one fact out of harmony with them should be emphasized. According to proper Freudians sex (in our terminology, love) is the principal emotion in which conditioned responses arise which later limit and distort personality. We wish to take sharp issue with this view on the basis of the experimental evidence we have gathered. Fear is as primal a factor as love in influencing personality. Fear does not gather its potency in any derived manner from love. It belongs to the original and inherited nature of man. Probably the same may be true of rage although at present we are not so sure of this.

The Freudians twenty years from now, unless their hypotheses change, when they come to analyze Albert's fear of a seal skin coat—assuming that he comes to analysis at that age—will probably tease from him the recital of a dream which upon their analysis will show that Albert at three years of age attempted to play with the pubic hair of the mother and was scolded violently for it. (We are by no means denying that this might in some other case condition it.) If the analyst has sufficiently prepared

[1] A work adder is a work-measuring device which sums up and indicates the total amount of work done by a series of muscular contractions.

[2] The stimulus to love in infants according to our view is stroking of the skin, lips, nipples, and sex organs, patting and rocking, picking up, etc. Patting and rocking (when not conditioned) are probably equivalent to actual stimulation of the sex organs. In adults, of course, as every lover knows, vision, audition, and olfaction soon become conditioned by joint stimulation with contact and kinaesthetic stimuli.

Albert to accept such a dream when found as an explanation of his avoiding tendencies, and if the analyst has the authority and personality to put it over, Albert may be fully convinced that the dream was a true revealer of the factors which brought about the fear.

It is probable that many of the phobias in psychopathology are true conditioned emotional reactions either of the direct or the transferred type. One may possibly have to believe that such persistence of early conditioned responses will be found only in persons who are constitutionally inferior. Our argument is meant to be constructive. Emotional disturbances in adults cannot be traced back to sex alone. They must be retraced along at least three collateral lines—to conditioned and transferred responses set up in infancy and early youth in all three of the fundamental human emotions.

---

3. The Laws of Learning*

Related selection: 1

A GENERATION of American teachers and teachers of teachers were nurtured on the psychology of Thorndike. His books on educational psychology are monumental and were, at the time of publication, a synthesis of knowledge about learning. In the selection that follows he reviews the laws of learning from an earlier book and then sets forth the position that learning is making connections. The ideas contained in these two short excerpts shaped the practices of many teachers for years and are still an important force in American education.

THE INTELLECT, character and skill possessed by any man is the product of certain original tendencies and the training which they have received. His eventual nature is the development of his original nature in the environment which it has had. Human nature in general is the result of the original nature of man, the laws of learning, and the forces of nature amongst which man lives and learns.

In a previous volume the original tendencies of man as a species were listed and described. It was shown that these constitute an enormous

* From Edward L. Thorndike, *The Psychology of Learning, Educational Psychology*, vol. II (Teachers College, Columbia University, 1913), pp. 1–5, 54–56. Reprinted by permission of the publisher.

Professor Thorndike (1874–1949) was for over thirty-five years Professor of Educational Psychology at Teachers College, Columbia University. He served as president of the American Psychological Association in 1912.

fund of *connections* or *bonds* of varying degrees of directness and strength between the *situations* furnished by physical forces, plants, animals and the behavior of other men and the *responses* of which the human creature is capable. Many of these tendencies are notably modifiable; and some of them—such as vocalization, manipulation, curiosity, "doing something to have something happen," and "making a variety of responses to an annoying state of affairs which continues in spite of this, that and the other responses"—are veritable hot-beds for the growth of learned habits.

These original human tendencies include also certain ones whereby modifiability or learning itself is possible. These are best thought of in the form of the three laws of Readiness, Exercise and Effect. The Law of Readiness is: When any conduction unit is in readiness to conduct, for it to do so is satisfying. When any conduction unit is not in readiness to conduct, for it to conduct is annoying. When any conduction unit is in readiness to conduct, for it *not* to do so is annoying. By a satisfying state of affairs is meant one which the animal does nothing to avoid, often doing things which maintain or renew it. By an annoying state of affairs is meant one which the animal does nothing to preserve, often doing things which put an end to it.

The Law of Exercise comprises the laws of *Use* and *Disuse*.

The Law of Use is: When a modifiable connection is made[1] between a situation and a response, that connection's strength is, other things being equal, increased. By the strength of a connection is meant roughly the probability that the connection will be made when the situation recurs. Greater probability that a connection will be made means a greater probability for the same time, or an equal probability, but for a longer time.[2] This probability in any case would be for the recurrence of the connection, supposing all other conditions—of general health, general or special fatigue, interest, time of day, distraction by competing tendencies, and the like—to be equal. Furthermore, in certain cases, where the probability that the connection will be made as the result of the mere presence of the situation is zero, the connection still may exist with a measurable degree of strength, shown by the fact that it can be remade more readily.[3] Also, in

[1] The vigor and duration of each "making" of the connection count, as well as the number of times that it is made.

[2] Thus, a certain greater strength of the connection between the situation "*What is the square of 16?*" and the response "*256*" may mean that the probability of that response to that situation is now ninety out of a hundred instead of sixty out of a hundred; or that it is ninety-nine out of a hundred for fifty days hence instead of for twenty days hence.

[3] Thus, though a man was utterly unable to give the English equivalent of a hundred Greek words, both on January 1, 1905, and on January 1, 1910, he might have been able to relearn them in thirty minutes in 1905, but only in sixty minutes in 1910.

certain cases in each of which the probability that the connection will be made is 100 per cent, the connections still may exist with different degrees of strength, shown by the fact that the probability of 100 per cent will hold for a week only or for a year; will succumb to a slight, or prevail over a great, distraction; or will otherwise show little or much strength. Thus, if the reader will read and repeat *miscob raltof* once or twice he may be apparently as able to supply the *raltof* when *miscob* is presented as if he had read and repeated these words a thousand times: but the future history of the two connections would reveal their differences in strength.

Ultimately degrees of strength of a connection in behavior will be defined as degrees of some anatomical or physiological fact whereby synapses between neurones differ in intimacy.

Varying symptoms that we now refer to the "strength" of a connection will then each appear as a consequence of this difference in the neurones concerned. For the present, greater strength has to mean either a greater percentage of occurrence under equal conditions outside of itself; or an equal percentage of occurrence for a longer time, or against greater competition; or a readier reëstablishment to equal strength (tested in any of the above ways); or some even more subtle and indirect effects on behavior.

It should be borne in mind also that the connection is often a compound of several connections each having possibly a different degree of strength. Thus, the connection between the situation, *Understanding of and desire to fulfill the command, "Write that man's full name,"* and the response of writing *Jonathan Edwards Leighton* is multiple. One of the names may be remembered and the other not; the bond productive of the general structure of the name may be strong, but all the others very weak, with the result that *Timothy Williams Damon* is the best that can be done; similarly for many variations in completeness, spelling, and so on. The actual physiological bond in even the apparently most single connections is doubtless a compound, and subject to variation by varying unevenly in its different parts as well as by an equal strengthening or weakening of them all.

The Law of Disuse is: When a modifiable connection is *not* made between a situation and a response during a length of time, that connection's strength is decreased. The explanations and qualifications stated in connection with the Law of Use apply here also.

The Law of Effect is: When a modifiable connection between a situation and a response is made and is accompanied or followed by a satisfying state of affairs, that connection's strength is increased: When made and accompanied or followed by an annoying state of affairs, its strength is decreased. The strengthening effect of satisfyingness (or the weakening effect of annoyingness) upon a bond varies with the closeness of the connection between it and the bond. This closeness or intimacy of association of the satisfying (or annoying) state of affairs with the bond in question may be the result of nearness in time or of attentiveness to the situation, response and satisfying event in question. "Strength" means the same here as in the case of the Law of Use.

These laws were briefly explained and illustrated in the previous volume. By their action original tendencies are strengthened, preserved, weakened, or altogether abolished; old situations have new responses bound to them and old responses are bound to new situations; and the inherited fund of instincts and capacities grows into a multitude of habits, interests and powers. They are the agents by which man acquires connections productive of behavior suitable to the environment in which he lives. *Adaptation, adjustment, regulative change,* and all other similar terms descriptive of successful learning, refer to their effects.

A man's intellect, character and skill is the sum of his tendencies to respond to situations and elements of situations. The number of different situation-response connections that make up this sum would, in an educated adult, run well up into the millions. Consequently, in place of any list of these detailed tendencies to make responses r_1, r_2, r_3, etc., to each particular situation, we may summarize the man in terms of broader traits or functions, such as "knowledge of German," "honesty," "speed in writing," "love of music," "memory for figures," "fidelity of visual images of faces," and the like.

In educational theories of human learning, and still more in the actual control of it by school practice, these larger traits or functions—these knowledges, powers, conducts, interests and skills rather than the elementary connections and readinesses of which they are composed, are commonly the subjects of discussion and experiment. Psychological theory and experimentation have also been engaged with traits or functions each of which denotes a group of elementary tendencies, though the traits or functions or abilities which have been investigated by psychologists are usually narrower than those just listed. For example, amongst the functions which have been somewhat elaborately studied are "rapidity in tapping as with a telegraph key," "the delicacy of discrimination of pitch," "ability to grasp and retain a series of nonsense syllables," "skill in tossing balls," and "interest in puzzles."

Facts concerning the nature of such "traits" or "functions" or "abilities" and their improvement by practice have been accumulating very rapidly in the course of the last fifteen years. To present and interpret these

facts is the second task of this volume, and the one to which the majority
of its pages will be assigned.

.   .   .   .   .

MENTAL FUNCTIONS

Learning is connecting, and man is the great learner primarily because
he forms so many connections.   The processes operating in a man of
average capacity to learn, and under the conditions of modern civilized
life, soon change the man into a wonderfully elaborate and intricate system of connections.   There are millions of them.   They include connections with subtle abstract elements or aspects or constituents of things and
events, as well as with the concrete things and events themselves.

Any one thing or element has many different bonds, each in accordance
with one of many "sets" or attitudes, which co-act with it to determine response.   Besides the connections leading to actual conduction in
neurones, there are those which lead to greater or less readiness to conduct, and so determine what shall satisfy or annoy in any given case.

The bonds productive of observable motor responses—such as speech,
gesture, or locomotion, are soon outnumbered by those productive, directly and at the time, of only the inner, concealed responses in the
neurones themselves to which what we call sensations, intellectual attention, images, ideas, judgments, and the like, are due.   The bonds productive of motor responses also include a far richer equipment than we are
accustomed to list.   Man's life is chock-full of evanescent, partly made,
and slurred movements.   These appear in so-called "inner" speech, the
tensions of eyes and throat in so-called intellectual attention, and the like.

The bonds lead not only from external situations—facts outside the
man—to responses in him, and from situations in him to acts by which he
changes outside nature, but also from one condition or fact or event in
him to another and so on in long series.   Of the connections to be
studied in man's learning an enormous majority begin and end with
some state of affairs within the man's own brain—are bonds between
one mental fact and another.

The laws whereby these connections are made are significant for education and all other branches of human engineering.   Learning is connecting; and teaching is the arrangement of situations which will lead to
desirable bonds and make them satisfying.   A volume could well be
written showing in detail just what bonds certain exercises in arithmetic,
spelling, German, philosophy, and the like, certain customs and laws,
certain moral and religious teachings, and certain occupations and amuse-
ments, tend to form in men of given original natures; or how certain de-

sired bonds could economically be formed.   Such would be one useful portion of an Applied Psychology of Learning or Science of Education.

The psychology of learning might also properly take as its task the explanation of how, starting from any exactly defined original nature, the bonds have been formed which cause the man in question to make such and such movements, attend to this rather than that feature of an object, have such and such ideas in response to a given problem, be satisfied with some of them and reject others, enjoy this picture, abstract numerical relations from a certain state of affairs, and so on through all the acquisitions which his life of learning comprises.   Psychology might seek to list the bonds and elements of bonds which account for his habits, associations of ideas, abstractions, inferences, tastes and the rest, might measure the strength of each, discover their relations of facilitation and inhibition, trace their origins, and prophesy their future intrinsic careers and their effects in determining what new bonds or modifications of old bonds any given situation will form.   As a geologist uses the laws of physics and chemistry to explain the modifications of the earth's surface, so a psychologist might use the laws of readiness, exercise, and effect to explain the modifications in a man's nature—in his knowledge, interests, habits, skill, and powers of thought or appreciation.   This task is, however, one for the future.

The process of learning is one of simple making and keeping connections and readinesses to conduct, but the result is a mixture of organized and unorganized tendencies that, even in an average three-year-old child, baffles description and prophecy.   No one has ever even listed the tendencies to respond of any one human creature above that age and of average capacity to learn, nor even begun to trace the history of their acquisition.

What psychology has done is to consider certain vaguely defined groups of tendencies, describing them roughly and observing how they change in certain important respects, notably in their efficiency in producing some desired result in living.   The terms, *intellect, character, skill,* and *temperament,* thus more or less well separate off four great groups of connections in a man.   Within the sphere of intellect, the terms, *information, habits, powers, interests* and *ideals,* go a step further in delimiting certain groups of connections.   The terms, *ability to add, ability to read, interest in music, courage,* and *business honesty,* are samples of compound tendencies or groups of connections much narrower than those listed above, and cutting across them in many ways.

4. Perception Research and Audio-Visual Education*

Related selections: 10, 17, 29

RECENT research in perception has caused students in education to re-examine much of what they formerly believed not only in respect to use of audio-visual aids to learning but also in other aspects of learning.   Although this article is chiefly concerned with the implications of perception studies for the use of audio-visual materials, it shows that perception is a governing factor in all learning.   If one perceives even material objects in terms of his prior experiences, then how individualized must be his view of himself, of others, and of the complex situation in which he finds himself and others?   The influence of the demonstrations described here and others like them has been felt in the development of personality theory.

PSYCHOLOGICAL research in the field of perception is obviously of great importance to the scientific development and use of visual materials in education.   Visual education rests upon the assumption that people learn from what they see, that visual experience influences behavior, and that instruction can be improved by enabling people to look at objects and pictures under appropriate circumstances, and in connection with other varieties of experience.   We have experimental evidence to show that broadening the base of perceptual experience improves learning.   Why this is so can perhaps be explained, crudely, although we are frequently inclined to take it for granted.   But we still have much to learn before visual presentations can be used as precision tools in communication and teaching.   In order to gain a better understanding of visual education we must first know what happens when we perceive.

Perhaps at no time in the past have psychologists shown greater and more wide-spread interest in the problem of perception.   Much experimental work is going on, and along with it, much discussion of the theoretical issues involved.   Various approaches and lines of development are represented.   Experimental psychologists still support a constant line of interest in the physiological aspect of perception, but a recent and

* Kenneth Norberg, "Perception Research and Audio-Visual Education," Audio-Visual Communication Review, vol. I (Winter, 1953), pp. 18–29.   Reprinted by permission of author and publisher.   Pictures and diagrams reprinted by permission of Franklin P. Kilpatrick, Institute for Associated Research, Princeton.
    Dr. Norberg (1909—) is Associate Professor of Education and Coordinator of Audio-Visual Services, Sacramento State College, California, and was formerly Director of the Audio-Visual Center, University of Chicago.

prominent trend seems to be toward an emphasis on a broader construction in which perception is viewed as an aspect of the total behavior of man
in the course of purposeful action.   One interesting and widely noted
example of the broader approach to perception is the development center-
ing in the work of the Hanover Institute and the well-known demonstrations which have grown out of the earlier experimentation of the Dart-
mouth Eye Institute.   The Hanover Institute is located at Hanover, New
Hampshire.   Adelbert Ames, Jr., is the director.

It is the purpose of this article to discuss the Hanover Institute demonstrations in perception with regard to possible implications for audio-
visual research.   In this brief analysis we shall rely mainly on the reports
and interpretative writings of a small cluster of men including Adelbert
Ames, Jr., Hadley Cantril, Merle Lawrence, Earl C. Kelley, and Ross
L. Mooney.   These sources have been selected and used either because
they were directly instrumental in the development of the demonstrations,
or have been actively concerned in their interpretation and/or educational
use.

Because the Hanover Institute experiments have already been widely
reported there will be no attempt to present a comprehensive description
here.   Instead, we shall describe very briefly a few representative demonstrations, mainly for purposes of orientation, and then proceed to the interpretation.

THE "CHAIR" DEMONSTRATION

The subject looks through a peep-hole in each of three different screens,
"A," "B," and "C."   Behind each of the screens he sees a chair, or what
appears to be one.   It is noted that behind each of the three screens the
observer sees an upright chair at a specific distance, of a specific size,
three-dimensional in form, with legs parallel and at right angles to the
seat.   Now, if the observer looks behind screen "A" he will find strings
arranged to give an outline of a chair.   Behind screen "B" he will see a
number of disconnected strings of different lengths and at different angles.
Behind screen "C" he will see strings in a plane which constitutes a perspective projection of a chair-shaped object.   What one sees if he looks
behind each screen (what is "actually there") is quite different from what
he sees as he looks through the several peep-holes.   (Figure 1.)

Now, it should be noted that the Hanover Institute demonstrations are
not merely experiments, in the usual sense.   They are actually demonstrations designed to bring out facts of perception, and to interpret and relate these facts in a gradually developing theoretical structure.   In the
case of each demonstration an interpretation is offered, and the interpre-

tations of the several demonstrations are fitted together in the cumulative development and elaboration of a theory of the nature of perception.

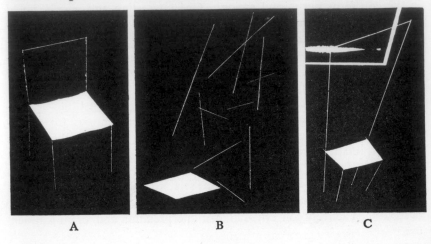

A   B   C

FIGURE 1

In the case of the "chair" demonstration the interpretations offered in the manuals and other writings connected with the Hanover Institute point out that the characteristics and qualities of the "chair" behind each of the three screens are obviously not in the object, itself, i.e., the arrangement of strings. The same stimulus pattern, or retinal image, may be produced by any one of an infinity of external conditions. Moreover, what is perceived, or seen, is not determined by the physiological stimulus pattern. Two conclusions are drawn: (a) The characteristics and qualities of things seen cannot be derived from the immediate outside world. (b) They cannot be derived from immediate physiological stimulus patterns. "This means, then, that the explanation of the nature of sensations must be looked for in the prior events that are related to the immediate events."

THE STAR-POINT DEMONSTRATIONS

In a completely dark room two star-points are viewed from a stationary position. These illuminated points are the same distance from the observer. One point is brighter. It appears to be nearer. The interpretation is that under these conditions the observer "assumes" the star-points to be identical and interprets the difference in brightness as a difference in distance from him.

In another demonstration the observer looks down (at an angle) at two star-points of equal brightness, one vertically above the other.   The observer senses the upper point as farther away.   If the situation is reversed so that the observer looks up at two points, the lower point will appear farther away.   "The apparent explanation of this phenomenon is that when we look down there is a probability that objects in the upper part of the field are farther away than objects in the lower part.   When we look up, the opposite is true."   (Figure 2.)

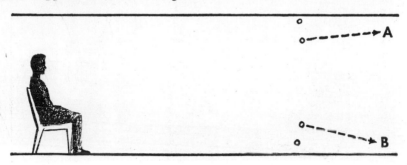

FIGURE 2

Although the star-points are actually equidistant from the observer, assumption from past experience causes A and B to appear more distant.

DEMONSTRATION WITH LINES

In a darkened room two vertical lines of different length, at the same distance from the observer, appear as though the shorter line were farther away, if the lines are positioned so that their middle points are on a level, B, Figure 3. However, if the shorter line is arranged below the longer one, it will appear closer, A, Figure 3.   "The apparent explanation of this phenomenon is that in the first relationship there is a greater probability that the two lines might represent identical things, e.g., telegraph poles, than in the second relationship where the longer line might represent a telephone pole and the shorter line a fence post."

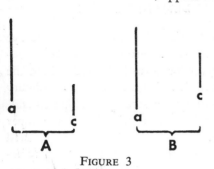

FIGURE 3

Now, if we repeat the first demonstration of the lines with the middle points on a common level, and give the observer a stick with a light on the end of it, directing him to touch the lines (first the shorter and then the longer) the following will result: the observer, after touching the shorter

FIGURE 4 A

line with the end of the stick, will at first fail to touch the longer line. After some experimental trying he will be able to touch the longer line, also. But by this time the two lines will appear to be at the same distance from him.

THE DISTORTED ROOM DEMONSTRATION

A distorted room is so designed that when it is viewed with one eye through a hole at a certain position in a screen the room appears rectangular and normal. (Even if the observer has already looked behind the screen and knows the room is distorted, it will still look like an ordinary room when he views it with one eye, through the screen.) (Figure 4.)

Now, if the observer takes a stick and tries to touch a ball in the upper left hand corner of the room after touching a ball in the upper right hand corner, he will be unable to do it, at first. After repeated tries he may become fairly successful in touching both balls. As this occurs *the appearance of the room will change.*

GENERAL INTERPRETATION OF THE DEMONSTRATIONS

Many of the Hanover Institute demonstrations have not been mentioned here. However, with this very brief introduction to the demon-

FIGURE 4B

strations we may now examine some of the main hypotheses which have
been advanced in explanation.

1. What is perceived is not determined by objective or environmental
conditions, in their own right.

2. What is perceived is not determined by the physiological stimulus
pattern.

3. *Given objective conditions and associated retinal stimulation, the
observer perceives whatever represents, for him, the most likely prognosis
for action based upon his experience.*   This prognosis is not a deliberate
judgment or consciously formed hypothesis.   Neither is it an arbitrary or
capricious fantasy without any necessary connection to what is "there."
But it is definitely something the perceiver makes for himself out of his
past experience and the present circumstances.   "The nature of what is
experienced is not a true portrayal of the existing physical environment; it
is only a 'guess' based upon all the previous experience the observer has
had with the impingements he has confronted."

4. What the observer brings to any particular occasion by way of his
perceptions reflects an "assumptive form world" built up out of his past
experiences.   This "assumptive form world" is modified as the prognoses
or predictions which we call perceptions are acted upon, and thereby
tested.

5. To understand perception we must look upon human behavior as a

"transaction" in which neither the individual nor the environment is regarded as an independent entity merely affecting or conditioning the other.

The functional character of perception which is brought out in the preceding statements is emphasized in the following definition of perception
given by Cantril:

> On the basis of the demonstrations, not to mention everyday life obser-
> vations, we may define a perception as an implicit awareness of the probable
> consequences an action might have for us with respect to carrying out some
> purpose that might have value for us.   Perceptions are conceived and given
> birth to in purposeful action that results from value-judgments.   And for
> whatever reason a perception may return to consciousness, it has in it im-
> plicitly the factors of action, purpose, and awareness of value.

Thus, at some risk of over-simplification we might sum up by saying
that the theory of perception developed in connection with the Hanover
Institute demonstrations insists first of all that perceiving be considered
always in the context of purposeful behavior, and that the question "what
is perceived?" must be answered as a directive for action reflecting some
set of assumptions as to what will happen if such and such actions are carried out.   Our perceivings are not merely guides for actions, or invita-
tions; they are essentially phases of purposeful action, itself.   They have
various degrees of reliability, but they are never direct copies of some
"reality" which is merely and independently "there."   Hence, they are essentially dynamic attitudes in constant change.

SOME POSSIBLE IMPLICATIONS

What are the implications of the Hanover Institute demonstrations for
audio-visual education?   This is a difficult question, and we will only attempt to suggest a partial answer. Perhaps the best answer, at this time,
is to indicate some questions that seem to arise out of the Hanover Institute demonstrations and the associated theoretical development.

1. *Can we actually learn anything from visual presentations as such?*
In the demonstration of the distorted room it has been noted that the observer can never get to see the room in its "true" shape just by looking at
it.   Merely looking, from a constant position, changes nothing—results
in no change in perception, no learning.   It is only when the observer
changes his position of observation, looks behind the screen, or attempts
to manipulate objects inside the room that some learning (involving
change in perception) results.   In more general terms, this would seem to
mean that we do not learn by merely seeing, but in the action, or course of
action, in which seeing is involved.   (It should be added that this would

not rule out learning *at the time* of visual presentation, nor the possibility that an appropriate visual cue might be critical to the carrying out of some action, or course of action, from which learning occurs.)

Of course, if the generalization just given follows from the demonstration of the distorted room, we would have to inquire what happens when something more than a single static perception is involved. True, nothing can be learned if we continue to stare at the room from a fixed perspective; we must actively explore the situation to gain new understanding. But what if we substitute for direct and active exploration a series of still pictures taken from different points of view? In this case behavior is still limited to merely "seeing" but it is apparent that some learning—some progressive change in understanding—might occur anyway. This is not difficult to explain, nor does it seem to contradict our generalization that merely looking at something does not constitute a learning experience. Would it be appropriate to say that we learn from a "look" at something only when this "look" stands in a *series* of experiences linked together in a course of purposeful action? This would take into account the fact that perception, itself, is a form of action, and that experiences that are primarily, or merely, visual, may (and very frequently do) assume critical value in carrying forward a line of purposeful action which results in learning. To say that learning may result from a visual presentation, as such, seems consistent with the Hanover Institute demonstrations *if* we include the presentation in question in a time-series of other experiences (not necessarily or exclusively visual), in which case we assign the learning effect to the series, primarily, and to the specific visual presentation only in so far as it represents a genuine link or culmination of that series.

2. *Is perception a cause of learning, or a dimension of the learning process?* This question is really a corollary to the first question. The Hanover Institute demonstrations bear out the thesis that our perceptions are learned. They are *results* of past experiences and present concerns. This, of course, does not rule out perception as a casual factor in learning, but it does suggest that we should not think of perception *merely* as cause, *nor* merely as a result of learning. The Hanover Institute demonstrations help to remind us that learning occurs in the course of purposeful action, involving the full range of behavior, over time.

It is probably more accurate and more fruitful to think of perception as an aspect or as a *dimension* of the learning process than merely as a "cause." A simple example may help to illustrate the point. Every child learns in due course of time that certain objects are dogs. This ordinary learning process involves a series of experiences during which certain sensory-motor, lingual, emotional, and other responses are developed. During the same series of experiences the child learns to perceive and to deal with certain external events as dogs. The child does not first perceive dogs and then learn to deal with dogs, or talk about them, although he may have crude perceptions of moving things, or animals-of-some-sort, prior to perceptions of dogs in a full and meaningful sense. The development of the perception is actually concurrent with the development of the interrelated motor habits, emotions, thinking, and talking that adds up to the "dog" behavior of the child. It is evident that children would not learn about dogs without sensory contacts with this animal. But what is more important is that there must be a *continuity* of perceptional experiences over time, during which there is constant interplay of sensory experience with the full range of other factors or "levels" of experience.

The implications for audio-visual research and theoretical development should be obvious.

3. *Are our visual perceptions of things more concrete than words?* Our "common sense" tells us our perceptions, including presentations of objects and events, come closer to the "concrete" than words. The Hanover Institute demonstrations seem to throw some doubt on this assumption. (Actually, a simple logical analysis reveals that words, *in general,* can hardly be regarded as less concrete than visual perceptions *in general.*) The theory growing out of the Hanover Institute demonstrations holds that every perception is a kind of summing up, a "weighted average," of the meanings of a vast number of particular sensory impingements, or stimulus-patterns, so that what we perceive at any given moment is not just a "concrete" object, in the sense of an independently existing thing, "out there," but a meaning which we derive from the past as appropriate to the present situation. In this sense, every perception is a kind of abstraction: a *pulling out* from the available fund of past experiences (the "assumptive form world") the "weighted average" meaning which represents the present "hypothesis" for action.

Now if perception is regarded in this way, it would appear that the differences between perceptions and words, as viewed by "common sense," should be reconsidered. Ross L. Mooney has commented on this problem as follows:

We are quite likely to assume that words and perceptions are two quite different sorts of things. However, it becomes quite clear, when we stop to think about it, that words and perceptions are the same kind of phenomena. Indeed, words are perceptions.

When we hear a spoken word, our ears are receiving sound waves; when we see a written word, our eyes are receiving light rays. As children, we come to know the "meaning" of a spoken word with the same operations we use to come to know the "meaning" of a squeaking door, a barking dog, or a clap of thunder. Similarly, we come to know the "meaning" of a written word with the same operations we use to come to know the "meaning" of a red ball, a square room, or a moving human figure.

This seems to outline a significant attitude to be taken into account by audio-visual specialists and research workers when dealing with the differences between visual and verbal methods of presentation. If words and perceptions are regarded as the same kind of psychological phenomena, it would follow that we must be careful in making any general assumptions about their relative abstractness or concreteness. It may be that all perceptions, including those we call "words," involve abstraction. Also, it may be that certain levels or kinds of abstractions necessarily involve lingual expression. But it seems overly crude, and possibly misleading, to generalize that perceptions (in the limited sense) are necessarily "concrete" as opposed to words. This is a highly complex problem which cannot be discussed in the limited space available here. However, it might be noted that so long as perceptions are regarded as yielding only prognoses for action they can hardly be regarded as providing the ultimate grasp which is considered to be the concrete object. In this sense, the concrete always lies one step beyond perception. It is not the object of present perception, and can be realized only by reconstruction of some event that has already occurred in the past.

4. *What are some of the larger implications of the Hanover Institute demonstrations?* One of the most striking features of the theoretical discussion growing out of the work of the Hanover Institute is the emphasis on wider application of the principles (hypotheses) revealed by the demonstrations. It is clear that those who have been associated with the Hanover demonstrations think of perception in very broad terms, and feel that the implications of the experiments cannot be limited to some range of experience regarded as merely or purely sensory in character. Cantril, for instance, points out that our social perceptions are governed by certain requirements brought out in the demonstrations, and his whole discussion of social perceptions in *The Why of Man's Experience* seems to reflect the assumption that the attitudes involved in social behavior can be interpreted along lines suggested by the demonstrations. The same general approach is observed in Earl C. Kelley's book, *Education for What Is Real,* which deals specifically with the educational implications of the Hanover Institute demonstrations. The more general implications of the demonstrations are also mentioned by John Dewey in the foreword to Kelley's book.

. . . There has been developed an experimental demonstration of the principles which govern the development of perceiving, principles which are formed, moreover to operate more deeply in the basic growth of human beings in their distinctive human capacity than any which have been previously laid bare.

Thus we are reminded that perception, in this general framework of interpretation, cuts across the entire range of human behavior including the social and the symbolic, that the story of our developing perceptions is also the story of learning. We are reminded that perception is never merely an appeal to the senses, while at the same time the effective engagement of the learner in lines of continuous action, by which his perceptions are changed and enriched, calls for an optimum level of carefully selected sensory contacts with whatever is pertinent to his developing purposes and interests.

The implications for audio-visual research and practice should not be too obscure. These seem to be some of them: We cannot say what an individual will learn from any discrete visual presentation, as such, and aside from a context of other experiences, in time. Learning results from a *series* of purposeful acts carried out with continuity of purpose and direction. All action is not overt or "physical," but to maintain and carry forward a line of purposeful action, in time, requires adequate conditions of sensory contact with the environment. We learn *from* visual presentations in so far as they make it possible, or easier, for us to carry out our purposes. As we learn *from* perceptions, and *to* new ways of perceiving things, our "assumptive form" world changes and this involves the most complex organizations of our behavior including social attitudes and conceptions.

We cannot learn without acting. We cannot act without perceiving.

---

5. The Idea of Learning as Development of Insight*

Related selections: 1, 6, 10

THE FOLLOWING article by Bayles is selected from a number of articles that have centered their attention on the study of insight in learning situations and have concluded that the development of in-

---

* Ernest E. Bayles, "The Idea of Learning as Development of Insight," *Educational Theory*, vol. II (April, 1952), pp. 65–71. Reprinted by permission of author and publisher.

Dr. Bayles (1896—) is Professor of Education at the University of Kansas. He has written widely in the field of education and is the author of several basic texts in high school science.

sight is the major factor in learning.   Is Bayles's position adequate for all kinds of learning?   Contrast the discussion of the role of repetitive drill and practice with Skinner's discussion in Selection 6.   A teacher's answers to the questions raised are crucial, for they will give direction to much of his effort in guiding learning in the classroom.

THEORY regarding the nature of learning lies close to the heart of teaching theory.   Lack of clarity regarding the former, whether in high degree or low, leads to corresponding lack of clarity regarding the latter.   This is not to say that learning theory is the whole of teaching theory; far from it. Theory regarding social organization and theory regarding the nature of subject matter are equally essential.   But, with the confusion which still surrounds current professional thinking regarding the nature of learning, further discussion of the question seems much in order.

Lack of clarity of the bond theory—of psychological connectionism— was brought home to me early in the twenties.   As a supervisor of practice teachers, I was supposed to help beginners achieve competence in handling the learning process.   But connectionist principles always pointed to wrong procedures.

Repetitive drill was obviously wrong.   Yet the path-wearing, bond-forming principle of conditioning, leading to supposedly lowered synaptic resistance along preferred neural pathways, pointed inexorably to that. Both the logic of the theory and the nature of teaching materials available at the time led inevitably to repetitive drill.

Then Gestalt theory, and relativism as a clear-cut psychological principle, began to present themselves for consideration.   Threads of clarity began to penetrate the confusion in thought, and order began to emerge. The books of Koffka, Koehler, and Wheeler appeared; then Bode's penetrating *Conflicting Psychologies of Learning*.   Afterwards, Thorndike reported that, on the basis of his research findings, repetition (*per se*) has little, if any, effect on learning and, although making no attempt to define the term, proposed the concept of "belongingness."

Looking at the matter through mid-twentieth century eyes, individuals appear to behave on the basis of the principle of least action; *to act in such a way as to try to achieve an adopted pattern of goals in the quickest and easiest way that they sense or comprehend as available under existing circumstances.*   In other words, we seem to be inherently lazy; to seek always the easiest way to get done what appears necessary or desirable. Laziness seems no longer to be intrinsically vicious.   It seems merely the wise thing to do something the easy instead of the hard way.   If we see an acquaintance taking a long way home, we are likely to suspect either his motives or his judgment.

INSIGHT AND THE PRINCIPLE OF LEAST ACTION

Reliance upon the principle of least action in the interpretation of behavior means that we base it upon three factors: *goal,* or what a person wants or intends to do; *confronting situation,* or what he will meet in proceeding to attain the goal; and *insight,* the way he sees or sizes up the situation with which he is confronted.   You will note that we do not say the quickest and easiest way available; we say the quickest and easiest way which is sensed or comprehended *as* available.   We do not take paths that we know nothing about.

What does this interpretation of behavior mean for learning?   Learning is repeatedly defined as a change in behavior.   And, when a person learns, he indeed undergoes a change in behavior.   He is likely to act quite differently from before.   But does every behavioral change mean learning?

A change in action or behavior will accompany a change in goal, even though no learning may have occurred.   Likewise, a change in behavior will accompany a change in confronting situation, even though no learning may have occurred.   Evidently, and this seems to be amply supported by experimental and experiential evidence though as yet not so recognized in psychological literature, learning represents and is confined to *a change in insight.*

The view that learning means development of insight, and that alone, is decidedly revolutionary.   Very few textbooks in educational psychology yet take this stand in a clear-cut way.   However, comparison of today's texts with those of a quarter-century ago or even a decade ago shows that they are coming to it.   About the last step in the transition is to argue that, although conditioning may be the way in some learning situations, that kind occurs very rarely, if at all, in school work.   Let us examine the idea of learning as development of insight.

THE MEANING OF "INSIGHT"

First, what do we mean by the term insight?   We do not mean any linguistic expression.   We refer to what lies back of any word statement; to that which one catches even before he has words to express it, such as the swing of a ball bat or an idea for which one cannot quite find the right word.   Perhaps insight should be defined as *a sense of, or feeling for, pattern.*   We may have words for it or we may not; it may be clear or it may be more or less confused; it may be true or it may be false, fruitful or unfruitful.   It is on the basis of what we see as being required by a situation that we design behavior.   That is what, for us, constitutes reality;

the real basis upon which we act in any and every case of intelligent behavior.

How does learning as development of insight differ from the notion of
learning as establishment or alteration of neural pathways?   To wear a
path requires continuous traversal of an area by way of a given line, without deviation.   That is the precise meaning, neurologically speaking, of
the so-called Law of Use.   Through use, resistance across a given synapse
is lowered and impulses cross it more easily afterwards.   This point is
vital to the path-wearing idea of conditioning, regardless of whether a
commitment is hazarded as to the nature of the resistance.   It was
neural paths of this kind which Lashley sought and failed to find.   Repeating a line of action always the same way until it is "stamped-in" is
what the concept has to mean if it means anything.   Repetitive drill is
another word for it.

On the other hand, development of insight means establishment of a
sense of, or feeling for, pattern.   It may require looking sharply into a
confronting situation, but imaginatively, in order to make the pattern
"jump out at you," as when we used to look for hidden faces in a cleverly
designed drawing or for stange animals in fleecy clouds.   Or it may require closing the eyes and trying intently to visualize a situation, possibly
not yet fully observed.   Then, catching the point, we act with precision
and exactitude.   It is less of learning by doing and more of learning by
seeing, even though with the mind's eye.   Emphasis, in the process of
learning, shifts from going through motions to conceptualization.

In working on a difficult violin passage, a learner needs first to study
the passage, figure out fingering which will lie best for the hand, imagine
the "feel" of the passage as a whole; then swing into execution.   Repeatedly have I had music teachers report to me with amazement the
results of tryouts of this kind on the parts of their students.   It was an
attack different from any used before, and the "hang" of it came with a
rush that they had never before witnessed.

A workman has to get the "heft" of an object before proceeding to move
it.   A batsman gets the feel of his bat before advancing to the plate and a
golfer the swing of his club before stepping up to the tee.   A child, approaching the multiplication process, needs to "get the sense of the matter"
before any attention whatsoever is given to speed in producing answers
for particular combinations.   The thought line probably needs to go from
addition to multiplication; first see multiplication as a form of addition.
If you add five fours together, how many will you have?   Therefore, five
fours make what?   Or, five times four equals what?   Take it easy; not
this fast.   Let each step "sink in" before taking the next.   Insights do
not form at the word, "Go!" although when they do form they practically

always come suddenly.   James employed the phrase, "flyings and perch-
ings."

THE PLACE OF PRACTICE

But, I am asked, shall we dispense with practice?   The answer is, of
course, that we shall not.   Because practice is to be something other than
repetitive stamping-in, does not mean no practice.   From the point of
view of learning as development of insight, the repeated efforts of practice
represent each time doing the thing differently from the way it was done
before.   Try it; see what happens; try to diagnose why it did not turn out
as intended; modify procedure in light of the diagnosis; try it again.   Each
trial is distinctly different from the previous ones; a step in a search for
the best way to do a thing.   Once that best way is caught—done with
a realization of *why* the doing achieved the desired end—then the matter
may be permitted to rest for a while.   Come back to it some time later—
a day, two days, a week, or more—just to see whether it still goes right.
If the point was really caught, later performances are very likely to be even
better than that or those at the time of arrival of insight.   If not, it is probable that the point was not really caught when it was thought to be.

It is not how many times a thing is done that counts.   It is the grasp the
learner has of it that makes the difference.   And this "grasp" is very much
of a mental phenomenon, whether the subject is basketball, woodwork,
appreciation of an art object, or mastery of a proposition in mathematics
or science.   Once one "gets the hang of a thing," the feel for pattern, one
does not have to repeat and repeat and repeat in order to make perfect.
There may, of course, be much else yet to be learned; more work to do.
But that should be analysed in terms of the additional insights to be gained,
and each subsequent insight attacked in the way just indicated.   We need
to get completely away from repetitive drill.   The present writer feels
thoroughly justified in insisting that, *whenever repetitive drill is invoked,
learning will suffer*.

Practice, which represents a search for insight, means persistently working with something new.   In spelling, for example, the policy of working
on a particular list of words until all of the words are known is to be almost,
if not completely, abandoned.   Instead, particular words are always to be
approached as typifying a certain spelling pattern, the pattern being what
is sought rather than a word for its own sake.   In the earlier stages, word-
lists need to be chosen on the basis of spelling patterns which they ex-
emplify.   Study will then represent a search for the hidden pattern and,
once discovered, other words will be sought which also conform.   Later,
words will be sought which seemingly should conform to the pattern, but

do not.   These, then, should be studied to see wherein they are divergent, to find why if possible, and to see whether the divergence is typical of other words as well.   If so, a statement of the divergence and something of when to expect it may possibly be incorporated in the original rule; e.g., *i* before *e* except after *c,* etc.

It will be noted that this represents a return to spelling rules, a practice abandoned during the teens.   It may well be that the abandonment worked to the detriment of instruction in spelling but, be that as it may, it should also be noted that there is a vital difference between former practice and the one here contemplated.   Formerly, the rule was learned more or less by rote.   Then the following list of words supposedly exemplifying the rule was learned, also more or less by rote.   Many were the pupils who failed to note the connection between the rule and the words which followed.   We propose that the words come first and that whatever rule is adopted be one worked out by the students and held only so long as it performs in a fairly satisfactory manner.   When, as vocabulary expands, an adopted rule becomes unsatisfactory, a new study is inaugurated and a new rule formulated.   And it must be remembered that, although we speak of "rules," we are really meaning basic insights, as previously defined.

It is true, of course, that the English language is bothersomely nonphonetic.   But this is far from completely so, in spite of what many so-called experts used to insist.   It is likely that at least 95 percent of words likely to be used can be handled in the above manner.   If the rest must be learned by rote, so be it; but even then a sound-pattern or a visual pattern can be sought.   It will be much better to learn only five percent by rote, if that be necessary, than to learn all in that manner.

We have dealt with spelling for what it typifies rather than for its own sake.   Study is focused upon "getting the idea," particular cases merely serving as a vehicle by way of which an insight is gained.   Once a child catches the phonetic signification of "at," he can handle "at" words whether he has met them before or not.   The kind of spelling instruction inaugurated under the aegis of connectionism took a child's attention completely away from sound-letter relationships.   If they were to be discovered at all, it had to be done by a child entirely on his own, in spite of his instruction rather than because of it. Small wonder we turned out a generation of poor spellers.

And here we may well inject a point of theory with reference to transfer of training.   Our suggestion is that an individual will transfer previous training (insights gained) if and whenever he sees a confronting situation as presenting an opportunity for transfer, and if his purposes at the time

make the transfer appear to him desirable.   Thus, again, it is not how
many times a thing is done that counts.   We re-employ an insight whenever we discover an opportunity and are disposed to take advantage of it.
Training will not transfer, even though opportunity offers, if the individual
does not recognize it as an opportunity, or if indisposed to take advantage
of the opportunity when recognized.   Therefore, training for transfer
requires, first, development of widely generalizable insights.   But it requires considerably more than that.   It also requires fertility of imagination, in order to wrest old learnings out of the limbo of forgotten things and
see them as again useable.   And it requires a set of suitable dispositions
(or goals), one being the disposition to search one's memory—to be self-
reliant and resourceful—when confronted with a situation seemingly new.

BELONGINGNESS AND REPETITION

Early in this paper we mentioned Thorndike's concept of *belongingness*.
His proposal, early in the thirties, was that belongingness must accompany
repetition; by itself, repetition has little if any effect.   But what is belongingness?   Thorndike did not say.   That it can, and should, mean insight
as we are using the term seems highly reasonable.   It may, in fact, seem
so reasonable or obvious that we may be thought by many as hypercritical
to say or imply that its original user should have defined it.   Yet here is a
case which shows exactly why words need to be defined with operational
clarity.

Thorndike's *operations* with reference to learning, even after his ad-
mission of belongingness, continued to include repetition—repetition in
the path-wearing sense.   In fact, it was *repetition with belongingness;*
repetition came first, belongingness was an adjunct.   Thus, the S-R*, re-
flex-arc principle remained intact, and connectionism remained in force.

It is exactly at this point that the insight theory parts company with connectionism, even though belongingness may be included. *Insights may be
gained without repetition,* and when they do no repetition is needed.
How many of us, who have sufficient insight to refuse to jump from a 50-
foot height, gained that insight by even a single repetition?   It may be
true that we learned it from lesser jumps, but the learning was by transfer
nonetheless.   Moreover, this is not an isolated case.   It is typical of the
bulk of human activity.   It represents the heart of habit-level action.
Whenever a confronting situation, and its meaning in terms of desirable
action, occur simultaneously in experience, correct action is possible
the first time; even though the action may not be taken.   If there is
any validity to the truism that life is forever new—that no line of action

* Stimulus-response.

is ever exactly twice the same—then we are continually having to act correctly the first time or be hopelessly incompetent. This is the point of R. H. Wheeler's repeated assertion that any psychology which fails to explain correct action the first time fails to explain human behavior at all.

There are many times, of course, when a situation and its meaning do not occur simultaneously in experience. This is a problem-case and reflective thought is in order. Or the anticipated meaning of a situation— the line of action first considered as appropriate thereto—does not turn out as anticipated. Then an alternative has to be sought. But the procedure in each case is much more accurately described by Dewey's "complete act of thought" than by Thorndike's "trial and error" process as Thorndike originally described it. Dewey's description was of a search for insight; Thorndike's was of gradual stamping in of a correct line of action through chance repetition of chance acts which later proved to be the right ones.

PROOF OF THE THEORY

Finally, we shall probably be asked what proof we have of the correctness of the insight theory of learning. Our answer is fairly simple. We rely upon the operational test. We deduce from the generalized theory the observable facts which, in given or particularized cases, the theory logically implies. *In the degree to which the facts turn out as anticipated* or deduced, the theory is taken as proven; proven in the sense of being demonstrated as dependable. Any theory which weathers this test better than competing theories is taken to be the better or best of those under consideration.

That the insight theory of learning has, so far, weathered this test is, I believe, a reasonable statement. Whenever, in connection with studies which have been made, sharp and precise deductions disclose the possibility of experimentally or experientially observable differences, the findings have consistently been such as to favor overwhelmingly the insight theory. It seems that the more painstaking or meticulous the analysis, the more convincing is the showing.

In summary, then, it seems that, if teaching is to be most effectual, the learning theory which should be employed is that which seeks consistently to develop insight. Procedural emphasis shifts from repetition to conceptualization, from learning by doing to learning by "seeing." Learning is not a function of the number of times an act is repeated. It is the feeling for pattern which is caught during a performance—the insight gained —that counts. Ten performances may have no effect and the eleventh one turn the trick. A teacher needs to look always for the "Oh! I see!"

response in whatever form it may become manifest. And it often comes after rehearsal periods are over; during a time of no performance at all. Many a time, of course, a learner or his teacher may feel that he has it when indeed he does not. But this merely indicates a need for caution against unjustified optimism. It does not deny the principle. Learning as development of insight does not mean elimination of practice, although over-all reduction of practice time—often marked reduction—may reasonably be universally expected if repetitional procedures have previously been employed. Learning as development of insight does mean that repetitive drill shall be eliminated completely; that it shall be no more.

---

6. The Science of Learning and the Art of Teaching*

Related selections: 1, 5, 7

SOME OF the work of Skinner on the need and value of reinforcement in learning is presented in this selection in such a way that it must be taken into account by all teachers. In view of what this research tells about reinforcement and in view of our ability to make machines and electronic devices capable of accomplishing so many tasks, the reader may well ponder the lack of such devices as teaching aids in our classrooms.

SOME PROMISING advances have recently been made in the field of learning. Special techniques have been designed to arrange what are called "contingencies of reinforcement"—the relations which prevail between behavior on the one hand and the consequences of that behavior on the other—with the result that a much more effectice control of behavior has been achieved. It has long been argued that an organism learns mainly by producing changes in its environment, but it is only recently that these changes have been carefully manipulated. In traditional devices for the study of learning—in the serial maze, for example, or in the T-

* B. F. Skinner, "The Science of Learning and the Art of Teaching," *Current Trends in Psychology and the Behavior Sciences* (Pittsburgh: University of Pittsburgh Press, 1955), pp. 38–58. Reprinted from *Harvard Educational Review,* vol. XXIV (Spring, 1954), pp. 86–87. Reprinted by permission of the author and publisher.

Dr. Skinner (1890—) is Professor of Psychology at Harvard University and a former president of the Eastern Psychological Association. His most recent books include *Walden Two* and *Science and Human Behavior.* He has conducted extensive research in the area of learning.

maze, the problem box, or the familiar discrimination apparatus—the effects produced by the organism's behavior are left to many fluctuating circumstances.   There is many a slip between the turn-to-the-right and the food-cup at the end of the alley.   It is not surprising that techniques of this sort have yielded only very rough data from which the uniformities demanded by an experimental science can be extracted only by averaging many cases.   In none of this work has the behavior of the individual organism been predicted in more than a statistical sense.   The learning processes which are the presumed object of such research are reached only through a series of inferences.   Current preoccupation with deductive systems reflects this state of the science.

Recent improvements in the conditions which control behavior in the field of learning are of two principal sorts.   The Law of Effect has been taken seriously; we have made sure that effects *do* occur and that they occur under conditions which are optimal for producing the changes called learning.   Once we have arranged the particular type of consequence called a reinforcement, our techniques permit us to shape up the behavior of an organism almost at will.   It has become a routine exercise to demonstrate this in classes in elementary psychology by conditioning such an organism as a pigeon.   Simply by presenting food to a hungry pigeon at the right time, it is possible to shape up three or four well-defined responses in a single demonstration period—such responses as turning around, pacing the floor in the pattern of a figure-8, standing still in a corner of the demonstration apparatus, stretching the neck, or stamping the foot.   Extremely complex performances may be reached through successive stages in the shaping process, the contingencies of reinforcement being changed progressively in the direction of the required behavior.   The results are often quite dramatic.   In such a demonstration one can *see* learning take place.   A significant change in behavior is often obvious as the result of a single reinforcement.

A second important advance in technique permits us to maintain behavior in given states of strength for long periods of time.   Reinforcements continue to be important, of course, long after an organism has learned *how* to do something, long after it has acquired behavior.   They are necessary to maintain the behavior in strength.   Of special interest is the effect of various schedules of intermittent reinforcement.   Charles B. Ferster and the author are currently preparing an extensive report of a five-year research program, sponsored by the Office of Naval Research, in which most of the important types of schedules have been investigated and in which the effects of schedules in general have been reduced to a few principles.   On the theoretical side we now have a fairly good idea of why a given schedule produces its appropriate performance.

On the practical side we have learned how to maintain any given level of activity for daily periods limited only by the physical exhaustion of the organism and from day to day without substantial change throughout its life. Many of these effects would be traditionally assigned to the field of motivation, although the principal operation is simply the arrangement of contingencies of reinforcement.

These new methods of shaping behavior and of maintaining it in strength are a great improvement over the traditional practices of professional animal trainers, and it is not surprising that our laboratory results are already being applied to the production of performing animals for commercial purposes. In a more academic environment they have been used for demonstration purposes which extend far beyond an interest in learning as such. For example, it is not too difficult to arrange the complex contingencies which produce many types of social behavior. Competition is exemplified by two pigeons playing a modified game of ping-pong. The pigeons drive the ball back and forth across a small table by pecking at it. When the ball gets by one pigeon, the other is reinforced. The task of constructing such a "social relation" is probably completely out of reach of the traditional animal trainer. It requires a carefully designed program of gradual changing contingencies and the skillful use of schedules to maintain the behavior in strength. Each pigeon is separately prepared for its part in the total performance, and the "social relation" is then arbitrarily constructed. The sequence of events leading up to this stable state are excellent material for the study of the factors important in nonsynthetic social behavior. It is instructive to consider how a similar series of contingencies could arise in the case of the human organism through the evolution of cultural patterns.

Cooperation can also be set up, perhaps more easily than competition. We have trained two pigeons to coordinate their behavior in a cooperative endeavor with a precision which equals that of the most skillful human dancers. In a more serious vein these techniques have permitted us to explore the complexities of the individual organism and to analyze some of the serial or coordinate behaviors involved in attention, problem solving, various types of self-control, and the subsidiary systems of responses within a single organism called "personalities." Some of these are exemplified in what we call multiple schedules of reinforcement. In general a given schedule has an effect upon the rate at which a response is emitted. Changes in the rate from moment to moment show a pattern typical of the schedule. The pattern may be as simple as a constant rate of responding at a given value, it may be a gradually accelerating rate between certain extremes, it may be an abrupt change from not responding at all to a given stable high rate, and so on. It has been shown that the performance characteristic of a given schedule can be brought under the control of a particular stimulus and that different performances can be brought under the control of different stimuli in the same organism. At a recent meeting of the American Psychological Association, Dr. Ferster and the author demonstrated a pigeon whose behavior showed the pattern typical of "fixed-interval" reinforcement in the presence of one stimulus and, alternately, the pattern typical of the very different schedule called "fixed ratio" in the presence of a second stimulus. In the laboratory we have been able to obtain performances appropriate to *nine* different schedules in the presence of appropriate stimuli in random alternation. When Stimulus 1 is present, the pigeon executes the performance appropriate to Schedule 1. When Stimulus 2 is present, the pigeon executes the performance appropriate to Schedule 2. And so on. This result is important because it makes the extrapolation of our laboratory results to daily life much more plausible. We are all constantly shifting from schedule to schedule as our immediate environment changes, but the dynamics of the control exercised by reinforcement remain essentially unchanged.

It is also possible to construct very complex *sequences* of schedules. It is not easy to describe these in a few words, but two or three examples may be mentioned. In one experiment the pigeon generates a performance appropriate to Schedule A where the reinforcement is simply the production of the stimulus characteristic of Schedule B, to which the pigeon then responds appropriately. Under a third stimulus, the bird yields a performance appropriate to Schedule C where the reinforcement in this case is simply the production of the stimulus characteristic of Schedule D, to which the bird then responds appropriately. In a special case, first investigated by L. B. Wyckoff, Jr., the organism responds to one stimulus where the reinforcement consists of the *clarification* of the stimulus controlling another response. The first response becomes, so to speak, an objective form of "paying attention" to the second stimulus. In one important version of this experiment, as yet unpublished, we could say that the pigeon is telling us whether it is "paying attention" to the *shape* of a spot of light or to its *color*.

One of the most dramatic applications of these techniques has recently been made in the Harvard Psychological Laboratories by Floyd Ratliff and Donald S. Blough, who have skillfully used multiple and serial schedules of reinforcement to study complex perceptual processes in the infrahuman organism. They have achieved a sort of psycho-physics without verbal instruction. In a recent experiment by Blough, for example, a pigeon draws a detailed dark-adaptation curve showing the characteristic breaks of rod and cone vision. The curve is recorded continuously in a single experimental period and is quite comparable with the curves of human subjects. The pigeon behaves in a way which, in the human case, we would not hesitate to describe by saying that it adjusts a very faint patch of light until it can just be seen.

In all this work, the species of the organism has made surprisingly little difference. It is true that the organisms studied have all been vertebrates, but they still cover a wide range. Comparable results have been obtained with pigeons, rats, dogs, monkeys, human children, and most recently, by the author in collaboration with Ogden R. Lindsley, human psychotic subjects. In spite of great phylogenetic differences, all these organisms show amazingly similar properties of the learning process. It should be emphasized that this has been achieved by analyzing the effects of reinforcement and by designing techniques which manipulate reinforcement with considerable precision. Only in this way can the behavior of the individual organism be brought under such precise control. It is also important to note that through a gradual advance to complex interrelations among responses, the same degree of rigor is being extended to behavior which would usually be assigned to such fields as perception, thinking, and personality dynamics.

From this exciting prospect of an advancing science of learning, it is a great shock to turn to that branch of technology which is most directly concerned with the learning process—education. Let us consider, for example, the teaching of arithmetic in the lower grades. The school is concerned with imparting to the child a large number of responses of a special sort. The responses are all verbal. They consist of speaking and writing certain words, figures, and signs which, to put it roughly, refer to numbers and to arithmetic operations. The first task is to shape up these responses—to get the child to pronounce and to write responses correctly, but the principal task is to bring this behavior under many sorts of stimulus control. This is what happens when the child learns to count, to recite tables, to count while ticking off the items in an assemblage of objects, to respond to spoken or written numbers by saying "odd," "even," "prime," and so on. Over and above this elaborate repertoire of numerical behavior, most of which is often dismissed as the product of rote learning, the teaching of arithmetic looks forward to those complex serial arrangements of responses involved in original mathematical thinking. The child must acquire responses of transposing, clearing fractions, and so on, which modify the order or pattern of the original material so that the response called a solution is eventually made possible.

Now, how is this extremely complicated verbal repertoire set up? In the first place, what reinforcements are used? Fifty years ago the answer would have been clear.   At that time educational control was still frankly aversive.   The child read numbers, copied numbers, memorized tables, and performed operations upon numbers to escape the threat of the birch rod or cane.   Some positive reinforcements were perhaps eventually derived from the increased efficiency of the child in the field of arithmetic and in rare cases some automatic reinforcement may have resulted from the sheer manipulation of the medium—from the solution of problems or the discovery of the intricacies of the number system.   But for the immediate purposes of education the child acted to avoid or escape punishment.   It was part of the reform movement known as progressive education to make the positive consequences more immediately effective, but any one who visits the lower grades of the average school today will observe that a change has been made, not from aversive to positive control, but from one form of aversive stimulation to another.   The child at his desk, filling in his workbook, is behaving primarily to escape from the threat of a series of minor aversive events—the teacher's displeasure, the criticism or ridicule of his classmates, an ignominious showing in a competition, low marks, a trip to the office "to be talked to" by the principal, or a word to the parent who may still resort to the birch rod.   In this welter of aversive consequences, getting the right answer is in itself an insignificant event, any effect of which is lost amid the anxieties, the boredom, and the aggressions which are the inevitable by-products of aversive control.

Secondly, we have to ask how the contingencies of reinforcement are arranged.   When is a numerical operation reinforced as "right"?   Eventually, of course, the pupil may be able to check his own answers and achieve some sort of automatic reinforcement, but in the early stages the reinforcement of being right is usually accorded by the teacher.   The contingencies she provides are far from optimal.   It can easily be demonstrated that, unless explicit mediating behavior has been set up, the lapse of only a few seconds between response and reinforcement destroys most of the effect.   In a typical classroom, nevertheless, long periods of time customarily elapse.   The teacher may walk up and down the aisle, for example, while the class is working on a sheet of problems, pausing here and there to say right or wrong.   Many seconds or minutes intervene between the child's response and the teacher's reinforcement.   In many cases—for example, when papers are taken home to be corrected —as much as 24 hours may intervene.   It is surprising that this system has any effect whatsoever.

A third notable shortcoming is the lack of a skillful program which moves forward through a series of progressive approximations to the final complex behavior desired.   A long series of contingencies is necessary to bring the organism into the possession of mathematical behavior most efficiently. But the teacher is seldom able to reinforce at each step in such a series because she cannot deal with the pupil's responses one at a time. It is usually necessary to reinforce the behavior in blocks of responses—as in correcting a work sheet or page from a workbook. The responses within such a block must not be interrelated. The answer to one problem must not depend upon the answer to another. The number of stages through which one may progressively approach a complex pattern of behavior is therefore small, and the task so much the more difficult. Even the most modern workbook in beginning arithmetic is far from exemplifying an efficient program for shaping up mathematical behavior.

Perhaps the most serious criticism of the current classroom is the relative infrequency of reinforcement. Since the pupil is usually dependent upon the teacher for being right, and since many pupils are usually dependent upon the same teacher, the total number of contingencies which may be arranged during, say, the first four years, is of the order of only a few thousand. But a very rough estimate suggests that efficient mathematical behavior at this level requires something of the order of 25,000 contingencies. We may suppose that even in the brighter student a given contingency must be arranged several times to place the behavior well in hand. The responses to be set up are not simply the various items in tables of addition, subtraction, multiplication, and division; we have also to consider the alternative forms in which each item may be stated. To the learning of such material we should add hundreds of responses concerned with factoring, identifying primes, memorizing series, using short-cut techniques of calculation, constructing and using geometric representations or number forms, and so on. Over and above all this, the whole mathematical repertoire must be brought under the control of concrete problems of considerable variety. Perhaps 50,000 contingencies is a more conservative estimate. In this frame of reference the daily assignment in arithmetic seems pitifully meagre.

The result of all this is, of course, well known. Even our best schools are under criticism for their inefficiency in the teaching of drill subjects such as arithmetic. The condition in the average school is a matter of wide-spread national concern. Modern children simply do not learn arithmetic quickly or well. Nor is the result simply incompetence. The very subjects in which modern techniques are weakest are those in which failure is most conspicuous, and in the wake of an ever-growing incompetence come the anxieties, uncertainties, and aggressions which in their turn present other problems to the school. Most pupils soon claim the asylum of not being "ready" for arithmetic at a given level or, eventually, of not having a mathematical mind. Such explanations are readily seized upon by defensive teachers and parents. Few pupils ever reach the stage at which automatic reinforcements follow as the natural consequences of mathematical behavior. On the contrary, the figures and symbols of mathematics have become standard emotional stimuli. The glimpse of a column of figures, not to say an algebraic symbol or an integral sign, is likely to set off—not mathematical behavior—but a reaction of anxiety, guilt, or fear.

The teacher is usually no happier about this than the pupil. Denied the opportunity to control via the birch rod, quite at sea as to the mode of operation of the few techniques at her disposal, she spends as little time as possible on drill subjects and eagerly subscribes to philosophies of education which emphasize material of greater inherent interest. A confession of weakness is her extraordinary concern lest the child be taught something unnecessary. The repertoire to be imparted is carefully reduced to an essential minimum. In the field of spelling, for example, a great deal of time and energy has gone into discovering just those words which the young child is going to use, as if it were a crime to waste one's educational power in teaching an unnecessary word. Eventually, weakness of technique emerges in the disguise of a reformulation of the aims of education. Skills are minimized in favor of vague achievements— educating for democracy, educating the whole child, educating for life, and so on. And there the matter ends; for, unfortunately, these philosophies do not in turn suggest improvements in techniques. They offer little or no help in the design of better classroom practices.

There would be no point in urging these objections if improvement were impossible. But the advances which have recently been made in our control of the learning process suggest a thorough revision of classroom practices and, fortunately, they tell us how the revision can be brought about. This is not, of course, the first time that the results of an experimental science have been brought to bear upon the practical problems of education. The modern classroom does not, however, offer much evidence that research in the field of learning has been respected or used. This condition is no doubt partly due to the limitations of earlier research. But it has been encouraged by a too hasty conclusion that the laboratory study of learning is inherently limited because it cannot take into account the realities of the classroom. In the light of our increasing knowledge of the learning process we should, instead, insist upon dealing with those realities and forcing a substantial change in them. Education is perhaps the most important branch of scientific technology. It deeply affects the lives of all of us. We can no longer allow the exigencies of a practical situation to suppress the tremendous improvements which are within reach.   The practical situation must be changed.

There are certain questions which have to be answered in turning to the study of any new organism.   What behavior is to be set up?   What reinforcers are at hand?   What responses are available in embarking upon a program of progressive approximation which will lead to the final form of the behavior?   How can reinforcements be most efficiently scheduled to maintain the behavior in strength?   These questions are all relevant in considering the problem of the child in the lower grades.

In the first place, what reinforcements are available?   What does the school have in its possession which will reinforce a child?   We may look first to the material to be learned, for it is possible that this will provide considerable automatic reinforcement.   Children play for hours with mechanical toys, paints, scissors and paper, noise-makers, puzzles—in short, with almost anything which feeds back significant changes in the environment and is reasonably free of aversive properties.   The sheer control of nature is itself reinforcing.   This effect is not evident in the modern school because it is masked by the emotional responses generated by aversive control.   It is true that automatic reinforcement from the manipulation of the environment is probably only a mild reinforcer and may need to be carefully husbanded, but one of the most striking principles to emerge from recent research is that the *net* amount of reinforcement is of little significance.   A very slight reinforcement may be tremendously effective in controlling behavior if it is wisely used.

If the natural reinforcement inherent in the subject matter is not enough, other reinforcers must be employed.   Even in school the child is occasionally permitted to do "what he wants to do," and access to reinforcements of many sorts may be made contingent upon the more immediate consequences of the behavior to be established.   Those who advocate competition as a useful social motive may wish to use the reinforcements which follow from excelling others, although there is the difficulty that in this case the reinforcement of one child is necessarily aversive to another.   Next in order we might place the good will and affection of the teacher, and only when that has failed need we turn to the use of aversive stimulation.

In the second place, how are these reinforcements to be made contingent upon the desired behavior?   There are two considerations here —the gradual elaboration of extremely complex patterns of behavior and the maintenance of the behavior in strength at each stage.   The whole process of becoming competent in any field must be divided into a very large number of very small steps, and reinforcement must be contingent upon the accomplishment of each step.   This solution to the problem of creating a complex repertoire of behavior also solves the problem of maintaining the behavior in strength. We could, of course, resort to the techniques of scheduling already developed in the study of other organisms but in the present state of our knowledge of educational practices, scheduling appears to be most effectively arranged through the design of the material to be learned. By making each successive step as small as possible, the frequency of reinforcement can be raised to a maximum, while the possibly aversive consequences of being wrong are reduced to a minimum. Other ways of designing material would yield other programs of reinforcement. Any supplementary reinforcement would probably have to be scheduled in the more traditional way.

These requirements are not excessive, but they are probably incompatible with the current realities of the classroom. In the experimental study of learning it has been found that the contingencies of reinforcement which are most efficient in controlling the organism cannot be arranged through the personal mediation of the experimenter. An organism is affected by subtle details of contingencies which are beyond the capacity of the human organism to arrange. Mechanical and electrical devices must be used. Mechanical help is also demanded by the sheer number of contingencies which may be used efficiently in a single experimental session. We have recorded many millions of responses from a single organism during thousands of experimental hours. Personal arrangement of the contingencies and personal observation of the results are quite unthinkable. Now, the human organism is, if anything, more sensitive to precise contingencies than the other organisms we have studied. We have every reason to expect, therefore, that the most effective control of human learning will require instrumental aid. The simple fact is that, as a mere reinforcing mechanism, the teacher is out of date. This would be true even if a single teacher devoted all her time to a single child, but her inadequacy is multiplied many-fold when she must serve as a reinforcing device to many children at once. If the teacher is to take advantage of recent advances in the study of learning, she must have the help of mechanical devices.

The technical problem of providing the necessary instrumental aid is not particularly difficult. There are many ways in which the necessary contingencies may be arranged, either mechanically or electrically. An inexpensive device which solves most of the principal problems has already been constructed. It is still in the experimental stage, but a description will suggest the kind of instrument which seems to be required. The device consists of a small box about the size of a small record player. On the top surface is a window through which a question or problem printed on a paper tape may be seen. The child answers the question by moving one or more sliders upon which the digits 0 through 9 are printed. The answer appears in square holes punched in the paper upon which the question is printed. When the answer has been set, the child turns a knob. The operation is as simple as adjusting a television set. If the answer is right, the knob turns freely and can be made to ring a bell or provide some other conditioned reinforcement. If the answer is wrong, the knob will not turn. A counter may be added to tally wrong answers. The knob must then be reversed slightly and a second attempt at a right. answer made. (Unlike the flash-card, the device reports a wrong answer without giving the right answer.) When the answer is right, a further turn of the knob engages a clutch which moves the next problem into place in the window. This movement cannot be completed, however, until the sliders have been returned to zero.

The important features of the device are these: Reinforcement for the right answer is immediate. The mere manipulation of the device will probably be reinforcing enough to keep the average pupil at work for a suitable period each day, provided traces of earlier aversive control can be wiped out. A teacher may supervise an entire class at work on such devices at the same time, yet each child may progress at his own rate, completing as many problems as possible within the class period. If forced to be away from school, he may return to pick up where he left off. The gifted child will advance rapidly, but can be kept from getting too far ahead either by being excused from arithmetic for a time or by being given special sets of problems which take him into some of the interesting by-paths of mathematics.

The device makes it possible to present carefully designed material in which one problem can depend upon the answer to the preceding and where, therefore, the most efficient progress to an eventually complex repertoire can be made. Provision has been made for recording the commonest mistakes so that the tapes can be modified as experience dictates. Additional steps can be inserted where pupils tend to have trouble, and ultimately the material will reach a point at which the answers of the average child will almost always be right.

If the material itself proves not to be sufficiently reinforcing, other reinforcers in the possession of the teacher or school may be made contingent upon the operation of the device or upon progress through a series of problems. Supplemental reinforcement would not sacrifice the advantages gained from immediate reinforcement and from the possibility of constructing an optimal series of steps which approach the complex repertoire of mathematical behavior most efficiently.

A similar device in which the sliders carry the letters of the alphabet has been designed to teach spelling. In addition to the advantages which can be gained from precise reinforcement and careful programming, the device will teach reading at the same time.   It can also be used to establish the large and important repertoire of verbal relationships encountered in logic and science.   In short, it can teach verbal thinking.   As to content instruction, the device can be operated as a multiple-choice self-rater.

Some objections to the use of such devices in the classroom can easily be foreseen.   The cry will be raised that the child is being treated as a mere animal and that an essentially human intellectual achievement is being analyzed in unduly mechanistic terms.   Mathematical behavior is usually regarded, not as a repertoire of responses involving numbers and numerical operations, but as evidences of mathematical ability or the exercise of the power of reason.   It is true that the techniques which are emerging from the experimental study of learning are not designed to "develop the mind" or to further some vague "understanding" of mathematical relationships.   They are designed, on the contrary, to establish the very behaviors which are taken to be the evidences of such mental states or processes.   This is only a special case of the general change which is under way in the interpretation of human affairs.   An advancing science continues to offer more and more convincing alternatives to traditional formulations.   The behavior in terms of which human thinking must eventually be defined is worth treating in its own right as the substantial goal of education.

Of course the teacher has a more important function than to say right or wrong.   The changes proposed would free her for the effective exercise of that function.   Marking a set of papers in arithmetic—"Yes, nine and six *are* fifteen; no, nine and seven *are not* eighteen"—is beneath the dignity of any intelligent individual.   There is more important work to be done—in which the teacher's relations to the pupil cannot be duplicated by a mechanical device.   Instrumental help would merely improve these relations.   One might say that the main trouble with education in the lower grades today is that the child is obviously not competent and *knows it* and that the teacher is unable to do anything about it and *knows that too*.   If the advances which have recently been made in our control of behavior can give the child a genuine competence in reading, writing, spelling, and arithmetic, then the teacher may begin to function, not in lieu of a cheap machine, but through intellectual, cultural, and emotional contacts of that distinctive sort which testify to her status as a human being.

Another possible objection is that mechanized instruction will mean technological unemployment.   We need not worry about this until there are enough teachers to go around and until the hours and energy demanded of the teacher are comparable to those in other fields of employment. Mechanical devices will eliminate the more tiresome labors of the teacher but they will not necessarily shorten the time during which she remains in contact with the pupil.

A more practical objection: Can we afford to mechanize our schools? The answer is clearly yes. The device I have just described could be produced as cheaply as a small radio or phonograph. There would need to be far fewer devices than pupils, for they could be used in rotation. But even if we suppose that the instrument eventually found to be most effective would cost several hundred dollars and that large numbers of them would be required, our economy should be able to stand the strain. Once we have accepted the possibility and the necessity of mechanical help in the classroom, the economic problem can easily be surmounted. There is no reason why the school room should be any less mechanized than, for example, the kitchen. A country which annually produces millions of refrigerators, dish-washers, automatic washing-machines, automatic clothes-driers, and automatic garbage disposers can certainly afford the equipment necessary to educate its citizens to high standards of competence in the most effective way.

There is a simple job to be done. The task can be stated in concrete terms. The necessary techniques are known. The equipment needed can easily be provided. Nothing stands in the way but cultural inertia. But what is more characteristic of America than an unwillingness to accept the traditional as inevitable? We are on the threshold of an exciting and revolutionary period, in which the scientific study of man will be put to work in man's best interests. Education must play its part. It must accept the fact that a sweeping revision of educational practices is possible and inevitable. When it has done this, we may look forward with confidence to a school system which is aware of the nature of its tasks, secure in its methods, and generously supported by the informed and effective citizens whom education itself will create.

7. Are Theories of Learning Helpful?*

Related selections: 1, 8, 35

RECENTLY there have been numerous objections to the belief that learning theory is the major contribution of psychology to education. Teachers and students in education have maintained that because of the confusion and conflicts in learning theory, they have found it of little help in understanding how to organize a teaching-learning situation. As a result, much of our classroom method is based upon a trial and error technique. This article points up the task of educational psychology in selecting from all fields those data relevant to schooling.

THERE has been concern about learning "since the memory of man runneth not to the contrary." The volume of theories has filled many volumes of books, and shows no indication of losing momentum. After centuries of thought and millions of words, nobody really knows the nature of the learning process. Theories follow theories; contradicting, replacing, modifying, ignoring, supplementing or re-verbalizing their predecessors. Students in the field become protagonists, presenting statements that describe the phenomenon without actually explaining causes and effects. Even the best friends of these theorists are showing signs of worry. In 1948, Ernest R. Hilgard' closed his excellent "Theories of Learning" with these words, "The erroneous impression may be left that little is known about learning. The factual knowledge does in reality bulk large. . . . It is the consistent ordering of this voluminous material into a compact and agreed-upon systematic structure which is lacking. . . . The time is ripe for a concerted attack upon the major points of disagreement within facts and theories. The next twenty years may well lead to a clearing of issues. . . ." Six years have passed, but this hope is not being realized. It may not be feasible to attempt an attack on the learning problem along the same lines as the present studies in cancer research; but it may be time to declare a moratorium on theories and to devote more energy to experimentation, as well as to correlation of data.

It was quite logical for the early students to concern themselves with problems of *individual* learning. The person who acquires, modifies, retains and forgets concepts is the basic unit to be studied. Since this is

* Samuel A. Kramer, "Are Theories of Learning Helpful?" *Educational Forum*, vol. XIX (January, 1955), pp. 227–235. Reprinted by permission of author and Kappa Delta Pi, copyright owners.
Dr. Kramer (1906—) is Educationalist, Office of Higher Education, U.S. Department of Health, Education, and Welfare, Washington, D.C.

so obvious, the questions of learning that relate to a member of a group were overlooked until very recent years. Most psychologists and educators simply accepted the "fact" that all learning is alike, and the same laws must apply to a child in a slum area, an ape, a Comanche Indian, a laboratory rat or a research scientist. Yet, there has never been any doubt about learning differences, quantitatively and qualitatively, under varying social conditions. In 1919, Floyd H. Allport experimented with groups of upper classmen and graduate students at Harvard and Radcliffe, and found marked differences between "working alone" and "working in groups."[1] The psychologists of that period and later years completely ignored the implications of such experiments. In what, then, were these learning theorists absorbed? Mainly, the answer is "Thorndike."

Although it was not the first important proposition, being preceded by the concepts of mental states and formal discipline, Thorndike's association theory is notable for its powerful and lasting impact on educational practices and related social phenomena. From 1898 to the present time, the S-R bond has been considered an integral factor in learning, as clearly a part of any animal as the digestive system. It is a peculiar but easily observable phenomenon that educators who give lip service to Gestalt and other field psychologies, write and use "How To Study" manuals that emphasize the concepts (without the language) of Thorndike's laws of readiness, exercise and effect. Further, they adopt wholeheartedly his six aids to improvement in learning: interest in the work, interest in improvement, significance of the problem, problem-attitude, attentiveness and the absence of irrelevant emotion and worry. They may now be called concentration, organization, memory, health, motivation, recreation, social adjustments and absence of personal problems; but this does not change them. Possibly there is no quarrel with this as a practical procedure, but it must be admitted that it stems directly from the educational psychology of Thorndike. His law of effect seems to have been most eagerly accepted, and to have left a lasting heritage in the form of punishments, promotions, school marks, substantive rewards and other incentive devices.

Thorndike was almost a messiah. Other doctrines developed in psychology, but at best they merely evaded his work; and, more frequently, the new schools did little more than paraphrase his findings. Until 1926, no one had the temerity to make a point-by-point refutation. Then was published "Aspects of Thorndike's Psychology in Their Relation to Educational Theory and Practice," by H. Gordon Hullfish.[7] His approach can be understood from this quotation. "How, then, can an intelligible answer be furnished to such questions as habit formation, interest, concept formation, the place of aims, and other kindred problems? The answer is necessarily colored by the underlying assumptions; and when these are not water-tight, the opinion advanced as a reply must remain questionable."

Hullfish pointed out that one important difficulty is Thorndike's vacillation between behaviorism and mentalism. On the one hand he admits ideas, such as satisfaction, annoyance and readiness, just as the Herbartian school did. On the other hand, he insists that "Whatever exists at all exists in some amount. To know it thoroughly involves knowing its quantity as well as its quality." Hullfish comments, "There is no measure of patriotism, confusion or the concept 'dog'; there is, simply, a measurement of products of reactions to these stimulating conditions. . . . Thorndike's dictum reduces education to a proposition in physics, and those who accept the thesis must frankly admit that they are of the behavioristic school." This paper is not the place to go more deeply into the evaluative criticisms. One other interesting point denoting further inconsistencies may be quoted, however. "Tests of native ability and achievement, as actually employed, likewise lean towards the stimulus-response position. The expressed conviction that native ability is being measured connects quite naturally with the assumption that the body is the whole thing. This point of linkage, however, is not always evident . . . the assumption has been made that a certain something, quite unknown, has been measured; whereas, as the behaviorist puts it, all that has been measured is behavior. And since the testor proceeds on the basis of the S-R bond hypothesis, he has no ground for claiming that he has measured anything more than a particular response to a particular stimulus."

This definitive critique seemed to open the floodgates of attack, some direct and some circumlocutionary. Naturally, the true behaviorists were at the forefront. Now that the first well-aimed stone had been thrown, other hurlers promptly appeared. One of the first casualties in Thorndike's system was the law of exercise, when Edwin R. Guthrie[4] announced his theory concerning the relationship between stimulus and response. He started with an apparent restatement of Pavlov's conditioned reflex theory that any combination of stimuli accompanying a movement will on its recurrence tend to be followed by that movement. However, he soon reached the conclusion that, "*A stimulus pattern gains its full associative strength on the occasion of its first pairing with a response.*" The italics are mine. Clearly he says that practice is a waste of time, although he hedges somewhat in the complete discarding of the value of repetitive action.

Closely following the lead of Clark L. Hull,[6] who developed a thorough and systematic presentation of behaviorism applied to learning theory,

Miller and Dollard[13] have determined that there are just four factors in learning.

1. *Drive*; the strong stimulus which impels to action.
2. *Cue*; the determinant of when, where and how the response will be made, serving as a goal or signpost.
3. *Response*; the result of acceptance of a cue, so that a major task of training is so to arrange the situation that the desired response will occur.
4. *Reward*; which develops a tendency to repeat the desired response.

Transfer of training is recognized, on the ground that the more similarity there is between one stimulus and another, the more nearly it can substitute for the other in arousing conditioned responses.

One other point must be made about the behavioristic approach. Sometimes, when a situation seems to be inadequately explained, an entity is posited which, if it were not a heresy to say so, seems to be an atavism strongly pointing to mental states. B. F. Skinner, a "descriptive behaviorist," has contributed the concept of a "reflex reserve" from which operant or learned responses are emitted over a period of time. *He claims emissions can exhaust the reserve.*[14] It is not difficult to envision the army of ants emptying the warehouse of wheat when each ant takes one grain; but is this "reflex reserve" the same thing? There is no clarification of what constitutes this reserve, or where it is located. It actually seems like a "deus ex machina," which may be unusual for a behaviorist.

It must now be evident that behaviorism was not as wide a departure from Thorndike's theory of association as was claimed during the late twenties and early thirties. The S-R bonds remained unbroken as the basis of all learning, and human beings and other animals were considered as only placid receptors, reacting stolidly to the changes in environment. The most intelligent animal, therefore, was merely the one who had the highest number of receptors. Although Watson and his cultural offspring emphatically announced that they were creating a new school of thought based on "mechanism," the freshness was more obvious in the claimants than in the claim. The school did little more than present a re-emphasis of existing ideas. The concept of mental states had been effectively destroyed by Thorndike and Woodworth; and their propositions had been clearly exploded by Hullfish and others. A "coup de grace" from the behaviorists was unnecessary.

A few years before the advent of behaviorism in the United States, an entirely different approach to research in human and other animal behavior was being born in Germany. About 1910, Max Wertheimer developed the Gestalt theory which was later expanded into the school of field psychology. The significant feature of Gestaltism is the recognition that man acts with a purpose or motive and that, therefore, he develops an "insight" toward the solution of his problems. Wertheimer had an overwhelming conviction that even a complete knowledge of sensory elements and all possible combinations of these elements— numbering in the millions—must be inadequate to explain perception. The fact that he and his two assistants, W. Kohler and K. Koffka, used facts from the physical sciences as illustrations and analogies was necessary, but highly unfortunate. This mention of physical facts created misunderstanding of intent, definition and application, and presented opponents with ready-made arguments that delayed acceptance of basic principles. They started with visual sensations that were not in agreement with physical phenomena, such as "seeing" a continuous moving picture that is really a series of discrete elements. Obviously, the whole was *more* than the sum of its parts. Something new had been added. The physical scientists could describe the manifestation but could not explain it. The social scientists could observe it, but could neither describe it as a social phenomenon nor explain it by accepted psychologies. What made the discrete phenomena appear to flow together?[8]

Wertheimer clearly intended to present this case of a visual perception as a starting point or springboard for its application to psychology. However, he was not credited with this purpose, so that early scholars in the field became enmeshed in a consideration of Gestalt as a physical approach to the problem of learning.

The general viewpoint of Gestalt psychology is expressed in the statement that the laws of organization apply equally to perception and to learning. Since they have demonstrated that perception is based on past experience, their "trace theory" is significant. Its essential features are: (a) a trace is assumed to persist from a prior experience, so that it is part of the present; (b) the present process can select, reactivate or in some manner communicate with the trace; and (c) there is a resulting new process of recall or recognition.[9]

What happens when new traces are formed? The aggregate trace system resulting from repetition is constantly being transformed and preceding traces are disrupted. The value of repetition lies in the fact that the trace *systems* become consolidated even while the individual traces are being destroyed. Gestaltists refer to such consolidated trace systems as being increasingly available (much as what associationists call a habit system ready to function). They warn, however, that if this is overdone, the trace system becomes too available for one process and not available for another; as too much drill in a school subject may have a narrowing or "blinding" influence. These psychologists are not at all disturbed by the similarity to associationism, because the important distinguishing concept cannot possibly be ascribed to anyone but the Gestaltists. This is "insight," or the perception of a relationship which leads to the solution of a problem. Insight depends upon capacity, relevant previous experience, experimental arrangements to make all parts necessary to insight readily available, and finally a period of fumbling and search. Insightful solutions can be readily repeated and can be used in new situations. In memorization and retention, insight is more important than drill, this being the best alternative to trial-and-error.[10, 15]

SOCIAL PSYCHOLOGY ENTERS THE FIELD

Just as the Gestaltists created consternation among the individual psychologists by insisting that the whole is more than the sum of its parts, the social psychologists have caused a revolution by showing that the individualists are not moving forward and, probably, have been causing harm. Most expressive of this attitude is that of Solomon E. Asch, professor of psychology at Swarthmore College, who remarks on page 24 of his "Social Psychology,"[2] "Modern psychology has often drawn, I suspect, a caricature rather than a portrait of man. As a result it has introduced a grave gap between itself and the knowledge of men that observation gives us and from which investigation must start." Nor is social psychology free from suspicion. As a relatively new system, it has leaned heavily toward acceptance of ideas from other sciences and popular beliefs, and has not yet fully adopted a cautious and experimental approach. However, the great value lies in its examination of the human element in social affairs, of studying man among men as something different from an ape among apes or an ape among men. In the field of learning, social psychology is *testing* the theories that have heretofore been blindly accepted or only theoretically adopted.

In his presidential address in 1950, W. J. Brogden said this to the Division of Experimental Psychology. "The advancement of knowledge in other areas of psychology depends upon the advancement of our understanding of learning. General laws of learning, then, are the goal. Although laws in the last analysis have their origin in experimental results, theory development can assist materially in such progression. A theory may organize the results of many researches, it may bring new relations to light, or it may serve as a catalyst for fruitful experimentation. On the other hand, a theory of learning may impede advancement seriously. It may fail to consider existing experimental evidence that does not support it; it may encourage research to proceed in non-productive channels; or it may define problems verbally that cannot be attacked experimentally.

There are other ways in which theories can hinder advancement or accelerate it. Each of our present-day theories is probably doing both."

This danger is further emphasized by Norman R. F. Maier.[12] "Changes in an individual imply learning, and in this sense therapy becomes closely associated with learning. Problems of learning, however, are very complex and many variables influence learning progress. Hence the association of therapy with learning does not simplify the views on therapy. Rather confusion may be created because varying learning theories have given clinical theory as well as clinical practice different types of emphasis."

The individual psychologist "naturally" considers all of learning as a personal affair, since his science is rooted deeply in biological thinking. The social world is considered as a one-way street in which the individual affects society but society does not basically affect the individual. In this view, capitalism exists because people are acquisitive and not because of social conditions. Consciously departing from the theorists, the experimental psychologists have nevertheless continued this individualistic approach. People have been studied without regard to the social conditions in which they developed. It is inferred that the sum of individual responses is all that needs to be known to understand society; and that social situations are merely end results and not causal factors. It is true that a knowledge of man's perceptions and conceptions is necessary to understand how he learns; but it is not true that such studies can be made without regard to the social atmosphere. Another statement by Asch will be found helpful.[3]

"We conclude that to discover the full potentialities of men we must observe them in the social medium, that the basic problems of psychology require the extension of observation into the region of social processes. The study of social processes must base itself on what is known about the relation of individuals to the physical surroundings, but it should in turn deepen and extend this knowledge. The region of social events should provide a body of facts and a testing ground for theories formulated under more restricted conditions, but it should also furnish problems for general psychology. Only in this way will psychology achieve a unified conception of the place of man in nature and society, and realize its mission as a natural and social science."

This refutes, or at least challenges, the proposition that a study of learning is entirely or even mainly the province of the individual psychologist who paid no attention to performance under such social stimuli as mass hysteria or authoritarian compulsion. A human being cannot be understood or properly studied as a hermit or a Tarzan. This is "learning" about man in a non-human environment, and therefore is not learning about him at all.   To understand *how* man learns, we must know *where,* *when,* and *under what conditions* he learns.   This is the function of the social psychologist; to evaluate the transformation of man in and by social relationships, and to study how his apparent individual limitations have been expanded by the fact of his living among men.   It will be remembered that even the Gestaltists, despite their emphasis on insight, spoke of "capacity" as being determined by age, species and individual differences within a species.   Nothing was said about the effect of social interaction on capacity.

Experimentation has developed at a great pace during the last ten years, by social psychologists as well as individual psychologists.   This is all to the good.   If an experiment studies man in a vacuum, there will likely be another experiment producing incompatible results—and someone is bound to raise questions.   The answer will probably be found in that the social conditions were different, and the perceptions could not be the same.   Yet it seems difficult to escape from the individualistic approach.   James J. Gibson[3] insists that learning is strictly a biological function rooted in the nervous system.   This was written in 1950, and we may expect less of this as experimentation continues.

The viewpoint of the social psychologist may be judged from the questions he asks.

1. Why do different human beings perceive situations in different ways?

2. Why does a human being perceive situations in different ways at different times?

3. What needs or values drive an individual to particular perceptions?

4. Since needs and values modify perceptions, how can these modifiers (hunger, desire for success, release from tensions, etc.) be measured?   This is a basic problem for the attitude researchers interested in *how* attitudes develop.

5. How can perceptions be differentiated from conception?   To the individual psychologist, this is not a problem, especially if he is a non-Gestaltist; but the social psychologist may well prefer to consider both as "cognition."

6. Is there any difference, in kind or degree, between man and other animals, and, if so, is it profitable to study animals in order to understand man?

7. Is there any original human nature, other than such simple reflexes as the patellar and salivary?   Since it is now commonly accepted that most behavior is learned, and depends very little on original nature, *the method of learning becomes a dominant social problem.*   For example, the desire for war may be learned, and not depend at all on innate human aggressiveness.

8. Is "learning" a single process or a group of many processes, so that different things are learned in different ways?

9. What is the importance of social and physical environments in learn-

ing? Is a man among men different from a cat among cats, or a cat among men?

10. If learning can be explained by a drive-reduction *or* a drive-increase (the more we learn the more we want to learn), what prevents these drives from being constantly reinforced to an overpowering point? Do social conditions and the institutional order prevent such an imbalance in most people?

11. If reinforcement is accepted as a central doctrine in learning theory, and people do things because they are rewarding or useful, how do persons learn to carry on survivals that have no apparent utility, beauty or other social function?

12. Is learning molar or molecular? This is simply asking whether the Gestaltists have a point.

13. Admitting that drives, needs, rewards and punishments are connected with learning among men and other animals, how does the capacity for rational thought fit into the picture?

14. With what material should we study the learning process? Krech and Crutchfield[11] claim that, "If we are interested in the general operation of the cognitive processes of one's social world, then data collected with almost any cognitive material will do." If this is true for the collection of data, does it also apply to the learning process? Is it a return to mind as an apperceptive mass?

15. Must there be any theories of learning? Would it be practicable simply to accept learning as any other behavior to be studied as a social phenomenon?

These are but a few of the questions that need answers. The inferences are clearly seen in the many writings and experiments in this field. If the proper study of mankind is man, it must now be realized that the proper place to study man is among men. This is the great task for the social experimenter, to give his work a definite and momentous import. Experimentation carried on in the social structure is possible and essential. Man is much more than a storehouse of fluid ideas or a mechanical entity dependent only upon habits formed by repetitive action. It is not enough to say that "We learn to do by doing."

From an immediate utilitarian viewpoint, a knowledge of the learning process is of the utmost importance to the educator. How has he been affected by these disputed approaches? The situation described in 1926 by Hullfish[7] still exists, although the entrance of social psychology may have made it more hopeful. He said in the preface, "The development of an educational psychology today cannot fail to be an interesting, though a precarious, undertaking. Interesting, because of increasing opportunities for research and study; precarious, because of the changes in psychology which have been taking place with a startling swiftness. There have come about radical shifts in the approach to this science; undeniable differences in fundamental positions now exist, and any educational psychology which is worthy of the name must needs account for the conflicts existing between present-day points of view.   In short, the student of to-day who engages in a study of psychology must find that his undertaking is far from simple; must realize, indeed, that his is truly a study of psychologies and not of a psychology. . . .   If the study does no more than suggest definitely, and clearly, that a basic and consistent approach is imperative, and that this must be made by first evaluating the psychologies now available, it will have served its purpose." At that time, the startling weakness of the "psychologies now available" lay in the fact that social phenomena were disregarded.   Educators have a stronger support now.

An eclectic approach is probably the only feasible attack.   The present knowledge of human learning requires an integration of data derived from such diverse fields as biology, sociology, chemistry, psychology, physics, education, and many more; aided by the techniques of statistics, attitudes research, mathematics and philosophy.   In developing a whole picture, no aspect must be overemphasized or underestimated.   There must be a fair sampling of each ingredient in the learning process.   Unilateral approaches are valuable only if no fixed and pat conclusions develop, and the findings are acknowledged to be just a part of the final pattern of explanation.   When this is learned by the scientists, they will be able to unfold the nature of the learning process.

BIBLIOGRAPHY

1. Allport, Floyd H.   *Social Psychology*.   New York: Houghton Mifflin, 1924.
2. Asch, Solomon E.   *Social Psychology*.   New York: Prentice-Hall, 1952.
3. Gibson, James J.   "The Implications of Learning Theory for Social Psychology," in Miller, J. G., ed., *Experiments in Social Process*.   New York: McGraw-Hill, 1950.
4. Guthrie, Edwin R.   "Conditioning," in National Society for the Study of Education, 41st Yearbook, Part II, 1942.
5. Hilgard, Ernest R.   *Theories of Learning*.   New York: Appleton-Century-Crofts, 1948.
6. Hull, Clark L.   *A Behavior System*.   New Haven: Yale University Press, 1952.
7. Hullfish, H. Gordon.   *Aspects of Thorndike's Psychology in Their Relation to Educational Theory and Practice*.   Columbus: Ohio State University Press, 1926.
8. Koffka, K.   *Growth of the Mind*.   New York: Harcourt, Brace, 1928.
9. Koffka, K.   *Principles of Gestalt Psychology*.   New York: Harcourt, Brace, 1935.
10. Kohler, W.   *Gestalt Psychology*.   New York: Liveright, 1947.

11. Krech, D. and Crutchfield, R. S. *Theories and Problems of Social Psychology.* New York: McGraw-Hill, 1948.
12. Maier, Norman R. F. *Frustration.* New York: McGraw-Hill, 1949.
13. Miller, N. E. and Dollard, J. *Social Learning and Imitation.* New Haven: Yale University Press, 1941.
14. Skinner, B. F. *The Behavior of Organisms.* New York: Appleton-Century, 1938.
15. Wertheimer, M. *Productive Thinking.* New York: Harper, 1945.

---

8. Counseling as a Learning Process*

Related selections: 7, 28, 29, 30

COUNSELING service for pupils with personal and educational problems has become widespread in our schools. Dr. Combs states his belief that since to be effective counseling must result in learning for the counselee, counselors must study learning and how it takes place. He believes that learning theories have not been helpful in education and that educators have turned to the educational philosophers for assistance (see Section B, "Educational Philosophy as Learning Theory"). He suggests personality theory as a substitute for learning theory not only in counseling but in teaching.

THERE can be little doubt that counseling is, in essence, a learning process. When counseling is successful, the client learns a new and better relationship between himself and the world in which he lives. Counseling badly done may, equally well, result in learning a poorer, less effective way of living. Whatever happens in counseling, the client learns something from the experience, even if it is nothing more than the idea that counseling is not much help to him. In this respect, counseling is no different from any other life experience. Counseling, however, should be a situation expressly designed to assist the client to learn more effectively and efficiently than is possible in most other life experiences. If not, counselors had better close up shop.

Assuming that counseling is fundamentally a learning experience, it

* Arthur W. Combs, "Counseling as a Learning Process," *Journal of Counseling Psychology,* vol. I (Winter, 1954), pp. 31–36. Reprinted by permission of the author and publisher.

Dr. Combs (1912–), formerly Director of Clinical Training at Syracuse University, is currently Professor of Education at the University of Florida. With Donald Snygg he is author of *Individual Behavior.* He is a Diplomate in clinical psychology.

would appear logical that our existing theories of learning should apply to the problem. Unfortunately, this does not turn out to be the case. The fact that counseling is a learning process does not mean that existing theories of learning automatically become useful in solving the problems of counseling. The writer has been forced to the conclusion that traditional learning theories seem to have little to offer to the improvement of counseling. Indeed, the attempt to apply them to the problem of counseling may even be fraught with considerable danger.

Our existing learning theories, for the most part, are concerned with small bits of the problems encountered in counseling. They seem to have little application beyond the simplest behavior, while the behavior of clients is complex and involving entire personalities. Most of our traditional theories apply to the *process of learning* rather than to *people who learn*. Counseling is unquestionably a process of learning, but a much broader process of learning than we have usually considered under that heading. What appears to happen to clients in counseling is a matter of personality reorganization calling for much broader concepts of learning than most present theories of learning even attempt to deal with.

This discussion does not mean to suggest that existing learning theories have no application to learning in counseling. They *do* apply, but to such small and isolated aspects of the problem of personality organization as to make them almost useless for any practical purpose.

THE EXPERIENCE OF EDUCATION WITH LEARNING THEORY

Educators have been dealing with problems of learning for a long time. Modern education has taken as its goal "the optimum development of the individual" and that objective could serve equally well as a goal for counseling. Counseling, like education, is a learning process. Perhaps we can learn something for our problem by observing the contributions traditional learning theory has made to education.

If there is any place where one would expect learning theory to have proved of value, it would be in the field of education. Yet, interestingly enough, learning theory has provided little or no leadership in solving problems of educational method. Leadership in education, almost exclusively, has come, not from learning theorists, but from educational philosophers. One looks in vain to find any great educational movement arising from learning theory. As a matter of fact, learning theory in some instances has even had a regressive effect on education. At the very time when education is moving to a holistic concept of teaching, many educators are still hammering away at methods of drill and rote learning growing out of the Ebbinghaus experiments of three generations ago.   Because such learning theory seems to be "scientific," furthermore, many teachers find great comfort in continuing to teach by methods long since outdated.

Modern education has shifted its emphasis from subject matter to children, from processes to people.   As a result, the theory of greatest use to educators is not learning theory but personality theory.   The mental hygienists have taken over a very large share of the former functions of learning theorists in many a school of education.   The unpleasant fact of the matter is that modern schools of education find little that is helpful in the average course on learning for the training of beginning teachers.   Teachers have discovered long since that children are people with feelings, beliefs, attitudes, personal meanings, and convictions.   Learning theory, which does not help to deal with these facets of child behavior, seems to the average teacher far out of touch with reality.   She needs a broader, more inclusive approach to her problems.   Education tried to gear itself to learning theory but found it to be a mistake.   It would be unfortunate were we to make the same error in counseling.   Counseling, too, is a problem of people rather than processes.   Perhaps we have something to learn from the experience of education.

THEORY LEVEL AND APPLICATION

There is nothing sacred about theory.   Theory in any field of endeavor is nothing more than a systematic explanation of events useful to the purposes one has in view.   Theory, which holds for one frame of reference or one problem, may be totally inadequate, even misleading, in another. Theory can be constructed on many levels and for many different purposes, but is maximally efficient only for those levels and purposes for which it is designed.   Atomic theory is useful in dealing with problems of atomic energy.   At that level and for those purposes, it is relevant and essential. Theories of organic and inorganic chemistry are useful and pertinent for the pharmacist when he makes up a doctor's prescription.   He knows little or nothing about atomic theory, however, and carries on his job quite effectively without it.   This is not to imply that atomic theory does not hold for the chemicals with which he deals.   Indeed, they do, but the pharmacist does not need to know them to carry on his profession adequately.   On still another level, colleges of home economics have developed theories of cake baking quite without reference to chemical or atomic physics.   While it is true that chemical and atomic theory is at work in the batter along with the hands of the cook, the cook does not need to guide her behavior by them, or even to know they exist.   This is as it should be. Society needs its atomic physicists to make atomic bombs, but most of us would rather our cakes be baked by cooks!

This same relationship of theory to function is true of learning theory as well. The learning theory one finds useful for his purposes depends upon the number of variables one attempts to control in studying a process. For example, theory may be constructed for purposes of understanding what happens to a client in the counseling situation. To do this it is necessary to deal with people as they are with a large number of variables left uncontrolled. Nevertheless, it is quite possible to construct effective theories extremely helpful for our purposes. This is the kind of study many educators carry on in the classroom to discover better methods of inducing learning-in-life situations. Such studies, however, make some people very uncomfortable. Too many variables remain uncontrolled. Accordingly, one may seek to study learning on a level wherein more of the variables may be controlled. He can, for instance, study learning in the laboratory instead of the classroom, where theories of learning can be developed from experiments using tachistoscopic exposures. One can go further and control the material being learned by removing all meaning from it as in the use of nonsense syllables. In short, one can repeat the Ebbinghaus experiments and find new theories of learning applicable to the "purer" situations constructed under such laboratory conditions. It is possible to eliminate even more variables and study a single stimulus-response unit as Pavlov did with his dogs. Here, too, it will be feasible to construct learning theories applicable to the kind of situations studied. Unfortunately, when learning is examined under these restricted conditions it is no longer people who are being studied but an isolated process.

Dynamic personality theory is expressly designed to aid our understanding of behavior outside the laboratory, in free situations where few, if any, variables are likely to be in the control of the observer. The fact of many variables left uncontrolled makes some psychologists feel that such investigations are somehow less "scientific." This is an unfortunate attitude which equates science with minuteness rather than understanding. Teachers have long since discovered how inadequate minute theories are in providing guides to classroom learning. In the writer's experience, they have proved equally fruitless as approaches to understanding what happens in the counseling process.

The major problems of our time are problems of human relationships. In solving these problems, psychology must, of necessity, play an ever more important role. To do this effectively, we need theories about behavior at every level which help us understand behavior. It is difficult to conceive, however, how we can live up to our tremendous birthright by an atomistic approach to holistic problems. Too great an insistence upon such an approach may make it difficult or impossible to contribute significantly to the great social problems of these times.

Although the writer's basic training in psychology was thoroughly behavioristic, he has been increasingly disappointed in traditional approaches to learning theory as they apply to the counseling process. Though these theories have explained certain isolated aspects of what seems to be happening to clients, they have generally failed to explain the kinds of changes any counselor observes daily in the course of his practice. Even more disappointing, they do not offer much help in improving practices or in providing guides to behavior when problems arise for which no ready answers are available. The counselor must live and work in a world where variables can seldom be controlled or held constant. Theory which applies only under laboratory conditions is of little help in solving his practical problems.

PERCEPTUAL FIELD THEORY AS A GUIDE TO
COUNSELING PRACTICE

More and more the writer has been forced to adopt a field theory of personality organization based upon our growing understandings about the nature and function of perception and the concept of self. Perceptual theory seems eminently more satisfactory in explaining what we can observe about human behavior. It seems more helpful, too, as a personal guide to behavior in our never ceasing attempts to become effective individuals whether it be in counseling or any other aspect of human relationships. This theory has been stated on several other occasions. The writer would certainly not presume to claim it as the answer to all our counseling problems. It is only an approach to personality which has proved satisfying, logical, and helpful in organizing thinking and guiding practice. That, after all, seems to be the purpose of any theory—to give meaning to the events we observe and to make possible the prediction and control of events still in the future. There is not room here for an exposition of this theoretical position. Let us, therefore, look only at its fundamental assumptions and point out a few of its implications for counseling theory.

Briefly, this theoretical position begins with the assumption that all behavior is a function of the individual's field of perceptions at the instant of behaving. In other words, people behave according to how things *seem* to them. If a man believes oysters can be eaten only in months with an R, he will avoid eating them in June and July. If he does not know about this concept, or if he does not believe in the "R" fiction, he will eat them anytime. How each person behaves at any moment is a function of the

organization of his perceptual field at the moment of behaving—or mis-
behaving.

This perceptual field has the feeling of reality to the individual and is
always organized with respect to the concepts he holds of himself. As the
field of perceptions changes, so, too, does behavior. When we perceive
differently, we behave differently. When perceptions are vague and
indistinct, behavior is correspondingly vague and inexact. When perceptions are clear and accurate, behavior is similarly precise and efficient.

This is the frame of reference within which an increasing number of
psychologists are basing their thinking and research. It is a broad frame
of reference capable of integrating and giving meaning and order to a
large amount of our accumulated research and thinking. It is consistent
with client-centered therapy and much of psychoanalysis. It seems to apply equally well to the problems of vocational and educational counseling
and to the problems of classroom teaching. Many of the seemingly diverse points of view, as those of Freud, Rogers, Murphy, Allport, Snygg
and Combs, Frank, and a host of others interpreted in this framework, fit
into a meaningful and useful theoretical structure. A tremendous amount
of recent research similarly finds effective interpretation in this setting.
Research on perception, for example, is directly applicable to such a
theoretical position. So, also, is a large amount of current research on
such problems as threat, rigidity, discrimination, and the whole field of
research on projective instruments.

If it is true that behavior is a function of perception, then the goal of
counseling must be to assist the client to change his perceptions. Effective, efficient, and satisfying behavior both from the viewpoint of the
client and of society requires a maximum freedom of perception.
Rogers, for example, has described the adjusted person as follows: "It
would appear that when all of the ways in which the individual perceives
himself—all perceptions of the qualities, abilities, impulses, and attitudes of the person and all perceptions of himself in relation to others—
are accepted into the organized conscious concept of self, then this
achievement is accompanied by feelings of comfort and freedom from
tension which are experienced as psychological adjustment."

In perceptual terms, the goal of counseling thus becomes one of aiding
the client to achieve a perceptive field as rich, varied, accurate, and free
of distortion as possible. If the perceptive field is organized about the
concept of self, this theory would imply further that counseling must concern itself with assisting clients to clearer, more accurate perceptions of
self and the relationship of self to the world in which the client lives.

If it is true that behavior is a function of perception, it follows that to
change behavior it will first be necessary to find ways of changing per-

ception. The perceptual field of the client is, however, a personal, internal organization not directly open to manipulation from outside. This means that counseling must be seen, not as a place where something is done *to* the client, but as the provision of a situation in which the client can be helped to change his ways of seeing. Counseling in this sense becomes a process of assisting, facilitating, and encouraging change in perception. It seems, furthermore, to reverse the usual doctor-patient role in which the doctor is the one who knows and the patient does not. In counseling, it is the client who knows and the counselor who does not. The counselor in this frame of reference is a catalyst in a process of growth. His task becomes one of supplying for his client a special kind of experience which will assist his client to explore and perceive a more adequate relationship of self to life.

VARIABLES OF PERCEPTION AS THE FACTORS OF COUNSELING

Finally, if it is true that behavior is a function of perception, then the variables of the process of counseling become the factors affecting perception. To understand and control the process of counseling, it becomes necessary to understand and control the factors which encourage or impede perception. Once these factors are well understood it would seem possible to design the counseling process in the light of these understandings. There is much yet to be learned about the variables of perception, but a fine start has been made. The literature already includes a considerable body of knowledge about some of these variables and every day brings new understanding about some further aspect of perception.

To this point there are at least six variables of perception about which a good deal is already known and which have immediate bearing upon the counseling process. Applying what is known about these variables has possibilities of helping improve the counseling process. These are:

1. Perception is a function of the state of the physical organism in which the perception occurs. Perception both affects and is affected by the physical organism which serves as the vehicle for perceiving.

2. Perception takes time. Effective perception requires sufficient exposure to make perceiving possible.

3. Perception cannot occur without opportunity for experience. This opportunity for perceiving may be of a concrete character or may be purely symbolic. In any event, there must be some form of opportunity provided for perceiving to happen.

These first three variables of perception are already well known and understood. They have been more or less intensively studied for a number of years. The last three have been far less subjected to experimental study but continue to grow in importance every day. They are:

4. Perception is a function of the individual's values and goals. The values and goals of the individual have a selective effect upon the individual's field of perceptions. Other factors being equal, people perceive more sharply and effectively those aspects of themselves and of life which have greatest value for them.

5. Perception is a function of the self concept of the perceiver. The concept of self has a selective effect on the perceptual field. People perceive that which is appropriate for persons with their concepts of self to perceive. Children who perceive themselves as poor readers read poorly. We are only beginning to understand the tremendous importance of the self concept upon every aspect of human behavior. It appears to be the very core around which all the rest of our perceptions of reality are organized.

6. Perception is seriously affected by the experience of threat. These effects seem to be of two kinds: (a) When a person feels threatened his field of perceptions is reduced to the object of threat producing the well-known effect of tunnel vision; and (b) when threatened, the individual seeks to defend his existing self-organization. Both of these effects seem to have extremely important bearings upon the counseling process.

A good deal is already known about these six important variables. Much of this information has a direct bearing upon the kind of counseling situations we need to construct. What is already known of these variables is highly useful in guiding the counselor in his task. These seem like fruitful fields for further experimental exploration. It is conceivable that there are a number of other important variables affecting perception with equally important implications for the counseling process waiting to be uncovered.

Counseling is indeed a function of learning. Learning in counseling, however, is never an isolated process. It is *people* who learn in counseling. Counseling could not exist without them. A theoretical position which can help us very effectively in improving our understanding of the processes the counselor sets in motion or the methods he devises to help his clients must be a theory which deals with people.

Learning theory applies to some parts of the problems of counseling. We cannot afford, however, to jump to the conclusion that because it is partly applicable it is a sufficient or an adequate avenue of explanation or exploration. There seems nothing more dangerous in human thought

than ideas which are partly true.   The danger of theory partly right is
that it encourages people by its partial provision of answers to the vain
hope that with a little more effort, a little more trying, they can find
answers to the whole problem.   Sometimes this works but sometimes,
too, it is better to find a better premise as a framework from which we
may evaluate and improve our practices.   An adequate theory for
counseling must *include* learning theory but must also extend beyond it.
This seems to require a personality theory in which traditional learning
theory would play but a very minor role.   The writer of this article has
here indicated the direction of his own bias, but the fact of the matter
seems to be that *almost any* personality theory is a more effective guide
to practice than the best our traditional learning theories have so far produced.

B. EDUCATIONAL PHILOSOPHY AS
LEARNING THEORY

9. Experience and Thinking*

SINCE the publication of *Democracy and Education* in 1916 educators have turned to Dewey for insight into many phases of education; even for those most familiar with his work, there are new dis-
coveries upon each rereading.   Most people agree that a major
objective of schooling is to teach people to think.   Disagreement
comes over how this is to be accomplished.   In this selection Dewey
sets forth the nature of thinking and how the processes called thinking and experiencing are related to each other.   Beginning students
may find this selection difficult, but it is worth careful reading and
study.   It may be helpful to organize a small group of classmates to
read it and discuss its meaning.

* John Dewey, *Democracy and Education* (The Macmillan Company, 1916), ch.
XI, pp. 163–178.   Reprinted by permission of the publisher.
    John Dewey (1859–1952) America's most eminent philosopher, was Head of
Department of Philosophy and Education at the University of Chicago before
becoming Professor of Philosophy at Columbia University.   He held this latter
position for over a quarter of a century.   He was made Honorary Life President
of the National Education Association in 1932.   His writings explored all aspects
of philosophy and education.

THE NATURE OF EXPERIENCE

THE NATURE of experience can be understood only by noting that it includes an active and a passive element peculiarly combined. On the active hand, experience is *trying*—a meaning which is made explicit in the connected term experiment. On the passive, it is *undergoing*. When we experience something we act upon it, we do something with it; then we suffer or undergo the consequences. We do something to the thing and then it does something to us in return: such is the peculiar combination. The connection of these two phases of experience measures the fruitfulness or value of the experience. Mere activity does not constitute experience. It is dispersive, centrifugal, dissipating. Experience as trying involves change, but change is meaningless transition unless it is consciously connected with the return wave of consequences which flow from it. When an activity is continued *into* the undergoing of consequences, when the change made by action is reflected back into a change made in us, the mere flux is loaded with significance. We learn something. It is not experience when a child merely sticks his finger into a flame; it is experience when the movement is connected with the pain which he undergoes in consequence. Henceforth the sticking of the finger into flame *means* a burn. Being burned is a mere physical change, like the burning of a stick of wood, if it is not perceived as a consequence of some other action.

Blind and capricious impulses hurry us on heedlessly from one thing to another. So far as this happens, everything is writ in water. There is none of that cumulative growth which makes an experience in any vital sense of that term. On the other hand, many things happen to us in the way of pleasure and pain which we do not connect with any prior activity of our own. They are mere accidents so far as we are concerned. There is no before or after to such experience; no retrospect nor outlook, and consequently no meaning. We get nothing which may be carried over to foresee what is likely to happen next, and no gain in ability to adjust ourselves to what is coming—no added control. Only by courtesy can such an experience be called experience. To "learn from experience" is to make a backward and forward connection between what we do to things and what we enjoy or suffer from things in consequence. Under such conditions, doing becomes a trying; an experiment with the world to find out what it is like; the undergoing becomes instruction— discovery of the connection of things.

Two conclusions important for education follow. (1) Experience is primarily an active-passive affair; it is not primarily cognitive. But (2)

the *measure of the value* of an experience lies in the perception of relationships or continuities to which it leads up.   It includes cognition in the
degree in which it is cumulative or amounts to something, or has meaning.   In schools, those under instruction are too customarily looked upon
as acquiring knowledge as theoretical spectators, minds which appropriate
knowledge by direct energy of intellect.   The very word pupil has almost
come to mean one who is engaged not in having fruitful experiences but
in absorbing knowledge directly.   Something which is called mind or
consciousness is severed from the physical organs of activity.   The
former is then thought to be purely intellectual and cognitive; the latter
to be an irrelevant and intruding physical factor.   The intimate union
of activity and undergoing its consequences which leads to recognition
of meaning is broken; instead we have two fragments: mere bodily action on one side, and meaning directly grasped by "spiritual" activity on
the other.

It would be impossible to state adequately the evil results which have
flowed from this dualism of mind and body, much less to exaggerate
them.   Some of the more striking effects, may, however, be enumerated.
(*a*) In part bodily activity becomes an intruder.   Having nothing, so it is
thought, to do with mental activity, it becomes a distraction, an evil to
be contended with.   For the pupil has a body, and brings it to school
along with his mind.   And the body is, of necessity, a wellspring of
energy; it has to do something.   But its activities, not being utilized in
occupation with things which yield significant results, have to be frowned
upon.   They lead the pupil away from the lesson with which his "mind"
ought to be occupied; they are sources of mischief.   The chief source of
the "problem of discipline" in schools is that the teacher has often to
spend the larger part of the time in suppressing the bodily activities which
take the mind away from its material.   A premium is put on physical
quietude; on silence, on rigid uniformity of posture and movement; upon
a machine-like simulation of the attitudes of intelligent interest.   The
teachers' business is to hold the pupils up to these requirements and to
punish the inevitable deviations which occur.

The nervous strain and fatigue which result with both teacher and
pupil are a necessary consequence of the abnormality of the situation in
which bodily activity is divorced from the perception of meaning.   Cal-
lous indifference and explosions from strain alternate.   The neglected
body, having no organized fruitful channels of activity, breaks forth,
without knowing why or how, into meaningless boisterousness, or set-
tles into equally meaningless fooling—both very different from the normal
play of children.   Physically active children become restless and unruly,
the more quiescent, so-called conscientious ones spend what energy they

have in the negative task of keeping their instincts and active tendencies suppressed, instead of in a positive one of constructive planning and execution; they are thus educated not into responsibility for the significant and graceful use of bodily powers, but into an enforced duty not to give them free play. It may be seriously asserted that a chief cause for the remarkable achievements of Greek education was that it was never misled by false notions into an attempted separation of mind and body.

(b) Even, however, with respect to the lessons which have to be learned by the application of "mind," some bodily activities have to be used. The senses—especially the eye and ear—have to be employed to take in what the book, the map, the blackboard, and the teacher say. The lips and vocal organs, and the hands, have to be used to reproduce in speech and writing what has been stowed away. The senses are then regarded as a kind of mysterious conduit through which information is conducted from the external world into the mind; they are spoken of as gateways and avenues of knowledge. To keep the eyes on the book and the ears open to the teacher's words is a mysterious source of intellectual grace. Moreover, reading, writing, and figuring—important school arts—demand muscular or motor training. The muscles of eye, hand, and vocal organs accordingly have to be trained to act as pipes for carrying knowledge back out of the mind into external action. For it happens that using the muscles repeatedly in the same way fixes in them an automatic tendency to repeat.

The obvious result is a mechanical use of the bodily activities which (in spite of the generally obtrusive and interfering character of the body in mental action) have to be employed more or less. For the senses and muscles are used not as organic participants in having an instructive experience, but as external inlets and outlets of mind. Before the child goes to school, he learns with his hand, eye, and ear, because they are organs of the process of doing something from which meaning results. The boy flying a kite has to keep his eye on the kite, and has to note the various pressures of the string on his hand. His senses are avenues of knowledge not because external facts are somehow "conveyed" to the brain, but because they are *used* in doing something with a purpose. The qualities of seen and touched things have a bearing on what is done, and are alertly perceived; they have a meaning. But when pupils are expected to use their eyes to note the form of words, irrespective of their meaning, in order to reproduce them in spelling or reading, the resulting training is simply of isolated sense organs and muscles. It is such isolation of an act from a purpose which makes it mechanical. It is customary for teachers to urge children to read with expression, so as to bring out the meaning. But if they originally learned the sensory-motor technique of reading—the ability to identify forms and to reproduce the sounds they stand for—by methods which did not call for attention to meaning, a mechanical habit was established which makes it difficult to read subsequently with intelligence.   The vocal organs have been trained to go their own way automatically in isolation; and meaning cannot be tied on at will.   Drawing, singing, and writing may be taught in the same mechanical way; for, we repeat, any way *is* mechanical which narrows down the bodily activity so that a separation of body from mind—that is, from recognition of meaning—is set up.   Mathematics, even in its higher branches, when undue emphasis is put upon the technique of calculation, and science, when laboratory exercises are given for their own sake, suffer from the same evil.

(c) On the intellectual side the separation of "mind" from direct occupation with things throws emphasis on *things* at the expense of *relations* or connections.   It is altogether too common to separate perceptions and even ideas from judgments.   The latter are thought to come after the former in order to compare them.   It is alleged that the mind perceives things apart from relations; that it forms ideas of them in isolation from their connections—with what goes before and comes after.   Then judgment or thought is called upon to combine the separated items of "knowledge" so that their resemblance or casual connection shall be brought out. As a matter of fact, every perception and every idea is a sense of the bearings, use, and cause, of a thing. We do not really know a chair or have an idea of it by inventorying and enumerating its various isolated qualities, but only by bringing these qualities into connection with something else—the purpose which makes it a chair and not a table; or its difference from the kind of chair we are accustomed to, or the "period" which it represents, and so on.   A wagon is not perceived when all its parts are summed up; it is the characteristic connection of the parts which makes it a wagon.   And these connections are not those of mere physical juxtaposition; they involve connection with the animals that draw it, the things that are carried on it, and so on.   Judgment is employed in the perception; otherwise the perception is mere sensory excitation or else a recognition of the result of a prior judgment, as in the case of familiar objects.

Words, the counters for ideas, are, however, easily taken for ideas. And in just the degree in which mental activity is separated from active concern with the world, from doing something and connecting the doing with what is undergone, words, symbols, come to take the place of ideas. The substitution is the more subtle because *some* meaning is recognized. But we are very easily trained to be content with a minimum of meaning, and to fail to note how restricted is our perception of the relations which confer significance.   We get so thoroughly used to a kind of pseudo-idea, a half perception, that we are not aware how half-dead our mental action is, and how much keener and more extensive our observations and ideas would be if we formed them under conditions of a vital experience which required us to use judgment: to hunt for the connections of the thing dealt with.

There is no difference of opinion as to the theory of the matter. All authorities agree that that discernment of relationships is the genuinely intellectual matter; hence, the educative matter. The failure arises in supposing that relationships can become perceptible without *experience* —without that conjoint trying and undergoing of which we have spoken. It is assumed that "mind" can grasp them if it will only give attention, and that this attention may be given at will irrespective of the situation. Hence the deluge of half-observations, of verbal ideas, and unassimilated "knowledge" which afflicts the world. An ounce of experience is better than a ton of theory simply because it is only in experience that any theory has vital and verifiable significance. An experience, a very humble experience, is capable of generating and carrying any amount of theory (or intellectual content), but a theory apart from an experience cannot be definitely grasped even as theory. It tends to become a mere verbal formula, a set of catchwords used to render thinking, or genuine theorizing, unnecessary and impossible. Because of our education we use words, thinking they are ideas, to dispose of questions, the disposal being in reality simply such an obscuring of perception as prevents us from seeing any longer the difficulty.

REFLECTION IN EXPERIENCE

Thought or reflection, as we have already seen virtually if not explicitly, is the discernment of the relation between what we try to do and what happens in consequence. No experience having a meaning is possible without some element of thought. But we may contrast two types of experience according to the proportion of reflection found in them. All our experiences have a phase of "cut and try" in them—what psychologists call the method of trial and error. We simply do something, and when it fails, we do something else, and keep on trying till we hit upon something which works, and then we adopt that method as a rule of thumb measure in subsequent procedure. Some experiences have very little else in them than this hit and miss or succeed process. We see *that* a certain way of acting and a certain consequence are connected, but we do not see *how* they are. We do not see the details of the connection; the links are missing. Our discernment is very gross. In other cases we push our observation farther. We analyze to see just what lies between so as to bind together cause and effect, activity and consequence. This extension of our insight makes foresight more accurate and comprehensive. The action which rests simply upon the trial and error method is at the mercy of circumstances; they may change so that the act performed does not operate in the way it was expected to. But if we know in detail upon what the result depends, we can look to see whether the required conditions are there. The method extends our practical control. For if some of the conditions are missing, we may, if we know what the needed antecedents for an effect are, set to work to supply them; or, if they are such as to produce undesirable effects as well, we may eliminate some of the superfluous causes and economize effort.

In discovery of the detailed connections of our activities and what happens in consequence, the thought implied in cut and try experience is made explicit. Its quantity increases so that its proportionate value is very different. Hence the quality of the experience changes; the change is so significant that we may call this type of experience reflective—that is, reflective *par excellence*. The deliberate cultivation of this phase of thought constitutes thinking as a distinctive experience. Thinking, in other words, is the intentional endeavor to discover *specific* connections between something which we do and the consequences which result, so that the two become continuous. Their isolation, and consequently their purely arbitrary going together, is cancelled; a unified developing situation takes its place. The occurrence is now understood; it is explained; it is reasonable, as we say, that the thing should happen as it does.

Thinking is thus equivalent to an explicit rendering of the intelligent element in our experience. It makes it possible to act with an end in view. It is the condition of our having aims. As soon as an infant begins to *expect* he begins to use something which is now going on as a sign of something to follow; he is, in however simple a fashion, judging. For he takes one thing as *evidence* of something else, and so recognizes a relationship. Any future development, however elaborate it may be, is only an extending and a refining of this simple act of inference. All that the wisest man can do is to observe what is going on more widely and more minutely and then select more carefully from what is noted just those factors which point to something to happen. The opposites, once more, to thoughtful action are routine and capricious behavior. The former accepts what has been customary as a full measure of possibility and omits to take into account the connections of the particular things done. The latter makes the momentary act a measure of value, and ignores the connections of our personal action with the energies of the environment. It says, virtually, "things are to be just as I happen to like them at this instant," as routine says in effect "let things continue just as I have found them in the past." Both refuse to acknowledge responsibility for the future consequences which flow from present action. Reflection is the acceptance of such responsibility.

The starting point of any process of thinking is something going on, something which just as it stands is incomplete or unfulfilled. Its point, its meaning lies literally in what it is going to be, in how it is going to turn out. As this is written, the world is filled with the clang of contending armies. For an active participant in the war, it is clear that the momentous thing is the issue, the future consequences, of this and that happening. He is identified, for the time at least, with the issue; *his* fate hangs upon the course things are taking. But even for an onlooker in a neutral country, the significance of every move made, of every advance here and retreat there, lies in what it portends. To *think* upon the news as it comes to us is to attempt to see what is indicated as probable or possible regarding an outcome. To fill our heads, like a scrapbook, with this and that item as a finished and done-for thing, is not to think. It is to turn ourselves into a piece of registering apparatus. To consider the *bearing* of the occurrence upon what may be, but is not yet, is to think. Nor will the reflective experience be different in kind if we substitute distance in time for separation in space. Imagine the war done with, and a future historian giving an account of it. The episode is, by assumption, past. But he cannot give a thoughtful account of the war save as he preserves the time sequence; the meaning of each occurrence, as he deals with it, lies in what was future for *it,* though not for the historian. To take it by itself as a complete existence is to take it unreflectively.

Reflection also implies concern with the issue—a certain sympathetic identification of our own destiny, if only dramatic, with the outcome of the course of events. For the general in the war, or a common soldier, or a citizen of one of the contending nations, the stimulus to thinking is direct and urgent. For neutrals, it is indirect and dependent upon imagination. But the flagrant partisanship of human nature is evidence of the intensity of the tendency to identify ourselves with one possible course of events, and to reject the other as foreign. If we cannot take sides in overt action, and throw in our little weight to help determine the final balance, we take sides emotionally and imaginatively. We desire this or that outcome. One wholly indifferent to the outcome does not follow or think about what is happening at all. From this dependence of the act of thinking upon a sense of sharing in the consequences of what goes on, flows one of the chief paradoxes of thought. Born in partiality, in order to accomplish its tasks it must achieve a certain detached impartiality. The general who allows his hopes and desires to affect his observations and interpretations of the existing situation will surely make a mistake in calculation. While hopes and fears may be the chief motive for a thoughtful following of the war on the part of an onlooker in a neutral country, he too will think ineffectively in the degree in which his preferences modify the stuff of his observations and reasonings. There is, however, no incompatibility between the fact that the occasion of reflection lies in a personal sharing in what is going on and the fact that the value of the reflection lies upon keeping one's self out of the data. The almost insurmountable difficulty of achieving this detachment is evidence that thinking originates in situations where the course of thinking is an actual part of the course of events and is designed to influence the result. Only gradually and with a widening of the area of vision through a growth of social sympathies does thinking develop to include what lies beyond our *direct* interests: a fact of great significance for education.

To say that thinking occurs with reference to situations which are still going on, and incomplete, is to say that thinking occurs when things are uncertain or doubtful or problematic. Only what is finished, completed, is wholly assured. Where there is reflection there is suspense. The object of thinking is to help *reach* a conclusion, to project a possible termination on the basis of what is already given. Certain other facts about thinking accompany this feature. Since the situation in which thinking occurs is a doubtful one, thinking is a process of inquiry, of looking into things, of investigating. *Acquiring* is always secondary, and instrumental to the act of *inquiring*. It is seeking, a quest, for something that is not at hand. We sometimes talk as if "original research" were a peculiar prerogative of scientists or at least of advanced students. But all thinking is research, and all research is native, original, with him who carries it on, even if everybody else in the world already is sure of what he is still looking for.

It also follows that all thinking involves a risk. Certainty cannot be guaranteed in advance. The invasion of the unknown is of the nature of an adventure; we cannot be sure in advance. The conclusions of thinking, till confirmed by the event, are, accordingly, more or less tentative or hypothetical. Their dogmatic assertion as final is unwarranted, short of the issue, in fact. The Greeks acutely raised the question: How can we learn? For either we know already what we are after, or else we do not know. In neither case is learning possible; on the first alternative because we know already; on the second, because we do not know what to look for, nor if, by chance, we find it can we tell that it is what we were after. The dilemma makes no provision for *coming* to know, for learning; it assumes either complete knowledge or complete ignorance. Nevertheless the twilight zone of inquiry, of thinking, exists. The possibility of *hypothetical* conclusions, of *tentative* results, is the fact which the Greek dilemma overlooked. The perplexities of the situation suggest certain ways out. We try these ways, and either push our way out, in which case we know we have found what we were looking for, or the situation gets darker and more confused—in which case, we know we are still ignorant. Tentative means trying out, feeling one's way along provisionally. Taken by itself, the Greek argument is a nice piece of formal logic. But it is also true that as long as men kept a sharp disjunction between knowledge and ignorance, science made only slow and accidental advance. Systematic advance in invention and discovery began when men recognized that they could utilize doubt for purposes of inquiry by forming conjectures to guide action in tentative explorations, whose development would confirm, refute, or modify the guiding conjecture. While the Greeks made knowledge more than learning, modern science makes conserved knowledge only a means to learning, to discovery.

To recur to our illustration. A commanding general cannot base his actions upon either absolute certainty or absolute ignorance. He has a certain amount of information at hand which is, we will assume, reasonably trustworthy. He then *infers* certain prospective movements, thus assigning meaning to the bare facts of the given situation. His inference is more or less dubious and hypothetical. But he acts upon it. He develops a plan of procedure, a method of dealing with the situation. The consequences which directly follow from his acting this way rather than that test and reveal the worth of his reflections. What he already knows functions and has value in what he learns. But will this account apply in the case of the one in a neutral country who is thoughtfully following as best he can the progress of events? In form, yes, though not of course in content. It is self-evident that his guesses about the future indicated by present facts, guesses by which he attempts to supply meaning to a multitude of disconnected data, cannot be the basis of a method which shall take effect in the campaign. *That* is not *his* problem. But in the degree in which he is actively thinking, and not merely passively following the course of events, his tentative inferences will take effect in *a* method of procedure appropriate to *his* situation. He will anticipate certain future moves, and will be on the alert to see whether they happen or not. In the degree in which he is intellectually concerned, or thoughtful, he will be actively on the lookout; he will take steps which although they do not affect the campaign, modify in some degree *his* subsequent actions. Otherwise his later "I told you so" has no intellectual quality at all; it does not mark any testing or verification of prior thinking, but only a coincidence that yields emotional satisfaction—and includes a large factor of self-deception.

The case is comparable to that of an astronomer who from given data has been led to foresee (infer) a future eclipse. No matter how great the mathematical probability, the inference is hypothetical—a matter of probability.[1] The hypothesis as to the date and position of the antici- pated eclipse becomes the material of forming a method of future con- duct. Apparatus is arranged; possibly an expedition is made to some far part of the globe. In any case, some active steps are taken which actually change *some* physical conditions. And apart from such steps and the consequent modification of the situation, there is no completion of the act of thinking. It remains suspended. Knowledge, already at- tained knowledge, controls thinking and makes it fruitful.

So much for the general features of a reflective experience. They are (1) perplexity, confusion, doubt, due to the fact that one is implicated in an incomplete situation whose full character is not yet determined; (2) a conjectural anticipation—a tentative interpretation of the given ele- ments, attributing to them a tendency to effect certain consequences; (3) a careful survey (examination, inspection, exploration, analysis) of all at- tainable consideration which will define and clarify the problem in hand; (4) a consequent elaboration of the tentative hypothesis to make it more precise and more consistent, because squaring with a wider range of facts; (5) taking one stand upon the projected hypothesis as a plan of action which is applied to the existing state of affairs; doing something overtly to bring about the anticipated result, and thereby testing the hypothesis It is the extent and accuracy of steps three and four which mark off a dis- tinctive reflective experience from one on the trial and error plane. They make *thinking* itself into an experience. Nevertheless, we never get wholly beyond the trial and error situation. Our most elaborate and rationally consistent thought has to be tried in the world and thereby tried out. And since it can never take into account all the connections, it can never cover with perfect accuracy all the consequences. Yet a thoughtful survey of conditions is so careful, and the guessing at results so controlled, that we have a right to mark off the reflective experience from the grosser trial and error forms of action.

SUMMARY

In determining the place of thinking in experience we first noted that experience involves a connection of doing or trying with something which is undergone in consequence. A separation of the active doing phase from the passive undergoing phase destroys the vital meaning of an ex-

---

[1] It is most important for the practice of science that men in many cases can calculate the degree of probability and the amount of probable error involved, but that does not alter the features of the situation as described. It refines them.

perience. Thinking is the accurate and deliberate instituting of connections between what is done and its consequences. It notes not only that they are connected, but the details of the connection. It makes connecting links explicit in the form of relationships. The stimulus to thinking is found when we wish to determine the significance of some act, performed or to be performed. Then we anticipate consequences. This implies that the situation as it stands is, either in fact or to us, incomplete and hence indeterminate. The projection of consequences means a proposed or tentative solution. To perfect this hypothesis, existing conditions have to be carefully scrutinized and the implications of the hypothesis developed—an operation called reasoning. Then the suggested solution—the idea or theory—has to be tested by acting upon it. If it brings about certain consequences, certain determinate changes, in the world, it is accepted as valid. Otherwise it is modified, and another trial made. Thinking includes all of these steps,—the sense of a problem, the observation of conditions, the formation and rational elaboration of a suggested conclusion, and the active experimental testing. While all thinking results in knowledge, ultimately the value of knowledge is subordinate to its use in thinking. For we live not in a settled and finished world, but in one which is going on, and where our main task is prospective, and where retrospect—and all knowledge as distinct from thought is retrospect—is of value in the solidity, security, and fertility it affords our dealings with the future.

---

10. Education from a Pragmatic Point of View*

Related selections: 4, 5, 9, 17

IN THIS chapter from *How We Learn,* Professor Bode draws upon the classic work of Koehler on the behavior of apes that demonstrated the importance of insight in learning. Bode analyzes the characteristics of this kind of learning, relates it to a conception of mind, and points out that the learner's feel for the total situation comes prior to his understanding of relationships. The implications for schooling are discussed.

* Boyd Henry Bode, *How We Learn* (D. C. Heath and Co., 1940), chap. XV, pp. 233–246. Reprinted by permission of the publisher.
Professor Bode (1873–1953), philosopher and teacher, was for many years Professor of Philosophy of Education at the Ohio State University. At the time of his death he was a visiting professor at the University of Florida.

IT IS to be expected that [one's] conception of mind . . . will have significant bearing on educational outlook. If mind is a function, there can be no room for a faculty psychology. If this function is a function of a "field," then education cannot be a process of organizing mental states. Lastly, if this function is a process of progressively shaping up the environment so as to bring an ongoing activity to a successful termination, then education cannot be identified with a mechanistic stamping in of S-R bonds.

In approaching the problem of learning, our clue must come from the idea that mind is such a process of "progressively shaping up the environment." This process was illustrated earlier by the example of the pedestrian making his way along a difficult path. He picks and chooses, as we say; which means that a whole field, consisting of environmental relationships and bodily reactions, is in continuous reorganization. This process of reorganization is not, indeed, the same as learning, since no new elements may be involved. The case is different if our pedestrian discovers, as a result of his experience, that clay is slippery, whereas sod or gravel affords a firm footing. He learns about clay, for example, provided that he notes the connection between the appearance of clay and what the clay does to him when he tries to walk on it. To note the connection is to learn something, and the learning takes the form of changing the experience. The clay now *looks* slippery; it has acquired meaning. Such change in an experience whereby it becomes more serviceable for the guidance of behavior is what is meant by learning.

In this illustration learning is an intellectual affair, since it is identified with the perception of significant relationships. This kind of learning naturally occupies a prominent place in formal education. Instruction in golf, for example, is possible because the reason why a beginner "hooks" his drives or fails to get distance can be analyzed out. The significant relationships can be brought to the attention of the learner. Where such analysis is difficult, instruction is correspondingly difficult, as, for example, in teaching a boy how to balance himself on a bicycle, or to wag his ears, or to be at ease in a social gathering. Such accomplishments are also classed as learning, but they are generally acquired by trial and error, and perhaps without any perception of significant relationships. The result may be achieved without any knowledge of how it was done. But, even so, the learning is a process of getting the "feel" of the thing; which is to say that the experience is changed so as to provide better control for behavior.

To what extent relationships are clearly perceived in learning is sometimes open to doubt. If a baby touches a hot stove and thereafter avoids the stove, we are tempted to assume that the baby sees the relationship between "stove" and "hot." It is evident that the experience of being burned changes the infant's response to the stove, and the inference is warranted that there has been a change in his experience of the stove. The precise nature of this change, however, is not so clear. Psychologically there is a vast difference between seeing the stove as "stove-meaning-burn" and seeing it merely as "bad" or "hot." In the former case there is a clear distinction between the object and the thing meant or pointed to; in the latter case the meaning is so completely incorporated that there is no clear distinction. This complete assimilation of the meaning to the thing is exemplified in all cases of simple recognition. Persons seeing a lemon will sometimes "make a face"; they react to the object as sour, but they may not make the distinction which we ordinarily make when we infer that a person broken out with rash has measles or smallpox. That is, we do not distinguish between "thing" and "meaning"; we "recognize" the thing without this internal distinction. Recognition, however, implies a change in the perceived object; a lemon *looks* different after we have had experience with it. Moreover, the lemon thus seen controls behavior in terms of future consequences; we decline, for example, to bite into it. Hence the lemon exercises the function which we have identified with mind. But this is mind in its lowest terms, so to speak; the "sour" is not definitely marked off as something symbolized, or indicated, or pointed to. The function is performed, but it is not definitely intellectualized.

In the case of the lemon it is easy enough for the average person to distinguish between "lemon" and its meaning, "sour," if there is occasion to do so. There are many situations, however, where we are unable to draw a satisfactory contrast between "thing" and "meaning." An experienced physician, for example, may "sense" that a patient stands no chance, before he has even started to make a diagnosis; a lawyer may "sense" that there is something crooked about the case that is brought to him, even if it baffles him to find anything wrong. The expert has learned to "size up" situations in advance of tangible evidence. Cases of this kind are not wholly devoid of the contrast between thing and meaning; but they suggest how thing and meaning can run together and blend, and they suggest why we speak of being guided by "intuition." They also suggest the possibility that there are experiences where the *contrast* between "thing" and "meaning" is not present at all. Sometimes the contrast is lacking because it has gradually faded out. The child learns at one stage that the man in uniform *means* letters; later on he simply recognizes the man as the mailman. But there may be other instances when the experience may undergo an adaptive change without the clear intervention of this contrast at any point.   The case of the baby and the stove may perhaps be explained either way.

A reference to the learning of the lower animals may serve to emphasize the fact that there are different varieties of learning and that careful interpretation is necessary.   There is a story of a cat eating from a dish of codfish under which a mischievous boy had placed a large lighted firecracker.   According to the story, that cat would never touch codfish again, no matter in what form it might be offered.   Did the cat remember the original experience and relate the codfish specifically to explosions, or did the learning consist in a simple transformation of the experience so that the codfish did not look good any more?   Then there is the familiar experiment with the pike, which was placed in a glass tank inside a larger tank, for the purpose of ascertaining whether the pike could learn to keep away from the small fish swimming around outside the glass tank.   The pike finally learned, but only after countless collisions with the walls of his glass tank.   In this case the learning presumably consisted simply in a change in the appearance of the small fish, so that they no longer looked inviting or appetizing.   It is related that the pike did not offer to molest these fish even after the inner glass tank was removed, but that it unhesitatingly pursued other kinds of small fish when these were introduced into the tank.   This bears out the supposition that the learning was confined to a change in the appearance of those kinds of fish with which its experience had been unfortunate.   There was no evidence of anything resembling what, on the human level, is called analysis and generalization.

By contrast the experiments of Koehler with apes do provide evidence of this kind.   These experiments were so devised as to require a comprehension or "insight" into relationships, if the apes were to solve their problem, which consisted in each case in adapting ways and means for securing tempting fruit.   The situations were so arranged that the ape would at least stand a chance to "figure out" the solution.   That is, the difficulty was, from a human standpoint, relatively simple, yet it required some kind of new adaptation of means to ends, such as fetching a box for the purpose of standing on it so as to reach an object overhead.

The experiment provides a situation in which the direct way to a goal is barred, but in which an indirect way is left open.   The animal is introduced into this situation, which has been so planned that it is fully comprehensible. The animal is then left to indicate by its behavior whether or not it can solve the problem by the indirect means that have been provided.[1]

---

[1] W. Koehler, *The Mentality of Apes,* by permission of Harcourt, Brace and Company, Inc., p. 4, quoted by K. Koffka, *The Growth of the Mind,* p. 81.

It is not necessary for our purpose to do more than to make brief mention of some of these experiments.   In one experiment, fruit was placed beyond reach outside the cage, but a string was attached to it which was in easy reach; in another there was no string, but a stick was placed inside the cage with which the fruit could be reached.   One variation of this experiment consisted in placing in the cage, not a stick, but a part of a dead tree from which a branch could be broken off to be used as a stick.   In another variation two bamboo sticks had to be fitted together by inserting one into the hollow end of the other so as to make the stick of adequate length.   In still another experiment the fruit was hung from the ceiling of the cage, but so high that a box which was in the cage had to be placed under it.   As a variation of this experiment the box was filled with stones which had to be taken out before the box could be moved.   Again the fruit thus suspended could be reached by swinging towards it with a rope, which was likewise suspended from the ceiling at a distance of two meters. In a subsequent experiment the rope was laid on the floor, and it had to be replaced on the hook—which was accessible to the ape—before it could be used for purposes of swinging.

In struggling with these situations the apes naturally made errors, some of which Koehler calls "clever," and others he labels "stupid."   For example, on one occasion an ape brought in a box and placed it against the wall above the floor where it was in a position from which the fruit could easily be reached, if only the box could be made to stick to the wall. Koehler calls this a clever error because it showed a comprehension of the problem, even though an essential factor had been overlooked.   This epithet applies also to the procedure of the ape who tried to obtain the fruit by means of two short sticks, his method being to lay the two sticks endwise, instead of inserting one into the other; so that by pushing with one of the sticks he made the other stick come into contact with the fruit.   In this way the ape succeeded in reaching the fruit with the sticks, although this did not help him in bringing the fruit into the cage.   By contrast a stupid error is illustrated by the behavior of a cat in Thorndike's experiments. The cat had learned to pull a string so as to release itself from the cage; and having learned this it went to the same spot and made the motion of pulling the string, in spite of the fact that the string had been hung in another part of the cage.

It may be remarked that the methods by which the apes sought to solve their problems were sometimes quite unexpected.   In one instance the two sticks to be fitted together were too nearly of the same size, so the ape proceeded to whittle down the end of one with his teeth, apparently for the purpose of making it fit.   This resulted in his breaking off a large splinter, which caused a change of plan.   The splinter was inserted into the other uninjured end of the pole, which made it long enough to serve the purpose of reaching the fruit.   On another occasion the ape led the keeper by the hand under the fruit, with the evident intention of using the keeper as a stepladder by climbing on his shoulder, as he had done on previous occasions.   This time, however, the keeper knelt down at the critical moment, so that, after the ape had climbed up, the fruit was still beyond reach.   The ape, as Koehler tells the incident, "climbs on to the man's shoulder after he has dragged him underneath the object, and the keeper quickly bends down.   The animal gets off complaining, takes hold of the keeper by his seat with both hands, and tries with all his might to push him up.   A surprising way of trying to improve the human implement."

With one exception, all of the experiments mentioned, and others besides, were successfully performed by some one or more of the apes.   As was perhaps to be expected, some of the apes proved to be distinctly superior to others in intelligence.   The experiment in which all the apes failed required that a rope lying on the floor of the cage be hung on a hook in the roof of the cage so that it might be used as a means of swinging the animal within reach of the fruit.   In these experiments there was no gradual sloping downward of the time-curve, as in the case of Thorndike's experiments with the cats, the reason being that Koehler's experiments were so arranged as to enable the animal to pick out the essential relationship beforehand.   Ordinarily the successful performance meant that the animal was master of the situation at once.   He could do the right thing on the next occasion with a minimum of fumbling.   In terms of curves, his learning was represented, not by a gradual downward slope, but by a straight drop.

It is of interest in this connection to observe that the experiment in which stones had to be taken from a box before the box could be moved was performed in a way that exhibited a curious limitation of insight. Instead of removing all the stones, the ape took out only as many as were necessary to make the box movable.   The labor involved in moving the box with a quantity of stones still left inside was considerable, but the ape apparently did not grasp the fact that his labor would be lightened by the removal of the remaining stones.   The stones were regarded as an obstacle to moving the box only as long as the box was too heavy to move. As soon as the box was movable, the remaining stones were ignored.

Learning, then, is a term that covers a variety of meanings.   Sometimes the emphasis is on the co-ordination that is acquired, as in the case of the batsman who learns to hit the ball safely, or the golfer who learns to correct a fault, without, in either case, knowing how it has been done.   All we can say is that there is an improvement in skill, together with a difference in the "feel" of the thing. Then there is the kind of learning in which the emphasis falls on this change in the "feel" or the quality of the experience; as when we learn to judge the speed of an automobile or to distrust certain persons, without being able to specify the clues on which we rely. Lastly, there is the kind of learning which is based on some trait of fact or relationship that can be analyzed out and offered as evidence, as when we infer from the appearance of a lawn that it needs sprinkling or when we abstain from coffee because it keeps us awake at night. The clear perception of relationships is what is sometimes designated as insight.

These differences in kinds of learning derive whatever significance they may have from the fact that they are connected with corresponding differences in the procedure by which they are acquired. They are primarily differences of emphasis. It seems safe to assume, on the one hand, that all learning involves some perception of relationship, however dim, and, on the other hand, that analysis, or insight into relationship, however extensive, never keeps abreast with the adaptive changes in our experience. Mind, as Dewey has told us, is "the power to understand things in terms of the use made of them." Understanding has to do with relationships. This understanding, however, may take various forms. It seems fair to describe the experience of the benighted pike in the tank as an obscure comprehension that the little fish were "to-be-let-alone." Some such quality of "futurity," therefore, inheres in all learning. It is worth noting that the expert who devotes himself to the business of analysis or the picking out of relationships does not thereby diminish the area of his unanalyzed experience. On the contrary, he increases it; he develops a kind of sixth sense or "instinct" or "intuition" which constantly outruns his ability to make clean-cut analyses and which guides him in situations that he cannot handle adequately by analysis. In other words, the expert never gets away from a certain resemblance to the pike. All this is reminiscent of the familiar advice given by an old judge to a young colleague, to the effect that a judge should make his decisions without giving the reasons therefor, because "the decisions are likely to be right, but the reasons are bound to be wrong."

All forms of learning, then, have a common element. They all involve a change in the experiential situation which gives greater control in relation to subsequent behavior. To the boy who has learned to swim, water has become a different medium, to which he responds differently. To the veteran salesman the reactions of his "prospects" when he approaches them take on the same kind of difference. The experiential situation has changed for them as truly as for the automobile mechanic who discovers that the trouble with an automobile is due to a defective carburetor. This change finds expression in the control of behavior, whether or not there is a *specific* reference to the future, in much the same way that the visual perception of a flame as "hot" controls behavior, without any such specific relationship as "flame *means* burn." All learning, then, is a change in experience such as to provide for increased control of behavior.[2]

We can now plot the curve of learning as it ordinarily goes on. It starts on the level of everyday living and it has to do with the changes made in things by our responses. These changes are speeded up and made more extensive by the process of analysis, or insight into relationships—a process in which the relationship of meaning or "pointing" is prominent and which aims to bring new elements into the picture. With familiarity this relationship of pointing drops out; the new elements become increasingly absorbed into the original experiences; recognition takes the place of inference. The experiences as thus modified become the basis for a repetition of the process; and thus experience continues to grow or to become enriched without any assignable limit.

This process of inference giving way to recognition is exemplified rather strikingly by language. When we first start to learn a foreign language, we rely extensively on the relationship, "this means that," (e.g., *cheval* means *horse*). If we reach a point, however, where we can speak and think in terms of the new language, this relationship disappears. The words begin to *look* different and to *sound* different. This change in the quality or *feel* of words takes place in much the same way in the case of our mother tongue. As William James remarks:

> Our own language would sound very different to us if we heard it without understanding, as we hear a foreign tongue. Rises and falls of voice, odd sibilants and other consonants, would fall on our ear in a way of which we can now form no notion. Frenchmen say that English sounds to them like the *gazouillement des oiseaux*—an impression which it certainly makes on no native ear. Many of us English would describe the sound of Russian in similar terms. All of us are conscious of the strong inflections of voice and explosives and gutturals of German speech in a way in which no German can be conscious of them.[3]

The inference to be drawn is that the term "meaning" has different applications. In one sense the term denotes the function of pointing

---

[2] "We thus reach a technical definition of education: It is that reconstruction or reorganization of experience which adds to the meaning of experience, and which increases the ability to direct the course of subsequent experience." John Dewey, *Democracy and Education,* copyright 1916 by The Macmillan Company, p. 89.

[3] From *Principles of Psychology,* vol. II, by William James. By permission of Henry Holt and Company, Inc., p. 80.

or symbolizing.   To make a clear contrast between the thing and whatever is pointed to is to "intellectualize" the experience of the thing. When this contrast drops out, the thing is still considered to retain the meaning, but the term meaning is now used in a different sense.   It is now a name for a certain quality of the total experience.   To use an illustration, we avoid an onrushing automobile, and we ordinarily do so without the help of a specific relationship, such as "automobile means danger." The quality of danger has become a part of the automobile, in the same way as its shape or color; it remains, indeed, just as effective in the control of behavior, but meaning is now better described as "appreciation" rather than "pointing."   In the language of Dewey:

Definiteness, depth, and variety of meaning attach to the objects of an experience just in the degree in which they have been previously thought about, even when present in an experience in which they do not evoke inferential procedures at all.   Such terms as "meaning," "significance," "value" have a double sense. Sometimes they mean a function: the office of one thing representing another, or pointing to it as implied; the operation, in short, of serving as a sign.   In the word "symbol" this meaning is practically exhaustive.   But the terms also sometimes mean an inherent quality, a quality intrinsically characterizing the thing experienced and making it worth while. . . .   In the situation which follows upon reflection, meanings are intrinsic; they have no instrumental or subservient office,—because they have no office at all.   They are as much qualities of the objects in the situation as are red and black, hard and soft, square and round.[4]

If we turn now to the consideration of the implications contained in this general point of view for school procedures, we are at once confronted with what Dewey calls the principle of the continuity of experience.   All learning, whether in school or out of school, has to do with the transformation of experience in the interest of better control.   In order to bring about this transformation, it is necessary to do something that will produce the desired change.   This contradicts the familiar assumption that pupils should go to school in order to draw upon a storehouse of knowledge, in somewhat the same way that a railroad car goes to the mine in order to take on a load of coal.   The school, from the present point of view, is simply a place which is especially designed to facilitate the business of securing the desired transformation of experience.   It is a place where new experiences are provided in such a form as to best promote that recon-

---

[4] Reprinted from *Essays in Experimental Logic* by John Dewey.   By permission of the University of Chicago Press, copyright 1916 by the University of Chicago.

struction or reorganization of experience which is identified with education.

---

11. We Learn What We Live*

Related selections: 9, 10, 31

IN THE folk thinking of America, there has been a disparagement of "book learning." This represents a belief that unless an endeavor is reflected in changed and improved behavior, it cannot be of much consequence. In this selection Kilpatrick sets forth the principles that learning involves changed behavior and that the change in behavior is what we learn. He also enumerates four principles as a basis for spiritual education. The statements regarding learning and those on the basis of spiritual life offer material for reflection and discussion.

WHAT THIS title means may not be quite clear to all. Just what does this transitive use of the verb *to live* mean? And is the theory thus asserted psychologically true? And if true, what does it mean for teaching? These questions we shall consider in the order given.

1. What does it mean *to live* anything that is to be learned? What does it mean for example, *to live persistence?* Can we not agree that actually *to live* persistence in any instance means (1) that one faces a life situation which itself calls for persistence; and (2) that one does then in his own heart accept the idea of persisting; and (3) accordingly does indeed so persist? When all these three things concur, then one has on that occasion *lived* persistence. If with this positive instance we contrast a negative one, the meaning may come clearer.

Certain pupils were asked to write out the words of their morning flag salute. Among the various replies received the following were noted:

I pejur legens; I plaig alegins; I pledge a legion; to the Republicans; one country invisable; one country inavisable; with liberty and jesters.

Is it not at once clear that these pupils did not adequately *live* the meaning of the words used in the salute? Whatever else they may or may not have lived, it stands clear that they did not in any full or adequate degree *live* the meanings which the words were supposed to carry.

* William H. Kilpatrick, "We Learn What We Live," *New York State Education,* vol. XXXIII (April, 1946), pp. 535–537. Reprinted by permission of the author and publisher.
Professor Kilpatrick (1871—) is Professor Emeritus of Education, Teachers College, Columbia, and a renowned teacher and scholar.

It may be added that we can live things in many different degrees. Take feelings, for example; some we may live so slightly that we hardly think of them at the time, and soon forget all about them. Others we live so deeply and poignantly that we can hardly banish them to give due attention elsewhere needed.

So much for the meaning of the transitive verb *to live*.

2. Is it psychologically true that we learn what we live?

The fact of internal *acceptance* we saw as an essential part of *truly living* anything. We can now say that different people will *live* the same thing differently if they accept it differently, differently for behavior purposes. Two women hear a child scream; both so accept it, the one as the scream of an unknown child, the other as the scream of her own child. Both are concerned; but the first one does nothing overt, the other hurries to rescue her child. Each woman lived the scream as she accepted it, accepted it for behavior purposes.

What now does *learn* mean? Consider this mother. After the screaming ceased, did not the matter remain with her—remain as she had accepted it? And as accepted, did it not help determine her further behavior? And determine it appropriately?

This then is what we mean by *learn:* When, after something has been lived, it does not die, but stays with one to get back, sooner or later, appropriately into one's further behavior—when these things happen, we say learning has taken place.

The full principle of learning may thus be stated:

We learn what we live as we accept it to live by, and we learn it in the degree that we live it.

For proof of this principle the reader is asked to apply it to his own life and see whether it fits, whether it does not pick out the strong instances of learning from the weak; and also to apply it to children and their living and learning in the home and in the school. Is it not true that one learns anything *as* he accepts it? Jacob accepted that the bloody coat was Joseph's and learned—falsely as to fact, but truly as to psychological learning—that Joseph was dead: "some evil beast of the field hath devoured him." And it stayed with him; "he refused to be comforted."

As to "degree of living"—and consequently of learning—there are two subprinciples that apply. (1) We live anything in the degree we count it important to us. So Jacob lived deeply the (supposed) death of Joseph and it stayed strongly with him to affect his further behavior. (2) We live more vividly and so learn stronger anything in the degree that it fits well in with what we already know and live. If a man tells me that he has moved next door to me, I shall remember his house number easily. In general, we learn easier what we understand well.

3. What difference in teaching does this learning theory demand?

First, it demands a kind of school different from the old one of merely assigned lessons in books; this must be a school of living.   If a child inevitably learns what he accepts in his heart to live by, then the quality of that living becomes the essential factor.   For all he lives, even his private heart reactions, he builds at once into character; and out of his character comes all his future behavior.

It is the learning of spiritual values that here concerns us.   Four typical samples will illustrate all such values: consideration for others, regard for their rights and feelings, appreciation, as for example of literature; persistence (in a worthy cause); and acting on thinking.   If these four are to be learned they must each be lived, lived (a) in some natural setting, as in life; and lived (b) in such variety of settings that the cumulative result is a dependable trait, well founded and many sided.

Let us conclude by considering the building of the four named typical traits.

Consideration of Others.   No true regard for others can come by mere compulsion, but only as the heart's own response to how others will feel justly considered.   True enough, compulsion may prevent positive habits of disregard.   How now shall we stir the youthful heart to regard others? The school life must be largely shared living, with abundant opportunities at co-operative creating and effecting. Each such sucessfully managed instance of shared effort makes *implicitly* for mutual regard.   But temptation to the contrary will arise; and besides the *implicit* regard must become *explicit* and critically judged.   When, then, conflicts occur, the resourceful teacher will mobilize the impartial public opinion of the group.   Nothing is more effective.   Next time the temptation will be better resisted, while the discussion has helped to build the conscious ideal.

Appreciation.   We must of course build many appreciations; for each is in range limited.   Can I build an appreciation of Whittier's "Barefoot Boy" by saying "I give you till next Monday to appreciate this, or else"? Clearly not.   Appreciation, like "the quality of mercy," is "not strained." We cannot command it. The only way is to help each youth find in the poem something that "clicks" within, something that rouses appreciation in him.   And the public opinion of the class must be closely watched; it can fortify and so strengthen a shared appreciation, but it can build a hurtful conformity instead of honest appreciation.   And note: Many varied cumulative appreciations are necessary to build a reliable "appreciation of good literature."

Persistence.   This we discussed at the outset.   How then shall we develop that crucial inner attitude, the wish to persist?   Here "nothing succeeds like success and nothing fails like failure." The wise teacher will know the strength and weakness of each pupil and see that each new enterprise, while difficult enough to be challenging, still lies within the area of possible success. The appreciative regard of the others in connection is a most powerful aid, as the same wise teacher will know. Persistence here is both effect and cause, effect of past success, cause of further and stronger effort, with the still further effect of increased self-respect and felt security.

Acting on Thinking. If there is any one trait which best promises to take care of all spiritual values, this is it. Consideration for others, persistence, proper sensitivity, self-respect, sense of security—these and a host of other spiritual traits are likely to come out of well-directed acting-on-thinking. In fact, this fourth trait of acting on thinking furnishes the twin highway for building, alike, both intelligence and strength of character. It builds intelligence; for acting on thinking is practically the only process for building trustworthy knowledge, reliable conceptions, effective principles of attack and of critical judgment. Acting on thinking likewise builds strength of character; for it alone can build sound and reliable attitudes and convictions, defensible ideals, and trustworthy principles of action.

The single principle to guide all teaching is that our pupils learn what they live as they in their hearts accept it.

II

Understanding the Learner

A. THE PROCESS OF GROWTH AND DEVELOPMENT

12. *The Nature of Organic Wholeness**

Related selections: 13, 32, 33, 47

RESEARCH in child development provides evidence that the growth of the individual tends to be unified and that the school must be concerned with the organic wholeness of children if desirable educational objectives are to be achieved. The growth demands of any child are a function of the totality of the organism and may or may not be the same as the growth demands of other children. The following selection by Professor Gilchrist clarifies the concept of organic wholeness. The entire original article, of which this selection is but the introduction, could be read with profit by students who are familiar with biological concepts and terminology.

WE HAVE become so accustomed to building toy houses of blocks, or constructing automobiles from accurately machined parts, that we think of wholes as formed by putting pieces together. It comes therefore as somewhat of a struggle to picture to ourselves a process, such as the molding of

* Francis G. Gilchrist, "The Nature of Organic Wholeness," *The Quarterly Review of Biology*, vol. XII (September, 1937), pp. 251–253. Reprinted by permission of the author and the Williams and Wilkins Company.

Dr. Gilchrist (1895—) is Professor of Zoology at Lewis and Clark College, Portland, Oregon.

a vase from a lump of clay, in which the whole precedes the parts and gives to the parts their meaning. Yet it is this latter analogy and not the former which we must have in mind if we are to comprehend aright the nature of the organism and the processes of its becoming.

If one would understand a machine he will take it apart, either actually or in his imagination, and will study it piece by piece, noting the characteristics of each piece and the relations of each piece to each other piece. Then by synthesizing the knowledge thus obtained, he will understand the machine. On the other hand, if one would understand the vase or organism, he must begin by first comprehending the thing as a whole. Only then will he be able to discern the significance of the parts. Indeed, he may fail to discern discrete parts at all; yet his appreciation of the whole will not thereby be impaired.

But how does one comprehend a whole except by knowing the parts and observing their relations to one another? Can one know a whole directly? Yes. Indeed, it is the natural thing to do. The child knows a cat before it distinguishes a head. It knows its mother's face before it discerns her eyes. It would be very unnatural indeed for a child to reconstruct its concept of a face by piecing together its various anatomical structures or its characters. It is just as unnatural for a biologist to construct his concept of an organism by adding together entities of any sort, be they organs, germ layers, unit characters, cleavage cells, or organforming stuffs. It is only a habit of mind which we have acquired through familiarity with houses and machines which leads us to think that way.

But admitting that one might form some general concept of a whole before discerning parts, is it nevertheless not true that a whole is nothing more than the sum of its parts plus whatever interrelations may exist between its parts? This is indeed true with regard to some wholes; namely, the artificial wholes which men construct; but it is not true of organic wholes such as we commonly find in nature. Certainly it is not true of organisms. Let us examine this assertion from the standpoint of a part.

A thing may become a part in one or the other of two ways: (a) It may begin as a discrete and independent unit and then by integration with other units secondarily find itself a part of a whole. Thus the brick becomes a part of a house. Thus also a balance-wheel becomes a part of a watch. Houses and watches as thus fabricated are merely the sums of interrelated parts. Their wholeness, or had we not better say, their togetherness, is the result of a "creative synthesis" which has taken place. Their special properties depend upon the special relations between their constituent parts. (b) In organic wholes, on the other hand, the whole exists first, and the part arises by differentiation within the pre-existing whole.

Homogeneity precedes heterogeneity. At first the parts are indistinguishable from one another except, perhaps, by future reference. Thus a "part" of a lump of clay may be described as the prospective handle of a vase, or a part of an amphibian egg may be termed "presumptive neural plate"; but the part is not yet handle, nor neural plate; nor is it entirely certain that it will become such.

Organic wholes, then, are not primarily composed of parts, or even of inter-related parts. They are not the result of an integration or of a "creative synthesis." Quite to the contrary, they precede their "parts" in time, and remain superior to them in space.

It is likely that the reader is not convinced. Perhaps he is a morphologist and is engaged in dissecting organisms and studying their structures, dead or alive. To him the organism is a definite pattern in space; or indeed a succession of such patterns, if he be an embryologist. But the morphologist's organism is, of course, not the whole organism. It is only that aspect of the organism which he has chosen to abstract and study. Perhaps the reader is a physiologist, and concerns himself with the functioning of organs or the rôles of forces. He, no doubt, has become much interested in the interrelationships of processes, and has noted the remarkable self-regulating devices within the functioning system. But his organism, like the organism of the morphologist is an abstraction from the whole.

To study the oragniom as an organic whole, one must be interested not merely in the organism which is and does; but he must know also what under other conditions and in other relationships this same mass of living matter will be and do. He will want to know how and why the organism came to be what it is and to do what it does. Indeed, he will go further and will seek to comprehend, if possible, the nature of the organic wholeness in itself; that is, the wholeness which precedes the being and the doing and which gives to parts their significance.

Let us illustrate this by reference to a very primitive animal, the freshwater polyp *Hydra*. A piece of the body stalk of this animal is morphologically only a piece of the body stalk. As such it may be killed, sectioned, reconstructed, and described. Physiologically it is an organization of more or less specialized cells carrying on the numerous functions of living. But isolate this piece of the stalk (the following is true of the central portions of the stalk), and immediately these same cells commence to reorganize themselves; and in a short time a whole new polyp has been formed. It is therefore true that what a part of a polyp is and does is a function of its position in a whole; and the whole must be understood first, if the structure and functioning of the part is to be comprehended.

13. Concepts of Growth—Their Significance to Teachers*

Related selections: 12, 14, 15, 32, 33

IF THE school is to provide the experiences necessary for the optimum development of children, teachers and administrators must be concerned with appraising and understanding the growth of individual children.   The concepts of growth held by teachers will influence both classroom practice and administrative policy.   The research of Olson and Hughes calls into serious question many of the common practices in education, particularly those relating to comparative marking, methods of reporting, promotion policies and attempts to force growth.

THE GROWING body of data and principles about human growth and development offers an ever more secure foundation for the adoption of philosophies of growth in the classrooms of the nation.   On the technical side, generalizations are increasing in number and proceeding toward greater precision and scope.   On the practical side, more teachers are attaining the fundamental understanding that enables them to meet new problems at a high level of professional competence and confidence.

The literature that definitely attempts to bridge the gap between the laboratory and the classroom is meager.   The resources for such a literature are enormous.   The writers will attempt to present concepts and illustrations that to them appear to be of peculiar importance in the classroom.   The illustrations are drawn from research at the child development laboratory of the University Elementary School at the University of Michigan.

While maintaining the importance of the point of view of the child as a whole, the writers have selected examples of historical and immediate concern to teachers.   This article will stress factors of significance in understanding the growth of individuals and the implications of these factors for school practices.   A series of studies made in the laboratory school stress the relationships that exist among members of classroom groups. Both individual and group concepts are needed for complete understanding.

* Reprinted by permission of the Association for Childhood Education and the authors.   "Concepts of Growth—Their Significance to Teachers," by Willard C. Olson and Byron O. Hughes.   From *Childhood Education,* October, 1944, vol. XXI, pp. 53–63.

Dr. Olson (1899—) is Dean of the School of Education, University of Michigan, and Professor of Education and Psychology.   He is a Diplomate in clinical psychology.   Dr. Hughes (1906—) is Professor of Education at the same institution.

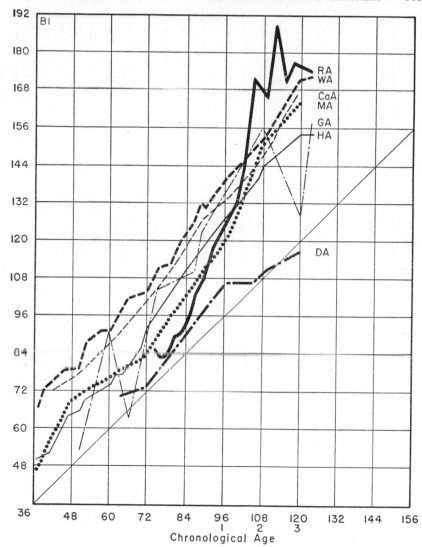

FIGURE 1

Growth of a boy at a high level (B1).

CHILDREN DIFFER IN RATE AND LEVEL OF GROWTH

Every classroom teacher is impressed with the fact that children are not alike.   If tests have been administered at any given time these impressions have been confirmed in an objective manner.   Research in child development gives added knowledge of the nature of the differences and how

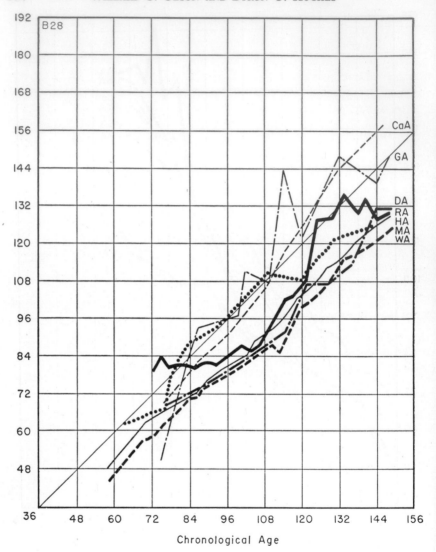

FIGURE 2

Growth of a boy at a low level (B28).

they persist through time.   By following growth in a number of characteristics more understanding of total significance is secured than by studying
one attribute.

Figures 1 and 2 illustrate how two boys grew through time.   Repeated
measures were made and the original units were translated into an age
scale as described in other publications.   Thus in the figures height in

inches has become height age (H.A.); weight in pounds, weight age (W.A.); number of permanent teeth erupted, dental age (D.A.); extent of ossification of hand and wrist bones, carpal age (Ca.A.); and strength of grip in kilograms, grip age (G.A.). In the conventional manner success in intelligence tests is described by mental age (M.A.), and achievement in reading by reading age (R.A.).

The figures are constructed by plotting growth ages for a particular attribute above the chronological age at which it was obtained and by connecting the points. Thus the record for the boy in Figure 1 (B1) starts at about 36 months of age in the nursery school while the record for the boy in Figure 2 (B28) starts in the kindergarten at about 60 months of age. These boys were selected because they represent the extremes in organismic age of 28 boys being given intensive and systematic study. Organismic age is a coined name for the average of all available growth ages at a point in time. A straight diagonal line has been drawn through the intersection of the scales for choronological and growth ages as a convenient reference point for average growth—12 months of growth for 12 months of living.

It will be observed that most of the curves for B1 remain above the line of average development throughout the period while those of B28 remain below the line. The various attributes of growth tend to cluster together and there is some continuity throughout the years. The numbers on the base line indicate that Child B1 had pubic hair at 108 months which was pigmented at 120 months. Pubic hair has not yet appeared in Child B28 at 150 months. The differences between Child B1 and B28 are deep seated. The first menstruation for the mother of B1 occurred at 11 years of age while that for the mother of B28 was at 15. B1 weighed 9 pounds at birth while B28 weighed 4¼ pounds. B1 was breast-fed 5 months and B28 not at all. B1 had his first tooth at 6 months and B28 had a tooth at 12 months. B1 reverses the trend by delaying talking until 20 months while B28 talked at 15 months.

Detailed case records are available for these boys showing interesting differences in health, behavior and personality. The inescapable fact of persistent individual differences in growth as illustrated by B1 and B28 must be taken into account in implementing a program based upon the philosophy of growth. Policies and practices that take differences into account will be elaborated elsewhere.

GROWTH HAS SOME UNITY WHEN VIEWED AS A WHOLE

Since growth as expressed in a child is a result of the action of the environment on the potential that originally existed in a single cell, it is not surprising that some tendency toward unity continues to exist through the years of growth. The research literature has demonstrated this tendency in a number of ways. The most common method is to calculate coefficients of correlation between the various attributes of growth. Such research rather regularly reports positive intercorrelations. In a few attributes and in some samples of children, the values may drop very close to zero. An accidental negative correlation may at times appear. The trend of the evidence, however, supports the conclusion of some tendency toward unification in childhood.

The writers currently are investigating another approach to the problem in which various aspects of growth are viewed simply as interchangeable samples of total growth, finding one expression in one individual and another in another. The essential conclusion is the same, i.e., that the various attributes in an individual tend to cluster about a center of gravity of growth of that individual and that the freedom to vary is restricted. The detailed support has been worked out, but the manuscript has not been printed. The thought can be illustrated by Figures 1 and 2 by pointing out that any measure collected for B1 tends to cluster with the others and that the same is true for B28. The finding is important for education in that achievement in school, illustrated by reading in the diagrams, tends to be an expression of total growth.* Consideration of the whole child thus becomes more vital and expectancies for a given child are modified accordingly.

CHILDREN DIFFER IN THE PATTERN OF GROWTH

Children vary in the growth curves that they present both in changes with time and in the arrangement of various aspects within the pattern. Thus in Figures 1 and 2, the children differ not only in the general level at which they are growing, but also in detail. In Figure 1 reading age is finally at the top of the pattern while in Figure 2 reading age is near the middle.

Figure 3 gives a more dramatic illustration of variations in pattern and the significance of these variations for education. The attributes of growth for this girl are somewhat more scattered than for most children. The physical assets are particularly high with height, weight, carpal development and strength above the line of average growth and with intellectual factors such as mental age and reading age several years below. If attention is focused on the mental age and reading, it would appear that

---

* The reader should note that the case illustrated by Figure 3 is atypical in that reading age lags behind all other indices of growth.

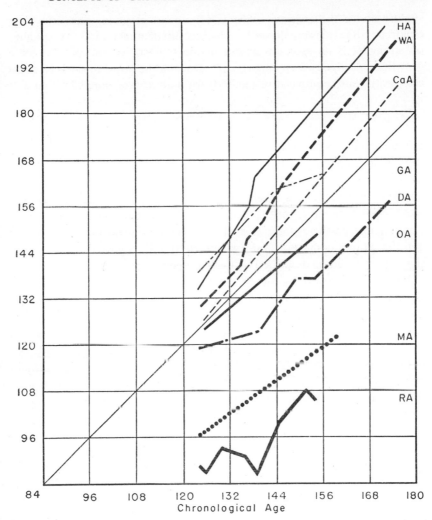

FIGURE 3

Pattern of growth for a socially competent, mentally retarded girl

this child has borderline intelligence.   No observer is likely to reach this conclusion if the behavior as a whole is viewed.   This child in the elementary period was one of the best baseball players and runners in the room, could sing well, and had artistic talents beyond the average.   As she went on into high school she did well in these areas.   Her organismic age is not markedly retarded and a measure of social age, not shown in the figure, is slightly above the average. She is very good at taking care of young children. She does not do well at abstract intellectual tasks. "Capitalize on strength" is an essential aspect of the philosophy and practice of a growth point of view in a classroom. It would be a sad mistake to stress competitive and comparative methods for a child growing as in Figure 3.

GROWTH WITH TIME IS A HIGHLY INDIVIDUAL MATTER

Differences in the level of various attributes of growth have been stressed in connection with Figure 3. The changes that occur in children with time are also important in a consideration of patterns. When the results of tests secured at a particular time are made available without the growth point of view, serious mistakes of interpretation may be made. For example, in the examination of 56 individual growth curves in reading, the writers could not find a single child with a growth curve of the shape that would be described by the average values or norms.

[When we trace] the growth in ability to read in 28 boys, [and in] 28 girls, the lines are so intertwined as to be indistinguishable in detail. However, problems of level and direction become apparent. The total group of girls presents a more compact picture than the boys and it is obvious that the girls most delayed in reading tend to start upwards between 9 and 10 years. The boys who are delayed, however, may remain at low levels even to 10 or 11 years of age. It is not an accident that boys supply a disproportionate number of cases for reading clinics.

A quantitative analysis of some of the reasons for the differences in the growth curves of individual children is being pursued. One of the writers has already reported in some detail on the differences between G7 and G24 called A and B in Figure 4. Although intelligence quotients have fluctuated slightly year by year, the average for each over the period is 118. Detailed study explains some of the reasons why their pattern of growth in reading has been so different. Child A had an earlier maturing mother (menarche at age 14) and is maturing early herself. Child B had a later maturing mother (menarche at age 17) and is maturing later than Child A. When total organism is taken into account, including all of the various attributes described elsewhere, Child A is actually an older organism, age for age, than Child B. Child B rejected reading experiences violently during the period of plateau and sought them avidly during the period of spurt. According to the growth philosophy and data it would be quite incorrect to call Child B a case of "reading disability" in spite of the retardation before age 9 and the discrepancy between reading and mental age.

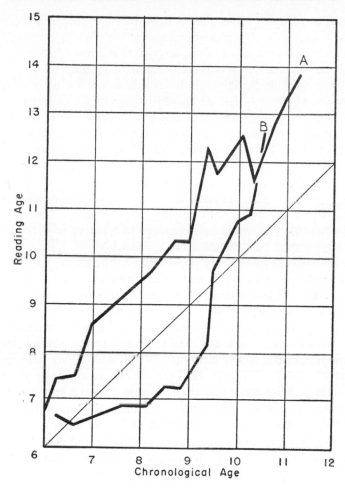

FIGURE 4

Contrasted patterns of growth in reading in two girls of equal mental ability but unequal total maturity. (Reproduced by permission of the Michigan Education Association.)

MEMBERSHIP IN A GIVEN FAMILY IS INFLUENTIAL IN DETERMINING THE PATTERN OF GROWTH

In the previous discussion the writers have noted that the reasons for differences in the growth of children are deep seated. The nature of some of these differences has been indicated in discussing the two girls of approximately the same intelligence who presented such diverse patterns of growth in reading. The writers have recently prepared the growth records in reading for 46 pairs of children where each pair comes from a given family. It becomes evident at once that a very important factor in the shape of a reading curve is membership in a family.

Pairs of curves illustrating high, intermediate and low achievement are presented in Figure 5. The chronological age of the children is on the base line and the growth in reading along the vertical axis. A and A′ are brothers born 25 months apart. B, B′ and B″ are three brothers born at intervals of 27 and 25 months, and C and C′ are brothers born at an interval of 36 months. By the longitudinal method it is possible to compare them as if they were twins advancing together. The rate and level of advancement in reading for A and A′ and C and C′ are, of course, strikingly similar. B and B′ cling rather closely. At 10 years of age B″ drops several years below in reading as compared to his older brothers and converges toward them near the close of the record.

These curves are particularly provocative to the person who may have been inclined to feel that level and rate of progress in reading were primarily a matter of instruction. It is true that these children would not read at all in a culture which did not provide the experience. The examination of the whole body of the material, however, makes it apparent that cases of extreme delay such as C and C′ cannot be understood simply by assuming that instruction is at fault. While reading has been used for illustrative purposes other aspects of growth behave in similar manner.

It should be pointed out that the 7 boys in Figure 5 encountered substantially the same school environment but their reactions in reading have been strongly influenced by the fact that they came from a given family with all that that implies for differences in heredity and nurture. Teachers should not expect the same effects from the same instruction or from the best possible adaptation of instruction to the individual. The folly of a common expectancy on the part of teacher, administrator, or parent is obvious since achievement is only partially under the control of the educational process.

GROWTH HAS STABILITY AND CONTINUITY AND MAKES ITS DEMANDS FOR NURTURE

If the reader will reexamine Figures 1 and 2 he will be impressed by the general picture of stability of the level of growth with time. Although detailed items in each pattern of growth show periods of plateau and spurt there appears to be some unifying factor in rate of energy available for growth which keeps the individual on his course.

It is interesting to study the curve of growth when organismic age is

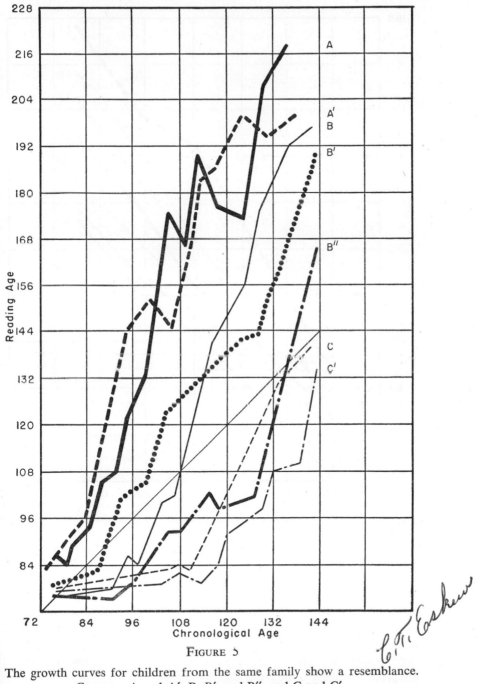

FIGURE 5

The growth curves for children from the same family show a resemblance.
Compare A and A′; B, B′, and B″; and C and C′.

111

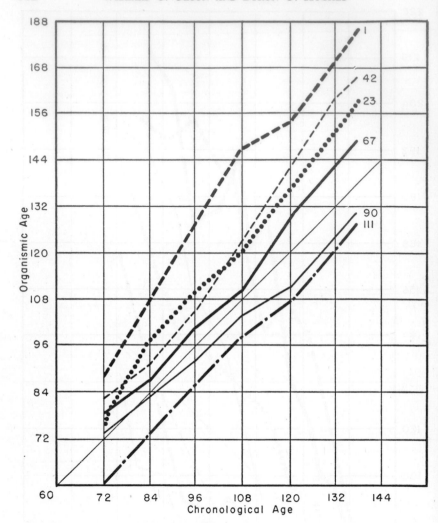

FIGURE 6

Regularity of growth in organismic age for illustrative children ranking 1, 42, 23, 67, 90, and 111 in a sample of 111 ranked at 96 months of chronological age.

taken as the best single expression available to us of the average growth for an individual. One hundred eleven curves were plotted and arranged in order of magnitude of organismic age as of chronological age 8. Children numbered 1 (Boy), 23 (Girl), 42 (Boy), 90 (Girl), and 111 (Boy) are given in Figure 6 for illustrative purposes.

It is probable that the age unit method and the use of averages make the curves unusually straight and smooth. The fact remains that the individual differences in total growth are highly predictable and continuous with time and even tell much about the achievement of the child in the years that follow the ages that have been plotted. The data also suggest some balancing mechanism which releases energy for the production of growth in an orderly fashion. Growth itself is a demanding process impelling the individual to seek nurture to supply it. A slowing down in growth alters attitudes and feelings. In a free environment in school, level of growth makes for differences in the number and difficulty of books consumed. Schools traditionally have emphasized the stimulating conditions and the learning process. Growth studies are giving a better understanding of the learner.

CHILDREN VIEWED AS WHOLES ARE MORE ALIKE THAN CHILDREN VIEWED AS PARTS

Curriculum materials and teaching methods once took an extreme swing in the direction of adaptation to individual differences in some one attribute of interest in schools. At the height of the enthusiasm many methods were proposed for the sectioning of classes, for classification according to special abilities, and for adjustment through promotion and retardation. For the most part the attempts were disappointing in that individuals with similar characteristics seemed to make the same progress regardless of the administrative plans. This is not surprising to the student of growth.

Individual differences among children are most impressive when one segment of total growth is viewed. For example, if we calculate the average deviation for reading age for the group of 56 children described elsewhere we find that it varies with age but averages 18 months. If we calculate the same measure for organismic age we find it to be only 8.5 months. Thus as we move toward the objective of total growth in the elementary period we may emphasize those things in which children are alike as well as those things in which children differ more widely.

SOME IMPLICATIONS OF GROWTH STUDIES FOR TEACHERS

"Seeking" behavior. Differences in growth among children of the same age make for differences in reaction to the environment that is supplied. The child is not a passive recipient of stimulation. He reaches out for it according to the maturity of his total and partial growth and the energy at his disposal. He reacts selectively to the surroundings that are sup-

plied and creates his own world of experience within them.   He tends to reject the experiences for which he is not ready.   Teachers may make full use of "seeking" behavior by providing a school environment in which children may find suitable experiences of a wide variety in kind and difficulty.   No narrowly conceived curriculum of fixed content can attain this goal.

Seeking behavior also underlies a principle of method—children should participate in the determination of their curriculum experiences both individually and in groups.   The planning period, continuous interaction, or observation of behavior thus give the teacher her safest guide as to the experiences for which the group as a whole is ready and the way each individual may be expected to relate himself to them.   These techniques on the part of the teacher also give the children experience in cooperative planning.   Growth does not occur in a vacuum and seeking behavior and environmental stimulation are interactive processes.   The problem is one of relative emphasis.

Pacing, forcing, and delaying.   When the teacher insures an environment adequate to the needs of all the children and adjusts his expectancy for each child according to the level and pattern of growth the technique may be called "pacing."   This simply means that the teacher meets the "seeking" level by an expectancy and experience in close harmony with it.   The child's aspirations and performance are not in conflict with the expectancies of the teacher.

A segment of the general and teaching population continues to have large confidence in specific instructional techniques and experiences as a means of achieving a high level of performance in a child.   This confidence was supported originally by laboratory studies of learning.   According to this idea a clever teacher with a clever method, excellent material, and time and persistence can produce achievement in a child beyond that which he would attain by seeking and pacing.   Thus someone might attempt to justify the early introduction of school subjects on the basis of this point of view.   This is sometimes called "forcing" in the sense that there is an attempt to push up the level of the growth curve. The writers admit that the total evidence is still inadequate but they are skeptical whether a forcing method produces anything more than a temporary effect of very limited size.

Their study of the effects of special instruction, feeding, and the administration of special growth substances supports the idea that deprived children show some responsiveness to special treatment, that well-nurtured children do not, and that the special effects do not materially upset individual differences or persist for a very long period of time.   They prefer "pacing" to "forcing" theory.

It has been advocated that schools should make a deliberate attempt to delay experiences. The experiments rather regularly demonstrate that the gains that subsequently follow when the experience is introduced will be very rapid and that there will be no permanent impairment of the objective desired. The more systematic studies of delayed experience in reading, stair-climbing, and language, as well as more informal studies of delay in arithmetic suggest that this will be true. The writers are more inclined to stress "seeking" and "pacing." If this results in delay, delay there should be. If on the other hand, some rapidly growing children seek reading and number experiences at an early age in nursery school and kindergarten, there seems no good reason to exclude them. Growth, after all, occurs in a context supplied by the total environment.

Administrative implications. What administrative policies and practices affecting children and parents should prevail in a school that has accepted the data, principles, and philosophy of growth? A few may be suggested for illustrative purposes. The strong tendency for achievement in school to reflect total growth and family patterns calls into question the policy of competitive and comparative marks and formal report cards. Elementary schools rapidly have been giving up such techniques as ineffective and incompatible with modern knowledge. Formal marking practices persist as a cultural survival where communities lag in in-service and parent education or where conservative and reactionary groups have attained dominance. The investment in time necessitated by the newer techniques of conferencing and mutual education brings returns in the long run. At times administrators have hoped that schools and teachers could be appraised by measuring the growth of the children. The idea sounds logical but there is nothing in the growth studies that gives much reassurance that such a measure can be used and properly interpreted.

Classification and promotion problems are of continual interest for administrative policy. Growth in achievement, just as in height and weight, appears to be independent of how children are grouped. It is obvious that a thoroughgoing growth philosophy finds the criteria for placement in the growth of the individual and his social relations rather than in arbitrary grade standards. The growth philosophy and data justify much experimentation with the nature of the groups that are to be maintained and how individuals should be placed in them. The growth philosophy tends to bring children through the elementary grades without failure. If reclassification is necessary after individual study because of extreme immaturity, retention is not thought of or acted upon as a failure on the part of the child.

It is probably fair to say that secondary schools, on the whole, have been relatively more committed to the selective philosophy than the elementary schools. The struggle of philosophies sometimes creates problems of articulation at the seventh grade level or the ninth grade level, depending on the type of school organization. There is evidence for reapproachment.

SUMMARY

Research in child development is providing working generalizations for the classroom teacher. Children differ in their rate and level of growth and the acceptance of these differences permits policies which make schools happier places for parents, teachers, and children.

Growth tends to be unified. Schools may properly take the view that they must be concerned with the whole child to accomplish even intellectual objectives.

The total competence of children is made up by different details of pattern. Building on these differences within the individual is an important aspect of curriculum planning, method, and guidance.

Growth is an individual matter and must be appraised from the point of view of the nature of the individual. There can be no common expectancy for achievement when it is conditioned by sex differences, the total maturity of the child, and the family from which he comes.

It is reassuring that growth has stability and is not easily deflected by the efforts of others to alter it. The stability of growth has great survival value for the race and the individual.

Children as they present themselves in schools have more things in common when viewed broadly than when single attributes are studied in detail. Similarities as well as individual differences deserve attention in classrooms.

The imperative demands of the organism for growth cause children to seek for the environmental supply of nurture and this behavior offers teachers an important clue to the provision of environmental experiences and the use of effective techniques.

Where the data, generalizations, and philosophy of growth have become the common property of the professional staff and patrons, classroom practices and administrative policies in the treatment of individuals and groups tend to be less rigid, competitive, and frustrating, and more flexible, social, and satisfying.

14. Life and Learning: Introduction to the Developmental Task Concept*

Related selections: 15, 16, 24

ONE OF the more recent developments in educational thought is the emphasis being given to the concept of developmental tasks. A developmental task is defined by Dr. Havighurst as "a task which arises at or about a certain period in the life of the individual, successful achievement of which leads to his happiness and to success with later tasks, while failure leads to unhappiness in the individual, disapproval by society, and difficulty with later tasks." Recognition of the particular tasks upon which the child is working at any given time is essential to an understanding of individual growth and behavior and to the proper timing of educational experiences. In this selection from *Human Development and Education*, Dr. Havighurst introduces the concept of development tasks, briefly discusses their origin, and indicates the usefulness of the concept for educators. The reader will find the entire book valuable for getting a picture of the developmental tasks of individuals at different age levels.

LIVING is learning, and growing is learning. One learns to walk, talk, and throw a ball; to read, bake a cake, and get along with age-mates of the opposite sex; to hold down a job, to raise children; to retire gracefully when too old to work effectively, and to get along without a husband or wife who has been at one's side for forty years. These are all learning tasks. To understand human development, one must understand learning. The human individual learns his way through life.

The lower animals rely more than human beings do on maturation, or "doing what comes naturally," to meet the problems of growing up. Apparently, playing with a mouse comes naturally to a kitten, without learning, and so does the salmon's long journey back to the waters of his birth, and the ways of the ant to the young graduate from the larval stage to adult anthood. Human beings are not built this way, with almost fully developed action patterns emerging as their nerves and glands and muscles

* Robert J. Havighurst, *Human Development and Education*, Longmans, Green, and Co., Inc., 1953, Chapter I, pp. 1–5. Reprinted by permission of the author and publisher.

Dr. Havighurst (1900—) is Professor of Education and member of the Committee on Human Development, University of Chicago. He was formerly Professor of Physics and Chemistry at Miami University and the University of Wisconsin. He is a scholar and author in the fields of the social sciences, human development, and education.

grow.   Very little of human behavior is such a crude product of maturation unformed by learning.

Nature lays down wide possibilities in the developing of the human
body, and which possibilities shall be realized depends on what the individual learns.   This is true even of such crude biological realities as feeding habits and sexual relations, while the more highly social realities of
language, economic behavior, and religion are almost completely the product of learning at the hands of society.

The path of learning is not one long slow uphill climb with something
to learn every new day, but consists of steep places, where the learning
effort is severe, interspersed with plateaus where one can speed along
almost without effort.   For instance, the little boy works hard to learn
how to throw and catch a ball, but once he has mastered this skill he may
coast along on it for years without further improvement.   The little girl
works hard to learn to form her letters into a neat feminine script.   She
learns this during the years from age five to ten, and then has mastered the
task.   In simple unchanging societies, the young adult has mastered most
of the learning tasks of his life.   He knows the solutions to most of life's
problems.   For him, learning is just about over.   Not so in the modern
changing society where social life changes so rapidly that the individual
must continually learn to adapt himself to changed conditions.

Living in a modern society such as that of the U.S.A. is a long series
of tasks to learn, where learning well brings satisfaction and reward, while
learning poorly brings unhappiness and social disapproval.

The tasks the individual must learn—*the developmental tasks* of life—
are those things that constitute healthy and satisfactory growth in our society.   They are the things a person must learn if he is to be judged and
to judge himself to be a reasonably happy and successful person.   *A developmental task is a task which arises at or about a certain period in the
life of the individual, successful achievement of which leads to his happiness and to success with later tasks, while failure leads to unhappiness in
the individual, disapproval by the society, and difficulty with later tasks.*

The prototype of the developmental task is the purely biological formation of organs in the embryo.

In this development each organ has its time of origin and this time factor
is as important as the place of origin.   If the eye, for example, does not arise
at the appointed time "it will never be able to express itself fully, since the
moment for the rapid outgrowth of some other part will have arrived, and this
will tend to dominate the less active region, and suppress the belated tendency for eye expression."

After the organ has begun to arise at the right time, still another time
factor determines the most critical stage of its development: "A given

organ must be interrupted during the early stage of its development in order to be completely suppressed or grossly modified. . . . After an organ has arisen successfully from the anlage, it may be lamed or runted, but its nature and actual existence can no longer be destroyed by interrupting the growth."

The organ which misses its time of ascendancy is doomed not only as an individual, it endangers at the same time the whole hierarchy of organs. "Not only does the arrest of a rapidly budding part, therefore, tend to suppress its development temporarily, but the premature loss of supremacy to some other organ renders it impossible for the suppressed part to come again into dominance, so that it is permanently modified. . . ." The result of normal development is proper relationship of size and function among the body organs: The liver adjusted in size to the stomach and intestine, the heart and lungs properly balanced, and the capacity of the vascular system accurately proportioned to the body as a whole. Through developmental arrest one or more organs may become disproportionately small; this upsets functional harmony and produces a defective person.

These purely biological developmental tasks of the body illustrate the essentials of the bio-socio-psychological tasks with which we are concerned. If the task is not achieved at the proper time it will not be achieved well, and failure in this task will cause partial or complete failure in the achievement of other tasks yet to come.

Consider the task of learning to talk, for example. Sometime between the ages of one and two most children master the essentials of human speech and language. They still have much to learn at the end of the second year, but they are well started. *They have learned to talk.* There is some evidence, from the few cases on record of children who were denied human companionship during their first few years of life and therefore did not learn to talk, that the task of learning to talk is extremely difficult and may never be accomplished well if it is not achieved in the second year of life. This is the crucial period for this particular task. And, if the task is not learned, the failure will stand in the way of learning a series of later tasks which depend greatly upon language.

THE ORIGIN OF DEVELOPMENTAL TASKS

As the individual grows, he finds himself possessed of new physical and psychological resources. The infant's legs grow larger and stronger, enabling him to walk. The child's nervous system grows more complex, enabling him to reason more subtly and to understand the complexities of subjects such as arithmetic. The individual also finds himself facing new demands and expectations from the society around him. The infant is expected to learn to talk, the child to learn to subtract and divide.

These inner and outer forces contrive to set for the individual a series of developmental tasks which must be mastered if he is to be a successful human being.

Some tasks arise mainly from physical maturation, such as learning to walk, learning to behave acceptably to the opposite sex in adolescence, and (for women) adjusting to the menopause in middle life. Other tasks, arising primarily from the cultural pressure of society, are learning to read, and learning to participate as a socially responsible citizen in society.

There is a third source of developmental tasks—namely, the personal values and aspirations of the individual, which are part of his personality, or self. The personality, or self, emerges from the interaction of organic and environmental forces. As the self evolves, it becomes increasingly a force in its own right in the subsequent development of the individual. Already by the age of three or four the individual's self is effective in the defining and accomplishing of his developmental tasks.

Examples of tasks arising primarily from the personal motives and values of the individual are: choosing and preparing for an occupation, and achieving a scale of values and a philosophy of life.

Thus developmental tasks may arise from physical maturation, from the pressure of cultural processes upon the individual, from the desires, aspirations, and values of the emerging personality, and they arise in most cases from combinations of these factors acting together.

THE TEACHABLE MOMENT

There are two reasons why the concept of developmental tasks is useful to educators. First, it helps in discovering and stating the purposes of education in the schools. Education may be conceived as the effort of the society, through the school, to help the individual achieve certain of his developmental tasks.

The second use of the concept is in the timing of educational efforts. When the body is ripe, and society requires, and the self is ready to achieve a certain task, the teachable moment has come. Efforts at teaching which would have been largely wasted if they had come earlier, give gratifying results when they come at the *teachable moment,* when the task should be learned. For example, the best times to teach reading, the care of children, and adjustment to retirement from one's job can be discovered by studying human development, and finding out when conditions are most favorable for learning these tasks.

15. The Fundamental Needs of the Child*

Related selections: 13, 14, 23, 31

THE NATURE of the human organism and its processes is such that every individual has certain basic needs that, in a measure, are with him continuously and that must be met if he is to develop into an adequate person. Such requirements consist of the things, the activities, the experiences and the conditions that are basic to permanent adjustment. Lawrence K. Frank's discussion is a synthesis that draws upon the findings of many studies of physiological and psychological needs.

EVERY society and every generation uses children for its own purposes. It is significant that to-day we are beginning to speak of the needs of the child as entitled to consideration in his nurture and education or even as the controlling factor in child care. Contrast this emerging conception of the child's nature and needs with the practices all over the world, among so-called civilized people and so-called primitive people, in which the nurture and education of children are dictated by religious, ethical, and moral ideas, by political and economic requirements, by social class lines, indeed by an extraordinary variety of ideas and purposes all more or less remote from the child himself. The children in all these cultures are molded by the dominant ideas and beliefs and the group purposes into greater or less conformity in which they may sacrifice much or little.

Consider also the variety of practices in regard to the physical make-up or form of children. Among certain Indian tribes, the infant's head is flattened to a board. Among certain African tribes, the lips or ears may be stretched or the neck encased in coils of brass. Everyone is familiar with the ancient Chinese practice of binding the feet of female infants. As children grow older, many peoples have puberty rites involving tattooing, skin incisions, various forms of mutilation of the male and female genitals, and the inculcation of rigidly prescribed motor patterns of action that may involve anatomical deformities. The catalogue of practices that deform, distort, or otherwise manipulate the physical structure is endless, but all are regarded by those who use them as essentially necessary to make

* Lawrence K. Frank, "The Fundamental Needs of the Child," *Mental Hygiene*, vol. XXII (July, 1938), pp. 353–379. Reprinted by permission of author and publisher.

Dr. Frank (1890—), distinguished scholar and author in the field of mental hygiene of children, is the recipient of many awards and honors and has served in an advisory capacity to a score or more government and philanthropic agencies.

over the child into the image prescribed by the culture as the only right form for a man or a woman. In their cultural context these practices and beliefs may be purposeful and valid.

Not only is the physical structure of the child made over into the patterns of the culture, but so are the physiological functions, as we see in the diverse standards imposed upon the young child by different societies. In the matter of nutrition, for example, every group teaches the child to like the food of its traditional choice, which means developing an appetite for an incredible array of foodstuffs, or supposed foodstuffs, and abhorring other foodstuffs of equal or greater nutritive value. Many of these food choices represent a wise, economical use of available animal and vegetable resources, while others are obviously dictated by various beliefs in sympathetic magic, by rigid taboos, and by religious convictions that have little or no relation to the nutritional requirements of the growing child or even of the adult. Every society, again, imposes some kind of training upon children with respect to elimination. In some cultures the requirements are minimal, but in others they may be so severe and so rigorously imposed upon the very young child as to create lifelong impairment of physiological efficiency. Even breathing, in some cultures, is subject to special training, and sleeping patterns, peculiar to each group, are inculcated at an early age.

It is safe to say that most of these traditional patterns of child training and nurture derive from ideas and beliefs and strong convictions that have little or no relevance to the immediate needs of the child. Civilized man in many cases has survived *despite,* not because of, these methods of child care, as we are now beginning to realize in the light of recent investigation.

Curious as are these practices of physical and physiological training, the variety of practices in psychological training are even more astonishing, since here we find methods and procedures for bringing up children in the most fantastic, distorted patterns of conduct and feeling. The belief in using the child for social purposes is revealed here more convincingly than in the realm of physical care, where the organic limits of deformation impose some restraint; whereas in the area of conduct and belief there apparently are no limits to the grotesque, the cruel and brutal, the diabolical ingenuity of man in warping and twisting human nature to cultural patterns which originally may have been useful or even desirable, but which have become rigid and perverse.

When we reflect upon these various beliefs and practices that are imposed upon the child to make him conform to group-sanctioned patterns, we can begin to understand how extraordinarily significant it is to-day that we are discussing the needs of the child as a basis for his nurture and education. We can also see how questions of education and training become the focus of bitter conflicts, as contending factions in a society struggle to direct the nurture of children in order to control the group life. As we meet to-day to discuss programs of education for the young child in the home and in the nursery school, we are not concerned merely with questions of technique and procedures, with this or that pedagogical device; we are faced with the major issues of the future of our culture and the direction of our whole social, economic, and political life, since an effective program of early-childhood education based upon the needs of the child will inevitably change our society far more effectively than any legislation or other social action.

We must, therefore, be humble and deliberate in our discussion, not only because of the gravity of the larger social issues involved, but also because we know so little about the needs of the child.   It is safe to say that whenever you hear any person or group speaking with strong convictions about specific needs of the child and how to meet them, that person or group is probably sustained more by emotional fervor and loyalty to cultural traditions than by dependable knowledge of actual children.

Anyone who is prepared seriously and fairly to consider the question of the child's needs must begin by trying to be honest about his or her own personality bias and beliefs, emotional attitudes, religious loyalties, and social-economic and political leanings, because these often unconscious feelings and values play so large a rôle in our attitudes toward the child and in our willingness to recognize some of his needs or our strong denial of them.   Probably the most general statement that we can make about the child's needs is that he should be protected from distortions, from unnecessary deprivations and exploitations by adults—parents, teachers and nurses, physicians, psychologists, and others engaged in dealing with children.

It is difficult to realize the extent of these often subtle coercions and pressures exerted upon the child.   Before the infant is born, the parents may have built up a picture of the kind of child he or she is to be, with a pronounced bias toward the male or the female sex, or toward a certain kind of temperament, physique, and ability.   The infant, having within him the genes of countless previous generations as well as the characteristics of his parents, enters into a family situation that even at birth may be threatening and out of harmony with his peculiar, idiosyncratic temperamental make-up and needs.   Parents who are eager to minister to the infant's need for warmth, food, and safety may be doggedly determined to deny the child's sex and his many personal, temperamental characteristics, which gives rise to needs as important and urgent as the need for physical care.

It is not without reason, therefore, that we stress this primary and inalienable need of the child to be accepted as a unique individual, or, if the parents cannot or will not accord that acceptance, the need to be protected and reinforced against the destructive, warping influence of these parental biases.   Every child suffers to a greater or less extent from this denial of his own personal, temperamental individuality, because even the most emancipated parents are not wholly free from the desire to see their children conform to the images they have constructed.   Moreover, every teacher has these partialities, often unconscious, which incline her toward one child and away from another.   Further, the child himself is subject to the strong desire to be like the parents, however out of harmony with his own make-up such an identification may be.   It is interesting to see how the recognition of individual differences is resisted even by professionally trained persons, such as teachers, who will accept the fact of such differences with respect to mental capacity, as shown by standardized mental tests, but deny it with respect to personality, temperament, physical maturity, and other obvious characteristics.

The infant, as he grows into childhood and youth, faces a series of life tasks that cannot be evaded or denied.   The way in which he meets those life tasks and his attempts to master them give rise to the various needs for which we to-day believe his nurture and education should provide. It is obvious that we have only a fragmentary knowledge of those needs, since we have studied so briefly the process of growth and development and the life tasks presented by our culture.   But it is highly significant, as we suggested earlier, that we are genuinely concerned with understanding child growth and development and are trying to discover the child's needs, as a basis for his education and nurture.

The processes involved in living and growing create needs for warmth, nutrition, and bodily care concerning which we are gaining more knowledge and technical competence.   Much of the research in the field of nutrition and its results are still in terms of uniform standardized rules based on pure-strain rat colonies, with no allowance made for individual differences in vitamin and mineral requirements, so that, in the name of scientific standards, we may create serious deficiencies in the individual child as contrasted with the standardized laboratory animal.   Even rats in the same litter differ, as Streeter has recently shown, in their susceptibility to rickets.   The nutritional and other physical needs of the individual child are to be viewed dynamically, not statically, in terms of continuing growth and development rather than fixed height-weight standards which are purely statistical averages.   Moreover, these needs should be viewed in terms of physiological functioning, not merely of structural size and shape, since it is functional efficiency, not structure, that is important.

How many problem children, hypochondriacs, and psychoneurotics have been created by blind adherence to these standardized tables which physicians and nurses, health educators, and teachers have given to mothers as scientific laws and which mothers have then used on their children!   Surely we should allow for individual differences in children and not increase parental anxiety in this area of physical needs by insisting upon these standardized height and weight tables for chronological-age groups. The child's need is for food, rest, sleep, and play, so that he will continue to grow and develop *at his own rate*.   The emphasis should be upon the growing, not upon fixed dimensions for chronological ages based upon the assumption that all children grow at the same rate.

The same criticism may be made of other chronological-age standards, such as prescribed hours for sleeping, where again failure to make allowance for individual differences has created many distraught mothers and problem children.   The sleep needs of children vary greatly, and the loss of a nap is often much less undesirable than conflict, rebellion, punishment, and other consequences of a rigid sleep regimen.

If we are to gain a better understanding of the child's needs in terms of the life tasks he faces, we should envisage the physiological processes involved in what we call socialization.   First in order of impact upon the infant is the regularization of feeding, involving a fixed interval of three or four hours between food intake, to which the infant must adapt despite individual differences in the reduction of blood sugar that creates hunger and in the capacity to endure hunger.   Prolonged hunger and crying, often while the mother keeps her eye on the clock to see when the precise minute for feeding arrives, create in the child a condition of tension that may in some cases initiate persistent personality difficulties.

In feeding we are confronted with something more than just a need for nourishment.   In early infancy, the whole body of the infant is receptive and in need of comforting, cuddling warmth and opportunity to suckle. In breast-feeding these needs may be adequately filled, through the warmth of the mother and the close tactual contact with her through nourishment and suckling, wherein the baby receives much of his needed sense of security and feeling of being protected.   Tactual contacts and soothing are primitive, but highly necessary forms of reassurance.   We never outgrow the need of them, but it is especially great in infancy and childhood. In this respect the human infant is like the young of all mammals, who thrive when nursed and cuddled and derive much needed emotional security from the oral activity of sucking and the close contact with the mother.

By many students of personality, it is said that if the infant is given adequate breast-feeding and affectionate cuddling, his future attitude toward the world will be outgoing, generous, and trusting, whereas if he is denied these satisfactions, he will be suspicious, niggardly, and resentful.   Dr.

David Levy is quoted with approval by Dr. James S. Plant as stating "that satisfactory breast-feeding [cuddling] experiences do more than whole dictionaries of later words in the establishment of security in the family group"—what Dr. Plant calls "belongingness." Since so many children nowadays are deprived of breast-feeding, it is necessary to consider the acceptance of that deprivation as a life task that is imposed upon the dependent infant, thereby creating specific needs which may persist throughout life. The seriousness of this deprivation could be diminished if the bottle-fed infant were held by the mother and cuddled while taking the bottle, so as to receive the warmth and security of her close presence during the feeding.

But even the breast-fed infant must sooner or later lose that happiness and comfort and face the process of weaning, which may create anxiety and irritability if too abruptly or roughly handled. During weaning the child needs additional reassurances and comforting to prevent acute feelings of insecurity and anxiety and to lessen the loss of sucking. Every deprivation is a threat to the child, a source of anxiety which can be mitigated by affectionate reassurance which makes him feel that the deprivation is not a punishment and that he is still loved. The important question for nursery schools to ask is what can they do for the children who have been deprived of breast-feeding or unwisely weaned, and who need to be reassured and protected, helped to outgrow their anxiety, and aided with affectionate reassurance.

Eliminations and their regularization present two more life tasks that may create persistent needs. In discussing and teaching toilet training, we are apt to forget what a profound physiological disturbance we are imposing on the child. The physiological process of elimination of urine and feces are marvelously well organized, so that automatically the sphincters of the bladder and the rectum respond to accumulated pressure within. This physiological autonomy the child is asked to surrender when toilet training begins. Instead of functioning in accordance with his physiological needs, he is asked to inhibit the sphincter response to pressure, responding instead to an external stimulus—vessel, place, and so on—presented by the adult. Furthermore, he is asked to respond at a fixed time, whether or not he needs to do so physiologically. In this training, the child is expected to subordinate his processes to outside events and times, giving up his own physiological autonomy, often months before he is sufficiently mature to make such an adjustment. Maturity does not mean chronological age or size or weight; it means that the child has had enough of an activity, such as sucking or unrestricted elimination, to be able to go on to something else without a persistent feeling of deprivation or an unsatisfied infantile longing.

The widespread prevalence of enuresis and of constipation are not unrelated to the way in which toilet training has been imposed upon children who find in this process a serious nervous and emotional strain. During toilet training the child needs constant reassurance and comforting to stand the anxiety he so often feels. When failure to be continent elicits scoldings and punishment, the emotional stresses are increased and reinforced by feelings of guilt and inadequacy, often expressed in various symptoms of misbehavior. Evidence of how precariously the little child is balanced during toilet training is seen in the relapses that follow any emotional shock or family disturbance, or in the appearance of misconduct suddenly in the midst of peaceful, engrossing play, when the child is made uneasy and restless by a full bladder of which he is not yet fully aware. The evident over-concern of parents and nurses with toilet training raises for nursery schools the question of what they can do to provide reassurance for the anxious child, and to make toilet functions an unemotional subject and action. It is probable that some nursery schools themselves are guilty of aggravating the child's insecurity by their rigid overemphasis upon toilet training and the fuss made over "slips" or the teachers' unconscious reaction toward feces.

Here it is necessary to point out that the emotional tone or attitude of parents, nurses, and teachers toward toilet training is the important thing, not their actions, for the child reacts to the tone or attitude and feels the tenseness or overemphasis or dislike in the adult's voice and handling. The importance of the manner and tone of voice lies in the child's feeling that he is being deprived by this training. Any anger or impatience, then, may become an occasion for anxiety and feelings of guilt. How else is the child to understand and interpret the adult's treatment of him? Since many adults carry over from their own childhood a feeling of anxiety or disgust at feces, it is clear that they are not able to treat the child under their care without emotional stress when faced with this process, which for the child is entirely normal and unconnected with emotion until adult interference begins. Since few children pass through toilet training without some stress, we may include among the needs of the child the need for reassurance and often for release from the effects of this process upon the personality. It is appropriate to raise the question about toilet training: Are we concerned only with character training and the conformity it implies, or are we concerned with personality development and the kind of human being we are helping to foster? We can instill good habits or foster a personality; in the latter case, the habits will usually be established without difficulty. Weaning and toilet training, as often handled, are important sources of personality twists and biases, and may give rise to persistent needs in the child.

The arrival of a younger child in the family also may create acute anxiety when the older child has not been prepared for it.   The shock of waking up one morning to find the mother absent, to be told that she has gone to the hospital to have a baby, and then to have her return with an infant who engrosses her time and attention, is the unhappy fate of many children whose parents either ignore their need for preparation and reassurance or else deny it because they cannot face the questions about sex and procreation involved.   So many children suffer unnecessarily from the arrival of a younger brother or sister when that arrival could be the occasion for happy expectations and enjoyment!   Here we have an excellent illustration of how children are sacrificed to religious and moral traditions that insist upon denying sex and hiding procreation as something shameful and obscene.

The symptoms of sibling rivalry, often aggravated by overt favoritism for the new baby and rejection of the older child, are many and various. The young child is faced with the necessity of accepting a place and a rôle for which he needs much affection and reassurance, which he may not receive at home or at school.   Often this shock comes just as the child is striving to learn toilet habits, so that he is under a double load of anxiety which may lead to "slips" or persistent enuresis.

The frequency of rejected children—children not wanted or not acceptable as personalities or temperaments to the parents—is so great that special mention should be made of the need of such children for something to compensate for their unhappy fate.   In this group must be numbered the children of oversolicitous mothers who are hiding their rejection of the child under an effusive care and atoning for their guilty feeling by "smothering" the child.   Nursery schools have a great opportunity to meet the acute needs of these children.

The little child is frequently disturbed physiologically by emotional reactions such as anger, rage, and grief which clamor for expression or release in overt behavior.   In a very real sense these physiological disturbances or upheavals seize control of the child and often impel him to act violently and destructively against things and people and even himself. One of the most important of life tasks for the young child is to learn how to manage these emotional reactions and thereby to free himself from this overwhelming experience.   It is difficult for adults to conceive or to understand the panic that these emotional reactions may arouse in the child, who finds himself helplessly carried on a tide of feeling so strong that he cannot resist it unaided.   If at the same time he meets with a violent response from adults, who strike him or forcibly restrain him, the emotional disturbance may be aggravated cumulatively until terminated by exhaustion.   Such an experience teaches the child nothing constructive or helpful, and it may make him so afraid of himself that he begins to be anxious about this behavior and less and less prepared to meet the next provocation. Although the adult may forcibly control the child at the moment, what the child needs is help in controlling the emotional disturbance himself, so that, instead of a persistent conflict within the child between himself and his emotions, he can bring these emotional reactions into the pattern of his own living. The situation is in many respects like that in the case of hunger and elimination, where physiological processes are initially dominant, but are gradually transformed into regulated functional activities over which the individual has, as we say, control, because those functional processes are subject to the culturally sanctioned times, places, and objects.

In other words, the emotional reactions of the child are normal psychological functions that call regulation and patterning, so that the child may be freed from their urgency and disturbance. They are not, as our tradition teaches, moral or ethical problems, and when handled as such, they only increase the child's guilt and resentment and serve to fixate him at that infantile level, as in toilet training when it is made a moral issue. Anger and rage, like fear, have had a great biological value in the past, but in group living they may, as persistent infantile reactions, seriously interfere with the individual's capacity for peaceful, coöperative adult living, just as persistent incontinence of feces will restrict an individual's activities.

The child, then, needs help in bringing his emotional responsiveness under regulation. Some children are more prone to anger and rage, others to fear and pain, so that each child requires highly individualized help in meeting his peculiar personal reactions. Unfortunately we have little knowledge of how to provide this help in a constructive, rather than a repressive, manner, because we have treated the problems as moral issues, meeting them with threats, punishment, shame, and often equally violent emotional reactions. There is need for much experimentation here in terms of physiological processes that need to be regulated and integrated into the child's total personality make-up through the help we can give him in his handling of these internal upheavals.

Perhaps the greatest need in these situations is for sympathetic reassurance that will allay the child's panic and so help him to meet the situation more effectively. If not helped early in life, the child may go forward with a capacity for violent reaction that his increasing size and strength make potentially dangerous, especially since he may, at the same time, be developing an increasing resentment toward others because of the way frustrations and deprivations are being inflicted upon him—a resentment that may later take the form of a persistent hostility and aggression, repeatedly reinforced by the revival of the infantile emotional reactions.

Fear and grief are also difficult reactions for the child to handle, but again we usually fail to provide really constructive help and only too often aggravate these feelings by our clumsy or careless attempts to dissipate them. Both fear and grief are physiological reactions that more or less paralyze or restrict activity, unless the fear activates flight. The child needs reassurance and reinforcement in meeting the strange, unknown, and apparently threatening experiences that confront him, and if we will accept the child's view that a situation is terrifying, even if we see that it is not, we can avoid the usual mistakes. Nothing is so helpful as learning some effective method of dealing with a fear-producing situation, since a learned motor response displaces the panicky fear of helplessness, as we see in the training of firemen, policemen, soldiers, and others. But many of the fears of children are not really physiological fears, but rather a disguise for other needs which the child cannot or does not reveal. It is the insecure, anxious child, the child who is not sure of himself or his place in the family or group, who appears fearful of situations that have no terrifying character, so that our earnest explanations and reassurances of safety are wholly irrelevant. Then, too, many children are reared under a constant threat of danger, the parents instilling fear before the situation arises in their efforts to protect the child, or the environment itself may be constantly terrifying. Again, many children have suffered really shocking accidents or exposures to danger which have been indelibly impressed upon them, so that they are ever apprehensive of a repetition and live in dread. Children from such a background need a long experience of peace, of safety and security, to escape from the terror that dominates their lives. In some cases only repeated rehearsals of the shock will enable them to escape from their hysterical reactions.

In view of the frequency of fears in little children, fears that often persist throughout life and handicap the individual, we should recognize as of the utmost importance the child's need for help in dissipating them. But we must be alert to the difference between fears and the persistent anxieties that derive from ill treatment and neglect and that are exhibited as fears of specific situations only because the child must find occasional release.

Grief is another pervasive emotional response for which we have little adequate treatment. Children lose beloved parents, siblings, and nurses through death, divorce, or the inevitable changes in relationship, and something happens to them that we can only guess at, for the child has no comforting philosophy or belief to assuage the acute sense of loss. He can then only mourn, as we see a dog mourn a beloved master, inaccessible to our proffered sympathy or reassurance, because what is missed is that idiomatic, personal relationship that can rarely be regained with another. Children who are well loved can often find in the non-verbal response of those they love some comfort, but if they have lost some one of value in their lives, that loss may never be forgotten. The facing of death or deprivation, the acceptance of the inevitable, is one of the life tasks which mankind has never found a satisfactory method of meeting. To-day children are increasingly obliged to face another kind of loss that is more perplexing and difficult than death—the separation or divorce of their parents, which is so hard to explain to the child and almost impossible to render innocuous. In meeting this situation the child has needs that we can scarcely understand, but we must try to provide some kind of helpful assistance, because the experience is so devastating to the young child and so persistently disturbing throughout childhood and especially adolescence. The conflict of parents, the frequent accusations and impugning of motives, all the bitterness and the competition for the child's favor, act as a psychological poison that, especially in the case of girls, may ruin the individual's capacity for adult mating, for one of the child's great needs is to build up images of the husband and wife, the father and mother, as guides to his or her own future rôle in marriage.

Another task of the child that is a source of anxiety, creating an acute need for reassurance and understanding help, is that of accepting his or her own sex and the many taboos that surround this subject. The traditional view of childhood is that children have no awareness of sex differences and no concern over their genitals, while the cumulative clinical evidence indicates that they are often greatly worried about sex differences and puzzled, if not greatly preoccupied, by their genitals. It is hard for a child to envisage the process of procreation, to accept his maleness or her femaleness, and to see any meaning or sense in the confusing "explanations" given, at the same time striving to understand the violent reactions of adults to exposure of the genitals, manipulation, and so forth.

Little children need constant reassurance and simplified enlightenment on questions of sex and procreation if they are to escape prolonged anxiety and possible lifelong unhappiness. In so far as nursery schools and other schools can provide children with an understanding and wholesome attitude here, we can see how the education of children may change our whole culture, for undoubtedly our culture is warped and distorted by our inherited traditions of uncleanliness, obscenity, and wickedness in regard to sex. We cannot expect to dispose of the child's curiosity and concern by purely biological explanations, since, as Otto Rank has pointed out, adults themselves are not satisfied with merely biological answers. Moreover, the exigent questions about sex, for the child and the adult, are not concerned with gestation, but with the uses of sex in living, in feeling, in intimacy and affection.

It is not too much to say that the ability of men and women to marry and to find happiness in marriage and family life is largely conditioned by their experience and acceptance of their masculine or feminine rôles and sex differences during the pre-school years. If the boy is to grow up as a psychologically potent male, he must during the pre-school years develop his maleness and focus his future sex interests and needs in the genitals, since failure to do so at that time, as clinical evidence amply shows, will compromise his adolescence and prevent his achievement of a wholesome heterosexual adjustment toward women. Likewise it is clear that the little girl, during the pre-school years, must get a clear idea of her future feminine rôle, must accept her essential biological, physiological, and anatomic difference from the male and begin to look forward to her psychological differentiation as a female, with unique capacities for mating, procreation, lactation, and maternal and feminine rôles.

Children find these tasks, which should be simple, wholesome, and natural stages of pre-school development, matters of extraordinary difficulty and stress. Their parents, especially the mother, are so often suffering from anxiety, disgust, or fear about their own sex functions and needs that they cannot tolerate the child's natural curiosities and activities, nor can they permit the child's efforts to make these early life adjustments. Unfortunately many nursery-school teachers suffer from the same unfortunate conditioning, and so are unable to give the child the understanding and help he or she needs. It is not going too far to say that in some nursery schools the difference between boys and girls is ignored or rigidly suppressed, with serious consequences for the personality of the children.

As we gain more insight into the process of personality development and realize how crucial these pre-school sex interests and adjustments are for the subsequent adult life, we can and must work out nursery-school procedures designed to help the child to meet these tasks with courage and happiness, free from the distortions and anxieties that are now so prevalent, able and ready to give and to receive affection.

Another life task confronting the child is that of learning to recognize and observe the inviolabilities that every culture establishes with respect to objects, persons, places, and times. We are so accustomed to think of private property in things and animals, of the sanctity of the physical person of individuals, of the great number of special places and days consecrated to particular purposes which must not be profaned, that we fail to realize that private property and the sanctity of the person are not entities or mysterious powers, but learned ways of behaving toward things and persons, taught to children often with severe penalties for evasion or violation. These lessons as to the inviolability of things and persons are painfully learned by the young child as he begins to explore the world about him, seeking occasions for satisfying his needs and expressing his impulses, and being more or less forcibly restrained, rebuffed, and frustrated. He finds that everything and every person is protected by an invisible barrier of inviolability ("don't touch," "don't look," "don't eat," "don't go near," "don't handle") which he may not disregard except in duly sanctioned ways, such as buying and selling and making contracts or agreements. He must also learn to uphold the inviolability of his own person and property.

These lessons are not simple, since there are many fine distinctions to be made. What is freely accessible in the home is taboo outside; certain persons may be freely invaded, as in fighting with siblings, while others, such as strangers, are inviolable; certain persons are receptive to physical contact, such as parents or near relatives, while others not in the family group are untouchable; actions that may be performed in one place or at one time are forbidden in other places and at other times. Then, too, the child confronts the magical power of money, whereby small pieces of metal or paper render freely accessible what is otherwise inviolable.

These lessons are indeed formidable, and the young child struggling with the complicated customs of group life faces a heavy task for which he needs endless patience and sympathetic teaching. How often a little mistake over private property, which he is just beginning to understand, evokes sudden and immediate punishment, with accusations of "thief" and "liar" and other terrifying characterizations. When we realize that these early lessons in observing the inviolabilities are the most essential steps in preparation for group living, perhaps we shall devise more desirable and effective methods of teaching them, and shall remember to provide toleration and reassurance for the bewildered child who is attempting to assimilate the cumulative customs of thousands of years. It is little wonder that the learning of these inviolabilities, involving as they do repeated frusstrations and a form of negative conditioning that inhibits the response to biologically adequate stimuli of objects and persons, should so frequently impair the child's whole adult life, causing him to face every encounter and every negotiation with timidity or anxiety, or to be intensely preoccupied with getting the better of every one in all situations.

Besides learning to inhibit his responses to things and persons who are inviolable, the child must also learn to perform those acts which his parents insist upon as the required actions in various situations. These actions include the traditional manners and customs, the etiquette and the moral duties which the parents especially cherish and respect and which they are compelled to teach their children as the essentials of life. These lessons are difficult for the child because, like the inviolability of things and persons, the required conduct has no natural, biological relation to the situations in which it is demanded of the child. He must, therefore, be repeatedly shown what to do, and prompted and compelled to do it, with a greater or less amount of verbal and often physical punishment. The outcome of this training is the establishment of more or less automatic conduct, according to the required pattern, which is always a variation, peculiar to the family, of the general socially approved pattern.

As in the teaching of inviolabilities, parental instruction as to the performance of these required actions involves the exercise of authority, often by the father, who rarely has as close and affectionate a tie with the child as the mother and who, therefore, relies more upon coercion to exact obedience, while the mother relies upon the child's desire for her love and approval. Thus the child experiences authority and coercion for the first time, and only too often it is administered severely and arbitrarily, arousing in the child fear, resentment, and hostility toward the father.

These disturbing emotional reactions toward the parents, especially the father, are of crucial importance for the future of the child. As a member of a group, he has to learn to acknowledge and to accept authority, to recognize outside himself a regulator, controller, and arbiter of conduct that is largely traditional, not reasonable or based upon anything but custom. He must learn to observe in his conduct the repressions and frustrations required by the inviolability of things and persons; and equally he must learn to perform various acts, from small courtesies to the greater, more important duties appropriate to his sex, status, class, position, and so on, accepting all these complicated and largely ritualized acts as necessary and desirable and as duly sanctioned by the law and the prescribed rules of social living. The development of such conduct involves the constant recognition and willing acceptance of the authority of the state, which, to be really effective, must function, not in physical coercion and police supervision, but within the individual himself. Authority, then, like private property, is merely a way of behaving toward individuals and situations; it is an attitude or effective reaction toward what is expected or demanded.

Now if the young child experiences authority for the first time as coercive, severe, and brutal, as something that arouses fear, anxiety, and resentment, his socialization will be compromised. He cannot calmly and gracefully accept that which is expected or demanded, performing acts or refraining from responses, but rather he will feel tension, will resent the parental authority, and will develop a persistent hostility toward the parents, especially the father, and all others who attempt to direct his conduct.

Instead, then, of accepting the inviolabilities or the required perform-ances, the child who has been thus treated will fail to build those conduct patterns into an integrated whole, in which his behavior and his personality are at one.   He may outwardly conform to what is demanded or pro-hibited, but only because of fear and anxiety.   The learned conduct, es-sential to group life, is never assimilated or made wholly automatic, and so the child becomes preoccupied with the conflict between what he must do and not do and what he feels.   Often he releases his feelings in misbe-havior that is difficult to understand, for it gives the child nothing of value or advantage and usually is wholly incongrous with the situation.   These aberrant actions are symptoms of conflict, modes of expressing resent-ment or hostility against authority that has made him fearful and un-happy.

With so many children exposed to this destructive experience of au-thority, destined by their persistent feelings of fear and resentment to un-happy adult lives, if not to more serious outcomes in mental disorders and criminality, the nursery schools are confronted by the urgent need of these children for help in accepting authority and in escaping these initial disturbances.   Can we devise experiences in the nursery school that will enable the child to accept authority and to find freedom from the emo-tional conflicts and resentments that his previous experiences have en-gendered?   The need is for ways of inculcating acceptance of authority without aggravating the already serious conflicts so many children have when they come to nursery schools; and this calls for reformulation of the problem, as discussed above, so that the authority will be transferred to the situation and divested of the personal element that evokes the resent-ment and conflict.   Paradoxically, this depersonalization of authority de-pends upon a personal relation of the parent to the child wherein the exer-cise of authority is benevolent and helpful, not antagonistic and repressive.

This brings us to another life task of the child, who must create for himself, out of his experiences and the teaching he receives, an image of himself and of the kind of person he would like to be.   This ideal of self will embody all the feelings of inadequacy and guilt that the child has ex-perienced and must somehow express.   Such feelings may lead to aspira-tions for constructive achievement, to altruistic, helpful conduct, and to other forms of expiation and atonement which, if not exaggerated into a neurotic drive for perfection, make the individual personality into a friendly, coöperative adult.   Or they may lead to hostility and aggression, which take the form of intense competitive striving or coercive conduct; to delinquency, so that the individual may obtain punishment; or to mental disorders, in which the individual punishes himself.   All these adjustment patterns are exhibited in childhood, when the child already has adopted his "style of life," and if we had enough insight and understanding, these adjustments might be treated in the nursery-school group in such a way as to mitigate, if not actually to revise, these personality trends. No one can prescribe a general method or procedure for all children, but undoubtedly the largest single element in the situation is the kind and extent of affectionate personal interest shown by an adult toward the child, who thereby may find much needed help toward a constructive, not a self-defeating, ideal of self. The process of identification, wherein the child strives to emulate an admired and loved adult, makes the teacher-child relationship of crucial importance. Lack of sympathetic understanding, of tenderness and patient toleration, may turn the child toward hostility and aggression, from which he can be reclaimed only by long and difficult therapy later, if at all.

One of the most important problems facing students of personality today is this question whether hostility and aggression are inborn characteristics of all individuals or whether they are the reactions of individuals who, as infants and pre-school children, were deprived of needed love and affection and security and so were driven by the unrelieved pressure for socialization to hostile, aggressive, destructive conduct. This question is of the utmost importance socially and educationally, since the answer involves the future of our society and of the civilized world. If man is innately hostile and aggressive, prone to destructive antagonisms and rivalries, then the prospects for a better, more humanly desirable society are not very bright. If human nature, as theological tradition and many of our contemporary students of personality tell us, is born wicked, sinful, and hostile and must be forced to be social, coöperative, and altruistic, the task of education is essentially a coercive one, that of curbing the hostility, of teaching individuals to "handle their aggressiveness." If, on the other hand, human nature is essentially plastic, subject to educational direction toward friendliness, coöperativeness, gentleness, and genuine group or social activity, then the task of education is to prevent the early distortions and unnecessary deprivations that arouse resentment and aggressiveness, by providing as much affectionate reassurance and toleration of individual, temperamental differences as possible for the children who have been ill treated or neglected by their parents. Here pre-school education has an immense opportunity and responsibility for the future course of our culture.

But here we must ask whether we know enough now to meet this issue of resentment and aggressiveness wisely. The policy of restraint and repression in many schools may prevent fighting and disorder for the moment, but it does nothing to release the child from inner tensions and frustrations of which his aggressions are but symptoms. Perhaps we have to face a mixed answer to the earlier question and realize that tensions and resentment are probably present in all children in the early years, as a necessary consequence of the process of deprivations and coercions they undergo during socialization. Whether these tensions will become persistent, life-long hostile attitudes toward the world, or be replaced by friendly, coöperative, attitudes, may be the critical issue of pre-school education. No permanent good is achieved by a repressive policy, nor is any constructive end attained by permitting the children to fight it out, with the risk of damage to all concerned. What is needed is an imaginative, insightful handling of conflicts and aggressions on an experimental basis, addressed to the underlying anxiety, guilt, and frustrations and the need for reasurance and security. There is also need for methods of handling situations in such a way that the initial hostility or aggression of the child may be rendered unnecessary by opportunities for friendly, helpful responses. Many children do not know how to act coöperatively and need the skillful guidance of an adult to encourage them in friendly conduct and sympathetic actions. It must be realized that repeated rebuffs and frustrations may transform love into hatred and aggression, so that the child can only attack what he has most desired.

This brings us to the exigent question of freedom and self-expression, over which there has been so much controversy and often hasty action. It may help us to obtain some perspective on this question if we will remember again that the child faces a series of unavoidable life tasks, including the persistent problem of how to get along in an organized group life. To the young child the world around him is indeed precarious and ambiguous. He faces a natural world often dangerous and always puzzling even to adults; his own organism, with its many functions and needs which must conform to parental and social patterning; obscure, often unconscious, impulses that impel him to actions that frequently he cannot understand, and that others usually resent, rebuke, and often retaliate for; a social or cultural world organized into patterns of behavior and regulated by symbols, such as language, that are subtly differentiated and variable; a constellation of human relationships, in the immediate family, the wider kinship group, the neighborhood, and the school, among which he must find personality fulfillment and security despite the capricious and disparate character of all these impinging personalities; and finally an immense body of tradition and folklore, knowledge, skills, and play.

Faced with such a welter of confusing, conflicting adjustments, the young child desperately needs the security of stable, persistently uniform situations, of dependable human relations, and of endless patience and tolerance. The frequent cry against any repression of the child involves a confusion that is often tragic for the child. Every culture involves deprivations and repression, the patterning and regulation of physiological functions and human behavior, which, if wisely handled, are only redirections and modulations of impulses. The young child especially needs a wisely administered regulation or direction because he cannot sustain the immense burden of making individual decisions on all the aspects of life and of learning unaided to manage his impulses. Few adults can do this, as we see in the overwhelming need for guidance, for precepts, for legal, ethical, and religious direction. Moreover, the regularization of hunger and elimination and the respecting of the inviolabilites leaves the individual free for other activities and interests that would not be possible if he were continually driven by hunger, beset by impulses to elimination, and at the mercy of every provocative personal contact or sexual stimulus. These learned patterns and repressions are the chief factors in man's ability to go beyond a purely organic existence. It is not the ordering of life that damages the child, but the distortion, the fears, anxieties, and permanent frustrations and inhibitions that parental and educational practices unnecessarily inflict upon the child in the process of establishing these socially and individually necessary repressions.

It is also the confusion and anxiety and insecurity of capricious, vacillating teaching that damages the personality in search of something stable and constant to build upon. Children love order, regularity, repetition of the same pattern endlessly, and they need consistent adult guidance and help in learning these patterns of what is essential to their adult life and social living. But they do not need, nor can they safely endure, the fears, the anxieties, the feelings of inadequacy and of guilt that so many parents and teachers instill during this socialization process. Indeed fear seems to be the chief psychological instrument in early child-rearing —either the arousal of fears by cruel and coercive treatment or the inculcation of fears of experience, of people, of living, which cripple the child for life. Fear, and the resentment or hostility it often generates, are indeed the major emotional drives in our social life and give rise to much unsocial and antisocial behavior. What the child needs, but seldom receives, is a clear-cut definition of the situation and of the conduct appropriate therein, so that he can and will learn what conduct is permitted and what is not permitted without the emotional disturbances he now experiences during these lessons. Practically, this means that the teaching by parents and teachers should stress the desirability or undesirability of the action without imputing blame to the child, so that instead of the usual admonishment, "You are a bad, naughty boy!" the statement should be, "That action is not desirable or not kind, not generous or not permissible, and I don't like it." The important difference is in the personal imputation of guilt and the emotional disturbance it creates in the child.

As many writers have pointed out, the child accepts socialization and the inevitable frustrations and repressions involved largely because he wants love and security from the parent and teacher. The long-popular method of asking the child to do this or that "if you love me," is especially damaging because it fails to create a recognition of impersonal authority in situations. The love for parents should never be exploited to control the child whose anxiety lest he lose that love is already great. The traditional manner of teaching, by calling the child bad or wicked when it is the behavior that should be defined as undesirable, makes the child fearful, guilty, and unhappy, and, if continued, may establish a persistent feeling of guilt and inadequacy and of being rejected. To assuage that feeling of guilt and to overcome the sense of inadequacy and rejection, the child may commit more antisocial or forbidden acts to get the punishment he needs for his guilty feelings or to prove that he is not worthless. As Dr. William Healy and Dr. Augusta Bronner have recently shown in their study, *New Light on Delinquency,* the delinquent generally has had an unhappy childhood, characterized by feelings of rejection, inadequacy, and guilt, and by lack of affection.

This point about the necessity of socialization for the child without undue emotional stress and strain during the process is being emphasized here because it has such great consequences for our social life. If we could persuade parents and teachers to avoid characterizing the child as bad or naughty, while defining the behavior, and then give the child ample reassurance when receiving such lessons, undoubtedly we could make an immense contribution to the reduction of delinquency, criminality, and other non-criminal, but socially destructive conduct on the part of those who spend their adult lives proving by the acquisition of property, prestige, and power that they are not as guilty or as worthless as they were repeatedly told in childhood.

This question of socialization of the child without distortion and emotional disturbances must be seen in the light of the great individual differences among children in intelligence, temperament, rate of maturation, and need of reassurance, so that each child may be treated individually. The professional urge to standardize, to routinize, to substitute academic training for sympathetic interest and insights into children and to look for uniformities and generalizations that will save thinking, all must be critically reëxamined by nursery-school educators who are aware of these large social responsibilities. Especially is there a need for questioning the well-established principle that nursery-school teachers should be impersonal and should repress all affective responses to and from children. This principle came into vogue in the 1920's when behavioristic theories of child-rearing were dominant. The ideal of education was seen as that of almost complete emotional anesthesia and continually rational conduct, which is the ideal of the neurotic who is afraid of life and is seeking to suppress all feelings, of which he is fearful. As we realize how much the child is in need—as indeed all adults are also—of warm personal, human relations, of affectionate interest and real concern, and of opportunities to give and receive affection and to *feel* we must challenge this old principle as directly contrary to the deepest need of the child and as destructive of human values, which can be preserved only by sensitivity and feeling tones toward people and situations.

Here it is necessary to ask why are we so afraid to recognize that the child needs mothering, not only at home, but in the nursery school, and that nursery-school teachers, by the very nature of their work, must be mother surrogates, ready and capable of giving affection and tenderness and warm emotional response to the children and of accepting them from the children. Is it because mothering does not seem scientific that we have tried to exclude it from the nursery schools or because—and I say this in no critical spirit, but as a statement based upon the actual situation —so many of those in nursery school education are unmarried and childless and have unconsciously projected their own personal life adjustment into the training of nursery-school teachers? When we reflect upon the number of children in all classes of society who are raised by fear, terror, punishment, and other sadistic methods, with little or no experience of love and affection, we may well ask whether mothering (not smothering) may not be the most important service the nursery school can render to little children. Mothering does not mean babying or pampering, but rather giving a feeling of being liked and wanted, of belonging to some one who cares, and of being guided in the conduct of life with benevolent interest and confidence.

Dr. David Levy, a year or so ago, told this story at a meeting of the American Orthopsychiatric Association. He said that the social workers in the Bureau of Child Guidance were having unusually successful results with problem children, just because they were being maternal to these boys and girls so frequently denied real mothering. But they gave up this procedure because, said he, it did not seem scientific and was so hard to record! Perhaps if the nursery-school teacher were to consider her function as not only educational, but clinical, it might be easier to accept what the psychotherapeutic clinician accepts—namely, the rôle of parent surrogate, who gives the child individual personal interest and attention and tries to help that child work out a design for living by providing direction and deprivation, but always with interest and helpful concern.

Finally, we must look at the question of socialization in the light of the cultural changes through which we are now living, which are bringing about the destruction of so many of our traditional ideas, beliefs, and older certainties.   The men and women of to-morrow will have to live in a shifting, uncertain world, of rapidly changing ideas and conceptions, with few or no absolutes or certainties.   What is to guide their lives, to help them find fulfillment and a design for living sanely, wholesomely, and coöperatively?   Probably no previous generation has had to face such acute personal problems without help from religion, custom, and tradition.   Either they will demand an authoritarian state because they cannot endure uncertainty or tolerate the destructive hostility and aggressions of unhappy individuals, or they will learn to seek in constructive work and recreative play, in the warm human relations of marriage, parenthood, and the family, a way of life that will permit realization of the enduring human values.

The nursery school, in close and coöperative relationship with the home and parents, is the primary agency for mental hygiene.   The opportunity in pre-school education to build wholesome, sane, coöperative, and mature personalities, and to determine the future of our culture, is unlimited. The discharge of that responsibility lies in helping the young child to meet the persistent life tasks and to fulfill his insistent needs.   But the nursery school cannot do this alone.   It must have collaboration from the kindergarten and the grade schools, and it must find some way of coöperating with the home and the family, despite the frequent blindness and resistance of the parents.   If nursery-school teachers were to realize that they are like parents, with their personal peculiarities, their emotional resistance and susceptibilities, their ignorance and rigid convictions—which may be just as undesirable for the child as the home practices they deprecate— perhaps such a realization would make them more tolerant and more willing to seek a basis of collaboration in meeting the fundamental needs of the child.   The family can and does provide the child with a place, a status, with "belongingness" and often much needed love and affection.   Can the nursery school organize its procedures and prepare its teachers to meet these same needs and also those other educational needs which the family has difficulty in supplying?

The fundamental needs of the child are in truth the fundamental needs of society.

16. On the Theories and Problems of Adolescence*

Related selections: 14, 27

Is ADOLESCENCE a single phenonmenon the characteristics of which
are much the same for all individuals, or is it a period during which
many different behavior patterns are manifested? Is it, as G.
Stanley Hall and later psychologists have described it, a period of
emotional storm and stress? Does adolescent behavior have its
origin in the biological changes occuring at puberty? Luchins
believes that the so-called emotional disturbances of adolescence
may be more related to factors in the social scene than to physiological maturity.

A. DISAGREEMENT CONCERNING THE MEANING
OF ADOLESCENCE

WHEN THE man in the street speaks of "adolescence," he generally knows
what he means by the term and is probably quite confident that the next
fellow using the expression has the same referrent in mind. The experts,
however, are not in agreement concerning the meaning of adolescence.

1. The Period of Adolescence

Some psychologists refer to adolescence as the period between 12 and
17 years of age, but others refer to it as the teen age period, while still
others regard it as the entire second decade of life, or as extending until the
25th year of life, or even later. There are psychologists who are opposed
to this description in terms of age, maintaining that adolescence begins
with biological puberty.

But there are psychologists who claim that the beginning of adolescence
cannot clearly be characterized either in terms of biological maturity or
chronological age but should be characterized in terms of when the individual faces adult adjustments. Adolescence itself is then regarded as the
period of transition between childhood and adulthood. For example, in
a recent text on adolescence, Kuhlen writes that regardless of actual
chronological age or state of biological development, an individual is
adolescent to the extent that he is engaged in the process of making sexual-

* Abraham S. Luchins, "On the Theory and Problems of Adolescence," *Journal
of Genetic Psychology,* vol. LXXXV, First Half (September, 1954), pp. 47–63.
Reprinted by permission of author and publisher.
    Dr. Luchins (1914—), Professor of Psychology at the University of Oregon,
was formerly at McGill University and also at Yeshiva University where he was
Director of the Guidance Bureau. He is a Diplomate in Clinical Psychology.

social adjustments, ideological adjustments, vocational adjustments, and adjustments relating to achievement of freedom from parents.   One is preadolescent in the years before he is concerned with such problems, and he is adult to the extent that he has successfully solved these difficulties and eliminated them as problems.   It must be emphasized that even among psychologists who define adolescence as the period between childhood and adulthood, there are differences of opinion as to the criteria determining the cessation of childhood and those determining the onset of adulthood.

2. The Characteristics of Adolescence

a. Storm and stress.   Not only is there a lack of agreement among psychologists as to when the period of adolescence begins and when it ceases, but there is not even general agreement concerning the *characteristics* of adolescence.   One of the characteristics sometimes referred to is that of emotional disturbance and instability.   G. Stanley Hall, who pioneered in the study of adolescence, in 1904 described adolescence as a period of emotional storm and stress. In line with Hall's theory of recapitulation —the theory that every individual in his development parallels the history of evolution of his species—he maintained that development in adolescence is suggestive of some ancient period of storm and stress for the species when old moorings were broken and a higher level attained. While the theory of recapitulation has largely been abandoned, the notion of adolescence as a period of storm and stress has persisted to the present day, exercising considerable influence not only on the layman's thinking but also upon that of many psychologists.

Yet this notion has not remained unchallenged.   Psychologists and anthropologists, among them Ruth Benedict and Margaret Mead, have emphasized the differences in adolescent behavior patterns prevailing in different cultures.   They note that in some so-called primitive cultures, for example, Samoa, emotional disturbances do not seem to accompany biological puberty or the teen-age years or the second decade of life or the attainment of adult status.   On the basis of such evidence it would not be valid to generalize that adolescence is everywhere an emotionally stressful period.

One might seek to limit this generalization to adolescence in our society but even this conception has been challenged.   Thus Kuhlen, after assessing the available evidence, concludes that adolescence in our society does not seem to be an unduly stressful period, that it is not a period of general storm and stress.

b. Reinforcement of sex drives.   Another supposedly general characteristic of adolescence pertains to the reinforcement of sexual drives. This aspect is emphasized by psychoanalysts who relate adolescence to the reawakening of the sex drives, particularly the drive for heterosexuality which is assumed to be rather latent in the period from about 6 to 10 years of age. A recent text by Harsh and Schrickel *defines* adolescence as that period during which sexual motivation reaches its peak, when psychosexual drives and emotions are probably more intense than at any earlier or later period of life. But actual observation and investigation do not support the contention that sex drives and emotions are for every individual necessarily more intense beginning with puberty or in the teens or during the second decade of life than at other periods. For some individuals, sex drives seem to become highly active before overt signs of puberty are noted or before the ages of 10 or 12 or 13 or any other of the various criteria considered to mark the beginning of adolescence; while for other individuals sex drives and emotions seem to become active or to be particularly intense only long after puberty or even after the second or third decade of life.

Thus, in this area also it does not seem possible to draw a conclusion which is generally valid.

c. Changes in personality development. Consider now another characteristic sometimes attributed to adolescence. G. Stanley Hall emphasized that marked and rapid changes occur in all aspects of *personality development* during adolescence, the changes being so dramatic that he referred to adolescence as a rebirth or a new birth. This conception has been challenged on the grounds that personality development constitutes a gradual and continuous pattern which generally does not reveal any striking deviations at or about the time of adolescence. In Hollingworth's words, the notion that every child is a changeling who at puberty comes forth as a different personality is but a widespread myth.

3. The Biological Origin of Adolescent Behavior

A particularly persistent belief exists that the characteristics of adolescence are biologically generated, that they result from the biological changes occurring at puberty. This point of view was set forth by Hall and has been reaffirmed by many other psychologists. For example, Blanchard, writing from a psychoanalytically oriented point of view, concludes that reinforcement of the drive for heterosexuality, of the drive for independence, and possibly, of the drive for aggression, are *direct results* of the physiological changes accompanying puberty.

a. Cross-cultural comparisons. Evidence against this viewpoint may be found in the reports of certain cultural anthropologists and psychologists. They indicate that the same physiological changes tend to be accompanied by different behavior in different cultures. They have emphasized the influence of different culturally-determined attitudes toward the same physiological and morphological characteristics. Thus, in certain parts of Africa, females desirous of becoming attractive enter a fattening house whereas in our society females having the same desire go on a starvation diet. To cite another example: Among the Carrier Indians of British Columbia at the time of the first menstruation the girl is considered to be seized by evil spirits and is treated as a social pariah who must live apart from the others, whereas among the Apache Indians the girl at puberty is considered to be possessed by good spirits and is regarded as a direct source of supernatural blessing.

b. Influence of socio-economic conditions. The thesis of biological determinism becomes even more tenuous if we consider the results of studies of the effects of socio-economic conditions on adolescent behavior. In our own culture, the great grandfathers of our present-day youth were generally considered adults, with adult responsibilities, at an age at which the youth of today often manifests so-called adolescent behavior. Surely the average chronological age of biological puberty has not advanced. As a matter of fact, the available evidence seems to indicate that the average age of physiological maturity of the studied samples tends to be somewhat lower nowadays than it was several generations ago. Another example may be found in the general differences among adolescent behavior in urban districts as compared to rural districts when presumably the same physiological changes occur in urban youth as in rural youth.

c. Physical-behavioral correlations. Finally, against the thesis that behavioral phenomena of adolescence are caused by pubertal changes, I should like to present the conclusions of a psychologist such as Wayne Dennis who is admittedly strongly biologically oriented. Dennis defines the beginning of adolescence as coinciding with biological puberty and conceives the central aim and interest of the psychology of adolescence to be the portrayal of the effects of pubertal changes upon behavior. To study these effects, he examines what he describes as certain sets of mental-physical correlations, bearing on the relationship between physical maturity and such a variety of behavioral phenomena as: sexual behavior, various play activities and interests, religious activities and interests, delinquency, suicide, and so on. His finding is that the available studies are generally inconclusive with reference to the causal relationship between psychological phenomena and physiological changes accompanying puberty. It would seem that even a biologically oriented investigator can at the present time find little evidence to support the thesis that biological changes accompanying puberty *cause* any given behavioral phenomenon.

d. To summarize. I have attempted thus far to show that there is a lack of agreement among psychologists with regard to the definition of the period of adolescence, the characteristics of adolescent behavior, and whether or not the behavior is biologically determined.

B. NEGLECT OF THE INDIVIDUAL CASE

Even after allowance is made for the varying definitions of adolescence, valid generalizations holding for all adolescents seem to be rare.   Perhaps this is not as unfortunate a state of affairs as it may appear at first glance. Perhaps there has been an overemphasis on the attempts to derive generalizations valid for all or most adolescents and too little emphasis on the study of the adolescent as an individual.   In support of this contention I should like to review some of the major approaches to the study of adolescence and to note how their very methodology involves a neglect of the individual case.

One of the approaches, which has already been referred to, seeks to correlate behavioral phenomena and physiological phenomena.   Whatever else may be said for or against this approach, it seems to be clear that the individual is of necessity lost in the correlations, that the correlations may portray *trends* but cannot portray what actually occurs in a particular case. Another approach, sometimes described as culturally-oriented, seeks to compare prevailing patterns of adolescence in one culture with that in another culture.   While the merits of this approach are not denied, it must not be overlooked that it concentrates on gross cultural differences, on general patterns and attitudes which seem most prevalent in a particular culture.   But the approach thereby tends to neglect or to minimize individual differences within any one culture.   A third approach is concerned with the influence of various social conditions and institutions in our society on adjustment to adulthood.   Adherents of this approach may note that adjustment to adulthood was somewhat different several generations ago than it is today or that even today the adjustment is somewhat different in rural than in urban districts.   Noteworthy as such observations are, they do not reveal individual differences in adjustment patterns which presumably existed for young people several generations ago and which exist today, even within any particular urban or rural district.

It seems to me that it is time to cease this rather futile chase after generalizations valid for all adolescents or for all adolescents of a particular culture or generation or locality.   It is perhaps time to concentrate on intensive studies of individual adolescents.   It may be time to cease attempting to explain the phenomena of adolescence exclusively in terms of biology or culture or society or psychoanalysis, or what have you.

Rather, we should perhaps suspend judgment as to the how and why of adolescent behavior.   We should momentarily put aside our theories and hypotheses, and seek to look as unbiasedly as possible at some examples of this behavior, permitting the behavior itself to suggest possible hypotheses for explanations.

C. SOME OBSERVATIONAL DATA

I shall now turn to some observations which I made during a seven year study of a group of boys of Brooklyn, New York.   The techniques used included participation with the boys in some of their activities, naturalistic observations, individual and group discussions with the boys, and discussions with their parents, teachers, siblings, and others in the neighborhood who knew them, as well as analysis of diaries kept by the boys.   All the boys were of bright-normal or superior intelligence and of about the same socio-economic status.

In 1931, when the study began, their ages ranged from 10 to 14.   Let us consider now the behavior manifested by three of the boys in the period between 1935 and 1936, when each of them was about 14 or 15 years of age.

1. Description of Behavior

When I first met Robert he seemed to be a happy, even-tempered youngster.   But at the age of 14 he was displaying what has been described as typically adolescent behavior.   He was depressed, moody, irritable, emotionally unstable, and difficult to get along with.   His parents and other adults frequently attributed this behavior to his adolescence.   In short, Robert seemed to fit the stereotype of the adolescent in our society.

Ted at 14 was well-poised, essentially happy, and emotionally stable, showing little of the turbulence manifested by Robert.   His teachers and other adults commented on his social poise and maturity.

Lester's behavior was closer to that displayed by Robert.   Lester was moody, irritable with parents, siblings, and almost everyone else.   He was inclined to think deeply and often about his own misery and the world's misfortunes.

2. Attempts at Understanding the Behavior

Should the behavior of these three boys be attributed to pubertal changes or to adjustment to adulthood or to the culture in which they live? Will any of these generalizations yield an understanding of the dynamics underlying each case? Will any of them give insight into the reasons for the differences and similarities in overt behavior?

To begin with, it should be noted that both Lester, the unhappy, brooding individual, and Ted, the happy, poised individual, were at 14 years of age manifesting an accepted sign of puberty, pigmented pubic hair, and were about equal in other signs of physical maturity. Robert, on the other hand, had at this age not yet shown any overt signs of pubertal change. Blond, slight of stature, and shorter than the others, he looked like a "kid," to use the label which members of the group sometimes applied to him in a derogatory manner.

Thus in two of the boys similar physical changes were accompanied by very different behavior patterns. Nor can the change in Robert's behavior from his earlier emotional stability to the storm and stress variety he manifested at the ages of 14 and 15 be correlated with any concomitant signs of overt physical maturity. Indeed, study of the relevant facts seem to indicate that Robert's change in behavior might more accurately be traced to his *lack* of physical maturity. Robert had previously been the acknowledged leader of the gang; but at 14 and 15, with the growing interest in females and social events, the group found him somewhat of a hindrance. They were afraid that his youthful appearance might hurt their chances with the girls and lessen their possibilities of making "pickups." Moreover, Robert's older brothers were prone to boast about their amorous exploits and Robert once told me that he wished that he were as manly-looking and attractive to girls as his older brothers.

What had happened to Robert? It might be said that he had lost status in the group, that he no longer had a sense of group-belongingness, that he no longer had a well-structured behavioral world, and that there were sharp discrepancies between his aspirations and his achievements. Incidentally, as Robert grew older and became physically mature, he joined another group, became their leader, and displayed considerably less behavior of the turbulent type. It would seem that physiological maturity in this case did not foster adolescent conflicts but was one of the factors helping to decrease emotional disturbance.

What about Lester? May his behavior be attributed to pubertal changes? As a matter of fact, acquaintance with Lester's life history reveals that he had for years been moody, irritable, concerned with the world's troubles. He had been struggling to find answers to such questions as: What is life? What is man? Who am I? He regarded as inadequate the answers given to him, directly or indirectly, by his teachers or by books he read. Although accepted and respected by members of the group, who were rather proud of his erudition, he often preferred being by himself and confided to me that he did not really feel that he belonged to the gang or that he could fully share the other members' interests.   What is important to note here is that the behavioral patterns and emotional tone manifested by Lester at or about the time of puberty were not very different from those which he showed in the years preceding overt pubertal change or, for that matter, from those which he showed in the years which followed.   Until his death in World War II at the age of 22, members of the group who were then with him later told me, he was always the same moody, irritable, philosophical Lester.   And yet, a psychologist attempting to study Lester's behavior only at about the time of puberty might have concluded that the moodiness and concern with ideological matters which he then revealed were a unique development accompanying biological puberty.   From the vantage point of a knowledge of Lester's history for several years prior and subsequent to pubertal change, it seems to me that he was seeking for a meaning in life, that he was attempting to develop a clearly structured world, and that there were sharp discrepancies between his ideals and reality, as well as between his aspirations and achievements with regard to a purpose for man's existence.

Let us return to Ted, the third of the trio.   Ted, the well-poised, emotionally stable youth was that way until about the age of 19 when a severe financial setback in his father's business necessitated his leaving college and obtaining a rather menial position to help support his family.   He became irritable, argumentative, displayed extreme mood swings and found it difficult to get along with his family and others.   He was, in short, manifesting at 19 the kind of turbulent behavior which Robert had shown at 14.   Analysis of my records on Ted made one thing clear.   As early as his elementary school days, he had made definite vocational plans.   He knew that he wanted to be a medical doctor, was confident of his mental ability and of the financial support required to achieve his goal.   But the financial reverses made it impossible for him to reach his goal and frustrated his ambition.

3. Inferences from the Three Cases

What can be inferred from these three cases?   Firstly, it would seem that youths living in the same locality and having similar socio-economic backgrounds may manifest strikingly different behavior patterns.   Secondly, similar physiological changes may be accompanied by different behavior patterns.   Also, individuals who are far apart with regard to physical maturity may display similar behavior patterns.   While the issue of whether or not pubertal changes may directly induce behavioral changes is still a moot one, it would seem that behavior may be a consequence of the *attitudes* possessed by the individual himself and others regarding physical changes or *lack* of such changes.   Thirdly, the kind of emotional storm and stress which is sometimes considered as characteristic of adolescence may not be manifested at all, may occur long before or only long after pubertal changes, may be momentary or of rather limited duration, or may be generally characteristic of the individual.

As a hypothesis for future research it is suggested that emotional instability may tend to be manifested at any chronological age when the individual lacks a clear frame of reference with which to meet reality, when his behavioral world is not clearly structured, and when there are marked discrepancies between his aspirations and his achievements.

4. Conclusions Drawn from Study

The inferences drawn from the three cases are not sufficient to account for the behavior of the other 12 boys who were studied.   Some of the boys, although behaving as typical adolescents, did not seem to have any serious emotional involvements.   Rather, it seemed to me that they had simply adopted the characteristic *stereotype*.   They were playing the rôle called for by this stereotype.   They were exhibiting the kind of behavior which they and others expected of adolescents of this day and age.   Still others of the boys behaved like impulsive children who were gorging themselves on new experiences in an irresponsible carefree manner.   The behavior of one of the boys seemed to be related to a deficiency of social skills, such as the skills of dancing and getting along with girls.   Once he acquired these skills, there was a noticeable change in his behavior.

In brief, adolescence does not seem to constitute one phenomenon. An analysis reveals a variety of different behavior patterns.   Moreover, the different phenotypical patterns are not caused by one genotype.   In other words, overtly similar behavior may be brought about by different conditions and overtly different behavior may be brought about by similar conditions.   In view of this, it is not surprising to find a diversity of contemporary descriptions and explanations of adolescent behavior.   One way to minimize the contemporary confusion of concepts and terminology may be to study the individual adolescent as a person instead of merely regarding him as a source of information which can confirm or infirm a hypothesis stemming from a general theory of adolescence.

D. SOME SOCIAL FACTORS WHICH MAY INFLUENCE ADOLESCENT BEHAVIOR

Regardless of the shape which future studies or theories of adolescence may take, there is an immediate and practical problem which must be faced. It is obvious to parents, teachers, and even the youths themselves that many individuals go through an adolescent stage characterized by turbulence and conflict. On the basis of the data collected in the study referred to above I was led to conclude that there are certain social field conditions which operate to produce or aggravate such turbulence and conflict. It is not denied that temperamental and experiential factors may make one more or less susceptible to the influence of these conditions. What follows should be taken as preliminary hypotheses to be tested by future research.

1. Uncertainty Concerning Adult Status

I have already hypothesized that emotional difficulties may tend to occur under conditions in which the individual lacks a clear frame of reference with regard to his status and function. There are factors in the social scene which are conducive to an unstable frame of reference concerning the achievement of *adult status*. Unlike what occurs in some other cultures, in our society there is no one initiation rite or ceremony or fixed pattern of activities in which one must participate in order to be regarded by himself and by others as having donned the mantle of adulthood. The physically mature youth may be treated as a child by those about him, either consistently or intermittently. At other times he may be reminded that he has no business behaving as a child. Indeed, there are individuals, regardless of chronological age, who are never quite certain of whether they have attained adult status.

Whether or not the individual ever attains adult status, either subjectively or objectively, depends on a host of socio-economic factors and on the nature of his inter-personal relations. Depending upon the individual circumstances and, to some extent, on such general conditions as whether it is a time of war or of peace, of depression or prosperity, there tend to be considerable differences with regard to the age of occurrence, the ease, and the mode of locomotion involved in the crossing of that nebulous threshold leading to adulthood. The existence of such differences may help to account for the various age limits which different authorities ascribe to the adolescent period. It may also help to account for the wide variety of behavior patterns observed during adolescence. Moreover the uncertainty which often accompanies the attainment of adulthood may help to account for the prevalency of emotional difficulties during adolescence.

Incidentally, I should like to refer here to the observation that adolescence in rural districts is by and large a less stressful experience than in urban districts. This may be related to the fact that the youth on the farm may be able to attain relative independence and other signs of adult status more readily than his urban cousin. Similarly, the observation that adolescence tended to be a less stressful experience several generations ago than it is today, may be related to the fact that adult status, including marriage, was generally attained at an earlier age in former years.

2. Institutional Complexity and Conflict

There are other factors which may contribute to an unstable frame of reference, to a lack of clearly structured behavioral world.   As the child becomes older, he may become more aware of contradictions between what is preached and what is practiced.   He may realize that his parents and their beliefs are far from perfect.   He may realize that his idols have clay feet.

Moreover, as he grows older, he comes into contact with more and more institutions and practices other than the primary institution of the home. Several generations ago the home was the center of life activities, with business, recreational, religious, educational, and vocational training activities centered in the home. Today there are separate institutions each specializing in an activity which was once the function of the home.   By and large, these institutions lack the intimate, personal relationship which may have prevailed in the home.   The very structure of these institutions may rule out the possibility of a warm, genuine interest in its members. The youth may be upset by what he regards as a cold, impersonal attitude towards him.

Each institution may think of the individual primarily as a tool for the fulfillment of the institution's goals and objectives.   It may demand of him that he play a certain rôle regardless of the individual's own needs. Or it may be interested in the individual only in so far as he is capable of playing this rôle.   A middling example of this is the practice of placing an individual into a vocational school because test results indicate that he has little chance of successfully playing the rôle of a student in an academic institution.   This may occur in spite of the individual's desire to attend an academic school and in spite of social pressures exerted by family and friends that demand that he be an academic student.

The demands which one institution makes on the individual may conflict with the demands made upon him by other institutions. Moreover, the various demands may clash with the values and purposes learned in the home.   Thus there may be a clash between what the home teaches and what the school teaches, what the church wants and what the street gang wants, and so on.   Confronted by these conflicting demands, the individual may have some difficulty in meeting them and yet maintaining his integrity as an organized, whole being.   He may have to struggle against becoming a mere collection of selves—a home self, a school self, a street self, a business self, and so on.   He may be aghast at the thought that he is expected to play a rôle and be able to don and cast off rôles as one might change masks.   Moreover, he may have difficulty in achieving a self-concept, in knowing just who he is.   All this may contribute to adolescent conflict.

In short, the youth must learn to dance in harmony with many different tunes while still attempting to maintain some degree of harmony within himself.   For some individuals, the conflicting demands may be extremely upsetting.   They may find that the personal and rather clearly structured world of childhood is replaced by a cold, disorganized, and unstable world.   They may not be quite certain of just who they are, whether they are being themselves or merely playing rôles, and just what rôle they are expected to play at any particular time.   Herein may lie some clues to the emotional turbulence which has come to be associated with adolescence.

3. Gaps between Aspirations and Attainments

Reference was previously made to the possible effect on behavior of a discrepancy between aspirations and achievements.   It seems to me that there are factors in our social fabric which, in some cases, make for a considerable discrepancy between the ideals and aspirations associated with adulthood and the actual achievements attained by the youth once he is "grown up."   As a child he may have been led to believe that when he grows up he will be allowed entrance into the wonderland hitherto denied to him, the world of privileges, immunities, status, worthwhile responsibilities, independence, and fulfillment of numerous dreams.   Yet, the physical signs of being grown up may be attained without the fulfillment of even one of the goals which had been intimately associated with being grown up.

For example, in our culture a premium is placed on economic independence.   Yet, scarcity of positions, the need for lengthy educational training or lengthy apprenticeship may make it necessary to postpone such independence for many years.   In some professions, economic independence cannot be secured until one is well past the second decade of life or well into the third.

Ideals and aspirations with regard to dating, romance, and marriage are fostered by the home, movies, and magazines.   But these ideals may be quite impossible of attainment or may be interfered with by finances or physical unattractiveness or simply by the fact that the available candidates for romance are quite different from those portrayed in the movies.

Youth is bombarded by stimuli which arouse or intensify various kinds of needs, particularly those involving status and sex. The radio, television, movies, magazines, newspapers, and even the home serve to over-stimulate certain needs. But at the same time there may be little or no opportunity for the youth to gratify these desires in socially accepted ways. For example, the boy or girl who is expected to abstain from sexual activity is at the same time exposed to stimuli which play up sex. The result may be that these over-stimulated desires become central in the youth's view of the situation and that obstacles to these needs loom very large. Consequently, the youth may feel that he is blocked and hemmed in on all sides. One might draw an analogy between the situation he faces and that faced by the rat in Norman R. F. Maier's experiments on neuroses. Forces arousing and overstimulating the various needs may be compared to the airblast aimed at making the rat jump; but, like the rat, the youth may have no way of reacting to these forces without encountering punishment. It is therefore small wonder that what is akin to neurotic behavior may be noticed in some adolescents.

4. Some Other Hypotheses

Thus far I have suggested that the emotional difficulties often associated with adolescence in our culture may in part be the resultant of a gap between the youth's goals and achievements or of his lack of a stable frame of reference with which to view his rather disorganized world. It is also interesting to speculate to what extent the youth who is seemingly manifesting emotional storm and stress may simply have adopted the stereotype of behavior which he and others associate with this period. I should also like to refer to the interesting hypothesis advanced by Kuhlen—namely, that the stress commonly attributed to the adolescent may in part be a projection of the emotional stress experienced by parents and other adults dealing with youth.

E. WHAT CAN BE DONE ABOUT THE EMOTIONAL TENSIONS OF ADOLESCENTS?

I have described some social field conditions which may produce emotional tensions in the adolescent. The problem arises as to what can be done to minimize these tensions. Before dealing with this problem, I should like to draw a distinction between two kinds of tensions. Every living system experiences tensions; these are necessary for the life activities of the organism, for its development and growth, and for the attainment and maintenance of its equilibrium. The late Max Wertheimer, founder of Gestalt Psychology, used to refer to these as tensions with a small t.   In contrast to the tensions with a small t, he referred to tensions with a capital T; by the latter he meant those tensions whose direction of operation is opposed to that of the organism, tensions which interfere with adequate functioning of the organism, hinder development, and even alter the organism's essential structure.

This distinction seems to me to be applicable to the tensions experienced by the adolescent.   Some are related to the youth's striving toward equilibrium under changing conditions and are necessary to further his growth both as a physical organism and as a social being.   Specifically, tensions may be said to have positive value insofar as they awaken the youth from a kind of lethargic slumber, arouse some self-analysis and introspection, and set him to seek for values and purposes in life.   Because of tensions, the youth may be led to question, to evaluate critically, and perhaps to strike out in new directions, to find new ways of doing things.   It might even be argued that the stresses and strains experienced by the younger generation help them to work for social change and social progress.   To such tensions we may refer as those with small t's.   But there are tensions with capital T's: tensions whose direction and nature of operation interfere with the youth's growth and development, which hamper his functioning at an adequate level, which keep him in continuous disequilibrium and may even creat mental illnesses.   These latter tensions are what I have in mind in what follows.

1.   There is a need to decrease somewhat the gap between the youth's goals and desires, on the one hand, and what he can accomplish, on the other.   Perhaps a step in this direction can be made by realistically evaluating the ideals and standards which our culture propagates with regard to adult status.   For example, completion of education and economic independence on the part of the male are often regarded as prerequisites for marriage.   Scholarships, fellowships, and apprenticeships may require the single status.   Under present-day conditions this often means late marriage which in turn makes more difficult the satisfaction of sexual needs within moral bounds.   If our society holds that present day sex standards have definite and positive value, then something should be done to make it easier for the physically mature youth to live up to these standards.   Somewhat less ballyhoo about sex in our movies, radios, magazines, may held to dim the spotlight currently focused on it and perhaps decrease the severity of youth's sex problems.   Another solution might be earlier marriage.   The success of married veterans who attended school after World War II seems to provide ample testimony that formal education and marriage are not necessarily incompatible.   Undoubtedly early marriage will raise problems of its own, including the very pragmatic issue

of finances; it may be necessary that financial assistance be given to the young couple by parents or perhaps private or government agencies. Notwithstanding the above something should be done to decrease the discrepancy between youth's sexual needs and his possibilities for gratifying them in a socially acceptable manner.

There is a broader issue involved here.   Many of our ethical standards may be seen by youth primarily as taboos, as limitations.   But just as a road facilitates travel even though it deters the traveler from other possible paths, so a social standard is not solely a taboo but often has a positive function.   Greater emphasis on the positive function of social and ethical standards rather than emphasis on their limitations to actions, as well as greater opportunity for young people to realize the positive values of these standards in their own life situations, may help to make youth more willing to accept and comply with the moral standards of our society.

It is appropriate to refer here to the matter of independence, quite aside from financial independence.   The mature individual in our society is expected to stand on his own feet, to make decisions on his own.   But such intellectual and emotional independence, if I may refer to it as such, does not suddenly spring into being at any one time of life.   Although the capacity for such independence may be related to personal endowment, the exercise of this independence hinges on previous training and on suitable conditions.   Parents must be made aware of the importance of training for emotional and intellectual independence, of allowing and encouraging ever-increasing opportunities for independent judgment on the part of the child.   They must, so to speak, allow for loosening of the proverbial apron strings.   Our schools can make an important contribution by placing an emphasis *not* on rote drill, memorization, and blind following, but on *understanding* and productive thinking.   The child should not merely learn a collection of facts and skills but should learn to learn.   Moreover, participation in the formation of value judgments in the school, as well as opportunities to evaluate these judgments, may help to create an individual who can make intelligent judgments outside of the school situation.

2. I have referred to the possible rôle of institutional conflicts in fostering emotional difficulties.   Here there seems to be a decided need for discussion and coöperation among representatives of various institutions in the community, among parents, teachers, other educators, religious leaders, people who determine policies in recreational and advertising media, and so on.   They should consider how they may contribute to the problems faced by adolescents.   They should consider their goals and practices in relation to youth and the demands which they make of youth. The aim should be to minimize intra-institutional and inter-institutional

conflict.   This calls for community planning, for the utilization of social action research in the community as well as for the utilization of other group dynamic techniques which have been successfully applied by Kurt Lewin and his students to various community problems.

3. It is important to find socially useful functions for youth, socially productive uses of youth's vast sources of energies.   Totalitarian movements have made use of the potential energy in youth and have taken advantage of youth's needs for group-belongingness, and need for a definite rôle and function in life.   Democracies have yet to channelize youth's energies into socially productive paths so that the young person knows and feels that he belongs and is needed.   The picture of groups of teen age youngsters, lolling idly about, seeking to kill time, seems to me to symbolize our tendency to be wasteful of our human resources.

In every community, worthwhile projects can be organized in which young people, either with their peers or together with other age groups, can serve in some worthwhile socially useful activity.   Such experiences might help to develop a feeling of belonging and being useful.   Since our social structure is of such a nature that there seems of necessity to be a long period between childhood and adulthood, we must learn to make those who are going through this period feel more than simply in-betweens, marginal individuals who are too old to be children and who are not yet adults   These young people are capable of dealing with certain community problems and projects, precisely because they are more mature than younger children and are not yet weighed down with all the time-consuming responsibilities of adulthood.   In short, adolescence can be made into a worthwhile, socially productive period of life rather than being merely a waiting period.

F. CONCLUDING REMARK

After criticizing others for talking in generalities rather than studying specific adolescents, I too have indulged in some generalizations and theorizing.   Of course there is nothing intrinsically wrong in promulgating general hypotheses concerning adolescence.   But, it seems to me, only by studying the individual case will we gain deep understanding of the particular field conditions which are operating to produce the specific kind of adolescent behavior.   Theorizing should not be a substitute for observation and study of the particular individual.   Nor should a theory or a hypothesis or a generalization predispose the investigator to look only for or at certain aspects of the phenomenon under study.   In conclusion, I should like to stress the importance—for parents, teachers, clinicians, and others who deal with adolescents—not to allow any *theory of* adolescence to blur their vision of the particular youth with whom they are dealing.

B. MENTAL ABILITY

17. Intelligence from a Perceptual Point of View*

Related selections: 4, 18, 29, 34, 50

HAS THE time-honored static conception of intelligence and human capacity proved more restrictive than constructive in educational practice?   Dr. Combs suggests that it has and explores the idea of intelligence as a function of an individual's perceptions.   If this view is tenable, it follows that the school, having the opportunity to influence appreciably some of the factors that affect perception, can thereby better educate most students, even those formerly believed to be operating near "capacity."

THERE is a growing trend in psychology toward viewing behavior as a function of perception.   More and more we have come to understand that the individual's behavior is not so much a function of the physical stimulus as it is a function of his perceptions of the events to which he is exposed. It is the meaning of events to the individual rather than the externally observed nature of events which seems crucial in behavior.   As a result, psychologists in increasing numbers are turning their attention to the problems of human perception and are attempting to observe behavior, not from an external point of view, but from the point of view of the individual who is behaving.   This paper is an attempt to relate this method of observation to the problem of intelligence.   The question we wish to explore in this paper is: "What is the nature of intelligence viewed from a perceptual or phenomenological frame of reference?"

* Arthur W. Combs, "Intelligence from a Perceptual Point of View," *Journal of Abnormal and Social Psychology,* vol. XLVII (July, 1952), pp. 662–673.   Reprinted by permission of author and The American Psychological Association.
    Dr. Combs (1912—), formerly Director of Clinical Training at Syracuse University, is currently Professor of Education at the University of Florida.   With Donald Snygg he is author of *Individual Behavior.*   He is a Diplomate in clinical psychology.

Intelligence as a Problem of Perception

By the term *intelligence* we ordinarily refer to the effectiveness of the individual's behavior. In a personal frame of reference the individual's behavior is described in terms of the perceptions that he can make in his own unique perceptive field. This perceptive field has been called by Snygg and Combs *The Phenomenal Field* and has been defined by them as "the universe of experience open to the individual at the moment of his behavior." In other words, the behavior of the individual will be dependent upon the perceptions that the individual makes in his phenomenal field at the moment of action. The effectiveness of his behavior will necessarily be a function of the adequacy of those perceptions.

If an entity in the perceptive field is vague and ill defined, the behavior of the individual will be correspondingly vague and lacking in precision. Until the child has clearly differentiated that 2 plus 2 equals 4, this function is comparatively meaningless and his behavior in arithmetic is correspondingly inaccurate and ineffective. Thus, the precision and effectiveness of the individual's behavior will be dependent upon the scope and clarity of his personal field of awareness. Intelligence, then, from a perceptual point of view becomes a function of the factors which limit the scope and clarity of an individual's phenomenal field.

The perceptions that could be made of any given situation, such as looking at a stone wall, for example, are, theoretically, practically infinite in number and quality. As a matter of fact, however, we are strictly limited in our perceptions of a stone wall to those which we, as human beings, can make. The perceptions possible to us are only those that people can make. We cannot, for instance, perceive the wall as it would appear to a man from Mars, or from the interior of an atom, or as it would appear to a centipede. What is more, we cannot even perceive it as it would appear to all people. Different people will perceive different aspects of the wall differently, even at the same instant. I can only perceive the wall, and hence behave toward it, in terms of the perceptions that I, as an individual, can make regarding it. I may, for instance, perceive it as a fine, sturdy fence enclosing my property, while a stone mason friend might perceive it as having been poorly designed or as having been built with too little cement in the mortar mixture. The perceptions open to my mason friend are the result of his unique experience. I, not having such experience, am incapable of those perceptions at this moment.

Potential and Functional Perceptions

Before proceeding further with our discussion of the limiting factors in perception, it is necessary for us to pause for a moment to distinguish between potential and functional perceptions. By potential perceptions I mean those perceptions that exist in the individual's unique field of awareness and that, given the right circumstances at any particular moment, *could* occur. The fact that a perception is potentially possible to any individual, by no means, however, means that it will occur at the moment of action. Even those perceptions that I can make potentially may not be active for me at any given moment. Potentially, I might be able, for instance, to perceive the wall that we have just been using as an example as a barrier to be gotten over, as an eyesore to be beautified, as composed of 687 bricks costing me $80.27, or as providing pleasant shade on a hot day. These are all potential perceptions I am capable of making about the wall. They will affect my behavior, however, only when they are active or functioning in my field of perceptions. When I am beating a hasty retreat pursued by a neighbor's angry dog, perceptions about the shade, beauty, or cost of the wall, though potential, are not functional in affecting my behavior. I behave only in terms of my functioning perception of the wall as something to get over—and quickly. The fact that particular perceptions may exist potentially in the phenomenal field of an individual is by no means a guarantee that they may exist functionally at the moment of action.

While the potential intelligence of the individual is of interest in judging his capacities, it is practically always a matter impossible to measure with any degree of accuracy. We can only sample those parts of a phenomenal field that *we* happen to feel are important. Obviously the measurement of a person's potential perceptions in these terms is open to extremely grave sampling error and improves in accuracy only as the individuals tested have common experience in the materials chosen for testing. It seems probable that an intelligence test cannot accurately measure the potential differentiations that the individual can make in his phenomenal field. Rather, what we usually measure are the subject's functional perceptions. That is, we measure what differentiations he can make when confronted with the necessity to do so for one reason or another. We may define these functional perceptions as: those perceptions in the field experienced by the individual at the moment of behaving.

From a perceptual viewpoint, if intelligence is the capacity for effective behavior, *the intelligence of an individual will be dependent upon the richness and variety of perceptions possible to him at a given moment.* To understand and effectively to foster intelligent behavior, it will be necessary for us to be concerned with the limiting factors upon the perceptions of an individual. We need to know not only what the individual *could* perceive, but what he *would* perceive at a given moment of behaving.

SOME LIMITING FACTORS UPON PERCEPTION

Physiologic Limitations on Perception

Certainly the physical limitations upon the organism affect the differentiations possible in the phenomenal field. Some forms of prenatal anomalies, like mongolism, microcephalia, and similar disorders, indubitably reduce the level of operation at which the individual can function and seriously impair the ability of the organism to make adequate perceptions. Similarly, there seems good reason to believe that some types of mechanical or disease injury to the central nervous system may result in impaired functioning, such as occurs in cerebral palsy, birth injuries, prefrontal lobotomy, the aftermath of such diseases as encephalitis or, even, in common childhood diseases accompanied by prolonged high fever. Various forms of endocrinopathics, particularly cretinism, also appear to have limiting effects upon differentiational capacity for some individuals. Such physical or biological limitations upon the organism have been widely studied but account for only a small proportion of those persons operating at impaired intelligence levels.

Other less dramatic forms of physical handicaps may also have important effects upon the perceptions possible to the individual, however. This is particularly true of individuals suffering impairment of various sense modalities which may inhibit the clarity or even the existence of some perceptions. We need to remind ourselves, however, that such persons may have as rich and varied a perceptive field within their own limitations as we have within ours. Testing persons living in one frame of reference with tests based on those of another can easily lead us astray, a fact well known to the makers of some tests for the handicapped. The limitations imposed upon perception by such physical handicaps as the loss or impairment of locomotion or the use of arms or hands are also important in limiting certain kinds of perceptions. These people experience different, but not necessarily fewer or poorer perceptions of events than so-called "normals."

Perhaps less well recognized in their effects upon perception are such factors as malnutrition, focal infections, and chronic fatigue, which may reduce both the need for and the ability to make adequate perceptions. It is well known in industrial psychology, for example, that fatigued workers are more likely to have accidents, perhaps because of failure to make the right differentiations at the right time. It is conceivable that persons suffering from chronic fatigue over long periods similarly fail to make differentiations useful to them on later occasions.

Certainly such physical factors as these have important effects upon the ability of the individual to make adequate differentiations in his perceptive field.   The more dramatic of these have often been recognized and studied.   Others, such as the effects of malnutrition, fatigue, and the like, have been less adequately explored.   In spite of the lack of research in respect to some of the physical limitations upon intelligence, far more work has been done in this area, however, than in some of those to be discussed below.

Environment and Opportunity as a Limitation upon Perception

The differentiations in the phenomenal field that an individual can make will, of course, be affected by the opportunities for perception to which he has been exposed.   To appear in the perceptive field an event must have been, in some manner, experienced by the person who perceives it.   Environmental effects upon perception appear to be of two types, actual or concrete and symbolic or vicarious.

Exposure to Actual Environmental Events.   In the first place the perceptions possible to any individual will be limited, in part, by the actual environmental factors to which he has been exposed.   Eskimos ordinarily do not comprehend bananas, nor African Bushmen snow, since neither has had the opportunity to experience these events in their respective environments.   It is not necessary to go so far afield for illustration, however.   In our own country our experience with the testing of children in various parts of the nation has shown that perceptions are highly limited by the environmental conditions surrounding the individual.   Mountain children, for example, often give bizarre responses on intelligence tests. Sherman and Henry found intelligence test results on such children arranged themselves in order of the opportunities provided by their environment.

There are differences also between the perceptions of rural and urban children, children from the North and children from the South, mountain and valley, seaboard and plains.   Nor are such differences confined only to children.   Adults, too, are limited in their perceptions by environmental factors.   During the war I worked for a time in an induction station receiving men from the mountains of Kentucky, West Virginia, and southern Ohio.   An intelligence test in use at this station was composed of a series of five pictures with instructions to the subject to cross out that one of each series of five objects that did not belong with the others.   One set of five pictures showed four stringed instruments, a guitar, harp, violin, bass fiddle, and a trumpet.   Large numbers of these back country men crossed out the harp because they had never seen one or because "all the others are things in our band."   We cannot assume that these men were less able to make differentiations or had perceptive fields less rich than their examiner on the basis of these tests.   We can only suggest that their perceptions are different from those who made the test.   Presumably, had they made the test and administered it to the psychologist, the psychologist would have appeared rather dull!

Exposure to Symbolic or Vicarious Events.   Differentiations may occur in the perceptive field upon a symbolic basis as well as from exposure to an actual event.   That is, perceptions may occur in the individual's field through indirect exposure to experience as in reading, conversation, movies, and other means of communication.   Although I cannot directly perceive that it is dangerous to expose myself to rays from an atomic pile, for example, I can differentiate this notion through what others whom I respect have told me.   Ideas and concepts are largely differentiations of this sort and it is probable that many of our perceptions are acquired through a symbolic rather than an actual exposure.   Certainly most of our formal schooling falls in this category which may explain in part, why so little of it is effective in our behavior.

It will be recognized at once that exposure to events in no sense completely determines the perceptions that the individual will make.   Exposure to events is only one of the factors involved in determining whether or not an event will be differentiated.   Even with equivalent exposure, the perceptions we make are not alike.   Perception is not an all or none proposition but a selective process.   The same person in the same situation at different times may perceive quite different aspects of the situation and behave accordingly.   The provision of opportunity to perceive is by no means a guarantee that a particular perception will occur, a phenomenon of which teachers are only too aware.   The personal field of the individual is always organized and meaningful and, even with exposure to events, only those aspects that have meaning for the individual in his own unique economy will be differentiated with permanence.

The individual in a particular culture perceives those aspects of his environment that, from his point of view, he needs to perceive to maintain and enhance his self in the world in which he lives.   This does not mean he makes fewer perceptions than an individual in another culture; he makes only *different* perceptions.   Thus, intelligence tests made in one culture and applied in another do not measure the ability to differentiate, nor do they measure the richness of the individual's field.   Perhaps what they really measure is no more than the difference between cultures.   American-made intelligence tests applied to other cultures generally show the following arrangement of nationality groups in decreasing order; British Isles, Germany, France, Italy, the Balkans, Asiatic countries.   It will be noted that these nationality groups are also roughly arranged in order of the degree of commonality with our own culture.

Time as a Limitation of Perception

Differentiation requires time. The richness of perception, therefore, will be in part a function of how long the individual has been in touch with experiences. While it is true that a perception is possible only when confronted by an experience, it is also true that this exposure must be long enough to make differentiation possible. This principle is familiar to anyone who has looked at a painting for a period of time. The perceptions which can be made are almost limitless if one looks long enough.

In thinking of the effect of time upon differentiation, it is necessary for us to keep in mind that we are speaking of the duration of the individual's experience with an event and not of the observer's experience. Thus, while it may appear to an outside observer that an individual is confronted by an experience, from the individual's own point of view, he may have no contact with it whatever. A child may sit in school all day, apparently exposed to the curriculum, but may actually be experiencing and perceiving quite different aspects of the situation. Perception is an internal, individual phenomenon and may be quite different from that of another person, even in the same situation.

Most perceptions that the individual makes are functions of previous differentiations he has made in his phenomenal field. For example, before one can perceive the mechanics of multiplication he must have perceived addition. In the same way, before he can perceive the function of a sand dome on top of the locomotive he must differentiate the fact that locomotive wheels sometimes slip. Clearly this process of differentiation takes time. It seems axiomatic that to make differentiations an individual must have lived long enough to do so, a fact we recognize in the construction of intelligence tests calibrated for various age levels, and which teachers recognize in the concept of readiness.

Differentiations in the phenomenal field seem to be occurring continuously as the organism seeks to satisfy its needs in the myriad situations of life. In this sense, intelligence never ceases to develop but is continuously increasing so long as the individual remains alive and operating. That intelligence seems to level off at age sixteen or later is probably a mere artifact of our method of observation. So long as the individual remains in school we have at least a modicum of comparable experience which can be tested in different persons. After the school years, when individuals are free to go their separate ways, this modicum of comparable experience rapidly disappears. The older one gets, the more diverse is his experience.   Intelligence tests based upon comparability of experience may thus fail to evaluate properly the effectiveness of adults.

The Individual's Goals and Values as a Limiting Factor in Perception

Up to this point in our discussion we have been dealing with factors affecting perception that are widely discussed in the literature and for the most part are well understood.   In the remainder of this paper let us turn our attention to several factors less well explored as they appear in a phenomenological setting.   The first of these has to do with the effects of the individual's own goals and values as a limiting factor on perception.

From a phenomenological view the individual is forever engaged in a ceaseless attempt to achieve satisfaction of his need through the goals and values he has differentiated as leading to that end.   These goals and values may be explicit or implicit, simple or complex, but they are always unique to the personality itself.   The goals of an individual will vary in another respect as well.   The individual's goals and values may be either positive or negative.   That is, in the course of his experience, the person may differentiate some things as matters to be sought, while other things may be differentiated as matters to be avoided.   What is more, although there is a considerable degree of stability in the major goals and values of a particular individual, there may be great fluctuations in how some goals are perceived from time to time, depending upon the total organization of the perceptual field at any moment.

The goals and values an individual seeks have a most important effect upon the perceptions he can make.   Once goals have been established by the individual they continue to affect his every experience.   Thus, the person who has differentiated good music as a goal to be sought, perceives music more frequently.   His entire experience with music is likely to be affected.   Certainly his experience will differ markedly from the person who has formulated a goal to avoid music at all costs.   In the same way the experiences of children who perceive schooling as something to be sought are vastly different from those of children who try to avoid all aspects of schooling.   If the fundamental thesis of this paper is accurate, that intelligence is a function of the variety and richness of the perceptive field, then the individual's goals must have a most important effect upon intelligence.   A considerable body of research has been accumulating over the past several years, demonstrating this controlling effect of goals and values on the individual's perceptive experience.   Such studies as those of J. M. Levine, R. Levine, Postman, and Bruner are fascinating cases in point.

This effect of goals on perception is by no means limited to the subject whose intelligence we wish to measure. It is equally true of the intelligence test constructor. It leads to the very confusing situation wherein the test constructor with one organization of goals perceives certain experiences to be marks of intelligence for another person who may or may not have similar goals. Indeed, the likelihood is that he, almost certainly, does not have similar goals. Intelligence tests thus become highly selected samplings of perception in terms of what the testers consider important. Low scores do not necessarily mean less rich and varied fields of perception; they may mean only fields of perception more widely divergent from those of the examiner. A young man whom the writer tested at an induction center during the war illustrates the point very well. This young man was a newsboy on the streets of a West Virginia city. Although he had failed repeatedly in grammar school and was generally regarded as "not bright," he appeared on a national radio hook-up as "The Human Adding Machine." He was a wizard at figures. He could multiply correctly such figures as 6235941 × 397 almost as fast as the problem could be written down. He astounded our induction center for half a day with his numerical feats. Yet, on the Binet Test given by the writer he achieved an IQ of less than 60! People in his home town, who bought his papers, amused themselves by giving him problems to figure constantly. When not so occupied this young man entertained himself by adding up the license numbers of cars that passed his corner. He was a specialist in numbers. Apparently as a result of some early success in this field, he had been led to practice numbers constantly, eventually to the exclusion of all else. This was one area in which a poor colored boy could succeed and he made the most of it. His number perceptions were certainly rich and varied but other things were not. Although he was capable of arithmetic feats not achieved by one in millions, he was classified as dull! I do not mean to argue that variety of perception is unimportant in effective behavior. I do mean to suggest the importance of goals in determining perception.

Cultural Effects on Goals and Perceptions

We have stated here that the richness of the individual's perceptive field is in part a function of the goals he has differentiated as important or threatening to him. But, clearly these goals are themselves the result of the individual's experience. The culture one grows up in deeply affects the goals one holds. Cultures both restrict and encourage, approve and disapprove the formulation of goals in the individual. This selective effect of the culture in large measure determines the goals sought and avoided by the individual. These goals in turn must exert important effects upon the perceptions that become part of the individual's perceptive field.

I remember the Kentucky moonshiner to whom I once administered the Wechsler-Bellevue. This man could not tell me "how many pints in a quart" although he had certainly been taught this fact in his early schooling. Knowing that my client did a considerable business in bootleg liquor, I framed the question differently and asked "Well, how do you sell your liquor?" He smiled tolerantly and replied, "Oh Boss, I just sell it by the jug full!" In his community to have done otherwise would have been to risk bankruptcy. In a culture where a jug is standard container for spirits, what need to know about quarts?

It is conceivable that low intelligence may be, at least in part, no more than a function of the goals an individual is striving to reach in achieving his need satisfaction. The well-known phenomenon in which intelligence tests give best results in the school years, when experience and goals have a degree of commonality, and break down badly following those years would seem to corroborate this point. Perhaps by concerning ourselves with human goals we can affect perception, and thus intelligence, much more than we believed possible. Can it be that the child of low apparent intelligence is not so much a problem of an unfortunate heredity as an unfortunate constellation of goals or values? We could do a great deal about intelligence if that were true.

The Self-Concept as a Factor Limiting Perception

We are just beginning to understand the tremendous effects of the individual's concept of self upon his perceptions and behavior. Lecky, for instance, reports the effect of a change in self-concept in improving the ability of children to spell. Other researches have reported similar effects of the self-concept upon the perceptions which the individual may make. Clinical experience would tend to bear out such observations. Any clinician is familiar with numerous instances in which a child's conception of his abilities severely limited his achievement, even though his real abilities may have been superior to his perception of them. One needs but to go shopping with one's spouse to discover again how one's conception of himself as a male or female affects the things he sees and the things he hears.

Perception is a selective process and the conception one holds of himself is a vital factor in determining the richness and the variety of perception selected. It makes a great deal of difference, for example, how one perceives the president of our country if one conceives of himself as a democrat, a republican, or a communist. One needs but to observe a group of children to become aware that little boys perceive things quite differently from little girls. Professors do not perceive like truck drivers, although when I have had to ride with professor automobile-drivers, I have often wished they did.   Thousands of people in our society avoid perceptions having to do with mathematical functions by their firm concept of themselves as people who "cannot do mathematics."   The self-concepts we hold have a very vital effect in selecting the perceptions which become part of our perceptive fields.   If the effectiveness of behavior is dependent on our perceptive fields, it follows that the self-concepts we hold must affect the "intelligence" of our behavior.

There is another factor in the effect of the self-concept upon perception that makes it even more important as a selector of experience.   That factor is the circular effect of a given concept of self.   Let us take, as an example, the child who has developed a concept of himself as "unable to read."   Such a child is likely to avoid reading and thus the very experience which might change his concept of self is by-passed.   Worse still, the child who believes himself unable to read, confronted with the necessity for reading, is more likely than not to do badly.   The external evaluation of his teachers and fellow pupils, as well as his own observations of his performance, all provide proof to the child of how right he was in the first place!   The possession of a particular concept of self tends to produce behavior that corroborates the self-concept with which the behavior originated.

Every clinician has had experience with children of ability who conceive of themselves as unable, unliked, unwanted, or unacceptable and perceive and behave in accordance with their perceptions.   And this effect is not limited to children alone.   It seems to me one of the great tragedies of our society that millions of people in our society perceiving themselves as able to produce only X amount, behave in these terms.   Society, in turn, evaluates them in terms of this behavior and so lends proof to what is already conceived by the individual.   Compared to this waste of human potential in our society, our losses in automobile accidents seem like a mere drop in the bucket.   It is even conceivable in these terms that we create losses in intelligence.   If, in our schools, we teach a child that he is unable and if he believes us and behaves in these terms, we need not be surprised when we test his intelligence to discover that he produces at the level at which we taught him!

It is conceivable that psychology has unwittingly contributed to this situation by the widespread publication of a static conception of intelligence and human capacities.   The concept of severe limits upon the capacities of the organism simply corroborates the self-concept of the man in the street and decreases the likelihood of change in his concept of self.   Even more important must be the effect upon our educational system.   Teachers who believe in an unchanging character of child capacities provide the attitudes and experiences that produce and maintain a child's conception of self and his abilities.   It is notorious that children's grades vary very little from year to year through the course of schooling.   This continuous and little-changing evaluation must have important effects on the self-concept of the child.   If the school system in which the child lives is thoroughly imbued with the notion that a child's capacities are comparatively fixed, it is even conceivable that the system may in large measure produce a child's intelligence level by the circular effect we have mentioned above.

Threat as a Factor in Perception

The last of the factors I should like to discuss as a possible factor in intelligence is the effect of threat upon the perceptive field.   If our fundamental assumption that intelligence is a function of the richness and breadth of the phenomenal field is correct, the effect of threat on this field becomes a most important consideration.   Although these effects have been so widely understood by the layman that they have been made a part of his every day speech, it is interesting that until very recently the phenomenon has been given little attention by psychologists.   The perception by the individual of threat to himself seems to have at least two major effects upon the perceptive field.

Restriction of the Perceptive Field Under Threat   The first of these effects is the restrictive effect that the perception of threat to self seems to have on the individual's perception.   When he feels himself threatened, there appears to be a narrowing of the perceptive field to the object of threat.   This has often been described in the psychology of vision as "tunnel vision."   The phenomenon is extremely common and almost everyone has experienced it at some moment of crisis in his lifetime.   One hears it described in such comments as "All I could see was the truck coming at us," or, "I was so scared I couldn't think of a thing."   There seems reason to believe that this effect is not limited to traumatic experiences alone, but exists in lesser degree in response to milder threats as well.   Combs and Taylor, for example, have demonstrated the effect under extremely mild forms of threat.

Such limiting effects on perception must certainly have a bearing upon perceptions available to the individual in his phenomenal field.   Subjects who have participated in food deprivation experiments report uniformly that when threatened by hunger, food becomes an obsession.   Recently, at the dinner table, I asked my young daughter what she had learned at school that day.   "Oh nothing," said she with much feeling, "But was our teacher mad!   Wow!"   It would appear from her remarks that, feeling threatened by an angry teacher, it was difficult for her to perceive much else. Her perceptions of the day were apparently entirely concerned with the nature of anger. No doubt these are valuable perceptions to possess, but I know of no intelligence test which measures them.

I recall, too, the behavior of two little girls whose mother was taken to a mental hospital at the beginning of the summer. The matter was kept a deep secret from these two children for fear they "would not understand." The children spent most of the summer with the writer's daughter in an incessant game of "hospital." From morning to night this game went on outside our living room window. Apparently, this preoccupation was the direct outcome of the threat they felt in the loss of their mother, for with the mother's return the game ceased as suddenly as it had begun. To the best of my knowledge it has not occurred since. Under threat there seem to be severe limits imposed upon the breadth and character of perception.

Defense of the Perceptive Field Under Threat. There is a second effect of threat upon the individual's perceptions. This effect has to do with the defense reactions induced in the individual on perceiving himself to be threatened. The perception of threat not only narrows the field and reduces the possibility of wide perceptions, but causes the individual to protect and cling to the perceptions he already holds. Thus, the possibility of perceptual changes is reduced and the opportunities for new perceptions or learning are decreased. Under threat, behavior becomes rigid. The fluidity and adaptation which we generally associate with intelligent behavior is vastly decreased. A number of interesting experiments in the past few years have demonstrated this phenomenon. Cowen, for example, illustrated this effect in problem solving.

Our own experiment previously mentioned also demonstrated this effect with even very mild forms of threat. This rigidity or resistance of perception to change under threat is well known to the layman and is well illustrated in some of the sayings of our culture. Such aphorisms as "Nobody ever wins an argument" or "You can lead a horse to water but you cannot make him drink" seem to be illustrations of a vague understanding of the phenomenon in the public mind. It is surprising that this principle has been so long overlooked.

I think it will be generally agreed that intelligent behavior is quite the antithesis of rigidity. In the terms we have used in this article, intelligent behavior is a function of the variety and richness of perception in the phenomenal field. Whatever produces narrowness and rigidity of perception becomes an important factor in limiting intelligence. If this reasoning is accurate, or even partly so, one is led to wonder about the effects of long continued threat upon the development of intelligence. What of the child who has suffered serious threats to himself for long periods of his life, as in the case of the delinquent, for example? Or what of the child who has been seriously deprived of affection and warmth from those who surround him over a period of years? Is it possible that we have created low intelligence in such children? Axline has reported a number of cases in which intelligence scores improved considerably under therapy. We have observed similar changes in our own clinical practice.

It may be argued that, although threat seems to reduce perception, some people under threat apparently produce more effectively. I think, however, it is necessary for us to distinguish between "threat" and "challenge." In threat, the individual perceives himself in jeopardy and feels, in addition, a degree of inadequacy to deal effectively with the threat perceived. In challenge, the individual perceives himself threatened but feels at the same time a degree of adequacy to deal with the threat. It would appear that whether an event is perceived as threatening or challenging is a function of the individual's feeling of competence to deal with it. If this analysis is correct, it would explain why a situation that appears threatening to a person, from the viewpoint of an outside observer, might one time produce rigidity and another highly effective behavior. This description of events seems characteristic of the history of civilization as well as of individuals, if Toynbee's explanation can be given credence. He points out that the most productive (more intelligent?) societies are those in which the society faces some crisis within its capacities to cope with the situation (challenge), while societies without crisis or in which the crisis is overwhelming produce very little or collapse entirely.

SOME IMPLICATIONS OF THIS CONCEPTION OF INTELLIGENT BEHAVIOR

If the conception of intelligence we have been discussing in this paper should prove accurate, it seems to me to raise serious questions about some of our common assumptions with respect to intelligence and, at the same time, opens some exciting new possibilities for the treatment or education of persons we have often assumed to be beyond help. It implies that our conception of the limiting factors of intelligence may have been too narrow. It would suggest perhaps that our very point of view with respect to intelligence may have resulted in our own tunnel vision, such that we have not been able to perceive other factors given little attention to this point. Perhaps we have been too impressed with the limitations upon growth and development which we observe in physical maturation. We may, for instance, have jumped too quickly to the assumption that intelligent behavior was limited as severely as physical growth and that we have explored to exhaustion other factors that may limit intelligence.

I am not suggesting that physiologic limits do not exist in respect to intelligence. I am suggesting that we may have conceded too early that we had approached those limits. There is no doubt that we can demonstrate in some cases, such as mongolism, cretinism, and the like, that physical factors severely limit intelligence. But these cases are comparatively few compared to the so called "familial" cases of low intelligence that we often assume are hereditary in origin. What evidence do we really possess that would lead us to the position that an individual of "normal" physical condition and vigor may be limited in his capacity for effective behavior by some physical condition? We assume there must be such factors operating because we cannot explain his handicap otherwise. That biological science has not yet been able to demonstrate such physical bases has not deterred us in this. On the contrary, we have simply deplored the lack of sufficient advance in that discipline to demonstrate our conclusion! I should like to suggest that this may not be their failure but ours. Until it can be definitely established that limitations exist as biological functions, our task as psychologists is to assume that they may just as well be social or psychological in character and to work just as hard exploring the matter in our discipline as we expect the biologist to work in his.

Let us, for example, explore to the very fullest the possibility that in those cases where we cannot demonstrate biologic impairment, the limitations upon intelligence may be psychological. If it turns out not to be true, we shall find out in time. I do not believe we can afford to limit the places where we look by the pre-perceptions we have about the matter. Our responsibility here is too great. Education, to name but the most obvious of our social institutions, has in large measure predicated its goals and methods on a concept of humanity with certain static limitations on intelligence. If these limitations are not static, it is up to us as psychologists to find out. The task of the scientist is to question, not to be content with answers. We cannot afford to accept an undemonstrated point of view that prevents us from asking questions.

Some Implications for Intelligence Testing

If the concepts of intelligence we have been discussing prove accurate, another area of psychological thought toward which we must cast a quizzical eye is the area of intelligence testing. This is particularly important at a time when our culture has come to accept these instruments as trustingly as the family doctor's prescription. If our approach to intelligent behavior as a function of the variety and richness of the perceptual field is a valid consideration, we need to ask regarding these tests at least the following questions:

1. Is our sampling of the perceptive field truly adequate? If I lived for years in a prison cell, I presume I should become expert in perceptions about that cell. Unfortunately, they would be of little value outside the prison walls, but can it truthfully be said that my perceptions are less rich or varied, or only that they are less rich and varied about things I have not had opportunity to experience? Is the delinquent, with rich and varied perceptions on how to elude the police, less intelligent or has he simply not perceived things society wishes he had?

2. Since perceptions are always closely affected by need, by whose need shall we sample perceptions—yours, mine, society's, the subject's own? I suspect that in terms of his own needs and perceptions the subject might be deemed quite brilliant, though he might or might not appear so from the point of view of society. For the most part our tests are based on the assumption that academic, upper middle-class, intellectual perceptions are important. But are they? Can we assume that the expert machinist, who can perceive things "out of this world" for most of the rest of us about a piece of stock on his lathe, is less intelligent than a diplomat who perceives many things about foreign affairs? Can we be so sure of our values as to call one bright and the other dull? Can we blame the machinist for his lack of perception about foreign affairs without asking the diplomat to be equally skilled in the machinist's field of perceptions?

3. Finally, if perceptions are affected by the factors we have discussed in this paper, is it fair to sample intelligence irrespective of the control of such factors? Shall we, for example, examine the child who has lacked opportunity to perceive, has possessed a concept of self or been so threatened over a long period of time so as to have been unable to perceive what we wish to sample without consideration of those factors? Shall we overlook such factors and be satisfied that the perceptions important to us are not there, or shall we seek for ways to make it possible for the child to have them? Shall we assume that our failure to discover a particular perception present in the field is, *ipso facto,* evidence of lack of capacity; or seek to discover why it is not? On the positive side of the picture, if the concepts we have here been discussing are sound, there is reason to believe that intelligence may be far less immutable than we have thought. It may be that we can do far more than we have dreamed we could. Perhaps we may even be able to create intelligence!

Implications for Constructive Action

Who can say, for example, what results we might be able to achieve by a systematic effort to remove or decrease the effectiveness of the limitations on perception discussed in this paper?   It is fascinating to speculate on the possibilities one might try in constructing a situation for a child, or adult, consciously designed to minimize the limitations imposed on perception by physical condition, environment, goals, the individual's self concept, and the effects of perceived personal threat.

If the position we have taken is accurate, it would suggest that there is much we can do (a) to free individuals from the restraints upon perception and (b) to provide the opportunities for perception to occur.

1. First and most obviously, we should be able to discover and make available to far more people the means to achieve better physical condition.   We have already done a good deal in this area but much needs yet to be done.   Who can say, for instance, what completely adequate medical care for all our people might mean a generation hence?

2. If this discussion has merit, there lies the possibility of providing experiences for people that will make adequate perceptions possible.   We have tried to do this in our schools, but have not always accomplished it. We have succeeded very well in gathering information and in making it available to students.   We have not succeeded too well in making such information meaningful.   Can it be that the decreases in school success with advance through the school years is more a function of lack of meaning for students than lack of intelligence?   Is it enough to assume that experience provided by us to the student is truly provided when he is free to experience it?   Has the child in school, who is so worried about his relationship with his peers that he cannot perceive what his book is saying, truly been provided opportunity to perceive?

In our training of children of "low intelligence," we often provide situations wherein they are carefully taught to perform repeatedly a simple act.   Is it possible that in so doing we may be further narrowing their fields of perception and building self concepts that produce even narrower perceptive fields?

What kinds of environments could we construct that might more effectively result in increased perception?   Such experiments as Lippitt and White have carried on with democratic and autocratic environments suggest some possibilities, but we need to know much more.   Perhaps we could learn to build such environments from observing with greater care and understanding the methods of good teachers.

3. Who can say what possible effects might occur from a systematic release of the individual's perceptions by the satisfaction of his most pressing needs or goals?   We college professors insist we can produce more, which is another way of saying perceive more, when we have the leisure time to do so, when we are freed from the necessity of spending our time satisfying our needs for sheer existence.   Can this be less true of others?   It is pos-

sible that the child with needs of love, affection, status, prestige, or a girl friend might also be freed to perceive more widely and richly, if we could but find ways of helping him satisfy his needs.   Ordinarily, we pay a good deal of attention to the physical needs of a child, understanding that with these needs unfulfilled, he makes a poor student.   Is there any good reason to suppose his psychological needs are less pressing or less important in freeing him to perceive widely and accurately?   We spend much time and energy trying to find ways of "motivating" people or blaming them for not being motivated to do what we need them to do.   We assume that if permitted to seek their own needs, people will not satisfy ours. Perhaps we should get further by helping them satisfy their needs; they might then be free to satisfy ours.

4. Most of our educational methods are directed at the provision of perceptions for the student.   He is lectured, required, shown, exhorted, and coerced to perceive what someone thinks he should.   It seems possible that with equal energy devoted to the matter of creating needs, goals, and values in students, rich and varied perceptions might be more efficiently produced.

What effects might we be able to produce by providing experiences that build adequate concepts of self in children and adults?   What differences in the richness and variety of perception might result from a generation of people with "I can" rather than "I can't" conceptions of themselves? What possibilities of increased perceptions and hence of increased intelligence might accrue to such a program?   Clinical experience has demonstrated frequently how a changed perception of self as a more adequate personality can free children for improved school performance, for example.

What would happen if we were consciously and carefully to set about the task of providing experiences that would lead people to conceptions of themselves as adequate, worthy, self-respecting people?   If freedom to perceive is a function of adequate perceptions of self, it should not surprise us that the child who perceives himself as unwanted, unacceptable, unable, or unliked behaves in rigid fashion.   It should be possible, too, to reverse this process and produce more adequate perceptions by systematic efforts at producing more adequate definitions of self.   The possibilities seem tremendous but we have scarcely scratched the surface of this problem.

Finally, if threat to the individual has as important effects as seem indicated in this discussion, the removal of threat would seem a most important factor to consider in the release of the individual to perceive more adequately.   The work of Rogers and his students in client centered therapy has already illustrated to some degree what possibilities freeing the individual to perceive more adequately may accomplish through the provision of a permissive nonthreatening relationship between counselor and client. We have already mentioned the effects Axline has reported following a permissive, nonthreatening form of play therapy.

Such effects do not seem limited to the therapeutic situation, however. A number of workers have applied this principle of permissiveness to the classroom situation with equally gratifying results. Experiments in student centered teaching at Syracuse have led many of us to believe in the tremendous educational possibilities in the removal of threat.

This paper has asked many questions. Indeed, it has asked far more questions than it has presumed to answer. That, it seems to me, is the function of theory. The picture of intelligence presented here as it seems from a phenomenological viewpoint may be accurate or false or, more likely, partly true and partly false. Only time and the industry of many observers can check its adequacy or inadequacy. It seems to me to pose problems that are both exciting and challenging. If it proves as stimulating to the reader as it has to the author, I shall rest content that a theory has achieved its purpose.

---

18. Some Implications for School Practice of the Chicago Studies of Cultural Bias in Intelligence Tests*

Related selections: 17, 21, 34

THE CLASSIC "nature versus nurture" debate of several decades ago failed to settle to everyone's satisfaction the question of the relative importance of heredity and environment in determining human intelligence. Recent years have seen an approach aimed at discovering whether the differences in intelligence between children from homes of unlike socio-economic status are true differences or whether the measuring instruments used are biased in favor of a particular group. In this article Dr. Eells discusses the meaning of the work which he and others did at the University of Chicago on the cultural bias in intelligence tests.

* Kenneth Eells, "Some Implications for School Practice of the Chicago Studies of Cultural Bias in Intelligence Tests," *Harvard Educational Review*, vol. XXIII (Fall, 1953), pp. 284–297. Reprinted by permission of author and publisher.

Dr. Eells (1913—) is psychologist and Head, Criterion Development Center, U.S. Naval Personnel Research Unit, San Diego, California. He was formerly at the University of Chicago where he collaborated with Dr. Allison Davis and with him developed the Davis-Eells Test of General Intelligence.

LET US suppose for a moment that you have a friend in Australia and that you have gone to visit him in his home country. He has told you that he is to take an intelligence test that afternoon and suggests that you take it too, just for the fun of it. You agree to do so. When you first open the test booklet you say to yourself, "Well, I'm in a foreign country, but since they speak English, I shouldn't have any special difficulty with this." But soon you are in trouble. Some of the items deal with Australian history and local social conditions about which you know almost nothing. Then you come to some questions that have to do with mutton. You know something about mutton, but suddenly it occurs to you that your friend probably knows more about it than you do. A little further on in the test you wish you'd paid more attention to the kangaroo when you visited a zoo several years ago. The questions are all in English, of course, but you find that some of the words seem to have a little different significance, and occasionally you come across a word which is completely strange to you. You wonder whether this is a word you just happen not to know or whether it is a local term that you could not be expected to know.

However, it is an interesting experience—until your friend, half in fun, says, "Well that was one of our best intelligence tests. How did you do?" As you think back over the test you are glad that the papers have not yet been scored. You realize that because of the mutton and the kangaroo, the strange words, the local information, and the variations in word connotations your friend had an advantage over you. If he thinks this is a good measure of your intelligence you are glad that he cannot compare your score with his.

Before leaving this somewhat informal introduction to the problem of cultural bias in intelligence tests, it would perhaps be well to point out that if your Australian friend had not called the test an "intelligence" test but had said instead that it was a test designed to measure your ability to read Australian newspapers and to converse with educated Australian persons effectively, you would have had no quarrel with the presence in the test of materials peculiar to the Australian culture, or with the test's use of words and grammatical construction which were strange to you. As a measure of your ability to get along in a certain portion of the Australian culture the test might be excellent, and you might willingly accept your low score as an accurate reflection of your "current ability." It is the labelling of the test as an "intelligence" test, with its accompanying implication that this is somehow a measure of some basic ability or potentiality of yours, that disturbs you. You have the feeling that if your friend could see your score he might decide you aren't very "intelligent" and that by this he might really mean that you aren't going to be able to solve effectively many of the major problems that you are faced with in living a full and successful life. You wouldn't object to being told you couldn't understand Australian newspapers very well; but to be told you're not very "intelligent" implies something more serious, doesn't it?

The comparison is not as farfetched as it may seem at first. The child who has been brought up on the "wrong side of the tracks" in an American community goes to a school presided over by administrators and teachers who are practically all drawn from a life different from the one he knows. They have grown up in different kinds of families, with different kinds of friends, and with different kinds of experiences. Now they ask the child to take a test to determine how intelligent he is, so that the school can plan properly a school program for him. He finds that the test is written in English, forunately, but he also finds that it is a kind of English which is quite different from that which he has learned at home and which he hears in his own neighborhood. He is probably not asked for information about Australian history and mutton, but he *is* asked to answer test items dealing with symphony orchestra instruments, with typewriters, with fire-places, with animals which he might have seen in a zoo if he had been brought up in another part of the city. He is asked about all sorts of things which he may or may not have ever seen and with which he almost certainly has had no chance to be really familiar. It all seems a little strange to him—perhaps even silly—since it has no very obvious importance for the kind of problems that are important to him. So he doesn't try very hard. Perhaps he marks the items rather quickly to end the painful process. Later his test paper is scored, and he is found to be somewhat below average in intelligence. His school program is arranged accordingly and the teachers are warned not to expect too much from him. This, in brief, is the problem of cultural bias in intelligence tests.

THE APPROACH

Most of what has been published thus far has dealt with problems of intelligence-test methodology. How much cultural bias is there in intelligence tests currently in use? If undesirable, how can the amount of it be reduced? Such questions have been investigated and discussed more fully than questions dealing with the implications for educational practice of the existence of such cultural bias. Assuming there is *some* cultural bias in present intelligence tests, what implications does this have for the actions of school administrators? What implications does it have for the classroom teacher? What does it mean for the guidance counselor? Such questions have received comparatively little attention thus far.

In the present article, some of these questions of practical implication are discussed. In this analysis, it is not assumed that all the methodological problems have been solved. Nor is it assumed that there is any way of measuring, at present, just how much cultural bias there is in intelligence tests. It is not even assumed that *all* of the differences which are known to exist between the scores of high-status children and of low-status children on intelligence tests are due to cultural bias in the tests. This may be true, and there are those who firmly believe it to be so. At present, however, there are no conclusive data to prove that it is so—nor, for that matter, to prove that it is not so.

One assumption, however, is made: that sufficient evidence is available to justify the conclusion that *at least a substantial part* of the known group differences in I. Q.'s of children from different sub-cultural groups may be accounted for by cultural bias in the intelligence tests. The writer believes that the evidence for this somewhat conservative statement is convincing enough to make an analysis of its implications for practical school purposes a worthwhile undertaking.

It would be comparatively simple to outline some of the specific implications—to provide a sort of list of cookbook rules for an administrator, teacher, or counselor to follow if he wished to make allowances for cultural bias in intelligence tests. However, this kind of approach would be likely to be misleading. It would leave many specific applications untouched, and it would be an insult to the intelligence of those responsible for different phases of the educational process. What will be attempted, instead, is to clarify the basic nature of cultural bias in intelligence tests and its relation to the school's objectives, and to leave to the reader the important task of making the necessary specific applications to a wider variety of specific school situations than would be possible to discuss by the first approach.

Once the essential nature of cultural-bias in tests is seen clearly—along with its effect on scores, or I. Q.'s—school administrators, teachers, and guidance counselors will have little trouble in seeing a multitude of specific applications. Administrators will see the implications for establishing school objectives in terms of the abilities and needs of pupils, and for curriculum revision and teaching-method development based on the measurement of student ability. They will recognize a need for setting up in-service training activities for teachers and counselors. They will see implications for the assignment of teachers to schools, or to school-rooms, where children from low status homes predominate. Teachers will see the need for looking at the "low I. Q. pupil" in a different light; they will see more clearly that some of the pupil's apparent lack of capacity is only a challenge for teacher exploration of new areas and new methods. Teachers will recognize even more vividly than before a need for greater individualization of instruction—and for every teacher to prepare himself to understand sympathetically and intelligently the many differences which separate his "way of life" from that of many of his pupils. Guidance counselors will see important implications for interpreting the I. Q. scores of pupils who are seeking their help on academic, vocational, or personal matters.

Most of the specific applications to school practice will probably fall into three general categories: (a) the need for considerable caution in arriving at judgments of individuals or groups based on traditional intelligence-test scores, or I. Q.'s—especially in the case of children coming from sub-cultures other than the "middle-class" one from which most teachers and school administrators come, (b) the need for a new type of intelligence test, along lines suggested later in this article, in order to have a basis for sounder and more defensible decisions in those school areas where tests of basic mental ability are helpful, and (c) implications, for basic school reorganization, of previously unidentified abilities in pupils.

The first application is largely an individual matter, and one where little difficulty will be encountered in making the necessary allowances and interpretations when the nature of culture-bias is better understood. The second kind of application—the development of a new type of intelligence test—involves technical problems which would not be appropriately discussed here. The balance of this article is concerned almost entirely with the last of these three types of applications—with the broad area of basic school organization. What are the implications for curriculum development, for teaching methods, for guidance practices, of the fact that our present intelligence tests probably underestimate, to a substantial degree, the abilities of a large proportion of our school children?

Let us consider first a few basic ideas related to what is meant, and what is not meant, by cultural bias in tests. Discussion in this general area has sometimes been somewhat beside the point when the discussants have failed to make clear precisely what they mean by the terms "cultural bias" or "intelligence." Several straw men have been set up and knocked down.

WHAT IS MEANT BY "CULTURAL BIAS" IN INTELLIGENCE TESTS?

Current controversy and doubts regarding possible cultural bias in intelligence tests have arisen in a number of places, and from different sources. For many years individual teachers, principals, and superintendents have had serious doubts as to the adequacy of the intelligence tests they were using. More recently an increasing body of research knowledge has become available which suggests the possibility that the scores on most intelligence tests are influenced substantially by the nature of the cultural material contained in the test. Much of this research has been carried on by Dr. Allison Davis, of the University of Chicago, and his colleagues and students. It is probably natural, therefore, that the point of view underlying such studies has come to be known in some quarters as "the Chicago point of view." This labelling is, however, an over-simplification and may be misleading.

In the first place, there is no single "Chicago point of view." While those most closely associated with Davis' research probably have certain basic points of view in common, they differ among themselves in the degree of emphasis which they attach to the factor of cultural bias in intelligence tests and to some extent in their interpretation of it. In the second place, much research in this area has been and is being carried on at other places than the University of Chicago.

Basic Definition. The general thesis underlying the Chicago studies of cultural bias in intelligence tests may be stated very briefly: most presently used intelligence tests (both individual and group) are so constructed and so administered that scores on them are influenced by the cultural backgrounds of the children taking the test, in such a way that children from certain kinds of cultural backgrounds receive scores that are not accurate reflections of their basic "intelligence." "Intelligence" is defined, for the present purpose, in terms of problem-solving ability. The more "intelligent" child is one who can, when operating under conditions of maximum motivation, solve problems which seem (and which actually are) real and important to him more effectively and more expeditiously than can the less "intelligent" child.

The meaning of the concept of "cultural bias in intelligence tests" may be clarified by (a) placing it in the larger context of the heredity-environment controversy which has plagued psychological and educational literature for many decades, (b) noting the effect of cultural bias on group and on individual differences in intelligence, (c) differentiating the idea of a "culturally fair" intelligence test from the idea of a "culture free" intelligence test, and (d) differentiating an "intelligence" test from a "scholastic aptitude" test.

Relationship to the Heredity-Environment Controversy. The problem under consideration has an important relationship to the time-worn heredity-environment controversy regarding the causes of differences in intelligence, but the exact nature of that relationship is easily misunderstood. The relationship may be most clearly seen in the context of differences known to exist on traditional intelligence tests between children from high-status homes and those from low-status homes.

Alfred Binet made the first known study in this area, in 1910. He found that children of physicians, university professors, lawyers, etc., in a private school in Belgium did systematically better on his new intelligence-test items than did children from public schools in working-class neighborhoods of Paris. The superiority amounted to about a year and a half on the Binet Scale.

More than eighty similar studies have since been carried out, always with the same kind of results. In these studies a wide variety of intelligence tests, both individual and group, have been examined. Many different methods of measuring social status—occupational level of the parents, income level of the family, dwelling areas within cities, and specially devised scales—have been used. A variety of statistical techniques has been utilized. Without a single exception, these studies have shown that, on the average, children from high-status homes do better on standard intelligence tests than do children from low-status homes. When average I. Q.'s for children from professional and managerial homes are compared with average I. Q.'s for children from unskilled labor backgrounds, the I. Q. difference is usually in the neighborhood of 15 to 25 I. Q. points. When the relationship between social-status and I. Q. is studied by correlational techniques, the correlations are typically in the neighborhood of .35, with half of the studies yielding correlations between .25 and .48. A comprehensive summary of the findings of these studies is available elsewhere.

While the existence of this social-status difference in average I. Q. is a well-established fact, the interpretation of its possible significance has led to much controversy. For many years this controversy was largely bipolar. Some psychologists and educators inclined to the view that the difference was due largely to hereditary factors. Their argument, in somewhat oversimplified form, claimed that the more intelligent parents gravitated to the occupational fields carrying higher status (professional, managerial, and to a lesser extent, skilled labor) while the less able parents gravitated to the lower status occupations, especially semi-skilled and un-skilled labor. These superior parents then passed on their superior intelligence to their children through genetic processes. The findings of the research studies were taken as support of the hypothesis that intelligence is inherited genetically.

Other psychologists and educators inclined to the view that the difference in average I. Q. for children from high status and from low status homes was due largely to environmental factors. Their argument—again in somewhat oversimplified form—claimed that the parents in the higher status occupations were able to provide more favorable and more stimulating environments for their children than were the parents in the lower status occupations. Since the environments were more stimulating for the children from high-status homes these children developed more nearly to their full capacities, whereas children from low-status homes were stunted and did not develop fully.   The findings of the research studies, it was pointed out, were consistent with this hypothesis and therefore supported it.

During the early years of the 20th century this controversy flourished somewhat vigorously, with ardent advocates of each point of view claiming research support for their view, and with only an occasional voice pointing out that the nature of the research evidence available made it impossible to arrive at any definitive answer to the controversy.   Since the homes in which the hereditary intelligence of the parents was supposed to be highest were also the same homes that were supposd to be environmentally the most stimulating, it was impossible to use the higher I. Q.'s of the children in these homes as evidence for either one of these two hypotheses.

As the years passed, the line of demarcation between these two extreme positions softened somewhat, with people on both sides conceding that the intelligence of children is probably a result of the dynamic interaction of both hereditary and environmental factors.   While probably few today would claim that either hereditary or environmental factors are *totally* responsible for all I. Q. differences, there is still wide variation in the degree of emphasis assigned to the different kinds of factors by different psychologists, sociologists and educators.

While these two traditional points of view differ markedly in their assignment of causes to the observed I. Q. differences, they have in common an acceptance of the fact that there *are* genuine differences in basic intelligence between children from high-status backgrounds and children from low-status backgrounds.   They differ only in the kinds of reasons which they believe explain these differences.

More recently, a third point of view has been expressed with increasing frequency.   This point of view side-steps the heredity-environment controversy and questions, instead, whether the differences in average I. Q. found for high-status and for low-status children represent the real differences in intelligence that they have been assumed to represent.   The persons taking this point of view point out that children from high-status homes have substantially different kinds of cultural experiences from children in low-status homes.   These experiences are different in the kinds of things with which the children deal, in the vocabulary and language with which the children will be familiar, and in the attitudes and values which determine what problems seem important and what problems seem unimportant to the children.   These people then point out that the usual intelligence tests draw more heavily from the content, the language, and the attitudes and values of the high-status culture than they do from the low-status culture. From this point of view, the differences in I. Q.'s, or scores, on the tests may be a reflection merely of this bias in the test materials, and not of basic differences in the real abilities of children from the different backgrounds.

In brief, while the discussion during the earlier part of the century revolved largely around the question of *why* children from high-status homes were more consistently found to be higher in mental ability (intelligence) than children from low-status homes, the present controversy deals more with the question of *whether* this apparent difference is a real one or whether it reflects merely a bias in the construction of tests.

This cultural-bias interpretation of intelligence-test results has long been generally accepted in the field of rural-urban differences. It has been recognized widely that when a test draws largely on experiences peculiar to urban life, it will penalize rural children and that lower scores of the rural children on such a test should be taken as indicating a deficiency in the test and not as indicating a genuine deficiency in mental ability of rural children. It seems strange that this same line of reasoning was not applied earlier to the I. Q. differences found between children of different sub-cultural levels within the urban culture. Perhaps this application had to await the development of more definitive research information on the extent of the difference in the cultural patterns to which children in different parts of the urban community are exposed. Warner and his colleagues, in particular, have contributed much to a clearer understanding of the extent of these differences.

Group and Individual Differences in I. Q. Some misunderstanding has arisen through failure to differentiate between the effect of cultural bias on individual differences in I. Q.'s and its effect on the average performance of groups of children.

Although there are substantial differences in the average I. Q. of high-status children and the average I. Q. of low-status children, wide variation of I. Q. is always found among the individuals in any one status group. Even on the traditional intelligence tests not all the "brighter" children will be found in the high-status group, nor all the duller children in the low-status group. In one study, for example, it was found that eight percent of the low-status children were *above* the average of the high-status children and that seven percent of the high-status children were *below* the average of the low-status children. The implications of this wide variation of ability within each status group are frequently overlooked.

The cultural-bias argument, outlined above, is applicable only to systematic group differences. It is true that any individual child's performance on an intelligence test will doubtless be affected also by whether the items happen to sample particular experiences with which he has come in contact. However, the presence in the tests of a fairly large number of items probably assures a fair amount of averaging out of such discrepancies, *so long as the nature of the items is not systematically biased against a particular child.*

If, however, whole groups of children have certain kinds of experiences more frequently than do other groups of children, and the test items are drawn mostly from the kind of material with which one group is familiar, group differences in intelligence-test scores would be expected.

Suppose that it could be conclusively demonstrated (which it cannot at present) that *all* the difference in average I. Q., as between high-status and low-status children, is due to cultural bias in the test. A wide variety of individual scores would still occur even if the systematic bias were somehow eliminated. In this area of *individual* variation of I. Q.'s, the old controversy of hereditary and environmental causes—and a dynamic interaction of the two—is still applicable.

Is a "Culture Fair" Test a "Culture Free" Test? It is not surprising that some confusion has arisen between these two terms which sound as though they might be synonymous or at least closely related. However, these two terms presumably are intended to refer to two quite different ideas. If by a "culture free" intelligence test is meant one in which the "intelligence" of a child is somehow measured entirely apart from the impact of any cultural experiences on the child, the term is practically a nonsense term. Psychologists and sociologists have long pointed out that all human beings are the product of an interaction between certain inner genetic characteristics and the forces which come from outside, usually called "cultural" or "environmental." From the moment of conception the development of any living organism is inescapably influenced by its environment—by "cultural" factors, in short. To attempt to devise test items to which a child can respond without being in any way influenced by the environment or culture in which he has been brought up is a task at least as hopeless as separating a baked pudding. Some test authors have apparently tried to construct "culture free" tests—at least they have so labelled them—by using arbitrary geometric figures which would be new to all children. Unless, however, the lines and elements which make up such designs, and the instructions which accompany them, are in some way tied in closely to the past experiences of the child, he will not be able to do anything with them. Furthermore, the very fact of requesting the children to work with material that looks meaningless to them introduces problems of culturally-determined work habits and attitudes.

Those who have proposed "culture fair" intelligence tests are not trying to eliminate all cultural material from the intelligence test. They are interested only in having tests which measure fairly the basic problem-solving ability of children from different kinds of cultural background. They are attempting to construct and administer tests so that children from each sub-group in the culture will have equal opportunity for being familiar with the materials and methods required for successful answering of the test items.

In summary, if an intelligence test is to be freed of "cultural bias," if it is to be fair measure of genuine problem-solving ability of children from different sub-cultural groups, three criteria must be met: (a) the tests must be composed of items which deal with materials common to the various sub-cultures in which it is to be used, (b) the test must be expressed in language and other symbols which are equally familiar to the children growing up in the different sub-cultures, and (c) the test must be so organized and administered as to stimulate equal degrees of interest and motivation for the children from the different sub-cultures. To the extent that an intelligence test does not meet these three qualifications, it cannot be said to be a culturally "fair" test. If it contains items which require familiarity with symphony orchestra instruments, with strange animals observable only in zoos and museums—or if it is expressed in academic, bookish words which are strange to children from the "wrong side of the tracks"—or if it is so uninteresting to children that the only children that will work hard at it will be those (mostly middle and higher status) who have been taught by their parents to do their best on anything the teacher asks—in any of these cases the test is characterized by "cultural bias."

What Is the Purpose of Measuring "Intelligence"? A serious problem arises in the measurement of intelligence because of the lack of any generally accepted definition of "intelligence." The term has been defined by some as the ability to adapt to one's environment, by some as the ability to think abstractly, and in a great variety of other phrases. Some of these definitions differ from each other only in their verbal expression, but others represent more basically different concepts.

One problem of definition has a particularly direct and significant bearing on the proper use of the intelligence test in the school situation. There are those who say that the main purpose of an intelligence test is to predict which pupils are going to do well in school—or in particular school curricula. For practical purposes, "intelligence" is defined as the ability to do school work.

According to this view, since the primary purpose of the test is to predict success in performing school work, the test should be judged empirically on the basis of how well it predicts such success. The question of whether the test is culturally biased or not is irrelevant, so long as the test actually does predict school success reasonably well.   It is possible that a culturally biased test will give a better prediction of school success in most schools, since most schools are based on curricular materials and teaching methods that are heavily loaded with concepts, language, materials, and values and attitudes that are characteristic of the middle-class or high-status culture.   It is, in this view, quite appropriate for low-status children to be penalized on the "intelligence" test, since they will also be handicapped in their attempts to master the school program.

With this basic point of view, the writer is in substantial agreement. If what is wanted is as good a predictor as possible of success in the school program *as it is now organized,* the test should be constructed and validated empirically, with those items being selected for the test which discriminate most sharply between pupils who succeed in the school as now organized and those who do not succeed, without any regard for *why* any pupil does poorly on the test or in the school.   The question of cultural bias is then irrelevant.   This is true even though the present tests are not very efficient predictors of school success (An intelligence test is considered as rather good which accounts for only about a quarter of the actual variance which occurs in school grades).

Acceptance of this view of an intelligence test as having as its chief purpose the prediction of success in the school as now organized requires a form of thinking, however, that is difficult to maintain.   The term "intelligence" has been used by so many people to mean so many different things that it is difficult to keep in mind while using a test developed in accordance with the definition of intelligence described in the preceding paragraph that the logic applies only if predicting school grades is the sole purpose for which the test is being used.

If the term "intelligence" had no prior connotations to trouble those who use it, one could define it as the ability to do school work in schools as now organized, just as one could invent any new word and arbitrarily define it in this way.   Probably it would be safe to say, however, that most persons not specifically trained in the field of intelligence testing and school-prediction problems will bring to the term a host of fairly vague connotations quite apart from the empirical definition just outlined.   To many, "intelligence" will automatically evoke thoughts of a generalized "mental power," probably "native" or "innate," although this is quite irrelevant, and potentially misleading, if intelligence is being defined empirically as scholastic aptitude.

When a test is designed to predict success in a particular occupation— stenography, for example—it is usually *labelled* as a stenographic aptitude test.   A test designed to predict successful performance in an algebra class is usually labelled as an algebra aptitude test.   If a test is to be used to predict success in school work generally, why is it not more consistent, more descriptive, and less open to misunderstanding, to label the test as a test of scholastic aptitude rather than to refer to it as an "intelligence" test?   This distinction is usually made at the college level.   This may be because the cultural content of these tests at the higher levels has been more generally recognized than is the cultural content of "intelligence" tests at the elementary-school level.

If a test has been constructed according to the usual empirical procedures for constructing aptitude tests, it can be used to predict which pupil will probably do well and which will not do well in the school, so long as the school's program is similar to those of the schools where the test-construction and test-validation work was carried out.   It is important to note, however—and this is frequently overlooked—that such a test cannot be used as a basis for planning school modifications or for evaluating school effectiveness.

One cannot legitimately say, "The intelligence test shows that certain of our pupils are bright and certain of them are dull.   The bright ones succeed well in our school so our school is doing a good job with bright pupils.   The dull ones are doing poorly, but the tests indicate they could not be expected to do any better, so we need not worry about them." Such an evaluative use of intelligence test results is utterly fallacious. One cannot justify securing poor educational results from "poor" students by saying the tests show them to be "poor" students; the tests were specifically constructed to do just this—to label as "poor" those students who do not do well in our schools as now organized.

Some may be willing to accept the present American schools as having the right kinds of school programs in all basic respects, and desire merely to identify those pupils who will fit into the existing school pattern successfully.   In this case, the present "scholastic aptitude" tests, constructed empirically and without regard for cultural bias, can be quite useful.   This is a legitimate use—and probably the only one—for these tests.   It is a use whose limitations would be more clearly understood and less easily overlooked if the tests were labelled by a term like "scholastic aptitude" which describes their actual function rather than by a term like "intelligence" which suggests a variety of irrelevant thoughts to many users of the term.

Suppose, however, a school administrator and his teachers are interested in identifying the abilities and potentialities of all the children which the school is suposed to be serving, and wish to use these abilities and potentialities as a basis for planning school programs which will develop to the fullest possible extent all these abilities and potentialities.   Tests of "scholastic aptitude" are almost worthless for this purpose.   When "intelligence" tests are used in this way the problem of cultural bias becomes particularly crucial. If whole groups of children are labelled by the tests as possessing less "brightness" or "problem-solving ability" than they really have, the real abilities of those pupils will be underestimated, and the importance of developing special programs for developing such abilities overlooked.

The writer has seen a number of school systems—probably many readers of this article have had the same experience—where certain schools are regarded as "poor" schools; it is assumed that there isn't really much point in trying to educate the children attending these schools. In some systems new teachers and new administrators are assigned to these schools, with the understanding that they will be "promoted" to more promising schools after they have served their "term" in the less desirable schools. Such schools become, essentially, custodial institutions. In some cases these children from whom little is expected and to whom little is offered constitute only particular rooms rather than whole schools. In some cases the distinction is made on an individual basis. In any case, however, the child, or the group of children, with low I. Q.'s on tests which are at least to some extent biased against them because of the particular cultural background from which they come—are labelled as relatively uneducable, and little is offered them.

There is no virtue in useless sentimentality. If these children really are uneducable, or if the educational achievement of which they are capable is really considerably below an "acceptable" level, an attempt to educate them would be silly—a waste of time and a waste of human resources. The same resources could better be utilized in improving the educational opportunities for children who are more capable of profiting from educational advantages.

But suppose that many children are shunted off to the side of the mainstream of education through a fallacy, through failure to realize that the school program is not geared to their particular abilities. The resultant loss to thousands upon thousands of individuals is tragic.

If good tests of basic problem-solving ability could be developed that would measure the ability of children to solve real life problems of the kind that are important to them, school authorities could use such tests as a basis for curriculum planning and as a basis for teaching-method evaluation. If certain students still turn out to have very little "intelligence" (or problem-solving ability), the school might as well face the fact that such children are relatively uneducable and that the most it can do is to provide some sort of custodial care for them. If, however, children now labelled as of low intelligence should be shown by such culture-fair tests actually to have a higher degree of problem-solving ability than formerly suspected, would not that be a great impetus and stimulation for the development of new kinds of curricula, new educational objectives, new teaching methods to capitalize on these previously undiscovered talents?

It will not be easy for most of us, whose whole personal orientation and background are in the "middle-class" tradition, to re-orient our thinking enough to devise ways of developing the problem-solving abilities of children whose cultural resources are of quite a different sort from our own. We will have to learn to understand children whose definition of what constitutes a "problem" is often quite different from our own use of the term, children whose interest in school work is already strongly negative because of the child's discovery that the school now has little to offer him. But that is the challenge of education in a democracy that is as heterogeneous as the United States. If we are to provide education for all children, must it not be education geared to the cultural backgrounds, the cultural needs, and the cultural motivations of each child? Can we be content much longer to attempt to fit children from the "wrong side of the tracks" into a school program not designed in terms of their interests or abilities or needs? Certainly we cannot justify our attempt to do so by using so-called "intelligence" tests to indicate that these children really aren't up to educational standard anyway. We cannot justifiably do so while we use tests which are really tests of scholastic aptitude and which were specifically constructed to identify as "poor" the child who will not do well in the present program.

On the basis of scores from tests designed only to predict success in schools as they are now organized, with their heavy emphasis upon curriculum materials, teaching methods, and values and attitudes drawn almost entirely from the middle-class culture, we are helping to shape children's lives. What human resources are we squandering? How many individual potentialities are we failing to develop? Dare we take the responsibility, as administrators, as teachers, or as counselors, for guiding children into educational dead-ends on the theory that they are not capable of better educational opportunities when the only evidence we have for this condemnation is the kind of intelligence tests at present available?

This is the question raised by the problem of cultural bias in intelligence tests.

19. Factors in Mental Retardation*

THERE is a growing recognition in our society of the need to help everybody, including the mentally retarded, to perform as near to capacity as possible.   In the selection below Dr. Jervis presents some basic information concerning the known and suspected causes of mental retardation.   Although this information is of particular importance to those who will work with the mentally handicapped, it has meaning for prospective teachers who wish to have an understanding of the broad spectrum of mental ability.

VARIOUS sciences have contributed to our present concept of mental deficiency.   For a long time sociologists have observed that there are individuals who, since childhood, have been socially incompetent and incapable of adequate self-support.   Psychologists, coming later, have noted that this social incompetence is often associated with defective intellectual development.   They have discovered ways of measuring the degree of intellectual deficit and of establishing certain correlations between intellectual endowment and social attainments.   Then as medical science advanced physicians became increasingly aware that some diseases occurring during fetal life or in infancy may result in lesions of the brain with consequent mental defect.   Finally, with the advent of the science of human genetics the relevance of genetic factors in determining deviations of intelligence emerged.

Mental deficiency may be defined as a condition of arrest or incomplete mental development existing before adolescence, caused by disease or genetic constitution and resulting in social incompetence.   This definition includes both the sociological concept which stresses the social inadequacy of the defective, and the psychological concept which is considered in the term "arrested" or "incomplete" mental development.   The biological viewpoint is embodied in the mention of genetic factors and diseases.

Intellectual impairment developing after adolescence is not usually known as mental deficiency but as dementia, a customary differentiation for more than a century in both legal and medical thinking, in spite of its dubious validity.

Thus defined, mental deficiency is not a single condition, but a symptom

* George A. Jervis, "Factors in Mental Retardation," *Children,* vol. I (November-December, 1954), pp. 207–211.   Reprinted by permission of the author and the Department of Health, Education, and Welfare, Social Security Administration, Children's Bureau.

Dr. Jervis (1903—) is Director of Clinical Laboratories, Letchworth Village, New York State Department of Mental Hygiene.

common to diverse conditions of disparate etiologies and of various manifestations.

In the recognition of mental deficiency, the results of psychological examination play the leading role. The mental age (MA) is determined by psychometric tests and the intelligence quotient (IQ) calculated as the rapport of the mental age to the chronological age (CA): $IQ = MA/CA \times 100$. Other factors besides intelligence quotient are taken into consideration, such as educational attainment, emotional reactions, general behavior, and social adjustment. The information from both familial and personal history is carefully evaluated. Finally, a complete medical examination is performed, using modern techniques of clinical and laboratory medicine. It is upon the evidence thus collected that the diagnosis is made.

Considerable difficulty is often experienced in diagnosing the borderline cases between "subnormality" and mental deficiency. The criterion of social adjustment is decisive in these instances.

INCIDENCE AND CLASSIFICATION

In estimating the incidence of mental deficiency, a great deal depends upon the criteria of diagnosis used in the assessment of defective individuals. For instance, if the criterion of social incompetence is adhered to, the incidence will be higher in a strongly competitive urban environment than in rural communities. If a purely psychological criterion is adopted, the test used and the arbitrary point of demarcation between the defective and the nondefective individual will determine to a large extent percentage figures. If one accepts an IQ of 75 instead of one of 70 as the lower limit for the nondefective, the percentage of defective population will be over twice as large. Estimates based on institutional censuses are obviously inadequate and always too low, since only a fraction of the mentally defective population is institutionalized. Those based on large-group testing of school children have their limitations and are perhaps too high. Accurate surveys using modern techniques of securing data and uniform criteria of evaluating intellectual and social development have been few in number and limited in extension.

On the basis of scattered and incomplete data collected from many sources, it may be assumed that the incidence of mental deficiency in the general population is around 1 percent, using IQ below 70 as the criterion. This figure yields a total of 1,500,000 mental defectives in the United States.

Defectives are usually classified into three groups—idiots, imbeciles, and morons, but the corresponding terms of low-grade, medium-grade, and high-grade defective are to be preferred. Defined in sociological terms and in the language of the English Mental Deficiency Act (1927), idiots are persons whose mental defectiveness is of such degree that they are unable to guard themselves against ordinary physical danger. Imbeciles are persons whose mental defectiveness, though less extreme than in idiots, still prevents them from managing themselves or their affairs, or, in the case of children, of being taught to do so. Morons are persons whose mental defectiveness, though not amounting to imbecility, is yet so pronounced that they require care, supervision, and control for their own protection or for the protection of others, or, in the case of children, appear to be permanently incapable of receiving proper benefit from instruction in ordinary schools.

In more precise psychological terms, an idiot is a person having a mental age of less than 3 years, or, if a child, an intelligence quotient of less than 20. An imbecile is a person having a mental age of 3 to 7 years, inclusive, or, if a child, an intelligence quotient from 20 to 49, inclusive. A moron is a person having a mental age of 8 to 11 or 12 years, or, if a child, an intelligence quotient from 50 to 70 (or 75).

Although of considerable value in dealing with practical problems of defectives, both sociological and psychological classifications present limitations, being purely descriptive in character. More comprehensive are medical classifications which follow mainly etiological criteria, grouping patients according to the cause of the defect. While this type of classification may offer considerable difficulty in individual cases, because of scanty and contradictory etiological data or the fact that more than one etiological factor may be responsible for the defect, it does bring about a better understanding of the problem in relation to preventive measures.

Etiologically, mental defect can be divided into two large groups— endogenous or primary, and exogenous or secondary. In the exogenous group the defect comes chiefly from environmental factors. This group can be subdivided into types according to the causative agent—infectious, traumatic, toxic, and endocrine. On the other hand, an endogenous defect is determined mainly by those hereditary factors known as genes. The group includes conditions due to the combined action of many genes each of which alone would have an insignificant effect, or to the action of a single dominant or recessive gene.

HEREDITARY DEFECTS

Multiple Genes

Mental defects determined by multiple genes are "undifferentiated" in that they carry no specific physical distinction and are "aclinical" in that they show no clinical manifestations other than intellectual impairment.

This group has also been designated by other terms: "residual" because it is composed of individuals who are left after a classification of specific forms; "subcultural" because so many of its members originate from low cultural environments; "familial" because of the high frequency of the condition in the patients' families. Since these cases can be diagnosed only by psychological and social adjustment criteria, differentiation between high-grade morons and dull-normal individuals may be difficult. While antisocial behavior and psychopathic traits occur in the group, they are far from universal.

Estimates of the incidence of undifferentiated mental defects run between 30 and 75 percent of all the mentally retarded, the lower figure probably running nearer to the facts. It includes defects of all grades, but high-grade morons predominate.

While the etiological factors determining the large number of undifferentiated cases of mental deficiency are still in dispute, it seems likely that they are similar to the factors responsible for general intelligence—in other words, genetic constitution. It seems reasonable to assume that most of these undifferentiated cases represent merely the lower part of the normal frequency-distribution curve of intelligence, known to statisticians as the Gaussian form. This means that a certain number of individuals are bound to appear in the range below the line indicating IQ 70. They are an integral part of the population as a whole, just as are individuals with superior intelligence with an IQ above 130. According to the curve, the majority of undifferentiated defectives are in the moron classification with IQ's between 50 and 70, and only a very few at the idiot level, with IQ's below 20—a picture which corresponds to observed fact.

Genetic constitution, however, is not the only source of all undifferentiated defectiveness, for environmental factors, such as subcultural milieu and poor hygienic conditions, undoubtedly play a causative role. The task of tracing the source of the defectiveness in individual cases is not easy, particularly when malnutrition and deprivation have been in the picture.

Single Genes

Some differentiated defects are determined by the presence of a single dominant gene transmitted from parent to child. Such defects are always traceable in the family history unless of a type that prevents reproduction. Frequently they turn up in severe form in alternate generations occurring in the intermediate generation only in incomplete form. Sporadic occurrences in families with no history of the defect are probably caused by a new mutation in a parental germ cell.

Data collected at Letchworth Village indicate that dominant genes probably account for only about 1 or 2 percent of all mental defects. These are always characterized by some physiological changes which make them classifiable into specific or clinically recognizable diseases. Among them are tuberosclerosis, neurofibromatosis, and nevoid idiocy —diseases in which mental deficiency is accompanied by skin lesions—and several forms of mental defect characterized by changes of bone structures.

There are also clinically recognizable defects caused by the presence of two similar genes, known as recessive genes, one from each parent.   Since persons of blood relationship are more likely to carry similar genes, such defects occur more frequently among the offspring of consanguineous marriages than in the general population.

In the great majority of the recessive cases the parents themselves are normal, being merely carriers of the gene, or, in genetic terms, heterozygous for the gene.   The defect is characteristically distributed among 25 percent of the sibs, and is sharply distinguishable.   While such defects are on the whole rare, they include a number of specific diseases: amaurotic family idiocy, a progressive and fatal disease accompanied by blindness which, according to type, may show up in infancy, childhood, or adolescence; gargoylism, a disease characterized by mental deficiency and grotesque bone changes; phenylpyruvic idiocy, the result of an inborn error in metabolism of an amino acid; hepatolenticular degeneration, a progressive form of mental deterioration caused by degeneration of nuclei at the base of the brain; and some forms of diffuse sclerosis, also a progressive disorder causing brain damage.

ENVIRONMENT-PRODUCED DEFECTS

A large but not yet clearly determined proportion of defectiveness comes from factors outside the hereditary constitution including infections, trauma, poison, glandular disorders, and physical or emotional deprivation.   Rough estimates, based on unpublished data from a number of institutions indicate that such factors may account for at least half of the mentally retarded population in the country.

Infection

Brain damage resulting from infection from the nervous system may occur in the womb or during infancy or childhood.   The type of infectious agent, the severity of its attack, and the age of the child when attacked determine the degree of damage.

One of the most prevalent of such infections used to be syphilis, transmitted during gestation from an infected mother through the placenta to the fetus and resulting in brain damage to the fetus and later mental defect in the child. While syphilis still is responsible for a small percentage of all defectiveness, the proportion of infected children has already been reduced by veneral-disease control programs and undoubtedly will be further reduced in the future. Especially effective has been the increasing adoption of routine serological tests of pregnant women, prescribed by law in many States.

One form of severe mental deficiency comes from rubella infection (German measles) in the mother during the first 3 months of pregnancy. Besides the intellectual impairment resulting from fetal brain damage the rubella virus's attack on the fetus often produces congenital deafness, anomalies of the heart and eyes, and microcephaly (undersized head and brain).

Facts about the effects of other virus infections of the mother on the fetus are not so definitely established. It is possible that some other viruses may act in a manner similar to that of the rubella virus.

Brain fever is estimated to be responsible for the mental defects of 10 to 20 percent of all institutionalized defectives, according to Letchworth Village data. Caused by one of the encephalitis viruses or by a bacteria, such as the meningococcus of meningitis, it often strikes in infancy and childhood. While many children recover from it completely and others die, some recover with permanent impairments, the most common of which is mental defect. Measles, scarlet fever, chickenpox, whooping cough, influenza, and other communicable diseases common in childhood also occasionally leave brain damage.

Patients whose mental defectiveness has resulted from acute attacks of these diseases are usually referred to as post-encephalitics. The degree of mental defect among them varies considerably with the individuals. Many of them exhibit a peculiar behavior pattern marked by episodes of overactivity, restlessness, impulsiveness, assaultiveness, and wanton destruction.

Trauma

While accidents resulting in injury to the brain may sometimes occur in infancy or early childhood they are insignificant in comparison to injuries at birth or in the neonatal period as a cause of mental defect. Cerebral trauma during birth has been variously estimated to cause from 10 to 50 percent of all defectiveness. However, the incidence in institutionalized defectives does not seem to be above 20 percent. According to data gathered by the United Cerebral Palsy from one-half to two-thirds of the children in the general population showing evidence of birth injury are not mentally defective.

Difficult labor and prematurity are the most frequent causes of brain damage during birth, the former because of the risk of mechanical injury and the latter because of the immaturity of the brain.   An immature brain is more prone to damage.

Brain damage at birth comes either by asphyxia or by hemorrhage. Asphyxia, which must be present for a relatively long period to produce irreversible damage, may result from premature separation of the placenta, cord complication, overdosage of the mother with analgesic drugs, or delayed breathing by the newborn.   Hemorrhage, which may be within the brain or its envelopes, comes from direct injury during delivery—by forceps, or by a tearing of the tentorium, one of the membranes of the brain, in compression of the head during its passage through the pelvic canal.

Toxic Causes

Little is known about the effects of toxic factors transmitted from mother to fetus during pregnancy, but evidence exists for suspicion that there are several ways in which fetal poisoning, resulting in malformation and mental defectiveness, may occur.   Eclampsia, a severe intoxication of obscure origin suffered by some pregnant and delivering women, may affect the child detrimentally.   Some toxic drugs taken by a pregnant woman may also damage the fetus but what these are and how great the dosage must be to be damaging are still mysteries.

X-rays, on the other hand, are definitely known to be damaging to the developing central nervous system.   Several cases are on record of mothers who after receiving deep X-ray therapy to the abdominal region during pregnancy have produced microcephalic children or children with other congenital abnormalities, including mental defect.   However, improved knowledge of the effects of X-rays has resulted in the routine testing of women of child-bearing age for pregnancy before radiation, and thus in the reduction of defects from this cause.

Blood incompatibility between mother and child also has a toxic effect upon the child.   This comes about most frequently as a result of the Rh factor, an entity present in the blood of about 85 percent of the population, but absent in the other 15 percent.   When an Rh negative mother (whose blood possesses no Rh factor) carries an Rh positive baby, toxic substances develop which may cause damage to the fetal blood, liver, and brain.   However, this condition is responsible for less than 1 percent of low-grade spastic defectives, as fortunately only 5 percent of Rh-positive children of Rh-negative mothers develop the disease, while some who do develop it recover completely.

Mongolism, or mongoloid idiocy, a condition with a characteristic physical appearance, may also be toxic in origin, although little is definitely known about its etiology. Some authorities believe that the condition appears in the fetus before the third month of pregnancy as a consequence of a variety of toxic conditions inherent in the mother and associated with advanced age, endocrine disorders, or pathological lesions of the uterus. Mongoloids comprise about 5 to 10 percent of all defectives. Their IQ usually runs between 15 and 40. Because these children are prone to infection, they have a higher mortality rate than other defective children.

Endocrine Disorders

While a certain percentage of mental defectives suffer from some glandular dysfunction, the proportion of defectiveness caused only by endocrine disorders is small. Cretinism is a form of mental defect definitely traceable to hypothyroidism or impaired function of the thyroid gland, either because of its lack of development or early destruction. This disease, which is also distinguishable by physical appearance, is endemic in areas where goiter is also prevalent, but it also occurs sporadically elsewhere. Dysfunction of the pituitary gland also causes mental defect, the most common type, Frölich's syndrome, being characterized by obesity, underdeveloped genitalia, and mild intellectual impairment.

Deprivation

Emotional deprivation, frustrations, and insecurity may not only bring about a condition among normal children resembling mental defect but may cause incorrect estimate of the intellectual abilities of high-grade defectives, especially those also physically handicapped. Pseudo-feeblemindedness is produced in normal children so deprived by an emotional blocking which responds to psychiatric treatment.

The most severe form of pseudo-feeblemindedness, infantile autism, is dramatic, if rare, evidence of the importance of emotional factors in the development of intelligence. Children so affected behave like idiots, do not talk, respond to stimuli, nor engage in any activity requiring intelligence, even though their intellectual capacity may be normal or better than average. Psychiatric examination shows that their apparent defect is a form of withdrawal.

The classical case of Kaspar Hauser exemplified the degree to which deprivation of the means of learning could impair intellectual development. Such extreme cases are not likely to occur today. Nevertheless, deprivation of cultural stimulation in some isolated communities still plays a role in producing the apparent low level of intelligence among the populace. More tragic are the effects of such deprivation on patients with disabilities interfering with academic learning. False diagnoses of feeblemindedness too often occur among children whose only impairments are in hearing, reading ability, word comprehension, minor motor handicaps, or other disabilities. In these children emotional factors are undoubtedly also contributing to the picture of apparent intellectual defeat.

THE INDIVIDUAL

In spite of the growing knowledge of the causes of mental defects few specifics are available for their treatment or prevention. As the foregoing shows, mental retardation is not an entity itself, but a characteristic of a variety of conditions, each with a different cause. Moreover, in each form there is a wide range of intellectual ability.

Prevention for some forms may lie only within the scope of eugenic measures, though more scientific knowledge in the field of human genetics would be required before such could be confidently prescribed.

Greater possibilities for preventing the exogenous forms through medical and public-health measures may be expected to be realized as knowledge of intrauterine life and development increases.

While treatment in the strict medical sense can be applied only to a small number of mentally defective individuals, in the broader sense of care and training it can be applied to all. But such a wide variation of conditions exist among children with mental defects that what kind of care and treatment each receives must be determined individually in line with a prognosis based on an accurate diagnosis of the case. While the goal can rarely be cure, it can almost always be improvement or the achievement of the maximum intellectual and social functioning of which the individual is capable.

20. Pupils Psychologically Absent from School*

Related selections: 31, 41, 45, 47, 50

THE FAILURE of some students to perform at the expected level indicated by measures of their academic ability is a persistent problem
facing teachers.   Often this seeming inability or reluctance to learn,
stemming from some emotional conflict, cannot be dealt with successfully by the classroom teacher.   In this paper Dr. Talbot and
Mrs. Henson report the results of social work treatment provided five
students who were referred to them because of learning difficulties.

CHILDREN who are present physically in school classrooms but absent
psychologically have always presented a problem to educators and are now
becoming the concern of orthopsychiatrists as well.

In this paper we propose to discuss only one component of this complex
problem: emotional conflict interfering with the continuous learning process.   The pupils herein represented had at least average intelligence and
had experienced no difficulty in mastering the rudiments of learning.
There was no clinical evidence of either physical or neurological involvement, or of school phobia.   The problem, briefly stated, was that certain
pupils continued to attend school but did not continue to learn.

Conspicuously absent was any involvement of other areas of their lives
on the reality or conscious level.   Outside of school, these children were
able to function and to gain some measure of satisfaction.   This delimita-
tion of the influence of neurotic conflict was brought out by Ernst Kris,
who quotes Hartmann: "He points to the fact that not all of the child's
achievements are related to his conflicts; that in physical and intellectual
life, and in growth and development, many steps are normally not affected
by conflicts."

The level of our treatment, which was psychoanalytically oriented social
casework in a school setting, revealed that these pupils were not otherwise
handicapped.   Our approach included not only the child, but also the
home and the school environment.   Ackerman and Neubauer have
stressed the necessity of considering the total environment in the treatment

* Mira Talbot and Isabelle Henson, "Pupils Psychologicallly Absent from
School," Presented at the 1953 Annual Meeting in a session on "Disability and
School Attendance."   Reprinted from the *Journal of Orthopsychiatry,* vol. XXIV
(April, 1954), pp. 381–390, by permission of the authors and the publisher.
Miss Talbot is Acting Supervisor of, and Mrs. Henson is Psychiatric Social
Worker in, the Queens Center of the Bureau of Child Guidance.   (William C.
Barger, Psychiatrist, is in charge of the Queens Center.   Other staff members who
participated in the study of pupils: C. John Mathias, Psychiatric Social Worker;
Hazel Wertman and Pauline Schwartz, Psychologists.)

of a child.   They emphasize the importance of the total approach: "To insure against failure, the therapist must have full knowledge of the child's environment as well as of the child.   He must have working contact, therefore, with the parents, the school, and other aspects of the child's daily reality."   Because our treatment was carried on in a clinic within an educational system, we had normal access to the child's life in the school as well as in the home.   Consultations were held with a psychiatrist, psychologists, and school personnel.

A discussion of the role of the social worker in the treatment of children suffering from academic failures is of particular significance because this type of problem is usually considered the province of psychologists and guidance counselors unless sufficiently complicated to demand the technique of psychiatry.

To illustrate the *social work treatment* of certain pupils psychologically absent from school, five examples are given.

Case 1.   In the case of Tim, treatment was not given at the onset of his difficulty.   The community clinic to which the psychologist had referred Tim did not accept Tim for treatment.   The worker made the common error of underestimating the possible seriousness of an isolated symptom of academic failure.

Initially, Tim was referred in 1950 when he was 13 years old and in the seventh grade.   At that time the complaint from the school was: "Although he has very good ability, he has no interest in school work and is failing in practically every subject.   No other problem."   He was again referred at 15, when he was in the second term of high school.   The complaint was identical: he was failing in every subject.

Tim was living with his widowed mother and older sister, both office workers, in an apartment of upper middle-class status   His father had died in the summer of 1947.   It was in the fall term of 1947 that his school marks first began to drop, and his general average was ten points lower.   He admitted to the Bureau psychologist that his feeling of frustration and futility first engulfed him directly following his father's death.   At that time, he had even left home for a few days.   However, family, church and school personnel had considered this a normal reaction to a great loss.   But Tim himself was worried because he found it impossible to complete his work.   Intellectually, he was within the superior range, and his reading achievement was at least four years beyond his grade placement.   His figures in the Person-Drawing Test were of a boy playing baseball and a girl diving.

Among his many interests enjoyed outside of school were swimming, football, photography, television, history and biography.   He also was a member of a neighborhood social group consisting of both boys and girls.

An outstanding characteristic was his deep concern for the underdog, and as a consequence he was consistently championing social causes. He could not pass by any wounded animal without giving it some care.

Physically, Tim was in excellent condition except for a slight visual defect and a slight tic of shoulder and head.

At the time of his second referral, the social worker offered him regular treatment sessions to be held in his school building. He responded: "I hope you can help me. There must be something wrong. I act as though I am stupid, but I know that I am not." Tim's own statement characterizes the description of a neurotic given by Dollard and Miller: "The neurotic, therefore, is, or appears to be, stupid because he is unable to use his mind in dealing with *certain* of his problems."

Tim took responsibility for keeping his weekly appointments—a total of 22 sessions—and also arranged for the therapist to see his mother several times. According to Tim, everyone thought his mother was perfect and therefore he felt ungrateful and disrespectful for not appreciating her. The reason he ran away after the father's death was that home was unbearable. The mother ran it like a business establishment: "Do for me, I'll do for you." Significantly, Tim did not mention the fact that his mother always called him "lover boy." Consciously, he perhaps was not aware of the intense emotional tie she admitted feeling for him, nor of his for her. He was aware of his hostility toward his mother. With bitterness, he told of his father's death. The morning he died, Tim was told by his mother that the father was sleeping; but later, while Tim was playing ball, he saw his father being carried out to a hearse and driven away. Somehow, he seemed to feel that his mother was accountable for his father's death.

Whenever schoolwork was mentioned, the boy repeated two episodes without any variation. First, he recounted his father's tragic life. In order to attain a college education, the father had studied nights and worked days. As soon as he had achieved his ambition, he became ill with cancer of the lungs, could hardly breathe for two years, and then suffered a painful death. Tim ended this story each time with "Look what happened to my father." Second, the boy described his mother's extreme perfectionistic standards, particularly in relation to schoolwork. When he was only in the first grade, she kept him up past midnight copying from a textbook. For the slightest error, he was made to recopy the entire page. He could not recall a single compliment, or word of praise or encouragement ever given him by his mother for his schoolwork.

Tim had concluded that his father's death was attributable to two causes: his mother and higher education. He was fearful of the same fate. On the other hand, his mother, who had practically no education, was determined that he should be as well educated as his father.   To achieve this, she was willing to scrub floors if necessary, although she suffered from spinal arthritis.   Unconsciously, the mother, by her negativism and persistence, was making it impossible for Tim to learn.   As a result of social work interviews, the mother was able to relinquish her ambitions for academic achievement and to allow him freedom to follow his own motivations.   Although he did no assigned schoolwork, he read selections from history and biography of his own choosing.

Despite the fact that the school personnel too discontinued all pressures, Tim still did absolutely nothing in the school setting.   He even lost his notebook.   There was no evidence of any resentment about his marks of zero in all major subjects.   On the contrary, his complete failure seemed to be the justification he needed to enforce his own wishes to leave school.   As soon as he became eligible, he obtained working papers.   At the present time, he is employed as a mechanic in a garage, which he enjoys; he has an active social life with both boys and girls; he has many interests including sports and reading; and he acts as though he has been relieved of an overpowering burden.

Preceding the termination of treatment, information and preparation were given him regarding mental hygiene resources, in case he should ever be ready psychologically to undergo psychoanalytic therapy.

When Tim was taken on for treatment, he had internalized his problem to such an extent that direct treatment on the conscious or preconscious level was ineffective.   In leaving school, he escaped from his neurotic involvement which was projected onto the school.   This case illustrates the adjustment made when Tim was relieved of the expectation of learning in a school setting: a relatively good adjustment from his point of view and his mother's; a failure in treatment from the social worker's point of view.

Case 2.   In marked contrast to the preceding case, Edward was treated at the first indication of regression in academic attainments.

Edward, 14, was referred in May 1950, when he was in the second term of high school.   He was failing in every subject and seemed to be "off in the clouds."   Outside of school, his interests were music, photography, electricity, and Boy Scout activities.   At the end of the first term, he was failing two subjects, although in elementary school Edward's achievement ratings had been well within the average range.

At home, there was no apparent difficulty except for fatigue, and he frequently went directly to bed after school.   A possible explanation of his fatigue is given by Pearson, who quotes Fenichel: "Even in those cases of children where fatigue results from insoluble intrapsychic conflicts . . . the physiological basis for the feeling of fatigue and its associated symptomatology is the result of excessive muscular action. Anxiety, the sign of an insoluble intrapsychic conflict, produces tension in the muscles. . . ."

Edward lived with his parents, twin sister, and a brother, seven years old. The family were American middle-class and "agnostic." Although the mother doubted the father's claim to a junior college experience, she boasted of her own college education. The father was employed by a large corporation as an electrician.

No pathology was indicated in Edward's physical examination. Psychological examinations given at the school in June 1950 corroborated the opinion of his teacher that Edward had the innate capacity to do passing high school work. His reading achievement was at the ninth grade level. On the Wechsler-Bellevue Full Scale, he attained an IQ of 123. The Rorschach examination revealed feelings of insecurity and a compulsive drive for intellectualization and organized planning. The projection data also revealed that he harbored hostility and occasionally gave vent to uncontrolled emotional outbursts. He disregarded authority, particularly that centered around the father concept, and continued to cling to maternal protection excessively.

The treatment program included the mother, father, and school personnel, in addition to Edward. His twin sister was not included in the treatment program in order to help him gain the feelings of an individual in his own right. When the twins first started school, mother, believing that the girl twin was precocious, had arranged for separate class placements. The parental feelings expressed at the birth of the twins had persisted without change throughout the years. To quote the mother: "Edward is my very own. The girl is extra." On the other hand, the father wanted to keep the girl and give the boy away. Until recently, Edward had not only been whipped by the father, but had also been called "stupid" and "a fairy."

It became apparent that the father punished his son for the feelings of inadequacy he harbored about himself: his wife rejected his love-making as adolescent and excessive, and on the job, the father felt inadequate also. As the father was resistive to any treatment for himself, a few interviews only were held with him for the purpose of maintaining his cooperation in the therapy of Edward. However, the mother in her treatment sessions, totaling 28, was helped to understand and to modify the tense interrelationships within the home.

Social therapy, 44 sessions, with Edward was carried on by a male social worker. During an interview, Edward expressed the wish that his father were more like the social worker: he had previously told his mother that he hated his father and wished he were dead. The boy was given oppor-

tunity to express his negativism, and was reassured that he was a competent person in his own right, independent of of his twin and his mother.

Concurrently with the boy's treatment, conferences were held with pertinent school personnel.   As an outgrowth of these interdisciplinary sessions, the teachers gained an understanding of Edward's failures.   One
male teacher took a special interest in Edward and even continued his interest after termination of clinical treatment.

Within the year, Edward's movement in the learning process was evidenced by renewed energy, interest, and passing marks.   He gained increased confidence in himself as a male, and when he showed interest in
a girl classmate, he gained her response.   His progress was attributable
partly to his mother's changed handling.   She relaxed in her high standards for him, and fostered his relationship with his father and maternal
grandfather.   As a consequence, a more harmonious family unit gradually evolved.   Upon termination of treatment, the mother thanked the
worker not only for the help to Edward, but also for strengthening her own
sense of worth both to herself and her family

Case 3.   The third boy's conflicts were on the threshold of consciousness and were treated before they were definitely internalized.   Accordingly, the major focus in treatment was on the situation.

David, 14½ and in the second term of high school, was referred in
1952.   The problem: "failing in schoolwork, and seems dazed."   Following corporal punishment by his stepfather for failing, David, for one
day only, truanted from school and stole a cigarette lighter.

David lived in a lower middle-class community with his mother,
stepfather, brother and sister.   The parents were American, Roman
Catholic, of Italian descent.   David's own father, of the same cultural
orientation, died of tuberculosis of the spine when David was three years
old.   Within two years, the mother married a healthy, domineering man
whose personality was the exact opposite of her first husband.   The stepfather did not "spare the rod," which gave the mother the excuse she admittedly desired for overprotecting and indulging her favorite child.
During her widowhood, the mother had been phenomenally successful in
business, and had even been able to save money for David's college education.

David, small for his age, was susceptible to colds, and had the habit of
biting his nails.   On the psychological examination given in June 1952,
David rated in the slightly above average group with an IQ of 111 on the
Stanford-Binet Form L.   He showed ability to reason with abstract material, to concentrate, and to persist.   In contrast, his work on the Wechsler Performance Scale was inferior.   Figure drawings indicated that he

was acting out his conflict with reality, particularly in relation to hetero-sexuality.

In addition to direct therapy with him, one of the goals was to effect a change in the emotional climate of the home environment. As the mother was the only member of the family reaching out for help, she was the major focus in treatment. The social worker had 22 sessions with her and several with the father. David was seen several times in the school setting. Teachers, like all other adults, were responsive to him, and willingly made adaptations in his program.

It became evident that the mother's handling of David—the most ap-pealing and vulnerable of their children—reflected not only the marital conflict, but also her own frustrated ambitions for a college education. She was envious of the stepfather's higher education, and determined that at least one of her sons would have the same advantage, and had selected David despite his own complete indifference.

Through her therapeutic sessions, the mother gained understanding of her part in David's problem. She came to appreciate that her overpro-tection of him started following her first husband's death. Since then, she had consciously thought that by her overindulgence she was protecting David from his stepfather's aggression. On the contrary, she learned that she was actually inciting her husband to be more punitive to her favorite son. When she gained insight into her repressed hostility toward her husband based on her competitive envy of him, the intense triangular conflictual situation began to disintegrate. At first the mother attributed the new serenity in the home to holidays and other external factors. In time, she faced the fact that she was more accepting of her marital status and her domestic role; this realization brought about a more harmonious family constellation.

Finally, the mother realized the impossibility of living her life over through David. The parents began to share recreational experiences with him and allowed him more freedom on his own. When the step-father ceased tutoring David, he was able to learn.

David himself showed renewed interest in learning, his grades im-proved, and there was not a single recurrence of any delinquent trends, such as his one experience of truanting and taking a lighter. Now he is permitted to assist the stepfather in his store. His own comment was, "There's no problem now because everything is better at home."

Case 4. Neither Jack nor his mother was treated directly. Owing to an unfortunate earlier experience with a psychiatrist, the mother ob-jected to any treatment allied with psychiatry. As a consequence, an understanding of the problem was obtained from one interview with the mother and a few with Jack, including a psychological examination; and the clinical insights gained were transmitted to the school personnel for their use in the normal education process.

Although Jack, a 14-year-old boy in the second term of high school, seems to have superior ability, his scholastic record was only mediocre. He seemed to lack interest.

On the psychological examination, Wechsler Intelligence Scale, given in February 1952, he rated well within the superior group in handling the more abstract, verbal material. He showed good social comprehension and also reasoning ability. His reading was well above high school level. Projective techniques showed him to be an aggressive and dependent person; his hostility was directed largely to the mother figure. It was felt that his deep feelings of hostility would undoubtedly make it difficult for him to make and maintain good human relationships.

The mother, a woman of limited education and background, was separated from her husband, a highly educated, successful scientist. She attacked and belittled the advanced education of her husband. She expressed the fear that if her son should become better educated than she, he would desert her also. She was fearful of rejection by the man who was partially supporting her. Her extreme guilt over her own extramarital affairs seemed to color all aspects of her life and to make her extremely defensive.

Many conferences were held with school personnel. Jack was changed to a class for intellectually gifted pupils, which gave him increased appreciation of himself and the motivation he needed to study. Confidence in his ability to learn was restored gradually through the understanding of his teachers and guidance personnel. A teacher and an administrative assistant—both males—gave him individual attention focused on his scientific interests. Jack became very much upset when his mother objected both to these contacts and to his renewed interest in schoolwork. It was pointed out to him that he might reassure his mother that he would not talk about her or be ashamed of her. His face lighted up. "That's what's been worrying her! I couldn't understand." There have been no objections on her part since his reassurance. Through modifications of the curriculum and special attention by school personnel, Jack's interest in school has been sustained, his marks have skyrocketed, and he has easier relationships on a limited basis with other pupils.

Case 5. Roy, who was taken on for direct treatment at a crucial point in his school life, has made phenomenally rapid progress.

At 14, in the second term of high school, he was brought to the social worker's office, crying. He was apprehensive about a test in science which he expected later that day. In the preceding term, he had been allowed to make up his failure in this subject.   His other marks were average.

He is the fourth of five children.   In the first session with the social worker, Roy compulsively gave dynamic understanding of his dilemma. All of the other children are bright and tall: he is short and dull.   His brother calls him "numbskull," and his younger sister is taller than he and might get ahead of him in school.   His father had trouble with his brains too, a brain lesion, and died the preceding summer after a long illness.   His father's symptom was dizziness and Roy feels dizzy too at times.   But his mother takes care of him, putting him to bed, bringing him food and comic books.   His only real pleasures are swimming, playing baseball, and associating with his girl friend and his dog.

Weekly treatment sessions were held with Roy as well as conferences with his teachers and his mother.   At his request, the content of the science course, including reproduction, was discussed with him.   He was able to recognize his apprehension about his intellectual inadequacies and his short stature, but his apprehension about his identification with his father's ailment was less readily understood.   In the beginning, he sat on the edge of his chair and frequently cried.   All concerned agreed to the plan that he remain in school and attend the science class regularly.   He did fail his first science test and his understanding teacher commented, "Not so bad to fail, is it?"

In subsequent sessions he became more relaxed and even whistled.   He admitted that his concerns were less overpowering.   He wanted to continue coming even though he was no longer afraid of science.   In fact, he was passing all tests and had received several marks of 100.   The fact that his father's condition was the result of an accident and not hereditary was discussed with him by both the social worker and the mother.

After only a few months of treatment, Roy acts like a different boy. According to him, "Science does not worry me any more."   In English class, he wrote a composition about his girl friend, labeling it, "The First Chapter of My Life."   He no longer complains of dizzy spells or asks to go home.   However, treatment is being continued because his underlying anxiety has not been completely allayed.

SUMMARY

This paper presents social work treatment of five boys whose emotional conflicts interfered with the continuous learning process.   The total situation, including the boy, the home and the school, was considered in the social diagnostic formulation in every case.   However, the focus in treatment varied from a total approach to a segmented one in which the school personnel carried the responsibility.

The social findings revealed that each boy was protecting himself against an anticipated impending disaster by the defensive mechanism of ceasing to learn.   The particular disaster feared on the conscious level was characterized by illness, death, divorce, passivity or femininity.   Had therapy on the deeper level been given, these dreaded disasters might have been revealed as anxieties relating to castration and unresolved oedipal complex.   Anna Freud has differentiated between the psychoanalytic and the psychiatric social work approach: "It [psychiatric social work] presents a picture of the psychoanalytic theory and practice shorn of their genetic content and approach." Genetic, here, means the exploration of the questions when, why, and how this particular form of behavior was *first* established.   Our treatment did not aim to uncover *earliest* memories or experiences, but did aim to discover the forces in the child's pre-consciousness and his particular social environment which were making continued learning impossible.   These forces proved to be:

1. All of the boys had experienced loss of their fathers.   Three fathers had died of serious illnesses: cancer of the lungs, tuberculosis of the spine, and injury of the brain.   One father, divorced, was living out of the home; and another, although living at home, was completely dominated by his wife.

2. All of the boys had been "pressured" by their mothers for academic success and, concomitantly, had been prevented from achieving.   The boys reflected the conflicts of their mothers, which were not fully described in this paper, however.

3. As an outgrowth of the first two experiences, all of the boys were afraid that academic success would bring upon them the fate suffered by their fathers.   As a defense against this disaster, they found it impossible to continue learning, yet they were expected to learn and at the same time prevented from doing so by their mothers.   Inevitably, they were in conflict.

We do not say that as a consequence of social work treatment the conflicts of these five boys were completely resolved.   We do say, however, that the internal conflicts of four boys were minimized.   This lessening of internal pressures was evidenced by movement on the reality level in the total growth process, including academic learning.   The degree of success in treatment was determined by the timing of therapy, preferably at the first manifestation of the learning block; an understanding early in the treatment process of the reality depth and breadth of the conflict; and utilization of the total forces influencing the learning process.

In conclusion, this paper shows how social findings revealed an explanation of the conflicting forces interfering with the continuous learning process; and how social work treatment diminished the power of these conflicting forces. Of significance to the authors is the fact that internal conflicts were affected by external and environmental treatment of relatively short duration.

---

21. Some Characteristics of Very Superior Children*

Related selections: 17, 22

THE LAST several decades in the United States have been brightened by the emphasis given to the conservation of our natural resources. Recently we have directed our attention to another underdeveloped and wasted resource—our talented youth. This new direction of effort is long overdue in a democracy dedicated to the optimum development of each individual. The two selections that follow give considerable insight into the problem of how to work with this segment of the school population. In the first article Mr. Lewis lays the ghost of the long-held notion that high intelligence in children is accompanied by poor adjustment. He shows that maladjustment is likely to occur only at the extremely high level of intelligence, and even then the maladjustment is most often to the school situation. In the second article (Selection 22) Miss Strang offers suggestions for teachers and school counselors who work with gifted children.

POPULAR opinion has long held the very superior individual to be some kind of freak, a very different and queer person who is likely to come to no good end, who can probably only look to a rather futile future at best. Psychologists have shown this popular belief to be erroneous, as they have done with so many popular ideas, but they have raised the question whether or not it is possible that very superior children may be too bright for their own good. The late Leta Hollingworth was quoted in the press on several occasions as having stated that the most desirable level of intelligence probably lies between *IQ*'s 125 and 145, that if one could choose his child's level of ability he should choose within this range since the best

* W. Drayton Lewis, "Some Characteristics of Very Superior Children," *The Journal of Genetic Psychology,* vol. LXII (June, 1943), pp .301–309. Reprinted by permission of the author and publisher.
Dr. Lewis (1901—) is Professor of Psychology at Southwestern Louisiana Institute.

adjustment, educational, personal, and social, appears to be made by children whose ability falls within this range and since those who possess intelligence quotients above the level may be so bright, may be so superior, and thus different from the children with whom they must associate in school and on the playground, that adjustment may be very difficult in the ordinary school and social situation.

Dr. Hollingworth also expressed the belief in various articles that the adjustment of superior children becomes increasingly difficult as the IQ's rise above 150.   This study is concerned with very superior children and endeavors to throw some light upon the educational and personality adjustments of children of varying degrees of superiority with the hope of determining, in some measure, whether or not adjustments do become increasingly difficult as the IQ rises above 145 or 150.

Coördinated Studies in Education, Incorporated, was able to collect a large amount of data on some 45,000 elementary school children in grades four to eight, inclusive.   These children were found in 455 schools and 310 communities in 36 states.   The children included in this survey were given the Kuhlmann-Anderson Test and these test results were made the basis of selection for the subjects included in this study.   Two methods of selection were used.   For some phases of this study all those who obtained an IQ rating of 145 or more were selected and they are compared with those whose IQ ratings were between 125 and 144 in order to determine whether those of the latter group were making superior adjustments to those of the most superior group at the time the tests were given. The second method of selection used was to choose the 10 with the highest intelligence quotients in each grade since the intelligence quotients did not run as high in some grades as in others, indicating, perhaps, that the Kuhlmann-Anderson Tests are not of equal difficulty at all grade levels.

The writer feels that he is justified in stating that the children included in these two groups possess very superior ability since each child represents approximately one in a thousand in ability as measured by the Kuhlmann-Anderson Test.   The purpose of this study is to investigate the home backgrounds and the personal and educational adjustments of these very superior children within the limits of the data available.

The methods of selection used in setting up the groups of superior children which have been publicized the most extensively in the literature have been such that some have expressed the opinion, which many have accepted almost without question, that superior children come from quite superior socio-economic levels.   A socio-economic rating scale was set up for the purpose of investigating the origins of the very superior children included in this study.   The socio-economic rating scale used takes account of the father's occupation, the presence in the home of a telephone, auto, radio, regular servant, and newspaper, and the room-per-person ratio. This scale gives a possible range of ratings from 0 to 18. The teachers also gave the home an economic rating of inferior, average, or superior—inferior to represent the lowest quarter and superior to represent the top quarter of the community economically.

The homes from which these very superior children come, that is, the children with *IQ* ratings of 145 and over, obtained ratings from 2 to 15, with a median rating of 8. The teachers were unable to give a rating relative to the economic status of many of the homes but 38 of the homes were rated. Seven were rated inferior, 27 average, and only four superior. This means that only four of the homes from which these very superior children came were judged to be on a par with the upper fourth of the community economically, whereas seven were rated as falling in the lower fourth economically, with approximately 70 per cent representing the middle half of the community economically. This means that some of the children come from homes where poverty is present, some from homes which are characterized by abundance, while the majority come from a wide range of middle class homes.

The highly significant finding, though, is that these very superior children can be expected in practically any type of home, as far as socio-economic rating is concerned. It is true that they tend to come from homes which have average ratings slightly higher than the average of the total population surveyed, but this fact can easily be over-emphasized and misinterpreted. It must be recognized that averages may be very misleading and that one gets an incorrect picture of the origins of these very superior children if emphasis is placed upon the average. The important finding is that these children can be expected in all kinds of homes, that the distribution of very superior ability is such that it might be termed a highly democratic distribution.

It is interesting to note that the median socio-economic rating for the group of superior children whose intelligence quotients range from 125 to 144 is slightly higher than that of the very superior group, 8.5 as compared with 8.0 Throughout this study the number of subjects, 930 for the 125 to 144 group and 50 for the very superior group, is too small to give statistically reliable results. For this reason, the writer does not believe that one is justified in interpreting the above results as indicating that the very superior group comes from homes which are inferior to those of the 125 to 144 group, but it does seem evident that they do not come from superior homes. The superiority of the homes of both of these groups is not very great when compared with the median rating for the entire population surveyed, which is 6.61.

The occupations of the fathers of the [very superior children] were listed. This listing, which is given in Table 1, emphasizes the fact that very superior ability may be expected in all types of homes.

TABLE 1

Professional group—5	Skilled labor—16
High school principal	Farmer—6
Captain—United States Army	Barber
Doctor	Printer
Minister	Mechanic—3
Designer	Mason
	Mail carrier
Business and managerial group—18	Plumber
Merchant—2	Sign painter
Salesman—5	Sergeant in army
Fruit broker	
Grocer—2	Semi-skilled and unskilled labor—12
Pharmacist	Road work—2
Jeweler	Mill hand—2
Security exchange commission	Miner
Aviator	Logger—2
Clerk	Truck driver
Insurance	Common laborer—2
Postmaster	Factory worker—2
Assistant superintendent of railroad	

One child was in an orphanage, and no information was available relative to the father, and the father of another child was an inmate of a state mental hospital.

A survey of the interests of this group of very superior children, as revealed by participation in the extra-curricular activities of the school and by their hobbies, gives no evidence of abnormality of interests for the group as a whole. They have, as a group, more extensive interests than average children and their interests in music and reading are very definitely superior to those of the total population surveyed. Three out of every five of these very superior children are designated as being interested in music, which is far greater than the interest of any other group in music. Equally significant is the fact that they have quite normal interests in all types of sports and games. The most significant finding here, we believe, is that the interests of this group of very superior children are quite normal in every sense of the term.

Most of the [very superior] children included in this study were given the *BPC Personal Inventory* and the scores obtained indicate that, as a group, their adjustment, as measured by this Inventory, is superior to that of any other group of children included in this survey [population of survey was approximately 45,000 children]. Their median score was 23.6, as compared with 27.8 for the group whose intelligence quotients lie between 125 and 144, 28.5 for the entire upper 10 per cent of this population, and 35 for an unselected group. This would appear to indicate that this very superior group has achieved a type of emotional stability, as revealed by this Inventory, which is quite superior to that of the other groups.

The entire population included in this study was rated on the basis of a list of 70 personality traits. It was suggested to those doing the rating that they pick out not less than five or more than 12 traits which they deemed to be most characteristic of each child to be rated. These personality ratings indicate that, on the whole, these very superior children have achieved personalities which are far superior to those of average children, or even to those of the upper 10 per cent. The data appear to justify a statement to the effect that very superior children, at least those included in this study, have superior personalities.

The characteristic which appears to differentiate this very superior group most definitely is *adventuresome*. One in three of these children is rated as being adventuresome whereas only one in 6.5 of the upper 10 per cent, and one in 10 of the total population surveyed are so characterized. Other personality characteristics which the teachers who did the rating believed to be particularly characteristic of this group are ambitious, dependable, energetic, friendly, happy, honest, investigative, leader, likes jokes, original, polite, and tidy.

Most individuals who have given any thought to the matter will concede that the very superior child, as judged by intelligence tests, is the most promising material which comes to the schools. It is important, therefore, to note any information, available in the data at hand, relative to the adjustment of the very superior children to the school situation which they must face. It would appear, offhand, that any teacher should recognize as possessing exceptional ability a child who rates one in a thousand on an intelligence test. It certainly is not to be expected that any of these would be rated as dull or mentally sluggish. Neither of these expectations is realized, if we are to judge by the ratings made by the teachers.

Only one boy in five and two girls in five are characterized as being *precocious* or *mentally quick*. It must be recalled that these children rate as one in a thousand on tested mental ability. When children of such unusual ability do not stand out in the ordinary classroom one would appear to be justified in assuming that the school is failing to challenge the child of exceptional ability. It is to be noted that this is even more the case with the boys than with the girls. It is equally significant to note that two of this group have been designated as *dull* or *mentally sluggish* by their teachers. While this is not a large percentage, it is hardly to be expected that teachers would so designate such brilliant children. The fact that a higher percentage of the group whose intelligence quotients are above 144 are so designated than of those with intelligence quotients between 125 and 144 might be interpreted as indicating some greater maladjustment relative to the school situation for the very superior group, but the subjects are too few to justify anything more than a hazardous guess since it may be wholly a chance distribution. There is nothing in these characterizations, however, to indicate that the schools are doing much for these very exceptional children.

There is some evidence that those with the highest intelligence quotients are somewhat more maladjusted than those who are slightly below them in intelligence. Of the 10 children who attained intelligence quotients of 160 or more, seven appear to be somewhat maladjusted as far as personality traits or educational achievement are concerned. On the basis of personality traits which are assigned to them by their teachers, six of the 10 appear to be suffering from personality maladjustments. That is, they are listed by their teachers as possessing several traits which mental hygienists rate as undesirable. The traits referred to here are "goody-goody," cute, destructive, domineering, day-dreaming, cruel, immature, nervous, over-sensitive about self, over-critical of others, too easily frightened, stubborn, inattentive in class, slovenly, suggestible, quarrelsome, lack of interest in work, pouting, unhappy, moody, or depressed, and self-conscious. If only one of these traits was ascribed to a child it was not considered to be particularly significant. The child was only considered maladjusted when the teacher believed that several of these traits were characteristic of the child. The Personal Inventory only indicated maladjustment in about a third of these cases and it should be noted that whenever the Inventory indicated maladjustment the teachers' ratings also indicated maladjustment. This would appear to indicate that the Inventory is not sensitive enough to detect maladjustment in all cases. A seventh of the 10 children mentioned above appears to have had a well-adjusted personality but was quite retarded educationally. That is, the educational age achieved on a battery achievement test fell below the mental age as indicated by the intelligence test. Twelve children obtained intelligence quotients between 150 and 160, and there is evidence of maladjustment in the case of only two of these.

Few of these very superior children who are maladjusted give evidence of aggressive behavior. Rather, they are characterized by behavior of the withdrawing or egocentric type. The characteristics most frequently attributed to them, as noted above, are day dreaming, nervous, moody, depressed, unhappy, over-sensitive about self, over-critical of others, suggestible, inattentive in class, lazy, self-conscious.

Unfavorable living conditions appear to react very powerfully, and even disastrously, upon these very superior children.   Ten of the 50 were shown as having come from homes of poverty.   All except one of the 10 appear to show the effects of this type of background and that one is well-adjusted both personally and educationally. . . .

Those with intelligence quotients above 145 show more educational maladjustment than those with intelligence quotients from 125 to 144. Sixty-four and five-tenths per cent of the former have educational ages which are below their mental ages whereas only 52.5 per cent of the latter have educational ages below their mental ages.

TABLE 2

A Comparison of the Percentages of Children with IQ's above 144 and Those with IQ's from 125 to 144 Whose Scores on Designated Achievement Tests Fell in Various Deciles as Shown

	Tenth Deciles		Ninth and Tenth Deciles		Lowest Five Deciles	
	IQ		IQ		IQ	
	125–144	145 Up	125–144	145 Up	125–144	145 Up
Reading	40.2	46.7	56.2	63.9	14.5	9.6
Geography	32.9	42.0	49.6	51.7	15.6	19.3
Arithmetic problem	33.8	42.8	52.4	52.3	17.2	22.3
Language usage	34.5	35.0	50.2	49.2	19.7	19.0

Decile scores were available for each grade of the total population on reading, geography, arithmetic problems, and language usage, the scores having been obtained from the *Unit Scales of Attainment Battery* which was administered to all of the children.   In order to determine how these very superior children were achieving relative to the entire population surveyed, their scores were scattered in the various deciles in which they fell. No consideration is given here to the fact that these children, if working up to ability, should obtain scores which would fall in the extreme upper ranges of the highest decile since they are one in a thousand in ability. Rather they are treated as if they were one in 10 in ability.

It is striking, indeed, that so many of these very able children are doing so little in the way of achievement.   As usual, they are doing better in reading than in other subjects, which again emphasizes that reading is more closely dependent upon intelligence than the other school subjects. It would appear to be a severe indictment of our present set up in the elementary school that less than half of these exceedingly able students, if we are to trust our measure of intelligence and achievement, are obtaining achievement scores which fall in the top decile and it is an even more severe indictment that so many of them are so low in achievement that they earn scores which fall in the lowest five deciles.   The comparisons shown in Table 2 indicate that the highest group, those with *IQ*'s of 145 or more, are achieving very little more than those with quotients from 125–144, in spite of their superior ability.   It is evident from Table 2 that as large a percentage, except for reading, of the latter group obtain scores falling within the two highest deciles as there are of the former group.

The latter part of this study has stressed the maladjustments of the very superior group.   Too much emphasis can be placed on this aspect of the study and there is a danger that the reader will conclude that these children represent a badly adjusted group.   The writer believes, after a careful study of all cases, that the only conclusion which can be arrived at is that, as a group, they are by no means as badly adjusted as some previous studies might lead us to believe.   Many, in fact the majority, have made excellent adjustments.   The data at hand indicate, we believe, that the majority are very normal children making normal adjustments and there is no evidence here that abnormality or queerness is the typical characteristic.   There is maladjustment to be sure, but it does appear to be evident that their very superior ability has enabled them to adjust, in the majority of cases, to an educational system which we know neglects them.   When maladjustment is present, especially in the very superior group, it indicates great social waste, and there is maladjustment.   This maladjustment appears to be slightly more prevalent in the very superior group as might well be anticipated.   All of this calls for a readjustment of our elementary educational program in order to serve more adequately the most promising material which comes to our schools.

22. Guidance of the Gifted*

Related selections: 17, 21

THE PRECEDING article by Lewis with its accompanying headnote should be read before this selection.

DO COUNSELORS have any special responsibility for the gifted?

Certainly counselors are very much concerned with the conservation of human resources, and recognize that neglect of the gifted represents an inestimable waste. At present an unknown number of gifted children, especially in the lower socio-economic groups, are falling far below their potentialities. Some drop out of school, not because of academic failure, but for social, economic, cultural, and other reasons. Counselors can help teachers to identify gifted individuals, to provide the educational experiences they need, and to help them choose and prepare for appropriate and socially useful vocations.

WHO ARE THE GIFTED?

They are children who are blessed with a fortunate combination of heredity and childhood experience. In general, they talk fluently, read fluently, and think clearly. Some may be especially talented mechanically or in art, music, dramatics, or the dance. Some are exceptionally gifted socially. In any of these lines their performance may be expected to be consistently superior. However, they need guidance to maintain this high standard.

HOW ARE THE GIFTED IDENTIFIED?

Too frequently teachers confuse conformity with intelligence. They may be unfavorably influenced by unconventional speech, manners, and appearance. These superficial judgments may affect a child's marks, or even lead to his leaving school.

The verbally gifted are identified fairly well by tests of intelligence and achievement. The best standardized tests are of value in predicting the

* Ruth Strang, "Guidance of the Gifted," *Personnel and Guidance Journal*, vol. XXXI (October, 1952), pp. 26–30. Reprinted by permission of the author and publisher.

Dr. Strang (1895—) Professor of Education at Teachers College, Columbia University, is the author of many educational books for children and adults. She has contributed greatly to the guidance movement in the United States and currently is editor of the National Association of Deans of Women Journal.

kind of education a child needs and the kind in which he is likely to succeed.

However, tests cannot be relied upon to detect all the gifted children; other clues must be obtained from observation and cumulative records. Present standardized tests are particularly weak in detecting critical and creative abilities. In interpreting test results, counselors should recognize that these may be influenced by extremes of environmental stimulation, the child's experience in taking objective-type tests, preliminary coaching (in some instances), inexcusable errors in administration and scoring, and emotional blocks or other factors which may cause fluctuations in the scores.

Many evidences of intelligence may be observed in daily contact with the child—for example, the vocabulary which he picks up naturally. Here, too, it is important to consider environmental conditions such as the child's opportunity to listen to and participate in conversation above the moron level. Other indications of mental ability are creativeness, quickness to see relations, intellectual curiosity, and enjoyment of reading. Teachers should observe such evidences of mental alertness.

The verbal intelligence tests do not always identify children with special talents. In the School of Performing Arts, New York City, a minimum intelligence was found to be necessary for superior achievement, but there was not a close correspondence between IQ and talent in art, drama, music, and the dance. The best method is to submit a sample of the child's work to an expert in the field and obtain his judgment of the child's talent.

Observation of socially gifted behavior can be made from preschool on. By observing the same child over a period of time, it will be possible to see whether his performance is consistently superior in this respect. There is need for longitudinal studies of children who early show unusual social sensitivity.

Early identification is important in order to help the child gain a sense of responsibility for his gifts, and to provide experiences which will bring them to fruition as part of his normal development. Though personality patterns develop at an early age, they may be modified if the environmental conditions are changed early enough in life. This is especially true of social behavior.

At Long Beach, California, Virginia Bailard has reported that the counselors are systematically studying the cumulative records of all the pupils, noting ratings on intelligence and achievement, and other clues of giftedness. They also ask teachers to list the gifted pupils in their classes. For each pupil thus identified, the counselors have prepared a special data sheet to be filled out and put in the child's cumulative record. The counselors are attempting to interview each of these pupils and their parents, and to confer with their teachers about ways of enriching their educational program. This plan represents real progress in the identification and guidance of gifted children and adolescents in a school system.

SPECIAL PROBLEMS OF GIFTED CHILDREN

Some years ago Leta S. Hollingworth interviewed some gifted children about their problems. One said, "The librarian is my problem. I wanted a certain book on electricity, and the librarian said, 'That's a book for adults, and you are a juvenile.'" Fortunately, such a situation is now rarely, if ever, met; librarians are keenly interested in the reading development of each individual. Another boy implied that teachers were his problems. Quite a few gifted children have complained that other children seemed unfriendly toward them; the gifted child feels rejected by less able pupils. Gifted children also mention as problems being held back by the rest of the class, being bored by the books and instruction offered them, and not getting the courses they want.

A fairly large number of gifted children and adolescents need guidance in the following problem areas:

Working up to capacity. Dr. Terman has said that too many gifted children "languish in idleness." In every school you will find students of high intelligence failing in one or more subjects; in many more instances you will find them barely "getting by" with passing grades. It is the counselor's job to identify these pupils and help them to think through the reasons for this discrepancy between ability and achievement. This is part of the developmental guidance that helps each individual understand himself and gain a sense of social responsibility for his gifts.

A smaller number of gifted children need guidance to avoid excessive emphasis on intellectual pursuits. Sometimes an exclusive interest in books and academic subjects is fostered by parents and teachers who have a high regard for that kind of achievement. This concentration on one field of interest is a problem only when the child uses it as an escape from other important adolescent tasks. A counselor can often suggest that the student add to his program another subject such as art, music, shopwork, handicraft, or typing. These subjects give the student creative outlets and certain skills that will be useful to him; they make a better balanced program, which he can easily carry. Extraclass activities serve a similar purpose and also provide valuable social experience.

Although the majority of verbally gifted children also make a good social adjustment, some definitely need help with social relations. A

senior with an IQ of 150 poignantly expressed her dissatisfaction with
her social adjustment:

When I entered high school (after a year spent with an invalid sister) I
found that I no longer knew how to get along with my contemporaries.   Trying to convince myself it didn't matter, I threw myself into my studies and
outside reading.   Unfortunately studies aren't a very good substitute for
friends, and I was extremely unhappy and lonely during my first three
years in high school.   Whenever I was particularly hurt or miserable, I
retired to my books—to forget.   This, as anyone can see, was not wise as it
made me even more out of place and self-conscious. If anyone was ever
heading directly for a nervous breakdown, it was I.
At the beginning of my senior year, I acquired a new teacher, who tried
to give me confidence in myself.   To a large extent, she succeeded, although
there is a great deal more to do.   I can at the moment carry on a conversation
without wishing to be on the other side of the world.   As yet I find it much
easier to get along with older people than with my own age group.
I think a great deal of suffering could have been avoided if someone had
taken some interest in me earlier, if someone had tried to bring me out of myself.   If someone had, I don't think I would have cried myself to sleep so
many nights during my first three years of high school.   If there had been
someone to help at the beginning, I don't think it would have been as hard as
it is now for me to get along with people.

Because of their wide interests, gifted children sometimes have difficulty
in choosing a vocation.   One boy described his varied vocational interests as follows:

At about the age of five, medicine appealed to me as a career and for
several years I persisted in this choice.   As the years passed, I wasn't so sure,
but I gave it little thought as the future seemed so far away.   In high
school I have discovered that I derive pleasure from writing.   I can say,
with no intention to brag or with conceit, that I have done fairly well in it.
Then again I have always been interested in science, especially chemistry.   In
my daydreams, I have seen myself a world-famous novelist or a great chemist
working unselfishly for humanity.   Although I have made no definite plans, I
now feel that I've had some experience on which to make a sound choice.

Conflict between the parent's ambition for the child and the child's own
vocational interest sometimes has profound emotional reverberations, as
in the following instance:

I feel sick and miserable when I think of the future.   My mother wants me
to teach.   She thinks teaching is a respectable and needed occupation, and she
tries to drive me into it.   I don't want a restricted life.   I want to be a musi-
cian.   But I'm scared to tell her.   She always seems to laugh when I'm

serious. I hate the sound of her laugh and almost hate her for trying to force her plans upon me. I don't want to hate her because she's really good and I love her, honestly. When I play my beloved piano, time passes unheeded. While I am playing, there is only one future for me: music.

Gifted children who come from subcultural and low socio-economic groups have special problems in realizing their potentialities. Their families and neighbors are often unsympathetic to their aspirations so they may have difficulty in financing the kind of education they should have, and in getting into the vocations for which they have prepared. Pritchard reported the case of a highly gifted Negro boy "who exhibited unusual inventiveness of thought as well as high creative and leadership ability"— the latter, indicated by his election to the presidency of the student government association of a specialized metropolitan high school. In both elementary and high school he made a good adjustment and was awarded a scholarship to a large metropolitan university. Here his gifts for leadership were not recognized by the college authorities. So he became a leader of an unorganized group—one of the so-called youth movements. He was sent by them to Czechoslovakia as a student representative. "When he returned he became more and more entangled with subversive movements and his activity in them finally brought him into serious difficulty. Although he was subsidized to the extent of a good education," his attitudes closed the doors of opportunity to him. "He reports vocational dissatisfaction and low personal life satisfaction—is cynical and bitter." With effective guidance he might have fulfilled his potentialities for personal happiness and social usefulness.

Among any gifted group there will be a few in need of intensive counseling and psychotherapy. Bettelheim described one of these complex emotional problems, apparently originating in emotional deprivation of the home. This case required intensive treatment in which unconscious motivations were brought to the surface so that the student could handle them rationally.

COUNSELORS' RESPONSIBILITIES

In addition to identifying the gifted and recognizing their problems, counselors can help administrators and teachers provide the experiences these pupils need, counsel individuals, and help parents to understand their gifted children.

Helping teachers create a favorable environment. Together, teachers and counselors will think of many ways in which they can provide worth-while and challenging activities for the gifted children in their heterogeneous classes. The following are some of the experiences which teachers have offered successfully:

Divide class into subgroups doing work suited to them, often on class projects to which each member contributes according to his ability.

Give homework that is creative and requires organization, and is not just boring "busy work."

Give many opportunities for discussion, giving talks, shouldering responsibility.

Give instruction and practice in effective study and reading methods, if students need it.

Provide creative activities and experiences in art and music.

Provide cooperative school work projects in science and other fields that will help gifted children finance their education as well as give them valuable vocational tryout experiences.

Give gifted young people opportunities to work with adults in the identification and solution of local problems.

Through individualized instruction and social experiences, gifted children will develop their capacities and learn to respect and accept people who are different from themselves.

Counseling individuals. The counselor has much responsibility for the educational and vocational guidance of gifted children. The decision as to whether to accelerate a gifted child should be made on an individual basis, with consideration of the child's physical and social as well as intellectual maturity. In general, some acceleration plus enrichment is a good policy. With respect to segregation, apparently the soundest practice is to keep the child in the heterogeneous group part of the day and give him opportunities to work in special groups with other gifted children the rest of the time. Each gifted child should have a program that enables him to develop his special abilities, but also includes subjects that will enrich his life as a whole.

Gifted children are frequently confused by a wide range of vocational possibilities. They need to learn how to narrow their choice on the basis of their capacities and interests, the need for workers in a particular vocation, and the opportunities which it offers. Having made a sound choice, they need help in preparing to enter the field. If their educational program, grade by grade, has helped them to develop their potentialities, they will be ready to make a vocational choice when the time comes to specialize.

As to counseling method, it would seem that the non-directive or client-centered approach would be particularly appropriate to gifted children. They have rich resources within themselves for gaining insights and solving their own problems. The large majority of them seem to do this without much help.   They might do it better with a little skillful guidance.   Perhaps they have a tendency to try to solve their problems on an intellectual level, neglecting the emotional aspects.   Intellectual understanding is often a step in the solution of an emotional problem; it may give one confidence in his ability to handle it emotionally.   With both children and parents, however, the counselor should not assume the problem is solved as soon as it is understood.

The school counselor also has the responsibility of referring seriously disturbed students to special guidance agencies.   At present a large number of children with IQ's over 130 are referred to child guidance bureaus; many of them are in difficulties because the schools are not making adequate provision for them.   For example, one boy was giving his teachers and parents a rough time.   The father, who was highly intelligent, was sure the boy was dull.   The teacher could not evoke the boy's interest in making any school progress.   When he was referred to the child guidance bureau, it was discovered that he had an IQ of 145.   Knowing this, his parents and teachers began to look at him in a different light, and he responded to their changed attitude toward him.

Guidance of the parents of gifted children is also needed to guard against two common extremes of behavior: (1) exploiting the child—valuing him more for what he can do than for his personal qualities; and (2) restricting the child's intellectual interests, with the mistaken idea that developing a gift or talent will handicap the child socially.   In conferences with parents and in programs of parent education, counselors can help parents understand their gifted children and provide the experiences they need.

The counselor can also see that creative and social activities as well as excellent library facilities and opportunities for discussion are available to gifted children, and help them take advantage of these opportunities.

The role of counselors in the guidance of the gifted is not radically different from their responsibility for the guidance of other individuals.   If, however, counselors help to identify the gifted and talented at an early age, and are aware of their special needs, they will, as Terman and Oden said, help "to bring the highest intellectual gifts to normal fruition and . . . to steer them clear of the dangers that threaten personality development."   This is of great social importance.

C. EMOTIONAL AND SOCIAL DEVELOPMENT

23. *Emotional Development in Early Infancy**

Related selections: 15, 26, 30, 46

INEXTRICABLY interwoven with all problems of personality and adjustment are problems of emotional development. In fact, the problems of one are essentially the problems of the other. All human adjustments and behaviors are permeated in varying degrees by feelings and emotions. How do we get our feelings and emotions, our affective processes? Are they present in any degree at birth? If not, what is their genesis and how do they develop? Dr. Bridges draws her conclusions from findings of one of the early studies of emotional development.

THE EMOTIONAL behavior of 62 infants in the Montreal Foundling and Baby Hospital was carefully observed and recorded daily over a period of three or four months. The circumstances attendant upon these reactions were noted, and the whole data was studied from the point of view of development from age to age. A summary of the findings will be presented in the following paragraphs. They will be seen to lend support to the writer's theory of the genesis of the emotions and to add further illuminating detail.

The babies under observation were in separate wards more or less according to age. In different rooms were infants under one month, one to three months, three to six months, six to nine months, nine to twelve months, and twelve to fifteen months. An older group of children between fifteen and twenty-four months of age played together in the nursery. The table below shows the number of children at the different ages whose behavior was observed for this study.

---

* Katherine M. Banham Bridges, "Emotional Development in Early Infancy," *Child Development*, vol. III (December, 1932), pp. 324–341. Reprinted by permission of author and publisher.
     Dr. Bridges (1897—) is an Associate Professor in the Department of Psychology, Duke University. Her research in emotional development was some of the pioneer work in this field. She is a Diplomate in clinical psychology.

Age in Months	Number of Children
Under 1	3
1–3	16
3–6	23
6–9	18
9–12	11
12–15	20
15–18	8
18–21	5
21–24	6
Over 24	2

Development in the emotional behavior of the young child comprises three main classes of change.   From birth onward there is a gradual evolution of the emotions taking place.   The earliest emotional reactions are very general and poorly organized responses to one or two general types of situation.   As weeks and months go by the responses take on more definite form in relation to more specific situations.   It seems to the writer, as already mentioned elsewhere, that in the course of genesis of the emotions there occurs a process of differentiation.   Coincident with the partial isolation of certain responses is a combining of the simpler reactions within the unit responses and the formation of bonds of association between these emotional syndromes and detailed aspects of the provoking situations.   In this manner slowly appear the well known emotions of anger, disgust, joy, love, and so forth.   They are not present at birth in their mature form.

In addition to the progressive evolution of the emotions, there is, going on at the same time, a gradual change in the mode of response of each specific emotion.   Muscles are developing, new skills are being learned. So that the anger, for instance, expressed by the eighteen-month-old differs in detail of form from the anger manifested by the ten-month-old baby.   Fresh bonds of association are being made between emotional behavior and the always slightly varying attendant circumstances.   Different situations come to have emotional significance for the growing child and subsequently provoke emotional responses.   Thus a gradual substitution takes place of the situations which prompt the emotions.   In the language of the behaviorists, emotional responses become conditioned to fresh stimuli.

EXCITEMENT, THE ORIGINAL EMOTION

After observing the behavior of babies *under one month* of age, the writer felt more than ever convinced that the infant does not start life with three fully matured pattern reactions, such as have been mentioned by behaviorists and named fear, rage and love.   Unfortunately the writer was not able to observe the infants within a few hours of birth, but this fact in no way invalidates observations made on children two or three weeks old. Moreover, if the above named emotional responses are really the three great primary emotions from which all our adult emotions are derived, surely they may still be observed a month or more after birth. And, even if the process of conditioning begins before or immediately upon birth, one may expect the original emotion-producing stimuli to elicit their natural responses at least for two or three weeks after birth.

It was observed in the hospital that, on presentation of certain strong stimuli the infants became agitated, their arm and hand muscles tensed, their breath quickened, and their legs made jerky kicking movements. Their eyes opened, the upper lid arched, and they gazed into the distance. The stimuli producing such agitation or excitement were: bright sun directly in the infant's eyes, sudden picking up and putting down on the bed, pulling the child's arm through his dress sleeve, holding the arms tight to the sides, rapping the baby's knuckles, pressing the bottle nipple into the child's mouth, and the noisy clatter of a small tin basin thrown on to a metal table whence it fell to the radiator and the floor.

The loud sound startled only four of the one- and two-months-old babies, while six others lay practically undisturbed.   None of the infants cried after hearing the noise.   The same experiment was tried upon children of successive ages up to fifteen months.   Under two or three months the reaction was one of sudden but rather mild general excitement as described above.   Children of three or four months and older gave more of a jump and looked definitely in the direction of the sound.   Afterwards they remained still with eyes and mouth open, and started towards the source of the commotion.   One baby of eight months stiffened and turned away on the second trial.   The corners of his mouth turned down, his eyes moistened and he looked to the adult for sympathy and comfort.   Another child of eleven months sat wide-eyed and still, the corners of his mouth drooping as if he were ready to burst into tears.   The older children merely stood, or sat, alert and attentive without further sign of distress.

Lowering the babies suddenly into their cribs, and in some cases lifting them quickly, also startled and excited them.   Sometimes they would cry following upon such a surprise.   Rocking a quiet child would cause him to open his eyes attentively.   But gently rocking a crying infant would often, though not always, cause him to reduce his activity, stop crying, and eventually become tranquil.   Gentle handling, slow patting, wrapping in warm blankets, and nursing easily soothed an agitated or crying infant, making him relax and yawn and become sleepy.

Light pinching of the arm left the three- or four-week-old baby unmoved. Deeper pressure caused him to kick slightly, breathe faster and move his arms. A sharp flick on the hand produced similar agitation, but a second rap resulted in a sudden check to breathing followed by a prolonged cry and other signs of distress. The first exciting experience had been found disagreeable and the second rap produced unmistakable distress.

Time after time on waking suddenly from sleep the infants were observed to wave their arms jerkily, kick, open and close their eyes, flush slightly, and breathe quickly and irregularly. Some grunted, some cried spasmodically for a moment or two, while others cried loudly for several minutes. The combined stimulation of light, of sounds, of damp or restricting bed clothes, and the change from sleeping to waking breathing-rate seemed to produce a temporary agitation and often distress. Waking apparently requires emotional adjustment.

The hungry child before feeding would often show restless activity, waving, squirming, mouthing and crying at intervals. The infant who had been lying in one position for a long time and the tired child before falling asleep would also show emotional agitation. Their breath would come jerkily, uttering staccato cries of "cu-cu-cu-ah," and they would thrust out their arms and legs in irregular movements. At the moment the nipple was put into the hungry baby's mouth he again breathed quickly, occasionally cried, waved the free arm, and kicked in excited agitation.

The emotional reactions of the tiny infant are certainly not highly differentiated. The most common response to highly stimulating situations seems to be one of general agitation or excitement. It is a question which word most aptly describes the behavior. The former perhaps conveys more the idea of general disturbance, although the two words are often used synonymously. This vague emotional response to a large variety of circumstances must surely be one of the original emotions, if not the only one.

A kind of general excitement over new and startling or other highly stimulating circumstances may be seen at any age. The behavior manifestations vary from time to time, but the main characteristics of accelerated response, alertness, slight tension or restlessness remain as constant attributes. In the babies, excitement is frequently manifested in kicking movements. The month-old infants kick jerkily with both feet at random. In another month or so, the kicking becomes more regular, the legs being thrust out alternately. By five or six months the babies express their emotions in combined leg thrusts, kicking with one foot, and in swinging the legs from the hips. At fourteen months when the children can stand they will hold on to a support and "mark time" with their feet or stamp. Stamping, jumping and running express excited agitation at a still later age.

Two- and three-month-old babies may be seen to suck their thumbs or fingers rapidly in moments of stress. At seven months and over, children bite, pull and suck their garments, as well as their fingers. This behavior seems to produce a gradual subsidence of the emotion. Body-rocking accompanied in many instances by rhythmic vocalizations is another expression of mixed emotion. Hungry, annoyed, excited or restless children will sit and rock for minutes on end. The five-month-old baby lies prone and pushes with his knees, or sways when lying dorsally. Seven-month-old infants support themselves on their arms and rock back and forth murmuring "m̅m̅-ŭm, m̅m̅-ŭm." After nine months they sit up and rock to and fro, or they kneel and bounce up and down holding on to the crib bars. Sometimes they sit and bump their backs against the side of the crib. This kind of behavior was observed in the nursery up to eighteen months of age.

Rhythmical movements were observed not only to be the outcome of emotional excitement or tension, but they were seen to have a soothing and pacifying effect. These must be attempts at adjustment on the part of the organism to reduce tension and restore emotional equilibrium or tranquility. In the light of these observations, it can be easily understood how long walks, games, field sports, singing, dancing, and sea-voyages are found to be so universally health-giving and positively curative for "nervous wrecks."

DISTRESS AND ITS DERIVATIVES

It is a moot question whether "distress" is an original emotion or whether it is a very early differentiated reaction to disagreeably painful and unsatisfying experiences. It may be that it is a part of the general emotional response of excitement which copes more satisfactorily with obnoxious stimuli. Tense muscles resist or remove pressure; activity warms a chilled body and reduces tension; and cries, at first reflex due to the rush of air in and out of the lungs, bring comfort and aid. These responses become differentiated from excitement, associated together and conditioned to the disagreeable stimuli as a result of experience. If such differentiation actually takes place, it must begin immediately after birth. For the two emotions of excitement and distress are already distinguishable in a three-weeks-old infant.

On the other hand, it is possible that there is a native emotional response to pain, particularly muscle pain. The sympathetic branch of the autonomic nervous system is predominantly active and the overt behavior is definitely that of distress. Other stimuli, such as loud sounds and sudden falling merely produce startled excitement. Blanton observed that the infant's cry of colic had a specially shrill character accompanied by rigidity of the abdominal walls. She also noted that infants during the first days of life cried from "(1) hunger; (2) in response to noxious stimuli (including rough handling, circumcision, lancing and care of boils, sores, etc.); and (3) possibly fatigue or lack of exercise." The writer has observed the same phenomena in three-weeks-old babies. But, hunger, rough handling, and fatigue were also noticed on many occasions to produce a restless excitement rather than specific distress.

It is not easy, in the case of the very young infant to distinguish distress from general agitation. Perhaps the most characteristic marks of the former are greater muscle tension, interference with movement and with breathing, closing of the eyes, and loud rather high-pitched crying. In children of two months and over, the eyes become moist and tears may flow. The crying of the infant *under a month* or even six weeks often seems to be part of the general activity in excitement. Breath comes more or less regularly, the cry emerging on both intake and expiration of air. There are no tears, and the skin does not flush. Movement is free though rather jerky; and the mouth is held open in an elliptic, round, or square shape.

The cry of distress, recognizable in the *month-old* baby, is irregular. There are short intakes of breath and long cries on expiration. The eyes are "screwed up" tight, the face flushed, the fists often clenched, the arms tense, and the legs still or kicking spasmodically. The mouth is open and square in shape or, more usually kidney-shaped with the corners pulled down. The pitch of the cry is high and somewhat discordant, and sounds something like "ah, cu-ah, cu-ah, cu-æh."

Cries of distress were heard from month-old babies in the hospital on the following occasions; on waking suddenly from sleep, struggling to breathe through nostrils blocked with mucous, when the ears were discharging, when lying awake before feeding time, after staying long in the same position, lying on a wet diaper, when the child's buttocks were chafed, and when the fingers were rapped. The three main causes of distress at this age, therefore, seemed to be discomfort, pain, and hunger.

Crying from discomfort and on awakening usually developed slowly, and sounded like "cu-cu-cu-cah-ah—." The cry of pain came suddenly, often after a holding of the breath. The sound was a loud shrill prolonged "ă-ă-ă," and lowered in pitch slightly from the first emission. The cries of hunger were rather like those of discomfort. The former came perhaps more in intermittent waves; the intervening moments being taken up with mouthing or suckling movements. Occasionally the hungry child would utter a sharp loud cry, as if in pain, and then whine or moan for a time.

Two-month-old babies cry less of the total waking time; but slighter discomforting stimuli seem to cause distress more frequently than in the case of the younger infants. They are more disturbed by a wet diaper, by flatulence, and by tight clothing which restricts movement and makes breathing difficult. Their movements are freer and they tend to move their heads from side to side when they are distressed. While one-month-old babies kick irregularly with jerky movements, the two-month-old kicks his legs alternately and more regularly. He waves his arms up and down when agitated or distressed, as well as in spontaneous play. The sound or sight of an approaching person will not quiet his distress; but being picked up will do so, or being fed if he is hungry.

By *three months* of age a child will cry and show other signs of distress when placed in an unusual position or moved to a strange place; as, for instance, when lain temporarily at the foot of another child's bed. He will wave his arms laterally as well as up and down, and will kick more vigorously. The hospital baby has learned to associate feeding time with the presence of an adult; for, when he is hungry he shows some excitement at the close approach of a person. He stares at the person's face, waves, kicks, breathes faster, and opens his mouth. If no food is forthcoming, he becomes more tense and jerky in his movements and begins to cry. He is distressed at the delay in normal proceedings.

Should the adult remain tantalizingly near for some minutes without either picking up the child or feeding him, his cry increases in intensity, his eyes become moist with tears, he holds his breath longer, and utters prolonged flat "ă-ă-ă" sound reminiscent of an older child's "paddy" or temper cry. The infant's motor responses were all set for being picked up and fed, and then he was thwarted and disappointed. His excitement changed into bitter distress with a semblance of angry vexation.

The slight change in vowel sound of the cry, the long holding of breath combined with more than usually vigorous leg thrusts and arm movements, seemed to suggest that the emotion of anger is beginning to evolve from general distress at about this age. Although for the most part the distress shown at discomfort differs almost imperceptibly from distress in response to disappointment, occasionally the latter includes, to a marked degree, those behavior elements peculiar to the emotion of anger. The situations which evoke these demonstrations of temper in the tiny infant are a stop or check in the progressive satisfaction of a physical need. In the above instance the child's appetite was aroused but not satisfied. Lack of even the first sign of a need being satisfied merely produces vague distress.

A *four-month-old* baby shows distress at the same general sort of situation that troubles the younger child.   He is, however, less frequently disturbed by bodily discomfort.   He moves about sufficiently to relieve tired muscles and local pressures, and to eliminate gas from his stomach.   He cries vigorously at delay in the feeding process and may show decided temper on such occasions.   His arms then stiffen and tremble; he screws up his eyes, flushes, holds his breath and utters prolonged and irregular cries on expiration of breath; he kicks violently, pushes with his feet and looks at any adult, presumably to see the effect.   He is getting very fond of attention at this age, and will show distress and often anger when a person leaves the room or ceases to pay attention and play with him.

At *five months,* the baby's interest in small objects, such as rattles, stuffed animals and, of course, his milk bottle, causes him to be distressed when these objects are removed.   He may express his displeasure as formerly by crying, squirming, waving and kicking, but he may also be heard merely to call out in a protesting tone of voice, "ah aye," without the half-closing of the eyes and the accompanying tensions of crying.

By this age the child may show slight revulsion for certain foods, coughing, spluttering, frowning and crying while he is being fed.   Chopped vegetables and soup too thick in consistency were specially disliked by some babies in the hospital.   Cereals, milk, and sweetish foods were almost always taken readily.   It was noted that babies under three months often refused to drink sterile water.   They just let it run out of their mouths without swallowing.   There was no emotion involved in this reaction.   Similarly, three- and four-month-old babies sometimes rejected their thin vegetable soup, but were not very disturbed about it.   A genuine emotional revulsion did not appear till five months or later.   Perhaps this is the beginning of the emotion of disgust.   Revulsion at nauseating sights and smells, the adult form of disgust, apparently does not develop until two or more years of age.

Several of the babies in the hospital *between six and eighteen months* were observed to splutter and choke, and refuse to swallow spinach more than other vegetables.   The mouthfuls that were rejected were usually, though not always, those containing large or stringy pieces of spinach. When the latter was chopped fine it was swallowed a little more easily; but only when it was mixed with other vegetables was it eaten without any protest.   There must be factors other than consistency and size of morsel to account for this objection to spinach.

It seemed to the writer that some cans of spinach tasted more bitter than others and were less palatable on that account.   In order to find how the children would react to a bitter taste, two teaspoonsful each of un-sweetened grape-fruit juice were given to nine children in the nursery. Four of them pursed or curled their lips, one turned his head away, and one frowned.   The others sat still and solemn, and kept tasting their lips attentively for some time.   There were certainly individually different re-actions to this bitter-sour, astringent taste.   Several of the children definitely disliked it and none of them seemed to like it.   It is possible then that there is a bitter taste to spinach which may in part account for children's aversion to it.   Another factor, that of the dark green colour of spinach may influence older children's and adult's feeling reaction towards it.   One two-year-old in the hospital on turning away and refusing to eat the vegetable was seen to point to it and say "dirty."

The *six-month-old* baby's attention is usually arrested by the presence of a stranger.   His movements are inhibited and he watches the new-comer intently.   He is not pleased and one could hardly say he is afraid. But he seems diffident and uncertain what to do, or utterly unable to move for a few moments.   At seven months he reacts in the same way to the approach of a stranger, though the general inhibition of movement is greater and lasts longer.   After a few moments or several seconds of ten-sion he may begin to cry slowly, or burst suddenly into tears.   The whole body is usually rigid and inactive.   The eyes, previously wide open, close tight and the head bends.   Should the stranger touch the child he will probably turn or draw away.   Here is the emotion of fear already dif-ferentiated.   Frightened distress results when the child through inhibi-tion, ignorance, or inability finds himself unable to respond at all ade-quately to the situation.

At *seven months* of age an infant calls out protestingly when a familiar person ceases to attend to him, instead of crying distressfully like a four-month-old.   He still cries and kicks angrily if some object in which he was deeply engrossed is taken from him.   He does so also after being highly excited by a playful adult when the latter goes away or stops play-ing with him.   He now makes prolonged attempts to get at objects out of reach.   If he fails to attain his objective he may give up and cry in helpless distress, or he may just grunt in protestation.

A *nine-month-old* child will struggle longer and make more varied at-tempts to reach the object of his desire.   Should he fail to do so after putting forth considerable effort he may become tense and red in the face with anger.   He will kick and scream and look for assistance, while tears flow copiously.   The cry at this age is becoming exceedingly loud, and tears flow more readily than at the earlier ages.   Prolonged crying at four or five months is accompanied by slight lacrimal secretion, but after six months of age tears often flow down the child's cheeks as he cries, especially after an adult's attention has been attracted.

Strangers are still quite terrifying to the nine-month-old baby. His movements are more completely arrested by the unfamiliar presence than those of the six-month-old. He will remain immovable for several minutes unless the newcomer approaches very close to him. In that case he will lie face down or bend his head and probably begin to cry. At ten months of age he may even be so frightened as to flop down suddenly on the bed and scream loudly. Then follows prolonged and tearful crying.

When children of *ten months* and over are hungry, uncomfortable, tired, or fretful and unwell, they will set up a whine or cry as the result of suggestion when another child cries. They do not, however, ordinarily imitate crying when they are occupied and happy. Under these circumstances they may call or babble in a pitch similar to that of the other child's cry. Small objects which can be manipulated interest them so intensely that they can be distracted from a distressing trouble fairly easily at this age. These objects need not necessarily be new so long as they are freshly presented.

Year-old babies often cry suddenly when they feel themselves falling, or when they lose their grip while climbing. If they miss the assistance of a helping hand they will also sit down and cry loudly. Sometimes their emotion is anger at the thwarting or failure of their endeavors. They scream, flush, and tremble in rage. At other times they sit motionless in fright and look for aid or comforting sympathy. When strangers approach the *twelve-or thirteen-month-old* baby he may hold his hand behind his ear in a withdrawing motion and stare apprehensively. He may actually hide his eyes behind his hands or look away so as not to see the awe-inspiring or annoying intruder.

At *fourteen months* or thereabouts we may see the real temper tantrum. At least, that is the age when it became noticeable in the hospital. If a child is not given his food or a coveted toy exactly when he wants it he may respond by throwing himself suddenly on the bed or floor. He then screams, holds his breath, trembles, turns red, kicks or thrusts his feet out together. Tears flow and he will wave away anything that is not the desired object. These outbursts may occur frequently for a few weeks, or only spasmodically for another year or eighteen months. The children under observation seemed to have their "off-days" when they were fretful and easily distressed or roused to anger. Such days were usually when they were incubating or recovering from colds, when the hospital routine was disturbed, or after the children had been excited by parents' visits.

Distressful crying becomes less common as the months go by. Extreme hunger and weariness after a long day or great activity may be accompanied by whining and intermittent outbursts of tears. Anger is expressed more in protesting shouts, pushing and kicking, but less in tearful screaming. So long as adults are present, however, the interference and rough handling of another child may bring forth cries and tears. A *fifteen-month-old* may show his annoyance by hitting a child who has taken his toy or who is holding on to the thing he most wants. He may even bite him or pull his hair without a preliminary scream or shout.

The attention of familiar and interested adults is much sought by children of *fifteen to eighteen months*. If such attention is given to another child there may be signs of deep distress. The neglected one may stiffen, stand motionless, bend his head and burst into tears. Here is perhaps the beginning of jealousy, distress at the loss of, or failure to receive, expected attention and affection. Some children will show aggressive annoyance when another receives the attention they covet. They do this usually by hitting the envied child.

A *twenty-one-month-old* child will show less mistrust of strangers than will a younger infant. He may, however, run away and watch the newcomer for a time at a safe distance. After eighteen months he shows anger at adult interference by obstinate refusal to comply with their requests. He may shake his head and refuse either to be fed or to feed himself. At two he will play with his food, throwing it about instead of eating it, as a spite against some offending or scolding adult. Distress is shown chiefly at pain and acute discomfort, though the child will cry miserably at much less discomfort if a sympathetic adult is close at hand.

The children in the nursery group, *between fifteen and twenty-four months,* were more or less unconcerned when being undressed for the annual physical examination. This part of the procedure was familiar and not unpleasant. Several of the children cried and stiffened somewhat when placed on the table in the examining room. One or two continued to show distress throughout the examination. Others smiled cheerily at the attendant nurse or the doctor, until they felt sudden and unexpected local pressure. All of the children cried at some time during the procedure. The most distressing events were when a flashlight was thrown into the eyes, and when the throat and ears were examined with the aid of the usual tongue-depressor and otoscope. The children had to be held firmly and their movements curbed during these operations.

It was patent to the observer that the children were undergoing rather different emotions according to their fast-developing individual idiosyncracies. Some were mainly startled and afraid, their movements were paralyzed. Some seemed to be just generally distressed at the unusual proceeding and the discomfort; while others were chiefly annoyed at the interference with their freedom. Several children showed signs of all three emotions.   These individual differences probably have their foundation in variants in the physical constitutions of the children, both hereditary and acquired.   They are certainly very much determined by the particular experiences the infants have gone through since their birth. A continuous study of behavior week by week reveals the actual differentiation and consolidation of individual traits of temperament.

Two or three of the nursery children over fourteen months developed fears for specific objects or persons.   Toy animals that squeaked frightened one or two, causing them to draw away, stare wide-eyed and perhaps cry.   This squeak could hardly be called a "loud low sound" such as Watson describes as one of the original fear-producing stimuli.   The sound is, however, rather unusual and comes at first as a surprise to the babies.   One child was afraid of a particular aggressive little boy.   No doubt he had gone up and hit her unexpectedly some time when the nurses were not watching.   One youngster showed fear of a dark grey dog with a rough fur, rather different from the soft teddy-bears and other stuffed animals in the nursery.

Parents often remark how their children may suddenly show fear of some surprisingly trivial and inoffensive object.   The answer to this may be found in certain partial associations with disturbing events of the past. It may also be found in the particular mental set of the child's mind and body when he came in contact with the object.   He may have become suddenly aware of its presence and perceived it as an unwelcome intruder upon an entirely different line of thought or action.   Still another phenomenon may account for the peculiar fears and objections of children. Timid behavior may be actually learned and preserved as a social asset, one of the numerous means of drawing attention.

The nursery child who cried and crawled away after touching the rough-haired, stuffed animal was flattered with the attention of all the adults in the room.   A nurse brought the dog up to the child, smiling and saying "nice doggie."   He looked up at her face, saw her kindly smile, then bent his head and began to whimper again.   Another nurse laughed appreciatively as he put his hand to his eye, and tried to coax him with a toy cat.   He turned away quickly, cried out again, then looked up to see the effect on the adults.   He was having a delightful time out of his apparent fear.

DELIGHT AND ITS DERIVATIVES

Delight is much later in becoming differentiated from general excitement than distress.   The baby under a month old is either excited or quiescent. Gentle stroking, swaying and patting soothe him and make him sleepy.

When satisfied after a meal he is no longer excited nor even distressed by hunger. And yet he is not positively delighted. He is just unemotionally content, and either tranquil or busy mouthing and staring at distant objects. When he is *over two weeks old* he will sometimes give a faint reflex smile upon light tapping at the corners of his mouth. This is hardly an emotional response.

One- and two-month-old babies cry and kick from hunger before they are fed, rather than show delight on presentation of the much desired food. They become calm, however, immediately when given their milk, but not at the mere approach of the adult who brings it. At two months infants will give fleeting smiles upon being nursed, patted, wrapped warmly, spoken to, tickled, or gently rocked. Perhaps this is the beginning of the emotion of delight.

By *three months* of age the emotion of delight is becoming more clearly differentiated from agitated excitement on the one hand and non-emotional quiescence or passivity on the other. The child kicks, opens his mouth, breathes faster, and tries to raise his head upon sight of his bottle. He gives little crooning sounds when being fed, nursed or rocked. He smiles when an adult comes near and talks to him; and he will even stop crying momentarily at the sound of a person's voice. He may also show delight in distant moving objects. One baby in the hospital, for instance, lay and watched the moving leaves of the creeper on the window for a minute or two at a time. Her eyes were wide and her mouth rounded and open. At times she would breathe fast, or inspire deeply, and utter murmurings of "uh-uh-uh." Her arms would wave up and down and her legs kick alternately.

The chief characteristics of delight are: free as against restrained movement; open eyes and expansion of the face in a smile as contrasted with the puckering of the forehead and closing of the eyes in distress; body movements or muscle tension of incipient approach rather than withdrawal; audible inspirations and quickened breathing; soft, lower pitched vocalizations than those of distress or excitement; more or less rhythmic arm and leg movements; prolonged attention to the object of interest; and cessation of crying. Although behavior varies in detail from child to child at successive ages, delight is always recognizable from certain general types of response. Free and rhythmic movements, welcoming and approaching gestures, smiles and vocalizations of middle pitch are most common features.

A *four-month-old* baby laughs aloud when some person smiles and frolics with him. He smiles in response to another's smile and even when anyone approaches his crib, whether they be strangers or not. He spreads out his arms, lifts his chin, and tries to raise his body in approach to the

attentive person.   He takes active delight in his bath, kicking and splash-
ing the water.   Food, though sometimes welcomed eagerly, is often neglected for the more interesting attendant who talks and smiles at him.

At *five months* a child vocalizes his delight in sounds of "uh-uh-ung" in
addition to waving, laughing, kicking and wriggling around.   He shows
special interest in small objects that he can handle and explore.   Musical
or noisy rattles are popular at this age.   When hungry he kicks, breathes
fast, and calls out eagerly at the first sign of the person who brings his
food.   His smiles are more transient, however, and his movements less
vigorous on approach of a stranger.

By *six months* of age a child will reach towards a familiar person but
will lie still and observe a stranger dubiously.   He crows and coos frequently, taking pleasure in his own movements and sounds.   In the hospital the babies of this age would watch each other through the bars of their
cribs, sometimes laughing and kicking in response to the sight of the other's
movements.   They would swing their legs rhythmically when lying on
their backs, or sway sideways when lying prone.

A *seven-month-old* baby is becoming increasingly interested in small
objects and in the act of reaching and grasping those close at hand.   He
will even struggle to attain things somewhat out of his reach.   When his
efforts meet with success he often smiles, takes a deep breath and expresses
his satisfaction in a sort of grunt.   After a moment or two spent in examination and manipulation of the object, he goes exploring again with fresh
vigor.   Possibly this is the beginning of the emotion of elation, exhilara-
ting pleasure in personal accomplishments.   Resting periods, after the delightful satisfaction of feeding or explorative activity, are often taken up
with a rhythmical rocking back and forth, the child supporting himself
on his hands and knees.

At *eight months* of age the child seems to take more delight than ever
in self-initiated purposeful activity.   He babbles and splutters and laughs
to himself.   Especially does he seem delighted with the noise he makes by
banging spoons or other playthings on the table.   Throwing things out of
his crib is another favorite pastime.   He waves, pats, and coos, drawing
in long breaths, when familiar adults swing him or talk to him.   He will
watch the person who nurses him attentively, exploring her, patting
gently, and often smiling.   Here are perhaps the earliest demonstrations
of affection.   The child will also pat and smile at his own mirror image.
But his behavior is rather more aggressive and inquisitive than really affectionate.

A *nine-month-old* baby is very popular with adults.   He laughs frequently, bounces up and down and tries to mimic their playful actions.
He pats others babies exploratively but does not show particular affection

for them. Strange adults may frighten him at first. But, after studying them for some time in the distance, he will smile responsively and join in play with them. By *ten months* of age the child is taking more interest in other babies. He will mimic their calls and even their laughter. The hospital babies of this age would pat and bang and laugh in imitation of each other.

An *eleven-month-old* baby takes great delight in laughter, not only his own but that of another. He will laugh in order to make another child laugh, then jump and vocalize and laugh again in response. At twelve months of age he will repeat any little action that causes laughter. He is becoming increasingly affectionate. He puts his arms around the familiar adult's neck, and strokes and pats her face. Sometimes he will actually bring his lips close to her face in an incipient kissing movement. He looks eagerly for attention; and may stand holding a support and changing weight from one foot to the other in rhythmic motion, as a solace when neglected.

Between *twelve and fifteen months* a child usually learns to walk with a little help. This performance, though often accompanied by panting and tense effort, causes great delight and even elation when a few steps have been accomplished. The child calls out, smiles and waves ecstatically (i.e. rapidly or jerkily). Without further encouragement from adults, he will then set out again with renewed fervor. When attentive adults are too enthusiastic in their appreciation, the little one may become positively tense with excitement. His efforts may consequently meet with less success, and then he cries in vexatious disappointment.

There is already a noticeable difference between the responsiveness of different *fifteen-month-old* children to demonstrated affection. Some children come readily to be nursed and petted, others require a little coaxing. One or two will kiss back when kissed, while others merely cling closely to the adult caressing them. At this age the children begin to show definite affection for each other. They take hands, sit close to one another, put their arms about one another's neck or shoulders, pat and smile at each other. Eighteen-month-olds will also jabber nonsense amicably together. Again, with regard to playmates as well as adults some children are more affectionate than others.

These variations in affection no doubt have a number of causal factors. They depend upon the child's physical constitution and his condition of health at the moment. Sick children may be very clinging and affectionate with adults, or, in some instances, refractory and irritable. They may be both by turns. Whether a child is affectionate or not also depends upon the nature of his dominant interest at the moment. Affection for a grown person depends upon the child's attitude towards adults in general; and that again is largely a matter of the amount of fondling or scolding the child has received. Affection for other children is considerably determined by the agreeable or exasperating nature of chance contacts.

Between *fifteen and twenty-one months* the children find increasing enjoyment in walking and running about. They chase each other laughingly and enjoy snatching one another's toys. They come back again and again to adults to be lifted high or swung round. The nursery slide is very popular at this age. One or two of the hospital children pulled away and watched apprehensively in the distance after the first slide. A little encouragement from the nurses and the eager shouts of the other children soon overcame their fear, and they joined the sliding group again.

Gramophone music was listened to intently by almost all the nursery children. Some of them responded by swaying or nodding motions to time. The children at this age were beginning to find individual interests in things and to express their enjoyment each in their own peculiar way. Absorbed preoccupation, tight clasping, biting, and varied manipulation of the attractive object were common expressions of interest. Some children would knock one object against another in play, some would collect things, and others would find pleasure in throwing and scattering toys about. These variations in appreciative interest in things and activities may be the precursors of the more mature emotion of joy.

Most of the eighteen-month-olds in the hospital were anxious to attract attention. They called out or came running to greet an adult. They would smile and hold out their arms to a familiar nurse in expectation of being lifted. A stranger they would watch solemnly for a while. Then they would approach slowly, touch and explore her clothes, or hit and watch for the effect. The children seemed to recognize their nurses at this age, whether the latter appeared in uniform or not. Babies of seven to twelve months, however, would sometimes turn away in fear or hostility when the nurses approached them wearing outdoor clothes.

Slight preferences for certain nurses were noticed as early as six months, but definitely affectionate attachments were observed chiefly between the ages of twelve and twenty-four months. One or two youngsters of eighteen months showed preferences for certain playmates. A twin boy and girl seemed especially fond of each other. The children would be more responsive and playful with those they liked, more delighted at their approach and very anxious to keep them close. Some children were friendly with almost everybody including strange visitors. Others showed more specific and decided likes and dislikes. When a terrifying stranger was present, some times a child would show more than usual affection for his familiar nurse, but at other times he would be restrained and aloof from everybody. Similarly when a beloved parent was nursing a child on visiting day he might be hostile to anyone else; but more often he would smile agreeably at everybody including awe-inspiring strangers.

A specific "like" does not necessarily enhance a specific "dislike" by force of contrast, though this does sometimes happen. If the disliked object threatens the satisfaction or enjoyment of the object preferred then the dislike becomes stronger. Similarly a preferred object may be enjoyed with greater intensity in the presence of, or following upon, something disliked. It is a comforting relief from distress. This effect of contrast is perhaps what Freud terms "ambivalence." There are situations, however, where it has no noticeable effect. For instance, as cited above, a child made happy by one person may like everybody for the moment, regardless of previous attitudes towards them. A troubled child may be annoyed with everybody, even his favorite playmates. Strong emotions may thus have a decided "halo" effect.

Although children between *eighteen months and two years* of age tease and hit each other frequently, they show more affection for one another than younger infants. They not only pat and stroke fondly, but they will kiss and hug each other on occasion. The older children in the nursery group were seen to direct the younger ones' activities and point out their errors by gesture and exclamation. There was no evidence, however, of the parental affection and almost self-sacrificing care shown by four-year-olds for their much younger playmates.

Noisy activities delighted the eighteen-to-twenty-four-month old youngsters. They took pleasure in tearing and pulling things to pieces and in lifting large but portable objects, such as their own chairs. They jabbered happily to each other at table. One child would repeatedly make strange noises to arouse the attention and laughter of another. With adults they would practice newly learned words and would seek to share their enjoyments. When the children received new toys in the hospital they would cling to them and guard them jealously from the other children. But they would hold them out for the nurses to share in their appreciation. Here is a mark of trusting friendship for their kindly guardians such as the children had not yet developed for one another. They would always rather share the other child's plaything than give up or share their own.

Affection, thus, begins as delight in being fondled and comforted by an elder. It becomes differentiated from general delight and manifested in tender caressing responses at about eight months of age. This earliest affection is essentially reciprocal in nature. Spontaneous affection for adults may be seen, however, by eleven or twelve months of age. Both reciprocal and spontaneous affection for other children make their appearance around fifteen months, but they are not as strong as affection for adults.

Specific affection for the grown-ups who give special attention may be manifested as early as demonstrative affection itself, i.e. eight or nine months. These preferences persist as long as the care and attention continue. Attachments between two children were not observed in the hospital till after fifteen months of age. They were usually very temporary, lasting only for a few hours or days. The behavior of a child-friend is so much more erratic and less dependable than that of an adult. Friendships between eighteen-to twenty-four-month-old children would sometimes last, however, for several weeks. There seemed to be no preference in these attachments either for the same or the opposite sex. Little girls would become friends together, or little boys, or a boy and girl would show mutual affection for one another.

SUMMARY AND CONCLUSION

The emotional behavior of young infants as observed in the Montreal Foundling and Baby Hospital seemed to lend support to the writer's theory of the genesis of the emotions. Emotional development was found to take place in three ways. The different emotions gradually evolved from the vague and undifferentiated emotion of excitement. The form of behavior response in each specific emotion changed slowly with developing skills and habits. Different particular situations would arouse emotional response at succeeding age-levels, although these situations would always be of the same general type for the same emotions.

The one-month-old baby showed excitement in accelerated movement and breathing, upon any excessive stimulation. He exhibited distress by crying, reddening of the face and tense jerky movements at painful and other disagreeable stimulations. But he was more or less passive and quiescent when agreeably stimulated.

By three months of age the child was seen to exhibit delight in smiles, deep inspirations and somewhat rhythmic movements when his bodily needs were being satisfied. Between three and four months angry screaming and vigorous leg-thrusts, in response to delay in anticipated feeding, were observed. A few weeks later anger was aroused when an adult's playful attention was withdrawn.

Distress and delight came to be expressed more in specific vocalizations with increasing age. General body movements gave place to precise responses to details of a situation. A four-month-old baby would laugh aloud with delight and cry tearfuly when distressed. A child of five months was seen to cough and reject foods of a certain taste and consistency in incipient disgust. He would reach towards objects that caused him delight. By six months of age he showed definite fear when a stranger approached. He remained motionless and rigid, his eyes wide and staring. It is possible that "non-institutional" children might show fear in response to other unusual or unexpected events a little earlier than this. There was little variation in the daily routine of the children under observation, and fear was a rare occurrence.

By seven months of age the child showed positive elation, and renewed his activity as a result of success in his own endeavours. At eight months he began to show reciprocal affection for adults, and by twelve months spontaneous affection. Delight was manifested in much laughter, bouncing up and down, and banging with the hand.

Between nine and twelve months of age the hospital babies would hide their heads, like ostriches, upon the approach of a relatively unfamiliar person. They would scream and become flushed with anger when their efforts or desires were thwarted; and they would cry out in fear and sit motionless after perceiving themselves falling.

It was observed that a child learns to kiss soon after twelve months of age, and by fifteen months he expresses his affection for other children. Anger over disappointment becomes more dramatic in its manifestation. The true temper-tantrum makes its appearance roughly about fourteen months of age. By eighteen months anger at adults is expressed in obstinate behavior; and annoyance at interfering children is manifested in hitting, pulling and squealing.

Eighteen-months-olds would constantly seek the attention of adults, and take great delight in running about and making noises. One or two children of this age showed depressed, and others angry, jealousy when another child received the coveted attention. A few specific fears were noticed; and several children developed particular affectionate attachments.

Thus it seems that in the course of development, emotional behavior becomes more and more specific, both as regards arousing stimuli and form of response. Distress, though more readily aroused, comes to find adequate expression in a variety of actions, and delight becomes sensitive appreciation and joy in numerous pursuits. The emotions evolve slowly, and the exact age of differentiation is difficult to determine.

A diagram showing the approximate ages of the appearance of the different emotions, as observed in the Montreal Foundling Hospital, is given in Figure 1. Study of a number of children in private homes might suggest a somewhat different age arrangement. Readers of the *Journal of Genetic Psychology* will note that a greater number of different emotions are attributed to the two year level than were suggested in a previously published diagram, based on a study of nursery school children.

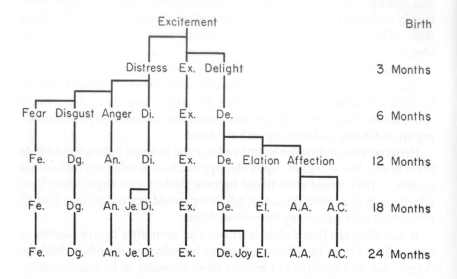

FIGURE 1

Showing the approximate ages of differentiation of the various emotions during the first two years of life. Key: A.A.=Affection for adults, A.C.=Affection for children, An.=Anger, De.=Delight, Dg.=Disgust, El.=Elation, Ex.=Excitement, Fe.=Fear, Je.=Jealousy.

Emotional behavior and development are very much determined by particular events and experiences and the routine of living. It is, therefore, to be expected that "institution babies" will show some deviations in their reactions from those of children at home. The former will probably exhibit fear of a larger number of things than other children, due to their very limited experience. On the other hand, they may show greater tolerance of interference, as a result of much practice in self-control in the nursery. They may also be more affectionate with other children, in consequence of the many happy play-hours spent together.

The daily round of feeding, washing, dressing and sleeping, however, has so many factors in common for all babies, that the observations made on the emotional development of a few hospital children, and the suggested inferences presented above, may have at least some general significance for infants brought up under other circumstances.

24. Building Secure Children in Our Schools*

Related selections: 14, 40, 41, 44, 50

SOME MENTAL hygienists estimate that from ten to twelve of one hundred children in school will spend part of their lives in jail and mental institutions and that perhaps fifty will be somewhat maladjusted. What part does the school contribute to this maladjustment? Certainly we are aware that classroom practice is not keeping pace with theories and facts in child development. Celia Burns Stendler questions certain current notions about how children develop and suggests positive ways in which teachers may contribute to the adjustment of children.

IN 1942, a study was published which had important bearings for classroom teachers in America. This was a study of the emotional adjustment of children in three large public schools of a midwestern city. On the basis of the evidence which Rogers presents, the average classroom teacher can expect that twelve per cent of the pupils in her classroom will have seriously maladjusted personalities and that as high as thirty percent will show evidence of being poorly adjusted to some degree.

Those who are raising eyebrows at these figures and questioning whether the situation with regard to mental health is as serious as Rogers pictures it may be interested to know that the judgment of other experts supports Rogers' estimates. Indeed, one mental hygienist has estimated that out of one hundred children in school, one or two will spend part of their lives in jail, eight or ten will be committed to mental institutions, and thirty to fifty will be maladjusted to a lesser degree.

Sociologists, too, are pointing out that the kind of social order in which

* Reprinted by permission of the Association for Childhood Education and the author. "Building Secure Children in Our Schools" by Celia Burns Stendler. From *Childhood Education*, vol. XXV (January, 1949), pp. 216–220.

Dr. Stendler (1911—) is Professor of Education, University of Illinois, and associate of the Bureau of Educational Research. She is author of *Children of Brasstown* and of texts in child development.

we live is creating serious personality disturbances.   James West argues that " 'rugged individualism' exacts a heavy toll in the security of the individual by compelling him to maintain defensive hostilities to all around him outside the family unit and even within it."   A social order which fosters extreme competitiveness, hostility, and envy is not conducive to the best mental health.

Many teachers will support Mr. Rogers and the other authors quoted who share his point of view.   Indeed, some teachers feel that the number of maladjusted children may be increasing.   There are primary teachers who report that they are dealing with more children in their classes who are emotionally disturbed than ever before.   There are junior high and senior high school teachers who are disturbed by the increasing number of difficult pupils with whom they come in contact.

Even if many teachers feel that predictions of the number of individuals who will have personality disturbances are exaggerated and that the situation is not as dark as has been pictured, nevertheless most of us will probably agree that many of the pupils with whom we are dealing have some peculiar quirks which keep them from functioning as efficiently as they might otherwise.   Unfortunately, we teachers frequently adopt a procedure for dealing with these quirks which only serves to make them worse.   Yet schools *can* promote better adjustment, can help to build secure children.   It will be the task of this article to point out first steps in the process.

One of the first steps we shall need to take in building secure children in our classrooms is to examine our theories of child development.   Whether we are a teacher of forty first graders or a science teacher in a junior high, whether we are a graduate of a two-year normal school or have a master's degree from a college of education, whether we have ever taken any work in the field of child development or not, we teach and treat children according to our ideas of how children grow and develop.

Most of these ideas are part of our culture and we learn them just as we learn habits of speech and attitudes toward other people.   Perhaps because these ideas are learned so painlessly, we rarely question their origin or their validity.   We may be surprised when we do so to find that recent research has proved some of our theories wrong and that we may be operating on a principle which stands in the way of doing an effective job in promoting the good adjustment of pupils.   Indeed, some of us may actually be adding to the burden of troubled youngsters.

Let us examine some of our notions of how children develop to see which ones are based upon poor mental hygiene and which ones contribute positively to the adjustment of children.

IF HE DOES IT ONCE

One of the most common misconceptions of how children grow and develop is the notion that if a child does a thing once, chances are he'll be doing it that way for the rest of his life. Therefore, in order to build correct habits, we must correct a child the first time he does something wrong. We don't want him to build up wrong ways of behaving or develop the notion that he can get away with something. Here are a few examples of how this principle looks in operation:

If a five-year-old has trouble with the letter "r" we must correct him every time he mispronounces a word so he won't be doing it that way forever.

If we find a thirteen-year-old smoking cigarettes, we should punish him severely so he won't learn the habit at that age.

If we tell John to remain at three o'clock to finish his work and he slips out to play baseball, we should call his home and have him return to school so he won't learn the habit of evading responsibility.

This notion undoubtedly represents a popularization of Watsonian behaviorism in its attempts to explain all actions in terms of the conditioned reflex. John would learn he could slip out after school if he did it once because the connection would have been made in his nervous system between (a) neglecting work and (b) having a good time after school. Similarly, the more a pupil says the "r" sound wrong, the stronger the improper connection becomes and the less likelihood is there of changing to the correct sound. But what John B. Watson left out of the picture were the two following principles:

As the child moves from one phase of development to another, he will revise many of the habits which have prevailed for a time. The nine-year-old who delights in blood-and-thunder radio serials may completely reject these same programs when he is thirteen. The pre-school child who says "I don't got any" will slough off such speech patterns of his own accord as he takes on the speech patterns of his social group. The dirty, unkempt preadolescent roughneck changes into a dandified gentleman when he first sees a girl as a girl. In other words, some of the traits which we see in children may be attributed to a particular phase of development and will disappear with age.

All behavior is caused, and in many cases the explanation may lie deep in the emotions. Bill may continue to be dirty and rough and unkempt even when the rest of his gang has dolled up and is dating the girls. But the reason he continues in his preadolescent behavior may not be because he was not corrected when he first began but because he may have grown up with the idea that he doesn't amount to much. He may feel so inadequate, have such a poor opinion of himself that he can't bring himself to revise his old habits. An overly-simple, superficial explanation of Bill's behavior in terms of habit-formation may stand in the way of planning a program for the boy which will really help him.

IF HE TRIES HARD ENOUGH

A second misconception which bears examination is the belief that if a child will simply try hard enough, he can do anything. "He could be an A student if he'd only try hard enough." "Johnny can do his arithmetic when he puts his mind to it." "If he'd make more of an effort, he could learn to read."

Many of us make statements similar to these about some of our students. Such notions about how children grow and develop undoubtedly had their origins in theories of the will—that man can, by the use of his will-power, develop his capacities to the fullest extent. But let us see how this works out with children.

In the first place, we grossly misjudge the intelligence of children in our classrooms. One writer shows that teachers may err in estimating intelligence quotients of pupils even to the extent of classifying as geniuses some children with intelligence quotients well below 90.

In Lewis Terman's famous *Genetic Studies of Genius* he reports that if one is allowed only one method of locating the highest IQ in a classroom, the chances of getting the right child are better if one picks the youngest child in the room rather than if one trusts a teacher's judgment. In other words, unless we have some objective evidence, we may be wrong when we assume that a child *has* the ability to do better work.

In the second place, a child may not be able to produce to the best of his ability not because he doesn't want to hard enough but because of an emotional barrier. A third grade pupil may not be able to learn to read because he's been told in not too subtle a fashion that reading is something he's no good at; he may have repeated the first grade because he couldn't learn to read and so he may look upon it as something he can't do.

A scunder approach to child growth would include recognition of the fact that feelings sometimes get in the way of a child's doing his best work academically. Notice the word *academically*. This means that a student may actually be doing his best in other fields. A high school English pupil may not be doing well in class but it may be because he is putting so much time and energy into learning how to get along with the other sex. This latter job, and very important one, he does very well but receives no credit for it on his report card. Indeed, as Havighurst has pointed out, unless the high school student sees the relationship between the academic task and his developmental task, the academic task will have to be policed.

IF HE KNOWS HE'S GOOD

Another misconception of child behavior which many teachers harbor is that we must never let the child know how good he is; we must always hold up higher standards than he can possibly meet. Too many of us operate on the notion that once a child knows he's good, he will immediately stop trying to learn. Therefore, a child is never good; he is only better than he was and on his way to becoming still better.

John has written a number of excellent compositions in the Fall but when report card time comes we give him a B so that he'll have the higher goal of A to shoot at in the next report. Giving him an A may keep him from trying to improve.

Mary comes up to show her booklet. "It's nice," we say unenthusiastically, "but let's see what we can suggest to make it better."

There is no quarrel with the notion that most of us may be capable of doing better work more efficiently than we are now doing, but there is argument against the theory that the way to get a child to raise his level of aspiration is to tell him continually he isn't good enough the way he is. Actually the task of helping a child choose a goal of a higher degree of difficulty is not so simple.

However, we do know that praise facilitates the rise of the level of aspiration. An experiment with young children shows that when they are praised for what they have done, they tend to choose a task of a relatively higher degree of difficulty the next time. We also know that it may be necessary for a child to feel that he *can* lower his level of aspiration.

Experiments by C. Anderson would seem to indicate that if the choice of a goal with a lesser degree of difficulty is made impossible, regression of the maturity of aspiration can be observed. In other words, if a child is made to feel he *cannot* lower his level of aspiration, he may act in a manner characteristic of a younger age level.

Not only do we block progress by withholding praise but we are frequently unrealistic in setting goals in terms of a child's ability. As has been pointed out above, we frequently misjudge an individual pupil's ability. Furthermore, we are inclined to encourage children to overshoot the mark rather than to choose a level of aspiration they are capable of attaining.

IF HE IS HAVING FUN

A fourth fallacy in our thinking about how children grow and develop is the notion that if a child is having fun, he isn't learning; learning is a painful experience.

Witness the kindergarten teacher who stops her class after fifteen minutes of "work period" where the children have been busy learning social skills in the doll corner, with the blocks, at the easel, at the workbench—the teacher who stops all this and calls her class together to start on a directed activity so that the children may begin to learn to work together.

Or the high school English teacher whose class is engaged in a gripe session on certain school regulations before the period officially begins. When the bell rings, the teacher briskly calls the class to order and organizes a group discussion so that the class may have practice in discussion skills.

The plain fact of the matter is that we don't always recognize learning when we see it; we are too prone to think children can only learn when they are working directly with the teacher at tasks which are either tedious or difficult. While we may enjoy seeing children have fun, there is a bit of the Puritan in many of us and we feel rather strongly that children must not enjoy themselves too much when they are supposed to be working.

HE'S GOING TO FAIL SOMETIME

Closely related to the fallacy discussed above is a fifth one: children must experience hardship, frustration, and failure. It is good for them not only because it prepares them for failure later on in life but also because it teaches them to take the consequences of their behavior. A child who doesn't learn to read in the first grade must repeat the grade so that he won't learn "he can get away with anything," and since he is going to fail at something later in life he might as well learn now.

Aside from the obvious criticisms of such a position in the light of what we know about how and when children learn to read, there is also the question one might raise regarding the advisability of experiencing failure. Does experiencing continual failure or failure in an area deemed very important really teach a child a constructive lesson? Does it inspire a teacher to do better work to have a superintendent tell her she is a poor teacher and that she compares most unfavorably with other teachers? Is a housewife a better housewife because her husband continually reminds her that the house is untidy, that his shirts are not properly ironed, that she is too extravagant, and that she is also a failure as a mother?

The process of growing up inevitably brings many frustrations. Rather than deliberately setting the same standards for all children which automatically condemns some to failure, the teacher who is interested in building secure children helps them to set a goal which they can attain and gives them a pat on the back on their way to attaining it. Having many opportunities to achieve success builds up in a child the feeling of power, that he can do things, that he amounts to something. When he feels good about himself, he is better able to take the inevitable frustrations he will meet in life.

There are doubtlessly many other stereotyped notions which we have about how children grow and develop. The list presented here is not meant to be exhaustive. It is hoped that it may be a starting point for us to examine our ideas about children, to accept those that stand up under critical examination, and to reject those that stand in the way of building secure children.

---

25. The Lonely Road of Unreality*

Related selections: 38, 39, 11, 17

WHAT IS the teacher's role in recognizing and treating the behavior problems of children? Evelyn I. Banning feels that, of the various adjustments the child makes in solving his problems, adjustment by withdrawal presents teachers with the greatest challenge. She describes some of the noticeable symptoms of prepsychotic behavior in children and mentions several things the teacher may do to help the preschizophrenic child.

OF THE varied processes of adjustment in response to the child's inner needs, the natural events of his life, and the presence and activities of those about him, adjustment by withdrawal presents the greatest challenge to the teacher, not only because withdrawal responses often escape notice, but mainly because such avoidant modes, more insidious than others, may become habitual and pathological before recognition. According to

* Evelyn I. Banning, "The Lonely Road of Unreality." Reprinted from *School and Society,* vol. 72, No. 1862 (August 26, 1950), pp. 132–33, by permission of the editors and of the author.
Dr. Banning (1903—) is a Professor at Wheaton College, Norton, Massachusetts, and was formerly a research associate at the Center for Field Studies, Harvard University Graduate School of Education.

Louttit, the boundaries between psychoneuroses and psychoses are no clearer than those between personality difficulties and psychoneuroses. In other words, between the child's seclusiveness and timidity, resulting from the withdrawing mode of behavior, and the borderlands of the functional psychosis of schizophrenia, there are no clearcut demarcations, no signposts that unquestionably indicate to the teacher that ahead lies the Lonely Road of Unreality. Nevertheless, the withdrawing, recessive personality, subjected to unbearable stresses and strains of his personal and social environment, may become the severely distorted and shattered personality of the psychotic.

Ten years ago Teresa, a slight, silent, and inactive child of seven completed grade one with a satisfactory record. The teacher's only comment at the time was, "Teresa is unsocial and shows no interest in playing with the other children." Today Teresa is institutionalized in a mental hospital, classified: schizophrenia, hebephrenic. And yet Teresa's behavior all through her eight years of public school received scarcely more than passing attention; indeed, no teacher considered her withdrawn manner or her extreme seclusiveness a matter of concern since she caused no disturbance in the classroom and showed great solicitation for teacher approval in the early grades.

Two questions immediately present themselves for our consideration of the teacher's role in recognizing and in treating behavior anomalies.

1. What are the symptoms of prepsychotic behavior observable in school children?

2. What help can the teacher actually give the child after recognizing these early symptoms?

The predisposing causative factors of schizophrenia are not definitely known; on the other hand, the precipitating factors, whether organic illness, physical discomfort, emotional trauma, psychic conflicts, or the developmental crisis of childhood or adolescence, merely evoke and exaggerate the schizophrenic response when the pattern has already been established. Bleuler states "There is nothing to be gained by listing the factors that have been implicated in the precipitation of the functional psychosis; obviously any incident toward which an individual may have become sensitized can tip the balance." For the teacher, therefore, the important consideration lies not in the etiology of the psychosis, either generally or in any specific case such as that of Teresa, nor in the therapy possible after the onset of mental deterioration, but rather in the recognition of the early symptoms of behavior disorders for the purpose of planning the best methods of improving the child's adjustment to reality. Likewise the full social significance of the value of early recognition is clear in view of the fact that schizophrenia is usually found among adolescents and young adults and that it accounts for approximately one fourth of all mental disorders.

Although sufficient data regarding prepsychotic behavior of the more serious disorders are unfortunately lacking, the preschizophrenic symptoms, in a broad sense, do resemble the introverted type of personality described by Jung and others. The most distinctive feature, according to Young, is the gradual and insidious development of inattention and emotional indifference to the world outside of the individual. Extreme seclusiveness, excessive daydreaming, regression of personal interests, and odd behavior are primary symptoms. The teacher needs to observe carefully the behavior of the shy, timid, and quiet pupil who may be overlooked, since he does not disturb class routine. Inasmuch as it is not always easy to determine whether the child's behavior is a normal striving for a satisfactory adjustment or an abnormal inability to meet regular daily experiences, the teacher should have a sound understanding of the psychology of adjustment and of human behavior.

The secondary symptoms are many and varied, depending upon the developmental stage, all symptoms that give evidence of a disordered contact with the environment. Out of the specific experiences, the individual comes to develop certain standard or habitual forms of reaction, substitute responses that in psychotics tend to involve the entire organization. Secondary symptoms include temper displays, a diminished breadth of general interest, emotional expressions, negativisms, psychomotor agitation, a variety of speech disorders, and overt sex practices. In these more severe cases, the teacher should not consider herself qualified for therapy, but should instead refer the child to a clinical specialist or psychiatrist. Such use of available resources for the treatment of severe behavior disorders is distinctly a credit to the professional alertness of the teacher.

The school and the teacher, however, do play a significant part in treating behavior problems before the developing personality of the child begins to deviate conspicuously from a normal path. Both through modifying the environmental factors of the school and through working directly with the child, the individual may be taught to meet social and cultural frustrations successfully and may be shielded from unattainable ideals of success. Work that is within the capacity of the child, that is meaningful, and that provides him with some sense of accomplishment is essential. Mental balance can also be aided by additional ambivalent activities that are approved outlets for deep and unsatisfied wishes: art, avocations, and hobbies. Most important of all, however, is the therapeutic attitude of the teacher, that teacher who, by her real understanding and knowledge of behavior anomalies, her resourcefulness, and encouragement, offers affectional security to the quiet, insecure child in a social setting not unduly exciting. Thus the teacher may be of help to the preschizophrenic child who is giving evidence of difficulty in making a reasonably adequate adjustment to the world of reality.

---

26. How Children Become Prejudiced*

How do children acquire their prejudices? What can be done to meet or counteract the impact of prejudice on children? These are questions to which psychologists and sociologists have given much thought and discussion in recent years. In this article Miriam Reimann reviews several important studies related to the question of prejudice in children.

A GROUP of seven-year-olds at a progressive school were reporting what they had done over their Thanksgiving vacation. A dark-skinned Negro boy, one of the most popular children in the class, said he had gone to watch television at the home of his uncle, Jackie Robinson.

"That's impossible! His uncle can't be Jackie Robinson," a white boy shouts out.

"Why is it impossible?" the teacher asks.

"Because Jackie Robinson is colored!"

This seven-year-old already knew that "colored" meant something to the world, but it meant nothing concrete to him; and his bizarre confusion is typical of children's awareness of race. But his ability to use such general terms as "colored" will grow as he grows; in a year or so he will know that Jackie Robinson is colored, and that his schoolmate is colored, too. Whether he will also be "prejudiced" toward Jackie Robinson and his schoolmate, and just what his "prejudice" will consist of—these are more difficult questions.

In the last fifteen years, psychologists and sociologists have been exploring the origins and development of children's attitudes to "minority" groups. In the long run, sound intercultural education programs, designed to reduce prejudice and increase the rational acceptance of differences, will have to be built on such knowledge. But the results of

* "How Children Become Prejudiced" by Miriam Reimann, *Commentary,* vol. XI (January, 1951), pp. 88–94. Reprinted by permission of the author.

Mrs. Reimann has studied the problem of prejudice, its causes and prevention. She has also given attention to the study of the problems of parents and children under different social orders.

research are now fragmentized into a great many articles published in scientific journals, much of it unknown to the thousands of teachers and community leaders concerned with developing intercultural education. Moreover, for all the effort so far expended, our knowledge is still very incomplete, and researchers' conclusions are, or appear to be, contradictory.

Four groups of questions are asked by those studying prejudice in children:

1. At what age do signs of prejudice appear among children? Does prejudice increase or abate with age? And what are the usual manifestations of prejudice at various age levels?

2. Is prejudice in children a social habit acquired from the culture, or is it largely a compensation for personal insecurity, springing from the needs and defects of the individual personality?

3. What social experiences most affect children's group attitudes? The conscious lessons in tolerance of a teacher? The unconscious lessons of prejudiced parents and other adults? The unthinking remarks of other children? How does the child handle the contradictions between the viewpoints of teachers, parents, and other children?

4. What can be done about children's prejudices? Does organized contact—in school or clubs—with members of minority groups prevent the acceptance of prejudiced stereotypes? What techniques might schools adopt for the prevention or elimination of childhood prejudices?

Some answers to the first set of questions can be found in Bruno Lasker's *Race Attitudes in Children* (Holt, 1929), an impressive collection of anecdotal material and speculations about children, assembled from adults in all parts of the country. This book was not an attempt to "measure" childhood prejudice, nor even a proof of anything—except that children are prejudiced, and in many confused ways. From all parts of the country, from school teachers, parents, social workers, and group leaders, came reports and examples of prejudiced behavior.

Lasker's informants found evidence that children were aware of other groups, and prejudiced against them, as early as in the kindergarten years. (Many educators to whom I have talked still maintain that few children under eight or ten even recognize group or color differences. Lasker's conclusions, however, have been supported by the work of later investigators in the field, notably that of Radke, Davis, and Trager, discussed below. And what many adults take to be innocence on the part of young children may be rather a sophisticated reluctance to exhibit what is officially forbidden.) Lasker observed that what we might consider prejudice is variously signified in various age groups: "The small child is more apt to exhibit signs of fear, the child of early school age teasing and combativeness, either associated with or soon followed by a sense of ridicule—more amused than malicious—for strangers in appearance, language or manners. . . ."

Prejudiced attitudes, Lasker generalized, are not deliberately taught but are transmitted without conscious intention to the growing child by parents and other adults, and children. (Later, Eugene L. and Ruth E. Horowitz showed that the parents of prejudiced children in Tennessee specifically disclaimed teaching their children prejudice, and that older children denied their parents had had any role in forming their attitudes—"Development of Social Attitudes in Children," *Sociometry*, 1938.)

Indeed, it appeared to Lasker that prejudice flourished *despite* the formal ideology of racial equality fostered in many public schools.   A Midwestern high school teacher, who is quoted often in the book, claimed that "it is quite practicable to eliminate race prejudice as an active force in school matters," but that even the complete absence of racial discrimination within the school had nothing to do with what the children did outside the school.   Colored and white boys formed distinct groups on the street during the noon hours.   "It is a question with me," this teacher concluded, "whether mixed education is likely to touch the social separation of the races."   Another Midwestern teacher reported the same phenomenon in the primary grades.   In their school games the children chose foreigners as partners as often as any others, but their choice of partners when they were unsupervised—while leaving the building or on the playground—was not so "democratic."   Thus, even at the ages of five to eight, these children had learned the niceties characteristic of prejudiced but well-mannered adults.

Among adolescents, Lasker found that the split between "official" and actual behavior widened.   On the one hand, adolescents have a deeper understanding of history and of the ideals of the American creed.   On the other, their more conscious competitiveness in scholarship and in sports, and their awareness of the sexual implications of intergroup mixing, predispose them to greater prejudice.

Lasker observed, on the basis of this and other evidence, that it is questionable whether individual contacts with members of other groups effectively offset other, prejudice-forming, influences.   And if they don't, "it is hardly worthwhile to engineer such contacts."   The public school system is commonly supposed to be America's great democratizing influence. But clearly the unsegregated school is not the only or major influence shaping the child's attitudes on race.   If Lasker's premise of the unconscious learning of prejudice is correct, one might have to borrow a concept from psychoanalysis and consider whether the best way to combat children's prejudices is not by revelation of the sources of their prejudices rather than simply by ideological counter-propaganda.   Or perhaps we should look toward a change in the social situation that creates these attitudes.

Dr. Lasker's book was frankly exploratory.   A later attack on this problem concentrated on the question: how does the child reconcile conflicting influences?   This study was R. D. Minard's *Race Attitudes of Iowa Children* (University of Iowa, 1931).   Minard gave a verbal questionnaire to 1,641 Iowa children from grades seven to twelve.   The questions asked were of two types: those requiring a judgment of the behavior of fictional persons, and those requiring the subject to indicate how he would act in hypothetical situations.

A typical question of the first category ran: "A young lady belonged to a sorority at a state university.   There was a faint trace of Negro blood in her ancestry, although no one would ever have suspected the fact from her appearance, and the young lady was herself unaware of the fact.   The truth was revealed by accident.   After the discovery it was suggested that she resign from the sorority, and she did so.   *Question:* Ought this young lady to have been asked to resign from the sorority?"

Questions of the second type inquired if the subject would just as soon have a trace of Negro blood that didn't show, or if the subject would just as soon marry a person who did have such a trace.

The interesting fact revealed in this study is that, as the children got older, their objective *judgments* of situations involving members of minority groups (that is, their answers to questions of the first type) became more tolerant, but their *personal responses* (that is, their answers to questions of the second type) indicated greater prejudice.   Apparently their personal emotional responses were somehow immune to their intellectualized attitudes.*

We can observe how the growing child's attitudes toward minority groups become immunized to official ideology by looking at another study, which tested the attitudes of some twelve-year-old children in Cincinnati in 1931, and retested them in succeeding years (Rose Zeligs, "Children's

* This study—and indeed, almost all those we will report upon—may raise in the reader's mind the serious question as to how one can distinguish *discriminating* behavior (rationally motivated) in reference to different ethnic groups from *prejudice* (motivated by emotional bias).   For example, if a young person is realistically aware that friendships with Negroes will lead to "trouble" with his family or hamper his success, and therefore does not become friendly with Negroes—is this prejudice?   All of these studies take it for granted that any expressions indicating that one would treat Negroes differently, or that one accepts a common view ("stereotype") of Negroes, are expressions of prejudice.   It is possible these may simply be means of accommodation to an environment which makes truly non-discriminatory behavior towards Negroes almost impossible.   The writer believes that the measures of "prejudice" usually resorted to in psychological studies really do measure prejudice and not this realistic type of "discriminating" behavior; yet it is perhaps worthwhile to raise this question in the reader's mind.

Intergroup Attitudes," *Journal of Genetic Psychology,* 1948). Dr. Zeligs concluded that race and nationality prejudices seem to be supported and perpetuated by patterns and stereotypes "deeply ingrained in our children's social environment and . . . molding their attitude." It is especially interesting to observe in the following series of responses how one girl's prejudiced feelings were rationalized and reconciled with other conflicting feelings and opinions:

"1931. The Negro isn't of my race of people. Most of the time white people don't associate with Negroes. They are not clean. Some of the girls are rough and not careful when they play.

"1933. I don't like the Negro race. I know the ones in our school are awful wild. They are unclean, unpleasant race to have around.

"1937. In some respects I dislike the Negro intensely because of their unclean ways of living, and yet, at times I pity them because people are so prejudiced against them."

At the age of twelve, this girl gave as her first reason a strong ingroup feeling ("the Negro isn't of my race"); as her second, social requirements ("white people don't associate with Negroes"); as her third, a popular stereotype ("they are not clean"); and finally, almost as an afterthought, her personal experience ("some of the girls are rough . . ."). At the age of fourteen, she raised her personal experience to first place. At the age of eighteen her childhood stereotypes remained in force, but she had developed some conflict about allowing them completely to dominate her, and we hear the echo of the conflict when her answer implies that unprejudiced views are supposed to be part of the "American way." This very awareness, however, permits her to remain prejudiced because she now feels she has taken the demands of tolerance into account. Her prejudice is legitimized by lip service to tolerance.

In recent years the personalities of prejudiced and unprejudiced persons have been studied, and significant correlations between personality and prejudice have been found. The most intensive study on this subject was done by a research group at the University of California at Berkeley, whose work on adults is reported in *The Authoritarian Personality* (Harper, 1950). One of the authors of this work, Else Frenkel-Brunswik, also studied a group of children aged eleven to sixteen ("A Study of Prejudice in Children," *Human Relations,* 1948). And for this group, too, she found that prejudice is not an isolated sentiment but part of a complex of attitudes toward men and society; and that this general complex is in turn related to the whole emotional orientation of the individual.

Fifteen hundred children were presented with a series of about fifty slogans relating to race attitudes as well as to more general social attitudes, and on the basis of their scores were divided into an upper 25 per cent of children considered "unprejudiced" or "liberal," and a lower 25 per cent considered "prejudiced" or, in the researcher's term, "ethnocentric."

The prejudiced children tended to have what might be called a conservative and self-oriented attitude toward society. For example, answering the questions, "What is wrong with America today, and how would you change America?" ethnocentric children gave such answers as:

"Taxes on everything, and the cost of living."

"Clean up the streets—all that garbage lying around! See that everything is in order."

The unprejudiced children, on the other hand, mentioned the "atomic bomb, the condition of the Negroes in the South, the need for world peace," and so on.

Ethnocentric children tended also to be conservative in their attitudes toward the roles of the sexes in society. Prejudiced girls and boys both tended to agree that "girls should only learn things that are useful around the house." An ethnocentric girl said that when girls are around boys, they should "act like a lady, not like a bunch of hoodlums. Girls should not ask boys to date. It's not ladylike." Ethnocentric children placed a high premium on good manners, order, social approval, cleanliness. The stress on social approval and on power converge to produce an attitude of awe toward money, which is considered as having an exaggerated power for good or evil. A typical comment of a prejudiced child was: "No dollar, no friend; have a dollar, got a friend"; and the reverse of the coin: "It [money] helps make enemies. Money is the root of all evil, they say."

The prejudiced children's aversion to weakness extended to those who have power over them, their parents and their teachers, from whom they demand harsh discipline and punishment for misdemeanors and failures. "For what should the hardest punishment be administered?" elicited the following replies from some of them:

"Naturally for murder, the next is for not paying attention to her mother and father. She should be sent to a juvenile home for not paying attention to her parents."

"Talking back, not minding; for example, if you are supposed to saw a certain amount of wood in one hour and don't do it you should be punished for it."

The ethnocentric children looked toward their parents as a source of power rather than of love. Liberal children stressed a comradely relationship to their parents.

In short, Dr. Frenkel-Brunswik concludes that the attitudes of ethnocentric children are outgrowths of their central personality, and indeed of the type of personality depicted (in adults) in *The Authoritarian Personality*—though in general it is less firmly established. Their prejudice stems from their effort toward rigid conformity to what they conceive to be the values of awe-inspiring and authoritarian figures. Their rigid conformism obstructs a flexible social attitude, and facilitates the acceptance of black-or-white group stereotypes, particularly those they see dominant in society.

This analysis applies only to the extremely prejudiced children on the one hand, and those most free of prejudice on the other. We should realize there has been no such exhaustive inquiry into the personalities and attitudes of the large group that falls into neither the upper nor the lower quarters, but is in the middle ground comprising 50 per cent of the children (although a study by Milton Rokeach, "Generalized Mental Rigidity as a Factor in Ethnocentrism," *Journal of Abnormal Psychology,* 1948, found a positive correlation among the entire population studied between prejudice and general mental rigidity). Conceivably, the study of milder prejudices might not reveal this psychological pattern linked with prejudice.

The conclusions to be drawn from the University of California study might indicate that the ethnocentric person requires psychotherapy for his prejudices. Other studies, however, suggest that the milder prejudices of children, as seen in verbal expressions and behavior, can be modified by a less intensive attack.

Virginia M. Axline has presented an extremely interesting report on a play therapy course conducted with four seven-year-old public school children, one of whom was colored. The children were what was formerly called "bad," now "disturbed," and were taken for a one-hour session once a week to a room for non-directed therapy under a trained therapist. The atmosphere was completely "permissive"—no behavior was prohibited except direct physical violence against persons.

The race problem came up five times, and did not arise at all during the last five meetings. Miss Axline reports the children's statements and actions in stenographic detail, and we see how the immediate hurt reaction of a Negro girl to verbal attacks by one of the boys eventually leads him to try to make amends. Miss Axline's conclusion was: "When one provides a situation wherein the children are given an opportunity to be themselves—and an opportunity to react in a very permissive situation, then it seems that they can more readily come to terms with their own attitudes and emotions; and in a face-to-face situation . . . they *can* and *do* assume responsibility for their attitudes. . . ."

But most children rarely if ever have the "opportunity to react" provided by the completely permissive situation of play therapy. It is a delicate task to elicit frank and uninhibited responses from children on a subject that is as embarrassing and taboo to them as sex used to be. To meet this problem, many psychologists have employed rather subtle and indirect approaches to the study of race attitudes.

Eugene Horowitz ("The Development of Attitude toward the Negro," *Archives of Psychology*, 1936) showed pictures of white and colored faces to comparable groups of New York City and Southern schoolboys and asked the subjects which they preferred: "Show me which you like best; show me which you would like to live next door to you," and so on.   He found a continuous development of prejudice from year to year, but no significant differences in prejudice scores between the Northern and Southern groups and no evident correlation of prejudice with the amount of contact by white subjects with Negro schoolmates.   Among the groups tested was a class which had a very popular Negro boy in it, and several other classes in mixed public schools, but these did not diverge from the general results obtained.   The only radically divergent results were found in a group of boys attending a Communist settlement house in New York, who showed no prejudice and possibly a slight pro-Negro bias.

Two years later, E. L. and R. E. Horowitz ("Development of Social Attitudes in Children," *Sociometry*, 1938) conducted another "show-me" study among Tennessee boys and girls, but this time pictures of both sexes as well as both races were shown.   To these children, race was a more important factor than sex in their choices; that is, a white boy, presented with a picture of a white girl and a colored boy, would be more likely to prefer the white girl, although in tests (written tests requiring the subject to state whom he would prefer to sit next to) given in Northern communities, sex had been found more important than race in comparable age groups.   In other words, among Northern children one's own sex is preferred to one's own race; among Southern children, one's own race is preferred to one's own sex.

The Horowitzes suggested ("Race Attitudes," in *Characteristics of the American Negro,* ed. Otto Klineberg, Harper, 1948) that while his earlier study indicates there is no apparent difference between Northern and Southern children in the prevalence of anti-Negro prejudice in the population, his later one suggests that there is a difference in the relative *weight* of prejudice in relation to other factors.

Summarizing the results of the studies reported to this point, it would appear that the questions asked at the beginning of the article might be answered in the following way:

(1) Prejudice appears during early childhood, perhaps in the pre-school years, and increases with advancing age (Lasker, Minard).

(2) Prejudice seems to be instilled by the unconscious example or teaching of the social environment formed by parents, adults, and other children (Lasker and E. L. and R. E. Horowitz, 1938).

(3) Prejudice is closely tied to the basic personality of the individual (Frenkel-Brunswik).

(4) Prejudice is on the whole stronger than the counter-propaganda of democratic teachers and the influence of democratic ideology, and becomes more organized and more rigid as the child grows older (Minard, Zeligs, Horowitz).   Further, prejudice does not seem to be closely dependent on personal contact with members of minority groups, for whether we study children in the North or South, or children in segregated or unsegregated classes, the pattern of prejudice is more or less the same (Horowitz).

What is implied for the educator by these theories of the source of childhood prejudices?   The implications of Frenkel-Brunswik's personality-and-prejudice correlation might be that the educator is powerless to alter the consequences of unsound parent-child relationships.   Another study, which adheres more closely to the social-influences line of Lasker, Horowitz, and Zeligs, however, has a more hopeful view, and offers positive suggestions for possible educational techniques to deal with children's prejudices.   This is the study of Marian Radke, Helen Trager, and Hadassah Davis, conducted under the auspices of the Bureau for Intercultural Education ("Social Perceptions and Attitudes of Children," *Genetic Psychology Monograph Series,* 1949).   The conclusions in regard to personality and prejudice made by these authors are directly opposed to those of Frenkel-Brunswik: ". . . conformity to environmental standards and expectations rather than individual securities or insecurities would appear to be the root of the child's earliest content and valences for social groups. . . ."

Radke, Trager, and Davis presented two hundred and fifty Philadelphia school children, aged five to eight, with a series of eight pictures about which they were asked to make up stories and express attitudes.   In one picture, for example, a colored child is seen standing aside from a group of white children playing together.   In another, two boys are seen emerging from a synagogue, while four boys stand down the street watching them.   The premise of the test is that the subjects project their own feelings and attitudes in discussing the pictures.

Many subjects at the beginning of the interview were uneasy and seemed to wish to avoid the questions of race and religion, but became actively interested when confidence in the interviewer was established.   Reserve and conflict were particularly apparent among the Negro children tested; at one moment, they rejected the white group and at the next rejected their own.   Jewish children valued their own group much higher than did Negro children, and expressed their valuations more emphatically than did Christian whites; they also referred to their group more frequently than did children of other groups, and almost half of the Jewish children projected "Jewish" into pictures where there was no such identification by the tester.

The study found an increase, with age, in the percentage of children expressing prejudice and showing an awareness of group tensions. The presence or absence of minority groups in the subjects' neighborhood or school had little effect on their attitudes. The authors concluded that it was not contact with minorities, but *contact with prevailing social attitudes* toward minorities, that was the foundation for prejudice.

Radke, Davis, and Trager found in the children's early inhibitions and later eagerness in regard to race discussions a clue to the kind of pedagogy required. Their fears, fantasies, curiosities, and misconceptions must not be suppressed but openly discussed. "A rule of silence about differences," they wrote, "not only fails the child in not helping him to achieve a better understanding . . . but the silence may also be perceived by the child as tacit agreement with societal prejudices." The authors also argued that the specific problems of prejudice which the child meets in his school, his neighborhood, and his home must be discussed frankly. The successes of the play therapy course by Axline reported above would seem to support such a program.

The author's own inquiries into New York City educators' attitudes toward intercultural education indicate that these suggestions are not widely followed. Whether because of fear of antagonizing some members of the adult community or because of the theory that such discussions only aggravate children's prejudices, many educators carefully refrain from mentioning to the children that there are significant differences among various groups, that there is some degree of prejudice in almost every community and institution in the nation, and that the children themselves are frequently the objects or the subjects (or both) of prejudice. In many schools there seems to prevail a kind of liberal over-optimism that may be as ineffectual in intercultural education as a reactionary fatalism. The ignoring of differences is expected to lead to the early disappearance of all the problems they create. In effect, the children are told there is no real problem, at least not where they are concerned—whereas, as a matter of fact, there is.

The Philadelphia experimenters concluded that prejudice is largely a matter of social imposition upon the individual; the California group, as we saw, held that it is a response of the individual personality to inadequate social and emotional satisfactions. Both studies were carefully conducted and in neither does it appear that there were unwarranted generalizations of the empirical conclusions.

However, there is one way of reconciling the apparent contradictions of the California and Philadelphia studies while accepting their results.

There is within our society a very wide range offered to the individual between tolerance and prejudice. He may choose any one of a number of positions, or several positions simultaneously or successively, without departing from what is regarded as the cultural norm. The "normally" prejudiced person accepts and perpetuates on the one hand a formal ideology of tolerance ("live and let live, equal opportunities for all, the American creed") and, on the other, a fluctuating set of invidious stereotypes. Which social attitudes he will accept as his own depends on personal as well as social factors. And within the "normal" range of prejudice and tolerance, it is probably not easy to distinguish the personality elements from the complicated interplay of social influences.

Thus for any random population—and such a random population was studied in the Philadelphia research—it is not easy to find a correlation between personality factors and prejudice. Most people will indeed pick it up "out of the air," from the "social atmosphere." And for these people, their prejudices will be virulent or mild, as the situation demands. But those persons who have really developed the kind of personality that *requires* prejudice to balance it—that is, the authoritarian personality—will develop more consistent and perhaps more violent attitudes, and will show up in studies as extremely prejudiced. Consequently, when we approach the limits of the scale of prejudice, we will find personality and prejudice linked together. From this point of view, the "liberal" child and the "ethnocentric" child, as they appear in Dr. Frenkel-Brunswik's study, are deviants from a norm of mild prejudice, since the completely secure and loving family held responsible for the former, the completely unprejudiced child, is probably as rare in our society as the completely hostile and rejecting family that is believed to produce the latter.

Whether "normally prejudiced" children can be taught finally to resolve the conflicts between a formal creed of tolerance and stereotyped prejudicial attitudes in favor of the former, is a question that educators like to answer in the affirmative, but that psychologists have not answered at all —unless we take their more general comments on attitudes. Thus, Gordon Allport writes ("Attitudes," in *A Handbook of Social Psychology,* ed. Carl Murchison, Clark University Press, 1935): "An attitude seldom contains all of the experience which is relevant to it, and seldom changes as rapidly as a faithful following of experience would require. . . . Because they save both time and effort, stereotyped attitudes offer great resistance to change. They resist the inroads of new contradictory experience and are retained as they satisfy and protect the individual."

In such a situation, what is the value of intercultural education, and what type of formal education is most valuable? To my knowledge, no follow-up tests have been made on children subjected to the various programs of intercultural education. The employment of such projective techniques as those used by Radke, Davis, and Trager, on a before-and-after basis, would seem to be an excellent means of testing the effectiveness of different pedagogical procedures—including the one suggested by these authors.

The subject of children's prejudices is also deficient in another type of study—one that would consider it in a non-laboratory atmosphere, in the ordinary relations of social life, in terms of *social behavior* (physical and verbal) rather than *verbalization,* i.e., the individual's report on his behavior. The laboratory emphasis may be responsible for the fact that more general social and economic causes of prejudices have only rarely been considered.

While a few studies have failed to discover any simple correlation between economic status and prejudice, no studies—that is, in the sphere of children's prejudices—have been made on the relation of change in economic status, and particularly loss of economic security, to prejudice. Indeed, the whole larger social background of prejudice—in the school, on the street, at home—is often filled in rather shallowly, if at all, in these studies. Yet many students believe that it is only in a time of economic crisis and general insecurity that prejudice becomes dangerous. A long-term study of the relation between economic factors and prejudice might give us some insight into the dynamics of the frightening shifts we have witnessed in our time from a relatively tolerant to a violently discriminatory social atmosphere. The fragmentary research we have summarized in this article will go on, we may hope, to fill in this social and economic setting.

---

27. Gang and Narcotic Problems of Teen-Age Youth*

Related selections: 16, 34, 35

CHILDREN and youth of today encounter more frustrations and anxieties, more uncertainties and confusions than youth have ever before experienced. In such a milieu it is not at all surprising that gang warfare and drug use and addiction, as well as other forms of social and emotional maladjustment, seem to be on the increase. Those who are interested in understanding the needs of youth and in working with their problems will find Dr. Dumpson's discourse a valuable source of information concerning the etiology of such problems.

INTRODUCTION

WITHIN one decade we have experienced in urban areas of this country two crisis situations among adolescent youth. During the period immediately following World War II, many communities were concerned about teen-age gang warfare. Early in 1950, we became aware of the increased use of narcotic drugs by teen-age youth. Probably more public concern has been expressed about these two behavior manifestations among adolescents than any other adolescent activities with which we are familiar in recent years.

In organizing my thinking and my experience in planning community programs to meet the needs of youth engaging in deviant behavior, it became clear to me that there are outstanding similarities in the description of the phenomena of gang boy and youthful addict and in the causative factors that precipitate their deviant behavior. Antisocial gang activity and drug addiction are types of behavior symptomatic of social and emotional maladjustment in the individual. Each of these two behavior patterns serves a function in the psychic economy of the teen-ager who is involved. In each, the etiology is deeply rooted in a multiplicity of interacting physical, social, and psychological forces.

For the gang boy and the teen-age addict, the frustrations and anxieties

* James R. Dumpson, "Gang and Narcotic Problems of Teen-Age Youth," *American Journal of Psychotherapy,* vol. VI, (April, 1952), pp. 312–328. Reprinted by permission of author and publisher.

Dr. Dumpson (1909—), formerly Child Care Consultant, Federation of Protestant Welfare Agencies and vice chairman of the committee on Use of Narcotics Among Teen-Age Youth, Welfare Council, New York City, is currently Director, Bureau of Child Welfare, Department of Welfare of the City of New York.

created by a world that has experienced a prolonged and seemingly unending state of war; the uncertainties of the future in terms of marriage, family, and productive living; the changing function of the family resulting in basic changes in child-parent relationship; the confusion that develops as a result of what is taught in the rearing process, in contrast to the practices they observe in meaningful adults in day-to-day living; the damage to self-esteem flowering from the practices of segregation and discrimination to minority groups—all of these characteristics of our present day world are important factors in the production of damaged and disturbed youth. These social factors become forces for antisocial behavior and set in motion a number of psychological processes. The extent to which these processes are activated depends on the individual's personality structure, the strengths and weaknesses of that personality. This backdrop of social psychological pathology reaps its toll with individuals as they accommodate to it. The behavior of the addict and of the gang boy is each's response to the pressures of his environment accompanied by resultant intermediary psychological processes.

Notwithstanding the commonality of precipitating causative factors, certain adolescents respond differently to them. Antisocial gang activity represents one response; drug use and addiction represents another. It is hoped that the discussion of these factors, as I have observed their interaction in the gang boy and the addict, will contribute eventually to the development by this and similar groups of a theory of therapy that will be practical and effective.

In considering the antisocial teen-age-gang, it is my purpose to suggest certain factors in gang structure and activity that were seen in the work of the Central Harlem Street Clubs Project of the Welfare Council of New York City during the three year period ending in March 1950, and to point up implications of gang membership and activity that may be pertinent to your interests as therapists. The material present here is based on the experiences reported by the Project as published in the book, *Working With Teen-Age Gangs* by Crawford, Malamud and your speaker. Major emphasis in my statement will be placed on administrative aspects of the problem and those treatment techniques that are within the function and skill of the casework process.

The gang is recognized as a specific type of structural division in associative life. Sociologically speaking, it is a primary group characterized by face-to-face contacts and direct inter-action, set up by common locality. In its genesis, the gang arises out of play groups from which it spontaneously develops. It is the next rung, after the family, in the social structure where the individual receives training in meeting his equal, in learning cooperation, and in struggling to express his own wishes. It is important to point out, however, that irrespective of its complex organization, in its full development, the gang is organized by the members themselves and not by adults interested in providing recreation or education for youth. In the course of contact with other play groups or gangs, and with the expression of adult authority, parents and police, the gang becomes formalized and structuralized. The impingement of certain social, physical and psychological pressures acting upon the individuals and the group produce antisocial behavior as one distinguishing characteristic of the gang.

The so-called "street gang" in its activity, may be classified as one of three types:

1. A group whose principal activities are antisocial. This is the criminal gang whose sole function and activities are antisocial in nature.

2. A group which occasionally engages in antisocial activities. This group is primarily a social unit engaging in activities common to all adolescents. In response to approprate environmental pressures, it may engage in antisocial or delinquent behavior.

3. A group which does not engage in antisocial activity, although individual members of the group may follow confirmed patterns of delinquent behavior.

The first type is a common form of organization in social life among adults. The other two types are usual among teen-age youth and are characteristic phenomena of modern urban life.

Only brief allusion needs to be made to the history of hostile, aggressive behavior that began among teen-age gangs in various sections of New York City during the early 1940's, that reached its height in 1947, and recently has flared up again in Brooklyn and the Bronx. The activities of these gangs were not just boyish escapades; they were carried on in dead seriousness. Instead of sticks and stones as weapons, gang boys used home-made guns, knives, and other lethal instruments. Instead of ending up with a few bruised shins, scratched faces or black eyes, these fights frequently resulted in serious casualties, including death to the participants and innocent non-participants. Instead of the typical corner fight between two adolescent boys, street gang fighters have involved as many as 100 or more boys in each opposing group. Stealing is a commonly accepted practice, ranging from petty thievery to more serious offenses such as purse snatching, breaking into stores, and armed robberies. While sex offenses, as commonly defined, occurred very rarely, some of the older boys engaged in "line-ups" and committed rape. Truancy, drinking, gambling, and narcotics use were all part of the pattern.

The boys involved in the project lived in a community of inadequate health, education and recreation facilities; overcrowding, poor housing, and low economic status.   The people reacted to segregation and discrimination with hostile and tense feelings which underlay many of their attitudes toward the value system of the community at large.   The ambivalence of the adults toward the values and patterns of the larger community should be seen as a dynamic environmental factor in the development of teen-age antisocial gangs.

A partial understanding of the motivation of the behavior of these boys was identified when we attempted to discern how they defined their own situation.   Some boys stated that they joined gangs out of their felt need for protection.   Others indicated that the gang provided avenues through which satisfying recreational experiences were obtained.   They all indicated that engaging in activities, considered antisocial by the community, was considered by them to be a normal way of relating to their environment.   The boys tended to see adults as "authorities," "hoodlums," or "suckers."   "Authorities" pushed them around, told them what to do and what not to do, moralized, made demands, threatened, condemned, and meted out punishment.   "Hoodlums" were smart guys who got along in the world by exploiting, cheating, and outwitting the other fellow. "Suckers" were "softies" who worked for a living, never stepped out of line, and always did what was right.   For these boys, most adults belonged to one of these groups.   The boys hated and feared "authorities"; had wary respect for "hoodlums," and expressed contempt for the "suckers"! Many boys felt that their fellow club members were the only persons in the world for whom they cared and on whom they could count.

The four gangs with which the Project worked were well organized on both a formal and informal level.   The broad base for the pyramidal structure of the club was the special interest club group, the social clubs, the baseball, basketball and football teams.   Practically all of the boys identified with a club were participating members of one of these subgroups or teams.   Their concept of the democratic process was built around a handful of powerful personalities that did the deciding.   They had their cliques, power blocs, and boards of strategy, which were powerful groups with high status rank in the gang structure.   One person, the gang leader, by virtue of his position, did most to determine the gang's structure, atmosphere, ideology, and activities.   He might even determine its goals, have the central role in coordinating the activities, exert discipline and the means of reaching the group's goals.   One gang leader was larger in physical stature than his followers and the only one to use his size and prowess to maintain control over the gang.   The other three retained control by establishing themselves as ideals for the boys.   Through their dash and daring, their cleverness and cunning, the impetuousness to act and to dominate, their drive to command and conquer, they maintained control over the group. While one leader was appointed, the others "topsied" into power. None was chosen by the democratic process, nor did any gain his position through the coup d'état. All were respected; all were feared. For the most part they were little men in quest of adventure and power!

Many workers with gang boys agree that these boys are psychologically sick, that their membership in and use of the gang, and the behavior that follows has its roots in seriously distorted personality structures and neurotic needs. We have been able to identify three basic forces that contribute materially to the emotional maladjustment of the gang boy: (1) damage to the boy's security feeling; (2) damage to the socialization process; and (3) damage to the self-esteem of the child. Cultural factors such as group prejudice, poverty, authoritarian family structure, and social disorganization are also identified as contributing to the individual's unhealthy ego development. Further, we identified factors in early childhood, such as parental rejection, family tension and disorganization, social isolation, and traumatic experiences as potent negative forces in the individual's development. Most workers with gangs also recognize the impact of current situational factors, such as chronic conflict in the environment, organic inferiorities, over-severe ideals, feelings of difference, and inability to meet cultural demands for masculinity or femininity. This formulation highlights, again, the bio-psycho-social aspect of delinquent gang behavior and suggests the need to discover whether there is a generic principle for treatment and preventing of such behavior.

As has been suggested, boys within the gang "interchangeably occupied the role of the persistent delinquent, occasional delinquent, and non-delinquent," reflecting frequently the alternative value systems virtually contained in each mode of conduct and reflecting, too, the duality of conduct norms of the area. The two-scale value orientation and its implications in the areas in which such gangs thrive need to be recognized and taken into consideration by therapists and caseworkers alike. Shifting adherence to the conventional value system and conduct norms and a deep motivation to change represent, frequently, the points at which the caseworker or the therapist may relate his role, his skills, and his function in treatment.

Out of our three year experience, we finally developed a conceptual scheme as a guide for working with antisocial street gangs. Basic to this conceptual scheme, I believe, is the need to recognize that the major determining factor in behavior is the need of the behavior. Only if we know the gang boy's needs and goals can we hope to affect change in his behavior. It is the need of behavior which gives it meaning, direction, and consistency. We have failed in our work with the "gang boy" and in handling similar deviant behavior to the extent that we have failed to find the answer to the question of what the boys need and why they misbehave. Behavior, delinquent or non-delinquent, is need satisfaction. Surely we find clues for treatment in recognizing that the gang boy, in his attempt to gain mastery over things and people, and his identification with the gang and the power inherent in such a group, is using mechanisms to defend his ego and to achieve a sense of self-esteem. The approach we developed recognized the technical limitations as well as the function of the casework process. While this theoretical framework is still provisional, I am certain that future efforts with teen-age gangs require staff persons who are psychiatrically oriented and should include the services of a psychiatrist to serve as a diagnostic consultant to the staff.

Three stages of relationship can be distinguished during the course of the worker's relationship with the boys. In the first, his primary emphasis was on overcoming the boys' distrust and gaining their acceptance. In the second, the worker focused on stimulating change in their attitudes and behavior. In the third, he aimed for a successful closing of relations. The stages overlapped and were interrelated; each presented its own opportunities and hazards, developed at different times for different boys or subgroups, and determined, at least partly, the kind of procedures that the worker followed. The following stages in relationships are suggested:

1. *Gaining acceptance:* It is axiomatic that the worker needed to gain the boys' acceptance before he could hope to effect constructive change. As their trust, respect, and affection for him grew, their amenability to his influence increased. They gave more careful consideration to his reasoning, interpretations, suggestions, insight-giving, and example-setting. They behaved in ways which they felt would please him and gain his approval, or they followed his example because they wanted to be like him. Techniques used successfully by the workers in establishing this first stage of relationship varied. For example, in order to "win" the boys, the workers attempted to satisfy their needs for affection, understanding and guidance. They did not condemn them for their behavior but showed confidence in the boys' capacity to work out their own problems constructively. They demonstrated their positive attitudes toward the boys not by words alone, but by spending time with them and sharing in their play, discussions, and planning. During this first stage, the workers learned all they could about the club's structure, its ideology, its activities, and its needs as well as evaluating the personality patterns of the individual members. They coped with such problems as gaining initial contact with a hostile, distrustful group, structuring their role with the boy and the group, and passing the boys' various "tests" of the worker. Obviously, the degree of success in this first stage of developing relationship influenced considerably the worker's effectiveness in subsequent stages.

2. *Stimulating change:* By the time the worker entered this stage, he had

achieved at least an approximate understanding of the dynamics underlying the boys' attitudes and behavior. Based on this understanding, he developed a systematic conception of the conditions under which specific changes can be expected. He acquainted himself with the range of possible methods for stimulating change and developed skill in the use of those which appeared most appropriate. In this stage he had to meet such problems as resistance, pseudo-change, anxiety following change, and relapses.

3. *Closing relations:* In contrast to most therapy situations, because we were on a time limited project, the termination of the workers' relations with the boys depended on a predetermined closing date rather than the degree of progress shown by the group. Therefore, unusually careful preparation of the boys for the workers' separation was required. Such preparation, initiated at the very outset of the relationship, was given special attention in the closing months of the project. During the final stage the worker, by tapering off his contacts and playing a progressively less prominent role in the affairs of the club, enabled the boys to test and gain confidence in their own capacity for responsible self-direction. In most instances, he encouraged the group to establish relations with other community adults or agencies, and referred for psychiatric or other specialized services those boys who needed it and were ready to use it.

This closing stage, too, presented a number of problems. Boys relapsed into antisocial behavior, some because they interpreted the worker's departure as betrayal or rejection, others because they had established a dependency on the worker and attempted to use their behavior to have him stay on. Members whose emotional ties to the worker were very deep frequently manifested their disturbance in the form of neurotic symptoms. Obviously, unless this stage is handled skillfully, the worker may nullify much of his previous accomplishment.

Working on this level of treatment with a group of 125 hostile, aggressive gang boys assigned to four male workers, none of whom were psychiatrically trained or oriented, after three years we assessed our results. What did we accomplish?

1. Each of the workers was able to establish a working relationship with a gang. While these relationships varied in quality and intensity, they placed the workers in a position to exert a constructive influence.

2. We did have a definite impact on the boy's aggressive behavior, but exerted much less influence on their escapist activities. From the time we established contact with the boys until the end of the project, there was no gang warfare in the project area. A decline in stealing was reported for three of the gangs, in sex offenses for one, and in truancy for another. There was, however, no significant change in the practice of narcotics use, drinking, or gambling.

3. The boys engaged in more organized recreational programs and won unprecedented opportunities for achievement and neighborhood recog-

nition.   Successful participation in planning, decision-making, and carrying out responsibilities gave the boys a new sense of confidence and self-
esteem.

4. New services were made available to these boys.   Individual counselling helped a few achieve a better personal and social adjustment.   A
few were referred for intensive psychiatric help.

Finally, however, without in any way detracting from the accomplishments listed above, I must point out what we failed to achieve: With
the possible exception of two or three members, we did not effect basic
changes in the boys' ideology.   True, their hostility and aggression
seemed to have diminished, their antagonistic attitudes toward the adult
world softened, and they began to view the future more constructively and
more hopefully.   Despite these changes, we believe that their basic attitudes towards themselves and others, although dormant perhaps, still
exist.   To these boys the world is still a dangerous jungle.   Yes, they
may grant the presence of sympathetic allies in this jungle, but a jungle it is
nonetheless.   It is still important to them to be tough.   Fearfulness and
weakness are still despised traits.   The exaggerated need for status,
the contempt for the law, exploitative attitudes towards girls—these and
other trends still operate virtually unmodified in most of the boys.

The second atypical group to be discussed in this paper is the teen-age
narcotic drug user and addict.   Actually, teen-age addicts do not organize
themselves into any social group with a structure and dynamic of its own.
We may refer to teen-age drug users and addicts as a group only in the
sense that they present a common course of development as far as their
addiction is concerned, and according to some studies, a common set of
characteristics including certain common personality traits.   My discussion of the teen-age addict here will be limited to a consideration of the
two aspects of the problem which most youthful addicts seem to have in
common—the course of development of drug use, and the characteristics
of the youth group involved in the problem.   We have had too little experience locally to discuss the effectiveness of treatment efforts of adolescent users and addicts and their results.   To this effort we hope that many
disciplines will contribute their thinking and experience.

It was in the spring and early summer of 1950 that we recognized the
existence of drug use and drug addiction to an alarming degree in New
York City.   Actually, of course, the use of narcotic drugs by teen-age
youth preceded the year 1950.   Pescor, in his statistical analysis of
hospitalized drug addicts in 1943, found "that while no age is exempt from
drug addiction, there is a heavy concentration of cases in the decade 20 to
29 years, more than half being victimized during this period."   16.5 per
cent of those studied, he found, were 19 years of age or less at the onset of

their addiction. Dr. Perry Lichtenstein reported in the New York Medical Journal of November, 1914, that "the number of young people addicted is enormous. I have come in contact with individuals sixteen and eighteen years of age, whose history was that they had taken a habit-forming drug for at least two years." In our contact with 125 teen-age gang boys we found that 79 or 42 per cent admitted to the use of narcotic drugs.

The startling fact about our current situation is the lowered age level and the increasing number of youth who are involved. In the past we were prone to identify drug use with individuals in particular social and economic strata of the community. Our experience clearly indicates that today, drug use among teen-agers cuts across all economic, social, racial, religious, and educational lines. Youth from all sections of the city are represented in the group of narcotic drug users or addicts.

The course of drug use and addiction among adolescents and the adaptation process involved are set forth in a preliminary study by Stanley K. Bigman, of the Bureau of Applied Research at Columbia University. Bigman describes the process by which adolescent addicts are made as having these phases:

1. *The phase of orientation:* The young person first goes through a process of learning which predisposes him favorably or unfavorably to the use of drugs. This orientation, we are told, comes from those who constitute the person's social world. There is substantial evidence that large numbers of boys and girls know about drugs in many sections of the city, and the ease with which it can be secured. The duality of conduct norms in many of these areas, previously discussed in connection with teen-age gangs, very likely condition the kind of orientation the youth receive.

2. *The phase of experimentation:* During this period, when narcotics are available for the first time, some youngsters will refuse to use drugs at all, some try their use intermittently, and some begin regular use culminating in addiction. The orientation to drugs of the key people in the lives of youth is an important factor in their orientation and the choice they will make concerning drug use.

3. *The phase of addiction:* With the experiencing of the symptoms of drug withdrawal, their interpretation as due to the absence of the drugs, and the resumption of drug use to alleviate them, addiction usually follows.

While Bigman's completed study of the adaptation of individuals to drug use leading to addiction, when considered in the light of psychiatric understanding, will be valuable to all of us, we already know that the youngster who plays with narcotics may be "hooked" before he is aware of it. For certain personality types, two or three experimentations with a potent drug, within a relatively short period of time may produce a mild physical dependency on the drug.

In addition to Bigman's sociological formulations concerning the adaptive process involved in adolescent drug addiction, other influential social and psychological factors must be considered. Any theory of therapy must recognize the search for status by many of these teen-age addicts (and a potent factor in motivating gang activity) who have had denied to them by institutions in the community the normal outlets for prestige and a sense of personal worth. Cognizance must be taken, too, of the fact that there is a concentration of teen-age addicts and users in the economically and socially deprived areas of our community. The socio-economic conditions of these areas represent important causative factors in the situation. They contribute to emotional instability and maladjustment and increase the addiction-prone characteristic of many of the youth in these areas. Zimmering, Toolan, Safrin, and Wortis, in a study of 22 consecutive adolescent boys admitted to Bellevue Hospital Psychiatric Division for heroin addiction in January and February, 1951, state that "all but one of our 22 patients have been Negroes or of Puerto Rican descent." They indicated that these boys all suffered psychologically from the discriminatory practices and attitudes directed against their racial groups. Their racial characteristics were considered to be a stamp of inferiority and they suffered injuries to their self-esteem. These authors state that "crime in its varied form flourished there (Harlem) and now the illegal drug traffic has become a major underworld activity." Bigman, not unlike other qualified observers, alleges that the orientation to drug use is unfavorable in the Negro community of Harlem. These two conflicting points of view about Harlem each contains a modicum of truth. They are illustrative of the dual value orientation and dual conduct norm of the area and have great importance to a full understanding of antisocial behavior in communities like Harlem.

How does addiction develop among teen-age youth? The Zimmering, Toolan, Safrin and Wortis study presents a composite picture of the development among the 22 boys studied. This picture is characteristic of the course followed among a majority in the adolescent group. The youth are initiated to drug use either by peddlers or addicted boys. Curiosity, experimentation, and group pressure facilitate the introduction of drug use by the youth. Reefer smoking, during the early stages of the current problem, preceded the use of other drugs. However, in a study of 151 youthful cases brought before the courts in New York City during March, 1951, we found that 66.4 per cent began their drug use with injections of heroin, indicating that reefer smoking and "snorting" the powder through the nose were by-passed for the subcutaneous ("skin-popping") and the intravenous method ("mainlining"). The intravenous method, widely popular among youth today, involves several rather simple steps. Heroin, the chief drug of choice, and a small amount of water are mixed in a spoon. This solution is heated over a flame and then drawn up in an eye-dropper. A hypodermic needle is fitted to the eye-dropper and the contents injected directly into the vein.

The Bellevue study and workers who have been in direct contact with the boys report that immediately after taking the drug, the user becomes a bit anxious followed by a feeling of complete well-being. This is described by the boys as a "charge" or "floating on a cloud." Interest in object relationships decreases; the sex drive is reduced; school, sports, and friends no longer hold interest for the young addict. The focus of their interest is obtaining and using the drug. The boys usually withdraw to a quiet dark room or go to a movie house and enjoy the effect as long as possible. They are irritable if disturbed, and are given to daydreaming and mild hallucinations. These youth do not participate in group activities and under the influence of heroin are not aggressive. The physical reactions that follow abstinence from the drug together with the depressed feeling produce the "yen" for larger and more frequent doses. They begin to sell and "push" the drug to other youth in order to secure funds to support the habit. Serious delinquent behavior is pursued in order to secure money with which to buy drugs. Physical and psychological dependency and tolerance to the drug establish the individual as a narcotic addict.

Planning for management of the problem is complicated by the conflicting evaluation of psychiatrists who have studied the addict. Dr. Herbert Wieder and others who have been associated with the U.S. Public Health Service Hospital at Lexington, as well as reports of psychiatric examinations in our local courts, state that the individuals who move into the addiction cycle may be classified as either psychoneurotics, psychopathic personalities, or as psychotics. On the other hand, the Bellevue study states "As a group they are not psychoneurotic. They do not suffer from crippling symptoms or character traits. Their condition can be described as Personality Disorders and under ordinary circumstances they make adequate adjustments."* In planning a local community program, we have moved on the theses set forth by the findings at Lexington. We recognize, however, that not all teen-agers exposed to drugs and those who are users

* *Note:* While the study presents many interesting facts, the inadequacy of the sample studied requires that generalizations based on the findings not be made concerning teen-age addicts and users.

of drugs will necessarily become addicts. We have proceeded on the theory that addicts either have constitutional make-ups that are conducive to addiction or their psychological problems precipitate addiction as a tool in their total psychic economy. For those who are addiction-prone, those with basic psychological problems, drugs solve internal conflict and put the individual in a state free of tensions. Our experience indicates that those youth who turn to drugs for the purpose of gaining status with the peer group, or for other "non-psychiatric" reasons, usually find it possible to give up drugs with little or no difficulty. The pleasure they receive is external, coming as it does from being like the group.

Of further significance are the findings of Zimmering, Toolan, Safrin and Wortis, concerning the common features of adolescent addicts. These authors describe them as soft spoken, and verbally adept. They are not the typical gang boy whom we have discussed earlier. "These boys are pleasant, likeable, and sociable, with a strong affinity for each other and seek each other out as friends." They lack aggression and the struggle for power and domination observed in the street gang boy. Again, unlike the gang boy, their friends are casual and they have no strong ties or buddies. While the gang boy is usually overtly rejecting of parental control, with a somewhat tenuous and loose relationship with his mother, the teen-age addict has a warm, close relationship with the mother. The father is described as a shadowy figure who has little meaning to the boy. It was interesting to note, again unlike the gang boy, that none of the boys studied at Bellevue as addicts had ever run away from home nor had the impulse to do so. The intellectual level of the addicts at Bellevue, as was true with the gang boy, ranged from borderline to high average I.Q. scores. Neither group can apply themselves successfully to intellectual tasks and both have difficulty in learning.

In summary, the Bellevue authors state that the 22 teen-age addicts seen at the hospital were characterized by a "lack of aggression, strong attachment to the mother, poor object relationships, omnipotent striving, and a tendency to regress." Wisely, they caution, however, that not all adolescents with these personality patterns will become addicts, nor has the experience of others established that these or any particular personality pattern is unique for all young addicts.

This paper, I believe, would not be complete if it did not indicate the proposals for treatment as proposed by the Welfare Council of New York City. In setting up a treatment and preventive program, one must know not only the nature of the problem but also the extent of it. Notwithstanding the wide publicity given to the subject in New York City and the numerous plans formulated to cope with it, no one knows, as yet, with any degree of reliability, the extent of the problem in New York. No systematic reasonably unduplicated count of teen-age users and addicts has been made. Indications from the records of police arrests, from the dockets of the courts, from the experiences of the public schools and social agencies, established without any doubt that there has been and continues to be an alarming increase in the use of narcotics by teen-age youth. It is known, for example, that the number of teen-age users or addicts committed to city correctional institutions in 1950 represent a 700% increase over 1946. If the rate of admissions for individuals under 21 for the first quarter of 1951 is continued, by the end of 1951 the increase will be some 900% over 1949. In the period 1947 through 1949, two minors secured voluntary commitment to city correctional institutions as addicts. In 1950, 45 minors were admitted on voluntary commitment. In the first quarter of 1951, 42 were admitted. In 1950, 10 of the 56 deaths due to narcotics and reported to the Chief Medical Examiner of the City of New York were of youths under the age of 21. Of the 22 deaths so reported for the first six months of 1951, 7 were 21 years of age or under.

In 102 narcotic cases of minors brought before the Courts for any reason in New York during the months of March, 1951, we found that 64 per cent were charged with offenses involving narcotics. An additional 42 cases were reported by the Children's Court for possession, sale, use or suspected use of narcotic drugs. 66.4 per cent of all the cases studied began their practice with heroin; and more than half had used narcotics for less than six months. Three hundred and forty admissions of teen-agers, of whom 298 were users of heroin, were made to Bellevue and Kings County Hospitals for the period January 1, 1951 and October 15, 1951.

These statistics, while indicating the trend of increase, are inconclusive. No systematic research on the teen-age user and addict has been done. We have recommended, therefore, as a first step, that an adequate registration and reporting system be set up by having the Health Department of the City define narcotics use and addictions as a reportable disease. We believe that this will give some reliable measure of the problem and, in addition, provide the controls normally exercised by health departments in such situations.

In considering a treatment program, as previously stated, we identified narcotics addiction as a symptom of personality disorder usually described as psychoneuroses or character disorder. The narcotic user, as distinguished from the addict, is an emotionally immature, unstable individual succumbing to strong social and environmental pressures. We recognize that any user can become an addict. We accept that therapy for these teen-age addicts or identifiable potential addicts can best be carried out in a custodial setting under the control of staff trained in various phases of treatment.   Such a facility should provide a program of good medical care, of occupational therapy, and where indicated, psychotherapy adapted to the needs and accessibility of the individual.   The decision to employ psychotherapy we consider a medical problem and determined in the main, by the personality characteristics of the individual and the level of emotional maturity he had reached prior to addiction.   The unavailability of psychiatrists to carry out psychotherapy for those who need it and can accept it, suggests the further exploration of group therapy techniques.

Within this formulation for treatment, we wholeheartedly support the announced plans of the Department of Hospitals to establish on North Brother Island a 150-bed school-hospital for teen-age youth.   This facility will operate as a "receiving, screening, and intermediate to long-term treatment center," designed to provide a long-term rehabilitation for those teen-agers who can profitably use it, and to provide a valuable opportunity for study and research on the teen-age narcotic problem.

CONCLUSION

An attempt has been made to have this statement point up that the gang boy and the teen-age narcotic user and addict are manifesting varying degrees of emotional disturbances and social maladjustment.   Neither the gang boy nor the teen-age addict represents a typical personality type.   The gamut of psychiatric illnesses may be found in each group.   I have attempted to point up the bio-social-psychological aspects of the behavior of each and have suggested the multidimensional treatment approaches that are demanded if these problems are to be corrected. Whether we focus on the pathology in the social milieu—bad housing, economic deprivations, faulty ethical and moral values; or whether we focus on the psychological factors of faulty ego development, emotional frustration, rejection and broken family life—we find conditions for the addict and the gang boy that precipitate feelings of insecurity, anxiety and inability to find need satisfactions.   For the gang boy it may be relief sought in aggressive reactions, guilt, anxiety and more aggression.   For the addict relief may be sought in escape from the internal and external pressures.   The aim of therapy for both is the rediscovery of inner security.   How to provide the kind of experience that will release the pressures whether they be internal or external, resolve the conflict, and fulfillment of need satisfactions, is the challenge that the gang boy and the teen-age addict present to all who are engaged in the helping process.

D. PERSONALITY ORGANIZATION

28. The Self-Other Process: How Self and Other Emerge Simultaneously to Consciousness*

Related selections: 8, 29, 30

How ONE acts or behaves in any given situation depends in large measure on his concept of self.   How the child feels about himself determines what his problems are and how he will attack them. One of the functions of the teacher is to assist the child in the enhancement of self and, when necessary, to help him change his self concept.   This introductory chapter to Professor Kilpatrick's book will contribute to one's understanding of the early beginnings of the self concept.

THE INTENT of the early chapters of this book is to defend the thesis that human personality, in any desirable sense, is inherently a social product; that only by the self-other process substantially as herein discussed has historic man been able to achieve his distinctly human attributes of language, critical thinking, sense of responsibility, conscience, and the use of standards.   And only by the same process can the growing child of today build these invaluable cultural achievements into his own character. In brief, the operation of the self-other process was essential alike to selfhood and civilization as historically achieved and is still essential in each individual case.

To make more explicit the general thesis just stated, the following specific theses are here set out, to be elaborated and argued later:

No one is born a self, nor is selfhood merely a matter of internal maturation (as this is now frequently used). Selfhood has to be achieved.

Man alone of all living organisms has been able to achieve selfhood. No brute can.

The process of achieving selfhood is an extended one, involving various stages and degrees.

* William Heard Kilpatrick, *Selfhood and Civilization* (The Macmillan Company, 1941), chap. I. pp. 1–10.   Reprinted by permission of author and the Bureau of Publications, Teachers College, Columbia University.

Professor Kilpatrick (1871—) is Professor Emeritus of Education, Teachers College, Columbia University, and is a renowned teacher and scholar.

This selfhood can be achieved only and necessarily in a social milieu, and the surrounding culture enters essentially into the process of achieving as well as into the resulting character achieved.

Consciousness of self and consciousness of others emerge simultaneously to the individual, each growing and contributing during the rest of life mutually to round out and implement the other.

At any one time after the process has been well begun, each, the self and the other, is inextricably composed of both self and other.

The selfhood thus achieved becomes a highly significant factor in and for the further life of the individual and for society.   Personality as such and civilization alike depend on it.

THE MEANING OF THE TERM "SELF": A FIRST DEFINITION

. . . We can here set down a first working definition [of self] in terms of the distinctions the child learns to make in ordinary social situations.   It will be clear, as asserted, that man alone learns to make these distinctions.

We say that a child has achieved selfhood, at least in working degree, when:

(1) he distinguishes himself clearly from others by the appropriate use of such pronouns as *I, me, my, mine; you, yours; he or she, him or her, his or hers;*

(2) he recognizes himself as an agent, one who can effect, bring to pass, and for this purpose uses such sentences as: "I didn't do it.   Mary did." "I can do it.   Let me do it all by myself",

(3) he has achieved a sense of time, past and present, including a notion of the continuity of his self, and for this will use such sentences as: "I am going to Grandmother's tomorrow.   I was there last summer.   Grandfather showed me the calf, but Mother says it is bigger now"; and

(4) he has built a sense of conscious intent and of accompanying accountability and responsibility, as shown by using such a sentence as, "I hurt John's hand, but I didn't mean to do it."

It will be noted that the definition as given is an instance of operational procedure: the defining procedure has to work in life in order to be accepted for thought.   The test as to whether selfhood has been achieved is that the pertinent words shall be used in an ordinary social situation to the satisfaction of competent observers.   The child is not only to use these words and sentences of his own motion; but he must also intend them in their ordinary meaning, and the other person must be able to see (within reason) from the life context that they are so understood and so intended.

All of which is to say that the words must function properly in ordinary communication.

.   .   .   .   .

THE PROCESS OF THING-MAKING

As a preliminary to the actual process of self-building, consider how the normal child comes to build a group of related experiences into a "thing." Such "thing-making" is so inevitable and is accomplished so early and easily that most have never thought of it as the personal achievement it is. The child's experience with his milk bottle will serve as an illustration.

A child ordinarily learns in time to suck from a bottle. From the use of the bottle and how it answers to felt want, the normal child learns to recognize how the bottle feels in his hand; he learns to shift it for more successful use; he associates pleasure with using it. Thereafter the sight of the bottle coming when he is hungry makes him expect handling and sucking and enjoyment. Now all these experiences, actual and potential, with more not here named, get somehow very closely associated in the baby's "mind"; he learns to recognize the bottle when he sees it or feels it and to expect the other experiences that are a usual accompaniment. These recurrent, associated experiences now constitute for the child a "thing"; the bottle has become differentiated from the "big, buzzing, blooming confusion"—to quote William James—of the environment around him, has become something more or less well defined in itself, something having a kind of existence of its own, suggesting certain meanings and arousing certain expectations.

This process of thing-making is, in its simpler and more concrete instances, inevitable with normal humans. However, names help with the process; frequent hearing of the words *bottle, milk* help to crystallize the situation. Helpful, too, is the fact that life in the family or group turns upon the common recognition of the thing under consideration. The child seeks to share in the common life process and so will in high degree accept from the others their practice, including specifically whatever of conception or distinction their practice may turn upon. It is under such circumstances that conceptions of things are built, each with its reliable unified abidingness. The milk bottle, for example, along with its name becomes for the child a means of entering into effective relationship with the family life going on about him.

Along with the milk bottle go also many other analogous "things," such as crib, carriage, cap, foot, finger. But chief of all the "things" that make up the child's world are certain moving objects which you and I, farther along life's road, call persons.   Mother early comes to be of strategic significance, especially if she herself nurses the child.   She is, to use our language, source and guarantee of security and protection, the reliable ever-present source and help in time of trouble.   When life appears darkest and the child is at the last gasp of pain and despair, she (or another of these mysterious things) suddenly appears out of the chaos and all is set right.   It happens not once, but every day and regularly.   Its very occurrence defines reliability and regularity.   Happy the child whose mother does so love him as to let him feel from the first thus secure in her sympathetic care!

In this way Mother comes to be the first object of call when the child learns to cry not simply as a reflex, but as a dawning means to his dawning ends.   No mother but knows this difference between cries.   Meanwhile other persons share also in this process.   In time several such moving objects come to have for the now growing child each its defined place and type of expectation.   The child is getting ready for a great advance.

ACHIEVING INTERNAL UNITY

While the "outside" world of things is thus taking on objective character, the child's internal life begins, so we believe, also to take on a certain interrelated unity.   Although this internal process is not open to the same observation as is the external thing-making, still its actuality seems probable.   The external process is subject to fairly definite observation; the internal remains more a matter of inference in the light of further developments.   Certainly, however, the child has a succession of wants, pains, wishes, and efforts.   Some of these recur sufficiently often to be recognizable even to the child—external movements seem to show this.   As already indicated, the child begins in time to cry in order to attract attention.   He will even get angry when attention is withheld.   Any observant person learns the signs.   This fact of agency, of using means to attain ends, grows as a defined part of the child's life and begins to be a "willed" affair.

It is easy then to believe, but not essential to the succeeding argument, that the normal child does in various ways build at this stage a preliminary conception of himself, of his internal life as some sort of abiding unity parallel with the abiding unity we call external things.   The full internal process can go on, it seems certain, only by contrast with other processes.   This fuller process comes in the next stage, but it seems probable that in this first stage some dawning unity begins, growing perhaps out of the feelings that accompany efforts.   The child continually meets obstacles.

Efforts follow. Some external things seem friendly, others unfriendly. The feelings connected with the mutually opposed external things stay with the child, favorable feelings with the friendly things, unfavorable feelings with the unfriendly, but all together forming an interrelated system. It is in the abidingness of this system and especially in the feelings of effort involved that William James (*Principles* I, 298 ff.) found the sense of abiding personal identity. It is easy to believe that some of this starts early.

THE SIMULTANEOUS COMING OF SELF AND OTHER

As the process of thing-making just discussed continues there comes a time when interaction begins more definitely between what may, with a certain exaggeration, be called the child's two worlds, the world of observed things, on the one hand, and the world of more immediately felt wants, pains, efforts, on the other. What he knows "externally" (as we say) begins to be so related with what he knows "internally" that a new kind of growth takes place: what he knows in one way begins to throw light on what he knows the other way.

What others call his hands and feet, he can move. Sister Mary also has hands and feet. They look like his; and hers, too, move. His and hers are small. Father's and Mother's are large. But they are all hands and feet.

He has a name, and Mary has a name.

He has his toys, and Mary has her toys. Mother will make Mary yield his toys to him and make him yield Mary's toys to her. It is an abiding distinction; Mother is herein again reliable and invariable. He hears Mary say, "It is mine, not yours." Eventually he says of his, "It is mine, not yours."

Mary falls, bumps her head, cries. Mother soothes her. Not long ago he, too, fell, bumped his head, cried. Mother soothed him. Now Mother says to him, "Poor Mary, she bumped her head. It hurts her, just as yours hurt you when you fell."

From such incidents consistently repeated, it gradually begins to dawn on this child that he (his body) is one among those other moving things and then that they feel pains like his. Enlightenment enters upon a higher stage. He now sees himself "from the outside": he has hands, feet, fingers, toes, head, just as Mary has. He now sees also that she, "on the inside," feels pains and cries, just as he does. Also she eats and he eats. She has little clothes, as he has little clothes. She and he are small editions of the same things that older people are.

In all of this a new self is in process of becoming, and these moving objects, persons, begin to emerge as other selves. His new compound self (composed in part of what he first saw in himself, in part of what he first saw in others) begins gradually to take over the conscious direction of his organism. He begins to act out of a self that knows itself. The factor of gradualness in the coming of this process must be emphasized. It is easy, but wrong, for us to read into the child's meager beginning the fullness of thought and distinction that we have achieved.

But once begun, the process grows continually throughout life. Until one has lived, any literature, even the simplest, is a closed book. Until one has felt love, one cannot understand it in others. Until one has suffered bereavement, one cannot in any full sense sympathize with the bereaved. Self and other thus continue to grow, each by what it learns from the other. The two emerge, for conscious consideration, simultaneously. The self is thus, as said before, a compound from both sources. One part has come directly from one's own immediate "internal" experiencing; the other part has come from observing the lives of others. After the first beginning, the two parts are inextricably interwoven. And a like compoundedness holds of my conception of others. Each other is for me composed of things that I have seen first or peculiarly in others but also of things that I attribute to the other because I know them in myself. As will be emphasized later, each human old enough and advanced enough to be a self has achieved a selfhood inherently and inextricably social in origin.

It may be well at this point to call attention to certain other features of self-other making that at times manifest themselves in even early life— some ugly, others good. All who know children have remarked upon a negativism often prominent in the early years, apparently the result of the first clear recognition of the fact of conscious consent or refusal. Gordon Allport tells of a child, not yet three who made a daily visit to his grandmother simply to announce, apropos of nothing in particular, "Grandma, I won't."

The exaggeration of an emerging trait is frequent. This self-insistent negativism appears to be simply an instance in point. Having got far enough along to refuse and negate, the child simply does so in excessive and exaggerated degree. Disagreeable as this may be to others, it probably serves to augment his nascent sense of selfhood through an aggressive exercise of self-determination where it seems, at that time, to count for most. Similarly some children build a pathological self-centeredness. They simply must, for the duration of this interest, hold the spotlight, occupy the center of the stage. Few things are more annoying, or more hurtful to healthy growth, than this maladjustment in its worst forms.

A more pleasing and more serviceable early development growing out

of the self-other process and helping it along is imaginative play.   In this
the child takes on now this character and now that in such fashion as to call
for the study and use of the characteristics assumed.

In all these varied ways, and in many more besides, is the individual advancing to a new and higher level of being.   Henceforth, in the degree
that selfhood has been achieved, will the child be able to see himself as
others see him, so that he can (and in some measure does and will) consider
his acts as he thinks others will judge them.   So achieved, this attainment
will enter as a positive factor in all conscious life thereafter.   Thenceforth
all that he consciously does is affected by the fact and existence of this new
compounded self.   It is not simply that he is conscious of himself in a new
light.   More than that, this consciousness itself enters with its compoundedness into the very constitution of the self to affect inherently all
that is done.   It is most literally true that the individual henceforth lives
on a new and higher level, a level to which none other of the animal world
can aspire.   This higher level is at least an essential part or aspect of, if
not scene and foundation for, all that we value most in human experience.

---

29. Some Observations on the Organization of Personality*

Related selections: 4, 8, 17, 28, 30, 50

TEACHERS everywhere are concerned with changing behavior, behavior that has to do with the whole gamut of children's experiences,
feelings and relationships—their work habits, their efforts, their
desires, the way they act and feel toward other people and things.
Clinical evidence indicates that efforts to change behavior should
be directly concerned with changing perception of self.   As Dr.
Rogers points out, changes in behavior occur as changes take place in
perception of self and perception of reality.   His discussion of the
conditions under which change occurs in perception of self holds
significant implications for educational practice.

* Carl R. Rogers, "Some Observations on the Organization of Personality,"
The American Psychologist, vol. II (September, 1947), pp. 359–368.   Reprinted
by permission of author and the American Psychological Association.
Dr. Rogers (1902—) is Professor of Psychology and Executive Secretary, Counseling Center, The University of Chicago, and writes on many aspects of counseling
and psychotherapy.   He is noted for his development of the theory and techniques of non-directive counseling.

THE RELATION OF THE ORGANIZED PERCEPTUAL
FIELD TO BEHAVIOR

ONE SIMPLE observation, which is repeated over and over again in each successful therapeutic case, seems to have rather deep theoretical implications.   It is that as changes occur in the perception of self and in the perception of reality, changes occur in behavior.   In therapy, these perceptual changes are more often concerned with the self than with the external world.   Hence we find in therapy that as the perception of self alters, behavior alters. Perhaps an illustration will indicate the type of observation upon which this statement is based.

A young woman, a graduate student whom we shall call Miss Vib, came in for nine interviews.   If we compare the first interview with the last, striking changes are evident.   Perhaps some features of this change may be conveyed by taking from the first and last interviews all the major statements regarding self, and all the major statements regarding current behavior.   In the first interview, for example, her perception of herself may be crudely indicated by taking all her own statements about herself, grouping those which seem similar, but otherwise doing a minimum of editing, and retaining so far as possible, her own words.   We then come out with this as the conscious perception of self which was hers at the outset of counseling.

"I feel disorganized, muddled; I've lost all direction; my personal life has disintegrated.

"I sorta experience things from the forefront of my consciousness, but nothing sinks in very deep; things don't seem real to me; I feel nothing matters; I don't have any emotional response to situations; I'm worried about myself.

"I haven't been acting like myself; it doesn't seem like me; I'm a different person altogether from what I used to be in the past.

"I don't understand myself; I haven't known what was happening to me.

"I have withdrawn from everything, and feel all right only when I'm all alone and no one can expect me to do things.

"I don't care about my personal appearance.

"I don't know *anything* anymore.

"I feel guilty about the things I have left undone.

"I don't think I could ever assume responsibility for anything."

If we attempt to evaluate this picture of self from an external frame of reference various diagnostic labels may come to mind.   Trying to perceive it solely from the client's frame of reference we observe that to the young woman herself she appears disorganized, and not herself.   She is perplexed and almost unacquainted with what is going on in herself. She feels unable and unwilling to function in any responsible or social way. This is at least a sampling of the way she experiences or perceives her self.

Her behavior is entirely consistent with this picture of self. If we abstract all her statements describing her behavior, in the same fashion as we abstracted her statements about self, the following pattern emerges—a pattern which in this case was corroborated by outside observation.

"I couldn't get up nerve to come in before; I haven't availed myself of help.

"Everything I should do or want to do, I don't do.

"I haven't kept in touch with friends; I avoid making the effort to go with them; I stopped writing letters home; I don't answer letters or telephone calls; I avoid contacts that would be professionally helpful; I didn't go home though I said I would.

"I failed to hand in my work in a course though I had it all done; I didn't even buy clothing that I needed; I haven't even kept my nails manicured.

"I didn't listen to material we were studying; I waste hours reading the funny papers; I can spend the whole afternoon doing absolutely nothing."

The picture of behavior is very much in keeping with the picture of self, and is summed up in the statement that "Everything I should do or want to do, I don't do." The behavior goes on, in ways that seem to the individual beyond understanding and beyond control.

If we contrast this picture of self and behavior with the picture as it exists in the ninth interview, thirty-eight days later, we find both the perception of self and the ways of behaving deeply altered. Her statements about self are as follows:

"I'm feeling much better; I'm taking more interest in myself.

"I do have some individuality, some interests.

"I seem to be getting a newer understanding of myself. I can look at myself a little better.

"I realize I'm just one person, with so much ability, but I'm not worried about it; I can accept the fact that I'm not always right.

"I feel more motivation, have more of a desire to go ahead.

"I still occasionally regret the past, though I feel less unhappy about it; I still have a long ways to go; I don't know whether I can keep the picture of myself I'm beginning to evolve.

"I can go on learning—in school or out.

"I do feel more like a normal person now; I feel more I can handle my life myself; I think I'm at the point where I can go along on my own."

Outstanding in this perception of herself are three things—that she knows herself, that she can view with comfort her assets and liabilities, and finally that she has drive and control of that drive.

In this ninth interview the behavioral picture is again consistent with the perception of self.   It may be abstracted in these terms.

"I've been making plans about school and about a job; I've been working hard on a term paper; I've been going to the library to trace down a topic of special interest and finding it exciting.
"I've cleaned out my closets; washed my clothes.
"I finally wrote my parents; I'm going home for the holidays.
"I'm getting out and mixing with people; I am reacting sensibly to a fellow who is interested in me—seeing both his good and bad points.
"I will work toward my degree; I'll start looking for a job this week."

Her behavior, in contrast to the first interview, is now organized, forward-moving, effective, realistic and planful.   It is in accord with the realistic and organized view she has achieved of her self.

It is this type of observation, in case after case, that leads us to say with some assurance that as perceptions of self and reality change, behavior changes.   Likewise, in cases we might term failures, there appears to be no appreciable change in perceptual organization or in behavior.

What type of explanation might account for these concomitant changes in the perceptual field and the behavioral pattern?   Let us examine some of the logical possibilities.

In the first place, it is possible that factors unrelated to therapy may have brought about the altered perception and behavior.   There may have been physiological processes occurring which produced the change. There may have been alterations in the family relationships, or in the social forces, or in the educational picture or in some other area of cultural influence, which might account for the rather drastic shift in the concept of self and in the behavior.

There are difficulties in this type of explanation.   Not only were there no known gross changes in the physical or cultural situation as far as Miss Vib was concerned, but the explanation gradually becomes inadequate when one tries to apply it to the many cases in which such change occurs. To postulate that some external factor brings the change and that only by chance does this period of change coincide with the period of therapy, becomes an untenable hypothesis.

Let us then look at another explanation, namely that the therapist exerted, during the nine hours of contact, a peculiarly potent cultural influence which brought about the change.   Here again we are faced with several problems.   It seems that nine hours scattered over five and one-half weeks are a very minute portion of time in which to bring about alteration of patterns which have been building for thirty years.   We would have to postulate an influence so potent as to be classed as traumatic.

This theory is particularly difficult to maintain when we find, on examining the recorded interviews, that not once in the nine hours did the therapist express any evaluation, positive or negative, of the client's initial or final perception of self, or her initial or final mode of behavior. There was not only no evaluation, but no standards expressed by which evaluation might be inferred.

There was, on the part of the therapist, evidence of warm interest in the individual, and thorough-going acceptance of the self and of the behavior as they existed initially, in the intermediate stages, and at the conclusion of therapy. It appears reasonable to say that the therapist established certain definite conditions of interpersonal relations, but since the very essence of this relationship is respect for the person as he is at that moment, the therapist can hardly be regarded as a cultural force making for change.

We find ourselves forced to a third type of explanation, a type of explanation which is not new to psychology, but which has had only partial acceptance. Briefly it may be put that the observed phenomena of change seem most adequately explained by the hypothesis that *given certain psychological conditions, the individual has the capacity to reorganize his field of perception, including the way he perceives himself, and that a concomitant or a resultant of this perceptual reorganization is an appropriate alteration of behavior.* This puts into formal and objective terminology a clinical hypothesis which experience forces upon the therapist using a client-centered approach. One is compelled through clinical observation to develop a high degree of respect for the ego-integrative forces residing within each individual. One comes to recognize that under proper conditions the self is a basic factor in the formation of personality and in the determination of behavior. Clinical experience would strongly suggest that the self is, to some extent, an architect of self, and the above hypothesis simply puts this observation into psychological terms.

In support of this hypothesis it is noted in some cases that one of the concomitants of success in therapy is the realization in the part of the client that the self has the capacity for reorganization. Thus a student says:

"You know I spoke of the fact that a person's background retards one. Like the fact that my family life wasn't good for me, and my mother certainly didn't give me any of the kind of bringing up that I should have had. Well, I've been thinking that over. It's true up to a point. But when you get so that you can see the situation, then it's really up to you."

Following this statement of the relation of the self to experience many changes occurred in this young man's behavior. In this, as in other cases, it appears that when the person comes to see himself as the perceiving, organizing agent, then reorganization of perception and consequent change in patterns of reaction take place.

On the other side of the picture we have frequently observed that when the individual has been authoritatively told that he is governed by certain factors or conditions beyond his control, it makes therapy more difficult, and it is only when the individual discovers for himself that he can organize his perceptions that change is possible.   In veterans who have been given their own psychiatric diagnosis, the effect is often that of making the individual feel that he is under an unalterable doom, that he is unable to control the organization of his life.   When however the self sees itself as capable of reorganizing its own perceptual field, a marked change in basic confidence occurs.   Miss Nam, a student, illustrates this phenomenon when she says, after having made progress in therapy:

"I think I do feel better about the future, too, because it's as if I won't be acting in darkness.   It's sort of, well, knowing somewhat why I act the way I do . . . and at least it isn't the feeling that you're simply out of your own control and the fates are driving you to act that way.   If you realize it, I think you can do something more about it."

A veteran at the conclusion of counseling puts it more briefly and more positively: "My attitude toward myself is changed now to where I feel I *can* do something with my self and life."   He has come to view himself as the instrument by which some reorganization can take place.

There is another clinical observation which may be cited in support of the general hypothesis that there is a close relationship between behavior and the way in which reality is viewed by the individual.   It has been noted in many cases that behavior changes come about for the most part imperceptibly and almost automatically, once the perceptual reorganization has taken place.   A young wife who has been reacting violently to her maid, and has been quite disorganized in her behavior as a result of this antipathy, says "After I . . . discovered it was nothing more than that she resembled my mother, she didn't bother me any more.   Isn't that interesting?   She's still the same."   Here is a clear statement indicating that though the basic perceptions have not changed, they have been differently organized, have acquired a new meaning, and that behavior changes then occur.   Similar evidence is given by a client, a trained psychologist, who after completing a brief series of client-centered interviews, writes:

"Another interesting aspect of the situation was in connection with the changes in some of my attitudes.   When the change occurred, it was as if earlier attitudes were wiped out as completely as if erased from a blackboard. . . .   When a situation which would formerly have provoked a given type of response occurred, it was not as if I was tempted to act in the way I formerly had but in some way found it easier to control my behavior. Rather the new type of behavior came quite spontaneously, and it was only through a deliberate analysis that I became aware that I was acting in a new and different way."

Here again it is of interest that the imagery is put in terms of visual perception and that as attitudes are "erased from the blackboard" behavioral changes take place automatically and without conscious effort.

Thus we have observed that appropriate changes in behavior occur when the individual acquires a different view of his world of experience, including himself; that this changed perception does not need to be dependent upon a change in the "reality," but may be a product of internal reorganization; that in some instances the awareness of the capacity for reperceiving experience accompanies this process of reorganization; that the altered behavioral responses occur automatically and without conscious effort as soon as the perceptual reorganization has taken place, apparently as a result of this.

In view of these observations a second hypothesis may be stated, which is closely related to the first. It is that *behavior is not directly influenced or determined by organic or cultural factors, but primarily* (and perhaps only), *by the perception of these elements.* In other words the crucial element in the determination of behavior is the perceptual field of the individual. While this perceptual field is, to be sure, deeply influenced and largely shaped by cultural and physiological forces, it is nevertheless important that it appears to be only the field as it is *perceived,* which exercises a specific determining influence upon behavior. This is not a new idea in psychology, but its implications have not always been fully recognized.

It might mean, first of all, that if it is the perceptual field which determines behavior, then the primary object of study for psychologists would be the person and his world *as viewed by the person himself.* It could mean that the internal frame of reference of the person might well constitute the field of psychology, an idea set forth persuasively by Snygg and Combs in a significant manuscript as yet unpublished. It might mean that the laws which govern behavior would be discovered more deeply by turning our attention to the laws which govern perception.

Now if our speculations contain a measure of truth, if the *specific* determinant of behavior is the perceptual field, and if the self can reorganize that perceptual field, then what are the limits of this process? Is the reorganization of perception capricious, or does it follow certain laws? Are there limits to the degree of reorganization? If so, what are they? In this connection we have observed with some care the perception of one portion of the field of experience, the portion we call the self.

THE RELATION OF THE PERCEPTION OF THE
SELF TO ADJUSTMENT

Initially we were oriented by the background of both lay and psychological thinking to regard the outcome of successful therapy as the solution of problems.   If a person had a marital problem, a vocational problem, a problem of educational adjustment, the obvious purpose of counseling or therapy was to solve that problem.   But as we observe and study the recorded accounts of the conclusion of therapy, it is clear that the most characteristic outcome is not necessarily solution of problems, but a freedom from tension, a different feeling about, and perception of, self. Perhaps something of this outcome may be conveyed by some illustrations. Several statements taken from the final interview with a twenty year old young woman, Miss Mir, give indications of the characteristic attitude toward self, and the sense of freedom which appears to accompany it.

"I've always tried to be what the others thought I should be, but now I am wondering whether I shouldn't just see that I am what I am."
"Well, I've just noticed such a difference.   I find that when I feel things, even when I feel hate, I don't care.   I don't mind.   I feel more free somehow.   I don't feel guilty about things."
"You know it's suddenly as though a big cloud has been lifted off.   I feel so much more content."

Note in these statements the willingness to perceive herself as she is, to accept herself "realistically," to perceive and accept her "bad" attitudes as well as "good" ones.   This realism seems to be accompanied by a sense of freedom and contentment.

Miss Vib, whose attitudes were quoted earlier, wrote out her own feelings about counseling some six weeks after the interviews were over, and gave the statement to her counselor. She begins:

"The happiest outcome of therapy has been a new feeling about myself. As I think of it, it might be the only outcome.   Certainly it is basic to all the changes in my behavior that have resulted."   In discussing her experience in therapy she states, "I was coming to see myself as a whole.   I began to realize that I am *one* person.   This was an important insight to me.   I saw that the former good academic achievement, job success, ease in social situations, and the present withdrawal, dejection, apathy and failure were all adaptive behavior, performed by *me*.   This meant that I had to reorganize my feelings about myself, no longer holding to the unrealistic notion that the very good adjustment was the expression of the real "me" and this neurotic behavior was not.   I came to feel that I am the same person, sometimes functioning maturely, and sometimes assuming a neurotic role in the face of what I had conceived as insurmountable problems. The acceptance of myself as one person gave me strength in the process of reorganization. Now I had a substratum, a core of unity on which to work." As she continues her discussion there are such statements as "I am getting more happiness in being myself." "I approve of myself more, and I have so much less anxiety."

As in the previous example, the outstanding aspects appear to be the realization that all of her behavior "belonged" to her, that she could accept both the good and bad features about herself and that doing so gave her a release from anxiety and a feeling of solid happiness. In both instances there is only incidental reference to the serious "problems" which had been initially discussed.

Since Miss Mir is undoubtedly above average intelligence and Miss Vib is a person with some psychological training, it may appear that such results are found only with the sophisticated individual. To counteract this opinion a quotation may be given from a statement written by a veteran of limited ability and education who had just completed counseling, and was asked to write whatever reactions he had to the experience. He says:

"As for the consoleing I have had I can say this, It really makes a man strip his own mind bare, and when he does he knows then what he realy is and what he can do. Or at least thinks he knows himself party well. As for myself, I know that my ideas were a little too big for what I realy am, but now I realize one must try start out at his own level.

"Now after four visits, I have a much clearer picture of myself and my future. It makes me feel a little depressed and disappointed, but on the other hand, it has taken me out of the dark, the load seems a lot lighter now, that is I can see my way now, I know what I want to do, I know about what I can do, so now that I can see my goal, I will be able to work a whole lot easier, at my own level."

Although the expression is much simpler one notes again the same two elements—the acceptance of self as it is, and the feeling of easiness, of lightened burden, which accompanies it.

As we examine many individual case records and case recordings, it appears to be possible to bring together the findings in regard to successful therapy by stating another hypothesis in regard to that portion of the perceptual field which we call the self. It would appear that *when all of the ways in which the individual perceives himself—all perceptions of the qualities, abilities, impulses, and attitudes of the person, and all perceptions of himself in relation to others—are accepted into the organized conscious concept of the self, then this achievement is accompanied by feelings of comfort and freedom from tension which are experienced as psychological adjustment.*

This hypothesis would seem to account for the observed fact that the comfortable perception of self which is achieved is sometimes more positive than before, sometimes more negative. When the individual permits all his perceptions of himself to be organized into one pattern, the picture is sometimes more flattering than he has held in the past, sometimes less flattering. It is always more comfortable.

It may be pointed out also that this tentative hypothesis supplies an operational type of definition, based on the client's internal frame of reference, for such hitherto vague terms as "adjustment," "integration," and "acceptance of self." They are defined in terms of perception, in a way which it should be possible to prove or disprove. When all of the organic perceptual experiences—the experiencing of attitudes, impulses, abilities and disabilities, the experiencing of others and of "reality"—when all of these perceptions are freely assimilated into an organized and consistent system, available to consciousness, then psychological adjustment or integration might be said to exist. The definition of adjustment is thus made an internal affair, rather than dependent upon an external "reality."

Something of what is meant by this acceptance and assimilation of perceptions about the self may be illustrated from the case of Miss Nam, a student. Like many other clients she gives evidence of having experienced attitudes and feelings which are defensively denied because they are not consistent with the concept or picture she holds of herself. The way in which they are first fully admitted into consciousness, and then organized into a unified system may be shown by excerpts from the recorded interviews. She has spoken of the difficulty she has had in bringing herself to write papers for her university courses.

"I just thought of something else which perhaps hinders me, and that is that again it's two different feelings. When I have to sit down and do (a paper), though I have a lot of ideas, underneath I think I always have the feeling that I just can't do it. . . . I have this feeling of being terrifically confident that I can do something, without being willing to put the work into it. At other times I'm practically afraid of what I have to do. . . ."

Note that the conscious self has been organized in "having a lot of ideas," being "terrifically confident" but that "underneath," in other words not freely admitted into consciousness, has been the experience of feeling "I just can't do it." She continues:

"I'm trying to work through this funny relationship between this terrific confidence and then this almost fear of doing anything . . . and I think the kind of feeling that I can really do things is part of an illusion I have about myself of being, in my imagination, sure that it will be something good and very good and all that but whenever I get down to the actual task of getting started, it's a terrible feeling of—well, incapacity that I won't get it done either the way I want to do it, or even not being sure how I want to do it."

Again the picture of herself which is present to consciousness is that of a person who is "very good," but this picture is entirely out of line with the actual organic experience in the situation.

Later in the same interview she expresses very well the fact that her perceptions are not all organized into one consistent conscious self.

"I'm not sure about what kind of a person I am—well, I realize that all of these are a part of me, but I'm not quite sure of how to make all of these things fall in line."

In the next interview we have an excellent opportunity to observe the organization of both of these conflicting perceptions into one pattern, with the resultant sense of freedom from tension which has been described above.

"It's very funny, even as I sit here I realize that I have more confidence in myself, in the sense that when I used to approach new situations I would have two very funny things operating at the same time. I had a fantasy that I could do anything, which was a fantasy which covered over all these other feelings that I really couldn't do it, or couldn't do it as well as I wanted to, and it's as if now those two things have merged together, and it is more real, that a situation isn't either testing myself or proving something to myself or anyone else.   It's just in terms of doing it.   And I think I have done away both with that fantasy and that fear. . . .   So I think I can go ahead and approach things—well, just sensibly."

No longer is it necessary for this client to "cover over" her real experiences.   Instead the picture of herself as very able, and the experienced feeling of complete inability, have now been brought together into one integrated pattern of self as a person with real, but imperfect abilities. Once the self is thus accepted the inner energies making for self-actualization are released and she attacks her life problems more efficiently.

Observing this type of material frequently in counseling experience would lead to a tentative hypothesis of maladjustment, which like the other hypothesis suggested, focuses on the perception of self.   It might be proposed that the tensions called psychological maladjustment exist when the organized concept of self (conscious or available to conscious awareness) is not in accord with the perceptions actually experienced.

This discrepancy between the concept of self and the actual perceptions seems to be explicable only in terms of the fact that the self concept resists assimilating into itself any percept which is inconsistent with its present organization.   The feeling that she may not have the ability to do a paper is inconsistent with Miss Nam's conscious picture of herself as a very able and confident person, and hence, though fleetingly perceived, is denied organization as a part of her self, until this comes about in therapy.

THE CONDITIONS OF CHANGE OF SELF PERCEPTION

If the way in which the self is perceived has as close and significant a relationship to behavior as has been suggested, then the manner in which this perception may be altered becomes a question of importance.   If a reorganization of self-perceptions brings a change in behavior; if adjustment and maladjustment depend on the congruence between perceptions as experienced and the self as perceived, then the factors which permit a reorganization of the perception of self are significant.

Our observations of psychotherapeutic experience would seem to indicate that absence of any threat to the self-concept is an important item in the problem.   Normally the self resists incorporating into itself those experiences which are inconsistent with the functioning of self.   But a point overlooked by Lecky and others is that when the self is free from any threat of attack or likelihood of attack, then it is possible for the self to consider these hitherto rejected perceptions, to make new differentiations, and to reintegrate the self in such a way as to include them.

An illustration from the case of Miss Vib may serve to clarify this point. In her statement written six weeks after the conclusion of counseling Miss Vib thus describes the way in which unacceptable percepts become incorporated into the self.   She writes:

"In the earlier interviews I kept saying such things as, 'I am not acting like myself,' 'I never acted this way before.'   What I meant was that this withdrawn, untidy, and apathetic person was not myself.   Then I began to realize that I was the same person, seriously withdrawn, etc. now, as I had been before.   That did not happen until after I had talked out my self-rejection, shame, despair, and doubt, in the accepting situation of the interview.   The counselor was not startled or shocked.   I was telling him all these things about myself which did not fit into my picture of a graduate student, a teacher, a sound person.   He responded with complete acceptance and warm interest without heavy emotional overtones.   Here was a sane, intelligent person wholeheartedly accepting this behavior that seemed so shameful to me.   I can remember an organic feeling of relaxation.   I did not have to keep up the struggle to cover up and hide this shameful person."

Note how clearly one can see here the whole range of denied perceptions of self, and the fact that they could be considered as a part of self only in a social situation which involved no threat to the self, in which another person, the counselor, becomes almost an alternate self and looks with understanding and acceptance upon these same perceptions. She continues:

"Retrospectively, it seems to me that what I felt as 'warm acceptance without emotional overtones' was what I needed to work through my difficulties. . . . The counselor's impersonality with interest allowed me to talk out my feelings. The clarification in the interview situation presented the attitude to me as a 'ding an sich' which I could look at, manipulate, and put in place. In organizing my attitudes, I was beginning to organize me."

Here the nature of the exploration of experience, of seeing it as experience and not as a threat to self, enables the client to reorganize her perceptions of self, which as she says was also "reorganizing me."

If we attempt to describe in more conventional psychological terms the nature of the process which culminates in an altered organization and integration of self in the process of therapy it might run as follows. The individual is continually endeavoring to meet his needs by reacting to the field of experience as he perceives it, and to do that more efficiently by differentiating elements of the field and reintegrating them into new patterns. Reorganization of the field may involve the reorganization of the self as well as of other parts of the field. The self, however, resists reorganization and change. In everyday life individual adjustment by means of reorganization of the field exclusive of the self is more common and is less threatening to the individual. Consequently, the individual's first mode of adjustment is the reorganization of that part of the field which does not include the self.

Client-centered therapy is different from other life situations inasmuch as the therapist tends to remove from the individual's immediate world all those aspects of the field which the individual can reorganize except the self. The therapist, by reacting to the client's feelings and attitudes rather than to the objects of his feelings and attitudes, assists the client in bringing from background into focus his own self, making it easier than ever before for the client to perceive and react to the self. By offering only understanding and no trace of evaluation, the therapist removes himself as an object of attitudes, becoming only an alternate expression of the client's self. The therapist by providing a consistent atmosphere of permissiveness and understanding removes whatever threat existed to prevent all perceptions of the self from emerging into figure. Hence in this situation all the ways in which the self has been experienced can be viewed openly, and organized into a complex unity.

It is then this complete absence of any factor which would attack the concept of self, and second, the assistance in focusing upon the perception of self, which seems to permit a more differentiated view of self and finally the reorganization of self.

RELATIONSHIP TO CURRENT PSYCHOLOGICAL THINKING

Up to this point, these remarks have been presented as clinical observations and tentative hypotheses, quite apart from any relationship to past or present thinking in the field of psychology.   This has been intentional. It is felt that it is the function of the clinician to try to observe, with an open-minded attitude, the complexity of material which comes to him, to report his observations, and in the light of this to formulate hypotheses and problems which both the clinic and the laboratory may utilize as a basis for study and research.

Yet, though these are clinical observations and hypotheses, they have, as has doubtless been recognized, a relationship to some of the currents of theoretical and laboratory thinking in psychology.   Some of the observations about the self bear a relationship to the thinking of G. H. Mead about the "I" and the "me."   The outcome of these might be described in Mead's terms as the increased awareness of the "I," and the organization of the "me's" by the "I."   The importance which has been given in this paper to the self as an organized experience and to some extent as an architect of self, bears a relationship to the thinking of Allport and others concerning the increased place which we must give to the integrative function of the ego.   In the stress which has been given to the present field of experience as the determinant of behavior, the relationship to Gestalt psychology, and to the work of Lewin and his students is obvious.   The theories of Angyal find some parallel in our observations.   His view that the self represents only a small part of the biological organism which has reached symbolic elaboration, and that it often attempts the direction of the organism on the basis of unreliable and insufficient information, seems to be particularly related to the observations we have made.   Lecky's posthumous book, small in size but large in the significance of its contribution, has brought a new light on the way in which the self operates, and the principle of consistency by which new experience is included in or excluded from the self.   Much of his thinking runs parallel to our observations.   Snygg and Combs have recently attempted a more radical and more complete emphasis upon the internal world of perception as the basis for all psychology, a statement which has helped to formulate a theory in which our observations fit.

It is not only from the realm of theory but also from the experimental laboratory that one finds confirmation of the line of thinking which has been proposed.   Tolman has stressed the need of thinking as a rat if fruitful experimental work is to be done. The work of Snygg indicates that rat behavior may be better predicted by inferring the rat's field of perception than by viewing him as an object. Krech (Krechevsky) showed in a brilliant study some years ago that rat learning can only be understood if we realize that the rat is consistently acting upon one hypothesis after another. Leeper has summarized the evidence from a number of experimental investigations, showing that animal behavior cannot be explained by simple S-R mechanisms, but only by recognizing that complex internal processes of perceptual organization intervene between the stimulus and the behavioral response. Thus there are parallel streams of clinical observation, theoretical thinking, and laboratory experiment, which all point up the fact that for an effective psychology we need a much more complete understanding of the private world of the individual, and need to learn ways of entering and studying that world from within.

IMPLICATIONS

It would be misleading however if I left you with the impression that the hypotheses I have formulated in this paper, or those springing from the parallel psychological studies I have mentioned, are simply extensions of the main stream of psychological thinking, additional bricks in the edifice of psychological thought. We have discovered with some surprise that our clinical observations, and the tentative hypotheses which seem to grow out of them, raise disturbing questions which appear to cast doubt on the very foundations of many of our psychological endeavors, particularly in the fields of clinical psychology and personality study. To clarify what is meant, I should like to restate in more logical order the formulations I have given, and to leave with you certain questions and problems which each one seems to raise.

If we take first the tentative proposition that the specific determinant of behavior is the perceptual field of the individual, would this not lead, if regarded as a working hypothesis, to a radically different approach in clinical psychology and personality research? It would seem to mean that instead of elaborate case histories full of information about the person as an object, we would endeavor to develop ways of seeing his situation, his past, and himself, as these objects appear to him. We would try to see with him, rather than to evaluate him. It might mean the minimizing of the elaborate psychometric procedures by which we have endeavored to measure or value the individual from our own frame of reference. It might mean the minimizing or discarding of all the vast series of labels which we have painstakingly built up over the years. Paranoid, pre-schizophrenic, compulsive, constricted—terms such as these might become irrelevant because they are all based in thinking which takes an external frame of reference. They are not the ways in which the individual experiences himself. If we consistently studied each individual from the internal frame of reference of that individual, from within his own perceptual field, it seems probable that we should find generalizations which could be made, and principles which were operative, but we may be very sure that they would be of a different order from these externally based judgments *about* individuals.

Let us look at another of the suggested propositions. If we took seriously the hypothesis that integration and adjustment are internal conditions related to the degree of acceptance or nonacceptance of all perceptions, and the degree of organization of these perceptions into one consistent system, this would decidedly affect our clinical procedures. It would seem to imply the abandonment of the notion that adjustment is dependent upon the pleasantness or unpleasantness of the environment, and would demand concentration upon those processes which bring about self-integration within the person. It would mean a minimizing or an abandoning of those clinical procedures which utilize the alteration of environmental forces as a method of treatment. It would rely instead upon the fact that the person who is internally unified has the greatest likelihood of meeting environmental problems constructively, either as an individual or in cooperation with others.

If we take the remaining proposition that the self, under proper conditions, is capable of reorganizing, to some extent, its own perceptual field, and of thus altering behavior, this too seems to raise disturbing questions. Following the path of this hypothesis would appear to mean a shift in emphasis in psychology from focusing upon the fixity of personality attributes and psychological abilities, to the alterability of these same characteristics. It would concentrate attention upon process rather than upon fixed status. Whereas psychology has, in personality study, been concerned primarily with the measurement of the fixed qualities of the individual, and with his past in order to explain his present, the hypothesis here suggested would seem to concern itself much more with the personal world of the present in order to understand the future, and in predicting that future would be concerned with the principles by which personality and behavior are altered, as well as the extent to which they remain fixed.

Thus we find that a clinical approach, client-centered therapy, has led us to try to adopt the client's perceptual field as the basis for genuine understanding. In trying to enter this internal world of perception, not by introspection, but by observation and direct inference, we find ourselves in a new vantage point for understanding personality dynamics, a vantage point which opens up some disturbing vistas. We find that behavior seems to be better understood as a reaction to this reality-as-perceived. We discover that the way in which the person sees himself, and the perceptions he dares not take as belonging to himself, seem to have an important relationship to the inner peace which constitutes adjustment. We discover within the person, under certain conditions, a capacity for the restructuring and the reorganization of self, and consequently the reorganization of behavior, which has profound social implications. We see these observations, and the theoretical formulations which they inspire, as a fruitful new approach for study and research in various fields of psychology.

---

30. The Relation between Psychoanalysis and Pedagogy*

Related selections: 8, 23, 28, 29, 45

IN THIS selection Anna Freud, daughter of the great Sigmund Freud, points out to a group of teachers in Vienna how Freudian psychoanalysis can aid pedagogy. She reviews its theory of personality and accuses education of "shooting at sparrows with cannonballs" in forcing children to repress instinctual behavior. On the other hand, she points out how the gratification of all instinctual sexual desire can arrest development and cause the individual to fail to develop enough inner restraint to allow the diversion of energy from sexual activity to other more socially approved activities.

WE MUST not demand too much from one another. You must not expect that in four short lectures I shall succeed in presenting to you more than the most important principles of a science the study of which would require many years. I, on the other hand, cannot expect you to remember all the details which I have put before you. Out of my summary, condensed from a great abundance of data and thereby probably often confusing, perhaps you will be able to retain for your guidance only three of the characteristic viewpoints of psychoanalysis.

* From *Psychoanalysis for Teachers and Parents,* by Anna Freud, published by Emerson Books, Inc., 1947, pp. 92–114. Reprinted by permission of the author and publisher.

Dr. Freud, (1895—) a psychoanalyst now living in London, has done extensive work in the area of child analysis and has contributed greatly to the solution of many of its technical problems.

The first of these ideas is concerned with the division of time.   Psychoanalysis distinguishes, as you have already learned, three different periods in the life of the child: early childhood up to about the end of the fifth year; the latency period to the beginning of the prepuberty stage, about the eleventh, twelfth, or thirteenth year; and puberty, which leads into adult life.   In each period there is a different emotional reaction of the child to those around him, and a different stage of instinctual development, each of which is normal and characteristic.   A special attribute of the child, or his method of reaction, cannot therefore be judged without reference to the specific period of his life.   An act of instinctive cruelty or shamelessness, for example, which belongs to the early period and to puberty, will cause anxiety to the observer if it occurs in the latency period, and if found in adult life will have, perhaps, to be judged as a perversity. The strong link with the parents, which is natural and desirable in the first period and in the latency period, is a sign of retarded development if it still exists at the end of puberty.   The strong urge to rebel and to have inner freedom which in puberty facilitates the emergence into normal adult life may be regarded as an obstacle to the right development of the ego in earliest childhood or in the latency period.

The second aspect is connected with the inner growth of the childish personality.   You have probably up till now pictured to yourself the child with whom you have to deal as a homogeneous being, and consequently have not been able to explain the difference between what he wants to do and what he is able to do, the clash between his intentions and his actions. The psychoanalytic conception shows you the personality of the child as of a three-fold nature, consisting of the instinctual life, the ego, and the superego, which is derived from the relationship with his parents.   The contradictions in his behavior are to be explained, therefore, when you learn to recognize behind his different reactions that part of his being which at this particular moment predominates.

The third principle is concerned with the interaction between these divisions of the childish personality; we must not imagine this to be a peaceful process, but rather a conflict.   The issue of such a duel, for example, between the ego of the child and an instinctive wish he knows to be undesirable, depends upon the relative strength of the libido at the disposal of the instinctive impulses compared with the energy of the repressing force derived from the superego.

But I fear, indeed, that these three principles for practical application which I have put briefly before you do not give you all that you hoped to get from psychoanalysis in the way of help for your work.   Probably you seek practical advice which will be a guidance to you rather than an extension of your theoretical knowledge. You want to know for certain which methods of education are the most to be recommended; which must be absolutely avoided if you do not want to imperil the child's whole development. Above all, you want to know whether we shall continue with more education, or give less than we have in the past.

In answer to the last question it should be said that psychoanalysis, whenever it has come into contact with pedagogy, has always expressed the wish to limit education. Psychoanalysis has brought before us the quite definite danger arising from education. You have learned how the child is forced to fulfill the demands of the adult world around him. You know that he conquers his first great emotional attachments by identification with the beloved and feared adults. He escapes from their external influence, but meanwhile establishes a court of judgment within, modeled on the authority of those beings, which continues to maintain this influence within him. This incorporation of the parent-figures is the dangerous step. When this takes place the prohibitions and demands become fixed and unchangeable. In place of living beings they become an historical background which is incapable of adapting itself to progressive external changes. In reality the parent-figures would be influenced by reason in their conduct and would be accessible to the claims of a new situation. Naturally they would be prepared to concede to the thirty-year-old man what was forbidden to the three-year-old child. But that part of the ego which has been formed from the demands and standards of the parents remains inexorable.

The following examples are given to elucidate these points. I know a boy who was extremely fond of dainties in his earliest years. As his passion for dainties was too great to be satisfied by legitimate means, he hit upon all kinds of unlawful expedients and dodges in order to procure sweets, spent all the money he possessed upon them and was not too particular as to how he procured more. Education was called upon to act; the boy was forbidden sweets, and his passionate devotion to his mother, who had interfered with his pleasure, gave special emphasis to the prohibition. His extreme fondness for dainties disappeared, to the great satisfaction of his elders. Yet today this lad, now an adolescent who has plenty of money at his disposal and the freedom to buy up all the sweetmeats of the Viennese confectionery shops, is not able to eat a piece of chocolate without blushing furiously. Everybody who observes him is at once certain that he is doing something forbidden—that he is eating things bought with stolen money. You notice that the restrictions imposed upon him earlier have not automatically yielded to the changed situation.

Listen again to another example, this time not so harmless. A boy loves his mother with special tenderness; all his desires are directed toward filling the place which actually belongs to his father, and toward being her confidant and protector and her best-beloved.   The child now suffers repeatedly the devastating experience that his father is the rightful owner of the position for which he is striving.   It is his father who has the power to send him away from his mother at any time and to show him his own childish helplessness and impotence.   The prohibition to aspire to his father's place is strengthened by his own fear of the father's great potency. Later, when he is an adolescent, this boy evinces a tormenting timidity and uncertainty which he feels as an unbearable obstacle when he finds himself in the same house as the girl he loves.   This basis of his fear is that somebody may come and declare that the place he is occupying belongs to another and he has no right to it.   To avoid this extremely painful situation he employs a great deal of his energy in preparing excuses which could plausibly explain to this other person his presence there.

Or take another case.   A tiny little girl develops an extreme pleasure in her naked body, shows herself naked to her brothers and sisters, and delights in running through the rooms stark naked before she goes to bed. Education steps in and again with success.   The little girl now makes a very great effort to suppress this desire.   The result is an intense feeling of modesty that continues in later life.   When the question of choosing a career arises somebody suggests an occupation which would necessitate sharing a room with companions.   She unhesitatingly states that this career is not for her.   Behind the rational motive the fear is ultimately revealed that she will have to undress before the others.   The question of qualification or preference for the career is of no consequence compared with the strength of the prohibition carried over from childhood.

The psychoanalyst who is engaged in his therapeutic work of "resolving" such inhibitions and disturbances in development certainly learns to know education from its worst side.   Here, he feels, they have been shooting at sparrows with cannon balls!   Would it not have been better perhaps to have given somewhat less value to decorum and convention in these various nurseries, and to have let the first child be greedy and the second imagine himself in the role of the father; to have permitted the third child to run about naked and a fourth to play with his genitals? Would these childish gratifications really have had any important adverse effect as compared with the damage wrought by a so-called "good education"?   Compare them with the division which is thus introduced into the childish personality; the way in which one part of him is incited against another; see how the capacity to love is diminished and the child grows up incapable, perhaps, of enjoyment and of accomplishing his life-work. The analyst to whom all this is apparent resolves, so far as he is concerned, not to aid such an education, but to leave his own children free rather than to educate in this way. He would rather risk the chance of their being somewhat uncontrolled in the end instead of forcing on them from the outset such a crippling of their individuality.

But you are, I feel sure, shocked at the onesidedness of my views. It is high time to change the standpoint. Education appears to us in another light when we have another aim in view—for example, when it is concerned with the neglected child, such as August Aichhorn deals with in his book *Neglected Youth*.

The neglected child, says Aichhorn, refuses to take his place in society. He cannot succeed in controlling his instinctive impulses; he cannot divert enough energy from his sexual instincts to employ them for purposes more highly esteemed by society. He refuses, therefore, to submit to the restrictions which are binding on the society in which he lives, and equally withdraws from any participation in its life and work. No one who has had to do with this type of child in an educational or psychoanalytical connection can fail to regret that in his childhood there had been no force from without which succeeded in restricting his instinctual life, so that these external checks would have been gradually transformed into inner restrictions.

Take as an example a child who for a little while occupied the attention of the Vienna Children's Court. This eight-year-old girl was equally impossible both at home and at school. From every educational institute or convalescent home she was unhesitatingly sent back to her parents after three days at the most. She refused to learn anything or to share in the activities of the other children. She pretended to be stupid, and so cleverly that in several places she was diagnosed as mentally defective. During the lessons she lay down on a bench and played with her sexual parts. Any interruption of this occupation resulted in a wild howling horrifying the grownups. At home she was ill-treated—this was the only idea the parents had of dealing with her. An analytic investigation showed two things. The external circumstances were peculiarly unfavorable to the development of any kind of emotional relations between the child and her environment. No one could offer a love that would have in any way compensated the child for giving up the gratification obtained from her own body. It also showed that the severe punishments from which the parents had obviously expected a restraining influence could not fulfill this purpose. Either owing to her own disposition or on account of significant early experience the little girl had developed such strong masochistic tendencies that each beating could only become once more a stimulus to sex excitement and sex activity. Compare this case of neglect with the one of repression which I described to you earlier. You can see that a free and self-reliant human being does not evolve from this child either. She is nothing but a cowed little animal whose further moral development has stopped simultaneously with her mental growth.

Aichhorn mentions in his book *Neglected Youth* another severe case of maldevelopment—that of a boy who from about his sixth year onward had found every kind of sexual gratification in his mother, and finally, after reaching sexual maturity, lived with her in actual sexual intercourse. He had thus actually accomplished what the other children had enjoyed only in fantasy. Neither has this boy developed into a self-reliant, harmonious, vigorous human being, as we might have expected, considering the evil effects of education described above.

A kind of "short-circuiting" had occurred in his development. By the actual fulfillment of his childhood's wishes he had saved himself the necessity of traversing the whole circle of "becoming grown-up." The wish to become like his father in order to attain all the possibilities of the gratifications permitted to his father was now superfluous. He had indeed escaped the "splitting" of his personality, but in return for that he had given up any further development.

But you will find that the problem is not so difficult as I have represented it to you, and that disturbances in development and delinquency may be merely extreme results, showing, on the one hand, the injurious effect of too great repression, on the other the lack of all restraint. The task of a pedagogy based upon analytic data is to find a *via media* between these extremes—that is to say, to allow to each stage in the child's life the right proportion of instinct-gratification and instinct-restriction.

Possibly a detailed description of this new analytical pedagogy should have been the content of my lectures to you. But for the present no analytical pedagogy exists. We have only as yet individual educators who are interested in this work, and having been analyzed themselves they now seek to apply to the education of children the understanding that psychoanalysis has brought to them of their own instinctual life. It will be a long time before theory and practice are complete and can be recommended for general use.

But in spite of this you ought not to say that psychoanalysis has done nothing beyond giving indications as to the future; that it certainly does not profit teachers engaged in practical work to study psychoanalysis, and that probably it would be better to dissuade them from having anything to do with it. Nor should you say that they had better make enquiries in ten or twenty years' time as to what has been accomplished meanwhile in the application of psychoanalysis to pedagogics.

I maintain that even today psychoanalysis does three things for pedagogy. In the first place, it is well qualified to offer a criticism of existing educational methods. In the second place, the teacher's knowledge of

human beings is extended, and his understanding of the complicated relations between the child and the educator is sharpened by psychoanalysis,
which gives us a scientific theory of the instincts, of the unconscious and of
the libido.   Finally, as a method of practical treatment, in the analysis of
children, it endeavors to repair the injuries which are inflicted upon the
child during the processes of education.

The following example illustrates the second point, i.e. it explains the
pedagogical situation by means of the unconscious background of the conscious behavior.

An excellent woman teacher began her career in her eighteenth year
when, in consequence of unhappy family circumstances, she left home to
take a post as governess to three boys.   The second boy presented a serious educational problem.   He was backward in his lessons and appeared
very timid, reserved, and dull; he played a subordinate part in the family,
and in contrast to his two gifted and attractive brothers was constantly
pushed into the background.   The teacher devoted all her efforts and
interest to this boy, and in a comparatively short time had obtained a
wonderful success.

The boy got very fond of her, was more devoted to her than he had ever
been to anybody before, and became frank and friendly in his ways.   His
interest in lessons increased, and by her efforts she succeeded in teaching
him in one year the subjects laid down for two years, so that he was no
longer behind in his work.   The parents were now proud of this child,
whom until then they had treated with but slight affection; they took much
more trouble about him, and his relations to them and also to his brothers
improved, until the little boy was finally accepted as a most valued member of the family circle.   Thereupon an unexpected difficulty arose.   The
teacher to whom the success was entirely due began now on her side to
have trouble with the boy.   She no longer gave him any love, and could
not get on with him.   Finally, she left the house, where she was greatly
appreciated, on account of the very child who had been in the beginning
the center of attraction to her.

The psychoanalytic treatment which she underwent nearly fifteen years
later for pedagogic reasons revealed to her the true facts of the case.   In
her own home, as a child, she had, with more or less justification, imagined
herself the unloved child—the same position in which she had actually
found the second boy when she began her work with him.   On the ground
of similar slighting treatment she had seen herself in this boy, and had
identified herself with him.   All the love and care which she had lavished
upon him meant that she was really saying to herself: "That is the way I
ought to have been treated to make something out of me."   Success, when
it came, destroyed this identification.   It made the pupil an independent

being who could no longer be identified with her own life.   The hostile feelings toward him arose from envy; she could not help grudging him the success which she herself had never attained.

You will say, perhaps, it was a good thing that this teacher, when she dealt with her pupil, had not yet been analyzed; otherwise we should have lost a fine educational success.   But I feel that these educational successes are too dearly bought.   They are paid for by the failures with those children who are not fortunate enough to reveal symptoms of suffering which remind the teacher of her own childhood and so make sympathy with them possible for her.   I hold we are right in demanding that the teacher or educator should have learned to know and to control his own conflicts before he begins his educational work.   If this is not so, the pupils merely serve as more or less suitable material on which to abreact his own unconscious and unsolved difficulties.

But in addition, the manifest behavior of the child is very seldom sufficient ground for a correct judgment.   I will now give you the following notes which a boy dictated as the first chapter of an extensive book.   As is so often the case with children, it remained a fragment.

Chapter I

THE WRONG THINGS GROWN-UP PEOPLE DO

Here, you grown up people, listen to me, if you want to know something! Don't be too cocky and imagine that children can't do everything that grown-up people do.   But they can do most of what you do.   But children will never obey if you order them about like this, for example: "Now, go and undress, quick's the word, get along."   Then they will never undress, don't you believe it.   But when you speak nicely, then they will do it at once.   You think you can do all you want to do, but don't imagine any such thing.   And don't ever say: "You must do this, you 'must' do that!"   No one "must" do things, neither therefore "must" children do things.   You think children "must" wash themselves.   Certainly not.   Then you say, "But if you don't wash everybody will say, 'Oh fie, how dirty he is!' and so you 'must' wash yourself."   No, he "mustn't," but he does wash, so that people won't call him dirty.

When you tell children what they are to do that's enough, and don't tell them so much about how they are to do it, for they do what they think right, just as you do.   And don't always say to them, "You 'mustn't' buy such and such a thing," for if they pay for it themselves they can buy what they like.   Don't always say to children, "You can't do that!" For they can do many things better than you, and you won't ever believe it, and afterwards you are astonished.   Don't always talk so much; let the children sometimes get a word in!

Now, suppose these written remarks were found in a school and taken to the head master. He would say to himself that this was a dangerous boy on whom one must keep one's eye. From further inquiry he would find out still more serious things about him. The boy was in the habit of making blasphemous remarks about God; he described the priests in language that can scarcely be repeated; he strongly urged his companions not to put up with any interference, and indeed he even planned to go into the zoological gardens and set free the animals whom he regarded as wrongfully imprisoned there. Now a conservative teacher of the old school would say: The rebellious spirit of this boy must be broken by some means or other before it is too late and he has become a serious menace to society. A modern educator, on the contrary, would have the highest hopes of this child's future, and would expect to see in him a future leader and liberator of the masses.

I must tell you that both teachers would be wrong, and all methods of training which they might base upon their knowledge of the manifest situation would be harmful and false. The eight-year-old boy is a harmless little coward, who is in terror when a dog barks at him, who is frightened to go along the dark passage in the evening, and certainly would not be capable of injuring a fly. His rebellious sayings come about in the following way. His early passionate emotional relations, accompanied by an intense preoccupation with his penis, were destroyed as the result of education and of medical treatment from which he experienced severe shock. As a safeguard against new temptations there remained an immense fear, that of being punished on the guilty part of his body, the fear which psychoanalysis names *castration-fear*. This fear caused him now to deny any kind of authority. When anybody has power, he says to himself, then he has the power to punish me. Consequently every possibility of a heavenly or earthly ruler must be removed from the world. The greater his fear of temptation the more he seeks to drown it by his quite harmless attacks on those in authority. This noisy method of protecting himself is, moreover, not his only one. Although he acts the part of an atheist, he kneels down in the evening and prays, secretly impelled by fear. He thinks: "There is indeed no God. But perhaps after all there might be one, and then it would be a good thing, in any case, to behave properly to Him." Now I take it this boy will become neither a menace to society nor a liberator of the masses. What he needs is, indeed, neither admiration of his efforts nor harshness and restrictions, but only—by some means or other—an abatement of his fear which will enable him, released now from his neurotic way of living, to obtain later on the capacity for enjoyment and work.

The psychoanalytic method of treatment which can achieve this is, then, the third service that psychoanalysis has rendered to education. But the description of this method, namely, child analysis, would go far beyond the limits of this course.

E. READINESS FOR LEARNING

31. When Are Children Ready to Learn?*

Related selections: 11, 15, 20, 32, 33, 34

THERE is ample evidence that all children of the same age or grade are not equally ready and able to learn the materials frequently expected of them. Yet thousands of classrooms are managed as if it were axiomatic that children of a particular grade or group have the same degree of readiness for certain experiences. This practice takes its toll in wasted effort on the part of teachers and in untold misery and maladjustment among children. Insight into how to evaluate or appraise children's readiness for learning may be gained from Professor Trow's discussion.

THERE is a tendency to think that children are "ready" to learn whatever happens to be in the course of study for the grade they are in. The result is that fruitless efforts are often made to teach children what they are not yet mature enough to learn.

When, then, *are* children ready to learn?

WHEN THEY ARE HEALTHY

While most classroom teachers know that the greatest possible freedom from physical defects is a sensible prerequisite for learning, the correction is not always complete. For example, parents who have been told their children need glasses, sometimes do nothing about it. But in spite of difficulties, physical examinations are important, and one has to follow through as best he can.

* William Clark Trow, "When Are Children Ready to Learn?" *NEA Journal,* vol. XLIV (February, 1955), pp. 78–79. Reprinted by permission of the author, the publisher, and the American Educational Research Association.

Dr. Trow (1894—) is Professor of Educational Psychology, University of Michigan, and author of widely used texts in this field.

Sometimes children need sleep more than they need instruction, and the child who does not pay attention, who is underactive or overactive, fidgety, cross, or tired, probably needs a physical examination more than a reprimand. Such children are not ready to learn anything; so, until something can be done about their physical condition, there is not much use trying to teach them.

WHEN THEY ARE WELL ADJUSTED

Everyone seems to be satisfied that the harsh punishments of a century and more ago have disappeared, but some self-appointed critics of modern education are dubious about the practices of better schools where children are not given failing marks and are promoted to the next grade whether they can "do the work" or not. Such critics say life is competitive, that children should get used to the idea that they have to work for what they get and should not be coddled.

People who talk this way overlook the fact that children are compelled by law to go to school. Also, these critics do not realize that when children—or older people—are forced to work at things they cannot do, and are then humiliated (with failing marks) for not doing it, they don't like it. They become resentful or aggressive, or perhaps they give up or escape (play truant). In any case, they don't learn—or at least they are not learning what they were sent to school to learn.

But bad school practices are not the only conditions that frustrate children unduly and produce undesirable attitudes and maladjustments of one kind or another. They may be the result of unsatisfactory home conditions, of constant quarreling and fighting between parents, of feeling unwanted, of shame for what their parents or other relatives have done, and of their own misfortunes either fancied or real. Children tend to carry over into school the anxieties and the aggressive or retiring behavior they have developed at home.

Children have difficulties and need to be carried along for a while until they begin to get straightened around. There is no need to expect much of them for a few days, or even a few weeks or months. When they find that they are "accepted" at school, they will begin to learn again.

WHEN THEY ARE MATURE ENOUGH

The familiar term, *reading readiness,* applies to physiological and psychological maturing. We know that it is very inefficient to try to teach children to read before their mental age gets up around 6.5. By that time most of them are ready to begin; before that, they are not.

So various kinds of prereading experiences are provided—listening to stories, looking at pictures, telling about things that happened, and the like.   Experienced teachers can tell when a child is ready to read, though tests may help, especially when classes are large.

But some children do not seem to be ready even when their mental ages hit the magic 6.5.   Sometimes emotional maladjustments are involved. Sometimes children prefer to be read to, and seem to be afraid to lose this sign of interest and affection, as they think they will if they learn to read themselves.   Or they may be uninterested in the simple reading they have to begin with as compared with the more mature stories that have been read to them.

Having rejected reading while the other children were learning, they may feel inferior because of their mistakes when they do try.   Or it may be that, although the mental-test score is high enough, other basic maturing has not taken place.

In any case, there is one thing we do know: that, while opportunity and encouragement are desirable, any form of pressuring works in the opposite direction.

But what of readiness for arithmetic, for geography, or history, or poetry?   The same principles apply to them.   Pupils mature gradually, each at his own rate.   Even those in the same grade are not equally ready to learn the same things.

A grade is a group of children of about the same age who are maturing at widely different rates and who are being provided with the kinds of experiences which it is believed will help them in the maturing process. Thus, it is not something children are promoted to if they have good marks, but instead it is a group in which the children who compose it can develop best.

They sometimes learn best if they drop back with the next younger group; i.e., by "repeating a grade."   However, many pupils who repeat a grade do no better the second time than they did the first.   More often they can learn more if they go along with their group.   Some would, no doubt, do better if they were placed in the grade ahead.

The point is, of course, that there is a wide range of ability in any one grade, whatever the promotion policy of the school—usually about a six-year range.

While attention should be given to the needs of the slow learner, it should also be given to the superior child, who is ready for something before it appears in the school program and is quite bored when the class discussion is on material with which he has long been familiar.   Such a child is likely to think up interesting ways to amuse himself that may cause some trouble for the teacher.   There should be opportunities for more advanced work for some, as well as for easier work for others.

But pressure on pupils to do what they are not ready for, not mature enough to do, does more harm than good, while encouragement and help when they *are* mature enough is often quite effective.

How can one tell whether a child is too immature, or whether he is "just lazy" and "doesn't work up to capacity"?

WHEN THEY ARE INTERESTED

These are difficult questions.   The answer seems to be a little complicated.   In the first place, we are not too sure of just what a child's capacity is.   Test scores are useful, but they are suggestive only.

And, besides, should children be expected to work up to capacity all the time when adults don't?   We work up pretty close to capacity on some things, but on others—say our knowledge of the theater, sports, modern music, or even politics—we are content to ride along, picking up a little here and there as we go.

In the second place, pupils who do not apply themselves as we would like to have them are not necessarily lazy.   They may not be healthy. They may have a low basal metabolic rate, or they may be disturbed and not well adjusted, so they don't feel like putting forth much effort.

As we have seen, these matters need separate attention.   But if children are healthy and welladjusted, they are not lazy, even tho they seem to be.

One teacher was persuaded to abandon traditional methods of assign, test, mark.   She tried a newer method the others were talking about— teacher-pupil planning, individual and group projects, and so on.   Suddenly the class became alive, the pupils began asking *her* questions, and she didn't know the answers.   It was terrible!   Things couldn't go on that way.   So pretty soon she got everything back in order again—assign, test, mark.   And after that, some of the children were "lazy."   They didn't work up to capacity!

The moral of this story, of course, is that, when children can work individually or in groups to find out something, they are more than likely to show unexpected enthusiasm, initiative, and perseverance.   But when the object is only to get a mark—well, that's something else again.

Of course, miracles do not always happen.   Pupil-teacher planning and setting up of projects (they don't necessarily go together) usually require wise guidance.   Otherwise children may attempt the impossible and then be disappointed.   Or they may prefer to let the teacher do the planning, the way some school faculties prefer to let the principal give the orders.   They feel secure that way because all they have to do is do what they are told, and it leaves them free to gripe if things don't come out right.

The well-prepared classroom teacher, who knows more of his subject-matter than is in the pupil's textbooks, can often suggest phases of work that are of interest to certain pupils who are not motivated to learn according to the routine procedure.

For example, a girl uninterested in the usual political history may be thrilled by the history of art or dress design, especially if there are illustrated books in the school library.   Or a boy not enamored of the regular science work may spend hours hunting and classifying sea or land shells.

A well-trained school librarian can be of tremendous help in suggesting books that interest and motivate pupils for further reading.   The materials of all sorts that are available throw the burden of proof on the teacher who says the children are not interested in school work.

32. Energy—Basis of Living and Learning*

Related selections: 12, 13, 31

CHILDREN are dynamic, going energy systems that are continu-ously capturing, transforming and using energy for growth and ac-tivity.   Whatever affects physical health will affect this process of free flowing energy and thus the person's ways of behaving.   How the child behaves in a given situation depends in part on his energy pool.   The teacher needs to recognize and understand individual variations in energy output and use.   In the following selections Dr. Dildine discusses how energy is used in living and learning and describes some of the differences in health and physical condition which affect energy output and energy use.

LIVING is *action*.   Anything alive moves, actively does things, responds with explosive power to changes inside and outside itself.   We are fascinated to watch an amoeba purposefully flowing around a clump of bacteria, or a robin searching all day for worms for her brood, or a child taking bump after bump in his need to learn to walk alone.

* Glenn C. Dildine, "Energy—Basis of Living and Learning," *NEA Journal*, vol. XXXIX (April, 1950), pp. 252–253.   Reprinted by permission of the author and publisher.
     Dr. Dildine (1909—) is Project Coordinator for the Research Project in Develop-mental Needs of Youth, National 4 H Club Foundation of America, Washington, D.C.   He was formerly a staff member of the Institute of Child Study at the University of Maryland.

Behind our fascination is wonder at ceaseless, kaleidoscopic ebb and flow of activity.   What whirring, changing dynamos living creatures are!

URGE TOWARD PERFECTION

Living is reaching for perfection.   The unfolding panorama of life through the ages reveals living things in increasing variety climbing toward greater complexity and directing their energy toward more effective adaptation.   In individual human development, children first revel in scattered, tumbling, bubbling play. Then they push their life-given activity onward into the miracles of adolescent awakening and adult achievement.

OBTAINING AND USING ENERGY

Living is capturing, controlling, and using energy.   Each human is designed to capture and transform the energy stored in foods into the complex processes of living, growing, and behaving.   Every organ in the body is planned to play some essential part in a regular, intricate sequence of internal energy flow and change.

Sense organs, arms and legs, mouth and teeth help to locate and get hold of food and pass it on to the digesting organs for chemical simplification and absorption.   The blood stream carries energy-rich products of digestion, together with oxygen extracted from the air by the lungs, to all parts of the body.   Each organ takes up from the blood the special products and the oxygen which it needs, burns enough to carry out its particular job, and changes this freed energy into forms essential to living.

The heart changes its energy into squeezing, pumping pressure on the blood.   Muscles change their energy into minutely variable amounts and directions of pull on the body's bony levers.   Brain and nerves change their freed energy into pulsing currents flowing in delicately patterned channels.   These currents serve to modify and direct all of the rest of the body's energy-transformations.

All processes eventually result in body activity.   And because man's superb brain is capable of such complex and efficient patterning of the energy at its disposal, human behavior can become amazingly effective.

FEELING

Living is also feeling.   Our deepest satisfactions come as energy surges through us and we succeed in the jobs we have set for ourselves.   If living is fundamentally energy flowing in intricately controlled patterns through a highly organized system, then emotion or feeling is our personal measure of the quality of our living.

If pleasure is anticipating, remembering, or actually experiencing efficient surge of internal power, then unpleasant feeling must be our warning of blocking or breakdown of normally free channels of energy flow.

To illustrate: A healthy youngster takes life head on, gleefully putting all he has into his fun. How violently he resents and fights against us if we suddenly force him to stop and then hold him quiet! We are halting his own free use of energy which he is spending for things he needs, wants, and enjoys. Also, we can remember personal bitterness when someone stopped something we liked to do.

Even physical pain is necessary, for it throbs with warning of injury and possible breakdown in some necessary part of ourselves. So unpleasantness and pain may be nature's way of telling us, "Something *here* challenges your very existence, for it threatens to disorganize or cut off vital flow of energy into and through your being."

Living depends on energy flowing on through into acting. Blocking a person's activity bottles energy up and dams it off and causes tension. Severe tension held too long gives way to inward or outward explosion, and inward explosion is breakdown or death. Energy channels have to be kept open.

URGE TO LEARN

Living is urge to learn. Being alive is really worthwhile when we feel we are growing more competent, better able to do things we want to do, learning to be the kind of person others expect. Children and adults are not naturally lazy or misbehavers.

We are coming to see that *our most basic human quality is an inborn urge and drive to push our own development and self-realization to their limits.* We long to learn to use our energy in more and more effective ways of feeling, thinking, deciding, and acting.

People of all ages, unless they have already been too severely wounded, will face up to severe physical, emotional, and mental threat for the joy of working on thru challenge toward greater competence and selfassurance. But this can happen only if the restrictions and demands from outside have not been too severe.

A child's own memory must consistently tell him, "I have succeeded more often than I have failed. The fun of growing up and learning has far outweighed the necessary pain and defeat and restriction along the way. How exciting and enjoyable it is to use my energy to grow and learn!"

What must adults have done to force so many growing children to deny this birthright? They have forced children to withdraw, already half-licked by life, into a tentative, hesitant shell for protection against any more wounding. They have forced children to become so aggressive, in tense defiance of too much blocking, that they lose much-needed affection, group acceptance, and opportunities for learning. The limitations and distortions which our culture forces onto children are a major problem.

ONLY ONE ENERGY POOL

Living requires balancing and directing the energy budget. The energy we have must be spent on several vital jobs: keeping body machinery in good working order; growing up into a maturing person; using and expanding our ability to feel; and learning to think, decide, and act more effectively. But each person has only one pool of energy to supply all these jobs—the energy he gets from the food he eats.

A grown man normally requires about 2800 calories of food energy per day, a woman about 2400. Approximately half of this is used just to keep alive—providing draft, stoking, cleaning out, carrying around, oiling and repairing the never-resting machinery of living. This maintenance energy is measured as *basal metabolism.* The other half of the energy pool is available for growing and learning.

Since all essential activities draw their energy from the common pool, they must be intimately and inseparably interrelated. We should expect that efficiency in one means more energy for the others, and that defects in one will detract from the others.

We can also anticipate that there must be some over-all control to insure that all energy available will be organized and used for the benefit and enjoyment of the whole person. From this viewpoint, the common denominator unifying all life activities is ever-flowing energy intertwined in increasingly intricate patterns, making breathing or thinking or acting from convictions or visioning the ultimate goals of man all part of a unified synthesis of flowing power.

HEALTH, GROWTH AND BEHAVIOR

Clearly, anything affecting a child's physical health will also affect his body growth and his ways of behaving as an individual. The changes occurring in growth have to build onto and into already working organs and systems *at the same time that these parts keep on working.* (Wouldn't it be miraculous if we could remake a Model T Ford engine into a 1950 V-8 motor at the same time we were driving the car at 60 miles per hour and simultaneously keep the motor in shape for decades of hard driving?)

Physical health affects behavior, but behavior also influences health and growth. The efficiency of our ways of organizing energy in the nervous system in order to control behavior (the nervous energy patterns behind our ways of feeling and thinking, our attitudes and goals, our hopes and values for right and wrong) will play a dominating part in physical health and growth. Good psychological adjustment is associated with healthy body and top-level growth, but psychological maladjustment can actually damage health and prevent growth.

We all know that stomach ulcers and heart disease increase with severe, prolonged emotional tension, and we have each sensed our own lost initiative and pep when we are struggling with a baffling internal emotional conflict. There is startling evidence to show that emotionally disturbed children fail to grow normally.

We conclude that all phases of energy flow are inseparably interwoven in any individual. What each of us will do with his total energy pool depends partly on the mechanical efficiency of body physiology, and partly on the more complex patterns of individual psychological organization, especially on *what life has come to mean to each person.*

If we are to understand any child, we must not only gain a clear picture of his body machinery, but we must also try to discover what this condition seems like to him. We must see how what he is and does matches up with the kind of person he feels himself to be and wants to become.

---

33. *"Motivated to Learn"**

THIS SELECTION should be read in conjunction with the preceding one by the same author.

THE FIRST article of this discussion described human life as ever-flowing energy, power surging in infinite variation and intricate pattern through a highly developed body and brain. This dynamic idea of human life helps in understanding behavior. It focuses on the core of an individual, on each person's internal, intimately personal pattern of controlling and using his own pool of energy.

A person's outward behavior (what he will actually do) is thus the final

* Glenn C. Dildine, " 'Motivated to Learn,' " *NEA Journal,* vol. XXXIX (May, 1950), pp. 356–357. Reprinted by permission of author and publisher.
For a brief biographical sketch of Dr. Dildine see the footnote for selection 32.

or outgoing phase of energy use. It will depend in part on the efficiency of his own body as an energy-transforming machine (the things his body actually could do). It will depend in part on how he feels and thinks and hopes about himself as a person, the kinds of things he likes to do (whether he thinks he is strong or weak; how much he wants to put out his energy).

Thus, any discussion of the effect of physical conditions on a child's behavior must include [1] knowledge of various physical processes in humans and physical conditions in a particular child, and [2] what this body seems like to the child.

HIGH VERSUS LOW ENERGY OUTPUT

It is astonishing how much more fun children become and how we improve our ways of working with them as we learn to recognize some of the reasons for differences in their energy output, their ways of using available energy, and their will to use the energy they have. For example, a child may have seemed "dull" to us, but more careful check shows that he has less energy to use than most of his classmates. Although he must go at living and learning more slowly, he shows that he can eventually learn well if we give him time.

Another child points up the gross difference in rate of living between adults and children. Not realizing that the years between have slowed our own energy output down by comparison, we may easily have described a certain child as "nervous," with a slight edge of distaste and rejection as we said it. Gradually deepening insight shows us that this child has a high energy efficiency, so his driving urge and need is to release a tremendous exuberance flowing thru a healthy body.

Realizing that his behavior is really normal and right for him, instead of trying to curb activity in order "to control nervousness," we now try to provide a variety of enjoyable and productive things for him to do. School seems more fun to him now; he is using his soaring energy productively, and we can be a little more relaxed around him.

PHYSICAL HEALTH INFLUENCES ENERGY OUTPUT AND USE

When we are sick, we not only lose efficiency of infected parts but also have to redirect much of the reduced energy we have left toward fighting the infection and replacing damaged tissues. When we recall how listless and irritable we get when coming down with a severe cold, we can sense how ill-health will rob children of energy, and of easy control of residual energy.   Listlessness and irritability may be signs that children need a doctor's care, not that they are lazy or bad.

Children react so differently to the same illness that one wonders what illness and health have come to mean to a child.   Is sickness so rare that it frightens?   Has previous illness been so painful or frightening that thought of nurses or doctor or sickbed is almost unbearable?   Has sickness been used as a substitute satisfaction to gain attention or love?   Has this child come to think of himself as a person who gets sick all the time, so he gives in easily?   Is he secure, confident, and independent enough to handle both illness and its emotional threats?

PHYSICAL DEFECTS REQUIRE REPATTERNING ENERGY USE

Injuries, defective eyes and ears, arm, leg, and spine deformities may reduce a child's actual efficiency and are often unrecognized causes for slow learning or "poor" behavior.   But we all know of people with gross bodily defects who have lived satisfying, productive lives.   Our bodies have amazing capacities for selfcorrection, for sharpening senses or strengthening the other leg.

But a child needs to know from everyday experience of being accepted, wanted, and helped that his defect does not make him shameful or ugly to others.   He then finds courage and can actually mobilize his energy to struggle through toward compensation and readjustment.   He needs help to see himself as a person, a bit different of course, yet able to do many things well and maybe some things even better than others.

ENDOCRINE EFFICIENCY IS BASIC IN ENERGY CONTROL

Chemicals (hormones) from ductless glands play a controlling part in our energy level.   Each gland has a special job, yet its effect is often modified by secretions of other glands.

The thyroid is a significant example.   The hormone thyroxin sets the body's rate of energy release by controlling the rate of burning body fuels, thus freeing energy from foods for change into nerve impulse, heart beat and blood flow, muscle action, and all the subtle variations in energy found in living systems.   If the thyroid is lazy, all body processes slow down.

Such a child may seem "lazy" because he has little energy left over from just keeping alive to use as he would like, or he may partially lose selfcontrol and become cantankerous because he hasn't energy enough left to keep himself focused, or he may gain excess weight because extra unburned fuel is stored away as fat. Lack of enough free energy will also slow down action of other endocrines, so hormone deficiencies may appear.

A basal metabolism test reveals thyroid condition. Doctors can frequently correct a malfunctioning thyroid and many other endocrine disturbances. But the effect on a child's picture of himself may continue, depending partly on how he was treated during the upset. If he became overweight, how did other people treat him? How much failure did he go through before the cause of low energy was discovered. Is this still a part of his estimate of present ability?

ENERGY VARIES WITH PLACE IN GROWTH CYCLE

Energy output changes with age. It is very high in young children, then tapers off. It spurts again during puberty, and then gradually declines. It will require a different home and school program to enable young children to control and use up their high energy output.

For young children, this means frequent change of activity, a minimum of such physical restraints as sitting quietly at a desk or talking in low tones, and chance for variety in much enjoyable physical action. We are just beginning to realize how right play is for children, how much they learn about growing up during play, in addition to releasing pent-up energy.

During the teenager's growth spurt, so much energy is shifted into growing that often little is left for home and school jobs. A boy or girl who had been fairly self-controlled and active may now show contrasting days of boredom, disorganized restlessness, and even hostility. It is significant to realize that during this growth spurt, energy may vary over 30% within a few days, but that stability returns during later puberty and that this will be reflected then in more consistent energy output and behavior.

Adolescent bodies change and grow so fast! A child may become quite accustomed to himself during the slow changes of late childhood, but all at once, "What is happening to me now? Will my feet ever stop growing? Is this the kind of nose I'll always have? Is this what a normal man is like? or woman? Why can't I be pretty?"

Our way of life puts such a high value on a particular, limited kind of beauty or handsomeness, screaming it from radio, billboards, magazines and movies! We reject deviations so strongly. How must it feel to Al or Caroline to be just their kind of young person, right now? Their answers to these disturbing questions may show very clearly in the ways they act in class or on the playground.

FATIGUE IS RELATED TO AVAILABLE ENERGY

Children (and adults) often get into trouble near the end of the day, losing self-control as energy dwindles. "Lazy" or "slow" or "stupid" children are often dead-tired from home chores or routine late hours or an extra-late visit the night before. Energy resources and the speed at which they can be used up are limited, vary for different children, and change through time in the same child. The amount of rest and sleep and the timing of alternate activity and rest also differ.

Some regimenting is necessary in schools and can be suited to the majority in a group, but many children will still need individual adjustment to suit their rhythm and their tiredness. Even though the others are expected to be actively at work, maybe one child today really should be sleeping instead.

EACH PERSON'S REALITY DETERMINES HIS ENERGY USE

Although many specific physical conditions vary widely between different children and in the same child at different times, these are relatively easy to discover. But what these conditions mean to a child is another matter, for each of us judges "what is real" by his own picture of it, by how it appears to him. This "seeing how things are" varies with our own peculiar psychological slant and differs for each person.

So it is hard for us to get even figuratively inside another person's skin in order to feel how they feel and see as they see. Instead, we are accustomed to interpreting any situation for others from how it would seem to us if it were happening to us. It takes time and conscious, continuous effort to develop sensitivity to the feelings of other people.

Why do so many healthy, good-looking, capable, well-coordinated, energetic young people take so little interest in schoolwork and even seem so antagonistic? Part of the answer lies in whether or not schoolwork and adult demands for behavior seem really good, worthwhile, important, and enjoyable to each child, as *he* sees it from *his* own personal feeling and ideas about himself and his own personal world.

The directions in which a child will use his energy wholeheartedly will depend on his attitudes and interests, the things he fears and hopes for, the goals he strives for and failures he has had all of which have been somehow included in his pattern of organizing and spending energy. The farther away his background of experience (especially at home and in his home neighborhood) is from the behavior the school expects, the less the chance that he will see much sense to the school program.

But if we can learn to tie the things we expect and demand (if only we can be sure our demands are important) to ideas and jobs that seem important to him and promise him pleasure, then he will move into the job cheerfully and profitably. He will be "motivated to learn."

---

34. The Structures of Rewards and Punishments in the Middle and Lower Classes*

Related selections: 17, 18, 27

THE GROWING amount of research on social-class structure in America indicates that not only does this structure operate in the schools but that it operates to the detriment of lower class children. Most public school teachers are from the middle class and need more understanding of the motivational structure of lower-class children and adolescents. What are the differences in basic drives of the lower and middle classes? What are the differences in their rewards and punishments? These are questions to which Dr. Davis has given much study. The student will profit from reading the entire Inglis Lecture, *Social-Class Influences Upon Learning,* of which the following selection is a part.

ANY ATTEMPT to trace the processes by which human beings in our society learn their social drives and social goals must face the problem of social-class differences in motivation. These differences occur in most of the basic areas of human psychology: in mental problem-solving, and in the motivational areas of hunger, sex, and aggression. The most urgent problem for the public schools is to learn the motivational structure of lower-class children and adolescents. About two thirds of our elementary school pupils have been trained in lower-class families and neighborhoods; at least one third of our school population comes from the bottom group within the lower class, the slum culture.

The fate of our nation, industrially, politically, and in case of war, depends primarily upon the ability of the public schools to help large numbers of children from these slum and farm-tenant groups to learn the basic

* Reprinted by permission of the publishers and author from Allison Davis *Social-Class Influences upon Learning,* pp. 23–37 (Cambridge, Mass.: Harvard University Press), Copyright, 1948, by The President and Fellows of Harvard College.

Dr. Davis (1902—) is Professor of Education at the University of Chicago and was a staff member in the division of child development, Commission on Teacher Education, American Council on Education. He is a student of the class and caste structure of American society and its effects on human development.

skills of our society.   The schools have not learned how to do this. Our public schools for the lowest third of our population, the schools in slums, are almost a complete failure.   The staffs of these schools generally are aware of their basic failure, and are demoralized.   Little serious effort has been made by our teachers, colleges, and universities to investigate this major problem in public education.   Our effort here will be directed primarily, therefore, toward examining the motivational structure as learned by the lower-class child from his family and other cultural groups.

To understand the socialization of slum children, one must first view the slum adult-world, and trace the motivational system which slum adults exhibit, as a group.   What are the basic social drives of slum adults?   To put this question more carefully, what experiences does the slum individual learn from his group to define as "pleasant," and what experiences does he learn to define as "painful" among the available experiences in his world?

This approach seems to be the quickest route to an understanding of the social motivation of any group.   For we know from cultural anthropologists that the primary function of all human cultures is to teach the members of the group to regard certain experiences as pleasant and others as painful.   That is to say, nearly all rewards and punishments, so-called, vary with regard to their particular form, intensity, and effect from culture to culture.   We wish to know, therefore, (1) what experiences seem, to the slum group, to be most attainable, pleasant, and free from anxiety, and (2) what experiences seem most unpleasant, or seem most dangerous to the physical survival or social acceptance of the individual.   Anyone who has tried to increase the motivation of slum individuals to work or study regularly knows that these are not simple questions.

One of the most basic differences in motivation between lower-class and middle-class people is their attitude toward eating.   Owing to the greater security of their food supply, middle-class people eat more regularly. They therefore have learned to eat more sparingly at any given time, because they know they are certain of their next meal.   They have also developed a conscientious taboo upon "overeating"; they feel some guilt about getting fat and about what they call "raiding the icebox."

Slum people, however, have a very uncertain food supply.   Their fear that they will not get enough to eat develops soon after the nursing period. Therefore, when the supply is plentiful, they eat as much as they can hold. They "pack food away" in themselves as a protection against the shortage which will develop before the next payday.   They wish to get fat for they regard fat as a protection against tuberculosis and physical weakness. Basically, the origin of this attitude toward eating is their deep fear of starvation.

Just as food-anxiety is far more urgent in lower-class than it is in middle-class society, so is the anxiety which is aroused by the danger of eviction from shelter, the danger of having too little sleep, the danger of being cold, and the danger of being in the dark. The middle-class individual is relatively certain that he will have enough coal or light; he buys his coal by the ton or the five tons; he burns five or ten electric lights. But the lower-class person's hold upon fire for heating is on a day-to-day or week-to-week basis. He buys coal by the bushel, or by the five bushels, or by one-ton loads. Every week or so, therefore, he has to face the fear of being cold, and of having his children cold.

Similarly with light, his anxiety is far more chronic and realistic. His evenings are spent in a gray light; if more than one or two bulbs are used, and those are not of the lowest candle power, he will not be able to pay the light bill. Therefore, the fear of not having so basic a necessity as light—a fear which middle-class people escape after childhood—is recurrent with the slum individual. Walk into any real slum housing at night. People are crowded together in a dingy, twilight world. Their streets and alleys likewise are full of darkness, so that their chronic expectation of assault or rape is increased.

Just as slum people have painful, anxiety-ridden associations with food, so they have with shelter, sleep, and darkness. To this list must be added the fear of being inadequately clothed in winter. Most slum men, Negroes and whites, have no overcoat in normal times. Most sharecroppers' children have no woolen clothes in cold winter weather.

Now, when these same people get relatively large increases in income— as they did during the late war—they spend their money "extravagantly," as middle-class people judge their behavior. What is the meaning of this "splurging" for fur coats, for expensive clothes for children, for new furniture, and so forth? Part of the motivation is a drive for prestige-symbols, an attempt to acquire some of the signs of middle-class status. Equally important, certainly, is its function as a defense against anxiety, which is similar to the function of their Gargantuan eating after payday. When one has money, he buys things which he will be able to buy only once or twice in his lifetime—such things as expensive, respectable, or warm clothes, and a "decent" bed. He burns all the lights he wants; he eats great quantities of meat.

Thus, lower-class people look upon life as a recurrent series of depressions and peaks, with regard to the gratification of their basic needs. In their lives, it is all or nothing, or next-to-nothing. When they have fire, their homes are stifling hot, and everyone sits as close to the fire as possible. For they remember anxiously what it was to be cold; to be too cold to sit in the house; so cold that the whole family must go to bed to keep warm. Just as their deep anxiety about starvation leads them even in good times to glut themselves, as middle-class people view their eating, so does the learned fear of deprivation drive lower-class people to get all they can of the other physical gratifications, "while the getting is good."

It would be more rational if they saved and budgeted their money, but human beings are not rational.   They are what their culture teaches them to be.   "Man is a reasoning, but not a reasonable animal."   Lower-class people cannot learn middle-class foresight and moderation unless they can participate socially with middle-class people, whom they may then learn to imitate.   So far, the public school is our only chance to teach lower-class people the middle-class motivational pattern.   But the schools do not yet understand how to reward lower-class pupils.   Furthermore, our economic system does not offer any prospect of a regular income to slum people; therefore, they lack the relative security which must underlie habits of saving, buying insurance, home buying, and so forth.   As the average slum worker says, "Why should I try to save?   The little bit I could put aside will be gone six months after the next depression starts."

Turning now to those experiences which are defined as painful chiefly by the social, as contrasted to the physical, environment, we find that the socially aroused anxieties are still more numerous.   The middle-class view that slum people have no sense of respectability, feel no pressure for social conformity, is simply ignorance of the facts.   Lower-class culture includes a vast number of social taboos, and therefore stimulates a great number of social anxieties.   First—to return to the so-called "physical" area of food, shelter, heat, and so on—slum culture has its own "decent" or "respectable" standards for food and housing.   Lower-class people learn their own group's cultural standard of "enough to eat," or "a good house," or "good furniture."   It is probably only when the culture goals for subsistence (as "subsistence" is defined by slum culture) are threatened, therefore, that the person experiences marked anxiety.   Lower-class people consider the same house or job as "good" which middle-class people regard as humiliating.   The same standard of living that raises the anxiety of middle-class people will greatly allay the anxiety of slum people in our present social system.

The socially defined dangers of slum life originate in the threat of disapproval, ridicule, or rejection of the individual by his family, play-group, gang, church, club, and so on.   All these lower-class groups make cultural demands of the child and adolescent, just as do the middle-class family, play-group, and so on.   But the demands are generally different than those of the middle-class group.   In other words, the lower-class individual is taught by his culture to be anxious about different social dangers. Whereas the middle-class child learns a socially adaptive fear of receiving poor grades in school, of being aggressive toward the teacher, of fighting, of cursing, and of having early sex relations, the slum child learns to fear quite different social acts. His gang teaches him to fear being taken in by the teacher, of being a softie with her. To study homework seriously is literally a disgrace. Instead of boasting of good marks in school, one conceals them, if he receives any. The lower-class individual fears *not* to be thought a street-fighter; it is a suspicious and dangerous social trait. He fears *not to curse*. If he cannot claim early sex relations, his virility is seriously questioned.

Thus society raises many anxieties in slum people also, but with regard to the attainment of what seem to middle-class people to be strange goals. For those who must live in a slum community, however, these goals are realistic and adaptive.

There is space here to consider only two areas of experience which are patterned by slum culture as chiefly pleasant. I do not believe that there is any evidence that these two areas, sex relations and physical aggression, are more basic physiologically than the food area or the heat-cold area of experience. But psychologically, the areas of sex and aggression are the most formative of middle-class personality, because middle-class culture teaches the individual, from childhood, that sexual responses and physical aggression, more than any other behaviors, must be either inhibited or very carefully controlled. The result of this middle-class training of children to fear their own sex impulses and their own rage is usually to make sex and aggression the chief problem-areas of the middle-class personality. The manifestations of these two types of problems are usually highly disguised, but the source is very simple. Sex and aggression (including stealing) become, if not "properly" controlled and guided according to the middle-class cultural standard, the most dangerous forms of behavior to a person of middle-class status. The middle-class child is taught this lesson by precept and example. For a large portion of middle-class people, therefore, sex has been stamped as "dirty," or "unimportant," and filled with anxiety, because in both their childhood and adolescence their own sexual responses were made to appear too dangerous socially by their parents and teachers.

In slum groups, on the other hand, both children and adults are permitted far more gratification of their sexual responses and of their rage responses. This "permissiveness," as it seems to middle-class people, extends into most of the basic areas of adolescent behavior in the lower class.

Before comparing middle-class and lower-class adolescents, however, a warning must be injected here. We recall that the long, indulgent nursing period of lower-class infants does not prevent their developing marked fear of starvation in later childhood and adulthood. This fact means that new situations, if strongly organized physically or socially, make new behavior. This is a cardinal principle of the new integrated science of social psychology. Basic learning can and does appear at any age level, provided that society or the physical environment changes the organization of its basic rewards and punishments for the individual.

Secondly, we should not be so naive as to think that lower-class life is a happy hunting ground given over to complete impulse expression. Slum people must accept in some form all of the basic sexual controls on incest, homosexuality, and marital irresponsibility. In fact, there is evidence to indicate that they are more observant of the taboos upon incest and homosexuality than is the upper class. Furthermore, the same pattern which holds in their food-intake—of deprivation, relieved by peaks of great indulgence—is typical of lower-class sexual life. Lack of housing, lack of beds, frequent separations of mates and lovers, the hard daily work of mothers with six to fourteen children, the itinerant life of the men, all make sexual life less regular, secure, and routine than in middle class. In the slum, one certainly does not have a sexual partner for as many days each month as do middle-class married people, but one gets and gives more satisfaction, over longer periods, when he does have a sexual partner. With this reservation in mind, one may proceed to examine adolescent behavior in the two classes.

The aggressive behavior of adolescents is a crucial case in point. In the middle class, aggression is clothed in the conventional forms of initiative, or ambition, or even of progressiveness, but in the lower class it more often appears unabashed as physical attack, or as threats of and encouragement for physical attack. In general, middle-class aggression is taught to adolescents in the form of social and economic skills which will enable them to compete effectively at that level. The lower classes not uncommonly teach their children and adolescents to strike out with fist or knife and to be certain to hit first. Both girls and boys at adolescence may curse their father to his face or even attack him with fists, sticks, or axes in free-for-all family encounters. Husbands and wives sometimes stage pitched battles in the home; wives have their husbands arrested; and husbands try to break in or burn down their own homes when locked out. Such fights with fists or weapons, and the whipping of wives, occur sooner or later in most lower-class families. They may not appear today, nor tomorrow, but they will appear if the observer remains long enough.

The important consideration with regard to physical aggression in lower-class adolescents is, therefore, that it is learned as an approved and socially rewarded form of behavior in their culture. An interviewer of ours recently observed two nursery-school boys from lower-class families; they were boasting about the length of their fathers' clasp knives! The parents themselves have taught their children to fight not only children of either sex but also adults who "make trouble" for them. If the child or adolescent cannot whip a grown opponent, the mother or father will join the fight. In such lower-class groups, an adolescent boy who does not try to be a good fighter will not receive the approval of the father, nor will he be acceptable to any play-group or gang. The result of these cultural sanctions is that he learns to fight and to admire fighters. The conception that aggression and hostility are neurotic or maladaptive symptoms of a chronically frustrated adolescent is an ethnocentric view of middle-class psychiatrists. In lower-class families, physical aggression is as much a normal, socially approved and socially inculcated type of behavior as it is in frontier communities.

There are many forms of aggression, of course, which are disapproved by lower-class as well as by middle-class adolescents. These include, among others, attack by magic or poison, rape, and cutting a woman in the face. Yet all of these forms of aggression are fairly common in some lower-class areas. Stealing is another form of aggression which lower-class parents verbally forbid, but which many of them in fact allow—so long as their child does not steal from his family or its close friends. The example of the adolescent's play-group and of his own kin, however, is the crucial determinant of his behavior. Even where the efforts of the parent to instill middle-class mores in the child are more than halfhearted, the power of the street culture in which the child and adolescent are trained overwhelms the parental verbal instruction. The rewards of gang social prestige, of freedom of movement, and of property-gain all seem to be on the side of the street culture.

Like physical aggression, sexual relationships and motivation are more direct and uninhibited in lower-class adolescents. The most striking departure from the usual middle-class motivation is that, in much lower-class life, sexual drives and behavior in children are not regarded as inherently taboo and dangerous.

There are many parents in low-status culture, of course, who taboo these behaviors for their girls. Mothers try to prevent daughters from having children before they are married, but the example of the girl's own family is often to the contrary. At an early age the child learns of common-law marriages and extramarital relationships by men and women in his own family. He sees his father disappear to live with other women, or he sees other men visit his mother or married sisters. Although none of his siblings may be illegitimate, the chances are very high that sooner or later his father and mother will accuse each other of having illegitimate children, or that at least one of his brothers or sisters will have a child outside of marriage. His play-group, girls and boys, discuss sexual relations frankly at the age of eleven or twelve, and he gains status with them by beginning intercourse early.

With sex, as with aggression, therefore, the social instigations and reinforcements of adolescents who live in these different cultures are opposites. The middle-class adolescent finds the roads to sex and aggression blocked by painful and intimidating experiences; the lower-class adolescent is frequently rewarded, both socially and organically, for these same behaviors. The degree of anxiety, guilt, or frustration attached to the behaviors, therefore, is entirely different in the two cases. One might go so far as to say that, in the case of middle-class adolescents, such anxiety and guilt, with regard to physical aggression and sexual intercourse, are proof of their normal socialization in their culture. In lower-class adolescents in certain environments, they are evidence of revolt against their own class culture, and therefore of incipient personality difficulties.

III

The Learning Situation

A. ORGANIZATION FOR LEARNING

35. *Psychology of Group Behavior: the Class as a Group**

Related selections: 7, 37, 43, 45, 46

THE PRESENT-DAY emphasis on group activity and the parallel concern with intra-group relationships mark one great area of difference
between the schools of yesterday and today.   Many teachers, however, still view their classes as aggregations of individuals and not
as functioning groups.   Others, intellectually committed to group
methods, find great difficulty in working effectively through such procedures.   This article by Professor Trow and his colleagues reviews
the research findings in group dynamics and describes how teachers
may utilize the dynamics of the group to further the learning process.

* William Clark Trow, Alvin Zander, William Morse, and David Jenkins, "Psychology of Group Behavior: The Class as a Group," *Journal of Educational Psychology,* vol. XLI (October, 1950), pp. 322–337.   Reprinted by permission of the
authors and publisher.
    For a brief biographical sketch of Professor Trow see the footnote for selection
31.   Professors Zander (1913—) and Morse (1915—) are members of the Department of Educational Psychology at the University of Michigan.   Dr. Jenkins
(1916—), formerly at the University of Michigan, is now with the Adult Education
Association, Chicago.

SOCIAL psychology has been experiencing a marked development in recent years; and because of the many implications for learning situations, those tilling the educational fields should be alert to the new points of view and new findings which are emerging.   This statement does not imply that individual educational pyschology is to be discarded, but rather that it is now directly complemented by the basic socio-psychological concept of the group and the consideration of intra-group relationships.   As long as sociologists confined their attention largely to such social groupings as crowds and mobs, criminals and delinquents, the family, and to census groups with racial and nationality characteristics, the help they could furnish to the classroom teacher was relatively slight.   But with the development of field theory and the study of interaction of individuals in a face-to-face group, and more specifically with the coming of the Iowa studies of democratic, autocratic and *laissez-faire* leadership, followed by the energetic labors of those in the field of group dynamics, the picture has changed.   To this has been added the later Freudian influence in the mental hygiene movement, its expansion in the area of inter-personal relationships, and the exploitation of such treatment techniques as those of group work and play therapy.   We are forced to ask ourselves whether the school class is a group, and, if it is, what this should mean to educational psychologists whose task it is to introduce teachers to the principles which should aid them in developing the best possible environment for learning in their classrooms.

DEVELOPMENTAL BACKGROUND

It should be recognized at the outset that educational psychology has from the beginning devoted itself almost exclusively to modifying the responses of individuals to more or less separate stimuli.   The principles of learning, derived from the performances of laboratory animals and sometimes of children, though the results were brought together statistically, have been applied to the individual learner; and his performance has been tested by presenting him with a series of tasks to perform, and measuring his success in performing them.   To describe the educational psychology of the past and the present in this way is not to belittle it.   Tremendous improvements have been made in instructional materials and methods as a consequence of this view.   We can well feel proud of the contributions of our colleagues and wish for their continuance, for there is much more to be done.   After all, individuals are individuals, and they are probably here to stay!

The single-line, teacher-pupil relationship, however, has other sources than the psychological laboratory.   There seem to have been changing patterns in our educational assumptions as to the most effective and desirable learning situations for the pupil.   At one time the tutorial arrangement, the scholar and the single student in a face-to-face relationship, was felt to be most nearly ideal.   And it may be for certain kinds of learning. But the practical situation in our public schools has not, of course, permitted this kind of teacher-pupil ratio; so we tried to make our classes of twenty-five or more pupils into twenty-five simultaneous one-to-one relationships.   At any rate we followed this pattern, in our classwork, of teacher control, assignment, and class discussion, all dependent on the teacher-pupil-teacher-pupil kind of interaction.   In this tradition we not only have emphasized the importance of the individual pupil of the subject-centered curriculum, but also of individualized instruction, and the child-centered school.

This arrangement tended to be strengthened by virtue of the fact that it provided a more direct system of control.   Any break in the line, with consequent spontaneous interaction among pupils might well mean that the teacher had lost that control which he felt it necessary to maintain. If the class were allowed to become an interacting group, the behavior of the pupils would presumably not be contributing to the learning goals which the teacher had in mind.   Thus, "groupiness" implied "bad discipline."

Two factors have probably contributed to the movement away from this tutorial conception of our classrooms: the increasing interest and attention being given to social learning, and the awareness that the classrooms are, potentially at least, social situations.   With the acceptance of the broader social goals of learning, no longer restricted to scholarly and intellectual activities alone, dependence on the tutorial tradition began to lessen, and the potentialities of the class as a medium for instruction in social learning became clearer.

The point where modern social psychology can offer desirable additions to the individualized approach lies in a recognition of the complex nature of what has in the past been rather loosely referred to as the stimulus situation when this situation is largely made up of other persons.   The exploration of this phenomenon, and of the function of perceptual and conceptual processes in relation to it, is the chief contribution of the gestalt psychologists, whose point of view the late Kurt Lewin was largely responsible for bringing over into the interaction field of social psychology. Teachers have long known that pupils responded to other stimuli than the words of wisdom emanating from behind the teacher's desk. But the teacher's task was to eliminate such distraction so far as possible.   And while this is still often desirable, we are now interested in these other stimuli also, in the interactions of the pupils among themselves and with the teacher. We are asking, what are the implications of viewing the class not merely as a number of individuals in the same room, but as a group?

The exposition of this point of view in education did not have to wait for the recent developments in social psychology. Although the tone is definitely authoritarian, beginnings are found for example in a volume entitled *School Discipline,* by William C. Bagley, published in 1917. In this volume Bagley discussed in some detail the problem of what he called the "unruly school." He pointed out twin antithetical causes: "harsh and unsympathetic treatment," and "indulgence and weakness of control," conditions not too far removed from frustrating autocracy and *laissez-faire,* respectively. He went on to indicate some of the "difficulties of reconciling the opposing ideals of individualism and collectivism." For transforming the unruly school he included among other conditions, "the importance of the objective attitude, and stimulating group responsibility."

Likewise many school practices, particularly in the extra-curricular field, have laid a foundation for group interaction. For a number of years group games and sports provided for coöperative as well as for individual effort, and teacher-sponsored "activities" of the hobby-club variety tended to promote more informed teacher-pupil relationships. The project method, while it chiefly emphasized individual performance, also had a place for group activities. With the activity program came the educational heyday of group participation involving the imitation of adult activities in stores, post offices and the like, but largely employed as a means for motivating learning and providing practice in the traditional subjects.

However, in nearly if not all of these situations, the teacher is set off against the class. His view of the class as a kind of unit is exemplified when the teacher asks a question and then says "Class," calling for all to respond more or less in unison. The teacher is boss, though at times he would tolerate some freedom of action on the part of the children that would permit some release of tensions. Even when an "audience situation" is provided for pupils to read or recite passages they had learned, the same condition maintains. Similarly in matters of student deportment, now usually referred to as citizenship, the teacher is the interpreter of the mores of the culture for the pupils, and serves as judge, jury, and lord high executioner, all bundled into one.

In some schools, the system of student government, with a student council, ideally shifts some of the responsibility to the pupils and permits pupil interaction and group decisions. Similarly, in what is referred to as teacher-pupil planning the teacher forsakes his antithetical position and becomes an actual group member in the rôle of a resource person. It becomes clear that there has been a long period of gradual change in theory which has been followed by practice in some schools, the majority however probably trailing far behind.   At any rate, it may be concluded that education is ready for a systematic overhauling of its theory and practice in dealing with the class as a group, and that it is the proper task of educational psychologists to lead the way.

CONCLUSIONS FROM RESEARCH IN GROUP DYNAMICS

First, in order to explore some of the possible directions that our inquiry might take, let us review briefly a few of the research findings that deal with group functioning and group interrelations in a wide variety of social settings.   Although teachers work with groups and are daily troubled or aided by group phenomena in their classrooms, there has been strikingly little research on the dynamics of classroom groups.   It is often difficult to identify and study the many forces at work in a classroom situation, but recent research in group dynamics indicates that it is possible to develop the necessary theoretical formulations, hypotheses, and measuring methods for testing these hypotheses.   The task remains to identify those areas in which we feel the presence of group phenomena is most relevant to the classroom setting.   We have much to learn about the forces involved in the relationships among students, and between students and teacher. Since the relationship between teacher and class-groups, for example, is by its very nature changing and flexible, it is important that the concepts employed be adequate to deal with the dynamics of relationships involving changing relationships among persons, and changing perceptions of the teacher and the class, as the members acquire new insights and learnings.

A number of assertions from recent research in group dynamics have both theoretical and practical value for the field of educational psychology and teaching methods.   This list is not exhaustive and there will be no attempt to describe the nature of the studies from which these data are derived.   Many of these findings are from laboratory investigations with groups, but a sufficient number of them were obtained in field-experiment settings to indicate that work of this nature can readily be done in the actual classroom setting, as well as in the laboratory.   Some of these assertions are well-tested and validated.   Others are less well proven.   All of them have relevance and promise for educational psychology.

1. The attitudes of an individual have their anchorage in the groups to which he belongs.   Present evidence makes it apparent that many attitudes can be changed more easily by making changes in certain properties of the group than by directly teaching the individuals, as individuals, even in a classroom audience situation.

2. The conduct and beliefs of pupils is regulated in large measure by the small groups within a classroom, such as friendship cliques, and the cohesive groups of students within a school.   These groups demand conformity from their members to certain group standards, and the more cohesive the group, the greater is its power over the member.

3. In some instances failure to learn may be advantageously conceptualized as resistance to change, using resistance here in the same sense as the therapist uses it in his relationships with a patient.*   For example, the group standards developed by persons who were learning a motor task quite similar to a previously perfected one, and who were simply told what they were to do, were entirely different from the group standards developed in a group in which the learners participated in a discussion and made group decisions about the necessity for, and the nature of, the new task to be learned.   Those who participated in the discussion learned much more, more rapidly, and with much less aggression and resentment toward the persons inducing them to make this change.

4. When frustrations are met, highly cohesive groups maintain their effort in movement toward the group goal much more vigorously and effectively than do groups of low cohesiveness.

5. Groups, especially those similar to classroom groups, can be disrupted into separate cliques; or this threat of disruption can be eliminated, by the alteration of forces which determine the attractiveness of the group for the members.   (For example, helping them to become aware of the strength of attraction they have for each other, or the degree to which membership in the group provides a way to achieve things they value highly.)   This condition can be brought about most easily when the members become aware of the forces influencing them, but it can also be effected by an outsider, such as a teacher, who adroitly helps the group to change the impact and strength of these forces surrounding and within their group.

6. The training of persons for effective social action such as performance in school or civic service, can lead to greater effectiveness of effort by the trainees if they are members of a group which is being trained to work as a group, than will result if they are merely individuals in an audience situation.

7. The amount of interaction among students in a class is determined in part by group factors.   For example, in highly cohesive groups arriving at a decision that has general approval, the person whose viewpoint is too different from that of the rest will be rejected—that is, ignored.   In a less

---

* It should be noted, however, that failure to change may be due to such "resistance."   There may be an inadequate set, unsatisfactory motivation, inability to comply with the demands of the goal or a rational non-acceptance of a new position.

well knit group, in which the discussion is not directed to a group decision, the deviate member is likely to get more comments directed to him than the person whose ideas are quite similar to those of the rest of the group.

8. When the members see themselves competing for their own individual goals which make coöperative effort impossible, there is disruption of the ready communication of ideas, the coördination of efforts and the friendliness and pride in one's group which are basic to class harmony and effectiveness. The competitive grading system commonly used today is an illustration in that it creates mutually exclusive goals among the members of a class group.

9. The group climate or style of group life can have an important influence on the members' personalities. One such style of group life can develop hostile, obedient, uncreative, 'goldbrickers'; another can produce confused, purposeless, competitive, drifters; and still another can mould coöperative, flexible, purposeful, turn-taking, we-spirited persons. The group climate that produces such effects is created by the resultant of a number of group properties which can be combined in various ways, among which are the leadership style of the teacher or that of those who function most as group leaders, the degree of cohesiveness, which has already been mentioned, the group-member-skills, the suitability of the group process for the task in hand, the techniques employed by the teacher to satisfy his ego and other needs, and the tension-release patterns used by the group.

10. The reasons for the occasional failure of project methods, and other teaching procedures which depend upon effectively functioning groups often lie in the ineffective use of group problem-solving methods, or in the unskillful handling of group procedures. Groups can help themselves to mature and improve their ability as a learning or producing team by diagnosing their own failures and planning ways of repairing their own deficiencies. Students of group development have devoted much attention to methods of group diagnosis, ways of presenting the findings to a group, and methods for alleviating a group's procedural difficulties.

11. Certain forms of classroom behavior may be recognized as mechanisms developed for relieving tensions somewhat similar to those employed by an individual in relieving his tensions. For example, they employ patterns of group behavior which help avoid difficult tasks or unpleasant situations. These mechanisms are often difficult to identify since they may either be wrongly perceived by the teacher as signs that the group is keeping busy, or they may be accepted as the usual troubles one gets into by the use of committee methods.

12. Difficulties in the transfer of verbal learning to social behavior can

often be overcome by the use of that form of rôle-playing referred to as reality practice, in which the participants try-out the behavior they are expected to use in a situation from which all threat has been removed. Inhibition blindnesses, or fears of 'learning' certain content, or behaving in unaccustomed ways can be removed by the use of a 'cultural-island,' a situation where new group standards are generated while away from the source of the inhibitions. This procedure is effectively used in excursions, conferences, summer camps, and other group activities in which the person is under the pressure of group standards that are different from those at home, and so he dares to adopt forms of behavior which might be quite desirable for him, but which he might hesitate to try out in his accustomed environment for fear of adverse criticism.

Thus we can safely accept the view that group phenomena definitely affect the progress of learning, as well as the kind of learning that takes place. The educational significance of this view derives from the fact that the pupil's attitudes as well as his behavior patterns are modifiable. Increased motivation in participating in the classroom activities, and consequently in learning, derives from several different potential sources in a group atmosphere where good mental hygiene prevails.

Three such potential sources of increased motivation will be considered. The first of these sources lies in method of *goal determination*—the extent to which the goals of the class are determined by the entire group including both pupils and teachers, in a truly co-participant sense. When this procedure is followed, the child will feel that he has some control over his own destiny and, therefore, is able to accept the group goals which he helped select as being his own personal goals. They are things which he himself wants to do and, therefore, he is more likely to follow through on them. The absence of such codetermined objectives does not mean the absence of group standards, but some of these standards are not likely to be the ones which the teacher would choose, or the ones which best promote learning. Such group standards as the 'gentlemen's mark' of C, and the group rejection of the student who is too 'eager,' are familiar to all. Thus group standards in a classroom may inhibit good learning as well as accelerate it.

The second source of increased motivation lies in the extent to which the teachers and the pupils build a *supportive atmosphere* in the classroom, one which helps each child to realize that he is an accepted group member. When this condition maintains, each child has his own 'area of freedom,' within which he is free to make his own decisions. This area can often be much wider than is ordinarily supposed by teachers who are constantly making pupils' decisions for them. Although the group may not approve of everything a pupil does, it still accepts him as a person.   In this kind of an atmosphere the child is able to develop a greater feeling of security with his fellows.   In addition—and this is the important contribution to learning—he is likely to feel freed from personal threat and criticism and, therefore, more willing to go ahead and try new things without fear, realizing that if he fails he will not be rejected either by the class or by the teacher.   Thus failure can be a very positive learning experience because, once the emotional threat is removed, the child can look at his abilities and limitations far more objectively and with greater awareness of what next steps are required for his learning.   It would seem that little learning can occur if the child is denied positive opportunities to make errors.

A third potential source of increased motivation lies in the extent to which the various members of the class are accepted as *participating members*.   When they are so accepted, each can benefit from the knowledge, skills, and abilities of all the other members.   They are no longer dependent primarily or solely on the teacher for all information and guidance. Besides offering the possibility of the development of broader understandings, this gives to each pupil the opportunity to be a contributor to the group, and the classroom becomes, then, a situation for mutual exchange, for mutual sharing.   Research is beginning to show the increased productivity of groups which have this coöperative pattern of relationship. Goal determination by the group, a supportive atmosphere, and a participating membership, then constitute three conditions of group organization of great effectiveness in developing motivation which contribute to the promotion of effective learning.

THE RÔLES OF A TEACHER

What can the teacher do to develop and maintain these conditions conducive to learning?   There are three fundamental rôles which cover the things a teacher does.   Actually these are not discrete parts of the teacher's job, but they do carry quite different implications.   The rôles that will be discussed are the following: (1) the instructional rôle, (2) the rôle of the democratic strategist, and (3) the rôle of the therapist.   Following this, we will ask how the teacher selects the proper rôle, and how the actual operation of this rôle can be evaluated.

First, the *instruction rôle*.   It is obvious that the concept of what a teacher should do has changed over the years.   To the Hoosier schoolmaster the matter was quite simple.   He was the drill sergeant.   The cadence of recitation was akin to the sound of marching feet.   As master of the drill, he called the steps.   This teacher also held the rôle of academic authority; not only did he choose the school experiences, but he was also revered for his great storehouse of information. His very person was the embodiment of learning, and he was categorically right. This fundamental instructional rôle has mellowed with the years. Now the teacher does not always have to know. He operates as an adult with superior learning to be sure, but serves more as a resource person explaining, telling, and demonstrating. His drill-master's uniform has been exchanged for the Socratic garb, for his instruction is more concerned with fostering the students' power to think and reason. This major 'informational rôle' of the teacher is often discussed and is perhaps quite well understood. But it should be clear that this rôle itself is not exclusively the property of the teacher. At times, especially as the content of the course falls within the experience of the students, the class members share or take over the instructional rôle. As we come to understand more about the dynamics of the classroom, we realize that the way in which this rôle is handled by the teacher has important effects on the total learning situation.

A second major rôle which the teacher must play is that of democratic strategist. This has been discussed by other writers under the heading of "group formation." With the goal of pupil participation the teacher must provide the occasion for the introduction of processes to facilitate teacher-pupil planning. To play this rôle successfully two things are required: a high regard for democratic values, and their implications, and a high level of psychological insight into group factors and individual personality. In the rôle of a democratic strategist, the teacher helps the group utilize various methods of progress evaluation, and the information about their progress which they secure. He further helps them see and clarify their accomplishments, blocks, and failures, as well as the values in democratic group action. Thus the task is more than that of being merely an exponent of democratic education. This rôle becomes one of activating democratic processes by helping the class to experience democratic goals and relationships in the design of their everyday classroom experiences.

Understanding the dynamic forces which are affecting the class as a group and those which the techniques bring into play makes possible a contribution to democratic learning because our democratic ethics have established the educational goals and values. Techniques are selected in terms of their potentiality for contributing to the democratic goals of the group at the particular time. It should be pointed out that on the basis of a different set of ethics for the same conditions in a group, different techniques would be selected in order to achieve the goals determined by these differing ethics. However, since it is a contribution toward democratic learning that is desired, it is essential that teachers become as skilled as possible in understanding and working with their classroom groups. For a lack of such skill is likely to result in conditions which are quite the opposite of democratic, even though democratic techniques were supposedly being used. Democratic techniques do not exist *per se;* a technique is democratic only to the extent that it serves as a means to help the group achieve its democratic goals at a particular time. For example, the democratic technique of voting has been used as a very effective method of imposing some small minority opinion on the group.

A third important rôle of the teacher can be subsumed under the title of therapist—a combination of clinician and group worker. Lest someone remonstrate at this obligation, let him be reminded that, willingly or not, every teacher plays this rôle. Sometimes it is somewhat separate from other functions, but more often it is embedded in the classroom life while other functions predominate. No teacher avoids being a group worker, although some are more successful than others and some do crude jobs to be sure. The rôle of therapist implies group management to the end of helping all of the children toward individual and social adjustment. This means a degree of permissiveness, the establishment of rapport with each child, and the conduct of the work without the teacher's ego becoming involved. Such masterful, objective, 'impersonal' human relationships are hard to come by. No one person is able to meet the differential needs of thirty-five or more children and serve as a cushion to soften the blows of harsh reality dealt out by the child's peer culture. But one tries. To do this the teacher must so act as to be the implicit embodiment of an acceptable code of behavior. Time and time again the mores of mental hygiene are illustrated as the teacher relates to the children, to their feelings and to their problems.

It is through the supportive atmosphere previously discussed that the teachers' therapeutic work is carried on. In a conflict situation pupils may come to the teacher as a judge or decision maker. The case need not be handled arbitrarily, but it must be handled. Teachers can never be neutrals but are continually interpreting 'the law' as it applies in individual cases. In the therapist rôle, the teacher shares insights concerning human behavior, helps to get at causes of conflict and to find methods of resolving it. Sometimes the teacher serves this end by just being a friend, or he may provide, or himself be, an example with whom the child can identify in the Freudian sense. At any rate, the teacher must be an expert in human relations, understanding both the group and the individual.

In general teachers play this rôle least adequately of all. They tend toward being moralists, policemen, or punitive agents expecting good character to be developed by decree. While we have much to learn in applying the therapist rôle to the teacher, we already understand enough to know that such a playing of the rôle spells failure. The reason for such failure may often be that the teacher, having personal needs, tends to exploit the situation to satisfy these needs. We have in mind the need to be loved, the desire to avoid conflict, or pressures from latent hostility as examples. A very common attitude is the desire for dependency, where the teacher is happy if the students remain attached and dependent. Redl has written a very interesting paper approaching this from a slightly different angle in which he shows how teachers tend to orient the whole atmosphere so that it plays into a masochistic or sadistic syndrome, to take only two examples. This is a complicated study in depth psychology, fraught with controversy. But it is not without point to us.

SITUATION AND CHOICE OF RÔLE

From the point of view we have been discussing, it will be seen that there is no single complex of rôles a teacher plays. The different legitimate objectives of a classroom demand different emphases. Certainly groups of children differ in their leadership qualities, and other individual and group factors need to be studied and understood. The question the teacher would then ask is: "What technique will contribute most effectively, in terms of the dynamics of my class at this time, to the goals and values which are held by the class (or myself, depending on who determines the goals)?" Two things are needed in selecting the techniques: (1) a knowledge of the dynamics of the technique itself, and (2) a knowledge of the goals and values of the group.

Knowledge about groups will help materially in gaining an understanding of the dynamics of a particular technique, and of the kinds of forces in the group which it brings into play in a positive (or negative) manner under specified conditions. To know these dynamics is important. Otherwise the teacher may fall into the trap of thinking that certain techniques are 'good' *per se,* forgetting that a technique will contribute to the group only as it is able to draw on the positive forces present in the group at the time. If the condition of the group is different at a particular time, the 'good' technique may bring out all that is 'bad' in the group, causing him to wonder why it didn't work, or to blame the group for 'not coöperating.'

SOME TYPICAL CUES FOR RÔLE CHANGES

How is it possible to determine which rôle to play at a particular time? What are the characteristics of a group which will serve as cues for shifting rôles? One such cue is group 'apathy.' If the group is lethargic and passive, one must start searching for reasons.   Is it the course content? The teaching methods?   A general atmosphere of repression?   Children who do not become boisterous at times are living under the control of teachers who are misers of freedom.

Another cue is to be found in the rapidity of 'spread of disorder.'   In a group with adequate morale and goal involvement, disturbances do not spread easily.   If one child upsets the room, individual work with that child is, of course, indicated.   But more important is the signal it gives about the group condition.   If a 'bad actor' is a source of rapid contagion, the bond of common purpose must be weak indeed.   This condition may be caused by such a simple thing as the need for a change of activity due to a requirement for overlong attention to a specific task.   It may be a tension for muscle discharge, or it may go far beyond this to a fundamental dissatisfaction with the teacher behavior.

Other cues for further diagnosis and rôle modification include the presence of isolates, cliques, scapegoating, exclusiveness, extreme competitiveness, and the like.   How much do teachers know about diagnosing these things?   Indeed, how much help can educational psychologists give?   Once the teacher really understands the situation and appreciates its deeper aspects, the rôle complex to meet the situation can usually be found.   The task of the educational psychologist is to see that teachers are so trained that they will understand the dynamics of that situation.

Understanding more about the dynamics of groups helps the teacher in a variety of ways toward increasing his effectiveness in the rôles that are appropriate in different situations.   As more is learned about the theory and research on groups, new ways of thinking about the classroom situation will at first be gained, ways which may have been overlooked before.   The importance of effective communication will come to be recognized in giving instructions and in expressing ideas.   The relationships between the various pupils in the class will be studied, how they feel about each other, and the leader-group relationships, and gradually the teacher will become aware of his own behavior in the class and the kinds of effect it has on the pupils.

Of course, it is not easy to take one's knowledge into the classroom and become immediately aware of these complex interrelationships.   Often it takes considerable training in observation and experience to be able to see, especially at the time it is happening, what is occurring in the group and what its causal relationships and potential effects are.   The transition from 'book learning' to 'observation skill' is a difficult one to make, but it must be made if knowledge about groups is to contribute to teaching effectiveness.

EVALUATION

How does one know one has effectively employed the correct rôle? Were the results in the true psychological sense, those which were described? Was there progress by the individual or the class in the direction of the goals which had been established, and was this progress as great as it might have been if some other teacher rôle had been used, or if this present rôle had been carried through more effectively? And were the dynamics of group relationships improved as a result of this particular rôle? Is the class in the 'healthier' condition and more ready to take forward steps toward whatever new goals may be established, or have they achieved some of their important goals at great cost to themselves and to their interrelations in the group?

Information about these questions can come from different sources. The teacher, by employing the same sensitivity and observational skill used in individual diagnosis of pupil difficulties will become accustomed to diagnosing the group. An examination of the condition of the group will be an examination, at least in part, of the way in which the rôle previously employed affected the group and their response to it. Diagnosis and evaluation, then, go hand-in-hand as a continuing process for the teacher. Evaluation of a previous step, in a large measure, provides the cues for the next step, and for the choice of the rôle to be employed.

Of course, the teacher is not the only source of evaluation data in the classroom. To overlook the students' contributions is to disregard not only a most important source of information, but it is to deny the students the opportunity of evaluating their experience in the class which is the basis for making decisions to improve themselves as individuals and as class members for future work. It is not an easy task, obviously, to carry through an effective evaluation as a group, but the process may be a most valuable educational experience for all.

A third source of evaluation data depends on the availability of outside persons who could be called into the classroom as observers. Someone who is not himself involved in the group is often able to note many important situations which the person who is trying to carry through an effective teaching job almost necessarily overlooks. The outside observer— whether he be a supervisor, principal, fellow teacher, or trained clinician— can note these situations. And to the extent that he has the personal skill in his relationships with those individuals to discuss his observations with the teacher freely and acceptingly, he can be of service in increasing the teacher's own skill in the classroom. He may also take the next step and open his insights to the group as a whole, helping them to see and comprehend more fully the processes of group interaction.

---

36. Research and Theory Regarding Promotion and Nonpromotion*

Related selections: 37, 42

"SOCIAL PROMOTION" is a term that may be depended upon to raise the emotional tone of any discussion among adults interested in modern school practice.   Happily, both those who do believe in nonpromotion and those who do not believe in it have only the welfare of the students in mind.   An intelligent position on this question can be taken only on the basis of an examination of the research.   Professor Goodlad's report, a summary of some of the findings of his and other research in this area, helps to put this problem in proper perspective.

BRING together a number of elementary-school teachers from anywhere in the country and ask them the question: "What are your ten most vexing educational problems?"   The problem of grade-to-grade promotion is likely to be included in all their lists.   There are no panaceas for taking care of the problem.   Blanket promotions for all children are not the answer.   Promotion on the basis of fixed minimum standards is not adequate.   What to do with the slow-learning child after he has been retained or sent along to the next grade is a problem that is at least as complex as the problem of whether to promote.   Present-day educators, in seeking solutions to such problems, pose the question: "What is best for the total development of this child?"   In answer, there are many opinions, some well-conceived theory, and, also, a considerable body of research worth examining.   This research and representative theory are the subjects treated in this article.

* John I. Goodlad, "Research and Theory Regarding Promotion and Nonpromotion."   Reprinted from *The Elementary School Journal,* vol. LIII (November, 1952), pp. 150–155, by permission of the University of Chicago Press and the author.
  Dr. Goodlad (1920—) is Professor of Education and Director of Teacher Education at Emory University and Agnes Scott College.

PROMOTION PRACTICES AND ACHIEVEMENT

Studies into the achievement of repeaters indicate that these children do no better than children of like ability who are promoted.   This was suggested by Keyes more than forty years ago, when he reported that only 21 per cent of a large group of repeaters did better after repeating a grade than before and that 39 per cent actually did worse.   Of course it is impossible to estimate how well the same children might have done had they been promoted.   Arthur sought to answer this question when she matched a group of repeaters with a group of nonrepeaters on the basis of mental age and discovered that the former learned no more than the latter over a two-year period.   She put forward the thought, however, that failure to eliminate the causes of retention, rather than the repeating experience itself may have been the more potent factor in determining subsequent achievement of the pupils.

The cause-and-effect relationship of a given factor can be clarified only by holding constant other factors likely to be influential.   Klene and Branson took cognizance of this fact when they equated children, all of whom were to have been retained in the grade, on the basis of chronological age, mental age and sex.   Half were then promoted, and half were retained.   Klene and Branson concluded that, on the whole, potential repeaters profited more from promotion than did the repeaters from nonpromotion, so far as achievement was concerned.   In this connection, Cheyney and Boyer observed that lack of readiness for the work of a given grade is largely due to a slow learning rate, which will not be improved by repeating a grade section.

Saunders summed up an extensive survey of studies into the effects of nonpromotion upon school achievement as follows:

It may be concluded that nonpromotion of pupils in elementary schools in order to assure mastery of subject matter does not often accomplish its objective.   Children do not appear to learn more by repeating a grade but experience less growth in subject-matter achievement than they do when promoted.   Therefore a practice of nonpromotion because a pupil does not learn sufficient subject matter in the course of a school year, or for the purpose of learning subject matter, is not justifiable.

PROMOTION PRACTICES AND HOMOGENEOUS GROUPING

For most teachers, to secure a class of children closely approximating one another in all areas of development would be the realization of a teaching utopia.   However, Keliher questions the social desirability and Elsbree doubts the feasibility of obtaining any such condition of general homogeneity. Burr points out that when groups are made nonoverlapping in achievement for one subject, or even for a phase of a subject, they overlap greatly in other subjects or other phases of the same subject. From a study of forty-six schools with varying rates of slow progress, Caswell concluded that variability in pupil achievement is no less for schools with high rates of nonpromotion than for schools with lower rates of nonpromotion—findings that are substantially in agreement with those of Akridge. Whether or not homogeneous grouping be desirable or attainable, nonpromotion does not appear to reduce the range of specific abilities with which the teacher has to cope.

PROMOTION PRACTICES AND HABITS AND ATTITUDES

Viele, arguing for the abandonment of no-failure programs, claimed that children will not put forth their best efforts when they know from the start that they are to be promoted. However, studies into the relative effects of various incentives upon school work tend to discredit this line of reasoning.

Both Hurlock and Gilchrist found that groups of pupils who had been praised for their work showed greater improvement over a period of time than did pupils who had been reproved for the quality of their work. Sandin found that the attitude of slow-progress pupils toward school was not commendable. He reported that approximately 40 per cent of these children wished to quit school as soon as possible and that a like per cent —as against 14 per cent of regular-progress pupils—indicated that they disliked school and school work. Of course, these children might have felt the same had they been promoted; Sandin set up no control factors, such as matched groups. However, the findings support Farley's conclusions that the failing child, receiving less satisfaction from his work, tends to become discouraged and frequently antagonistic.

PROMOTION PRACTICES AND BEHAVIOR

The question of the effects of promotion practices upon behavior has provoked considerable controversy. Robinson, for example, maintains that pupils' failure replaces their interest in school work with feelings of resentment that may be expressed in aggression. Jablow, on the contrary, maintains that the frustration produced by inability to perform the work of the higher grade leads promoted slow-learning pupils to become disciplinary problems. Research studies conducted by McElwee and by Sandin revealed a greater incidence of behavior considered troublesome among retarded children than among regular-progress pupils. Although these findings favor promotion over nonpromotion, further experiments with carefully controlled situations need to be conducted.

PROMOTION PRACTICES AND PERSONAL-SOCIAL ADJUSTMENT

In the field of promotion practices, the area involving personal-social adjustment probably is the area most barren of research. A study by Farley, Frey, and Garland indicated a significant correlation between retardation and a low score on a five-point character-rating scale but left open the question whether this was a cause or an effect relationship. Anfinson sought to determine the nature of this relationship by setting up controls. He matched 116 pairs of junior high school pupils on the basis of school attendance, chronological age, sex, intelligence, and socioeconomic status, one member of each pair having been promoted regularly and the other having repeated some previous grade. His findings showed a significant advantage for nonrepeaters over repeaters in social and personal adjustment as revealed by the Symonds-Block Student Questionnaire. As Anfinson pointed out, it would have been better to have tested these irregular-progress pupils soon after the failure occurred—in some cases several years had elapsed. In addition, the range of measuring techniques was very limited. The results of such questionnaires, when used without other sorts of evidence, must be handled with considerable reservation.

Sandin used sociometrics, rating scales, check lists, observations, and interviews to study aspects of social and personal adjustment. In general, he found that nonpromoted children tended to choose companions from grades higher than their own, to be pointed out by classmates as children who associated with pupils from grades other than their own, and to be discriminated against in the selection of study companions. This last finding did not hold true for the first grade, where nonpromoted children received significantly more than their expected share of choices. Sandin's findings concerning attitudes and feelings, described previously, disclosed a general outlook indicative of a less happy adjustment among slow-progress pupils than among normal-progress pupils. Since he made no attempt to equate the groups studied on other factors likely to affect social and personal adjustment, it is impossible to weight the contributing influence of the promotion factor. Sandin put his finger on this problem when he concluded:

It is necessary to conduct further study to discover to what extent children who might have been nonpromoted according to grade standards, but who actually were promoted, show a better picture of adjustment than those who were held back.

The writer conducted an investigation in an attempt to throw some light on the question raised by Sandin.   He equated a group of fifty-five promoted second-grade pupils with a group containing a like number of nonpromoted first-grade pupils on the basis of chronological age, mental age, and achievement.   Considerable preliminary research was done in order to secure equivalent conditions in regard to such matters as enrollment, urban-rural location of schools, physical normality of the selected children, and socioeconomic status of their families.   Two major hypotheses, tested as null hypotheses, gave direction to the study:

1. There are no differences in social adjustment between school children who repeat grades and those who do not.
2. There are no differences in personal adjustment between school children who repeat grades and those who do not.

The instruments for evaluating adjustment were chosen with three purposes in view: (1) to give the selected children an opportunity of rating themselves, (2) to give all children an opportunity to rate one another, and (3) to give the teachers an opportunity to rate the subjects selected.   These three purposes were fulfilled, in the order given, by administration of the California Test of Personality (Primary Series), utilization of sociometric "best-friend" questions, and administration of the Haggerty-Olson-Wickman Behavior Rating Schedules.   The California Test of Personality and sociometric questions were administered both at the beginning and at the end of the school year.   The Haggerty-Olson-Wickman Schedules were administered only at the end of the school year.

Since twenty-nine instances of significant difference were identified, the two hypotheses were clearly rejected.   Eighteen of the significant differences favored the promoted group, and eight favored the nonpromoted group.   The remaining three instances were not clearly to the advantage of either group.   A heavy concentration of those differences favoring the promoted group had to do with peer-group relationships.   All three sources of data pointed to the general difficulty of the nonpromoted children in making satisfactory social adjustments.   The promoted children, on the other hand, tended to be more disturbed personally over their school progress and their home security—concerns that appear to be closely related.

CONCLUSIONS

Throughout the body of evidence runs a consistent pattern: undesirable growth characteristics and unsatisfactory school progress are more closely associated with nonpromoted children than with promoted slow-learning children.   Conversely, slow-learning children who have been promoted tend to make more satisfactory progress and adjustment than do their peers who have been kept back.   Equally obvious, however, is the conclusion that not all the differences identified favor the promoted groups.   The greater incidence of differences favoring the promoted groups is counterbalanced, in part, by certain significant differences favoring nonpromoted groups or individual children.   It becomes clear that blanket promotion policies are not justified by the evidence.   Nevertheless, the evidence supports promotion over nonpromotion as the more defensible educational practice.

RECOMMENDATIONS

The findings of these studies suggest the following recommendations related to the classification of pupils in graded elementary schools.

1. Each child should be considered individually rather than in the light of system-wide policy.   When an affirmative answer, based on fact rather than opinion, cannot be given to the question, "Is nonpromotion likely to favor the all-round development of these children?" then children about whom there is doubt should be promoted to the next grade.

2. Teachers should adopt a broad, factual basis for making their decisions.   Facts related only to achievement and intelligence are not sufficient; nor is the division of a limited body of information into more categories adequate.   Needed are facts related to all phases of human growth and development, collected from a wide range of sources throughout the year rather than during the last few weeks of the school term, and analyzed in relation to sound principles of child growth and development.

3. Instructional needs of the pupil should take precedence over matters of administrative expediency in dealing with questions involving promotion and nonpromotion.   Determining and dealing with cause and effect are infinitely more important educational matters than making decisions regarding the immediate act of retaining or promoting.   School personnel must examine the curriculum out of which failure grows and is being perpetuated.   Then, matters of pupil classification are likely to emerge as by-products rather than as ends in themselves.

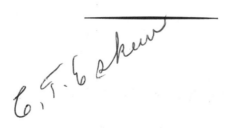

37. The Organization of the Elementary School and the Development of Personality*

Related selections: 35, 36, 40

ORGANIZATIONAL structure, established to facilitate the administrative function, has a way of assuming a sanctity and vested position that tend to obscure the very process that is being administered. In the public schools many illustrations of this phenomenon may be found; for example, the influence of the Carnegie unit on the high school program. In the elementary school certain organizational practices do not seem to agree with what we now know about personality development and learning. In the article below, Dr. Heffernan and her colleagues critically examine the elementary school structure in the light of the educational goal—"for every child a healthy personality."

"FOR EVERY child a healthy personality," the theme of the Mid-century White House Conference on Children and Youth, emphasized an important goal of education. One session of the 1951 California Conference of Elementary School Principals and District Superintendents of Schools was devoted to evaluating elementary school practices in relation to this goal. The practices evaluated were presented by the elementary education staff of the State Department of Education. The staff, basing its judgment on research and experience, chose for presentation the elementary school practices indicated by the following questions:

1. Does the practice of grade placement assure pupils opportunities to develop healthy personalities?
2. Does departmental teaching in the elementary school offer opportunities for pupils to develop healthy personalities?
3. Do current practices in reporting pupil progress to parents tend to give pupils good opportunities to develop healthy personalities?
4. Does the maintenance of grade standards assure opportunities for pupils to develop healthy personalities?
5. Does an articulated program of instruction provide superior opportunities for pupils to develop healthy personalities?

No brief was held for the selection of these questions in preference to others, but the staff believed that the questions cover areas that are of

* Helen Heffernan et al., "The Organization of the Elementary School and the Development of Personality," *California Journal of Elementary Education,* vol. XX (February, 1952), pp. 129–153. Reprinted by permission of authors and publisher.
  Miss Heffernan (1896—) is Chief, Bureau of Elementary Education, California State Department of Education.

concern to every principal and teacher who sees in healthy personality development the major purpose of modern child-rearing.

A HEALTHY PERSONALITY

Before approaching the problems set by the questions, common ground was sought for the meaning of the term "healthy personality." The concept of personality that was expressed during the White House Conference gave significant emphasis to the qualitative aspects of human relations and indicated that everyone who works in the service of children must take *children's feelings* into account. This way of looking at children leads inevitably to the conclusion that demeaning poverty, inadequate school and health services, and racial or ethnical discrimination not only are in and of themselves handicapping to children but also constitute a denial of the democratic ideal that every person is of precious and equal worth. As Allison Davis pointed out, these are serious considerations in a country which at this moment urgently needs all the skilled people it can get. More than 60 out of every 100 children in the United States live in families of low socioeconomic status. The ability represented in this large group of children is largely undiscovered and unused.

To be sure, emotional ill health may have many causes. Inadequate food and housing, racial discrimination, physiological malfunctioning, lack of guidance toward sound life values, and lack of love and affection of parents are all part of the pattern which may disturb or obstruct well-balanced development in children. The problem in the elementary school is to determine ways to be sure that none of its practices constitute hazards to sound development.

The origin of the word "personality" is interesting. The word comes from the Greek *persona* or "mask," something which an actor puts on to conceal his true identity. Many advertisers seem to use the word in somewhat the same sense—the "man of distinction" becomes associated with a commodity available in bottles; an irresistible epidermis can be attained by liberal applications of a gooey substance in a tube or jar; social acceptability is somehow connected with the advertiser's toothpaste or deodorant.

But these were not the meanings of "personality" basic to the White House Conference. Rather, the philosopher, the psychologist, the physiologist, the sociologist, the psychiatrist pooled their ideas and came out with another meaning of personality. They said, "By personality we mean the thinking, feeling, acting human being, who conceives of himself as an individual separate from other individuals. The human being does does not have a personality; he is a personality."

What then are the components of a healthy personality?   These components, said Erikson, are the sense of trust, the sense of autonomy, the sense of initiative, the sense of accomplishment, the sense of identity, the sense of intimacy, the parental sense, and the sense of integrity. These components will bear elaboration as bases for consideration of the organization of the elementary school.

The Sense of Trust

The first component of the healthy personality is the sense of trust. Trust can exist only in relation to something.   The baby begins at an early age to develop the sense of trust as he learns that there are adults in this world who will relieve his hunger, provide for his physical comfort, and give him the affection he needs.   Infants that are brought up in institutions in which the environments are unfavorable to their emotional stability show by listlessness, emaciation, pallor, immobility, unresponsiveness, poor appetite, poor digestion, and a wide variety of evidences of unhappiness that their experiences have not led them to develop a sense of trust. Fortunately most infants in our society find the comfort and affection that are essential to a developing sense of trust.   Both nature and culture are conducive toward making mothers motherly at the very time the child's personality is in need of the nurture which develops this basic component of the healthy personality.

The Sense of Autonomy

Next in chronological order of development is the sense of independence or autonomy.   The second and third years of life are roughly the beginning of the individual's struggle to establish himself as a human being with a mind and will of his own.   The young child must experience over and over that he is a person who is permitted to make choices.   Personal autonomy is an outstanding feature of the American way of life.   Every red-blooded American resents being bossed, being pushed around; he maintains vigorously that everyone has a right to express himself, has a right to control his own affairs.   The American people want each child to grow up to be the upstanding, look-you-in-the-eye kind of individual. That is the type of person Americans admire.

Although the beginnings of this sense of autonomy are important in the early years of life, independence is not established once and for all time any more than is the sense of trust.   The period during which these components of personality first emerge is crucial, but if we want youngsters to emerge into adulthood with healthy personalities, we must continue to nurture their sense of trust, respect their desire to assert themselves, help them learn to hold their desire for independence within bounds, and avoid treating them in ways to arouse any doubts in themselves or feelings of shame in connection with their accomplishments.

A Sense of Initiative

At four or five years of age, the young child wants to find out what kind of a person he can be.   He watches the activities of adults about him; he recreates their activities in his play and yearns to share in their activities. It is important for the child's developing personality that much encouragement be given to the enterprise and imagination which charaterize these years.   The child is ready and avid to learn.   This sense of initiative must be constantly fostered.   If it is restricted, resentment and bitterness and a vindictive attitude toward the world may develop as a functioning part of the child's personality.

A Sense of Accomplishment

If during the early years of life a child has developed the sense of trust, the sense of autonomy, and the sense of initiative, we may expect when he is about six years of age to see the beginning of great development of the sense of accomplishment.   While this sense is developing, a child wants to engage in real tasks that he can carry through to completion.   After a period of time characterized by exuberant imagination, a child then wants to settle down to learning exactly how to do things and how to do them well.   Much of this period of a child's life is spent in the elementary school.   Under reasonably favorable circumstances, this is a period of calm, steady growth, especially if the problems of the previous stages have been well worked out.   Although this is a rather unspectacular period in human growth, it is an important period, for during it there is laid the basis for responsible citizenship.   And during this period children acquire knowledge and skills that make for good workmanship, the ability to co-operate and to play fair, and otherwise to follow the rules of the larger social game.

The chief danger a child may encounter during this period is the presence of conditions which may lead to a sense of inadequacy and inferiority. If in the home or school too much is expected of a child, or if a child is made to feel that achievement is beyond his ability, he may lapse into discouragement and lack of interest.   It is important, therefore, that children have a feeling of successful accomplishment in connection with their school work.   Studies of delinquent children frequently show that they hated school—hated it because they were marked as stupid, awkward, and not able to do so well as other children.   Children who accept their inferiority passively are perhaps more damaged psychologically than those who react aggressively to frustrating experience.

A Sense of Identity

At the onset of adolescence an individual begins to seek clarification of his concept of who he is and what his role in society is to be. During this period a youth is preoccupied with his appearance in the eyes of others— particularly his peers. If the course of personality development has been healthy up to this period, the young person will have acquired a reasonable feeling of self-esteem which will carry him through the tensions and strains that are biologically or culturally imposed on adolescents.

A Sense of Intimacy

Only if the young person has acquired a sense of identity can he achieve the next component of a healthy personality in his relation to others—a sense of intimacy. The surer the young person is of himself, the more successfully can he enter into relations of friendship, love, and inspiration.

The Parental Sense

In its broadest meaning, the parental sense involves the qualities of creativity and productivity. As the individual advances into adulthood, this sense develops normally if the preceding steps have been achieved with reasonable success.

The Sense of Integrity

The final component of a healthy personality is the sense of integrity. Throughout the child's development, his home and school have been helping him to accept the dominant ideals of the culture—honor, courage, purity, grace, fairness, self-discipline. These are the core of integration of the healthy personality. The acquisition of these values and ideals is the ultimate goal of American culture.

With this abbreviation of the background concepts that the White House Conference used as a guide, present practices in elementary education may be examined to determine whether or not they contribute to healthy personality development.

THE EFFECT OF GRADE STANDARDS

Do grade standards contribute to the development of a healthy personality? Is the development of a healthy personality extended by a classification of pupils based on rigid grade standards? For those who accept the findings of research regarding individual differences, the answer is "No." Would healthy personality growth be furthered if the organization of the school provided a program of continuous learning and advancement in accordance with the growth patterns of individuals?

Research clearly indicates that the personality development of a child may be greatly affected by the maintenance of formal grade standards. Successful acomplishment gives the child confidence in himself, while retardation or assignment to slower groups tends to destroy the child's sense of personal worth and to cause him to have feelings of frustration. Rigid grade standards cannot be met by all members of any class.   To the child with strong academic interest and ability, who succeeds almost effortlessly in school, the grade standard has no threatening consequences. To the child whose limitations are greater than average, the grade standard constantly threatens defeat and thereby prevents wholesome personality growth.

Grade standards originated as an administrative device and not as an answer to the question, What is best for the child?   Can we justify the continuance of rigid grade standards as a basis for classifying pupils? Fixed grade standards are untenable in the light of what is now known about the best ways to meet the needs of children.   A plan for continuous growth is widely recognized as more desirable than the experience of annual evaluation followed by promotion or nonpromotion.   Learning is continuous and must progress according to individual rate and ability. Schools cannot, therefore, justify the continuance of annual promotion or retardation as sound practice.

An adult can never fully know how a child feels about school failure unless the adult has experienced such failure.   Were you ever failed? Who knew that you failed?   Did you lose status with your mother or your father, with big brother or sister?   Children have feelings about failure even though some teachers say that children do not mind failure.   How would you cover it up if you failed in your job?   The hurt is deep, it must be hidden.   To carry on, one must appear indifferent.   Children are courageous.   They are helpless in the face of adult decisions—decisions which so irrevocably affect their personality growth.

Can each of thirty-five children, all nine years old, make the third-grade standard on May 26?   Can each of the thirty-five youth, fourteen years old, be expected to pass the *same test* in United States history for graduation from the eighth grade?   Can thirty-five children, six-years old, each read all the same pre-primers, primers, and first readers?   Roma Gans in her book, *Reading is Fun,* says that "perhaps no subject has been taught with greater disregard for child development than has reading."   The eyes of all six-year-old children do not focus well; the children may not speak in complete sentences; their family may speak Spanish at home; Dad may have gone to Korea and Mother may be working. Are children in each of these circumstances equally ready to read?

Statistics show that teachers fail over one-seventh of the children in their classes. Are teachers aware that under such circumstances it is the school that has failed? Grade standards for subject and skill mastery do not promote the development of healthy personalities. Yet there appears to be something compulsive about the desire of teachers and school authorities to make all children alike even though they know that each child differs from all other children.

A basic democratic principle is violated when the school fails to recognize the worth of the individual. The educational principle of individual differences is widely accepted. Equally widely accepted is the knowledge that learning is an individual, not a mass, accomplishment. More than twenty-five years ago psychologists publicized information about individual rates of development, abilities, interests, and needs. For many years William Heard Kilpatrick has directed our attention to the fact that a child learns what he lives. If the child is to learn democracy, teachers and principals must make the school environment such that he lives democratically and successfully in accordance with his potentialities. Success motivates, failure frustrates children.

The child as a whole must be accepted. Intelligence, which is measurable to a degree, is but one of the factors which the child brings to the learning situation. To a high degree, ability to learn is conditioned by emotions, health, and past experiences as well as by native mental ability. Teachers must help children to grow, not attempt to force them nor to drive them down standardized roads to learning through slavish attention to the same book. Children must be helped to know themselves, and to build their destinies in terms of their strengths. No one ever had his personality developed by constant emphasis on his weaknesses. Since individuals are different, fixed standards are not conducive to healthy growth. In a flexible program, differentiated materials and opportunities permit each child to explore and experiment, to figure, to discuss, to share and collect, and to find answers at a rate that is commensurate with his ability and interest.

When individuals have purpose they can master arithmetic combinations, learn to write a business letter, and read for information material adapted to their level of achievement. They will move steadily ahead, even though they may move slowly. When the child knows his needs, knows the next steps to be undertaken, and has had a part in planning how to attain his objectives, he is ready to learn. Interest motivates the child to put forth effort. Opportunities for continuous growth are challenging and stimulating to him.   Attempts to force learning are not only unnecessary, but they are also futile unless the child is responding to inner drives of interest which encourage him to put forth effort.

Education to meet the needs of all children includes education to help parents understand their children and their children's problems.   Parents must be helped to understand that there are some things that the school cannot do for children.   Leaders in education to whom parents rightfully turn for information and guidance must help parents to understand individual differences and to accept their child and to love him as he is, even if he is a slow learner.   Parents must know that the school cannot teach the child to read before he is ready and that no amount of effort to do so will produce the results desired.   And parents must know that attempting to force a child toward mastery of a skill, before he is capable, produces frustration and delays learning.   Schools must prevent frustrations, emphasize prevention, and do away with the need for remedying problems that they have created.   Parents must realize that each child is unique; that his rate of learning, his ability, experiential background, health, and emotions strongly influence his learning.   The individual's ability to learn differs from that of others as does his personal appearance or physical strength.   Teachers must be honest and straightforward but kindly and understanding as they seek the help of parents.   Parents and school people must become a team that believes in and supports each child.

Expediency should never be the basis for determining the treatment that a child shall be accorded.   Democratic philosophy emphasizes the sanctity of individual personality.   Change requires effort.   When principals and teachers become dissatisfied with present practices in education they will willingly put forth the effort necessary to find improved ways of helping children.   If inflexible grade standards do not meet individual differences or provide for continuous learning, schools must find better ways to do these things.   The task of schools is to build, not to destroy, personalities.   Each child must be accepted as he is, where he is, and provided with opportunities for continuous growth.   Democracy needs confident, healthy personalities.   Schools must modify practices so that during each day each child has satisfying opportunities for growth toward the realization of his individual potentialities.

DEPARTMENTALIZATION AND PERSONALITY DEVELOPMENT

As part of the major topic—"Does the organization of the elementary school contribute to the development of a healthy personality?"—one subtopic to be considered is the following: "Does departmentalization of the elementary school or departmental teaching in the elementary school contribute to the development of a healthy personality?"

By departmentalization or departmental teaching we mean the type of organization in which a group of children has a different teacher for instruction in each subject or in a combination of subjects.

We will agree that any type of organization has advantages and disadvantages. Before a principal and a faculty adopt a program of departmentalization, they should weigh the advantages and disadvantages of such an organization in terms of the wholesome personality development of children.

Departmentalization has its roots in tradition. In the development of schools in our country there came into prominence, particularly in New England toward the close of the eighteenth century, the type of school organization known as the "departmental school." The chief characteristic of the departmental school was the vertical division of the course into a reading school and a writing school. Although the two departments were housed in the same building, each of them had its own master, its own room, its own set of studies. The pupils attended each department in turn, changing from one to the other at the end of each half-day session. This type of organization appeared to further the purposes for which schools were maintained at that time.

Another quick look at the organization of elementary schools in our country reveals that departmentalization passed out of the picture during the nineteenth century but was reintroduced in the New York City schools, particularly in the upper grades, in 1900. Various types of departmentalization were introduced into elementary schools during the next twenty years. During this period the "platoon school" reached full development.

The various types of organization in existence in the twenties and thirties gave rise to extensive research relative to the values of different types of organization. The chief claim of the advocates of departmentalization was in terms of better achievement in understanding subject matter. The advocates of the platoon school were the most ardent supporters of departmentalization. The studies which were made to evaluate the platoon school and various types of departmentalization failed to show unquestioned superiority of that form of organization in teaching subject matter. The research of such men as Stewart, Gerberich, Prall, Spain, Shepard, Courtis, and Bonser support this statement.

It would appear from the research evidence this group made available that by the early thirties departmentalization had ceased to grow. But the tendency at the present time for certain elementary schools to reintroduce departmentalization, especially in the seventh and eighth grades, makes it appear that the facts pertaining to departmentalization have to be rediscovered by each generation of educators. Let us look, then, at the advantages and disadvantages of departmentalization. As we consider the purposes of schools in a democratic society, the objectives of education, the needs of boys and girls, and the ways of learning that are psychologically sound and conducive to wholesome personality development as the basis for analyzing departmental organization, there appear the following disadvantages in departmental organization:

1. It organizes learning experiences in terms of areas of subject matter.
2. It disintegrates rather than integrates learning experiences.
3. It separates the tool subjects from the activities in which the tools are used.
4. It fails to utilize ways of learning that are psychologically sound.
5. It interrupts continuity and destroys the relatedness of learning experiences.
6. It requires a teacher to meet an exceedingly large number of children each day; thus no teacher knows each child well enough to perform important guidance functions.
7. It results in the situation where a number of teachers make demands upon one pupil.
8. It requires a rigid schedule, which interrupts activities and thus prevents purposes from being realized and interests satisfied.

The scales are heavily weighted against departmentalization. Except in a few instances, departmentalization appears to be unjustified in the first six grades of the elementary schools. Departmentalization might be justified in those rare instances in which certain teachers are unable to instruct pupils in such specialized areas as music and art.

In the seventh and eighth grades some departmentalization may be justified in the organization of learning experiences for young adolescents only if it permits these youth to satisfy their special interests and develop their abilities in such areas as art, music, physical education, and science. If a departmental organization making these provisions is used, it should permit the child to spend at least half his school time with one teacher. The social studies should constitute the core of his learning experiences. The social studies, language arts, science, and mathematics should be integrated in his learning experiences.

REPORTING PUPIL PROGRESS TO PARENTS

The answers to the question: "Do current practices in reporting pupil progress to parents contribute to the development of a healthy personality?" is "No," if the practice involves sending home at regular intervals one of several varieties of what have been called "nasty little status cards" as the sole means of acquainting parents with the social and academic progress of their children.

Analyze a few of the cards used to report pupil progress. The fairly innocuous one sometimes given to children in the kindergarten asks the teacher to respond to two items: (1) "He does his best," and (2) "He could do better." Perhaps the child is marked: "Does his best." Why? Does the teacher like the child? Does the family see that his physical and emotional needs are being adequately met? Do the school and the home work well together? He may be marked: "Could do better." Why he could do better is left out. Could he do better if his tonsils were out, if his mother prepared more nourishing meals, if he felt better about the new baby, if his mother and father got along without quarreling, if his father were home from the army, if the teacher gave him more chances to succeed, if the experiences of the school were closer to his out-of-school experiences and made sense to him?

The unanswered questions that arise in the minds of many parents as they read such a report cause them to lose confidence in the school program and to develop a feeling of separation from activities of the classroom. Such reports make it difficult for attitudes of confidence to develop between home and school.

In discussing another type of report card, one that is marked S and U, a mother remarked that these report cards were "U" to her. In one case a child received a U in physical education although both the parents and the teacher knew that the child's flat feet prevented him from running and playing games as well as the other children. On being questioned about this mark, the teacher said: "I couldn't give Tommy an S because it is apparent that he can't play the same games other children play. It wouldn't be fair to the others or keep up the standards. Besides, the children know that he doesn't play as well as they do. You can't fool them." And so a child is marked down for having a physical defect and is made to feel even more inadequate.

Another type of marking employs a series of numbers or letters—1, 2, 3, 4, or A, B, C, D, and F. One of the arguments for this kind of marks on a report card is that they are "so definite." Great importance is often given to the value of retaining the "F." The argument for it is that failure occurs in life and, therefore, children must be habituated early to experiences of failure. People holding this position are saying in effect that lessons in failure must begin when one is young and must be continuous; otherwise—to carry out this thought—the strength of the human spirit might triumph and a nonreader might grow up to think he amounts to something.

"A" marks may be bad for a child, too. They may cause him to have feelings of smugness or an exaggerated sense of intellectual power when he is only being rewarded for natural ability, docility, or skill in pleasing the teacher.

Marks are meaningless and unreliable. Try a little experiment to prove this fact to yourself. Mark a set of papers as efficiently as you know how. Put them away for three months. Mark them again. Compare the two sets of marks. The testimony in your own handwriting will be convincing.

Unreliable measures of achievement encourage destructive competition. Yet the evidence is clear that competitive systems are not effective in stimulating effort toward the attainment of desirable goals. A child who has done well feels that he has failed because someone else has surpassed him. Another child may be proud of mediocre achievement if he is ahead of others, and thus the levels of aspiration are lowered for both children.

Report cards on which a marking system is used do not contribute to the development of healthy personality. Their evil effect may be minimized by many factors; teachers who realize the harm which competitive and comparative marks do may mark accordingly, or strong feelings of friendliness and confidence between home and school may exist in spite of report cards only because both discount the importance of the report card.

Reporting to parents can be a positive factor in building mental health if parents are informed of their child's growth through frequent conferences with the child's teacher. In order to make these conferences successful, teachers should be given time within the school day for conducting them.

The 1950 yearbook of the Association for Supervision and Curriculum Development, *Fostering Mental Health in Our Schools,* will prove helpful to teachers conducting conferences with parents. The section on developmental tasks is especially useful. Clerical assistance in the typing of anecdotal records, in the preparation of cumulative records, and in preparing reports of conferences should also be available to teachers.

An important part of any parent-teacher conference should be the development of a plan of action outlining the next step in learning. A parent and teacher sit down together to consider the total development of the child, his strength, his weaknesses, and how home and school can best help him. A record should be made of the simple steps which parents and teacher plan to take to help the child. A part of such a record might read as follows:

THE PARENT'S PLAN

Mr. Jones will play ball with Jerry after school so that he will learn to catch better and will be willing to play with the other children. Mrs. Jones will invite small groups of children to play with Jerry after school so that he will not be alone so much. Billy was suggested as a good child to be included in this group.

Now that Mrs. Jones is busy with the new baby, she realizes that Jerry may be feeling rejected and left out; so she is planning to have her mother give him some special attention by taking him on trips and entertaining him. She also realizes that he needs to have some responsibility for the care of his little brother.

THE TEACHER'S PLAN

I will see that Jerry gets some playground success. I will also give him some special attention in the room. He might have charge of the hall exhibit box for the rest of the term.

What does this tell a teacher who may have the child the following year? This program for action indicates to the discerning teacher that Jerry has been feeling insecure because of a new baby brother in the family, that he needs more attention from adults, that he should develop playground skill, and that home and school share responsibility for helping him.

This child might have had a report card that would have read: "Deportment, U, Physical Education, U." What would either the child, the parent, or a new teacher have known about the child under these circumstances? It is possible that the new teacher would have pushed Jerry further from the attention he needed, that the mother would have felt that his bad behavior in school added one more burden to her problems at the time that she was much concerned with the new baby. Jerry's father may have looked at the U in physical education and wondered how in the world he could have a son who couldn't catch a ball. Jerry's new teacher would take a look at the report card and say with a sigh: "Another child who doesn't know how to behave and who can't do anything on the playground!" Clues to the underlying causes of behavior do not appear in the traditional report card, and no provision is made for suggestions as to remedial action.

Parent-teacher conferences can be supplemented by having the children prepare and take home statements of their own progress, by frequent classroom evaluations, by informal notes or phone calls, and by planned programs which acquaint parents with the purposes of education in a democracy and the specific ways in which the school is working to fulfill those purposes.

Parents have a right to know the facts about the progress of their children in school.   The cumulative record tells more than any report card. The major purpose of reporting to parents is to provide the information necessary for a sound working relation between them and school, and many avenues of communication should be opened to make this relation operate successfully.

GRADE PLACEMENT OF PUPILS

Does the grade placement of pupils contribute to healthy personalities? In answering this question regarding the effect of grade placement on personality, children who have been retained in a grade should be considered. Should judgment regarding the placement of a child be left to a teacher who may not be familiar with the research in the field or who may be operating on the basis of personal opinion and limited experience?   To answer these questions let us consider the problem of Larry.

Larry, a 13-year-old, is in the sixth grade.   Larry is of average size for his age, which means he is one of the larger boys in the class.   He was retained in the first grade because he seemed immature and did not learn to read.   He was retained again in the third grade because of poor progress and because he was not ready for fourth grade work.

Larry's ability is low average as measured by standardized tests.   His achievement is about two years below the norm for the class he is in and three years below his potential.   Larry wastes his time, fools around, and shows little interest in school activities.

Larry's father is a sheet-metal worker in the railroad yards.   He is disgusted with Larry.   "What that kid needs," he says, "is a job and the sooner the better.   He is wasting his time in school."   His father is disgusted with the school, too.   "It's this modern education," he says, "it's too soft.   They don't make the boy work.   The discipline is poor. Too much time is spent on frills and not enough on the three R's."

Larry says, "I don't like school.   It's not much fun.   I'd like to learn a trade if I ever get to high school, but I doubt if I'll ever make it."

The teacher asks the following questions: "Should I promote Larry this year?   Promotion would reward lack of effort.   Would that destroy the morale of the others who worked hard?   Would Larry believe that he could always get by without working?   Wouldn't promotion for Larry mean lowering standards—a soft education?"

The teacher says, "Larry is not ready for seventh-grade work.   To promote him would mean too wide a range of achievement for the seventh-grade teacher to handle. He would surely fail in the seventh grade. Shouldn't Larry understand that he has to work if he is going to get anywhere in this tough world?"

What does educational research show about Larry? Research shows that to dislike school, to waste time, to make little effort, to achieve below capacity is the behavior expected of a child who has experienced nonpromotion. Larry is running true to form.

The threat of nonpromotion, or nonpromotion itself, does not increase motivation but lowers the level of aspiration for most children. So it is with Larry. Larry has no fun in school because he is not well accepted by the others. The findings of research show that this is what usually happens to children who have experienced nonpromotion. The other children in Larry's grade either overtly state or tacitly think that he is stupid, which colors all their attitudes toward him.

Has Larry's nonpromotion reduced the range of achievement in Larry's class and thus provided a more homogeneous group? No, Larry is still at the tag end in achievement but he is the most mature boy in interests and physiological development. This heterogeneity in development and interests of the pupils is more of a problem to the teacher than the wide range of materials she must provide.

Will Larry straighten out when he gets to high school and learns a trade? The probability is that he will not get through high school. One research study showed that of 643 pupils who dropped out of high school, 638 had repeated the first grade. Research also shows that the most common characteristic of "drop outs" from high school is overageness.

How will Larry get along socially and emotionally as an adolescent? This is problematical. The correlation of school failure to delinquency is high. The effect of failure on personality is to develop either withdrawing behavior or compensating mechanisms which are usually unwholesome in their effect on social adjustment. Grade retardation has not been profitable for Larry nor has it eased the instructional problem in school.

Larry's problems have not all arisen from nonpromotion in school. A meager home background, limited ability, lack of understanding and encouragement by parents, and too little home guidance have been the roots of his problem. When it allowed Larry to fail in school work, the school relinquished its opportunity to guide, inspire, and help him, and to compensate for the inadequacies in his home. He has lost his trust in the school and in himself. His initiative, if he has any left, will never be directed toward improving himself through education. . . .

Would Larry have had a better chance of promotion had his name been Loretta? Yes, the facts show that among girls and boys of equal ability and achievement, girls are promoted more frequently. Why is this true?   Research regarding the causes has not been completed but a good guess is that a Loretta would have been more submissive and less annoying to her teachers than Larry was and thus her failure to meet standards might have been overlooked.

How many children in California schools raise similar questions in the minds of teachers?   The age-grade status of 234,000 children in 28 counties was studied in 1950.   In this study it was found that 51 per cent of the boys and 37 per cent of the girls were over the expected age by the time they had reached the eighth grade.   No doubt some of these children had entered school late, but it can be presumed that most of them had been retarded one or more years in grade placement.   The range in age in each grade was from five to ten years, and 19,528 of the children were more than one year overage.   Many youth 15, 16, 17, and 18 years old were found in the eighth grade.   Eighth-grade enrollment was significantly lower than other grades even when differences in birth rate were considered, showing that drop-outs occur in elementary as well as in high school.

Certainly individual cases exist in which nonpromotion is desirable. No truth is universal; there are exceptions to every rule.   There may even be individuals for whom grade failure could be a salvation.   But the mountains of research evidence against nonpromotion are so high that the burden of proof that a child should be failed rests with the school that fails him.   Only a psychologist qualified to evaluate the physical development of a child, to measure his maturity, to diagnose his personality needs, and to understand his home should say, "*This* child should not be promoted." The psychologists should be able to say with certainty: "All the bad effects of nonpromotion which we know happen to most children will not happen to this child because he is so different."   Only then is a school justified in running counter to well-established research evidence by insisting upon nonpromotion of any pupil.   And even in these circumstances, careful follow-up studies should be made to detect the onset of possible bad effects and to prevent permanent harm to any pupil through nonpromotion.

ARTICULATION OF UNITS OF THE SCHOOL SYSTEM

Does an articulated program of education contribute to the development of a healthy personality?   Recently an elementary school teacher who is unusually adept in establishing friendly rapport with her pupils and who is teaching children in a large elementary school from which pupils enter a departmentalized junior high school was reviewing certain of her observations during the past three years.   She said:

I have been teaching children in the sixth grade in this school for the past three years. The children who were with me during my first year in this position are now in the eighth grade of a highly departmentalized junior high school. Last year when they were in the seventh grade, and this year, too, they have invited me to their social gatherings which are usually held in a home of one of the group. Sometime before each evening is over they discuss their school activities. They tell one another and me, too, what they like about school. They also tell the things in elementary school that they miss, and one thing comes up over and over. It seems that in their junior high school the pupils not only have different teachers every hour on the hour but find themselves with different members of their group in the different classes. They miss most the opportunity to become acquainted with one another and with their teachers. They speak of one teacher as a home-room teacher but discern little difference between their home-room teacher and other teachers except that she appears to have more records to keep. They miss particularly a close association with one another. They enjoy and keep alive the social gatherings that were begun three years ago because they can meet with boys and girls they know well and with people who know them. They seek a sense of intimacy, friendship, love, and inspiration.

An eighth-grade teacher was talking about a boy who completed the eighth grade last June. She said:

I teach in a rural school. After students finish the eighth grade, they are picked up by a school bus provided by the high school district and ride many miles to the high school. I don't see them often after they start to high school because they leave early and get home late. Last week, however, one of the boys who finished the eighth grade last June came to talk with me. He was a good pupil in my class. I thought he was an unusually promising boy. While in the eighth grade, he had talked about taking courses in high school that would prepare him to work with the 'business part of getting fruit ready for the market,' to use his words. But now, after we had talked for a while, he said he was thinking about quitting school and getting a job. When I asked him why he was thinking about quitting he said, 'My grades aren't very good. We have a lot more homework to do now than we had last year and I don't get mine done. Last year we didn't have much homework and I got along fine. Whenever we did have homework last year, I didn't get mine done at home. You know there are three of us kids at home and we still live in the trailer. When I try to do my homework I'm in everybody's way and I don't get it done. I've thought about it for a long time now and believe the thing for me to do is to earn some money. Maybe after I have earned some money to help at home I will be able to go to school again. Then, too, I'll have enough money to buy clothes and go places like the others do.' I felt depressed after he left and began to wonder what I could do to familiarize his high school teacher with the problems confronting him.

This statement by the eighth-grade teacher raises several questions.   If feelings of discouragement persist in this once promising boy, can he have a healthy personality?   Will such feelings give him the help he needs to develop a sense of accomplishment, a willingness to settle down to learning how to do things and do them well?   Will they permit him to select desirable social goals and to feel reasonable security with his peers?

The two incidents mentioned are not isolated.   They are typical of statements by teachers regarding young adolescents in many elementary schools.

A program of education contributes to the development of a healthy personality if each administrative unit is articulated in a total, continuous program.   More specifically, schools which contribute to the development of a healthy personality are those in which the following statements describe school goals, planning, and procedures:

1. Twelve years of education are regarded as minimum preparation for citizenship in today's complex society.

2. School activities are guided by a unified philosophy of education which combines the guidance concept with intellectual education.

3. The objectives or goals for each administrative unit are arrived at with joint representation and mutual understanding of all administrative units which constitute the school system.

4. The curriculum is planned jointly by elementary and secondary teachers, particularly for grades 6–7 and 9–10 in the 6–3–3 systems and for grades 8 and 9 in the 8–4 systems.

Educators today are accepting the idea of separate elementary and secondary schools only as convenient administrative units in a continuous, total program of public education.   Educators today recognize that problems peculiar to elementary or secondary schools derive from the maturity levels of young people, not from any special institutional function or purpose.   The elementary, junior high, and senior high schools joined end-to-end should provide an articulated program for the child from the time he enters school until he is prepared for adult citizenship in our modern society.

A principal in an elementary school enrolling young adolescents in grades seven and eight reported the following incident which led to improved articulation in his school system.

One boy in the school was frequently referred to the principal because he did not always conform to the pattern of conduct expected of pupils.   The principal said that he had long ago become convinced of the value of looking at the cumulative record of individuals before talking about their personal problems.   He recalled that this youth was nearing his seventeenth birthday, was in the eighth grade, and was rated as average in ability by most of his teachers but below average by certain teachers. The boy was tall, well-developed physically, and would pass for a youth older than his actual age. The principal judged that the youth had a wide background of experience, responsibility, and association with older people. He had come to school by transfer from another state and seemed to get along satisfactorily most of the time.

The principal listened with interest whenever he succeeded in getting the boy to talk about himself, for then his hostility would diminish and before the end of the conversation he could analyze his present situation and his problems.

During one of these meetings, the boy said, "I like my home-room teacher very much. If it weren't for my home-room teacher I would quit school. It is lucky for me that I am in her room a half day every day and longer on some days. I could quit school, you know. I am old enough to quit."

The principal said, "Yes, you are old enough to stop coming to this school and go to continuation school, providing it is necessary for you to work and providing you find a job. But you haven't done that and there are reasons why. Would you mind telling me what they are?"

This is a part of the boy's reply: "No one in our family [and the principal remembered that there were two brothers and a sister] has finished the eighth grade. Where we lived before coming to California we did not have to stay in school until we were sixteen, so my brothers and sisters dropped out to work as soon as they could. My parents wish they had gone to school longer. They are getting along, but I see the need to get more schooling. I want to graduate. The thing that bothers me most is getting mixed up with the rules around the school. I'm careful about some things. I know that I shouldn't smoke around the school so I don't. All my after-school friends are in high school or out of high school. We are mostly interested in cars and ways to earn money. I'd sure like to be in that auto mechanics shop in the high school."

The principal concluded the discussion with this statement: "This boy and others like him caused us to examine our promotion policy in kindergarten through grade twelve. As a result we now have provision for steady progression through the twelve grades. The high school accepts children from the elementary school after they have gone through our school. They pass from grade eight to grade nine on the same basis as they go from grade three to four or five or six.

"Our high school recognizes the principles of human growth and development. The faculty knows that we have done our best to help each child achieve his fullest potentiality as he moved through our school. The high school teachers accept their guidance function and think of their great task as that of meeting the physical, social, and emotional needs of young people as well as their intellectual needs. We are working to provide educational experiences that will keep all or nearly all of the young people of our community in school for twelve years. We want children and youth to stay in

their normal social group and not acquire feelings of inferiority by being classified with younger and smaller children.   The problem of adjusting instruction
to the needs of individuals must be met in every group.   We are gradually
getting away from artificial grade standards as we understand children better."

Healthy personality will be promoted as the elementary and secondary
schools of a community put themselves through the process of developing
and employing an educational philosophy that will make education a continuous, developmental experience for boys and girls.

B. THE CLASSROOM ATMOSPHERE

38. Children's Behavior and Teachers' Attitudes*

Related selections: 24, 25, 27, 39, 49

TEACHERS are realizing that the most important aspect of behavior
is its significance in revealing what is happening in the development of the pupils. The two selections that follow show the
differences in attitudes and evaluations of teachers and mental
hygienists in respect to pupil behavior.   The first is the introduction and summary from a famous study by Wickman, and the
second is a follow-up by Stouffer that repeats the earlier study
and compares today's teachers with those of the earlier period.
The two selections should be read in sequence.

WHAT IDENTIFIES the problem child?   How do we determine that a child
is well adjusted, or maladjusted?   What kinds of behavior are undesirable in any child?   How "normal" is misbehavior in children?
The answers that teachers make to these questions are the subject of this
experimental study.
However perplexing the questions may be to the modern parent or
teacher, the immediate requirements of child rearing and training neces-

* E. K. Wickman, *Children's Behavior and Teachers' Attitudes,* The Commonwealth Fund, 1928, pp. 1–5, 129–130. Reprinted by permission of author and
publisher.
Dr. Wickman (1895—) is Director of the Division of International Fellowships
of The Commonwealth Fund, New York City.   He is a co-developer of the H. O. W.
Behavior Rating Schedules.

sitate definite answers. Such answers are to be found in the direct responses of adults to the distressing behavior of their children. Some customary responses to child behavior have lately been called in question, subjected to careful examination, and are being modified according to our growing knowledge of child life and child needs. But many everyday habits of regarding and treating problems in child behavior are so taken for granted that they are rarely formulated into words or held up to intellectual scrutiny. This study is an effort to analyze prevailing attitudes toward behavior problems of children.

The subject of child behavior has recently taken on a new significance. The relationship of behavior disorders of children to social-pathological problems of the adult is inviting careful attention. The importance of the social and emotional development of children is becoming recognized along with the need for their intellectual and physical training. Education is turning serious attention to preparing the child for life. With our concepts of child needs and child problems in a state of reorganization, it is appropriate to inquire at what point we have arrived in defining the issues of child behavior in our everyday practices.

That our study is concerned with teachers' viewpoints on these questions is the result of fortuitous circumstances. Facilities were offered in representative public schools of two cities for making experimental studies on the behavior problems of elementary school children. In carrying on these investigations it was necessary to appreciate the teachers' points of view toward the behavior disorders of their pupils. Though the original purpose of the investigations was to secure factual data on behavior-problem children, it seemed as the study progressed that the attitudes of teachers were fundamental to any study of the behavior disorders of their pupils. The experiments were forthwith turned in this direction. Later on it became desirable to extend the studies to a measurement of the attitudes of many groups of teachers.

Personal and social attitudes are important factors in the solution of any human problem. When physical ailments were considered the affliction of evil spirits, medical science was precluded. So long as insanity was regarded as demoniacal possession or punishment from God, those suffering from mental derangements were banished or abused. If behavior problems of children are defined in terms of "bad," "evil," "wrong" behavior, their natural causation cannot be appreciated. Fortunately, we are beginning to think more objectively about conduct disorders and to evaluate child behavior in terms of child welfare; unfortunately, the welfare of the child seems not infrequently to be confused with the convenience of the adult.

Whereas the influence of attitudes toward physical and mental disorders affects chiefly the treatment of those diseases, attitudes toward behavior are an integral part of behavior disorders.   Behavior, in the social sense in which it is here employed,* is a socially evaluated and socially regularized product; and behavior problems represent conflicts between individual behavior and social requirements for behavior.

It is to be noted that the very existence of a behavior problem is designated by personal or social attitude.   There can be no problems in behavior, in the active social sense, unless someone reacts to them as such. Moreover, any form of conduct in a child or adult may become a problem if it is regarded and treated as undesirable behavior by the social group in which the individual happens to live.

This definition of behavior problems in terms of personal and social attitudes is forced upon us as soon as we undertake a systematic study of social maladjustments in children.   Here we find ourselves so lacking in consistent standards of behavior evaluation that it is impossible to establish any criteria which will be serviceable in all social situations.   What is acceptable behavior to one parent, teacher, or school system may become unacceptable when the child passes into the control of another parent, teacher, or school.   No two families maintain exactly the same requirements for the behavior of their children.   The school may revoke the standards of conduct set up for a child in the home.   The parent in turn often criticizes the teacher's requirements for the child's behavior. Racial, religious, educational customs and practices contribute heavily to differences in attitudes toward individual behavior.   In so far as parents and teachers have different nervous constitutions and different experiential backgrounds there will be differences in the requirements they impose for, the responses they make to, the behavior of their children.

What constitutes a behavior disorder and why certain forms of behavior are "problems" are thus questions of personal and social attitudes.

However wisely or unwisely a parent or teacher may designate a behavior problem in a child, that designation must be the starting point of any study of the child's behavior disorder.   The problem is the maladjustment between the child and those who seek to regularize his behavior. The very designation of undesirable conduct, and the attitudes toward the child in consequence of this become stimuli for the child and determinants of his behavior.

In ordinary practice the factor of attitudes is often forgotten in the behavior equation.   When parent or teacher is distressed by the behavior

* Webster's definition: "Behavior applies to our mode of behaving in the presence of others or toward them."

of a child, the usual assumption is that the difficulty is with the child. From an objective point of view the issue becomes: (1) why is the adult distressed by the child's behavior, and (2) why does the child behave in a fashion that distresses the adult?   The first question is obviously one of adult or social attitude, and our interest is directed to the factors that determine the designation of unacceptable behavior.   The second question also involves the consideration of attitudes, for its answer is to be found in the child's behavior responses to the requirements of behavior which parent, teacher, school, or social order impose.   Any attempt to study and treat behavior problems of children, then, involves an analysis, first, of the child whose behavior is distressing, second, of the social order that declares the behavior unacceptable or unwholesome, and, third, of the interactions between them.   It is impossible to consider a child's behavior apart from the attitudes that are taken toward his conduct.   The two are intimately related and bound up in the same issue.

The dictionary defines the term attitude, in the sense in which it is here employed, as "any habitual mode of regarding anything; any settled behavior or conduct, as indicating opinion or purpose regarding anything."* In examining teachers' attitudes toward behavior problems of children we shall need to inquire into (1) their habitual mode of regarding child behavior with reference to the kinds of behavior which they consider undesirable or unwholesome, (2) their customary responses to these problems, (3) their opinions and purposes that lead them so to evaluate and respond to the behavior of their pupils.

The factual evidence secured in our investigation of teachers' attitudes relates chiefly to the first and partially to the second of these three items. An analysis of data secured with reference to the manner of the teachers' reactions to behavior problems in children affords some basis for an interpretation of the opinions and purposes that underlie these reactions.

In interpreting teachers' responses to child behavior as indicated in these studies, it will be necessary to bear in mind the particular nature of their teaching responsibilities and their special interests in child training. The professional responsibilities of teachers are in a large measure laid upon them by the school system and by the established aims of modern, public school education.   In so far as the functions of the school coincide with the concepts of child training held by parents, we may surmise that teacher and parental attitudes toward child behavior are in agreement; in so far as the school stresses special aspects of child training, we may expect teachers' attitudes to be peculiar to their profession.   In a sense, the

* This is the definition of the Standard Dictionary. Webster defines the term "Position or bearing as indicating action, feeling or mood."

measurement of teachers' responses to child behavior constitutes a measurement of the attitudes of the public school.

The conclusions that will be drawn from our study relate only to the most general, though possibly very fundamental, characteristics of prevailing attitudes toward child behavior.   It may be that this report contains nothing fundamentally new beyond bringing to conscious recognition some facts that reveal *how we behave* toward the misbehavior of our children.

.   .   .   .   .

The differences in attitudes toward behavior problems represented in the ratings obtained from mental hygienists and teachers should be interpreted as differences in stress laid upon the seriousness of the various problems.   Teachers stress the importance of problems relating to sex, dishonesty, disobedience, disorderliness and failure to learn.   For them, the problems that indicate withdrawing, recessive characteristics in children are of comparatively little significance.   Mental hygienists, on the other hand, consider these unsocial forms of behavior most serious and discount the stress which teachers lay on anti-social conduct.   Such differences in attitudes imply essential differences in methods of treatment and discipline.

In interpreting these findings it is essential to bear in mind that the clinicians, unlike teachers, were not laboring under pressure for educating children according to prevailing curricula and thus were not especially sensitized to those problems in behavior which disturb or frustrate the teachers' interests in the educational achievement of pupils.   Moreover, in making their ratings, the clinicians were influenced, both by their particular professional interests and by specific instructions, to consider (1) the effect produced on the future development and on the social, emotional adjustment of the child by the possession of any behavior problem which is allowed to run its usual course; and (2) the need for remedial work, and the nature of remedial efforts, in treating the behavior disorders in question.

.   .   .   .   .

[The following chart shows how teachers in the Wickman study regarded the seriousness of certain related types of behavior problems in children.]

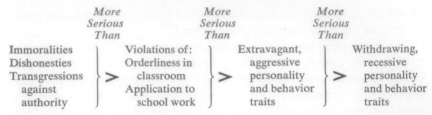

The ratings made by the mental hygienists are not quite as well arranged according to types of problems; but we may formulate the direction of their reaction to the importance of behavior disorders in contrast to the teachers' reactions, as follows:

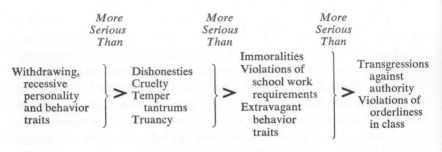

39. Behavior Problems of Children as Viewed by Teachers and Mental Hygienists*

A Study of Present Attitudes as Compared With Those Studied by E. K. Wickman

THE PRECEDING selection by Wickman with its accompanying head-note should be read before this article.

IN 1928 a study was published which has been described both as "a classic investigation" and as "one of the most illuminating and interesting studies in the field." This was E. W. Wickman's *Children's Behavior and*

* George A. W. Stouffer, Jr., "Behavior Problems of Children as Viewed by Teachers and Mental Hygienists," *Mental Hygiene*, vol. XXXVI (April, 1952), pp. 271–285. Reprinted by permission of the author and publisher.
Dr. Stouffer (1911—) is Director of The Psycho-Educational Bureau, The State Teachers College, Pennsylvania. He served as U.S. Navy Senior Psychologist, assigned to the 1st Division, U.S. Marine Corps, on duty in Korea.

Teacher's Attitudes. The study has been widely quoted and, as the author of this paper discovered, it is also very often misquoted, or variously interpreted. Even though it was conducted twenty-five years ago, the inclusion of data from it in recent books in the field of mental hygiene indicates that it still exerts considerable influence on contemporary thinking in that field.

So influential has Wickman's study been in shaping public and professional opinion that it was thought worth while to repeat it, in an attempt to ascertain whether the passage of twenty-five years had produced any measurable change in teachers' attitudes toward children's behavior, and whether any new problems of child behavior confronted to-day's teachers.

In the present study, which follows the pattern established by Wickman, rating scales were submitted to teachers in elementary schools and to mental hygienists—psychiatrists, psychologists, and psychiatric social workers—in child-guidance clinics. On these scales teachers and mental hygienists recorded their judgments as to the degree of seriousness of each of 50 behavior problems of children. The raters were directed to make their ratings at any point on a scale that was descriptively captioned to indicate an ascending degree of seriousness, from minimal concern on the part of the rater to judgment of the problem as a grave one. The calibrated rule contained twenty equal divisions, to facilitate statistical treatment of the data obtained.

One questionnaire—Form A—was administered to teachers, with a set of directions for completing it. This form duplicated in every respect the one completed by the teachers in Wickman's original study. A second questionnaire—Form C—was rated by the mental hygienists who coöperated in the study, duplicating the one submitted by Wickman to his group of mental-hygiene experts. The mental hygienists were furnished with their own set of directions and conditions under which they were to rate the various problems. These were different from those given the teachers. A third questionnaire—Form B—was administered to the same teachers who had completed Form A. In this form the directions and conditions for rating were the same as those under which the mental hygienists had made their ratings on the 50 problems.

A brief explanation may be in order as to how the directions and conditions for rating differed for the various forms. The conditions for rating the behavior problems on Form A included a time limit, and the directions were worded with the aim of obtaining the rater's immediate impression and, perhaps, emotional reaction to a current situation. On Forms B and C, which were identical, there was no time limit for completing the ratings and the wording of the directions was aimed at getting the raters' intellectualized attitude toward a problem, not as to its effect at the moment, but as to how they thought it would affect a child's future development. This modification of Wickman's procedure was made to meet criticisms of his findings growing out of the lack of uniformity in the directions and conditions for the rating of the scale by teachers and by mental hygienists. In brief, an attempt was made to find out whether the teachers' ratings differed when they used the two different sets of directions and conditions.

The 481 male and female elementary-school teachers who coöperated in the study were chosen as a representative sample of teachers from all parts of the country, teaching pupils of various racial extraction and socio-economic status, in rural and urban schools, with a variety of educational philosophies. The 70 mental hygienists participating included psychiatrists, psychologists, and psychiatric social workers on the staffs of thirteen child-guidance clinics throughout the country. The over-all sampling closely approximated the one used by Wickman.

When the data were collected and evaluated, the relationship between the rating of the 50 problems of child behavior by the teachers of Form A and by the mental hygienists on Form C was recorded as shown in Table I. Table II shows a rank-order comparison of to-day's teachers' ratings (Form B) and those of the mental hygienists when both groups were using identical questionnaires.

The results both of inspection and of statistical treatment showed that to-day's teachers, psychologists, psychiatrists, and psychiatric social workers were in much closer agreement as to the seriousness of certain problems of children's behavior than they were twenty-five years ago. This appears in our first comparison, Table I, in which we used Wickman's procedure of furnishing the teachers and the mental hygienists each with their own set of directions and conditions for rating the behavior problems; and an even greater similarity in attitude is found when both groups were given the same directions and conditions for rating.

The data on the ratings by teachers and by mental hygienists were organized to appraise the agreement of these two groups of people who are concerned with child behavior and mental hygiene. This was done by three methods of examination. First, we considered the relative position, in the rank-order arrangement as to seriousness, assigned respectively by the teachers and the mental hygienists of to-day to the various problems of children's behavior. Little in the way of agreement seems apparent in an examination of Table I. No item of behavior in the teachers' column is in juxtaposition with the same item in the mental hygienists' column. Of the ten problems rated the most serious by the teachers, and, therefore, appearing as the first ten in the rank-order arrangement,

TABLE I

A RANK-ORDER COMPARISON OF THE RATINGS BY TO-DAY'S TEACHERS
(FORM A) AND MENTAL HYGIENISTS OF THE RELATIVE SERIOUS-
NESS OF 50 BEHAVIOR PROBLEMS OF CHILDREN

Teachers (Form A)	Mental Hygienists
1. Stealing	Unsocial, withdrawing
2. Cruelty, bullying	Unhappy, depressed
3. Heterosexual activity	Fearfulness
4. Truancy	Suspiciousness
5. Unhappy, depressed	Cruelty, bullying
6. Impertinence, defiance	Shyness
7. Destroying school material	Enuresis
8. Unreliableness	Resentfulness
9. Untruthfulness	Stealing
10. Disobedience	Sensitiveness
11. Resentfulness	Dreaminess
12. Temper tantrums	Nervousness
13. Unsocial, withdrawing	Suggestible
14. Obscene notes, talk	Overcritical of others
15. Nervousness	Easily discouraged
16. Cheating	Temper tantrums
17. Selfishness	Domineering
18. Quarrelsomeness	Truancy
19. Domineering	Physical coward
20. Lack of interest in work	Untruthfulness
21. Impudence, rudeness	Unreliableness
22. Easily discouraged	Destroying school materials
23. Suggestible	Sullenness
24. Fearfulness	Lack of interest in work
25. Enuresis	Cheating
26. Masturbation	Selfishness
27. Laziness	Quarrelsomeness
28. Inattention	Heterosexual activity
29. Disorderliness in class	Restlessness
30. Sullenness	Inattention
31. Physical coward	Impertinence, defiance
32. Overcritical of others	Slovenly in personal appearance
33. Sensitiveness	Tattling
34. Carelessness in work	Obscene notes, talk
35. Shyness	Laziness
36. Suspiciousness	Stubbornness
37. Smoking	Attracting attention
38. Stubbornness	Thoughtlessness
39. Dreaminess	Imaginative lying
40. Profanity	Disobedience
41. Attracting attention	Carelessness in work
42. Slovenly in personal appearance	Masturbation
43. Restlessness	Impudence, rudeness
44. Tardiness	Inquisitiveness
45. Thoughtlessness	Disorderliness in class
46. Tattling	Tardiness
47. Inquisitiveness	Interrupting
48. Interrupting	Profanity
49. Imaginative lying	Smoking
50. Whispering	Whispering

TABLE II

A RANK-ORDER COMPARISON OF THE RATINGS BY TO-DAY'S TEACHERS
(FORM B) AND MENTAL HYGIENISTS OF THE RELATIVE SERIOUS-
NESS OF 50 BEHAVIOR PROBLEMS OF CHILDREN

Teachers (Form B)	Mental Hygienists
1. Unreliableness	Unsocial, withdrawing
2. Stealing	Unhappy, depressed
3. Unhappy, depressed	Fearfulness
4. Cruelty, bullying	Suspiciousness
5. Untruthfulness	Cruelty, bullying
6. Unsocial, withdrawing	Shyness
7. Truancy	Enuresis
8. Impertinence, defiance	Resentfulness
9. Cheating	Stealing
10. Easily discouraged	Sensitiveness
11. Resentfulness	Dreaminess
12. Destroying school material	Nervousness
13. Suggestible	Suggestible
14. Heterosexual activity	Overcritical of others
15. Domineering	Easily discouraged
16. Temper tantrums	Temper tantrums
17. Selfishness	Domineering
18. Nervousness	Truancy
19. Disobedience	Physical coward
20. Laziness	Untruthfulness
21. Impudence, rudeness	Unreliableness
22. Lack of interest in work	Destroying school material
23. Fearfulness	Sullenness
24. Sensitiveness	Lack of interest in work
25. Carelessness in work	Cheating
26. Masturbation	Selfishness
27. Overcritical of others	Quarrelsomeness
28. Quarrelsomeness	Heterosexual activity
29. Obscene notes, talk	Restlessness
30. Enuresis	Inattention
31. Slovenly in personal appearance	Impertinence, defiance
32. Sullenness	Tattling
33. Physical coward	Slovenly in personal appearance
34. Shyness	Obscene notes, talk
35. Suspiciousness	Laziness
36. Inattention	Stubbornness
37. Stubborness	Attracting attention
38. Tardiness	Thoughtlessness
39. Disorderliness in class	Imaginative lying
40. Dreaminess	Disobedience
41. Thoughtlessness	Carelessness in work
42. Profanity	Masturbation
43. Attracting attention	Impudence, rudeness
44. Inquisitiveness	Inquisitiveness
45. Restlessness	Disorderliness in class
46. Imaginative lying	Tardiness
47. Tattling	Interrupting
48. Interrupting	Profanity
49. Smoking	Smoking
50. Whispering	Whispering

only two are found in the ten rated most serious by the mental hygienists. At the other end of the rank-order arrangement of the problems, of the ten rated least serious by the teachers, only four are found in the last ten positions in the rating by the mental hygienists.

Further examination of the problems ranked in order of seriousness by the teachers and the mental hygienists reveals that the most marked differences in the ratings are in the following behavior items:

Disobedience	Smoking
Impudence, rudeness	Masturbation
Impertinence, defiance	Heterosexual activity
Disorderly in class	Obscene notes, talk
Profanity	Unsocial, withdrawing

It would appear that these problems, all of which seem to represent an objective type of behavior, might be thought of as problems that outrage the teachers' moral sensitivities and authority, or that frustrate their immediate teaching purposes.   According to the ratings by the mental hygienists, however, only the "unsocial, withdrawing" behavior could, with reasonable certainty, be considered as representing a serious future threat to the school child's stability.

Since this first appraisal of the relative seriousness assigned to the behavior problems of children by the two groups did not seem to be too productive, an examination of the data in a more precise fashion was made.

An evaluation for agreement or disagreement between the teachers and the mental hygienists was made by examining the means of their ratings on the same items of problem behavior for statistically significant differences.   This technique revealed that to-day's teachers and mental hygienists were in substantial agreement as to the importance of the following behavior problems of children:

Resentfulness	Physical coward
Nervousness	Restlessness
Domineering	Imaginative lying
Easily discouraged	Thoughtlessness
Suggestible	Lying
Sullenness	

In Wickman's original group of teachers and mental hygienists, only two problems, "cruelty" and "temper tantrums," were assigned about the same degree of seriousness by the clinicians and by the teachers.   Of the eleven items about which the mental hygienists and teachers now find

themselves in agreement, in Wickman's study there was complete disagreement as to the seriousness of "resentfulness," "easily discouraged,"
"suggestible," "physical coward," "imaginative lying," and "domineering." All of these problems, with the exception of "lying" and "thought-
lessness," were characterized by Wickman as "problems describing the
withdrawing, recessive personality and behavior traits" or as "extravagant, overdetermined personality and behavior traits."

The behavior problems that the clinicians rated as more serious than
did the teachers include:

Unhappy, depressed	Overcritical of others
Unsocial, withdrawing	Sensitiveness
Fearfulness	Shyness
Enuresis	Suspiciousness
Dreaminess	

Again it would appear that overt, objective behavior is rated as more
serious by the teachers, and a subjective type of behavior by the mental
hygienists. However, more agreement between the two groups than was
found in Wickman's original inquiry seems clearly to emerge.

In a third method of evaluation correlations were obtained by arranging the means of the ratings by the mental hygienists of the respective behavior problems of children in order of seriousness from the highest to the
lowest, and listing opposite the corresponding values for these behaviors
as judged by the teachers. The matched means were then converted
into ranks, which in turn were converted into per cent positions. The
per cent positions were changed to "scores" by the use of Hull's table. In
computing the coefficient of correlation between the above matched scores,
Pearson's product-moment formula was employed.

Wickman reported a coefficient of correlation of minus .11 between
the rank-order arrangements as to seriousness of the problems of child
behavior as rated by the mental hygienists and by the teachers. In the
present study a coefficient of correlation of plus .52 was secured when
Wickman's original procedure was duplicated (teachers' Form A and
mental hygienists' Form C), and a coefficient of correlation of plus .61
was obtained when Wickman's procedure was modified to provide both
groups with the same directions and conditions for rating the problems
(teachers' Form B and mental hygienists' Form C).

In a comparison of the ratings by to-day's teachers and by the teachers
of twenty-five years ago, shown in Table III, it was found that problems relating to honesty, sex, truancy, and to classroom order and application to

school tasks are rated among the most serious of the 50 problems of behavior by to-day's teachers, as they were by the teachers of Wickman's study. However, several of the problems concerned with withdrawing, recessive personality traits—*i.e.,* unhappiness, depression, unsociability, and withdrawing—have moved toward the top of the list as rated by to-day's teachers. Masturbation has dropped sharply in the teachers' estimation as a serious behavior problem. Interesting changes in position downward as to seriousness are those of smoking and profanity, in which there were striking shifts in position.

On the ratings for obscene notes, masturbation, and heterosexual activity there were large standard deviations of the means, indicating considerable variance of opinion among to-day's teachers as to the seriousness or importance of these three problems. Wickman's teachers had disagreed most markedly on "smoking" and "nervousness," as judged by the size of the standard deviations.

A separate evaluation of the ratings of the male elementary-school teachers was made. When the ratings of the male teachers were matched against those of the entire group, including these male teachers, no item was rated by the male teachers as being more serious than by the entire group of teachers. However, the following behavior problems were rated as less serious or less undesirable:

Heterosexual activity	Impertinence, defiance
Masturbation	Unreliableness
Physical coward	Disobedience
Smoking	Temper tantrums

This may indicate that there are measurable sex differences between male and female teachers in attitude toward certain problems of behavior.

It was discovered that while teachers have changed their attitudes toward the behavior problems of children in the past twenty-five years, there has been little change in the attitude of mental hygienists, as shown in Table IV. The change, however, can best be determined by examining the statistical significance of the difference of the means of the ratings of the two groups of clinicians. When this was done, it was found that the psychiatrists, psychologists, and psychiatric social workers of to-day's child-guidance clinics rated 37 of the 50 problems of child behavior exactly as had the mental hygienists of twenty-five years ago. On the remaining 13 items, there were few marked reversals of attitude or shifts in opinion, as measured by the evaluation of the seriousness or importance of certain problems. Of the 13 changes, Wickman's mental hygienists rated the

TABLE III

A Comparison of the Rank-Order Arrangement of 50 Behavior Problems of Children as Rated by 481 of To-day's Teachers (Form A) and 511 Teachers in E. K. Wickman's Study

Wickman's Study	Present Study
1. Heterosexual activity	Stealing
2. Stealing	Cruelty, bullying
3. Masturbation	Heterosexual activity
4. Obscene notes, talk	Truancy
5. Untruthfulness	Unhappy, depressed
6. Truancy	Impertinence, defiance
7. Impertinence, defiance	Destroying school material
8. Cruelty, bullying	Unreliableness
9. Cheating	Untruthfulness
10. Destroying school material	Disobedience
11. Disobedience	Resentfulness
12. Unreliableness	Temper tantrums
13. Temper tantrums	Unsocial, withdrawing
14. Lack of interest in work	Obscene notes, talk
15. Profanity	Nervousness
16. Impudence, rudeness	Cheating
17. Laziness	Selfishness
18. Smoking	Quarrelsomeness
19. Enuresis	Domineering
20. Nervousness	Lack of interest in work
21. Disorderliness in class	Impudence, rudeness
22. Unhappy, depressed	Easily discouraged
23. Easily discouraged	Suggestible
24. Selfishness	Fearfulness
25. Carelessness in work	Enuresis
26. Inattention	Masturbation
27. Quarrelsomeness	Laziness
28. Suggestible	Inattention
29. Resentfulness	Disorderliness in class
30. Tardiness	Sullenness
31. Physical coward	Physical coward
32. Stubbornness	Overcritical of others
33. Domineering	Sensitiveness
34. Slovenly in personal appearance	Carelessness in work
35. Sullenness	Shyness
36. Fearfulness	Suspiciousness
37. Suspiciousness	Smoking
38. Thoughtlessness	Stubbornness
39. Attracting attention	Dreaminess
40. Unsocial, withdrawing	Profanity
41. Dreaminess	Attracting attention
42. Imaginative lying	Slovenly in personal appearance
43. Interrupting	Restlessness
44. Inquisitiveness	Tardiness
45. Overcritical of others	Thoughtlessness
46. Tattling	Tattling
47. Whispering	Inquisitiveness
48. Sensitiveness	Interrupting
49. Restlessness	Imaginative lying
50. Shyness	Whispering

following problems of more importance than did the mental hygienists of
to-day:

Suspiciousness   Physical coward
Resentful   Sullenness
Overcritical of others   Selfishness
Easily discouraged   Stubbornness
Domineering

Problems regarded as more serious by to-day's clinicians are:

Enuresis
Destroying school materials
Restlessness (overactivity)
Disorderliness in class

The increased importance of enuresis might possibly be explained upon
the basis of the increased psychological significance attached to it as an
evidence of underlying emotional maladjustment, rather than as a purely
medical problem. It would seem that the problems that the mental
hygienists of twenty-five years ago found more important than do those of
to-day largely represent subjective behavior. Behavior that the present-
day group thought more important than did the group of twenty-five years
ago would seem to represent objective behavior. The coefficient of correlation between the rating by the mental hygienists in Wickman's study
and those in the present study was found to be a plus .87.

To determine whether to-day's teachers were confronted with any new
behavior problems of children, other than those reported by the teachers
of twenty-five years ago, 232 of to-day's teachers, of all grades, were asked
to report and rate the undesirable behavior of their pupils. The only
new problems of behavior were "reading comic books" and "watching
television." When teachers were asked to evaluate the problems they
had listed as to seriousness or importance, it was found that their ratings
of the problems were uniformly similar to the rating of the same problems supplied by the investigator.

The majority of the items listed by teachers as undesirable represented what children do rather than what they fail to do. In analyzing
the lists of problems, it would seem that the behavior-problem child in
school is still, as he was twenty-five years ago, identified chiefly by annoying, disorderly, irresponsible, aggressive, untruthful, and disobedient
behavior. Teachers of to-day, however, are not so oblivious to behavior
indicative of social and emotional maladjustment as were those reported
in Wickman's inquiry.

TABLE IV

A Rank-Order Comparison of the Ratings by the Mental
Hygienists of Wickman's Study and Those of the
Present Study on the Relative Seriousness of
50 Behavior Problems of Children

Wickman's Study	*Present Study*
1. Unsocial, withdrawing	Unsocial, withdrawing
2. Suspiciousness	Unhappy, depressed
3. Unhappy, depressed	Fearfulness
4. Resentfulness	Suspiciousness
5. Fearfulness	Cruelty, bullying
6. Cruelty, bullying	Shyness
7. Easily discouraged	Enuresis
8. Suggestible	Resentfulness
9. Overcritical of others	Stealing
10. Sensitiveness	Sensitiveness
11. Domineering	Dreaminess
12. Sullenness	Nervousness
13. Stealing	Suggestible
14. Shyness	Overcritical of others
15. Physical coward	Easily discouraged
16. Selfishness	Temper tantrums
17. Temper tantrums	Domineering
18. Dreaminess	Truancy
19. Nervousness	Physical coward
20. Stubbornness	Untruthfulness
21. Unreliableness	Unreliableness
22. Truancy	Destroying school materials
23. Untruthfulness	Sullenness
24. Cheating	Lack of interest in work
25. Heterosexual activity	Cheating
26. Lack of interest in work	Selfishness
27. Enuresis	Quarrelsomeness
28. Obscene notes, talk	Heterosexual activity
29. Tattling	Restlessness
30. Attracting attention	Inattention
31. Quarrelsomeness	Impertinence, defiance
32. Imaginative lying	Slovenly in personal appearance
33. Impudence, rudeness	Tattling
34. Inattention	Obscene notes, talk
35. Slovenly in personal appearance	Laziness
36. Laziness	Stubbornness
37. Impertinence, defiance	Attracting attention
38. Carelessness in work	Thoughtlessness
39. Thoughtlessness	Imaginative lying
40. Restlessness	Disobedience
41. Masturbation	Carelessness in work
42. Disobedience	Masturbation
43. Tardiness	Impudence, rudeness
44. Inquisitiveness	Inquisitiveness
45. Destroying school materials	Disorderliness in class
46. Disorderliness in class	Tardiness
47. Profanity	Interrupting
48. Interrupting	Profanity
49. Smoking	Smoking
50. Whispering	Whispering

All the evidence would seem clearly to indicate that the passage of years has brought changes in teachers' recognition, understanding, and practice in the area of the mental hygiene of the school child. The teachers' changed attitudes might be attributed to a change in the total social and, in particular, school situation as it exists to-day. If we accept the judgment of the psychologists, psychiatrists, and psychiatric social workers as an adequate criterion, we can authoritatively say that teachers have grown in their knowledge of how the school child develops and behaves.

While we may be gratified by the increased degree of similarity in attitude toward the behavior problems of children by the teachers and clinicians of to-day, we cannot ignore the fact that a difference still does exist. In comparing the attitudes of the mental hygienists and the teachers, one must recognize the differences in professional interests. The psychologist, the psychiatrist, and the psychiatric social worker are interested solely in the social and emotional adjustment of the individual child. Society has caused the chief interest of the teacher to be the educational achievement of the child. Does the public think that the teacher's job is that of a social engineer, engaged in promoting the all-round growth and development of pupils, or that of a filling-station attendant whose job it is to fill the tank in the child's mind with subject matter? All persons connected with schools know that children are sent to school to be "educated." Social pressures seem to operate to the disadvantage rather than the welfare of the child. The teacher cannot escape this pressure in determining his or her chief interest; and it is important to remember that no such pressure is brought to bear upon the psychologist, the psychiatrist, or the psychiatric social worker, who usually works in the seclusion of his office, isolated from the many potent and influential forces of the community.

In interpreting the comparative ratings in a study of this sort, it should be remembered that the teachers, in rating behavior items like "masturbation" and "truancy," were probably making their evaluations, particularly on our Form A of the rating scale, in terms of a larger perspective than the more restricted professional horizon of clinicians. Teachers are undoubtedly aware of the dire consequences for the child, the school, and the teacher if community opinion is outraged by a violation of conventional sexual taboos. Similarly, their concern about truancy is understandable. How can you reach the goals of education, largely community prescribed, if the pupils fail to attend classes?

In assessing the total picture of the attitudes of teachers and those of mental hygienists toward the behavior problems of children, one cannot but wonder if there are not in conventional school practices certain things that aggravate and promote the development of behavior problems. It would appear that our present tradition-bound school, with its regimentation and its regimented teachers, of necessity fosters behavior that is pathological from a mental-hygiene point of view. If this is true, who is to accept the responsibility for the teacher's attitude? The teachers in question make the natural mistake—owing, no doubt, to practical school-room conditions—of evaluating children's behavior in terms of good order and recognition of authority. On the other hand, the psychologist, the psychiatrist, and the psychiatric social worker think in terms of the effects of behavior in the long run. Teachers are expected to maintain reasonable order, and in doing this, at times make the mistake, from a mental-hygiene point of view, of favoring withdrawing behavior and ruthlessly suppressing overtly aggressive (symptomatic) behavior without thought of the consequences thereof.

Are the differences between the attitudes of teachers and mental hygienists toward certain problems of children due to social pressure rather than to a wide gulf between them in knowledge of the principles of mental hygiene and understanding of the child's welfare?

Considerable emphasis has been placed by Wickman and other investigators in similar areas upon the amount and significance of the disagreement between teachers and clinicians as to the importance of the symptoms of "shyness," "sensitiveness," "unsocial," and other withdrawing behavior in children, but the trend, the data would tend to indicate, is in the direction of eventual agreement or similarity of attitudes in the two professional groups. This, by the way, is not to imply that all shy, unsocial, sensitive, withdrawn children are of necessity headed for the neuropsychiatric hospital.

Certain implications for teacher-training institutions would seem to grow out of the findings of a study of this nature. The increased emphasis upon an understanding of child growth and development on the part of these institutions has undoubtedly been reflected in the changing attitudes of teachers. However, an increased fusion of the twin disciplines of education and psychology in the training courses of prospective teachers might conceivably increase their over-all knowledge and understanding of the physical, mental, social, and emotional life of the child.

There must be continued instruction of the teacher in the dynamics of child behavior. New knowledge must continuously be made a part of the teacher's understanding and approach to the child. Some teachers undoubtedly will need reëducation and eradication of fixed attitudes in regard to the emotional and experiential factors that produce behavior problems in children.

The public—and parents in particular—must be reoriented, where necessary, as to the rôle of the school and the teacher in the education of children and they must constantly be given information to assist them in understanding what could and should be accomplished in the best interests of the child.

Psychologists, psychiatrists, psychiatric social workers, and teachers need to exchange ideas and experiences in regard to the behavior problems of children. It would appear that these professional people have much to offer one another, and from their mutually increased knowledge would come marked advances toward the goal of complete understanding of the child. Continued and coöperative research in the multiple issues of child behavior is important. If education for life is to become a meaningful concept, we will need to know more about and constantly to investigate the social and emotional dynamics of behavior as well as the intellectual development of the child.

---

40. Education for the Development of Personality*

Related selections: 21, 24, 37, 44

SLOWLY BUT steadily over the past several decades the point of view that personality or character development must be placed high on the list of the school's objectives has been gaining acceptance. Some critics of the modern school have made this a central point of their criticism, alleging that attention to this phase of development has lessened the attention spent on enterprises that are more legitimately the function of the school, for example, learning selected subject matter. Other students of education feel that personality development and subject matter learning are not rivals for time in the school day, but that the time and energy spent in creating an environment and arranging experiences to enhance personality development pay good dividends in increased subject matter learning.

IN A study of adolescent fantasy extensive case records were gathered on 40 normal adolescent boys and girls. These records include not only the main data of the study—stories told in response to the pictures in the

* Percival M. Symonds, "Education for the Development of Personality," *Teachers College Record,* vol. L (December, 1948), pp. 163–169. Reprinted by permission of the author and publisher.
    Dr. Symonds (1893—) is Professor of Education, Teachers College, Columbia University, and a Diplomate in clinical psychology. He is a scholar and author in the fields of psychology and personality and developer of projective techniques in testing.

Symonds Picture-Story Test—but also the results of interviews with the pupils and their parents and teachers, autobiographies written by the pupils, personality questionnaires, and information available from the school records. It is believed that these data make it possible to form accurate impressions of this group of pupils—their backgrounds, present abilities, behavior and personalities, and their motivations and outlooks on life.

As each of these cases was reviewed the question was asked: What can the school do that will be of the greatest aid in furthering this pupil's personality development? Naturally, different pupils would apparently profit by different features of school life, so in planning a school program for personality development it should be recognized that no part of such a program would pertain equally to all pupils. Any school must be ready to relate its program to the individual needs of its pupils, but if a school provided each of the features suggested herein it would take care of the personality needs of most of its pupils insofar as this can be done in school.

SUGGESTIONS FOR A SCHOOL PROGRAM

The following is not a theoretical armchair program, but one that grew out of intimate acquaintance with 40 normal boys and girls as they were observed by teachers, parents, and fellow students, and as their own attitudes and inner tendencies were revealed by a projective technique, the Symonds Picture-Story Test.

Social participation. The greatest need among these adolescents was that of opportunity for social participation. Many of them seemed inhibited and withdrawn. This may seem strange in view of the democratic and social nature of schools and society today, but more intimate acquaintance with individuals shows that the greatest personality handicap still is social isolation. Boys need an opportunity to mingle in give-and-take with boys, girls with girls, and boys with girls. This opportunity would be provided in the classroom by a more democratic organization, by more occasions for free interchange of opinion in discussion, and by activities which call for sharing and joint participation. Too much of the work in the classroom is carried on in individual isolation. Classroom learning is too often thought of as an individual process rather than a group process. In addition, the school should provide opportunities for social participation outside the classroom. This can be done in passing from class to class and in the lunchroom, gymnasium, and assembly room, for example. Clubs and organizations should be democratically organized under pupil direction, with provision for group participation that will permit each individual to contribute according to his talents. Must schools relegate the clubroom to some building across the street, or would it be possible to provide something in the nature of a clubroom within the school itself?

Of special importance for some pupils—both boys and girls—is the opportunity to engage in the kind of competition provided by sports. Most boys would profit by participation in contact sports such as basketball, volley ball, soccer, or football.   It is surprising how many boys there are of whom it is said, "spends all spare time at home," "fusses in kitchen, cooks," "hobby-photography," "unobtrusive, childish, immature, inattentive," "is now taking up tap and ballroom dancing."   This problem is not solved merely by providing the opportunity for participation; these boys are the very ones who would not attend any social activities that the school might provide.   Nor would assigning them arbitrarily to activities or trying to force them to participate be successful.   They need patient, kindly encouragement to join a group, and should be led to feel that demands would not be made upon them that they could not meet.

Acceptance.   The second plank in the school's platform for personality growth and development is emotional acceptance of these boys and girls by their teachers.   Many come from homes in which they do not feel accepted.   Some are living in homes as state wards, as foster children, or as stepchildren; some are competing with brothers or sisters and feel that they are not favored by their parents.   Consequently, these cases especially need to feel that they are accepted by the school and by their teachers. They need to feel that they "belong" and are welcome.

This necessitates no elaborate machinery or organization.   The only requirement is accepting teachers; teachers who like boys and girls of adolescent age, who understand them, who can accept them with all of their aggression, carelessness, irregularity, guilt, and need of punishment. It is not necessary to have long individual conferences with pupils to accomplish this.   It can be done by a friendly smile, saying "Good morning," and by recognizing the child when his turn comes.   It can be done by judicious praise and encouragement instead of by adverse criticism. Some children need positive expressions of affection which teachers should be willing to give.   It increases a child's emotional security in school to know that he really belongs to the school, to his classes, and to organizations within the scool.

Freedom.   At least 10 of the 40 cases of this study need greater freedom in school.   They come from homes in which they are held under strict discipline.   The parents take the responsibility for the children's school progress and the children sabotage their efforts by various kinds of passive resistance.   What appears in many instances to be lack of ability or lack of interest is really part of an unconscious campaign of non-cooperation.   These children need the opportunity to manage themselves, to make their own decisions, to plan and execute their own work.   The transition period would be somewhat chaotic before the boy or girl accepted the challenge to assume responsibility for himself.   Fear of this transition period is obvious in the anxiety of both parents and teachers with regard to a child's school progress.

Firmness, strictness.   Not every child needs more freedom.   At least 9 of the cases would profit by stricter discipline.   These are the boys and girls who come from homes where too much freedom is allowed and there is not enough strictness in laying down requirements and adhering to them. These pupils would profit by being held more strictly accountable for requirements.   This should be accomplished by means of frequent and careful checks, not in a repressive, faultfinding way but, after eliciting the pupil's cooperation, with firmness and tact.   At least one boy definitely needs to be repressed.   He should be required to wait his turn, to be courteous in class, and in general to tone down his smart-alecky attitude. All of this group would benefit by being helped to plan a regular schedule and live up to it.

Opportunity to express emotions.   At least 7 cases would benefit by an opportunity to express their emotions.   These are children who have been overly repressed, with the result that their personalities are expressionless and colorless.   The school should provide opportunity for expression in writing, speaking, drawing, painting, modeling, singing, playing a musical instrument, play-acting, building or making things, and in social activities.   The choice of activity should be left pretty much to the pupil, so that he may follow lines of interest already partially developed.   It is of particular importance that these children be given freedom to express their hostilities and their loves, the two types of feelings most often repressed in this culture.

For some of these pupils much of the school's program could be looked upon as the constructive expression of aggression.   A boy who is described as quick-tempered, impatient, excitable, and having difficulty in personal relations has never learned to put his aggressive impulses to constructive use.   The school's program should provide such a boy an opportunity to carry through his work successfully, to construct things, and to take responsibility, so that some of his awkward, aggressive energy will be directed into more satisfying channels.   In the case of some girls, the school can help by encouraging them to express their feminine qualities, particularly if they wear severe clothes and tend to compete with boys.   A girl should be accepted and admired as a girl, and not made to feel she must be "first," or the dominant person in the group.

Success.   Schools should provide every boy and girl an opportunity to be *successful* in something, both in the classroom and outside.   In the classroom this consists, in large part, of adapting materials and methods to the ability of the individual; and in our big cosmopolitan schools this means more than anything else placing the boy or girl in the group where the work is adapted to his maturity.   But success is more than being confronted with a possible task, neither too hard nor too easy: it depends largely on the encouragement of the teacher and her capacity to find something gratifying in the work of a boy or girl.   The child who has had unfortunate school experiences, who has suffered by having to compete with a more successful brother or sister, who is spoiled and undisciplined, or whose parents are demanding and critical needs the taste of success in order to find satisfactions which can wean him from disappointment in other areas.

Avoidance of punishment.   In the case of at least 4 children in this group it would be essential for the school to avoid punishment or anything that could be interpreted as punishment.   These are in the group of pupils who would benefit from greater freedom—those who have been punished at home and held strictly to the parents' demands.   In general, punishment is to be avoided in school, control being maintained by more positive methods.   The boys mentioned above have been punished to make them conform to their parents' wishes, and in school they should receive encouragement, praise, and opportunities for self-expression.

Provision for responsibility.   Giving pupils responsibility, which has been mentioned before, now comes up for special discussion.   Responsibility is hard for teachers to give; concern with getting the task done seems to take precedence over development of personal growth.   But if pupils are to take responsibility they must be given it, even though the results are not always letter perfect.   Giving responsibility means keeping hands off until the task is completed, but holding pupils strictly accountable for what is assigned to them.   If the task is one which has meaning to the group as well as to the teacher, then there will be social pressure to see that it is completed: the child will be held accountable to the group as well as to the teacher.   If the group's goals are likely not to be met, then the pupil in charge of a project may have to be relieved, but this signal of failure is to be avoided, if possible, and every effort made to help the pupil who has been given the responsibility to carry it through successfully.   Much will depend on the insistence and enthusiasm of the teacher.

Encouragement.   Encouragement, which also has been mentioned previously, is needed particularly by those boys and girls who come from homes where they are rejected and feel that they are not loved.   These pupils need not only acceptance but also the boost that comes from their being encouraged and urged to do their best.   They need more than anything else the steady trust of a teacher who, believing in them, will encourage them to pick up after each discouragement and try again.

Opportunity for pleasure. In the case of two individuals, both girls, who seemed to be somewhat moody and depressed, it was believed that their school life could be made to compensate for the drabness of their homes by providing opportunities for fun. For such boys and girls the school at its worst is a haven and every activity is pleasurable. But schools should strive to make each activity enjoyable for *all* children. The curriculum should be adapted to the interests of the different ages, and it should be organized so as to present a challenge the successful meeting of which brings a thrill. Probably pleasure in school comes as much from being a member of a happy family with important tasks to perform as from any mechanical or organizational arrangement.

Freedom from competition. At least one of the group would derive benefit from a school program in which competition was reduced to a minimum. In the section on "Social Participation" it was pointed out that some boys and girls need the give-and-take of competition. But for others, particularly those already engaged in family rivalries, the competitive nature of many school activities only aggravates an unfortunate personality trend. If competition is introduced into school it should be in a spirit of play; competing for marks, awards, and promotion becomes too serious and threatening for many pupils and should be eliminated.

Provision for insight. It was believed that several pupils in the group would be helped by insight into their personalities. The mirror might be held up to their personalities so that they could see themselves as they appear to others. Each boy and girl could be helped to understand what purpose various personality trends serve and how each individual adjusts to circumstances in which he lives. This insight can be provided in two ways: in group guidance activities, through exercises of personality description and general discussions of mental hygiene and simple aspects of the psychology of adjustment; in personal counseling, through helping individual boys and girls to know themselves better and to understand the meaning of their adjustments.

Psychological help. At least two boys in the group needed professional help. Their adjustments bordered on the psychotic; their fantasies were gravely distorted, and they needed special assistance to bring them back to normal ways of thinking and of meeting their problems. This could be accomplished only if the parents, too, were acquiring saner and more normal attitudes. While only two boys (5 per cent) in the group were definitely in need of professional help (and this is perhaps a fair portion to expect in any school), more than this number could profit from individual professional psychological counseling. And every pupil in school needs the advantage of an educational and vocational counseling program. It is not suggested that all pupils need all aspects of the above program in the same degree. All aspects should, nevertheless, be provided by the school so that the needs of all individuals can be served. What the school program can contribute to each child must be determined for the individual separately by a detailed case study. Only by such a case study can it be determined whether a pupil needs more freedom or more strictness, more emphasis on social participation or on achieving success, more competition or less, more opportunity to express emotions, or more attention to fulfilling the obligations of a planned program.

It should be stated in all candidness that the suggestions which were blocked out for each pupil in this study came more from life material than from fantasy material. The life history material revealed lacks to be filled and trends to be corrected. The fantasy material did not show the nature of actual adjustments, but pointed out their meaning by revealing the wishes, hopes, desires, anxieties, and guilt feelings that lay beneath them. One boy needed more acceptance and more encouragement because (as revealed by the case material) he was rejected by his stepmother, an attitude which resulted in his continual backsliding in school. His aspirations and ambitions apparent in the fantasy material existed *only* in fantasy and needed the encouragement of his teacher to realize them. The fantasy material often indicated what was lacking, but seldom furnished a clue to how to supply the deficiency.

The school should reinforce the influence of the home in the case of well-adjusted pupils, and counteract and supplement its influence in the case of the poorly adjusted pupils. Actually, it would be difficult for a school to carry through such a program successfully. The parent who expends his aggression in overambition for and strictness with a boy expects the school to reinforce his efforts. For the school to give this boy more freedom would be a distinct threat to the goals of the parent, who would then criticize the school and bring pressure to bear on it to reinforce his own tactics with his boy. Any school, therefore, that genuinely proposes to institute a program of personality development must seek the cooperation of the parents of its pupils and, if necessary, arrange a program of guidance and counseling that will enable parents to adapt their attitudes to the needs of their children.

SUMMARY

After studying the needs of the 40 boys and girls and planning educational programs for them, the conclusion was reached that an understanding of the fantasy life has a secondary but nevertheless important role in determining the essential features of a program for personality development. It is of major importance to know the nature of the child's adjustments, as they can be observed, and something of his background. Knowledge of fantasy helps in discovering the meaning of a child's adjustments and the lacks in his personality development. Any teacher will achieve more sympathy with and understanding of a pupil through acquaintance with his fantasies. The program outlined provides for increased social participation, acceptance by teachers, freedom, firmness, opportunity to express emotions, opportunity to be successful, avoidance of punishment, pupil responsibility, encouragement, opportunity for pleasure, freedom from competition, personality insight, and psychological help. It is emphasized that no one pupil needs all aspects of such a program. Each pupil in a school should be studied intensively as an individual with a view to learning what the school can contribute to his optimum personality development.

---

41. Psychosomatic Illness and Emotional Needs*

Related selections: 20, 24, 25, 44, 47

THERE HAS been skepticism concerning the ability of the school to improve the mental health of pupils by giving attention to all aspects of the learning situation. The experiment reported by Fleming in the following selection indicates that schools, by taking into account the knowledge about the emotional needs of children, can arrange the learning situation in such a way as to lessen the emotional strain on children and the accompanying distress symptoms.

IF TEACHERS could know the innermost thoughts of many of their students, they would likely discover that often children are "crying from within." The concerns of some children are so great that they are likely to sit in classrooms brooding, thinking and worrying about the problems, anxieties, fears, tensions and frustrations which are so real to them. As teachers engage in their teaching of "subjects," many children are victims

* Robert S. Fleming, "Psychosomatic Illness and Emotional Needs," *Educational Leadership,* vol. IX (November, 1951), pp. 119–123. Reprinted by permission of author and publisher.

Dr. Fleming (1914—) is Professor of Education, University of Tennessee, and formerly Research Editor, *Educational Leadership.*

of emotional problems.   If these frustrations in children continue, and if the teacher strives to fulfill his academic objectives only, observable evidences of tension sometimes arise in the form of symptoms of physical illness.

Flanders Dunnbar has said, "A child may become ill because he is unhappy or bewildered."   This suggests the need for careful consideration of illness and its relation to behavior.

UNDERSTANDING EMOTIONAL NEEDS

For years there has been a growing emphasis upon understanding the nature of emotional needs.   The work of Prescott, Murray, Frank, Hymes, Baruch, and Raths has led to extensive research and interest in the meaning and the characteristics of emotional needs.   One finds numerous lists of emotional needs throughout educational literature.   Raths' classification of needs includes the following:

The need for belonging
The need for love and affection
The need for achievement
The need for economic security
The need for freedom from fear
The need for freedom from guilt
The need for sharing
The need for understanding

The needs theory developed by Raths and his associates also indicates that there are four possible consequences of unfulfilled emotional needs. This hypothesis is based in part on Dollard's Frustration-Aggression Theory.   Raths believed that as emotional needs are unfulfilled four major frustrations might develop.   They are:

The individual becomes extremely aggressive
The individual becomes submissive
The individual tends to withdraw from his group and to isolate himself
The individual becomes physically ill
Combination of these four

The relationship between unfulfilled needs and illness was the basis of a recent investigation.   Today one finds many evidences of a growing interest in an understanding of psychosomatic illness.   James Halliday describes the psychosomatic condition as bodily disorder whose nature can be understood only when emotional disturbances are investigated in relation to physical disturbances.   This new field has great implications for education.

AN EXPLORATORY STUDY

In order to study the nature of psychosomatic illness and its relationship to the emotional needs of children, the working hypothesis was formulated that as teachers attempt to meet the emotional needs of children, psychosomatic manifestations become less frequent and less acute.   The study was thought of as one of helping teachers to identify and to meet the emotional needs of children as a means of reducing certain forms of physical illness.   The study began with the identification of thirty-eight children in an elementary school in a metropolitan area who had a previous history of illness.   In fact, the children were first identified from existing health records in the office of the school nurse.

An in-service teacher education program was planned which was to help teachers determine ways of working with children with psychosomatic illness.   The in-service program consisted of frequent conferences to help teachers become sensitive to the eight emotional needs and their implications for working with children.   A series of human relations films were used.   When teachers were brought together to talk about their purposes it was not at all unusual to find them on the defensive. Over and over again teachers wanted to be told what to do with children showing psychosomatic symptoms.   Through the use of films and other impersonal media teachers were helped to focus their attention upon emotional needs.

The study was an exploratory, experimental one in which there was a comparison of a "before" and "after" nature.   An Experimental Group and a Comparison Group were set up in order to be able to draw some conclusions concerning the effects of the in-service program on the health of children in the Experimental Group.   It was assumed that teachers in the Experimental Group would work with their children in a manner quite different from the way the teachers in the Comparison Group worked.

The Experimental Group was composed of a group of twenty-six children whereas the Comparison Group consisted of twelve children.   The twenty-six children in the Experimental Group were represented by nine teachers in the in-service program.   The children in the study had such physical difficulties as: stomach upsets, allergies, metabolic difficulties, upper respiratory infections, kidney difficulties, "accident prone" children, "nervous children," and children with frequent headaches.   Care was taken to make sure that there were children in both the Experimental and the Comparison Group representing various difficulties.   Also, consideration was given to factors of sex, age, grade, and variety of psychosomatic disturbances.

All children in the study, Experimental and Comparison, were examined by a medical doctor at the beginning of the study and at the end of the study.   In addition, the teacher, school nurse, and the investigator kept a close check on the children and prepared extensive records on their health during the experimental period.   The nurse and the doctor were available throughout the study to observe the children and to make necessary records.   The crux of the design of this investigation lay in the effectiveness of the in-service program which was to be developed.

TESTS TO DETERMINE NEEDS

As an aid in determining unfulfilled needs, a Needs Test was given. *The Wishing Well* was used for grades 1, 2, and 3 and *Self Portrait N* was given in grades 4, 5, and 6.   These tests were thought of as sources of data which were to be used with all other available data.   This was of great importance since specific therapy for specific needs was thought to be required.   After the Needs Tests were given and the teachers had an opportunity to pool these results with all other available information concerning each child, a special program was designed for each person in the Experimental Group.   This "tailor-made" program was thought of as an attempt to meet the child's unfulfilled emotional needs.   That is to say, the specific suggestions were made in a setting in which the interest of the child, the work of the group, the materials available, and the setting of the school in its community were taken into account.   Such a plan was to be used as a basis for planning with the teachers the ways in which they might extend and apply the basic concepts of meeting emotional needs of children.

The teachers in this investigation sought opportunities to work with children in a manner which would free them, which would make them secure, which would help them like school, which would help them recognize success, which would help them work on things for which they saw purpose, which would give them opportunities to see more clearly what they were doing in school, which would help them become better participants in their group.   Such activities are often very simple activities for teachers to use in working with children.   The point seemed to become one of teachers relating themselves to children in a manner characterized by purposeful activity in a friendly, relaxed setting.   Such a method of relating oneself to children is of tremendous importance in maintaining the emotional security of boys and girls.

A few examples of the things a teacher did for a child who had a need for achievement were:

Provided an opportunity for him to list on the board the things that he had accomplished.

Provided an opportunity for him to learn some skill in art or music which he shared with other people in the group.

Congratulated him on his contributions to the class planning.

Complimented him on his accomplishments of the day.

Had him keep a folder with samples of work which would help him recognize growth.

Numerous other activities were thought of and were carried through, but this list suggests some of the ways in which the teacher attempted to meet this boy's need for achievement.

USE OF SUGGESTIONS

The importance of such suggestions as these seems to lie in their consistent use.   Each suggestion was not necessarily used daily and yet it was pointed out how important it is for teachers to work with children consistently day after day.   If one were to analyze the kinds of things which teachers did most frequently in meeting the emotional needs of children, they would likely fall under such ideas as: teachers did listen to children, they did relate the work the children were doing to things they could do, they helped children save face with their group, they worked in a calm, relaxed manner, they tended to avoid tension, they analyzed the situations which were difficult, they made special provision for certain individuals to extend their work, they were often careful to explain to children what was to be done, what was expected, details of situations.   They gave individuals opportunities to do many things.   They overlooked trivial situations which made for anxiety, worry, frustration.

The teachers in this study did not produce a formula for teaching. Neither did each teacher in the study employ the same procedures for any particular situation.   One would not expect all teachers to work in a common way.   Yet the common element in the work of the teachers in the Experimental Group seemed to represent a sincere effort on the part of all to help each child function consistently and continuously in a free, relaxed manner.   The dynamics of this process comes, not by any one plan or group of plans which teachers employed, but through the *consistent* use of the underlying philosophy which has been described.   That is to say, a child having a need for achievement must experience success many times a day, day in and day out, over a long period of time in order for frustrations caused by a lack of feeling of success to disappear.   One of the most crucial characteristics of the needs approach seems to be the consistent nature of its application.   One cannot help children overcome psychosomatic difficulties by trying to meet emotional needs unless he is willing to view the process as a long term one.

The very nature of the psychosomatic manifestations makes it impossible for one to study thoroughly a child with psychosomatic symptoms unless he attempts to consider all aspects of his day by day life. Psychosomatic therapy is not a simple procedure in which one takes "a pill for a pain." Instead, the identification and fulfillment of emotional needs is an intricate and a complex procedure. This calls for detailed information concerning the child, his background, his physical symptoms, the onset of the difficulty and the relationship of factors associated with the difficulty. Such information is of vital importance in helping the teacher plan the design for beginning her work to meet the needs of an individual child.

A summary of the progress of each child was important as a means of measuring the results of the study and of testing the underlying hypothesis. This included health, relationship with other children, attendance, general well-being and a daily log kept by the teacher.

FINDINGS OF THE STUDY

The intensity of the psychosomatic syndrome was described by the physician at the beginning and at the end of the exploratory period. The physician did not know which children composed the "Experimental Group" and which ones were in the "Comparison Group." In summarizing, 96.1% of the children in the Experimental Group showed significant improvement, whereas 50% of the children in the Comparison Group showed significant improvement. This comparison in improvement was judged by the medical doctor. According to the doctor's records, a consideration of emotional factors should be given major emphasis in working with all children in the two groups.

In terms of frequency, 80.8% of the Experimental Group were having symptoms, daily, or several times a day, at the beginning of the investigation, while at the close of the period 84.7% of the children in this group had symptoms described by parents and teachers as occurring occasionally. This gain was not true in the Comparison Group, since 41.6% of the children in this group continued to have symptoms daily.

Records of school attendance were kept for all children in the study. These records consisted only of absences due to illness. A comparison of the monthly attendance records of the children was made with the record of the same period during the previous year. An analysis of the data shows that significant improvement in school attendance was made in the Experimental Group with a gain of 49.7% in attendance during the

1949 school year over the same period during 1948. The reverse was true in the Comparison Group. The Comparison Group had a loss of 40.9% in attendance for 1949 over 1948.

Thus, it is shown that as teachers become sensitive to the nature of emotional needs, and as they attempt to meet specific needs of an individual child having psychosomatic manifestations, significant improvement in the child's health takes place. This occurs in terms of a reduction in both intensity and frequency of illness and makes for improved school attendance.

And so it seems that the teachers of America have the potential ability of working with boys and girls in a manner which contributes to the meeting of their needs and hence to the improvement of many health problems.

---

42. An Attempt to Evaluate the Threat of Failure as a Factor in Achievement*

Related selection: 36

A POINT often raised by critics of the mental health goal of schooling is that if the threat of failure is minimized in a school, then the children and youth, lacking that fear as a motivation, will not exert necessary effort to learn. Achievement will then be lowered. The experiment described below raises serious question concerning the necessity of this threat as a part of a teaching situation.

THE PROBLEM of pupil failure or non-promotion in school has been a crucial issue in school administration throughout the history of elementary education in the United States. Numerous statistical studies and a few experimental investigations regarding pupil failure have been made. Administrators and teachers everywhere have struggled to reduce the amount of non-promotion, and in some school systems the percentage of failure has been reduced to less than two or three and in a few cases almost to zero. Many and varied methods have been used in efforts to

* Henry J. Otto and Ernest O. Melby, "An Attempt to Evaluate the Threat of Failure as a Factor in Achievement." Reprinted from *Elementary School Journal*, vol. XXXV (April, 1935), pp. 588–596 by permission of the University of Chicago Press and the authors.

Dr. Melby (1891—) is Professor of Education and Dean of the School of Education, New York University. He is a member of the Educational Policies Commission. Dr. Otto (1901—) is Professor of Elementary Curriculum and Administration, University of Texas.

lower the percentage of children required to repeat the grade at the end of the school term.   One of the most disturbing elements in the general move to reduce failures has been the fear that the quality of school work would depreciate and that the standards of achievement of the schools would drop to scandalous depths if the failure rate should approach zero. School workers were perfectly willing that the percentage of failure should be lowered, but they were equally convinced that the practice of failing *some* pupils must be continued as an insurance against low standards of achievement.   In other words, the threat of failure must be retained to guarantee that every child will keep his shoulder to the wheel and will work to capacity.   The threat of failure is thus deemed essential as a motivating device in elementary education.

There are some educational workers, however, who believe that it is not necessary to hold over children's heads the whip hand of failure in order to bring pupils to achieve and to achieve willingly and to capacity. It is the contention of these workers that educational science has progressed far enough so that there are many ways of handling and motivating children which bring better results and which are more conducive to mental health of both teacher and pupil than is the threat of failure.   The study reported in this article was an effort to discover whether pupils threatened with non-promotion throughout the semester if they did not attain desirable achievement levels would make greater, less, or the same academic progress, as measured by standardized achievement tests, as did pupils who were told at the beginning of the semester that they would all be in the next higher grade in the following semester.   The study was conducted in four typical school systems of northern Illinois during the second semester of 1933–34 and involved 352 pupils and 18 classroom teachers.   One hundred and ninety-two pupils in Grade II A and 160 in Grade V A remained in the same school and class throughout the semester so that beginning and end tests could be given to them.   Eight sections or classes of pupils in Grade II A were taught by eight teachers, and ten sections of pupils in Grade V A were taught by ten teachers.

In organizing the experiment each superintendent selected two teachers of Grade II A and two teachers of Grade V A who in his judgment were among the most competent of his teachers and who were interested in participating in the investigation.   In West Aurora Superintendent Smith found it opportune to include six sections of Grade V A which had been classified into X, Y, and Z divisions.   The classes used in the study were taken just as they were found in the typical school situation; that is, the organization of classes and the classification of pupils normally found in a particular school were not disturbed.   It was thought that similar groups of children in the same grade would not reveal a sufficient number of statistically significant differences to influence the study. The accuracy of this supposition is borne out in the data which follow. The entire study was conducted in such a way as not to disturb the routine of administration in the least. For this reason teachers were not rotated. It was thought that the factor of teacher variation would be largely overcome by having four control-group and four experimental-group teachers in each grade.

At the beginning of the second semester the Kuhlmann-Anderson Intelligence Tests and the New Stanford Achievement Test, Primary Examination, were given to all children in Grade II A who were to be included in the study. The same intelligence test and the Unit Scales of Attainment were given to all pupils in Grade V A. Different forms of the two achievement tests were given before the close of the semester. In each of the four school systems one second-grade class and one fifth-grade class were designated as experimental groups, and one class in each of the two grades was designated as a control group, except in West Aurora as already explained.

Each teacher of an experimental group told her pupils at the beginning of the semester and several times during the semester that they would all be in the next higher grade the following term. Teachers were instructed (in most cases orally and by written statement by the writers) to make these announcements, not as sudden thunderbolts, but as statements of encouragement, and to make them so clearly that no pupil would lack a full understanding of the fact that there were to be no failures in his class during the term.

Each teacher of a control group informed her pupils at the beginning of the semester and several times during the semester that anyone who did not work hard and do well would have to repeat the grade. As in the experimental groups, the announcements in the control groups were not given in such an abrupt way that all or some of the pupils would become frightened about a sudden change in the academic requirements of the school; yet the announcements were made with sufficient clarity that every pupil would understand the proposition put before him. Doubtless in many instances the situation in the control groups was no different from the situation during any other semester with a particular teacher nor different from the setting in the majority of the elementary-school classrooms in the country.

Except for these announcements in the experimental and the control groups, no changes were made in the teaching situation. Each teacher was urged to carry on her teaching exactly as she would have done if no experiment were under way. Control-group teachers kept before their pupils the possibility of failure if good work were not done, while experimental-group teachers kept pupils aware of the fact that in the following term they would all be in the next higher grade.   Obviously, experimental-group teachers were denied the use of the threat of failure as a motivating device.

TABLE I

COMPARISON OF PUPILS IN GRADES II A AND V A IN EXPERIMENTAL GROUP WHO WORKED WITH NO THREAT OF FAILURE AND CONTROL GROUP WITH WHOM THREAT OF FAILURE WAS USED

	Experi-mental Group	Control Group	Differ-ence	Standard Error of Differ-ence	Critical Ratio
Grade II A:					
Number of pupils	93	99	—	—	—
Mean chronological age (in months)	92.5	91.4	1.1	0.7	1.57
Mean mental age (in months)	96.4	96.5	− .1	.8	.13
Mean intelligence quotient	104.4	105.9	−1.5	1.2	1.25
Mean initial educational age (in months)	99.0	100.3	−1.3	1.4	.93
Mean final educational age (in months)	107.0	107.2	− .2	1.1	.18
Mean gain	8.0	6.9	1.1	.8	1.38
Grade V A:					
Number of pupils	73	87	—	—	—
Mean chronological age (in months)	130.7	131.0	− .3	1.6	.19
Mean mental age (in months)	136.0	134.6	1.4	1.6	.88
Mean intelligence quotient	104.7	103.4	1.3	1.9	.68
Mean initial educational age (in months)	144.2	138.6	5.6	1.9	2.95*
Mean final educational age (in months)	150.4	144.1	6.3	2.1	3.00*
Mean gain	6.2	5.5	0.7	1.3	0.54

* Statistically significant differences.

The data for the experimental and control groups are summarized in Table I.   It will be noted that there are no statistically significant differences for Grade II A.   In this grade the mean gain of the experimental group is 1.1 months greater than the gain of the control group.   In Grade V A the initial and the final educational ages showed statistically significant differences in favor of the experimental group.   However, the difference in the mean gain is only 0.7 a month, and this gain is in favor of the experimental group.   In other words, in so far as these data show, there is no difference between the achievement of children (taken as groups) who have been threatened with failure and that of children who have been told at the beginning of the semester that they would all be promoted to the next higher grade at the end of the term.

In an effort to discover whether the threat of failure as a factor in pupil achievement might operate differently for children of different levels of intelligence, the children in Grade II A were divided into three groups: (1) pupils with intelligence quotients of less than 90, (2) pupils with intelligence quotients between 90 and 110, inclusive, and (3) pupils with intelligence quotients above 110. Within each intelligence group the data for the experimental and the control pupils were compared. In no instances were the differences statistically significant. As the number of second-grade children with intelligence quotients below 90 was small, the data for this group probably have little reliability, but the middle and the upper groups contained 140 and 46 pupils, respectively.

The children in Grade V A were similarly reclassified into three intelligence groups. The number of cases in the groups were as follows: intelligence quotients of less than 90, twenty-one pupils; intelligence quotients between 90 and 110, ninety-one pupils; intelligence quotients above 110, forty-eight pupils. Within each intelligence group the experimental and the control groups were compared, and no statistically significant differences were found in the final educational age and the mean gain of any of the intelligence groups. Such minor differences as existed were in favor of the experimental groups.

As a partial index to the way in which the two promotion policies represented in this study might operate under different teachers, the experimental and the control groups in each city were compared. There were eight teachers of Grade II A and ten teachers of Grade V A for which such comparisons could be made, four comparisons in Grade II A and five comparisons in Grade V A thus being possible. There were no statistically significant differences in the mean gains in the four comparisons made for Grade II A; in three of the four comparisons the minor differences existing were in favor of the experimental groups. For Grade V A there were no statistically significant differences in the mean gains in any of the five pairs of groups which were compared; in three out of the five comparisons the small differences found were in favor of the experimental groups. One might reasonably conclude, therefore, that in the total experiment variations due to teachers were not of sufficient importance in any one or a few classrooms to distort the general findings of the study.

At the end of the semester a one-page questionnaire was submitted to the participating teachers, on which they were asked to give their reactions to certain aspects of the study. Six teachers in each grade returned the inquiry blank. The first question was: "Did you notice any changes in the reactions, attitudes, or application of pupils which you believe are

due to the conditions imposed by the experiment?   If so, explain fully."
The following answers to this question were received.

Experimental-Group Teachers in Grade II A
    1. No.
    2. Perhaps the realization that they were working toward a higher goal made them put more conscious effort into their work.   I think there was a normal desire to improve, taking the group as a whole.
    3. Yes.   There seemed to be a little slacking up on work by a few, but, when they were reminded that the work in Grade III would be easier if certain work were accomplished in Grade II A, there was a better spirit of cooperation.   A happier and more satisfied attitude toward the work was noticed.

Experimental-Group Teachers in Grade V A
    1. No.
    2. Yes.   There was a general slump in attitude and quality of work.   It was difficult to arouse a feeling of pride in work well done.   It was necessary to do a great deal of checking up to bring in completed assignments and neat papers.
    3. I have in the past had the experience of an "I don't care, I'm not going to pass anyway" idea.   I have encountered no such attitude at the end of this semester.

Control-Group Teachers in Grade II A
    1. I really did not notice any definite reaction except possibly the real dislike of work in some children.
    2. No change was noticed because, being in the control group, the conditions before and during the experiment were practically the same.
    3. The children at all times seemed fully aware of the fact that they must reach certain standards in order to be promoted.

Control-Group Teachers in Grade V A
    1. No.
    2. There was a slightly greater application on the part of some pupils. There was an attempt to bring subjects in which they were weak up to a higher standard, but children are always trying to improve in those subjects for daily lessons.
    3. In most cases I think the pupil worked harder as many asked for home work.

The second question asked the teachers read as follows: "Did pupils seem to work harder, about as hard, or less hard during the experiment than groups ordinarily do, according to your past experience?"   The following replies were received to this question.

Experimental-Group Teachers in Grade II A
1. About as hard as usually.
2. I thought my pupils worked about as hard as they do ordinarily.
3. About as hard.

Experimental-Group Teachers in Grade V A
1. Just as hard.
2. Less hard unless it was a subject they liked.
3. I could see no difference.

Control-Group Teachers in Grade II A
1. Children seemed to work harder.
2. I think they may have worked a trifle harder when spurred on by a threat of failure.
3. The pupils seemed to work about as hard as usual during the experiment.

Control-Group Teachers in Grade V A
1. About the same in some cases, while in others much extra work was done at home and in the morning before school.
2. About as hard.
3. About as hard.

A third question asked teachers was: "After having spent the semester co-operating in this experiment, what is your opinion as to the desirability of conducting an experiment of this kind?" Typical answers to this question are as follows:

1. I think an experiment of this kind would have to extend over a period of years in order to be of value.
2. I liked the close follow-up work in testing which the experiment afforded, but I am not sure it stimulated the group to greater effort solely because of the emphasis on promotion.
3. It has been extremely interesting, and I feel that it will help in solving some of the problems about non-promotion which confront the elementary school.
4. Changing the control group in Grade II A to an experimental group next semester should give some interesting reactions, especially from four pupils who so far in their school life have been "jacked up" quite persistently by their teachers.
5. I don't see that it changed the work in the room.
6. I feel it is an excellent experiment.
7. Very desirable.
8. The child does not expect any drastic change from his past experience. If he has been allowed to go on before when he was not as good as the rest of the group, he thinks he may do so again.

Teachers were asked a fourth question; "Do you think the basic character of this experiment has sufficient significance for education and pupil welfare so that the study ought to be expanded and developed along several unexplored lines?" Nine of the twelve teachers answered in the affirmative, many of them giving excellent suggestions for steps which should be taken next in an effort to solve the many related problems suggested by the present study.

SUMMARY

This investigation represents a preliminary effort to evaluate the effect of the threat of failure as a factor in the achievement of children. Within the limited range of this study it seems fair to conclude that children who are told at the beginning of the semester that all will be in the following grade the next term do as well on a comprehensive achievement test as children who throughout the semester are reminded that they must do good work or suffer non-promotion. This generalization applies about equally well to the groups in Grade II A as to the groups in Grade V A. In general, the statements of experimental-group teachers are to the effect that the elimination of the threat of failure did not affect materially, either favorably or unfavorably, the quality of work, the attitudes, or the application of the pupils. These opinions of teachers are supported by the test results. Consequently, if the line of research represented here can be extended and expanded, there may be hope that within a short time the elementary school can be liberated from the undesirable aspects of non-promotion.

It should be clear to any reader that the study reported herein is only a preliminary step and that the experiment has many limitations. There are numerous questions raised by a project of this kind. What, for example, will be the ultimate effect on the attitudes of children toward success and failure if the policy of 100 per cent promotion is followed throughout a child's elementary-school career? Will six years in the absence of the threat of failure result in a total educational growth by the end of Grade VI as great as the growth attained under the constant pressure of the threat of failure? What differences will there be in the mental health, personality development, and social adjustment of children? How will children who have been permitted to go on regularly from grade to grade in spite of low attainment fit into the academic activities of typical achievers in the intermediate grades? Do teachers now have, or can they be taught, motivating devices other than the threat of failure which will cause each child to achieve to capacity? Is the threat of failure more useful and valuable in higher than in lower grades? What is the relation between promotion policies and report cards? These and many other questions must be investigated more fully before the policy of non-promotion can be generally eliminated in public-school practice.

---

43. Experiments on Autocratic and Democratic Atmospheres*

Related selections: 35, 40, 49

THE WORK of Lewin and his associates in studying the effects of social climate on the behavior of individuals has made a strong impact on the thinking of teachers, administrators and others who work in our schools. His work has focused attention on the human relations within the group as a determinant of behavior.

ARE GROUP actions against scapegoats always organized, or can such a situation arise as spontaneous group action? What are the conditions of such action and who is predestined to become the scapegoat? How does a democratic or an autocratic atmosphere influence the stability of group structure? What difference does it make whether intensive work is the outcome of strict order or spontaneous interest? The answer to questions such as these is approached experimentally in a study on democracy and autocracy carried on by R. Lippitt at the Iowa Child Welfare Research Station with clubs of ten- to eleven-year-old boys. At present he and R. White are repeating the experiment with other individuals and different leaders, and have extended their scope of "social climates" to include "laissez faire."

To attack experimentally such problems as democracy and autocracy may seem hopeless or even absurd for a number of reasons. Democracy, for instance, as a cultural and political pattern in the United States is something which has been built up gradually through hundreds of years, created a multitude of institutions, and formed political procedures. It has deeply influenced business as well as hospitality; family life as well

---

* Kurt Lewin, "Experiments on Autocratic and Democratic Atmospheres," *Social Frontier,* vol. IV (July, 1938), pp. 316–319. Reprinted by permission of the Progressive Education Association.

Professor Lewin (1890–1947), late Director of the Research Center for Group Dynamics, Massachusetts Institute of Technology, was the inventor of "topological" and "vectorial" psychology. His extensive writings touched upon many aspects of intra-group relationships.

as education.   In short, *it has affected all and every interrelation between persons.*

Is democracy then not much too large a subject for an experimental approach?   Would such an experiment not presuppose having the control of a full country with cities, streets, and factories and a hundred years to learn the outcome of the experiment?

Furthermore, is the question of democracy not much too "complicated" for a direct experimental attack?   Does not a scientific analytical study of such a phenomenon imply the necessity of breaking the problem up into smaller units to be approached one by one?

METHODOLOGY OF "FIELD" INQUIRIES

These questions remind me of some arguments the group of psychologists had to face who, around 1920, endeavored to study problems of will and emotion in a more serious manner than just measuring reaction time. They were told by their colleagues, by philosophers, and by practitioners, that it was foolish to study, for example, the problem of decision as long one could not create some "real events of life," such as telling the mother of the subject to study his reaction.   The issue of complexity too was raised: "real" emotions such as anger were said to be too complicated for direct experimental approach.   One should split them into emotional "elements" and study those.

Today these arguments are dead.   The experimental studies on will and emotion, although proceeding slowly, are definitely under way.   Psychology sees somewhat more clearly the general methodological issues involved.   In particular:

(1) Science has to be *analytical* in determining and measuring the factors influencing behavior.   However, that does not mean that the experiments have to split up objects and events into smaller parts.   An isolated ion behaves very differently than in its setting within an atom.   You cannot study the behavior of molecules by studying only the atoms in isolation, or more generally, you cannot study wholes without keeping them intact. Similarly, one cannot study group life or draw conclusions for group life by making experiments on isolated individuals.

(2) The absolute *size* and *intensity* of a psychological event or "object," like a group, is of course important in psychology.   More important, however, are the *type* of event and the *pattern* of the setting.   If an experiment is able to create the *constellation* it wishes to study, even though on a smaller scheme, it will go quite a way toward understanding the laws of this constellation.

(3) Psychology will have to get hold of such factors as "atmosphere" or "social climate" of a situation if it wishes to understand behavior. The concept "atmosphere" seems to be rather vague and not very scientific. On the other hand, every teacher knows that he will have no disciplinary difficulties if he can create the right atmosphere. If he is unable to create the proper atmosphere he might never overcome these difficulties, whatever single measure he might apply. Experiments on emotions (Dembo, Prescott), on regression and frustration (Baker, Dembo), on the effect of the pedagogical-cultural atmosphere in orphanages, foster homes, and nursery schools (Wellman and Skeels), and the findings of cultural anthropology in regard to so-called primitive societies (Mead) all show increasingly the importance of the social atmosphere.

As a rule, the general atmosphere of the situation can be said to be in the long run more important for behavior and for development than even a rather crucial single experience.

No one would attempt to understand the movements of a physical body without taking into consideration the character of the field of gravity (to speak in terms of classical mechanics) in which it is located. *Similarly, psychology will have to find a way of conceptually characterizing and quantitatively measuring the properties of the general field in which a person is located.* Doubtless the social atmosphere is one of the outstanding characteristics of that field: the group to which a person belongs, its culture and social climate. It is the *ground* on which the person stands. The character of the group and of the person's position within the group determines whether this ground is firm or shaky, whether the situation is clear or unclear, and therefore whether the person feels secure or insecure. Moreover, the ideology of the group determines to a very high degree the goals of the individual, his values, and his style of living.

EXPERIMENTING WITH MINIATURE SOCIAL "SYSTEMS"

The set-up in Lippitt's and White's experiments is about the following:

The personal interrelations between the children of two different classes were studied by means of the Moreno Sociometric tests, by observations, and with the help of the teacher. From the children who volunteered to be members of a club, the purpose of which would be to make theatrical masks, two groups were chosen which were matched according to leadership qualities, friendship-rejection, interpersonal relationships, etc. In Lippitt's experiment a democratic and an autocratic group under the same student leader were compared; in the experiment of Lippitt and White four different groups were chosen under four different student leaders, the atmosphere being democratic, autocratic, or "laissez faire."   Also the variety of club activities was extended greatly but equated within the different atmospheres as much as possible.   Group loyalty to the club was built up by permitting the children to choose the name of the club and to decorate and equip their own club rooms.   In this experiment, after a number of weeks a new leader came in and at the same time the atmosphere was shifted, for instance, from democracy to autocracy, or to laissez faire (or vice versa).   Thus the same group of children could be studied in all three atmospheres and in different orders of change.

It should be mentioned that no attempt was made to copy an extreme autocratic regime such as Nazism.   The autocrat always tried to be friendly and did not purposely suppress free expression.   He merely told the children what to do, with whom to work, and how to do it.   As a whole, this was an atmosphere not too different from that created by a friendly teacher who believes in strict discipline.   In the democratic group all problems of policy were put up to the children to decide.   The leader acted as fully as possible as a regular member of the group.   In laissez faire, no encouragement was given to cooperative decision.   The leader stood entirely apart from the group, but ready to give technical information when approached.

WHAT DIFFERENT SOCIAL STRUCTURES DO
TO THEIR MEMBERS

Lippitt's comparison of autocratic and democratic groups gave the following quantitative results:

(a) Probably the greatest quantitative difference is the amount of *hostility* expressed among the members of the group.   It is about thirty times as high in the autocratic group as in the democratic group.

(b) This is probably due partly to the greater *tension* which seems to prevail in the autocratic group.   This tension shows itself in the fact that the *total volume of social interaction* is 55 per cent greater in the autocratic group, in spite of the fact that objectively there is less need of communication in regard to the ongoing activity because it is directed by the autocratic leader.

(c) The autocratic group shows a *less stable group structure*.   In 38 per cent of the time the members of the autocratic group work each by himself (group structure 1–1–1–1–1), or only one of the children works with another (2–1–1–1), whereas, in the democratic group such structure occurs only in 18 per cent of the time.   The more cooperative group structures in which all or at least four of the five children worked together

(5, 4–1) occurred in the democratic group much more frequently: 56 per cent, against only 12 per cent in the autocratic group. In the autocratic group the more cooperative group structures had to be built up by the experimenter and had a tendency to break down rather quickly, whereas in the democratic group this cooperation developed spontaneously.

(d) The autocratic group shows *more dominating behavior* and *less objective behavior*. This difference was particularly great in relation to out-groups where the autocratic group showed 102 per cent more ascendent behavior than the democratic group.

(e) The democratic group showed 47 per cent more feeling of *"we'ness"* as expressed in language and in test situations; the autocratic group 27 per cent more feeling of *"I'ness."*

(f) It is in line with this that the democratic group showed *more cooperative* endeavor: more often cooperation was offered and asked for, and there were many more occurrences of praise and expression of friendliness.

(g) There was more expression of an objective, *matter-of-fact attitude* in the democratic group, as against more *personal feelings* in the autocratic one; many more constructive suggestions were offered in democracy and there was more give-and-take of objective criticism without personal involvement.

(h) The *constructiveness* was higher in the democratic group as shown in the superiority of the group products. Certain test periods where the experimenter left the room for a short while were introduced. In such periods, typically, the constructiveness of work in the autocratic group fell down very quickly, whereas in the democratic situation work went on with very little change.

(i) Feeling for *group property and group goals* was much better developed in the democratic group. The records show that the children at the close of the club had the tendency to destroy the masks or take them for themselves individually in the autocratic group, whereas in the democratic group they presented them to their leader and teacher.

(j) During the twelve meetings of the club twice the situation of a *scapegoat* arose, where the whole group ganged together against one of the members. At the fourth meeting most of the hostility was directed against one member. The next day he was still the center of hostility. As a matter of fact, he was treated so badly that he ceased to come to the club. A few weeks later another member was made the scapegoat. He too quit, saying that he had bad eyes and that he could not come because his physician said his eyes needed the fresh air.

As a whole one might say then that the autocratic situation was characterized by what one might call a state of higher "basic tension," less objectivity, and more hostile aggressiveness.   This aggressiveness was not directed openly against the autocrat (towards whom the children generally were rather submissive) but tended to find an outlet in the easy and less dangerous way of attacking a scapegoat.

ASSOCIATED PHENOMENA

Here is not the place to go into the specific dynamics behind this individual and social "mechanism," more than to say that it obviously has to do with the combination of the narrowing down of the space of free movement, the loss of status, and the resultant of forces in this constellation.

Sometimes the behavior in the autocratic group is such that overtly everything seems to go along smoothly, and that the children even seem to like the situation.   It was quite a revelation when the interviews with these children (which were conducted by a person not connected with the experiment) brought out a most intensive dislike of the autocrat.   Not infrequently the dominant note in autocracy is not so much an atmosphere of hostility as one of primitivation, lack of initiative, and listlessness.

This is shown, I think, rather effectively by one of our films which recorded the change of the same group of children from democracy to autocracy.   The last day of democracy showed the children lively and intensely working (independent of presence or absence of the leader), an atmosphere of friendly cooperation, and considerable conversation among the children   It is striking to see how quickly during the first hour of autocracy, the conversation between the children dies down.   Only the leader is approached if a question arises; the faces of the children become definitely less alive, more apathetic.   On the fifth day of autocracy the films show these trends firmly established.   When the autocratic leader leaves the room the intensive work going on in his presence quickly fades out, and that with the same children who have shown in democracy independent productive work in full swing.

The rapidity with which a shift in social atmosphere affects ideology and conduct is as impressive in some of the other transitions.   The last day of "laissez faire," for instance, as shown by the film, reveals the typical characteristics of that atmosphere: cooperative work between a few children might arise, but it usually disintegrates very quickly into individual undertakings, and ends generally in horse-play.   The difference between a democratic atmosphere and that of laissez faire is rather striking and speaks for the necessity of strictly distinguishing both social climates: namely, the one where decisions are made cooperatively and then carried out individually or collectively according to the nature of the project (democracy), from the climate of "total freedom" (laissez faire) where goals are set individually. The quantitative analysis of that situation is not yet available; however, the children often give the impression of feeling bored. *The actual space of free movement in our situation of laissez faire seems not to be greater but smaller than in democracy and insofar similar to that of autocracy.* The lack of time perspective of worthwhile goals for long-range actions seems definitely to narrow down the children's space of free movement, although the limitations are in this case not set by the ruling of an autocrat.

DEMOCRACY IN LEARNING AND TEACHING FUNCTIONS

When the new democratic leader enters the group a quieting down of the chaotic behavior is clearly visible even in the first hour. By unobtrusively listening-in and cooperating in the work of the children, without bossing them, the leader is able to build up a spirit of democratic cooperation more quickly than one might expect.

Naturally, it seems to take somewhat more time to establish democracy than to establish autocracy. *The democratic style of life presupposes active participation on the part of every member.* The members therefore have to experience this style and acquire a feeling for handling it before it will be well established. Besides, democracy depends much more upon every one of its members: one person out of line is apt to do more harm to the total atmosphere than in autocracy where the individuality of the members matters less.

One might think that the quickness with which conduct and outlook changes with the change in social atmosphere might be characteristic only for children and for experimental situations. However, reports on historical events, such as the recent shift to Nazism in Austria, seem to indicate that the conduct of an entire population can be changed over night rather deeply if the change in its social situation is sufficiently great. (In some respects, by the way, the shift to Nazism seems to have produced results similar to those which come up in the experiments of Lippitt and White.)

I do not like to conclude without cautioning the reader against a too quick generalization. It was not the purpose of these experiments to test "the" democracy, the "ideal" autocracy, and "the" situation of laissez faire. Obviously a great variety of each of these climates is possible. The purpose of the experiments is to study the dynamics of the factors involved rather than to copy historically-given examples. Nevertheless, certain conclusions as to the value of the different climates for education might readily be made.   In addition, one general outcome might be stressed:

These experiments point anew to the great possibilities vested in education, and to the responsibility given to moulders of young lives which are so sensitive to the present social climate and are so dependent upon it.

C. THE TEACHER'S ROLE

44. The Classroom Teacher and the Emotional Problems of Children*

Related selections: 25, 40, 41, 47

WE ARE reminded again and again that the "whole child comes to school."   Many teachers, however, ask if it is possible for them to foster desirable emotional development of children and provide help for those who have some degree of emotional disturbance.   Dr. Patterson makes specific suggestions for the teacher who desires to maintain a classroom environment that embodies the conditions for good mental hygiene.

INCREASINGLY it is being accepted that the classroom teacher is responsible for more than the academic development of the child.   Education now tries to supply the physical needs of the pupil as well, since it has been recognized that a child handicapped by a temporary or permanent physical disability is also handicapped in academic learning.   In comparison with the physically handicapped, relatively little has been done in the classroom for the emotionally disturbed or handicapped pupil.   But it is just as true, perhaps even more true, that the academic progress of the child is affected by his emotions and feelings.   As Dorothy Baruch and others point out, children bring their emotions, as well as their minds and bodies, to school with them.

* C. H. Patterson, "The Classroom Teacher and the Emotional Problems of Children," *Understanding the Child,* vol. XXI (June, 1952), pp. 67–72.   Reprinted by permission of author and the National Association for Mental Health.
Dr. Patterson (1912   ) is a counseling psychologist with the Veterans Administration, St. Paul, Minnesota.   He was formerly associated with the Fels Research Institute in Human Development, Antioch College.

It is true that much progress has been made since the study of Wickman, which revealed the disagreement between teachers' concepts of the seriousness of behavior characteristics and the opinions of mental hygienists. Since that time considerable effort has been made to help teachers recognize emotional disturbances when they exist. The well-behaved, overly-quiet child may be covering up a serious emotional disturbance.

The emphasis, however, has been upon the recognition, or diagnosis, of emotional problems. Many teachers have become quite skilled in detecting signs of emotional disturbances in children who should be referred for special treatment. This is well and good, since early treatment is desirable. But emotional disturbance is a matter of degree, and there are many less serious problems, or beginning problems, which cannot be treated by the limited number of psychiatrists and psychologists available. And there are the more or less normal or temporary emotional disturbances of the so-called "average" child. The teacher has a responsibility in these cases, so that emotional development will continue normally. That is, the teacher should be able to maintain a healthy environment for the emotional development of all of her pupils.

Little has been done to help the teacher meet this responsibility and opportunity. There has been much discussion of the problem, but not of how to handle it, except through referral of serious cases. More than this is necessary. The teacher must acquire and be able to put into practice the attitudes and techniques of good mental hygiene. This is necessary because, as suggested above, not all maladjusted children can be treated in a clinic; because there are many borderline cases for which there are no treatment facilities; and because the principles of mental hygiene which are effective with maladjusted children are equally good for the normal child, who also has emotions.

CHARACTERISTICS OF EMOTIONAL DISTURBANCE

As a background for dealing with emotional maladjustment, it is essential that the teacher understand what the emotionally disturbed child is like. There are several points which must be kept in mind.

1. *The emotionally maladjusted child is not a malingerer.* He is not faking, he is not pretending or feigning in order to gain something, inventing complaints for his own ends. He is not deliberately manufacturing excuses and alibis.

2. *Emotional maladjustment is not a willful or consciously developed condition.* It is not brought on by conscious design, but develops against the will of the child. It is not an indication of wickedness, stubbornness, laziness or perverseness. It is not true, as is sometimes thought, that an

emotionally maladjusted child can cure himself if he only wants to, if he will only "buckle down," try to control himself, or "snap out of it." Of course, maladjusted behavior serves a purpose, but it is not consciously developed as a clever trick to avoid something unpleasant.

3. *The physical complaints so common in emotional maladjustment are not imaginary.* Another mistaken notion is that the aches and pains of the emotionally maladjusted individual are not real. But the fact that a symptom or pain is of functional or psychological origin rather than of physical origin does not make it any the less painful or annoying. The nervous child actually suffers from his physical symptoms. A functional pain or symptom is just as real and painful and disabling as one due to organic disease.

4. *An emotional disturbance is not a sign of weakness.* It is trite to say that everyone has his breaking point, but it is true. The stresses and strains of military life were severe enough to cause many individuals to become emotionally maladjusted who might never have become so if they had continued in civilian life. There are many emotionally disturbed— or neurotic—individuals who are very successful in business, the professions, and the arts. Many are hard-working, ambitious, conscientious individuals, who perhaps take things too seriously at times. Emotional maladjustment is not something to be ashamed of; it is a misfortune, not a disgrace. The emotionally disturbed child is therefore not to be considered inferior, worthless, or untrustworthy. He is not of tainted heredity. He is not a slacker or coward. During the war the proportion of medals was as great among those who broke down in combat as among those who did not.

5. *Emotional maladjustment takes many forms.* It has been called the great imitator. It may manifest itself in tremors, headaches, backaches, other pains, shortness of breath, palpitation of the heart, rapid pulse, high blood pressure, excessive perspiration, anorexia, vomiting, indigestion, stomach upset, constipation, diarrhea, irritability, fatigue, restlessness, inability to concentrate, fears and phobias, functional blindness, deafness or muteness, stuttering, functional paralyses, as well as hostility, over-aggressiveness, etc. Because of the physical symptoms, it is important that a physical examination be given to check for any organic disease. However, if after thorough examination no physical basis for the complaint is found, an emotional disturbance is probably present. It has been estimated that from one-half to two-thirds of those individuals seen by the average doctor have a psychological, or emotional, basis for part or all of their complaints.

Many of these symptoms are present at times in all of us, without any physical basis. We are all familiar with the headache which develops—

on a purely unconscious level—when we face an unpleasant engagement. A temporary emotional disturbance may be responsible for a variety of physical and psychological symptoms, without, however, warranting the classification of the individual as a neurotic.

WHAT CAN THE TEACHER DO?

With the general understanding of emotional disturbances just discussed, what can the teacher do for the emotional needs of the child? Without being a psychologist or a psychiatrist, how can she handle emotionally disturbed children, or the temporary emotional upsets of the average child? We shall discuss briefly some of the attitudes and techniques which are important in such situations. First, there are several "don'ts" which follow from the characteristics of the emotionally disturbed individual just presented.

1. Since the emotionally disturbed child is not a malingerer, or pretending, he should not be treated as such. He shouldn't be accused of faking, of making up or exaggerating his complaints. He is honest and sincere in his claims, and should be respected as such, with belief, not suspicion.

2. Since emotional maladjustment is not willful, but is beyond conscious control, no one should be blamed for it. Don't condemn the maladjusted child. It does no good to tell him to use his will power, to "snap out of it"—he would if he could. Lectures, sermons, exhortations are usually useless. Avoid such comments as "you should know better"; "you're old enough not to do that"; "what if your mother knew about this?"; "you should be ashamed of yourself."

3. Since the pains and physical complaints are real, not imaginary, don't deny them, or tell him to forget them, or try to argue him out of them. Accept his aches and pains, recognize them as unpleasant and disabling. Don't deny him medical attention—if he doesn't need it, the doctor will tell him so.

4. Since the emotionally disturbed child is not a weakling or coward, he should not be condemned as one, or blamed or censored as if he had committed a crime. Anger, reproval, "telling him off," are harmful to his attempts to adjust. His feelings of self-condemnation, guilt, and failure are so strong that reproach or condemnation by others may drive him deeper into despair and hopelessness.

5. Don't diagnose or label, or classify the emotionally maladjusted child as abnormal, neurotic, or "a mental case." It is not necessary to be familiar with psychiatric terminology; applying a psychiatric label to the

child doesn't help him, but will probably hurt him.   The psychiatrist is the only one qualified to make a psychiatric diagnosis.

6. Don't talk about the child in his presence, to his parents or to anyone else.   Frequently teachers have been overheard talking about a child, in very uncomplimentary terms, while he is present but ignored, as if he weren't present, or didn't count—almost as if he weren't a person at all, but an inanimate object.   Such treatment is damaging to the child and to his self-respect.   He should be treated as a human being who has feelings.

The teacher should be able to do more than to avoid these mistaken attitudes, however.   She should be able to do something positive to foster the adjustment of the child.   Teachers frequently complain that they don't have training in mental hygiene, or that they don't have time to study each child as an individual.   But it is not necessary to have extensive training in mental hygiene to be helpful.   Nor is it necessary to have a detailed, complete case history, to know all the facts about the background, development, and home life of each child.   There are certain basic, fundamental attitudes and techniques that are applicable in all situations involving emotional expression which teachers can cultivate, with no more background in mental hygiene than has been just discussed.

1. The most essential element in handling emotional disturbances is that there be a real understanding and acceptance of the child, as he is, with his negative attitudes, hostility and aggression, destructiveness, etc. These emotional reactions are just as natural as the more positive ones— they are not bizarre, "crazy," shameful, but natural expressions under the circumstances.   Realizing this the teacher must avoid condemnation, criticism, and moralizing.   It is not necessary that the exact cause of the behavior be known; it is enough to know that it is natural under certain conditions.   These conditions almost always involve situations in which the child has been hurt, frightened, threatened.   It is only natural that resentment, aggressiveness, anger, and other negative emotional behavior result.   The test of the ability of a teacher to handle emotional disturbances constructively is whether or not she can accept such negative, hostile, emotions and resulting behavior as natural responses.

The most important need of the child is to be understood and accepted —to be able to share his thoughts, without fear, suspicion, or defensiveness.   The maladjusted child feels aggressive because he feels threatened.   He actually is threatened by others, usually the adults in his environment, when they criticize, condemn, exhort, or shame him.   He needs to feel understood, to feel that someone accepts him as he is for what he is, with all his faults, to feel that someone knows how he feels.

To be able to put oneself in the place of another helps in understanding that other person. It is in this way that empathy develops, which leads to the ability to understand the other person.

2. If one really understands the emotionally disturbed child, and accepts his negative, hostile behavior as natural under the circumstances, the next step is to realize that emotions, once stirred up, need to be expressed or released. This may seem to be contrary to the attitude of many teachers, who feel that negative behavior and emotions must be controlled. They believe that the child cannot be allowed to express hostility, anger, or hatred of others, including his parents and teacher. If he cannot control these emotions, the teacher attempts to suppress them. But such attempts to exert control result only in suppression, or perhaps gradually repression by the child himself—the emotions continue to exist, and to cause emotional maladjustment in the child. Contrary to general opinion, the freedom to express the emotions of hostility and hatred does not result in an increase of such negative emotions and behavior, after the initial period following such freedom. It rather allows the negative emotions to drain themselves off, so that the more positive, constructive emotions and behavior have a chance to show themselves. Discipline and punishment are thus not the answers to negative emotions and behavior. Expression rather than suppression or repression is necessary if the child is to reach a stage of better adjustment.

This does not mean that the child is allowed to be physically assaultive or destructive. There must be limits set to prevent injury to other children and adults, and damage to property. But while destructive behavior is prohibited when it injures others, there is no limit to the expression of destructive and aggressive thoughts and feelings, and if possible the expression of such behavior on substitute objects, such as rubber toys, especially dolls representing the individuals towards whom the child feels aggressive or resentful. Verbalization of feelings and emotions is to be encouraged, and accepted without surprise or shock. It is important that the teacher really be able to accept such feelings, without actually condemning or judging the child in her thoughts. Children are acutely aware of our feelings, and sense if they are really being understood and accepted, or if we are only pretending to do so. If it is the latter, the child will know it and be suspicious, afraid of being tricked into saying or doing something for which he will be punished. We must really prove to him that we are accepting and understanding. Being able to express in words those feelings which the child himself is unable to verbalize is often helpful in showing him that we do understand.

It is impossible here to go into the detailed methods and techniques of developing an understanding of the child, of encouraging the expression of his emotions, and of helping him handle them constructively. Rogers has developed this method as a means of therapy with adults. Baruch has applied the same principles to handling children in the home. They are just as applicable to dealing with children in the school. Student-centered teaching is the term used for applying the principles of client-centered therapy to teaching. Excellent discussions of this approach will be found in Axline, Rogers, and Snygg and Combs. The teacher who wishes to provide the best emotional environment for her pupils, and who feels that the emotional development of pupils is at least as important as their academic progress, will want to learn more about these new techniques and methods.

---

45. Education and Psychotherapy*

Related selections: 8, 29, 30, 35, 47

IT IS OFTEN said that teachers should help students to develop healthy personalities. This concern for the all-round development of children is evidenced by the reading and study that teachers are doing in the area of personality development and psychotherapy. Some see this as a desirable, constructive movement in present-day education. Others raise serious questions about the feasibility of relatively untrained persons attempting to apply the principles of therapy. Professor Symonds points out the basic similarities and differences between education and psychotherapy and clarifies many of the issues involved.

AT THE BEGINNING of the movement toward psychoanalytic education and the introduction of mental hygiene principles into education the aims and methods of education and psychotherapy were far apart. Psychotherapy was concerned with bringing mentally disturbed persons to normality; while education was concerned with imparting knowledge, helping in the formation of skill, and in general in assisting boys and girls to develop along lines that would help them to fit as responsible members into the

* Percival M. Symonds, "Education and Psychotherapy," *Journal of Educational Psychology,* vol. XL (January, 1949), pp. 5–20. Reprinted by permission of author and publisher.

Dr. Symonds (1893—) is Professor of Education, Teachers College, Columbia University, and a Diplomate in clinical psychology. He is a scholar and an author in the field of psychology and personality and a developer of projective techniques in testing.

society in which they were growing up. With the passage of years the function of psychotherapy is conceived to be that of assisting in belated personality development while education, too, has accepted greater responsibility for the all-round development of the individual instead of for isolated segments of his personality. Methods of the two disciplines, too, have become more and more alike until some writers suggest that they are almost identical.

Axline, for instance, says: "The basic principles of non-directive therapy seem to have far reaching implications for educators" . . . "the most important single factor in establishing sound mental health is the relationship that is built up between the teacher and his or her pupils." . . . "It is the permissiveness to be themselves, the understanding, the acceptance, the recognition of feelings, the clarification of what they think and feel that helps children retain their self-respect; and the possibilities of growth and change are forthcoming as they all develop insight. . . . It is in the establishment of this relationship that the basic principles of self-directive therapy loom up into an important position. . . . The teacher will accept each and every child exactly as he or she is. . . ." "The teacher will establish a feeling of permissiveness in the relationship so that the child feels free to express his feelings and to be himself. . . . The therapist-teacher is alert to recognize the feelings the child is expressing and reflects those feelings back to the child in such a manner that the child gains insight into his behavior. This can be done to a great extent in any classroom situation if the teacher has an understanding of her pupils and an insight into human behavior."

This lengthy quotation would imply that the distinction between psychotherapy and teaching has diminished so as to have reached the vanishing point. Perhaps the pendulum has swung too far and the time has come to point out in what way psychotherapy and education differ as well as how they are alike. One's attention is caught by the attitude expressed by Cantor who has suggested introducing progressive methods into college teaching. In discussing a conference with a student he says: "He [the student] wanted to talk about the backgrounds of his difficulty. It was a temptation to which I almost yielded since I felt that he would be immensely relieved if he could express what was troubling him. But talking about what led up to his poor work would have been another way of avoiding doing something about it.

I am not a therapist. My function is to deal with a student's difficulty only insofar as his work in the course is involved."

This raises the question: What psychotherapy and what education am I talking about? It is recognized that there are many differing points of view and shades of opinion about both education and psychotherapy.

However, a recent symposium designed to ventilate possible differences in point of view concerning psychotherapy concluded that there was more general agreement than disagreement on many issues. Agreement among educators may not be so apparent. The point of view taken in the following pages to represent education corresponds closely to what is known as Progressive education and may have little correspondence to education as it is found in actual practice up and down the land. The following discussion, however, explicitly recognizes and attempts to clarify many of the unsolved issues in both disciplines.

SIMILARITY BETWEEN PSYCHOTHERAPY AND EDUCATION

First let us review some of the points of similarity between psychotherapy and education.

1.—*Both teachers and therapists should treat children as individuals with potentialities for progressively taking over direction of themselves.* This principle certainly has not always been followed by teachers in practice. Many teachers, sensing so strongly the immaturity of children, do not have faith in their potentialities to take responsibility for themselves and hence exercise close restraint and control. And it must be admitted that it becomes difficult, if not impossible, to see the individual when he is one child in a class of forty. But this principle is being accepted more and more by progressive teachers for whom the conditions of teaching permit giving children greater responsibility.

2.—*Both teachers and counselors should be warm, friendly, outgoing, pleasant and kindly.* The exact attitude and relationship here must be defined carefully. It does not mean effusiveness, a bubbling-over approach, lavishing affection or sympathy. It does not consist of giving praise, or flattery. It exercises itself in such qualities as genuine interest, sensitivity to the feelings of others, willingness to listen to the other person, and being unhurried, sincere and genuine. It may mean little more than the friendly nod, the cheery "good-morning" or the sympathetic smile. Snyder who has discussed the meaning of warmth in non-directive counseling seems to find the essence to lie in the correct use of standard therapeutic procedures, minimizing the emphasis on emotional outgoingness. Perhaps the essence of what is meant by warmth cannot be defined in terms of what the therapist does, the feelings he expresses, or the attitudes he assumes, but rather is a less tangible quality which emanates from a personality which is free from tension and anxiety.

3.—*Both teachers and therapists are counseled to accept the child as he is—no matter how stupid, lazy, dirty, resistive, or disorderly.* One of the cornerstones of modern psychotherapy is the acceptance of the patient by the therapist. Accepting means more than tolerating. It means on the one hand avoiding negative feelings toward a child of dislike, contempt or disgust, and withholding criticism, censure, or blame; but it also means that there must be some genuine liking as might be shown when the teacher is glad when a boy comes to school and is sorry when he is absent. For the teacher this means accepting potentiality and promise in a child as well as the skills and habits actually present. A teacher may like a boy because he sees that he has potentialities for growth. Children are highly sensitive to minor indications of lack of interest, boredom, preoccupation with other matters and other attitudes of unconcern which the therapist or teacher may show.

Should the teacher accept negative behavior? Should the teacher accept breaking of the rules, destructiveness, hostile behavior? He may accept them no more than the therapist. A teacher is expected, as we have seen, to express what he as a person and as a representative of society does and does not stand for. But it is possible at the same time to accept the person who has broken these rules. It is possible to accept the person while at the same time rejecting what the person does. Many a child feels sure that his mother or teacher really loves him when the parent or teacher takes time to chide or reprimand him. A teacher may be disappointed in what a child accomplishes, to be sure, but faith and belief in his potentialities still persist. And both therapist and teacher must show tolerance, a willingness to overlook and be forgiving, with faith in the final triumph and emergence of the forces of good.

Acceptance, *per se,* does not mean approval, or disapproval; that is the valuation of behavior. But here is where teaching and therapy part company. Therapy, since it is not interested in directing change, does not evaluate. Education, since it is interested in directing change, adds to mere acceptance valuation through praise and criticism.

Should the teacher accept negative feelings? Yes, temporarily as a therapist for the purpose of helping the child to accept himself and eventually to reduce the need for negative feelings. But since teachers cannot work with negative feelings as teachers, these feelings must be discouraged so that positive feelings can operate in their place. Teachers may use the therapeutic method of dissipating negative feelings by recognizing them, sensing from whence they spring and recognizing the justification for them, and also helping the child to recognize them, but they can also be dissipated by disregarding them, or jollying and 'kidding' a person along about them.

But being accepting means a certain greater degree of emotional restraint by the therapist than the teacher, for the therapist avoids giving praise, rewards, gifts, advice and suggestions, in fact, any outgoing response that can be interpreted as a form of control.

4.—*Teachers and therapists may also be expected to be permissive—but to a degree only.* Teachers and therapists not only should accept the child in spite of his past behavior, but give the child permission to be himself, in feeling particularly, in behavior as far as possible. Both teachers and therapists believe in the practice of restraining dangerous and destructive behavior, and both believe in giving freedom for the expression of feeling. But the teacher is not merely a permissive person; he also positively encourages, stimulates and directs. A good teacher finds a happy balance between being permissive on the one hand, and using his influence in directing, acting, thinking and feeling on the other.

5.—*Both teachers and therapists have a responsibility to understand the child.* A therapist is expected to be particularly sensitive to unconscious motives and the mechanisms by which they are expressed. A teacher is expected to be particularly sensitive to conscious motives and interests, but the teacher who is also sensitive to unconscious motives may be better able to tolerate the bad in a child and hence to find opportunity for the release of negative feelings while at the same time he may appreciate untapped possibilities for constructive growth and be more courageous and patient in encouraging their expression.

6.—*Both teachers and therapists should be sensitive to feelings expressed by the child and should help the child to be aware of them.* This is one of the therapist's principal tasks, but only one of many angles of the teacher's task. Many teachers, however, would not dare to let pupils express their feelings openly and freely—to do so would be too great a threat to the teacher's prestige and authority. But children should learn at school not only about the world around them, but also about the world within, and this insight can be best acquired by permitting pupils to express their feelings freely and then directing their attention toward them.

DIFFERENCES BETWEEN PSYCHOTHERAPY AND EDUCATION

Having now pointed out six points which education and psychotherapy have in common, let us review the ways in which they differ.

1.—*A teacher is principally concerned with the world of reality and his task is to help children to become effective in the real world. A therapist, on the other hand,* according to Rogers, *gives his attention primarily to the feelings expressed by a child* and neglects or overlooks as of less importance the content of what a child says. Instead of helping a child to adjust to the real world, a therapist helps a child to accept himself with all his immaturity, limitations and shortcomings. This distinction, however, need not be too sharply drawn. The teacher, too, must give attention to feelings when feelings interfere with attention to the task at hand. The wise teacher selects some activities such as dramatics, painting and drawing, music, story-telling or rhythms to promote and encourage the release of feelings. Constructive activities in shop and laboratory may provide outlets for aggressive tendencies. When a teacher, however, has to pause to pay attention to the feelings which his pupils are expressing he is, strictly speaking, stepping out of his rôle as a teacher and temporarily functioning as a therapist. If the child responds readily to recognition of his feelings and returns quickly to the task at hand instead of having further to defend himself, the teacher can well afford this brief excursion into the therapeutic realm. If, on the other hand, the child is slow to respond and needs to have his attention called repeatedly to the feelings he is expressing, or if he lacks control even after he has given his attention to them, then the teacher is stepping out of his rôle as teacher for therapeutic ends. If the child is his only pupil then that may be the best use of his services, but if he is the teacher of a class then this one child may be usurping time which the teacher should be devoting to the educational interests of other children who are ready to use it.

2.—*A teacher feels and expresses love, but avoids hate; a therapist does not express either love or hate.* A teacher enters himself into the relationship emotionally—he gives of himself to his pupils. He cares for them, devotes himself to their needs and interests and uses his energies on their behalf. A teacher, to be successful, must like his pupils—like them well enough to work for them as well as for himself. He gives of himself freely and not only on condition that the child meets his expectations. It is in response to these expressions of love that a child learns; he learns in order to retain this love and to avoid anxiety lest love be withdrawn. The teacher cannot afford to hate, however, for hate stirs up antagonistic emotions in the child, which interfere with learning.

The therapist, on the other hand, neither loves nor hates but avoids becoming emotionally involved in the relationship. Hamilton says of this: "The 'love' of the therapist consists of warmth, concern, therapeutic understanding, interest in helping the person to get well. . . . The therapist does not give love in the ordinary sense, just as he must not disapprove of or dislike what the client is, says, or does." When the therapist enters actively into the therapeutic situation with tokens of love there is danger that the child will be encouraged to become more infantile and dependent than ever—just the opposite of the therapeutic aim. Ackerman has written at length on the problem of the therapist's "giving love." He says: "A large number of patients who seek the aid of psychotherapy are able initially neither to receive nor to give love. For them, the psychotherapist's aim must be not so much to 'give love' as to modify their characters in order to prepare them to accept love and then return it." And again: "Patients need love. They have suffered privations in their childhood and, especially, they have been denied love by their own parents. Nevertheless, certain important obstacles interfere with compensating for that original lack." Ackerman goes on to discuss at length mechanisms in the client that prevent him from being able to accept love and in the therapist from giving it.

With regard to the giving of gifts by the therapist to the child, Allen says: "Some therapists might feel like giving a child a present at the end, but I do not like the practice, as it seems false and confusing. At the end some children feel guilty about wanting to stop; giving a present can accentuate that feeling."

3.—*The teacher expresses himself boldly and readily.* He not only imparts information and guides in the formation of skill, but also expresses his stand on issues. *The teacher is a dynamic, vigorous, outgoing individual.* Society expects a teacher to direct and lead the way. In controversial issues a teacher may be expected to present fairly both sides and in any case he ought to present the bases and arguments for each point of view. But a *therapist is expected to be a more passive individual.* Although he should be warm, friendly, interested, tolerant and sensitive, he avoids exposing or exerting his personality too directly or openly on the client. His principal task is to understand the client, to be sensitive to his feelings and hence to help the client to accept and become more tolerant of his own feelings and tendencies to action. *The therapist believes that his task is not directively to influence or control his client,* indeed, he believes he will defeat his purpose of encouraging his client to self-expression if he exercises too much control.

4. *The teacher uses praise and blame, reward and punishment to aid in the education process.* Teachers that I have observed who have been most successful in their work have been extravagantly lavish with praise. The praise has been given warmly and with enthusiasm; but it has been genuine praise for acts or work that has been deemed praiseworthy and children have been sensitive to its sincerity. Children respond to praise with increased effort and the use of praise helps to establish the positive relationship mentioned above.

The teacher also uses censure or blame judiciously. Mild criticism probably meets Estes' criterion of a punishment that is mild and which actually influences unlearning. A severe punishment inhibits behavior and hence removes an act from the influence of either positive or negative learning. Mild criticism or blame may permit an act to be repeated without satisfaction or reward or reinforcement and, hence, satisfies the conditions for experimental extinction and unlearning. The wise teacher, however, does not criticize or blame without making sure that a positive love relationship has already been established, for it is only on the basis of a positive relationship that positive learning can take place to supplement the reaction that is being extinguished.

The therapist uses neither praise nor blame, reward nor punishment. The task of the therapist is to encourage response, to enable the subject to accept himself as he is, to reduce the necessity for continued use of defensive measures, to avoid encouraging a person to over-estimate himself, and to help a person to become self-directing. Praise certainly encourages a subject to follow the suggestion of the would-be therapist and may lead to over self-valuation. Criticism would force the continued and increased use of defensive measures and would defeat tendencies toward self-acceptance.

5.—*The teacher stimulates, encourages, directs, guides.* This is the teacher's recognized and established function. He has been employed by society to act as a leader and a guide. This does not mean that he need operate autocratically, or with use of coercion or force. His influence rather can be that of a kindly older person who can show the way that children want to go. And as he suggests or advises it is always with the child's interests in mind. As Rank points out, "The child will instinctively grasp the ideologies offered to him, because he needs them as props for the unfolding and justification of his individual ego." So the teacher uses influence without undue pressure. By stating his position and his likes and dislikes vigorously, the child who already loves, respects and trusts his teacher will want to go in the direction pointed out.

The therapist, on the other hand, consistently avoids using any influence in the form of suggestion, advice or encouragement. The therapist's task is to strengthen the ego of the child, to make the child more independent and more self-directing and self-supporting. To influence the child by suggestion or guidance is to interfere with the development of self-determination.

The teacher, too, is interested in helping children become more mature. Consequently he provides considerable genuine freedom, but the teacher is always there to offer suggestions or support, recognizing that the immature child may need guidance or support for his own emotional security.

These principles regarding the neutrality of the therapist are sometimes violated in the interest of the reality of the situation. When a child threatens violence and harm or damage either to persons (including the therapist himself) or to property, then the therapist may exert a restraining influence. A distinction is made between verbal (or fantasy) expression and motor expression. Motor expression can become so violent and disorganized that it loses any growth value it might have, whereas verbal or fantasy expression would seem always to be closer to the influence of judgment and reason. It would seem then that there are occasions when the therapist must broaden his rôle and act more like a teacher until the child regains his emotional equilibrium. On the other hand, these controls must not be placed too high for there is sometimes therapeutic value in the cathartics of strong emotional release.

It is of interest that the therapist in deciding to wield no directing influence himself depends on a principle of self-realization in the client to take care of direction. He posits an innate tendency toward self-direction in the client which will lead him to make wise choices and decisions. Rogers, who has elucidated this principle at length in recent papers, says concerning it: "One is compelled through clinical observation to develop a high degree of respect for the ego-integrative forces residing in each individual. One comes to recognize that under proper conditions the self is a basic factor in the formation of personality and in the determination of behavior. Clinical experience would strongly suggest that the self is, to some extent, an architect of self, and the above hypothesis simply puts this observation into psychological terms" . . . And again: "the client has a strong drive to become mature, socially adjusted, independent, productive" . . . "In most if not in all individuals there exist growth forces, tendencies toward self-actualization. . . . The individual has the capacity and the strength to devise, quite unguided, the steps which will lead him to a more mature and more compatible relationship to his reality." Rogers implies here that the subject not only has innate forces within him that lead him to seek a better integrated adjustment toward reality but that these same forces direct him toward that reality.

The following incident from one of Axline's cases would indicate that the direction of the adjustment is a product of education rather than of some internal force. Ernest who visits his mother with traumatic results comes to his next play session expressing his aggressive feelings with profanity. " 'They are the God-damnest nails. Bitty baby nails. Mama and papa nails. Look at this old bitch! Son-of-a-bitch if I ever saw one." Therapist: 'You've learned some new words that you want to show off.' [Beautiful handling of this situation by recognition of the attitude the child is expressing. Note again that the satisfactory classification of an attitude, in an accepting atmosphere, immediately dissolves the need for symbolic expression. It is this that accounts for the fact that accepted catharsis, that is, outgiving of feelings, alters behavior.] Ernest: 'Mrs. R. has a fit. She says I'll go to hell. They are bad words.' Teacher: 'Mrs. R. says they are bad words, but you still like to use them.' "

According to the report Ernest used no more profanity during the session. But can this be attributed to the result of an inner tendency of self-realization or ability to accept Mrs. R's judgment that these are bad words? It seems obvious that the direction of the behavior is determined in part culturally, that is, by the influence of education in the broad sense. Therapists believe that they defeat their own purposes if they themselves try to direct behavior, but it is obvious that they depend on society's offering very pronounced efforts to direct behavior. The task of psychotherapy is to assist in a reorganization of personality so that the individual is able to benefit by education.

6.—*A teacher should on occasion be firm.* He should take a stand and express himself with conviction with regard to many issues and stick to his stand with consistency. Firmness, however, need not involve the use of force and should not be confused with punishment. It would be of little use for a teacher to exert firmness if he had not already shown love and in turn won love from his pupils. If a positive relationship has been established, if pupils are sensitive and responsive to his expressions of approval and disapproval, then force is unnecessary, for the relationship will be sufficient to be effective.

A therapist, however, need not in general be firm, for he is actually not expected to take a stand on any issue, but to be neutral, accepting and permissive. However, to the extent that a therapist feels that he must enforce limitations in the subject's behavior in the interests of reality to prevent harm or damage to persons or to property, then a show of firmness would be appropriate. But the setting of limitations is not part of the therapeutic process—it sets conditions in the world of reality which permit therapy to take place. Setting limitations in therapy helps a child to control himself and reduces guilt. In setting practical limitations there is no intention on the one hand to restrict the expression of feeling or, on the other to coerce the child to follow a line of action which must come about eventually from his own inner choice and decision.

7.—*A teacher should have a program and be directive. A therapist should be non-directive.* This principle is by no means universally accepted either by all educators or by all therapists. While it is generally believed that schools should have courses of study and that some, if not much, learning should be laid out in advance, there are advocates of the child-centered school in which children not only determine or have a hand in determining day-to-day goals but also the larger objectives. Many teachers believe that self-determination of goals is an essential ingredient in the educational process. Even the most extreme of the child-centered advocates, however, would expect the teacher to exercise some leadership or at least be available for friendly counsel in the process. But whether one gives the teacher or the children the principal responsibility in deciding upon the program, a program there must be so that at the end of the year one can point to tangible results in the form of growth and learning.

Whether the therapist should or should not be directive has been the focus of another controversy. There are some like Thorne who believe that there are occasions when the therapist, like any physician, must step in with positive suggestions to wield his influence through persuasion if necessary to help a person work out better adjustments. The weight of opinion, however, follows Rogers that such methods are palliative only and that real personality change takes place when the therapist by his non-direction forces the client to take responsibility for himself.

It is clear that the rôles sometimes become confused on this issue. There are some therapists who simply do not trust the subject to have the intelligence, judgment and control to select the reasonable way, and feel that they must exercise the teacher's function of guiding and directing. And there are some teachers who have such a profound belief in the child's capacity to learn through the opportunity of making his own de-cisions that they adopt the therapists' non-directive rôle. But some-where, sometime children must learn the meaning of honesty, helpfulness, good sportsmanship, self-control, generosity and the like, and how will they ever learn these character traits unless someone in the rôle of the parent or teacher leads the way and directs them?

There are other less obvious and more subtle differences between the teacher and therapist.

8.—*The teacher works only through the positive forces in the child and the good teacher calls out only these positive forces.* Everything the good teacher does throughout the school day is designed to call forth posi-tive constructive attitudes and behavior from pupils. As Isaacs says, the teacher "must be a 'good' parent to the child, even though she be a strict one . . . I do not mean that educators have to be inhumanly perfect be-fore they can educate at all. Children readily forgive occasional out-bursts of anger and other real faults in an adult whose general attitude is reliable and friendly and understanding . . . But she must not, by her real qualities, attract to herself the negative explosive reactions of hatred and aggression."

It is not the teacher's task to have to deal with a child's hostile attitudes as such, for education cannot take place in an atmosphere of defiance, mis-trust, or rebellion. Teachers are expected to put a child's aggression to work in constructive channels, and the successful teacher is able to harness children's aggressive energies to the activities and tasks at hand. When the child displays hostility in the classroom through no fault of the teacher, then the teacher must temporarily step out of his rôle of teacher to act as therapist possibly by verbalizing the child's feelings and attitude, thus bringing them to his attention and helping the child thus to reduce the strength of his feelings and control his attitudes.   If simple measures do not work then the child is in need of more thoroughgoing therapy for he is at the moment uneducable.   Punishment is seldom called for in the control and reduction of hostility, for it only represses feeling, inhibits behavior, and does not get at the root of the difficulty.

The therapist, on the other hand, must be ready to deal with negative attitudes of the child.   Not that the therapist stimulates negative attitudes, but he must be ready to accept negative attitudes that will inevitably arise in the child who needs therapy.   The therapist has to be able to tolerate the child's aggression without adopting punitive attitudes of counter-aggression.

9.—The next point is one in which we are in a state of transition in our thinking.   It is obvious that the teacher's main concern is with conscious processes as they express themselves openly in interests and activities. He is also concerned with motivation in terms of conscious wishes and desires.   There is a question, however, of the extent to which the teacher needs to be aware of unconscious processes and motivation.   Isaacs says the unconscious lies outside the teacher's sphere.   "The teacher has no direct concern in her work as an educator with the fact that the child's love and wish to make may be covering his fear and hate and wish to destroy. That is the analyst's concern, not the teacher's. . . .   Unconscious wishes as such are not, and cannot be within the competence (of the teacher)—any more than the teaching and training of the child in skilful manipulation or understanding of the external world is within the competence of the analyst. . . .   The educator [teacher] can only make use of unconscious trends in so far as they are available within the field of the conscious life, and in the form in which they are available in conscious life."   Is it not possible that Isaacs has gone too far in this point of view?   Might not the teacher of the 'goody-goody' child who harbors unconscious hostility be more successful as a teacher if he knows of the child's unconscious hostility and provides occasions for the expression of it?   Might not the teacher of a delinquent be helped if he knew of the child's inner conflicts and struggles between the good and the bad, his potentialities for achievement so that the teacher could lend his strength to help the child choose the more socially-approved ways and exercise control against the socially unapproved? Granted, however, that the teacher should use his knowledge of unconscious forces to assist him in the selection of educational devices and not in direct interpretation of them to the child.

There are some who believe that teachers are not able to understand and make use of unconscious material because they themselves have not been analyzed, and because the point of view in terms of unconscious motivation is too far removed from a common sense interpretation.   This dogma has long gone unchallenged.   There is reason to believe that these points of view can and are being assimilated by teachers in courses in psychology emphasizing the dynamic point of view and by projects such as are reported in the book, *Helping Teachers Understand Children,* which makes a start at interpretation on a very elementary basis.

Unconscious forces are generally recognized as being the special province of the therapist or child analyst.—Just how these unconscious forces are to be handled is the subject of another unresolved controversy. Rogers believes that the therapist should not recognize them until they are verbally expressed by the subject (and hence have become to a degree conscious).   Many successful child analysts (Blanchard, Gerard, Isaacs and others) believe in the value of more direct interpretation of wishes and motives that are not conscious.   "At times, when the unconscious wish . . . comes near the surface, the anxiety of the child may mount up and take violent forms of defense by aggression, if it is not relieved by the analyst's immediate interpretation."   Isaacs believes that the analyst can work best through the transference, that is, attitudes that the child expresses directly toward the analyst.   "The analyst is at all times functioning also as an ego, since through all these character situations she makes clear to the child at each point what he, the child, is doing and why he is assigning this or that part to the analyst; and so assists the intelligence and judgment and sense of reality of the child himself to work upon the material of his own inner world."   It is clear, however, regardless of how a therapist operates, that the teacher and child analyst make quite different uses of unconscious impulses.   *The therapist tries to understand unconscious impulses, the teacher provides them opportunity for expression.*

46. The Teacher's Rôle in the Peer Group During Middle Childhood*

Related selections: 23, 26, 35

THE CHILD'S first social world is, of course, that of his family, but very early he begins to make forays into a broader social scene. He thus begins the process of growing out of the family and into the world of his peers. His roles and relationships with peer groups play a significant part in his socialization. Nedelsky describes some things the teacher may do to foster desirable peer relations in general and to help particular children establish relationships with their classmates.

IN MIDDLE childhood, it is in the company of other children, rather than in the company of his parents, that a child explores the world; that he tests the meaning of authority and the nature of his independence; that he experiments with adult rôles and adult behaviors. Throughout this period he is shifting from living in a world in which he depended almost entirely upon adults for orientation to a world in which his orientation grows out of being part of a group of other children whom he accepts as equals.

These problems are not unique to this age; they began in infancy and will continue into adolescence and maturity, but the child now needs the support that comes from being part of a group of equals if he is to achieve the learnings that are an essential part of this stage of development. Finding a place for himself in a society of equals is necessary for the child if he is to take the next step forward along the road to independence and maturity.

Adults, however, continue to be very important during this entire period. The child must look to adults for interpretation of reality even though it often is within the peer group that he tests his understandings of those interpretations. The child continues to be dependent on his parents for his basic sense of security, but now the parents share with the teacher the responsibility of giving him security. One can say that these adults form the background of a child's life at this age—a background which is essential to his well-being.

Being part of a peer group is not a separate compartment in a child's

* Ruth Nedelsky, "The Teacher's Role in the Peer Group During Middle Childhood," *Elementary School Journal*, vol. LII (February, 1952), pp. 325–334. Copyrighted by The University of Chicago Press. Reprinted by permission of the author and copyright holder.

Mrs. Nedelsky (1918—) was formerly on the Committee on Human Development, University of Chicago.

life.   It is a part of his everyday activities.   Children form groups as they
work and play together; they form groups in whatever kinds of situations
they find themselves.   A child spends a great deal of his time in school
in these middle years.   Consequently, the school is an important setting in
which children relate to one another.   If one accepts the theory that, as a
member of a peer group, a child is able to do the most effective job of working through the developmental tasks he faces in these years, then the question of the teacher's rôle in this process becomes important.

SETTING THE LIMITS OF GROUP ACTIONS

One of the most important groups in a child's life during the period of
middle childhood (seven to ten years of age) is the class in school to which
he belongs.   The school class becomes a group as the children react to
one another, and to the teacher, in the course of doing the assignments, living under the rules and regulations, and sharing the penalties and rewards
which are assigned by the teacher.   It is, in other words, the presence of
the teacher which enables some thirty or forty children to arrive at common feelings about themselves, to think of themselves as Miss Smith's
third-graders or Miss Thompson's fourth-graders.

Much as children may want to have a sense of belonging together, much
as they may need the support that comes from identifying with other children in a group, they are unable at this period to function constructively
for any length of time as a group unless there are clearly defined limits of
action within which they are to operate.   Sometimes, as in games, the
limits are inherent in the activity.   Usually, however, the children need
the help of an adult in establishing the limits.   This dependence on adults
to structure a group decreases as the children grow older.   One finds that
the seven-year-olds, even at play, are unable to sustain group activities for
any length of time by themselves.   The ten-year-olds can and do.

EFFECT OF TEACHER'S ATTITUDE ON THE GROUP

In the classroom, then, it is the teacher who must assume responsibility
for outlining the activities, for providing appropriate materials, for defining the goals, the penalties, and the rewards.   This is true regardless of the
philosophy of education under which the school system and the teacher
operate.   The assuming of this responsibility is inherent in her rôle as
teacher and, at the same time, is required by the needs of the children.

As she chooses certain activities in preference to others, as she sets up
certain standards and not others by which to judge the behaviors and the
achievements of the children, the teacher is structuring the group.   The
feelings that the children have about themselves as a group, the kinds of

situations in which they are likely to feel and act as a group, the extent to
which all the pupils in the class feel a part of the class group—all these follow from the choices the teacher makes.[1]

When the teacher makes choices of the kinds of activities and materials,
the kinds of procedures, the rewards and punishments that she will use,
she makes them with reference to her conceptions of what children are
like, how they ought to behave, what they ought to learn.   If the activities that a teacher plans and the kinds of behaviors she expects from the
children are in harmony with the kinds of behaviors normal for children of
that age, then the pupils are likely to feel at home in the classroom.   They
are likely to feel accepted by the teacher, and this feeling of acceptance
will carry over into their relationships with one another and with the
teacher.

The conceptions that children have of themselves affect the peer groups.
In the classroom these conceptions stem mainly from their feelings about
their work and from the way the teacher reacts to their behavior.   Let
us look at two classroom situations and see how the difference in the
ways the teacher conducts the class affects the child's feelings about himself and, in turn, the relations within the peer group.

A CLASSROOM EMPHASIZING BASIC SKILLS

In a number of schools, a teacher's rating depends, to a large extent, on
the academic achievements of her class.   Thus, a teacher must "get the
class through" so many readers, must have the class make a satisfactory
showing on a spelling test, and so on.   Consequently, the activities that a
teacher plans for the children may fall within a narrow range of academic
work: they may include drill in spelling and arithmetic, learning to pronounce correctly the words in the reader, finding in the geography or history books proper answers to set questions.   Within this range, many of
the children may not be able to find experiences in the classroom which
give them an inherent sense of worth or an adequate sense of achievement.
There are two reasons for this.

In the first place, there will be a wide range in the intellectual maturity
of the group, but the children will all be judged in terms of ability to
achieve a certain fixed standard.   To varying degrees, the children will
feel that their worth as persons is being appraised by their success in these
subjects.   It is unlikely that the children who consistently fall below the

---

[1] The teacher's choices are not the sole determining factor.   The particular
aggregate of children—their level of maturity, their interests and abilities, the particular personalities—also are important factors in the feelings the children will hold
about themselves in a group.

level of achievement that is acceptable to the teacher will have any real sense of security or adequacy as a result of being in the class.

In the second place, the tasks may have little real significance for the children. Consequently, if a child does such a task, he does it either because he wants the approval of the teacher or because he wants to escape punishment. The mastery of a task that is not accepted as meaningful by the child cannot in itself lead to an increased sense of adequacy. A child's sense of worth then is dependent on the teacher.

In such a situation there will be an endless struggle to achieve status, either with the teacher or within a peer group. Not being sure of their worth, children will compete with one another for whatever marks of status the children evolve. In such a situation it is unlikely that the children will be able to move freely from group to group. Entrance of a new child into a group may make every other child uneasy about his own group position. It is in such a climate that cliques, closed friendship groups, are most likely to occur. Efforts of the teacher to separate the group — by changing seats, by reprimanding the children, and so on—merely increase the insecurity of the children and usually result in making the clique a more tightly knit group than it was before.

Many children are likely to be deprived of any group status at all. Some children will just give up the struggle entirely. In a West Coast school system it was found that, after ability grouping within each classroom had been in effect in grade after grade, many of the children who were in the slowest group year after year finally lost all sense of their own worth. When given a sociometric test, these children were unable or unwilling to express any choice of a child to work with or sit next to.

Yet even within a school system where emphasis is placed on mastery of the three R's, such a situation can be modified. There are probably few, if any, classrooms today where the children spend all their time in drill. They are permitted to draw and color, to cut and paste. There is always time for children to tell of interesting things that have happened to them, for the class to write a story of something the children have done together. What matters is the teacher's attitude toward these activities. The children will welcome them whatever value the teacher assigns to them. If the teacher looks upon these activities only as something to keep the children busy in spare moments, then, for many children, these other activities can contribute little to their feelings about themselves in school. On the other hand, if the teacher believes that there are many important learnings beyond the mastery of the "basic skills," if she values and enjoys these extra activities, then for the children they become a bona fide part of the school day.

A CLASSROOM USING CHILDREN'S INTERESTS

Let us look now at a classroom where the teacher provides (1) a range of activities in keeping with the interests, concerns, and abilities of the children in her group; (2) materials which the children enjoy working with and can learn to manipulate; and (3) perhaps most important of all, an attitude of respect toward the different kinds of achievements that grow out of the different activities.   In such a situation it is likely that every child will find one or more areas in which he can achieve mastery.   Then with each task that he completes, the child will feel greater confidence in himself as a person and in his ability to master the tasks that are a necessary part of growing up in our culture.

As the child finds projects in which he can achieve success, he will also have the satisfaction that comes from making a contribution to the group. The very fact that the teacher feels respect for whatever task a child does, whether washing the blackboard, keeping charge of supplies, helping paint a mural for the classroom, dramatizing a favorite story, or drawing a fine map, makes the child feel that he is contributing to the whole group.   He feels that he *is a part* of the group.   To the extent that he takes for granted that he is a part of the group, he has no need to fight for status.

In such a climate, children will freely join one another in different activities.   The children are likely to choose to work with those groups that best meet their needs.   A child may choose a group in which he can make an important contribution, a group in which he can handle apparatus or material that he enjoys, a group in which he can practice a skill he is working on, or a group in which he can be with a child whose company he prefers.   In the course of a day he is likely to join in a number of different groups, each time getting different satisfactions and making different kinds of contributions.

STANDARDS OF CONDUCT

A group of children can live and work together only if there is a common understanding among the children about the kinds of things they may do, about the ways of expressing themselves that are permitted.   In the classroom it is the teacher who has the responsibility for defining the behaviors that are expected, those that are permitted, and those that are frowned upon or forbidden.   It is important for the children to know clearly the areas within which they may experiment as well as to understand just what is expected of them.   Having the boundaries sharply defined is a source of security for the child. He knows then what is expected of him and what to expect of the teacher.

This knowledge in itself is not enough to give a child a sense of security. He must feel capable of achieving the degree of control over his behavior that is expected of him while, at the same time, he feels free to experiment in a field that is broad enough to give him genuine satisfaction. Most important, though, are the feelings that the teacher has about the children and their ways of behaving. If the teacher is able to accept the children as they are, whatever their particular shortcomings, the children will feel at home in the classroom. To the extent that the children feel secure and accepted, to that extent will they be able to accept one another.

However, in many classrooms, children are expected to behave in ways that run counter to what can be called "normal" behavior patterns for children of their age. Children are expected to sit still, to keep quiet, for long periods of time. They may be required to stay at a task until it is completed. The day may be organized in such a way that many of the children feel the constant pressure of doing one job after another. The natural desires of children to talk together, to help one another with the work, to share secrets, may be frowned upon.

Besides that, the teacher may expect the children to be "good" children, that is, to be quiet, polite, and obedient. The teacher may be able to accept warmly and without reservation only those children who fall into the "good" category. The children are likely to feel the necessity of showing only their "good" side if they are to be accepted. The child who clowns, the child who seldom gets his work done, the child who is defiant or fresh, the child who often lies—all these fall short of the teacher's expectations, and the children cannot help feeling her rejection. If, however, the teacher realizes that the lying, the disobeying, the talking-back are all behaviors which are fairly typical of this age and which, given time and help, the child is likely to "grow out of," the teacher may change her attitude toward the child and her ways of dealing with him. The teacher will understand that these behaviors are his particular way of expressing the strains he is feeling as he tries to grow up and that he can be helped to find other ways of expressing himself which will not only be more satisfying to him but also be acceptable to society. A child, however, will not be able to accept help from a teacher who makes him feel unacceptable because of his behavior.

If the children feel that they must be quiet, industrious, polite, and obedient in order to have status with the teacher, then their doubts about their abilities to grow up to the expectations of the adult world are intensified. The effect on children of being expected to exercise controls they are unable to master at the time is to increase their anxieties about being able to conform to the standards of the adult world.

Children express their anxieties in different ways, but, whatever form the expression takes, it has its repercussions in the peer-group relationships. Some children may become more passive, more (rather than less) dependent on the praise and blame of adults for their own sense of worth. Others may retreat into a pleasanter world, a world of phantasy. These children are likely to find it difficult to face the tasks necessary to being part of a group.

Other children may act out their anxieties by rebelling against the standards that cause the anxieties. They may become erratic in behavior, challenging the authority of the teacher, behaving defiantly, and at times deliberately violating the codes the teacher has set up. Feelings of hostility against the teacher, dislike of the activities in the classroom, may be the feelings that begin to bind together either a small group or the whole class. If the codes established by the teacher make the children feel worried about being able ultimately to achieve adult status, then the codes that the peer groups will build up are likely to be at variance with those of the teacher.

Children become tense and irritable in situations in which they are able to achieve adult approval only by struggling for controls that are beyond their ability to manage easily, in which they can feel no certainty of being accepted by the adult. These tensions and resentments are often expressed against each other. Children may pick on the "teacher's pet," or they may "gang up" on some child who is particularly vulnerable. The groups that do spring up are likely to be closely knit, with strong loyalties within each group and little movement from group to group.

In a classroom where the children feel that the teacher does not accept the kinds of feelings, the kinds of behaviors, that are a very real part of them, they are likely to have very little sense of well-being. Communication between the teacher and the children is likely to be cut off, and the teacher will be excluded from the activities of the peer groups that have any real meaning to the children.

Thus the teacher, by the choices she makes in fulfilling her functions as a teacher, affects the peer group relationships within the classroom, whether or not she is aware of it. It is within the power of the teacher to establish a classroom climate in which children can freely associate with one another and can build up groups based on mutual acceptance and appreciation. There is every indication that the academic learning that the children are able to achieve increases as they work and play together in a friendly, accepting atmosphere.

DETERMINING THE COMPOSITION OF GROUPS

In a classroom in which the pupils are able to mingle freely with one another and to work together easily, children may be faced with the necessity of making choices daily of the pupils whom they are going to sit next to, walk down the hall with, eat lunch with, work with. The teacher may find that, for many a child, having to face the worry of whether he will be chosen or whether the child he chooses will agree to be his partner is not conducive to easy relationships.

Such procedures are not likely to make for group stability and cohesiveness, as it is difficult for a feeling of mutual trust to grow up if each day a child fears his place may be taken by another. Some sense of stability of arrangement must be communicated to the children, especially the younger children, if they are to be able to establish constructive group relationships. The teacher may find, too, that asking for a show of hands for volunteers on a work project is not always the most successful way of selecting a group. This does not mean that every activity must be organized by the teacher; merely that the experience may be more rewarding for the children if for some activities the groups are determined by the teacher.

The most effective groupings seem to be those which permit each child to be in a group with at least one of the persons he most wants to be with. (It should be noted that a child's playmates are not always the children he most wants to be with. Instead, they may be the available children, those who are willing to play with him.) A teacher can best learn the real choices of the children by asking each child to write, in order of preference, the names of the three children he most wants to be with for whatever specific situation the teacher is going to arrange the grouping. This device is commonly referred to as the sociometric test.

Obviously, every child cannot have his first choice, but each child is assured that he will be granted one of his choices. Usually the unchosen children are given their first choice (unless they should be rejected by the child they chose); for, according to the studies that have been made, a child's first choice is always a child more mature than he himself is, usually one who can serve as a model or a guide, as a source of confidence in the very area in which the child is having his greatest difficulty. (No clear pattern has yet emerged from second and third choices.) It is the unchosen child who most needs the support of his first choice. On the other hand, the children who are chosen by a number of children are likely to be those who are already quite successful in establishing relations with other children and who are likely to function in any group with success and with enjoyment.

Since the children's preferences are held in strictest confidence, no child knows the choices that other children made. An unchosen child knows only that he has been given one or more of his choices and that the others in the group have, too. Consequently, he feels that he has a right to be in the group. This in itself gives him a new feeling about himself, a new confidence. Under such circumstances, it has been found, the unchosen children make greater use of their capacities and act in a more mature manner.

VALUES OF TEACHER SELECTION OF PEER GROUPS

Thus, one of the values that can come from the teacher's using the children's choices as a basis for determining seating arrangements, or the composition of the groups in certain situations, is that those children who most need the help that comes from being part of a group are given an opportunity to be with one or more of the children they most want to be with. The extent, however, to which these aggregations of children will accept one another and will feel themselves to be a group will depend in part on the way the particular personalities of the children react to one another. Making sure that no child is put in a group with another child who rejects him increases the probability that the children will be able to accept one another. If the interest in the project is strong enough, the children may find enough in common as they carry through the project to establish genuine relationships among themselves. Most important of all, probably, is the kind of climate, the atmosphere in the classroom.

The second value is that, if these aggregations of children do grow into groups, if communication is established among the children within each group, the effect will be that of increasing the number of children with whom a child shares his thoughts, his feelings, his ideas.

This plan is not to be understood as an attempt by the teacher to arrange for a child who his associates shall be. It is not an attempt to break up a friendship cluster. It is an attempt, through one particular situation, to provide children with access to those children whom they most want to be with.

HELPING CHILDREN INTO THE PEER GROUP

We now come to the problems that particular children may have in establishing relationships with their classmates, and we present suggestions of things a teacher may do to help the child.

1. In Grade II a teacher may find children who still do not seem to know how to go about making friends, who do not seem sure enough of themselves to make overtures to other children, or who do not seem to realize that they would be acceptable playmates to some of the children. If a teacher can find work situations in which such a child feels at ease and in which he has at least a fair degree of competence, then he may be able to relate to another child (or children) in terms of the work. He may accept help from them and in that way establish a relationship. He may have good ideas to contribute and get acquainted with the others through an exchange of ideas. Sometimes he may establish a relationship by bringing something from home which is needed in the group work or something which the others enjoy looking at or playing with. With each successful contact that he is able to make with another child, his confidence in himself is likely to increase, and his ease with other children will grow as he experiments with different ways of approaching children.

2. A child may try to make friends, may try to get into a group, but be ignored by the other children. This frequently happens if a child has ways of behaving that are annoying to the other children. If the teacher can find some talent, some skill possessed by the child, and can create a situation in which the child may contribute his talent or skill in a way *that will be valued or appreciated by the other children,* they may see the child in a new light and may be willing to accept him, even if in a limited area or a limited way. As in the case above, with each success, with each new feeling of confidence, the child is likely to be able to establish better and better relations.

3. A child may be so torn by inner conflicts that he is unable to establish any constructive relationships with the other children. He may be unable to exercise a sufficient degree of control over his actions to make him at all acceptable to the other children. Probably each year a teacher has a child like this. Sometimes the child is so preoccupied by his own trouble that he does not even seem to be aware of his rejection by the other children. In such a case the most important thing the teacher can do is to help the child understand that the teacher can accept him as a person of worth, even with all his shortcomings. This, of course, may not always be possible. Teachers have feelings too, and sometimes a teacher just may not be able to feel sympathetic toward a child no matter what insights she has about his behaviors. In that case it has been found that the best thing may be for the child to be transferred to another teacher who can take this particular child in stride. This solution is not possible in every school system.

If the teacher, while assuring the child of her acceptance, can at the same time find ways in which the child can gain a respect for his abilities, either by doing jobs in the classroom, like cleaning the sink or washing the blackboards, or by mastering some of the assignments, the child may gradually get a changed conception of himself and eventually may be able to enter into some kind of relationships with the children, even if he never bcomes popular.

In helping any child establish better relationships with a group, all the teacher can do is to create a situation in which it may be possible for the group to see the child in a new rôle. It is not within the province of the teacher to dictate to the children whom they are to take into their groups, whom they are to like. This is the prerogative of the group. But, if the teacher, within the limits of her position, makes an effort to organize the classroom in such a manner that children have easy access to one another, if she creates an atmosphere in which each child feels confident of his worth, then it is likely that the children will freely form groups and will be able both to offer and to accept help from one another in their problems of growing up.

---

47. Function and Focus in the Learning Process*

Related selections: 20, 25, 41, 44, 50

CAN THE teacher teach the "whole child"? Is the teacher *directly* concerned with the personal development of his students? Professor Cantor answers these questions in the negative and calls for schools to re-focus their efforts in the learning process. The reader may note a difference between the viewpoint expressed in this selection and the position taken by certain other contributors to this volume of readings, for example, C. H. Patterson (Selection 44).

THE AIM of this essay is to clarify the function of the classroom teacher. The analysis of the teacher's function will apply, generally, to teachers on the primary and secondary levels and in the colleges of arts and sciences.

Much of the current thinking about the aims of primary and secondary education rests upon two related concepts, namely, "the whole child" and "life adjustment courses." Insufficient attention, however, has been given to the *process* by which these aims are to be realized.

* Nathaniel Cantor, "Function and Focus in the Learning Process," *Journal of Educational Research,* vol. XLV (November, 1951), pp. 225–231. Reprinted by permission of author and publisher.
Professor Cantor (1898—) is a sociologist specializing in criminology and is Department Head at the University of Buffalo. He has done special work in causes of crime, treatment of offenders, mental hygiene and education.

It is impossible, I think, to teach "a whole child" or to teach "life adjustment." One always teaches a child *something specific,* or helps a child to adjust to a *specific* problem rather than to "life." The rejoinder may be made that the above concepts refer to overall objectives and not to any specific content. If this be the case the problem is narrowed to discovering the most effective use of a teacher in furthering these over-all goals. To state objectives should not be confused with the process of realizing them. I submit that a professional teacher is most effective when he operates within carefully defined limits. The skilled teacher becomes sharply aware of his function and the focus of his effort. This requires explanation.

No one lives in a vacuum. Each of us lives in a world of people, objects, and situations with which or against which we must contend. We have to learn to accept limitations of time, place, persons, opportunities, talents, health, and so on.

We are in a constant process of adjustment *to* something or someone. We do not adjust generally once and for all. We cope with specific problems, at specific times, under specific conditions. In order to adjust to a given situation we must take into account what can't be helped so that we can judge what can be. Adjustment and development always occur in a given context, part of which consists of limitations with ourselves and obstacles about ourselves.

Teaching takes place in a given context. The particular school has its own peculiar organization; staff, standards, goals, governing board, curriculum requirements, physical equipment, and supporting community. The teacher's function will be qualified and limited by any or all of these several factors.

The particular school, then, through its administrative personnel articulates, more or less clearly, what services it offers and selects the teachers who are to offer *those* services through *particular* skills. The particular services and the particular skills are the stable, given factors in the educational context. What instructors and students do, the direction in which they move, will be defined by the declared objectives of the school and the specific skills of the teacher. Were this not so, teaching would become a glorified, chaotic eight-room circus. The teacher, otherwise, would be willing to help the student in anything, at any time, since "the whole child" is involved.

The student exposed to this kind of limitless confusion would never discover what he wants nor how to go about getting it. He would not know what the teacher stood for, nor what was expected from him.

By this time most readers have replied that no school actually operates in this fashion. The individual teachers, you say, are prepared to teach a specific subject. There are history teachers, social study teachers, economic citizenship teachers, home economic teachers and band leaders. The state departments of education or local boards do set limits (so many pages of history, so many units of credit, so many courses to qualify teachers, etc.) This is so. What, then, happens to teaching "the whole child"? How is the child helped in "life adjustment" through conjugating irregular Latin verbs or by memorizing the dates and routes of early explorers of the North American continent or by charting the distribution of metals in the United States?

Recently I met a physical education instructor of a very reputable high school in Western New York. I asked him what he did in the gym. He replied, "I teach basketball." "Why do you teach basketball?" I politely inquired. He smiled patiently and said, "You see, I'm the gym teacher." "Yes, I understand, but I'm interested in what you consider to be your function as a gym teacher. What do you really do for the kids in your gym classes?" "Oh, I see," he said. "I teach them the rules of the game and how to shoot baskets." "Oh, I see," I said, and I did.

The issue will be clarified, I think, if the double meaning of the term "function" is pointed out. A goal or function of education is to help students develop into competent citizens who understand the kind of world they live in and their relations to others. (The particular goals are unimportant in the present context. The above general goal merely illustrates the meaning of the function of education in reference to an ultimate purpose).

The function of a particular instructor, however, is to help the student to learn a *particular* content.

The individual courses, however far apart in specific content, acquire integration, if they do, in light of the general purpose of education.

When we speak of life adjustment or educating the whole child the reference is to the overall purpose of education. To confuse the general function of education with the particular function of the teacher leads to a misunderstanding of both. I should like to give an example of how the teacher through his particular course tries to carry out the general purpose of education.

Mr. Robin was called to a conference with me. He had failed to hand in several previous assignments. He came 45 minutes late for the appointment. Another time was arranged and he was 10 minutes late.

Robin: What did you want to see me about?

Instructor: I thought we might discuss your work in relation to the class. (Robin remained silent). How do you feel about the quality of work you are doing?

Robin: I'm very much interested in the course as you can tell by my discussions in class.

Instructor: Apparently your interest doesn't extend to handing in the written assignments.

Robin: Oh, those.   The reason for that is simple.   I don't like to hand in papers written in my sloppy handwriting, I prefer typing them.

Instructor: Yes, I find it much easier to read.   But I've received no typewritten papers.

Robin: I want to do good papers and haven't got 'round to complete them.

Instructor: I believe they were all due weeks ago.

Robin: Well, you wouldn't want me just to hand in a paper for the sake of being on time if I haven't anything to say?

Instructor: It may be that if you have nothing to say, the course isn't giving you enough, and you should resign from it.   That sometimes happens.

Robin: I don't want to do that, I'm getting lots out of the course.

Instructor: What are you giving to it?

Robin: You mean the papers, again?

Instructor: That is your responsibility.

Robin: I am interested in the course, but I carry three lab courses and am taking the course in flying.   The trips to and from the flying field take an awful lot of time, and I can't get around to writing the papers.

Instructor: You mean typewriting the papers.

Robin: Well, that was the original reason I gave.

Instructor: If you are too busy with other matters, I suppose the wise thing to do is to select what interests you most.   If you haven't time to carry the responsibility of this class, perhaps it's best that you drop it.

Robin: I don't want to drop out.   (I said nothing during the next half minute of silence).   Suppose I accept whatever penalty goes with not handing in papers?

Instructor: It isn't a matter of penalty, which should interest us, but whether you are doing the best kind of work of which you are capable.

Robin: Well, what do you want me to do?

Instructor: That's up to you.   What do you want to do?

Robin: What's the point of going through the motions and just handing in black scribbling on white paper—just to hand something in?

Instructor: There isn't much point to that.

Robin: Well, I could do that like others are doing.

Instructor: Perhaps some of the others who just hand in anything also aren't meeting their responsibility, doing their best work?   I suppose, too, that what they do is irrelevant to our problem.   (There was silence for about a minute).

Robin: Will you do something for me, Dr. Cantor?

Instructor: If I can.

Robin: I've been in a jam in my other work, too.   I don't know what's the matter. I'm having trouble with my girl and my parents. Can you understand what I mean? (Tears started to appear).

Instructor: I appreciate something of the difficulties which must be involved. And in addition you have the problem of doing something about your work in criminology.

Robin: You're the only professor I feel like talking to.

Instructor: What would you like me to do about helping you in your work in criminology?

Robin: Will you give me a week's time to think the whole matter over?

Instructor: What is there to think about?

Robin: I want to decide what to do about the course.

Instructor: Very well, suppose we meet a week from today at the same hour.

The papers he failed to hand in were relatively unimportant. It was important that I try to help Mr. Robin assume responsibility for a decision and the consequences which flow from that decision. I was interested in Mr. Robin and not the student in criminology. The college wants to help him to develop into a responsible citizen (general goal of education). I try to help him through my particular skill and the specific limits of the courses (specific function of teacher). Change and growth occur only as by-products of meeting specific challenges.

A surgeon shows interest in the *general health* of his patient not by operating generally (that is an autopsy), but by a specific operation for which he has skill. If the specific source of infection is removed, the entire organism makes a recovery. The function of medicine is to maintain and preserve the health of individuals. Preventive and corrective medical service is always specific.

To function in a limited way, through specific problems and skills, as they relate to the needs of the students in a particular course, while at the same time keeping in the teacher's *background* the goal of general education, requires the highest kind of professional teaching skill.

Consider the problem of grade or high school teachers assuming responsibilities for "child guidance." An eighth grade history teacher, let us say, observes that Richard isn't paying attention (to her!). Furthermore, he disturbs the class. A few minutes with the boy lead to the discovery of a very bad home situation. What should the history teacher do? There are several answers. She can "talk" to the boy. How long and how many times? Suppose there are five such "difficult" students out of a class of 36? Has she the time and energy to teach history and counsel students? Furthermore, what qualifies a history teacher to undertake the extremely delicate role of therapist? Meat-cleavers, ordinarily, are not certified to perform neuro-surgery. The knowledge and skill required to mend a broken heart are, to say the least, as involved as the knowledge and techniques required to set a shattered bone.   Turn the situation around.   Is the well developed guidance counselor ordinarily prepared to teach solid geometry or intermediate Spanish?

I do not mean to imply that the history teacher requires special development to learn how to greet the children with a spontaneous and friendly smile, or to offer friendly help in minor matters.   All teachers, during their professional development, should have acquired sufficient background in personality growth and mental hygiene to recognize serious student problems which they should not attempt to deal with.   This is the job of the professional counselor or therapist.   The teacher should have sufficient awareness to realize when the child should be referred to the counselor or the guidance clinic.   It is extremely regrettable that too few of the large urban schools and almost none of the rural schools provide professional counselling service.*   Regrets and practical difficulties, however, do not invalidate the logic of the case.

The teacher prepared to offer her services in a particular content-area is, I submit, not *directly* concerned with the whole student or with the student's personal development or with adjusting the life of the student. (How many of us are highly "successful" in adjusting our own lives?) Her limited function is to help to develop the meaning of the particular course.   That is what she is in the class for.   That is the particular service for which she was engaged.   The interpretation of the data in light of its meaning to the student is the factor which the teacher can consciously control.   Presumably she is competent in her limited, special field.   In so far as the student shows interest in, or has his interest awakened by a special subject he can be helped to develop or modify his understanding and attitudes *with reference to that limited course.*

Attitudes and adjustments are not developed in a vacuum.   They are acquired and made by facing and working through specific, limited problems which narrow confusion and define areas of challenge.   There must be a focus which enables the student to decide what, if anything, he can do about his particular responsibilities.   *The teacher focuses on her service to the student, not on the student.*   Interestingly enough, this focus provides the most effective means for the student's development as a person.

To function in a limited way, through the specific course as it is related to the problem of the student *in that course,* while keeping in one's *background* the goal of general education requires the highest kind of professional teaching skill.

Such skill cannot be effectively exercised unless the teacher is continu-

* This service, of course, has nothing to do with vocational guidance or testing services.   The reference is to therapeutic help for students.

ally and keenly aware of the general aims of education and of the way her limited specific function focuses on the realization of them. To discover and rediscover the way provides the challenge of a great profession and the opportunity for creative teaching.

---

48. How Invalid Are Marks Assigned by Teachers?*

IN ASSIGNING grades do high school teachers show partiality toward girls? Professor Carter reports a study which provides evidence that such is the case, and his conclusions are borne out by the literature he cites. While the statistical presentation and terminology in the selection may be difficult for many students, the findings can be easily understood by all. This article, in addition to the broader implications that it has for grading and evaluation practices, illustrates a type of research that contributes to our understanding of teachers and learners. The prospective teacher should learn to interpret most of the statistics presented.

WITH THE rapid development of objective testing procedures in the United States, it was to be expected that there would be numerous investigations concerning teachers' marks. Mathematics, traditionally a subject which lends itself to objective measurement, has come in for its share of these investigations. There is a scarcity of investigations of the validity of teachers' marks in beginning algebra. Most studies devoted to the question of teachers' marks have been carried out with respect to elementary school arithmetic or with plane geometry. The latter, usually an elective subject, is not necessarily subject to the same factors in teachers' assignment of marks. Of the research in the elementary school field, a great portion is devoted to a discusson of sundry philosophical aspects of the question or an evaluation of the theoretical implications of marks in general.

THE PROBLEM

The investigation was designed to determine whether or not teachers tend to favor one sex and whether the sex favored tends to be determined by the sex of the teacher. The study sought an answer to the problem:

* Robert S. Carter, "How Invalid Are Marks Assigned by Teachers?" *Journal of Educational Psychology,* vol. XLIII (April, 1952), pp. 218–228. Reprinted by permission of author and publisher.

Dr. Carter (1915—) is an Associate Professor in the Department of Psychology, Denison University.

With intelligence held constant, what is the relationship between the sex of the student and the sex of the teacher in the assignment of marks in beginning algebra?

REVIEW OF THE LITERATURE

Garner attempted to compare the marks assigned by men and women teachers. His data were obtained by investigating 5,152 marks assigned to boys and 5,132 marks assigned to girls. He made no attempt to differentiate school subjects. He concluded that both men and women give high marks to girls rather than to boys, that women sort students so that the boys get low marks. His study concluded that there is need for refining marks to make them more meaningful.

Swenson investigated the membership of the National Honor Society at Lindsborg, Kansas, High School for the years 1932 to 1941. In his investigation he found that even though boys out-numbered girls in class attendance for the ten-year period, girls outnumbered boys in the Honor Society by 2.75 to 1. He did not find substantial differences in the intelligence of boys and girls, but decided that membership was gained by inequalities in teachers' marks. He concluded that teachers were prejudiced against boys.

Three writers, Day, Douglass, and Shinnerer, in three separate studies, for the years 1937, 1938, and 1944, concluded that boys had more failures at the secondary-school level, girls had a consistent and generally substantial advantage over boys in obtaining honor ranks, but, in the light of the investigations, it seems probable that marks are determined by factors other than achievement, especially marks assigned by women teachers, and that these influences result in slight overrating of girls generally and the particular underrating of boys by women teachers.

Newton, in a study in 1942, reported that women gave higher grades than did men teachers in Central High School, Indianapolis, Indiana. He inspected the grades on two hundred forty-six permanent record cards which had been assigned by twelve women teachers and twenty-six men teachers. The total number of grades inspected was 4,255. He made no effort to account for the difference, nor did he state whether the differences were significant.

Edminston added additional evidence of sex differences in marks assigned by teachers. In the situation which he studied, the average grade for girls was 84.4 and for boys, 80.0. He further pointed out that women teachers gave the girls grades that averaged 5.4 points above those given to boys, while men teachers were less partial to the girls, giving them an average of only 3.4 points above those given to the boys.

Lobaugh, investigating the relationship of achievement and marks assigned by teachers, found that girls had a grade point average of 2.19 while the boys had a grade point average of only 1.97. When he compared the scores made on the Myers-Ruch High School Progress Test, the boys' median score was 46 while the median score for girls was 36. This ten-point differential was characteristic of all tests administered during the period from 1940 to 1945. Further, in 1940 the valedictorian, a girl, could do no better than rank number 36, while it was necessary to go down to number 105 to find the salutatorian. In 1941 the valedictorian ranked number 19 while the salutatorian ranked number 41. On the 1940 test, the boy who ranked number 1 on the achievement test failed to graduate and had to return to school for the fifth year in order to graduate. The results in 1940 showed that the top fourteen scores were made by boys. In 1941 and 1942 the results indicated that only three girls could be found among the top fifteen scores. Lobaugh accounted for the differences between achievement and marks on the basis of evidence that girls were more meticulous, more punctual, and neater about their work. He also recognized greater maturity among the girls and a tendency for the boys to compensate for their immaturity.

MATERIALS AND SUBJECTS

Results of an investigation of this type are of most value when they can be used for evaluation and interpretation over a wide area, or by a large number of individuals. With this in mind the investigation was undertaken in a city in western Pennsylvania. Two hundred sixty pupils took part in the testing program from which the basic data for this study were obtained. This investigation is based on two hundred thirty-five pupils taking high-school algebra for the first time. In all, nine classes were used, four classes being taught by women and five classes being taught by men. Of the students, one hundred thirty-five were boys and one hundred were girls. Since students are assigned to classes alphabetically, no known selective factors operate which would give a biased sample.

In the school in which the investigation was made, there are six teachers, three men and three women, teaching beginning algebra. The six teachers all hold valid Permanent High School Certificates issued by the Pennsylvania Department of Public Instruction. None of the teachers has had less than fifteen years of experience. The training of the three men and the three women used in this study was almost identical. Whatever effect factors of age, training, and experience may have on assigned marks was minimized.

During the last week of the first semester, the investigator administered the Otis Quick Scoring Mental Ability Test, Beta Test, Form A, and the

Colvin-Schrammel Algebra Test, Test I, Form A, to all students enrolled in the course in beginning algebra in the public school of a western Pennsylvania city.   One week following the end of the first semester the examiner inspected the permanent record cards for the subjects used in the investigation.   These cards were inspected in the office of the principal. From the cards, the examiner secured the necessary information concerning the marks assigned by individual teachers to each student as an indication of his level of achievement for the semester.

RESULTS OF THE TESTING PROGRAM

For the purpose of this investigation, the sample is divided into four groups: 1) Boys taught by men teachers.   2) Girls taught by men teachers.   3) Boys taught by women teachers.   4) Girls taught by women teachers.

In the presentation of the data which follow, the results of the testing program are presented so as to reflect these categories.

A. Intelligence Test Results

In Table I are shown the critical ratios of the differences of the various groups with respect to mental ability as measured by the Otis Test.   The differences for the various groups (range 1.62 to −.83), when treated statistically, give critical ratios that range from .91 to .13.   The largest difference shown, that between boys and girls taught by men (1.62), gives a critical ratio of only .91.   Differences as large as 1.62 might be expected by chance one out of five times.   It is important to realize, therefore, that with respect to intelligence, as measured by the Otis Quick-Scoring Mental Ability Test, there are no statistically significant differences between the groups in the present investigation.

B. Algebra Achievement Test Scores

The critical ratios of the differences between the means of the various groups based on the results of the Colvin-Schrammel Algebra Test are found in Table II.   Differences range from 1.69 (the difference in mean scores for boys and girls taught by men) to .17 (the difference between groups taught by men and by women).   It is to be noted that the average boy makes a better score on this test than does the average girl. The mean score for boys taught by men is higher than the mean score for girls taught by men.   On the other hand the average score of girls taught by women exceeds the average score for the boys.   The student whose sex is the same as that of the teacher makes higher mean scores than do the students whose sex is opposite to that of the teacher.

With respect to average achievement in algebra, as measured by the Colvin-Schrammel Test, the differences among the various groups in this investigation are not significant. The largest critical ratio, the critical ratio between the mean score for boys and girls taught by men, 1.13, indicates that differences as large as 1.69 could be expected by chance thirteen times out of one hundred. It must be concluded, then, that the small differences among the various groups could happen by chance, and, as far as ability in algebra is concerned, boys and girls, whether the teacher is a man or a woman, show equal algebra achievement within the limits of the present data.

TABLE I

DIFFERENCES AND CRITICAL RATIOS BETWEEN SCORES MADE BY BOYS AND GIRLS
ON THE OTIS QUICK SCORING MENTAL ABILITY TESTS, BETA TEST

Number	Sex	Mean	Standard Deviation	Standard Error of Mean	Difference $(M_1 - M_2)$	Standard Error of Difference	Critical Ratio
	Taught by men						
75	Boys	107.28	11.59	1.36			
58	Girls	108.90	8.84	1.16			
					1.62	1.79	.91
	Taught by women						
60	Boys	107.60	8.15	1.05			
42	Girls	107.38	9.14	1.41			
					.22	1.76	.13
	Boys (taught by)						
75	Men	107.28	11.59	1.36			
60	Women	107.60	8.15	1.05			
					—.32	1.72	—.19
	Girls (taught by)						
58	Men	108.90	8.84	1.16			
42	Women	107.38	9.14	1.41			
					1.52	1.83	.83
	Totals (taught by)						
133	Men	107.97	10.64	.92			
102	Women	107.51	8.57	.85			
					.46	1.25	.37
	Totals						
135	All Boys	107.42	10.34	.89			
100	All Girls	108.25	8.99	.90			
					—.83	1.26	—.66

C. *Marks Assigned by Teachers*

The critical ratios of the differences between the mean grades assigned to boys and girls by teachers of beginning algebra are found in Table III. Although it has been shown that no significant differences exist among the various groups in either intelligence or algebra achievement, significant differences are found in the marks assigned by teachers of beginning algebra.

The average mark assigned by men is 6.44 points lower than the average mark assigned by women. This difference is nearly six times the standard error of the difference. This cannot be attributed to chance factors. In all instances the girls receive higher average marks than do the boys. In the present investigation, the difference in marks assigned by men and women teachers indicates that men assign lower marks to boys and to girls.

TABLE II

MEAN DIFFERENCES AND CRITICAL RATIOS BETWEEN SCORES MADE BY BOYS AND GIRLS ON THE COLVIN-SCHRAMMEL ALGEBRA ACHIEVEMENT TEST, FORM A

Number	Sex	Mean	Standard Deviation	Standard Error of Mean	Difference $(M_1 - M_2)$	Standard Error of Difference	Critical Ratio
	Taught by men						
75	Boys	30.84	9.32	1.08			
58	Girls	29.15	7.74	1.02			
					1.69	1.49	1.13
	Taught by women						
60	Boys	29.51	8.42	1.09			
42	Girls	30.52	7.19	1.11			
					—1.01	1.56	—.65
	Boys (taught by)						
75	Men	30.84	9.32	1.08			
60	Women	29.51	8.42	1.09			
					1.33	1.54	.86
	Girls (taught by)						
58	Men	29.15	7.74	1.02			
42	Women	30.52	7.19	1.11			
					—1.37	1.51	—.91
	Totals (taught by)						
133	Men	30.10	8.70	.75			
102	Women	29.93	6.77	.67			
					.17	1.00	.17
	Totals						
135	All Boys	30.25	8.18	.70			
100	All Girls	29.73	7.54	.75			
					.52	1.02	.51

More specifically, the data show that boys are given lower average marks than are girls, regardless of the sex of the teacher assigning the marks; but, marks assigned by men are lower than those assigned by women. Consequently, boys get the lowest average marks when those marks are assigned by men. Girls, on the other hand, get the highest marks when those marks are assigned by women teachers.

458 ROBERT S. CARTER

D. Relationship between Teachers' Marks and Achievement Scores

In Table IV are presented the coefficients of correlation, both zero order or product moment r's and partial r's of the first order. The product moment r's reflect the relationship between teachers' marks and algebra achievement. The partial r's reflect the relationship between teachers' marks and algebra achievement with the effect of intelligence held constant.

TABLE III

DIFFERENCES AND CRITICAL RATIOS BETWEEN MARKS ASSIGNED TO BOYS AND TO
GIRLS BY TEACHERS OF BEGINNING ALGEBRA

Number	Sex	Mean	Standard Deviation	Standard Error of Mean	Differ-ence $(M_1 - M_2)$	Standard Error of Difference	Critical Ratio
	Taught by men						
75	Boys	76.61	8.19	.95			
58	Girls	79.50	6.60	.87			
					—2.89	1.29	—2.24
	Taught by women						
60	Boys	82.63	9.08	1.17			
42	Girls	86.71	8.67	1.34			
					—4.08	1.78	—2.29
	Boys (taught by)						
75	Men	76.61	8.19	.95			
60	Women	82.63	9.08	1.16			
					—6.02	1.50	—4.01
	Girls (taught by)						
58	Men	79.50	6.60	.87			
42	Women	86.71	8.67	1.34			
					—7.21	1.60	—4.51
	Totals (taught by)						
133	Men	77.87	7.67	.67			
102	Women	84.31	9.15	.91			
					—6.44	1.13	—5.70
	Totals						
135	All Boys	79.29	9.10	.78			
100	All Girls	82.53	8.34	.83			
					—3.24	1.14	—2.84

When intelligence is held constant and teachers' marks are compared with algebra achievement, the correlation for the first order r decreases in magnitude in all groups. Large changes are found in the totals (N equal to 235) when the product moment r is .52 and the partial r is .40, and among all boys (N equal to 135) when the value of the r changes from .59 to .47. The largest change, however, is observed in comparing the coefficients for girls taught by women (N equal to 42). When teachers' marks are compared with achievement scores, the zero order r is .35. When intelligence is held constant, and these two variables are compared, the coefficient is reduced to .18.

TABLE IV

COEFFICIENTS OF CORRELATION BETWEEN TEACHERS' MARKS AND ALGEBRA
ACHIEVEMENT AND BETWEEN TEACHERS' MARKS AND ALGEBRA
ACHIEVEMENT WITH INTELLIGENCE HELD CONSTANT

0. Teachers' Marks
1. Algebra Achievement Scores
2. Intelligence Test Scores

	Boys	Girls	Total
Taught by men			
Number	75	58	133
$r_{01.2}$	.70 ± .06	.47 ± .10	.57 ± .06
$r_{01.}$	.78 ± .05	.57 ± .09	.68 ± .05
Taught by women			
Number	60	42	102
$r_{01.2}$	.28 ± .12	.18 ± .15	.31 ± .09
$r_{01.}$	.37 ± .11	.35 ± .14	.43 ± .08
Totals			
Number	135	100	235
$r_{01.2}$	.47 ± .07	.36 ± .09	.40 ± .05
$r_{01.}$	.59 ± .06	.45 ± .08	.52 ± .05

When intelligence is held constant and teachers' marks are compared with algebra achievement scores, the reduction in the magnitude of the r's indicates that teachers' marks actually reflect not only achievement but also that the teacher assigns at least part of the mark on the basis of intelligence. This condition is not prevalent in the same amount under all groups. The grades assigned to boys by men teachers are not as greatly affected as are the grades assigned to girls by women teachers. As is to be expected, however, intelligence is a factor in the assignment of marks by both men and women teachers to both boys and girls.

SUMMARY

With respect to intelligence, no significant differences existed among any of the groups. In the results of the algebra achievement scores, small and, on the whole, insignificant differences favored the group whose sex was the same as the sex of the teacher. The differences in achievement were not significant at the one per cent level of confidence, indicating that the small differences which were present could have been accounted for by chance.

When the teachers' marks in beginning algebra were investigated, significant differences were observed. Girls made significantly higher marks than did the boys. Women teachers tended to give higher marks than did the men teachers. Specifically, when marks were assigned, boys were given lower marks than were the girls regardless of whether the teacher was a man or a woman; but, marks assigned by men teachers were lower than marks assigned by women teachers.

CONCLUSIONS

1. It was evident from the data, although no significant differences could be found in intelligence or in algebra achievement, that significant differences existed in the marks assigned by teachers, differences clearly not attributable to chance. The differences, generally, gave the advantage to the girls. It was made clear that the girls were no smarter, did not know any more algebra, but they did receive higher marks.

2. There were definite indications that intelligence was a factor in the assignment of marks. The correlation coefficient between teachers' marks and algebra achievement gave some indication that, theoretically, at least, they represent measurement of the same variable.

3. When intelligence was partialled out, and thus held constant, the relationship between teachers' marks and achievement declined. This indicated that the teachers' marks not only reflected achievement but also intelligence. Since the relationship was far from perfect, some other factors entered into the assignment of marks by teachers of beginning algebra.

4. It must be concluded that teachers' marks represent more than chance estimates of the pupils' achievement. The findings in the present investigation indicate that teachers' marks represent achievement, but, and this is important, they give evidence of the effects of intelligence upon the teacher.

5. It must also be concluded in the light of the data in the present investigation that the sex of the teacher was not so important in the investigation of marks as was the sex of the student. Regardless of whether the teacher was a man or a woman, boys were penalized in the assignment of marks. The penalty was not so great, at least so far as these data were concerned, if the teacher was a man. There was higher correlation between achievement and teachers' marks when the teacher was a man.

6. The data indicated a definite necessity for the refining of marks,

if these marks are to reflect true achievement.   The data used in this investigation proved that there is a slight overrating of girls generally and an underrating of boys, especially by women teachers.

RECOMMENDATIONS FOR FUTURE STUDIES

The evidence in the present investigation indicated that the mark assigned by teachers reflected more than algebra achievement.   From the evidence at hand it was impossible to account for all of the factors that affected the grading or marking situation.   In view of the data upon which the conclusions of the present investigations were drawn, further investigation should be directed toward finding answers to the following questions:

1. What are the effects of interest, socio-economic status and personality of the student on the assignment of marks by teachers of beginning algebra?

2. Are the factors mentioned above important in the grading situation when investigated in light of sex differences of student and teacher?

3. Of what significance are non-intellectual factors when teachers assign marks?

---

49. Teacher Behavior Liked and Disliked by Pupils*

Related selection: 43

THERE IS some indication that the personality characteristics exhibited by a teacher affect the personality development of the children with whom he works.   Although fundamental changes in personality structure are difficult to achieve, it is possible for most teachers to scrutinize their attitudes and behavior toward children. Such an examination, coupled with the results of Professor Leeds's study below, should provide clues for constructive changes that teachers might make in their relations with students.

* Carroll H. Leeds, "Teacher Behavior Liked and Disliked by Pupils," *Education,* vol. LXXV (September, 1954), pp. 29–36.   Reprinted by permission of author and publisher.

Dr. Leeds (1906—) is Professor of Psychology and chairman of the department, Furman University.   He has done extensive research in the area of pupil-teacher relationships.

RECENT years have witnessed a growing and enlightened interest on the part of both educators and laymen in the all-around personality development of children.   Forward-looking educators have for some time been stressing the idea that the *whole* child goes to school, not merely an intellectual one fourth.   Insightful parents are becoming increasingly cognizant of the developmental status of their children's social and emotional behavior.

Playing a significant part in the development of the child's personality are the personalities of those with whom he comes in contact.   One would suppose that the close and extensive association experienced daily by teacher and pupil in the classroom would make the personality of the teacher a decisive influence in shaping the personality pattern of the child. Evidence supporting this supposition has become available in recent years.

Maladjusted teachers and teachers whose personality patterns are not conducive to pleasant and harmonious relations with children are actually detrimental to the optimum personal growth of their pupils.   Inability to establish rapport with children leads to ineffective learning situations, disciplinary problems, and undesirable attitudes of both teachers and pupils.

It is with the attitudes of pupils toward teachers and teacher behavior that this paper primarily is concerned.   Research seems to point toward a reciprocal relationship between the attitudes of a child and his adjustment status; that is, the child's attitudes represent both a determining factor in his adjustment and a resultant factor.   If this is the case, the attitude of a pupil toward his teacher or teachers has a direct bearing on his adjustment status.   An undesirable attitude toward the teacher might indicate, then, not only possible maladjustment of the pupil but *the distinct probability that this attitude is contributing further* toward his maladjustment.

Granting, then, the responsibility of the school for the child's personal and social development, the influential part played by the teacher in the developmental process, and the intimate relationship between children's attitudes and their adjustment, we are led to the inevitable conclusion that the attitudes and reactions of pupils toward their teachers warrant far greater consideration and study than are customarily allotted them.   The rating of teachers by their pupils has been discussed rather extensively in the literature.   There is a growing tendency to endorse this type of rating. Even though a child's attitudes may change with increased maturity, it would seem that his *present* attitude would be of primary concern to the educator rather than his *future* attitude.   Furthermore, it would appear that the most significant factor in a pupil's attitude toward his teacher is the affective element of like or dislike.   It may be true that the elementary school pupil is not prepared to rate a teacher's instructional ability, but certainly he is qualified to reveal his feelings toward the teacher as a person.   It is this immediate attitudinal response that would seem basic to all teacher-pupil relationships, and it is with it that we are concerned in the present discussion.

THE STUDY

The purpose of this article is to present and discuss the reactions of some 1000 fourth-, fifth-, and sixth-grade pupils to certain aspects of teacher behavior.   These reactions were obtained in the course of other investigations described elsewhere.   Two hundred fourth-, fifth-, and sixth-grade public school teachers had been rated by their pupils by means of a 50-item questionnaire, devised by the writer, entitled *My Teacher*.[1, 2]   The items were simple questions adapted to the mental maturity and experience of fourth-, fifth-, and sixth-grade children, that could be answered simply by underlining "Yes," "No," or "?".   The content of the questions related to the teacher's disposition, her treatment of pupils, her teaching, her interest in children's activities, her status in the pupils' esteem, her sense of humor, and a number of other topics within the realm of teacher-pupil relationship.   The following items are cited as examples:

1. Does this teacher scold the pupils a lot?   Yes   No   ?
38. Does this teacher give you a chance to ask questions?   Yes   No   ?

Space was provided on the questionnaire for the pupil to comment relative to: (1) Why I Like This Teacher (2) Why I Don't Like This Teacher.

The questionnaire was administered in person, by the writer, to 200 groups (100 in each 2 studies) of approximately twenty-five pupils each. No one was present during the rating other than the pupils and the writer. It was made clear to the pupils that no one except the writer would ever see the papers and that their grades or school standing would in no way be affected by the way they answered the questions.   They were not to sign their names.

As a basis for discussion in the present article, an intensive study was made (for both the 1946 and the 1951 data) of pupil reaction to the ten teachers at the upper end of the distribution of pupils' ratings and the ten teachers at the lower end.   Table 1 indicates, for each item in the *My*

---

[1] Actually two separate but identical investigations had been conducted involving 100 teachers in each.   The studies were made in 1946 and 1951, respectively, in Pennsylvania and South Carolina.
[2] The reliability of the questionnaire was .94 (split-half technique).

Teacher questionnaire,[3] the relative frequency (in terms of per cent) with which pupils reacted unfavorably toward the ten teachers at each extreme of the distribution of pupils' ratings. Results are presented for both the 1946 and the 1951 studies. The data in Table I are interpreted as follows:

For Item 3, in the 1946 study, 10 per cent of the 281 pupils who rated the upper ten teachers, indicated that the teacher being rated failed to praise them "for doing good work"; whereas 49 per cent of the 265 pupils rating the lower ten teachers made the same indication. In the 1951 study, 5 per cent of the 257 pupils rating the upper ten teachers are contrasted, in the like manner, with 15 per cent rating the lower ten teachers. Data for the other items are interpreted in the same way.

DISCUSSION OF FINDINGS

Table I indicates several points of both importance and interest:

1. The proportion of undesirable reactions is considerably and consistently larger toward the lower ten teachers (only exception in Item 39 with the 1951 data). For the majority of items, the percentage figures relating to this inferior group are five to ten times as large as those relating to the superior group. In several instances, particularly in the 1946 study, the figure is twenty to forty times as large. In the earlier study, the total average percentage response per item is 7.3 for the superior group and 50.5 for the inferior group. These figures are 5.7 and 29.5 respectively, in the 1951 study.

2. It is of interest that the pupils in the South Carolina study (1951) are less critical of their teachers than those in the Pennsylvania investigation (1946). Particularly is this true of the lower ten teachers. The studies do not indicate the causal factors responsible for this difference. Of interest are three items (Items 8, 25, and 43) which prove an exception to this generalization, and indicate a more unfavorable attitude on the part of the South Carolina (1951) pupils: "unable to keep order," "detention during recess or after school," and "assigns 'lots' of homework." The differences are not great, but they are consistent with both superior and inferior teachers. Actually of greater import than the differences between the 1946 and the 1951 studies is their relatively close agreement.

3. Among those descriptive behavior traits which pupils mention as characterizing the teachers most disliked and which also seem to dif-

---

[3] Items 1 and 2 were not included in the scoring as they were not concerned directly with teacher behavior. The remaining items are not reproduced exactly, but their content is represented by ideas phrased in terms of undesirable teacher behavior.

ferentiate most noticeably the superior and inferior teachers are the following: "scolds pupils a lot;" "usually cross;" "often bossy;" "talks too much;" "always 'fussing at' the pupils;" "becomes angry at pupils' failure to under-

TABLE I

FREQUENCY OF PUPIL REACTION TOWARD UNDESIRABLE BEHAVIOR
OF THE TEN TEACHERS TAKEN FROM EACH END OF THE DISTRIBUTION OF
PUPILS' RATINGS (1946 AND 1951 STUDIES)

Item Number	Undesirable Teacher Behavior	Percentage of Pupil Reaction to Upper 10 Teachers		Percentage of Pupil Reaction to Lower 10 Teachers	
		1946 (N:281)	1951 (N:257)	1946 (N:265)	1951 (N:261)
3	Failure to praise	10	5	49	15
4	Scolds pupils a lot	4	7	71	50
5	Usually cross	3	4	59	20
6	Doesn't explain school work	0	2	19	6
7	Doesn't speak to pupil on street	0	1	20	6
8	Unable to keep order	5	7	30	48
9	Does not make school work interesting	1	1	39	21
10	Often "bossy"	2	4	58	32
11	Difficult to approach with problems	5	6	56	26
12	Forces ideas on pupils	12	8	44	24
13	Not usually kind to pupil	2	0	37	10
14	Does not keep promises	2	0	25	19
15	Does not participate in children's games	9	17	64	64
16	Thinks she is always right and pupil wrong	7	2	51	31
17	Has "pets" among the children	27	16	54	57
18	Scolds a pupil in front of other pupils	44	23	91	80
19	Difficult to please	7	4	64	33
20	Talks too much	5	3	63	40
21	Easily annoyed or bothered	17	11	70	61
22	Unfair with pupils	3	2	39	18
23	Always "fussing at" the pupils	6	2	58	31
24	Failure to acknowledge pupil's hand	5	4	48	34
25	Detention during recess or after school	16	30	69	87
26	Makes fun of pupils	6	3	38	15
27	Disliked by most pupils	2	1	68	30
28	Doesn't laugh with pupils at amusing incidents	11	10	44	20
29	Unfair in grading	3	2	33	9
30	Talks too loudly	1	1	43	21
31	Does not give everyone a chance to recite	2	5	40	29

TABLE I

(continued)

Item Number	Undesirable Teacher Behavior	Percentage of Pupil Reaction to Upper 10 Teachers		Percentage of Pupil Reaction to Lower 10 Teachers	
		1946 (N:281)	1951 (N:257)	1946 (N:265)	1951 (N:261)
32	Failure to explain school work	1	0	28	9
33	Becomes angry at pupil's failure to understand	5	3	59	33
34	Unwilling to help with school work	2	2	38	15
35	Doesn't seem to like children	1	0	42	16
36	Punishes whole class for 1 or 2 offenders	12	8	71	41
37	Scolds pupils for mistakes	4	2	55	22
38	Does not give opportunity for questions	0	3	34	21
39	Lowers grades for helping others	19	20	57	20
40	Will not permit making up work failed	13	9	54	18
41	Often becomes angry with pupils	7	4	74	61
42	Pupil afraid to ask for help	6	4	42	20
43	Assigns "lots" of homework	5	8	54	55
44	Punishes in front of other pupils	20	14	86	61
45	Unwilling to give extra help	1	2	31	10
46	Does not see things as children do	3	5	52	37
47	Uninterested in pupil's activities outside of school	33	9	63	39
48	Does not explain lessons clearly	1	1	31	11
49	Disliked by individual pupil	1	0	53	28
50	Disliked by other pupils	1	1	58	20
	Total average per item	7.3	5.7	50.5	29.5

stand;" "assigns 'lots' of homework;" "often becomes angry with pupils." It is of interest to note that practically all of these traits relate to the personality and disposition of the teacher and to the resulting affective and human relationships between teacher and pupil. It is probably true that a pupil's liking or disliking a teacher (see Items 27, 49, 50) is intimately related to, if not determined by, factors that are essentially affective, personal, and human. Such findings are in general agreement with the results of previous studies concerning why teachers are liked or disliked by pupils.

4. Of interest are those items in Table I with a relatively high percentage of response with reference to the "superior" teachers. This is especially true of Items 17, 18, 25, 44, and 47. Although in no case as high as 50 per cent, a relatively large proportion of the pupils indicate that

even the "superior" teachers "have 'pets' among the children," "scold a pupil in front of other pupils," "detain pupils during recess or after school," "punish in front of other pupils," and are "uninterested in pupil's activities outside of school." These same items also show high percentages of response with reference to the lower ten teachers.

Partiality or favoritism shown by teachers toward certain pupils has always been a source of resentment for most children. For the teacher it may represent a possible outlet for feelings of insecurity.

Whether verbal or corporeal, punishment of a pupil in the presence of his classmates is resented and dreaded by children. Apparently even our better teachers are too often guilty of this practice, especially in verbal form.

Detaining a pupil during recess or after school would seem to be at least a questionable practice when one considers the reaction of the child.

A rather common weakness among teachers is an apparent lack of interest in what their pupils do outside of the school environment. In the 1946 study as many as one-third of the pupils indicated that teachers of the "superior" group were guilty of this lack of interest. It is quite possible, however, that this item was interpreted by some pupils to refer to the trait of keeping one's "nose out of other people's business."

If space permitted, much could be written concerning the responses to the remaining items in the questionnaire. Careful study of the accompanying Table should cause any individual teacher to pause in her work and ask herself the question: "Am I treating these young human lives as I would like to be treated if I were in their position?"

Comments written by pupils as to why they liked or did not like certain teachers reveal in startling fashion underlying attitudes which would seem of extreme importance. Because of this significance a number of these comments are presented:

Reasons for Liking Teacher:
   "Because she is always friendly to the pupils."
   "She is very patient and kind."
   "I like this teacher because she is kind and not a boss."
   "I like her because she is interested in my hobby which is building airplanes, boats, and other models."
   "She considers herself one of us."
   "Because she is helpful. I can take problems to her. She understands. She is pretty (that helps out a lot)."
   "Because when I came to this school she was kind to me."
   "Because when I ask her questions she gives me a chance to tell her."
   "I like my teacher because she is interested in children."

"She tries to be very understanding. I think she is grand to put up with us."

"She is kind and not like most other teachers."

"Because she keeps her promises and takes us on trips and lets us ask questions without getting mad at us."

"She is kind and helpful and explains things carefully and listens to what you say."

"I like this teacher because she is fair and I feel free to ask her anything."

"She isn't cranky. She doesn't get angry when you don't get everything right."

"Because she'll stop and help anybody who needs help when she has important work to do."

"Because she is helpful and understanding in my work. And she is like a mother to all the children."

"Because she lets you laugh when something is funny and she has fun with children."

"I like this teacher because she's easy to get along with and I'm always at ease when I'm in her room."

"I like this teacher because she does not get angry. She does not embarrass us in front of the class."

"I like her for she is very nice, talks low, not too low, and she explains your lessons clearly."

"Because she likes all the children and not one or two."

"She goes skating like boys and girls and likes basketball and laughs when we do."

"Because she is humorous and laughs with the class and it makes school more fun."

Reasons for Disliking Teacher:

"Because when you ask her a question she will scream at you and tell you to sit down."

"She gets mad too easy."

"Because she fusses too much."

"Because she blames me for things I don't do and she hates me."

"I don't like her because she tries to boss everyone and she talks too much. And I wish she would shut up."

"Well the way I feel about it she gets too mean over just a little thing."

"She looks like a witch."

"I don't like this teacher because she hates me and I don't get to have part in most things."

"Because she does not keep her temper very good."

"She likes other pupils better."

"She has too many pets."

"When I first came to this school she called on me all the time but now I can sit and wave my hand for hours and she won't pay any attention to me. She embarrasses me in front of other pupils."

"Because she doesn't make jokes out of anything."

"Because sometimes she promises me I can do something and when I get ready to do it she says she never promised me."

"Because she yells too much."

"She is unfair with the pupils."

"Because she is mean to all of us when only one pupil is to blame for it."

"She just tells you what to do and doesn't explain the work."

"She seems to be always cranky."

"Because she is always picking on certain children."

"She thinks she is too smart. And she is too bossy. I hate her."

"When election time was here she took a badge off a pupil because she voted for Dewey."

"She's mean, crabby, cross. That's why I hate her."

"I don't like her sometimes because she scolds me when I miss a word."

"She always gets the paddle out and hollers for nothing."

"If she would be a little nicer I would do my work better."

"I just came to this school and she don't like me so I don't like her. If she would explain better I'd learn."

"Because she is always griping about something."

"Because she is always scolding us and telling us to keep quiet. She is really mean."

"Because she's cross when other teachers are around."

"Because she always keeps me in when I have to play basketball."

"One day she hit me across the back about fifteen times."

"She is MEAN."

"She puts chewing gum on our nose."

"She is too bossy and doesn't care for children of our age."

"She is too mean and always scolds at us when we make a mistake."

"I am afraid of her. She hit —— —— with a paddle and make his neck bleed. Blood was running down his neck."

"Because she hit me on my head."

"Because she does not go to our basketball games and does not take interest in sports."

"Because she hollers at you in front of the room."

"I have no reason otherwise than that she doesn't let me express my thoughts."

"She doesn't give every pupil a chance to ask questions."

The above comments certainly substantiate the view previously advanced that, in the elementary school classroom particularly, the simple emotional, personal, and human qualities are basic in teacher-pupil relationships. Children, as other humans, demand and appreciate friendliness, understanding, and simple courtesy in the treatment accorded them. Such thoughtfulness and consideration would seem to presuppose a teacher personality pattern characterized, principally, by a liking for children and interest in what they do, a disposition patient as well as kind, and a balanced outlook on life, involving such things as a sense of humor and a conscience not overburdened with rigorous perfectionism.

Assuming a liking for children, it would seem that basic to everything else is a kind and pleasant disposition. This might then imply certain other more specific characteristics. Conspicuous in the remarks of the pupils is a distaste for "bossiness' in teacher behavior. Isn't it just as human to resent being "bossed" as it is to always want to order others around? And who appreciates being reprimanded in the presence of others? Children are human!

Undoubtedly, many teachers in their behavior are "bossy," inconsiderate, ill-mannered, and lose their tempers easily because of an insufficient amount of patience. Working with children demands an undying patience!

Prominent also in pupil reaction to teacher behavior is an appreciation of a sense of humor. The teacher who can laugh at amusing situations, who can see things the way children do, and who does not take life too seriously would seem to have a philosophy of life in keeping with satisfying human relationships with young people. Closely associated with one's attitude toward life is one's reaction toward his own conscience. An overburdened conscience, especially when coupled with feelings of insecurity, is often manifested in meticulous attention to minor details and an overemphasis upon less important matters and processes. Such perfectionism in a teacher's attitudes and behavior inevitably leads to "nagging," with a consequent animosity on the part of pupils.

SUMMARY

Underlying this study was the multiple assumption that the social and emotional development of the child is a responsibility of the school, that the teacher plays a principal role in this development, and that the attitudinal reaction of pupils toward the teacher and her classroom behavior is of great significance in pupil adjustment.

Ratings of teachers made by fourth-, fifth-, and sixth-grade pupils indicated that affective, personal, and human factors provided the basis for differentiating teachers well-liked by pupils from those greatly disliked.

To be appreciated and liked, teacher behavior must stem from a personality basically well-adjusted and characterized by a sincere liking for children, a kind and pleasant disposition, and a balanced outlook on life.

50. Aspects of Mental Health in Teaching and Learning*

Related selections: 17, 20, 24, 29, 47

WHEN IS a person "mentally healthy"? What is the extent of the teacher's responsibility for improving the mental health of his pupils? How does the teacher's own mental health influence his work in the classroom? In answering these questions Blos discusses four attributes of a mentally healthy person and suggests ways of achieving this state of well-being.

WE MEET at a time when the world is full of strife, confusion, distrust, and fear. To describe the present condition of man, I like to borrow Julian Huxley's eloquence:

Our thinking is chaotic, our nerves are jumpy, we are prey to pessimism and depression, we seem frightened of our human selves. Our half of the world lacks a common faith; the other half has had imposed upon it a crude dogmatic faith which can never satisfy free men. Above all, we have lost our sense of continuity, our long-term hope, and seem only able to concentrate on prospects of immediate disaster or immediate methods of escaping from it.

The educator has to view his work from a different position. in his effort to bring up children, he extends his influence into the future, and only there will he be rewarded in his expectation of having contributed significantly to the formation of mature adults who are less susceptible to the disorganizing influence of fright and flight. After many years of disillusionment, we have come to realize that the accumulation of knowledge and the advances in technology—in short, the conquest of nature itself—have not automatically created a world that harbors happier people.

The latest science to come to fruition is the science of man himself. Not until our lifetime did the working of man's inner life become transparent. The potentials of the creative and destructive powers that lie in all of us, the conditions of life that lead best to man's most mature achievements—namely, his humanity—and, further, the intelligible and orderly progression of personality and character development—all these insights have filled our libraries during the first half of this century. It

* Peter Blos, "Aspects of Mental Health in Teaching and Learning," *Mental Hygiene*, vol. XXXVII, October, 1953, pp. 555–569. Reprinted by permission of author and publisher.

Dr. Blos is a psychotherapist associated with the Child Guidance Institute, Jewish Board of Guardians, New York City, and is a Diplomate in clinical psychology.

has become clear that since we conquered our natural environment, the sole disturber of our peaceful and creative pursuits is man himself. It has become apparent that our deepest suffering, our immense waste of human energies, are inflicted on man by man himself.

It is this awareness of the refractory effect of man's state of mind that found expression in the preamble to the charter of UNESCO. Its opening sentence reads: "Since wars are made in the minds of men, it is in the minds of men that peace will be established."

It is only good common sense to turn to the resources that the science of inner man has to offer and apply them to the bringing up of children. I should like to remind you that nothing has been more impressive, in all the voluminous research into the origins of attitudes and goals of man, than the repeated confirmation that these attitudes and goals are formed and anchored in childhood. A significant part of childhood's destiny lies in the hands of its teachers, and rests on the influence that they can bring to bear on the meaningfulness of school experiences, on good family life, and on sound community living.

We have come face to face with the fact that the 27 million children now in our elementary and secondary schools are poorly prepared indeed for adult life if we do not make their personality development the pivotal point on which to concentrate our efforts. Knowledge can be applied fruitfully and with social responsibility only when it operates in a human mind that is free from distorted emotions. This fact is demonstrated again and again in our guidance clinics and mental hospitals. We have to ask ourselves most searchingly: What are the essential needs of children in their formative years and how can we, as teachers, bring our influence to bear on the development of healthy personalities? We are asking, in effect, the question: What is mental hygiene?

To this question, I like to give the following answer: Mental hygiene concerns itself with all those influences on the individual which make the orderly unfolding of human capacities possible. This unfolding follows a natural sequence of maturational stages, physically and emotionally, and leads ultimately to a way of life that is fruitful to the individual and in harmony with the values of the group to which he belongs.

These values are man-made and vary in different societies. Our own democratic credo makes two attitudes the foundation of our spiritual existence—namely, respect for the individual and his dignity, and the responsibility that every one individually assumes for his actions. This formulation, as you can see, leaves room for the responsible dissenter or the responsible nonconformist. Mental health is, consequently, not synonymous with conformity.

The rest of my talk I want to devote to material more directly related to the educative process and the principles of mental health—in essence, to the interaction of the two. By way of introduction, I must say a few words about a basic problem—namely, the place of constitution or heredity in our present-day thinking about personality. Up to the turn of the century—and many people still are at that point—constitutional factors dominated our approach to personality development. It was generally believed that each individual possesses in his genes a set of hereditary characteristics that will determine the physical and mental dimensions of its bearer—in fact, that the destiny of the individual was fixed by his genetic pattern or his genotype.

Within the last twenty-five years a revolutionary change has taken place which has almost reversed the picture. Observations and research have revealed the incredible impressionability of the child in relation to his environment, for good or for ill. For example, children of feeble-minded parents, when reared in good foster homes, showed a most remarkable development in intelligence as compared to the children of a control group who continued to live with their feebleminded parents. Since we are in a better position to control the environment than we are to control the genes, these new findings promised to open up boundless horizons on the educational frontier. Overoptimism developed, and parents as well as teachers felt that it was in their hands to mold children into whatever they believed to be most desirable.

Research in the last ten years has struck a sobering note and brought constitutional factors back into our thinking, but with a different emphasis. The whole question has become more complex; the controversy of constitution versus environment, of nature versus nurture, has become an argument with false premises, because the two components interact and constitute reciprocal agents. We have come to see that certain patterns in the child—such as activity patterns, perceptual sensitivity, tempo and rhythms in bodily functions such as sleep, movements, eating, digestion, and so on—are constitutionally fixed and show a high degree of stability over the years. A very active child born into a family of more placid parents is constantly expected to behave in a fashion for which he is constitutionally ill equipped. In fact, such a child can develop nervous symptoms as a result of restraining his motility beyond tolerance from its natural flow.

It is of particular interest for teachers to apply these considerations to the problem of intelligence. Intelligence, once considered to be fixed by heredity, has been shown to be influenced decisively by environment, within, however, individual limitations. While on the one hand we have come to realize that every child has educable intellectual capacities, the degree of educability shows individual differences that are beyond our

power to alter.   Studies have shown that the I.Q. can be raised by stimulating experiences in childhood and particularly by emotional factors
usually summarized as motivation.   Attendance at nursery school, with
enriching experiences in toys, play space, social contact, language, and
perceptual stimulation, tends to supplement the limited stimulation that
prevails in many children's families.   This point of view has been given
recognition in the report of the Midcentury White House Conference on
Children with these words:

> It was, therefore, concluded that the intellectual differences between high
> and low economic groups are explainable on the basis of the limitations or
> advantages in education and other important conditions of life that necessarily
> accompany these groups.

In assessing children's intellectual functioning, the teacher, then, has
to differentiate between constitutional capacity, environmental deficiencies, and emotional interferences.   Should these three dimensions of
intellectual functioning be clarified by observation over a period of time
—possibly by testing also—then the teacher is in a position to base her
expectations of a child's learning as to rate and level on the solid basis of
differential findings.   This will enable her to bring to best fruition the
latent capacities that the child possesses.   If teaching can be done without
too drastically overtaxing or undertaxing the child's potential, a permanent contribution to his mental health has been made.

I want now to become more specific in my discussion of mental health
and the educative process.   In order to accomplish this, I asked myself:
What are the mental conditions that best help man to maintain a feeling
of well-being, to behave in a socially useful way, and to withstand the
unavoidable vicissitudes of life?   From my experiences with children,
adolescents, and adults, I have abstracted four conditions that seem to
me to embody what we refer to as mental health.   I will trace the genesis
of these conditions and will attempt to uncover the ingredients of experience that, through the years of childhood, have cumulatively led to a
mental state conducive to a way of life useful to others and to oneself.

The first condition I want to discuss with you can be summarized as
the sense of personal worth.   This refers to a subjective conviction that
it does matter in the world how I act, that my existence is of significance
and value, that I am, so to say, entrusted with myself, to take good care
of this trust, to protect its dignity, to cherish its hopes, and to assuage its
yearnings.   You realize already from the way I have phrased the description that the sense of personal worth is the indelible imprint in the self
that is made by the significant relationships of childhood.   This sense of
personal worth goes always parallel with a trusting attitude toward life,

a confidence in possible fulfillment and betterment. In contrast, the absence of the sense of personal worth leaves the growing child with a perpetual distrust, pessimism, and cynicism. Such a person will find any retaliatory and exploitative behavior, with its contempt for human dignity, irresistible. Such propensities eventually lead to character distortions, which make the individual an easy prey to illness, criminality, or ideological fanaticism. All these results are destructive either of the self or of others or of both. These grave consequences warrant careful scrutiny of the problem.

The child's concept of himself is the result of the attitudes that the significant persons of his life have had toward him. Acceptance and belongingness have in a real sense their origin at the mother's breast. This early beginning, however, is followed up by other influences, among which those of the teacher are of great significance. Unstable or shaky self-esteem is in large part traceable to the unstable and shifting attitude that adults have toward children. Children please the adult when they live up to expectation, and they are rejected when they disappoint their elders. This shift in the attitude of the teacher, whose own security is greatly enhanced by the conforming child, becomes indelibly manifest in the child's low self-esteem, in the shifting pattern of loving and hating himself.

A reasonable degree of stable relationship between teacher and child is essential for the maintenance of self-respect, without which a child cannot develop normally. Destructive practices and attitudes of teachers that creep easily—even if only in miniature editions or in latent phantasies —into the daily classroom life are those of shaming and belittling, distrusting and humiliating. These practices destroy the budding self-esteem in the child and lay the foundation for a self low in self-esteem and consequently low in the regard of others. The child who has the confidence that he can count on his teacher can also constructively accept criticism and blame from her.

I remember a ten-year-old boy, Freddie, who was brought up by his grandparents after his own parents had been divorced during his first year of life. One day his mother came to visit him after years of absence. The child told the principal that his mother had arrived, and that she had invited him to see her early in the afternoon. The principal asked Freddie whether he had completed his work, and Freddie answered truthfully that he had. The principal then asked the child to get a note from each of his teachers to confirm this. The child pleaded with the principal, saying that he would be late for the visit with his mother. The principal, interested only in the school routine, overlooked the rising anxiety in the child and told Freddie that he had to do as told.

The principal's distrust and disregard for the child's feelings so infuriated Freddie that he ran out of the school building to meet his mother. While passing through the entrance door he made a vow never to set foot in this school again. In fact, he never did. This story needs no commentary; it speaks for itself and high-lights the point I have tried to make.

We now come to the second condition of mental well-being—namely, *the capacity to distinguish between internal and external events, between feelings and facts.* This capacity enhances our ability to think rationally, to judge justly, and to act realistically. The division between our feeling life and the world outside is vaguer in most of us than we like to think. Phantasies merge with perception of the outside world and place our thinking easily on shaky ground. Thinking under such conditions is far from realistic. Only when we can clearly see which sensations arise within ourselves and which have external sources are we in a position to think realistically. This mental state carries a feeling-tone that can be described as a sense of mastery and sureness in response, a compactness as to the feeling of self, and a sure orientation in the ocean of physical and emotional events that engulfs us. Psychologists describe this condition in terms of ego boundaries. This concept, in fact, has become a cornerstone of the normal personality.

As you can see, the condition that I am describing here is closely related to the cognitive processes and is, therefore, of particular concern to teachers. The cognitive capacity to perceive correctly inner and outer events passes through several stages until it reaches its full development. The ability to think is not only useful in enabling us to add up our grocery bill correctly, but it represents a faculty that strengthens the division of self and outside, a division that does not exist in the young child. You are all familiar with the child's confusion of his own feelings with that of others, of blaming the mother for his pain and kicking the chair into which he bumped accidentally. Children, when angry, feel the other person is angry and act on that premise. Needless to say, such action has a high degree of self-reference; it is inappropriate and disrupts the communication between the individual and the people around him. It is surprising to see similar processes, however more subtle and devious, operating in older children and adults to the detriment of their personality integration.

To give a concrete example, let us take an every-day situation. We are all familiar with the fact that children—more than is usually realized—attach fears and phantasies to their school life and to the teacher in particular. These apprehensions in children—related to fears of failure, of inability to understand, of punishment, of parental disappointment, of competitive-aggressive behavior, or physical injury, and so on—these apprehensions in children can be used for conforming and controlling purposes by the teacher.   This, however, results in phantasy elaborations that blend with reality.   A loose grasp of reality represents always a serious threat to mental health.   What can be done?

The fact that children experience emotions in relation to learning and school life should be recognized and made part of the learning experience. In order to prevent unhealthy elaboration in children, their active participation in classroom life, their free expression of feelings, and their opportunity for creative activity are basic requirements of sound teaching.   The more real as a person the teacher can be in her relationship to the children she teaches, the more clearly they can see her, experience her, and test their opinions about her.   Under these conditions the teacher ceases to be the target for the projection of children's phantasies.   It follows that their grasp on reality will be more firm and, consequently, that they will be more interested in learning and more objective in relation to subject matter.   This, needless to say, is the state in which learning can take place best and most successfully.

The third condition that deserves our attention is *the capacity to tolerate a modicum of tension.*   You know that the threshold of tension tolerance in the young child is very low and that an uprising urge is not quieted until gratified.   The postponement of gratification and the substitution of primitive gratifications by socially valued activities is education's main endeavor.

Let me explain: It is quite normal for the one-year-old, when the sensation of hunger makes itself felt, to become absorbed by the wish for food. In the ten-year-old, we expect that slight hunger sensations will not absorb all his attention and render him unable to pay further attention to the task at hand.   We can expect that the knowledge that lunch time will come at the regular hour makes possible a suppression of disturbing and distracting sensations.

The same thing, of course, is true of all the inner urges and affects that continuously arise within us and threaten to disrupt our orderly activities. Some of these urges and affects—such as, for example, aggression—cannot find direct, uninhibited expression; they need a modified, socially acceptable outlet, usually called sublimation, as in organized games, in dramatic productions, in mastery of skills, and in the solving of problems. I might remind you that we speak of "tackling a problem" and "putting our teeth" into a difficult task.

What I am saying here is simply that the child has to experience anxiety in order to develop devices to master it.   It becomes a question of dosage and timing.   This runs counter to what you might have heard over many years—namely, that anxiety is an unhealthy affect and should be avoided at all cost.   Is it not a distortion of the realities of life when we pretend to children that there is nothing to be afraid of? "We have nothing to fear but fear itself," as F. D. R. once said? One fear that cannot be wholly eradicated is the fear of our inner conflicting desires.

In the effort to spare children the unpleasant feeling of anxiety, educators recommended self-expression as the safest road to emotional security. It was assumed that, with a maximum of gratification, the child would grow automatically into an individual not burdened by repressions. This has proved not to be true because the disintegrating interference of tension against which the child had not developed workable defenses left him weak and unstable. Conflict is part of life; to permit the child to experience conflict and, with the help of the teacher, arrive at a satisfactory solution, is part of the teacher's task. It is a most delicate balance that the teacher must maintain between the child's self-expression and adult direction, between giving immediate gratification and imposing postponement or suppression. As teachers, we should not be afraid of creating conflicts in children as long as they remain within the child's capacity to master productively.

One such experience of a fourth-grader I should like to tell you. Mike loved to read. His teacher was pleased by the boy's enthusiasm and whenever he wanted to go to the library, he got permission. What the teacher did not notice was the fact that Mike always was overcome by the urge to read when time for arithmetic came around. The teacher in the fifth grade realized that Mike had not the vaguest idea of the multiplication table. Since Mike was a bright boy, she gave him an ultimatum: either you know your tables by Christmas or you go back to the fourth grade. What did Mike do in this conflict? He learned his tables.

As a postscript to this story, I might add that Mike became an extremely able student of mathematics in high school and college.

I cannot leave this point without letting John Dewey speak. He warned the educator many years ago

. . . that the proponents of freedom are in a false position as well as the would-be masters and dictators. There is a present tendency in so-called advanced schools of educational thought to say, in effect, let us surround pupils with certain materials, tools, appliances, etc., and let pupils respond to these things according to their own desires. Above all let us not suggest any end or plan to the students; let us not suggest to them what they shall do, for that is unwarranted trespass upon their sacred intellectual individuality since the essence of such individuality is to set up ends and aims. Now such a method is really stupid. For it attempts the impossible, which is always stupid; and it misconceives the conditions of independent thinking. There are a multitude of ways of reacting to surrounding conditions, and without some guidance from experience these reactions are sure to be casual, sporadic, and ultimately fatiguing, accompanied by nervous strain.

Let us not forget John Dewey's admonishment that the teacher, even in the most modern conception, has a place as an active and directive adult in the child's life.

A fourth condition of man that is identical with mental well-being is *self-realization in an accepted role*. By this I mean the feeling of identity that a person possesses, which is to say,

the awareness of the fact that there is a self-sameness and continuity to the ego's synthesizing method and that these methods are effective in safe-guarding the sameness and continuity of one's meaning for others.

This sense of identity takes shape in adolescence, but preparatory steps precede its definite achievement. As educators, we must ask ourselves whether we are preparing children to use what they learn in the positions that they will assume in society. This does not imply that an adjustment to the *status quo* is to be favored, but rather that the recognition of social facts as they are is basic for intelligent action. Lucid awareness of one's social position is not identical with passive acceptance of it. It has, for example, contributed immensely to the feeling of frustration in women that they were in large numbers exposed to the stimulating experiences of college education and later were in no position to apply their learning in any socially useful rôle, but rather had to content themselves with the status satisfaction that they owed to their degree. Obviously, the remedy is not to stop educating women, but to make them aware of the problem that the highly educated woman in this society is bound to meet.

We have to see to it that a curriculum is related to the realities of the life of the children for whom this curriculum is devised. Otherwise, school and life lie far apart, and ideals of achievement are allowed to flourish in children's minds which outside the classroom are contradicted by the social organization to which they belong.

The discrepancy between individual aspirations and the restrictions and taboos of society can result only in frustration and resentment. The school—especially in the case of minority groups—has to acquaint children with the social realities of their caste and class and assist them in developing clear-cut attitudes, awareness, and behavioral techniques to cope with these. Only from a clear understanding of the social realities in which a person finds himself can a course of action develop that will bring about social change. Democratic institutions, which inherently favor the process of social evolution, can be used rationally only by individuals who are acquainted with the operation of such institutions.

These are processes that children can learn in the classroom in solving the difficulties of their own miniature societies, and this experience will lead later to a clearer recognition of the social rôle potential with which the adolescent can identify himself.   If the adolescent can do this realistically, without a feeling of failure, without self-deprecation or self-blame, then we have achieved our educational purpose.

The teacher cannot do this alone; society has to do its share also and adjust its organization to protect the self-development and the dignity of all of its members.   Social progress takes places through the wider distribution of knowledge, understanding, and awareness of individuals, which in turn forces social institutions to adapt themselves to these changing conditions.

You will be relieved to hear that the teacher is not expected to work miracles.   Nevertheless, in thinking back over what I have said, the task of the teacher seems gigantic.   It stands to reason that the teacher's task is a difficult one.   Therefore, the training for the teaching profession or the selection of prospective teachers is of the utmost importance in terms of the mental well-being of children.

It has often been asked what the motives are, why people choose to become teachers.   Do they love children, or do they love long vacations, or perhaps the status that goes with the profession and the fairly secure position?   I venture to say that only a person who is genuinely interested in children can exert a formative influence on a child that will outlast in significance most of the subject matter it has learned in school.   Just remember for a moment the teachers you had when you were a child.   We have all had a teacher who has made an unforgettable impression on us.

At this point I like to sound a note of caution.   Having a good relationship to children does not blow away all the teacher's troubles; indeed it creates new ones.   It is a known fact that children easily ignore the teacher who has no meaning for them and that they involve a beloved teacher in all the personal and intimate conflicts of their young lives.   To illustrate, let me tell you the story of Jack and his teacher.

Jack was twelve years old and his teacher, who had him for the second year in her class, had always got along splendidly with this often willful and impulsive lad.   They were on good terms and it seemed nothing could happen that they could not straighten out.   No wonder that Miss Jones was not overly alarmed when Jack started trouble.   He got into the habit of disturbing the class, of interrupting, of falling from his chair, dropping books, talking back and "being fresh" to the teacher.

Miss Jones talked to him kindly, but Jack did not change.   He got worse; he neglected his home work; he became sullen and indifferent.   Miss Jones ignored the disturbances that Jack created, but this tactic did not bring any noticeable improvement either.   She had been kind, understanding, tolerant, and patient—what had to come next? Obviously punishment. Correct. But punishment without effect. At this point, after many months of struggle, Miss Jones asked me to talk with Jack because she was at a loss what to do next.

Jack came to see me. I knew of his behavior difficulties, but I knew almost nothing about his life outside school. I knew only one fact which Miss Jones had told me—namely, that he had an older brother and no father; his father had deserted the family when the child was an infant.

Jack didn't mind talking to me. In response to my questions about the trouble in Miss Jones' room, he poured out a stream of accusations: Oh, Miss Jones! What a teacher! She had been nice once, yes, but she had changed. Now she doesn't care about her students; she only thinks of herself. Jack told me that he had seen her downtown—yes, running around with men. She has nothing else in her head but her own fun. So it went on and on.

Since I knew Miss Jones, I knew that Jack was phantasying about her. But he was saying something, he was accusing somebody, and I guessed who it was. I said to Jack: "Does your mother think of remarrying?" Jack looked at me with astonishment: "Who told you?"

We can see from this episode that Jack made himself so unpleasant with Miss Jones precisely because he was on such good terms with her. He lived out the conflict with his mother in relation to a mother-figure, his teacher. The good relationship between Miss Jones and Jack made it almost impossible for the teacher to resolve this conflict herself. Such incidents of sudden disruptions in a good relationship will always happen to teachers. The source of the trouble cannot always be found. The teacher has to understand that children will act out in relation to her; then it will be easier for her not to become personally hurt by the child's action, but to continue to feel toward the child as she did before the crisis.

One reason why it is so difficult to be a good teacher lies in the fact that some of our own childhood problems are still with us. There is nothing abnormal about this. The best we can do is to search ourselves and keep an observant eye on our own reactions as well as on those of the children in our care. How often, when I have discussed with a teacher her classroom problems, have we come to realize that her selective and severe reaction to children's behavior was due to the fact that such behavior confronted her with precisely those transgressions—be it lying or cursing or showing off or messing—which the teacher in her own childhood could control or suppress only with greatest difficulty.

These problems are not solved only by studying psychology; the teacher has to study her own reactions and try to understand herself. Since it is of such great importance to have mature and understanding teachers, training institutions may well consider facilities that will enable young teachers-in-training to receive help with those personal problems which interfere with their professional usefulness.   Counseling with a mature and experienced person can be of greater practical benefit than textbook studies in psychology alone.   The prospective teacher begins her training during the years of late adolescence, which are emotionally difficult years. Only as far as teachers can themselves arrive at a state of mental well-being can they lay the foundation in children for the growth of emotionally stable adults, with a sturdy capacity for love and for work.

In closing, I will read to you a passage from a lecture by General Chisholm, that great Canadian who has devoted himself passionately to the reëstablishment of a peacetime society.   He says, in his William Alanson White Memorial Lecture:

The most important thing in the world to-day is the bringing up of children. It is not a job for economic or emotional misfits, for frightened, inferiority-ridden men and women seeking a safe, respectable, and quickly attainable social and emotional status, nor for girls filling in their time before marriage. Fortunately there are recent signs of intellectual stirrings amongst teachers which give some hope.   To be allowed to teach children should be the sign of the final approval of society.

CORRELATION OF THIS BOOK WITH EDUCATIONAL PSYCHOLOGY TEXTS

	Bernard, Psychology of Learning and Teaching, McGraw-Hill, 1954	Blair, Jones, and Simpson, Educational Psychology, Macmillan, 1954	Cole and Bruce, Educational Psychology, World Book, 1950
Text chs.	Related Selections in *Readings for Educational Psychology*		
1	—	—	—
2	5, 11	2, 17–19, 34	—
3	43, 49	2, 12–16, 19, 23, 26, 28–30, 34, 46	12, 13
4	14–16, 30–34, 46	14, 16, 20, 22, 34, 40, 41	13, 16, 32, 33
5	12–16, 19, 29	1–11	17–22, 34
6	31–33	13, 17, 20, 31–34, 41, 48	2, 15, 16, 23–27, 30, 41, 44
7	1–11	6, 17, 28, 31–34, 36, 42, 43	14, 15, 31–34
8	9, 10	26, 34, 43	14, 16, 18, 28, 34, 43
9	—	5, 6, 9–11, 35–37, 43, 49	14, 28–30
10	23, 28–30, 38–45	—	1–11, 43
11	17–22	35, 37–40, 43, 46, 49	2, 6
12	18, 48	17, 19, 20, 24, 25, 41, 44, 45, 47	3, 4, 6
13	20, 24, 38, 39, 41, 43	15, 20, 24–27, 30, 41	1, 5, 8
14	16, 27	35, 38, 39, 43, 49	4, 9, 10
15	6, 11, 36, 42, 47	20, 24, 25, 37–40, 44–47	—
16	23–27, 37, 44–46, 50	17, 18, 34	8, 38, 39, 46, 49
17	—	18, 48	40, 45, 47
18	26, 27, 34, 35	18, 48	35–37, 42, 48
19	—	36, 37, 42, 48	38, 39, 49, 50
20	24, 37, 40, 44, 50	—	
21	35, 48	43, 45, 46, 49, 50	
22		43, 45, 46, 49, 50	

	Commins and Fagin, *Principles of Educational Psychology,* Ronald, 1954	Cronbach, *Educational Psychology,* Harcourt, 1954	Crow and Crow, *Educational Psychology,* American Book, 1948
Text chs.	Related Selections in *Readings for Educational Psychology*		
1	1–11	—	—
2	3, 5–7, 12–15, 28, 31–34	15, 27	43, 45–47, 49
3	13, 18, 19	1–8	12–16
4	12, 13	12–16, 28, 31–34	12–16
5	17–19, 21–23, 34	18–20, 34	19
6	14, 18, 34	31–34	2, 16, 23
7	2, 15, 17, 23–27	18, 21	16, 23–27, 35, 37
8	18, 48	35–37, 42	17–22
9	17–22, 37	9–11	—
10	15, 20, 24–26, 28–30, 38–41, 44, 45, 49	2–5	28–30
11	8, 22, 29, 36, 37	2, 8, 26, 27, 34	31–33, 37
12	1–8	3, 5, 6	1–11
13	2–5, 9, 10	6	23, 26, 27, 31–34, 36, 42
14	6, 34, 42	35, 36, 42	—
15	35, 38, 39, 42, 43, 49	35, 38–49	4, 9–11, 17
16	5, 9–11	37	9, 10
17	5, 6, 10	20, 23–25, 30, 40, 41, 44, 45, 47, 50	—
18	5, 7, 11	8, 29, 30, 38–40, 46, 50	18, 48
19	4, 9–11, 17	27–30, 50	—
20	5, 9–11		48
21	8, 20, 25, 27–30, 41, 50		—
22			
23			—
24			
25			
26			—
27			
28			20–22, 50
29			14, 15, 20, 25, 41, 50
			38–40, 44, 50

484

Text chs.	Ellis, *Educational Psychology,* Van Nostrand, 1951	Garrison and Gray, *Educational Psychology,* Appleton-Century-Crofts, 1955	Gates, Jersild, McConnell, and Challman, *Educational Psychology,* Macmillan, 1948
	Related Selections in *Readings for Educational Psychology*		
1	7, 8, 45	—	7, 8
2	13, 34, 36, 37, 48	12–16	2, 12, 13, 15, 23
3	31–34, 37	13	13, 16
4	27	2, 23–27, 30	2, 23, 49
5	1, 3, 5, 6, 38, 39, 44–49	17–22	21, 34, 35, 43, 46
6	4, 6	—	17
7	—	16, 23–27, 34, 35, 43, 46	17–22
8	5, 9–11	26, 34, 46, 47	18, 21
9	—	28–30, 40, 51	31–34, 43, 47
10	2, 23–27, 34, 43, 49	14, 15, 20, 25, 38, 39, 41, 43–45, 49, 50	1–11
11	17–22, 42, 48	1–11	6
12	17–22, 42, 48	31–36, 42, 48	3, 34, 36, 42
13	—	—	5, 9–11
14	20, 24, 25, 38–46, 50	4, 6, 9–11, 47, 49	9, 10
15	19–22, 25, 27, 40, 41	5, 9–11	—
16	8, 22, 29, 34, 47	—	18, 48
17	15, 16, 27, 30, 38, 39	18, 36, 48	26, 40, 46
18	35, 38, 39, 44–49	34	14, 15, 23–30
19		19, 21, 22, 25, 27, 38–41, 45, 49	20, 23–27, 30, 40, 41
20		8, 20, 22, 35, 37, 49	19–22, 34, 37–39, 44, 45, 49
21			20, 22, 40, 46, 50
22			—

	Guthrie and Powers, *Educational Psychology,* Ronald, 1950	Morse and Wingo, *Psychology and Teaching,* Scott, Foresman, 1955	Mursell, *Psychology for Modern Education,* Norton, 1952
Text chs.	Related Selections in *Readings for Educational Psychology*		
1	—	47, 49	7, 11, 28–30, 40, 44, 47
2	—	—	15
3	17–19, 21	17, 24, 28, 29, 40, 45, 47	3, 34–36, 42, 49
4	4, 11, 17	12–19, 30	14, 20, 31–34
5	2, 23–27, 31–34	2, 15, 23	1–11
6	12, 13, 32, 33, 41	26, 31–33, 46	1–11
7	1–11	16, 27	—
8	1–11	1–11	5, 9, 10, 17
9	1–11	35, 37, 43, 46	2, 20, 23–27, 38–41
10	15, 28, 30, 35–37, 42–49	20–22, 26, 34, 41	5
11	15, 28, 30, 35–37, 42–49	9, 10, 40, 45	12, 13, 17, 19
12	12, 47	2, 9, 10, 26, 43	12–16
13	4	25, 38, 39, 43, 44, 49	17–19
14	18–22, 36, 42	35, 36, 48	19–22
15	18, 37, 48	11, 24, 37, 42	5, 6, 37, 40
16	—		38–50
17	20, 31		
18	6		
19	36, 37		
20	47		
21	35–49		
22	—		
23	14, 24, 26, 27		
24	15, 16, 28–30		
25	15, 16, 28–30		
26	24, 25, 27, 38–45, 47, 50		
27	34, 43		
28	8, 22, 24		
29	—		
30	—		
31	44–49		

	Remmers, Ryden, and Morgan, *Introduction to Educational Psychology,* Harper, 1954	Simpson, *Fundamentals of Educational Psychology,* Lippincott, 1949	Skinner, *Educational Psychology,* 3rd ed., Prentice-Hall, 1951
Text chs.	Related Selections in *Readings for Educational Psychology*		
1	12–19, 23, 47, 50	12, 13, 21, 32, 33, 41	—
2	20–22, 25–30, 38, 39, 41, 43	17–22	12–16
3	17–19, 21, 32, 33, 41	31–34	2, 15, 20, 23, 28, 43
4	20, 34	2, 23–30, 38–41, 44, 45, 47, 49, 50	26, 34, 40, 46
5	24, 35–40, 43–47, 49, 50	14, 15, 26, 27, 34, 35, 38, 39, 43, 46, 50	17–22
6	16, 27, 50	8, 20–22, 41	17–22
7	18, 28, 34, 50	18, 20, 31–34	14–16
8	12, 13	18, 48	—
9	31–34, 42	1–11	15, 31–34, 42
10	1–11	4–6, 31–35, 37, 42	—
11	48	—	5, 6, 10
12	—	4	9, 10
13	—	6, 12, 13, 15–22, 31, 41, 42, 48	26, 43, 49
14		32, 33, 49	—
15		—	19, 20, 32–34, 36, 41, 43, 47
16		18, 36, 48	1–11
17			1–11
18			23, 24, 26, 28–30
19			20, 24, 25, 29, 38, 39, 41, 50
20			20–22, 24, 25, 27, 40, 41, 44, 45
21			17, 19, 41
22			18, 37, 48
23			18, 37, 48
24			8, 22, 29, 38, 39, 45, 49
25			8, 22, 29, 38, 39, 45, 49
26			24, 35, 43, 44, 46, 47, 49

	Smith, *Psychology in Teaching*, Prentice-Hall, 1954	Sorenson, *Psychology in Education*, 3rd ed., McGraw-Hill, 1954	Stephens, *Educational Psychology*, Holt, 1951
Text chs.	Related Selections in *Readings for Educational Psychology*		
1	47, 49	48	—
2	12, 13, 16, 32, 33	37, 48	1–11, 30
3	2, 15, 23–27, 43, 44	—	1–11, 30
4	14–16, 26, 27, 34, 46	12, 13, 16	—
5	26, 27, 34	14, 15, 30	—
6	17–22	23, 25, 28, 29, 41, 50	12, 13, 15, 21, 27, 32, 33, 41, 50
7	15, 20, 28–34, 36, 42	20, 24, 38–41, 43–47, 49	17–22
8	1–11	49, 50	18, 20, 41, 48
9	5, 6, 35, 43	26, 27, 34, 46	14, 16, 31, 48
10	17–22	17, 18	18, 34
11	—	17–22	5, 6, 26, 31–35, 42, 49
12	48	17–22	2, 3, 5, 6, 8, 22
13	14, 20, 25, 40, 41, 44–47	22, 37, 48	4, 5, 9–11
14	27, 34, 37–39	36, 37	1, 6, 36, 40, 42
15	8, 22	—	42
16	50	1–11	35–37, 44–49
17		1–11	14–16, 23–27
18		31–34, 36, 42, 43	20, 27–30, 37–40
19		3, 5, 6	14, 16, 27, 30, 34, 43, 46, 50
20		—	35, 37, 40, 41, 45, 47
21		32, 33, 50	24, 25, 38–46, 49, 50
22		35	47, 49, 50

Text chs.	Trow, *Educational Psychology*, Houghton Mifflin, 1950	Witherington, *Educational Psychology*, Ginn, 1952	Woodruff, *The Psychology of Teaching*, 3rd ed., Longmans, Green, 1951
	Related Selections in *Readings for Educational Psychology*		
1	—	—	—
2	35, 45–47, 49, 50	12–16	9, 10, 12, 13, 15, 17, 18, 28
3	27, 34, 35, 37–43	2, 15, 16, 23–27, 31–34, 44, 47	4, 32, 33, 41, 43, 44
4	15, 23, 29–34	6, 16, 20, 26, 27, 34, 41	8, 45
5	20, 23–27, 30, 41	12–16, 19	17, 28
6	20, 25, 26, 30, 38–41	17–22, 34, 36, 37	10, 11, 14, 15, 20, 41
7	12–16, 19	18, 19, 34	15, 16, 30–34, 40
8	17–22, 37	1–11, 31–34, 42	4, 5, 9–11, 28
9	18, 48	6	3, 4, 6, 17
10	4, 6, 8	9, 10	15, 16, 20, 23, 25–27, 34, 38, 39, 44
11	1–3, 6	—	12–14, 19, 34
12	9, 10	26, 27, 35, 43, 49	12–16, 31–33, 50
13	—	11, 28, 38, 39, 47	13, 14, 27, 28, 37, 44
14	1, 5, 9, 10	18, 34, 42, 48	14, 16, 27, 40
15	6, 7	20, 24, 25, 28, 40, 41, 43–46	1–11
16	—	5, 6, 10, 11	3, 5, 6, 9, 10
17	11, 22, 28, 34–44	24, 28, 30, 37–41, 47, 50	9–11
18		—	17–22, 31–34
19		—	12, 20, 32, 33, 41
20			34, 35, 37–40, 43, 49
21			20, 24, 25, 30, 36–41, 44–47, 49
22			20, 24, 25, 30, 36–41, 44–47, 49
23			20, 24, 25, 30, 36–41, 44–47, 49
24			28–34, 37
25			8, 22, 48
26			8, 22, 48
27			8, 22, 48

Index